Lecture Notes in Computer Science 10299

Commenced Publication in 1973
Founding and Former Series Editors:
Gerhard Goos, Juris Hartmanis, and Jan van Leeuwen

Editorial Board

More information about this series at http://www.springer.com/series/7411

Amr El Abbadi · Benoît Garbinato (Eds.)

Networked Systems

5th International Conference, NETYS 2017
Marrakech, Morocco, May 17–19, 2017
Proceedings

 Springer

Editors
Amr El Abbadi
Department of Computer Science
University of California, Santa Barbara
Santa Barbara, CA
USA

Benoît Garbinato
Université de Lausanne
Lausanne
Switzerland

ISSN 0302-9743   ISSN 1611-3349   (electronic)
Lecture Notes in Computer Science
ISBN 978-3-319-59646-4   ISBN 978-3-319-59647-1   (eBook)
DOI 10.1007/978-3-319-59647-1

Library of Congress Control Number: 2017940840

LNCS Sublibrary: SL5 – Computer Communication Networks and Telecommunications

Printed on acid-free paper

This Springer imprint is published by Springer Nature
The registered company is Springer International Publishing AG
The registered company address is: Gewerbestrasse 11, 6330 Cham, Switzerland

Preface

In May 2017, the 5th edition of the International Conference on Networked Systems (NETYS) took place in Marrakech (Morocco). For this edition, we received 81 submissions, which were reviewed by a Program Committee of 47 international experts in various fields related to networked and distributed computing systems. Out of these submissions, the Program Committee decided to accept 28 regular papers and six short papers. In addition, three renowned researchers accepted to give keynote presentations:

- Michel Raynal, from the University of Rennes
- Sergio Rajsbaum, from the National Autonomous University of Mexico
- Alexander A. Schwarzmann, from the University of Connecticut

As program chairs of NETYS 2017 and editors of these proceedings, we want to warmly thank again all the authors for their high-quality contributions and all the Program Committee members and external reviewers for their invaluable hard work. We also sincerely thank our three keynote speakers for sharing their precious insights and expertise. In particular, we are very grateful and happy that Michel Raynal accepted to give a keynote this year, since he will be officially retiring in 2017, after a rich academic career spanning more than *four decades* in the area of distributed computing! Last but not least, our special thanks go to the Organizing Committee and to all the local arrangements coordinators, and of course to Ahmed Bouajjani (Université Paris Diderot, France), Mohammed Erradi (ENSIAS, Rabat, Morocco), and Rachid Guerraoui (EPFL, Lausanne, Switzerland), the conference general chairs, without whom NETYS would simply not exist.

May 2017

Amr El Abbadi
Benoît Garbinato

Organization

Program Committee

Parosh Aziz Abdulah	Uppsala University, Sweden
Periklis Andritsos	University of Toronto, Canada
Najib Badache	USTHB, CERIST
Slimane Bah	Mohammed V University, Morocco
Rida Bazzi	Arizona State University, USA
Yahya Benkaouz	FSR, Mohammed V University of Rabat, Morocco
Ismail Berrada	L3I and LIMS
Mohamed Bettaz	Laboratoire Méthodes de Conception de Systèmes, ESI, Algeria
Silvia Bonomi	Sapienza Università di Roma, Italy
Aysu Betin Can	Orta Doğu Teknik Üniversitesi, Turkey
Antonio Carzaniga	Università della Svizzera italiana, Switzerland
Rachida Dssouli	Concordia University, Canada
Xavier Défago	Tokyo Institute of Technology, Japan
Amr El Abbadi	University of California, USA
Mohamed El Kamili	LiM, FSDM, USMBA, Fès
Patrick Eugster	Purdue University, USA
Pascal Felber	University of Neuchatel, Switzerland
Bernd Freisleben	University of Marburg, Germany
Roy Friedman	Technion, Israel
Eli Gafni	UCLA, USA
Benoît Garbinato	University of Lausanne, Switzerland
Mohamed Gouda	The University of Texas at Austin, USA
Seif Haridi	SICS
Maurice Herlihy	Brown University, USA
Kévin Huguenin	UNIL-HEC Lausanne, Switzerland
Zahi Jarir	Cadi Ayyad University, Morocco
Mohammed Jmaiel	ReDCAD, ENIS
Anne-Marie Kermarrec	Inria, France
Mikel Larrea	University of the Basque Country UPV/EHU, Spain
Miroslaw Malek	Humboldt University of Berlin, Germany
Louise Moser	
Achour Moustefaoui	Université Nantes (LINA), France
Guevara Noubir	Northeastern University, USA
Rui Oliveira	Universidade do Minho, Portugal
Meriem Ouedirni	IRIT/INP Toulouse/ENSEEIHT, France
Mohammed Ouzzif	ESTC
Stacy Patterson	RPI

Fernando Pedone	University of Lugano, Switzerland
Andreas Podelski	University of Freiburg, Germany
Shaz Qadeer	Microsoft
Michel Raynal	IRISA, France
Elad Schiller	Chalmers University of Technology, Sweden
Mohamed Sharaf	University of Queensland, Australia
Gregor von Bochmann	University of Ottawa, Canada
Fang Yu	National Chengchi University, Taiwan
Mohamed Zait	Oracle
Albert Zomaya	

Additional Reviewers

Ali, Muqeet	Ngo, Tuan Phong
Baccour, Nouha	Pereira, Óscar
Bendjoudi, Ahcene	Phi Diep, Bui
Bettaz, Mohamed	Reaz, Rezwana
Cheikhrouhou, Saoussen	Rezine, Othmane
Genkin, Daniel	Sebgui, Marouane
Guidara, Ikbel	Trinh, Cong Quy
Hatem, Bellaaj	Vilaça, Ricardo
Jmal Maâlej, Afef	Yahiaoui, Said

Keynote Presentations

Another Look at the Implementation of Read/Write Registers in Crash-Prone Asynchronous Message-Passing Systems

Michel Raynal

University of Rennes, Rennes, France
michel.raynal@irisa.fr

Abstract. Yet another work on the implementation of read/write registers in crash-prone asynchronous message-passing systems! Yes..., but, differently from its predecessors, this talk presents a communication abstraction which captures the essence of such an implementation in the same sense that total order broadcast can be associated with consensus. To this end, the talk introduces a new communication abstraction, named SCD-broadcast (SCD stands for "Set Constrained Delivery"), which, instead of a single message, delivers to processes sets of messages (whose size can be arbitrary), such that the sequences of message sets delivered to any two processes satisfies some constraints. The talk will then show that: (a) SCD-broadcast allows for a very simple implementation of a snapshot object (and consequently also of atomic read/write registers) in crash-prone asynchronous message-passing systems; (b) SCD-broadcast can be built from snapshot objects (hence SCD-broadcast and snapshot objects –or read/write registers– are "computationally equivalent"); (c) SCD-broadcast can be built in message-passing systems where any minority of processes may crash (which is the weakest assumption on the number of possible process crashes needed to implement a read/write register).

Reference

Imbs, D., Mostéfaoui, A., Perrin, M., Raynal, M.: Another look at the implementation of read/write registers in crash-prone asynchronous message-passing systems (extended version). Technical report, arXiv: ArXiv-1702.08176v1.pdf, 21 pages (2017)

Biography

Michel Raynal is a Professor of Informatics, IRISA, University of Rennes, France. His main research interests are the basic principles of distributed computing systems. Recognized as a world leading researcher in distributed computing, he is the author of numerous papers on this topic (more than 150 in int'l scientific journals, and more than

---

Joint work with Damien Imbs, Achour Mostéfaoui and Matthieu Perrin.

330 papers in int'l conferences). He is also well-known for his books on distributed computing. From a "purely numeric" point of view, his h-index is 54 and his i-10 index is 254. Michel Raynal is a senior member of the prestigious "Institut Universitaire de France", and a member of Academia Europaea. He was the recipient of the 2015 Int'l Award "Innovation in Distributed Computing" (also known as SIROCCO Prize). Michel Raynal is also "Chair Professor on Distributed Algorithms" at the Polytechnic University (PolyU) of Hong Kong.

Tasks, Objects, and the Notion of a Distributed Problems

Sergio Rajsbaum

National Autonomous University of Mexico (UNAM), Mexico City, Mexico
rajsbaum@matem.unam.mx

Abstract. The universal computing model of Turing, which was central to the birth of modern computer science, identified also the essential notion of a problem, as an input output function to be computed by a Turing machine. In distributed computing, *tasks* are the equivalent of a function: each process gets only part of the input, and computes part of the output after communicating with other processes. In distributed computing tasks have been studied from early on, in parallel, but independently of *sequential objects*. While tasks explicitly state what might happen when a set of processes run concurrently, sequential objects only specify what happens when processes run sequentially. Indeed, many distributed problems considered in the literature, seem to have no natural specification neither as tasks nor as sequential objects. I will concentrate on our recent work on interval-linearizability, a notion we introduced to specify objects more general than the usual sequential objects. I will describe the bridges we establish between these two classical paradigms, and our discussions about what is a distributed problem, and what it means to solve it.

Biography

Sergio Rajsbaum received a degree in Computer Engineering from the National Autonomous University of Mexico (UNAM) in 1985, and a PhD in the Computer Science from the Technion, Israel, in 1991. Since then he has been a faculty member at the Institute of Mathematics at UNAM. His research interests are in the theory of distributed computing, especially issues related to coordination, complexity and computability. He has also worked in graph theory, algorithms, and content management systems. He has published over 100 papers and book on the use of topology for a distributed computing theoretical foundation, a topic on which he is one of the world leading experts.

Atomic Shared Objects for Distributed Systems: Consistency, Latency, Reconfigurations

Alexander A. Schwarzmann

University of Connecticut, Storrs, USA
aas@uconn.edu

Abstract. Consistent shareable data services supporting atomic (linearizable) objects provide convenient building blocks for distributed systems. In general it is notoriously challenging to combine provable correctness guarantees with efficiency in networked systems subject to delays and processor crashes. To deal with crashes one must replicate objects at multiple network locations, and this creates the challenge of guaranteeing consistency. We survey work on specification and implementation of consistent read/write data objects and algorithms, focusing on fault-tolerance and latency. Then we describe a framework for dynamic consistent data services that can be tailored to yield implementations for various target network settings and that incorporates on-the-fly reconfiguration that only modestly interferes with on-going read and write operations. Here the goal is to guarantee safety (atomicity) for arbitrary patterns of asynchrony, crashes, and message loss, while enabling practical implementations. We describe examples of specification, reasoning about correctness, provable optimizations, and implementations of consistent data services in distributed systems.

Biography

Alexander A. Schwarzmann earned his B.S. from Stevens Institute of Technology in 1979, M.S. from Cornell University in 1981, and Ph.D. from Brown University in 1992, all in Computer Science, and he did his post-doctoral work at MIT from 1995 to 1997. His research is in fault-tolerant distributed computing and security of electronic election systems. Prior to pursuing his academic career he worked at Bell Labs and Digital Equipment Corp. From 1997 he is at the University of Connecticut, where he is now serving the Department Head of Computer Science & Engineering. He chaired and served on the Program Committees of more than 50 leading conferences, and he served as the Steering Committee Chair of both the ACM Symposium on Principles of Distributed Computing (PODC 2012–2015) and EATCS Symposium on Distributed Computing (DISC 2004–2007). Since 2006 he is also the Director of the UConn Center for Voting Technology Research (VoTeR). The Center provides technological expertise in security and integrity of electronic election systems. Schwarzmann is an Associate Editor of Information & Computation. He is an author of over 150 technical publication and three books.

Contents

Verification

Security and Privacy

Software Engineering

Concurrency and Specifications

Communication

Networking

An Innovative Combinatorial Approach for the Spanning Tree Entropy in Flower Network

Raihana Mokhlissi[1]([✉]), Dounia Lotfi[1], Joyati Debnath[2],
and Mohamed El Marraki[1]

[1] LRIT Associated Unit with CNRST (URAC No 29), Faculty of Sciences,
Mohammed V University in Rabat, 1014 Rabat, Morocco
mokhlissiraihana@gmail.com, {lotfi,marraki}@fsr.ac.ma
[2] Winona State University, Winona, MN 55987, USA
jdebnath@winona.edu

Abstract. The spanning tree entropy of a complex network provides a useful insight about its robustness. The most robust network is the network that has the highest entropy. In this paper, we represent construction of a complex network called Flower Network by using two combinatorial approaches: (1) Bipartition and (2) Reduction. We based both methods on geometrical transformation. We also develop topological properties of the network, obtain analytical expression for its number of spanning trees. In the end, we calculate and compare its spanning tree entropy with those for other networks having the same average degree of nodes for estimating a robust network.

Keywords: Entropy · Complex network · Flower network · Bipartition · Reduction · Number of spanning trees

1 Introduction

In nature, most of the complex systems in real life are represented by networks, where the nodes denote the basic constituents of the system and links describe their interaction. The Internet, electric, imaging, telephone calls, social networks and many other systems are now represented by complex networks [1]. There are many different types of these networks and this classification depends on the properties such as nodes degrees, clustering coefficients, shortest paths. Another concern in studying complex network is how to evaluate the robustness of a network and its ability to adapt to changes [2]. In general, the robustness of a network is correlated to its ability to deal with internal feedbacks within the network and to avoid malfunctioning when a fraction of its constituents is damaged.

In this work, we suggest a structural characterization of robustness in terms of network entropy [3], a structural property of the network. This concept is widely used in thermodynamics to measure the systems' efficiency. For complex networks, we use **the entropy of spanning trees** or what is called the

© Springer International Publishing AG 2017
A. El Abbadi and B. Garbinato (Eds.): NETYS 2017, LNCS 10299, pp. 3–14, 2017.
DOI: 10.1007/978-3-319-59647-1_1

asymptotic complexity [4] in order to quantify the robustness and to characterize the structure. It is related to the capacity of the network to withstand random changes in its structure. Graph theory has provided powerful combinatorial tool to calculate this entropy. This tool represented by **spanning tree** [5] helps us to focus on the relationship between the structure and the function of networks. To obtain the entropy of a complex network, first of all, we have to determine its number of spanning trees (The complexity). This number gives us an idea about how many possible topologies that a network can have. It is obtained by computing the determinant of a submatrix of the Laplacian matrix corresponding to the network (Kirchhoff's matrix-tree theorem) [6,7]. However, for a large network, the evaluation of this determinant is very difficult and even impossible. Most of the recent works have tried to find some alternative methods in order to avoid the arduous calculations of the largest determinant as needed by the algebraic method and enumerate the spanning trees for large and complex networks.

In this paper, we perform a process on a specific self-similar complex network, which is called the Flower network [8]. It consists of self-repeating patterns on all length scales. This network can be constructed by using two combinatorial approaches, which highlight the self-similarity of a complex network at different iterations. These techniques are based on geometrical transformations of the original network, by multiplying the number of nodes in the case of the **Bipartition approach** [9], or by multiplying the number of links in the case of the **Reduction approach** [9]. First, we define these combinatorial methods, we cite their properties, we study their complexity and we generalize these results to the case of k-partite and k-reduced networks. Then, we present two models of the Flower network, the first is characterized by two dimensions of self-similarity denoted by **2-Flower network** and the second is the general case denoted by **k-Flower network**. We examine their construction, we analyze their topological properties and we evaluate their complexity by combining Our approaches. Finally, we calculate their spanning trees entropy and we compare it with those for other networks having the same average degree of nodes in order to determine the most robust network between them.

2   Related Work

In this section, we present our approaches and we quote all the theorems, the definitions and the properties which we need to construct the network and calculate its complexity. We use the standard terminologies indistinctly as: "network" and "graph", "node" and "vertex" and "link" and "edge". Let $G = (V_G, E_G, F_G)$ be a simple planar connected graph with V_G is the set of vertices, E_G is the set of edges and F_G is the set of faces. Our approaches are presented as follows:

2.1   The Bipartition Approach

The bipartite graphs belong to one of the simplest families in the graph theory [9] and their representation helps to study and use in various areas such as semantic web, data mining and segmentation of images, etc.

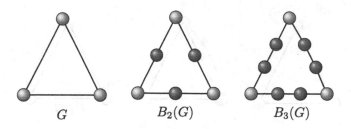

Fig. 1. A graph G, its bipartite graph and its 3-partite graph

Definition 1. *A graph becomes bipartite when we add a new vertex between two directly connected vertices, denoted by $B_2(G)$ (See Fig. 1).*

Lemma 1. *Let G be a planar graph and $B_2(G)$ its bipartite graph. The number of vertices in $B_2(G)$ is given by $V_{B_2(G)} = V_G + E_G$, its number of edges is given by $E_{B_2(G)} = 2E_G$, its number of faces is $F_{B_2(G)} = F_G$ and its average degree is*
$$<z>_{B_2(G)} = \frac{2E_{B_2(G)}}{V_{B_2(G)}} = \frac{4E_G}{V_G + E_G}.$$

Theorem 1. *Let $B_2(G)$ be a bipartite graph of a planar graph G. The number of spanning trees in $B_2(G)$ is given by:*

$$\tau(B_2(G)) = 2^{F_G - 1}\tau(G) \tag{1}$$

The main objective of the bipartite approach is to reduce the number of nodes of a network before finding its complexity.

Definition 2. *A k-partite graph of a planar graph G is defined by adding $k-1$ new vertices in each edge, denoted by $B_k(G)$ (See Fig. 1).*

Lemma 2. *Let G be a planar graph and $B_k(G)$ its k-partite graph. The number of vertices in $B_k(G)$ is given by $V_{B_k(G)} = V_G + (k-1)E_G$, its number of edges is given by $E_{B_k(G)} = k \times E_G$, its number of faces is $F_{B_k(G)} = F_G$ and its average degree is $<z>_{B_k(G)} = \frac{2E_{B_k(G)}}{V_{B_k(G)}} = \frac{2k \times E_G}{V_G + (k-1)E_G}.$*

Theorem 2. *Let $B_k(G)$ be a k-partite graph of a planar graph G. The number of spanning trees in $B_k(G)$ is given by:*

$$\tau(B_k(G)) = k^{F_G - 1}\tau(G) \tag{2}$$

2.2 The Reduction Approach

The reduction approach is another concept that is characterized by the presence of multiple edges [9]. It is an implementation method for functional programming languages.

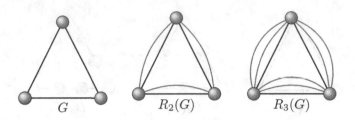

Fig. 2. A graph G, its reduced graph and its 3-reduced graph

Definition 3. *A graph becomes reduced when we add a new edge connecting two existing vertices of a planar graph G. It is denoted by $R_2(G)$ (See Fig. 2).*

Lemma 3. *Let G be a planar graph and $R_2(G)$ its reduced graph. The number of vertices in $R_2(G)$ is given by $V_{R_2(G)} = V_G$, its number of edges is given by $E_{R_2(G)} = 2E_G$, its number of faces is $F_{R_2(G)} = F_G + E_G$ and its average degree is $< z >_{R_2(G)} = \frac{2E_{R_2(G)}}{V_{R_2(G)}} = \frac{4E_G}{V_G}$.*

Theorem 3. *Let $R_2(G)$ be a reduced graph of a planar graph G. The number of spanning trees in $R_2(G)$ is given by:*

$$\tau(R_2(G)) = 2^{V_G-1}\tau(G) \tag{3}$$

The main objective of the reduction approach is to reduce the number of links of a network and that makes the complexity easy for computation.

Definition 4. *Let G be a planar graph. The k-reduced graph of G noted $R_k(G)$ is obtained when for each pair of vertices of G, we have k multiple edges connecting them (See Fig. 2).*

Lemma 4. *Let G be a planar graph and $R_k(G)$ its k-reduced graph. The number of vertices in $R_k(G)$ is given by $V_{R_k(G)} = V_G$, its number of edges is given by $E_{R_k(G)} = k \times E_G$, its number of faces is $F_{R_k(G)} = F_G + (k-1)E_G$ and its average degree is $< z >_{R_k(G)} = \frac{2E_{R_k(G)}}{V_{R_k(G)}} = \frac{2k \times E_G}{V_G}$.*

Theorem 4. *Let $R_k(G)$ be a k-reduced graph of a planar graph G. The number of spanning trees in $R_k(G)$ is given by:*

$$\tau(R_k(G)) = k^{V_G-1}\tau(G) \tag{4}$$

3   The Construction and the Topological Properties of the Flower Network

In this section, we introduce the construction of the Flower network which are built in an iterative way. We treat two types of flower graphs: **The 2-Flower graph** based on the reduced and the bipartite approaches (see Fig. 3) and **the k-Flower graph** based on the k-reduced and the k-partite approaches (see Fig. 4). Then, we discuss their topological properties.

3.1 The 2-Flower Graph

The 2-Flower graph denoted by C_n are constructed as follows: For the iteration $n = 0$, we have a simple edge that connects two vertices. For $n \geq 1$, first, we apply the reduced approach by adding a new multiple link for each edge of the graph in the previous iteration. Then, we apply the bipartite approach to this last obtained graph by adding a new vertex in the middle of each edge. We can denote this process by $C_n = h_2^n(C_0) = h_2(C_{n-1}) = B_2 \circ R_2(C_{n-1})$. For illustration, in Fig. 3, we present 3 iterations of the 2-Flower graph.

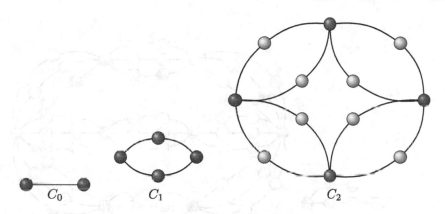

Fig. 3. The 3 iterations of the 2-Flower graph.

According to this construction, the number of edges of C_n is calculated as follows:

$$E_{C_n} = E_{h_2^n(C_0)} = E_{h_2(C_{n-1})} = E_{B_2 \circ R_2(C_{n-1})}$$

Using Lemma 1, we obtain: $E_{C_n} = 2E_{R_2(C_{n-1})}$

And using Lemma 2, we obtain:

$$E_{C_n} = 4E_{C_{n-1}} = 4^2 E_{C_{n-2}} = 4^3 E_{C_{n-3}} = \ldots = 4^n E_{C_0}$$

So the number of edges of C_n is: $E_{C_n} = 2^{2n}$

Similarly, we find:

The number of vertices of C_n: $V_{C_n} = 2 + \frac{2}{3}(2^{2n} - 1)$

The number of faces of C_n: $F_{C_n} = 1 + \frac{2^{2n}-1}{3}$

The average degree of C_n: $<z>_{C_n} = \frac{2E_{C_n}}{V_{C_n}} = \frac{2^{2n+1}}{\frac{4}{3} + \frac{2^{2n+1}}{3}}$

3.2 The k-Flower Graph:

The k-Flower graph denoted by G_n with n is a number of iterations can be created using the following iterative way: For n = 0, we have a simple edge that connects two vertices. For $n \geq 1$, first, we apply the k-reduced approach to obtain k multiple edges connecting each pair of vertices of the graph in the previous iteration. Then, we apply the k-partite approach to this last obtained graph by adding k−1 vertices in each edge. This process can be denoted by $G_n = h_k^n(G_0) = h_k(G_{n-1}) = B_k \circ R_k(G_{n-1})$. In Fig. 4, we illustrate 3 iterations of the k-flower graph with $k = 3$.

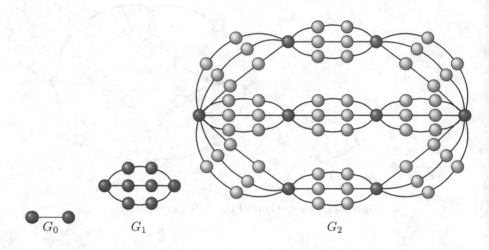

G_0 G_1 G_2

Fig. 4. The 3 iterations of the 3-Flower graph.

Using this construction, it is possible to give the exact values for the properties of the k-Flower graph. The number of edges of G_n is calculated as follows:

$$E_{G_n} = E_{h_k^n(G_0)} = E_{h_k(G_{n-1})} = E_{B_k \circ R_k(G_{n-1})}$$

Using Lemma 2, we obtain: $E_{G_n} = k \times E_{R_k(G_{n-1})}$

And using Lemma 4, we obtain:

$$E_{G_n} = k^2 \times E_{G_{n-1}} = k^4 \times E_{G_{n-2}} = k^6 \times E_{G_{n-3}} = ... = k^{2n} \times E_{G_0}$$

So the number of edges of G_n is $E_{G_n} = k^{2n}$

Similarly, we find:

The number of vertices of G_n: $V_{G_n} = 2 + \frac{k(k^{2n}-1)}{k+1}$

The number of faces of G_n: $F_{G_n} = 1 + \frac{k^{2n}-1}{k+1}$

The average degree of G_n: $< z >_{G_n} = \frac{2E_{G_n}}{V_{G_n}} = \frac{2k^{2n}}{2 + \frac{k(k^{2n}-1)}{k+1}}$

4   The Number of Spanning Trees of a Flower Network

Due to the large size of self-similar networks, their complexity is very difficult to compute, even if we use the theorem of Kirchhoff. For this reason, we use these combinatorial approaches that facilitate this computation. We choose the Flower network as a self-similar network because of its interesting topological structure. Using the above theorems and the proposed methods in the last section, we obtain the exact number of spanning trees in the 2-Flower network and the k-Flower network:

4.1   The Number of Spanning Tree of a 2-Flower Graph:

We combine Our approaches: First, we apply the reduction approach, then the bipartite approach to calculate the number of spanning trees of the 2-Flower graph.

Theorem 5. *Let C_n denote a 2-Flower graph where n is the number of itera-tions. The number of spanning trees of C_n is given by the following formula:*

$$\tau(C_n) = 2^{2[\frac{2^{2n}-1}{3}]} \tag{5}$$

Proof: This process can be presented as:

$$\tau(C_n) = \tau(h_2^n(C_0)) = \tau(h_2(C_{n-1})) = \tau(B_2(R_2(C_{n-1}))).$$

Using Theorem 1, we obtain:

$$\tau(C_n) = 2^{F_{R_2(C_{n-1})}-1} \times \tau(R_2(C_{n-1})) \text{ with } F_{R_2(C_{n-1})} = F_{C_n}$$

Using Theorem 3, we obtain:

$$\tau(C_n) = 2^{F_{C_n}-1} \times 2^{V_{C_{n-1}}-1} \times \tau(C_{n-1}).$$

Using the properties of the 2-Flower graph in Sect. 3, we obtain:

$$\tau(C_n) = 2^{\frac{2^{2n}-1}{3}} \times 2^{1+\frac{2}{3}(2^{2(n-1)}-1)} \times \tau(C_{n-1})$$
$$\tau(C_n) = 2^{2^{2n-1}} \times \tau(C_{n-1})$$
$$\tau(C_n) = 2^{2^{2n-1}+2^{2n-3}} \times \tau(C_{n-2})$$
$$\tau(C_n) = 2^{2^{2n-1}+2^{2n-3}+2^{2n-5}} \times \tau(C_{n-3})$$

$$\vdots$$

$$\tau(C_n) = 2^{2^{2n-1}+2^{2n-3}+2^{2n-5}+\dots+2^1} \times \tau(C_0) \; with \; \tau(C_0) = 1$$
$$\tau(C_n) = 2^{2[(2^2)^{n-1}+(2^2)^{n-2}+(2^2)^{n-3}+\dots+(2^2)^0]}$$
$$\tau(C_n) = 2^{2[\frac{2^{2n}-1}{3}]}.$$

4.2   The Number of Spanning Tree of a k-Flower Graph:

We combine Our approaches: First, we apply the k-reduced approach, then the k-partite approach to evaluate the number of spanning trees of the k-Flower network.

Theorem 6. *Let G_n denote a k-Flower graph where n is the number of iterations. The number of spanning trees of G_n is given by the following formula:*

$$\tau(G_n) = k^{k[\frac{k^{2n}-1}{k^2-1}]} \tag{6}$$

Proof: This process can be presented as:

$$\tau(G_n) = \tau(h_k^n(G_0)) = \tau(h_k(G_{n-1})) = \tau(B_k(R_k(G_{n-1}))).$$

Using Theorem 2, we obtain:

$$\tau(G_n) = k^{F_{R_k(G_{n-1})}-1} \times \tau(R_k(G_{n-1})) \; with \; F_{R_k(G_{n-1})} = F_{G_n}$$

Using Theorem 4, we obtain:

$$\tau(G_n) = k^{F_{G_n}-1} \times k^{V_{G_{n-1}}-1} \times \tau(G_{n-1}).$$

Using the properties of the k-Flower graph in Sect. 3, we obtain:

$$\tau(G_n) = k^{\frac{k^{2n}-1}{k+1}} \times k^{1+\frac{k(k^{2(n-1)}-1)}{k+1}} \times \tau(G_{n-1})$$
$$\tau(G_n) = k^{k^{2n-1}} \times \tau(G_{n-1})$$
$$\tau(G_n) = k^{k^{2n-1}+k^{2n-3}} \times \tau(G_{n-2})$$
$$\tau(G_n) = k^{k^{2n-1}+k^{2n-3}+k^{2n-5}} \times \tau(G_{n-3})$$
$$\vdots$$
$$\tau(G_n) = k^{k^{2n-1}+k^{2n-3}+k^{2n-5}+\dots+k^1} \times \tau(G_0) \; with \; \tau(G_0) = 1$$
$$\tau(G_n) = k^{k[(k^2)^{n-1}+(k^2)^{n-2}+(k^2)^{n-3}+\dots+(k^2)^0]}$$
$$\tau(G_n) = k^{k[\frac{k^{2n}-1}{k^2-1}]}.$$

Based on the Eqs. 5 and 6, we calculate the complexity of the k-Flower network based on its size:

Table 1. The numerical result of the complexity of the k-Flower network G_n.

k	n	$\tau(G_n)$
2	10	$1,0434 \times 10^{210435}$
3	7	$7,67435 \times 10^{855770}$
4	5	$1,0346 \times 10^{168348}$
5	4	$1,5099 \times 10^{56882}$
6	4	$1,5927 \times 10^{224056}$
7	4	$8,3606 \times 10^{710473}$

The numerical result: The below table presents some values of the number of spanning trees or the complexity of the k-Flower network G_n. These computations were performed using Maple by changing the value of the number of iterations n and the dimension of the Flower network k (Table 1).

5   The Spanning Tree Entropy in Flower Network

The entropy of spanning trees of a network or the asymptotic complexity is a quantitative measure of the number of spanning trees and it characterizes the network structure. We use this entropy to quantify the robustness of networks. The most robust network is the network that has the highest entropy. When the spanning trees number of networks grows exponentially with the number of vertices of G_n as $V_{G_n} \to \infty$, there exist a constant ρ_k describing this exponential growth, which is defined as:

$$\rho_k = \lim_{V_{G_n} \to \infty} \frac{\ln \tau(G_n)}{V_{G_n}}. \tag{7}$$

with $\tau(G_n)$ is the number of spanning trees of G_n and V_{G_n} is the number of vertices of G_n.

This formula provides the computation of the spanning tree entropy for the k-Flower graph.

Corollary 1. *The spanning trees entropy of the k-Flower graph is given by:*

$$\rho_k = \frac{\ln(k)}{k-1} \tag{8}$$

Proof: We calculate the spanning trees entropy of a k-Flower network by: $\rho_k = \lim_{V_{G_n} \to \infty} \frac{\ln |\tau(G_n)|}{|V_{G_n}|} = \lim_{V_{G_n} \to \infty} \frac{\ln(k^{[\frac{k^{2n}-1}{k^2-1}]})}{2+\frac{k(k^{2n}-1)}{k+1}} = \lim_{V_{G_n} \to \infty} \frac{\ln(k) \times (k+1)}{k^2-1}.$

Then, the result. Similarly, we can find the entropy of the 2-Flower graph:

$$\rho_2 = \ln 2 = 0.6931$$

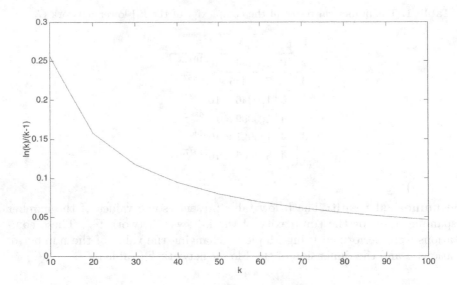

Fig. 5. The spanning tree entropy of the k-Flower graph

Knowing the number of spanning trees for the Flower network allows us to calculate its spanning tree entropy. In Fig. 5, we show that the entropy of spanning trees of the k-Flower graph varies with the dimension k and the increasing of this value leads to decrement the entropy of spanning trees. From this result, we deduce that the Flower networks with a higher dimension are less robust than those with a lower dimension.

6   Comparison with Other Networks Having the Same Average Degree

The value of ρ_2 is compared with the entropy of other networks having the same average degree (See the table below). The bigger the entropy value, the more the number of spanning trees, the network is more robust with the stronger heterogeneous topology because the increase of the number of spanning trees provides more possibilities of connecting two nodes related by defective links, that ensures a good reliability, robustness and availability of communication networks.

From the Table 2, we compare the entropy of the spanning trees of the 2-Flower network C_n with those of other networks with the same average degree. We notice the value of the entropy of the spanning trees of the 2-Flower network is the highest reported for the Koch networks and the Hanoi networks and it is the lowest reported for the 3-2-12 lattices, the 4-8-8 bathroom tile and Honeycomb lattice. This reflects the fact that the 2-Flower network has an average spanning tree rate compared to other networks with the same average degree.

Table 2. The entropy of several networks having the same average degree.

Type of network	$< z >$	ρ
Koch network [10]	3	0.549
Hanoi networks [11]	3	0.677
2-Flower networks	**3**	**0.6931**
The 3-2-12 lattices [12]	3	0.721
The 4-8-8 bathroom tile [12]	3	0.787
Honeycomb lattice [13]	3	0.807

This result proves that the 2-Flower network is more robust than the Koch networks and the Hanoi networks, on the other hand, the 2-Flower network is less robust than the 3-2-12 lattices, the 4-8-8 bathroom tile and Honeycomb lattice.

7 Conclusion

The concept of spanning tree entropy of a network is used to measure network robustness. In this paper, we have investigated a family of self-similar complex networks: A Flower network. We proposed two combinatorial approaches: The bipartition and the reduction to construct this network, to determine its topological properties and calculate its number of spanning trees. Finally, we evaluated its spanning tree entropy and compared it with those for other studied networks with the same average degree in order to estimate the most robust network between them.

References

1. Cook, A., Zanin, M.: Complex network theory. In: Complexity Science in Air Traffic Management, vol. 9 (2016)
2. Gao, J., et al.: Robustness of a network of networks. Phys. Rev. Lett. **107**(19), 195701 (2011)
3. Sorkhoh, I., Mahdi, K., Safar, M.: Cyclic entropy of complex networks. In: 2012 IEEE/ACM International Conference on Advances in Social Networks Analysis and Mining (ASONAM). IEEE (2012)
4. Lyons, R.: Asymptotic enumeration of spanning trees. Comb. Probab. Comput. **14**(04), 491–522 (2005)
5. Wu, B.Y., Chao, K.-M.: Spanning Trees and Optimization Problems. CRC Press, Boca Raton (2004)
6. Kirchhoff, G.: Ueber die Auflsung der Gleichungen, auf welche man bei der Untersuchung der linearen Vertheilung galvanischer Strme gefhrt wird. Annalen der Physik **148**(12), 497–508 (1847)
7. Merris, R.: Laplacian matrices of graphs: a survey. Linear Algebra Appl. **197**, 143–176 (1994)
8. Lin, Y., et al.: Counting spanning trees in self-similar networks by evaluating determinants. J. Math. Phys. **52**(11), 113303 (2011)

9. Lotfi, D., Marraki, M.E., Aboutajdine, D.: The enumeration of spanning trees in dual, bipartite and reduced graphs. J. Discrete Math. Sci. Crypt. **18**(6), 673–687 (2015)
10. Zhang, Z., et al.: Mapping Koch curves into scale-free small-world networks. J. Phys. A Math. Theor. **43**(39), 395101 (2010)
11. Zhang, Z., et al.: The number and degree distribution of spanning trees in the Tower of Hanoi graph. Theor. Comput. Sci. **609**, 443–455 (2016)
12. Wu, F.Y.: Number of spanning trees on a lattice. J. Phys. A Math. Gen. **10**(6), L113 (1977)
13. Shrock, R., Fa Yueh, W.: Spanning trees on graphs and lattices in d dimensions. J. Phys. A Math. Gen. **33**(21), 3881 (2000)

A Dynamic Genetic Algorithm Approach to the Problem of UMTS Network Assignment

Mohammed Gabli[1(✉)], Soufiane Dahmani[2], El Bekkaye Mermri[3], and Abdelhafid Serghini[2]

[1] Department of Computer Science, Faculty of Science (FSO),
University Mohammed Premier, BV Mohammed VI, Oujda, Morocco
medgabli@yahoo.fr
[2] LANO Laboratory, ESTO-FSO, University Mohammed Premier,
BV Mohammed VI, Oujda, Morocco
dahmani.soufiane@gmail.com, a.serghini@ump.ma
[3] Department of Mathematics, FSO, University Mohammed Premier,
BV Mohammed VI, Oujda, Morocco
mermri@hotmail.com

Abstract. The problem of the universal mobile telecommunication system (UMTS) network assignment is divided into two assignment sub-problems: the assignment of a set of Nodes Bs to a set of radio network controllers (RNCs), and the assignment of those RNC concurrently to a set of Mobile Switching Centers (MSCs) and a set of Serving GPRS Support Nodes (SGSNs). The objective is to find an assignment that minimizes the cost of such implementation.

This paper proposes, first, an improvement of the existing mathematical modelling. Second, it presents a solution method to the problem based on genetic algorithms with a dynamic approach. To compare our proposed model to the existing one, some numerical examples are given. The obtained results show the efficiency of our model and our approach.

Keywords: UMTS · Optimization · Cell assignment · Genetic algorithms

1 Introduction

The deployment of Universal Mobile Telecommunications System (UMTS) network involves a huge investment mainly related to the cost of infrastructure. It is therefore necessary to optimize these networks to reduce the cost of its investments, and ensure a good quality of service to users. In UMTS networks, the assignment problem takes into account three levels of equipments. The first level consists of Node Bs (one Node B per cell), whereas the second level consists of Radio Network Controllers (RNC), and the third level includes both Mobile Switching Centers (MSCs) and Serving GPRS Support Nodes (SGSNs) (see for instance [1]). As illustrated in Fig. 1, each Node B is connected with an RNC, and each RNC is permanently connected with an MSC and an SGSN. In this

© Springer International Publishing AG 2017
A. El Abbadi and B. Garbinato (Eds.): NETYS 2017, LNCS 10299, pp. 15–26, 2017.
DOI: 10.1007/978-3-319-59647-1_2

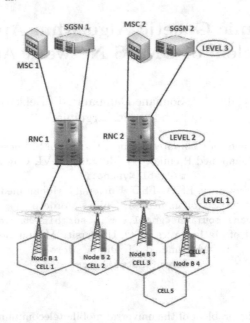

Fig. 1. Example of UMTS assignment problem

context, the cell assignment problem consists of assigning first, Node Bs to RNCs in an optimal way, then RNCs to MSCs and SGSNs in order to provide mobile users with simultaneous voice and data services.

On the other hand, two types of handoff are taken into account in UMTS networks.

– *Simple handoff.* It occurs when a user moves from one Node B to another Node B', as both Nodes B and B' are connected with RNCs that are served by the same MSC and the same SGSN.
– *Complex handoff.* It occurs when a user moves from one Node to another, and two MSCs and two SGSNs are involved in the process. So this type of handoff needs transferring data from one MSC to another MSC and from one SGSN to another SGSN.

Complex handoff is more costly than a simple handoff.

1.1   Related Work

UMTS networks planning problems have been the interest of many researchers. Indeed, Kumar et al. (2002) [2] presented a multi-objective genetic algorithm approach to design telecommunication networks while simultaneously minimizing network performance and design costs under a reliability constraint. Juttner et al. (2005) [3] used a combination of simulated annealing and a specific b-matching method to determine the cost-optimal number and location of the Radio Network Controller (RNC) nodes and their connections to the Radio Base

Stations (RBS) according to a number of planning constraints. Hashemi et al. (2008) [4] examined the same problem but this time by using the hybrid ant colony algorithm. Amaldi et al. (2003) [5] studied the UMTS base station (BS) location problem based on propagation models with power control. To solve the problem, authors proposed two randomized greedy procedures and a tabu search algorithm. St-Hilaire et al. (2006) [6] proposed a global approach for planning UMTS networks in the uplink direction using local search heuristic. Gabli et al. (2013) [7] proposed a genetic algorithm approach and a dynamic trade-off parameter to solve the UMTS base station (BS) location planning problem. To deal with the imprecise and uncertain information of prices (costs), Gabli et al. (2014 and 2016) addressed the same problem using fuzzy logic [8] and a possibility theory approach [9], respectively. However, all those approaches have only solved the problem of assigning Node Bs to RNCs. For solving the global problem, Mamadou et al. [1] among other, considered in the same formulation not only the assignment of Node Bs to radio network controllers (RNCs), but also the assignment of RNCs to Mobile Switching Centers (MSCs) and Serving GPRS Support Nodes (SGSNs). Moreover in [1], authors propose a model formulation and a solution which take the mobility aspects into account by integrating the handoff costs into the cost function.

In this paper we focus on the last problem which is divided into two assignment sub-problems: the assignment of a set of Nodes Bs to a set of RNCs, and the assignment of those RNC concurrently to a set of MSCs and a set of SGSNs. We describe, in Sect. 2, the problem and we present its mathematical modelling. In Sect. 2.2, we propose an improvement of the existing mathematical modelling. In Sect. 3, we present a dynamic approach using genetic algorithm. To compare our proposed model to the existing one, we give in Sect. 4 some applications of our approach, then we present the obtained numerical results. Finally, in Sect. 5 we give some concluding remarks.

2   Problem Statement and Model Presentation

Consider a territory to be covered by an *UMTS* service. Let $I = \{1, ..., n\}$ be a set of Nodes *Bs*, $J = \{1, ..., r\}$ a set of *RNCs*, $K = \{1, ..., m\}$ a set of *MSCs* and $L = \{1, ..., s\}$ a set of *SGSNs*. In this paper, we consider the same assumptions as presented in [1].

- The locations of Nodes *Bs*, *RNCs*, *MSCs* and *SGSNs* are known;
- Each Node *B* is connected with one *RNC* and each *RNC* is simultaneously connected with one *MSC* and one *SGSN*;
- The costs, types and capacities of links used to connect a pair of equipments are known;
- The connection costs between a pair of equipments are known. Such costs include both link and installation costs;
- The total capacities of the links connected with an equipment cannot exceed the capacity of that equipment, in terms of circuits, bits per second, and maximum number of interfaces that can be installed on that equipment.

Table 1. Notations

c_{12}^{ij}	Cost of connecting B_i to RNC_j
c_{23}^{jk}	Cost of connecting RNC_j to MSC_k
c_{24}^{jl}	Cost of connecting RNC_j to $SGSN_l$
w_2^{vj}	Circuit switching capacity of RNC_j
w_2^{dj}	Packet switching capacity of RNC_j (in bps)
w_3^{vk}	Capacity of MSC_k (number of calls per unit of time)
w_4^{dl}	Capacity of $SGSN_l$ (in bps)
f_{12}^{vi}	Amount of voice traffic from Node B_i
f_{12}^{di}	Amount of data traffic from Node B_i
f_{23}^{vj}	Amount of voice traffic from RNC_j
f_{24}^{dj}	Amount of data traffic from RNC_j
$h_3^{ii'}$	Reduced costs per unit of time of complex handoffs involving two $MSCs$
$h_4^{ii'}$	Reduced costs per unit of time of complex handoffs involving two $SGSNs$

In this section we will need the notations presented in Table 1. We see that

$$f_{23}^{vj} = \sum_{i=1}^{n} f_{12}^{vi}, \quad \forall j \in J \text{ such as } B_i \text{ is assigned to } RNC_j$$

and

$$f_{24}^{dj} = \sum_{i=1}^{n} f_{12}^{di}, \quad \forall j \in J \text{ such as } B_i \text{ is assigned to } RNC_j$$

2.1 Model Presentation

Let us define the three following classes of decision variables:

$$x_{12}^{ij} = \begin{cases} 1 \text{ if } B_i \text{ is assigned to a } RNC_j, \\ 0 \text{ otherwise.} \end{cases} \quad \text{for } i \in I \text{ and } j \in J. \quad (1)$$

$$x_{23}^{jk} = \begin{cases} 1 \text{ if } RNC_j \text{ is assigned to a } MSC_k, \\ 0 \text{ otherwise.} \end{cases} \quad \text{for } j \in J \text{ and } k \in K. \quad (2)$$

$$x_{24}^{jl} = \begin{cases} 1 \text{ if } RNC_j \text{ is assigned to a } SGSN_l, \\ 0 \text{ otherwise.} \end{cases} \quad \text{for } j \in J \text{ and } l \in L. \quad (3)$$

Let $z_{12}^{ii'j}$ and $y_{12}^{ii'}$ be defined as:

$$z_{12}^{ii'j} = x_{12}^{ij} \times x_{12}^{i'j} \text{ and } y_{12}^{ii'} = \sum_{j \in J} z_{12}^{ii'j}.$$

It is clear that $z_{12}^{ii'j} = 1$ if Node B_i and Node B_i' are both assigned to the RNC_j; and $y_{12}^{ii'} = 1$ if Node B_i and Node B_i' are both assigned to one and only one RNC. In the same way, we define $z_{23}^{jj'k}$, $y_{23}^{jj'}$, $z_{24}^{jj'l}$ and $y_{24}^{jj'}$:

$$z_{23}^{jj'k} = x_{23}^{jk} \times x_{23}^{j'k}, \; y_{23}^{jj'} = \sum_{j \in J} z_{23}^{jj'k}, \; z_{24}^{jj'l} = x_{24}^{jl} \times x_{24}^{j'l} \text{ and } y_{24}^{jj'} = \sum_{j \in J} z_{24}^{jj'l}.$$

Since we must consider two assignment sub-problems, the total cost function will be divided into two parts: the cost of assigning Nodes Bs to $RNCs$, which is denoted f_1, and the cost of assigning $RNCs$ to $MSCs$ and $SGSNs$, which is denoted f_2. In this case, f_1 and f_2 are expressed in [1] as follows:

$$f_1 = \sum_{i \in I} \sum_{j \in J} c_{12}^{ij} x_{12}^{ij} \tag{4}$$

and

$$f_2 = \sum_{j \in J} \sum_{k \in K} c_{23}^{jk} x_{23}^{jk} + \sum_{j \in J} \sum_{l \in L} c_{24}^{jl} x_{24}^{jl}$$
$$+ \sum_{i \in I} \sum_{i' \in I} \sum_{j \in J} \sum_{j' \in J} h_3^{ii'} \times (1 - y_{12}^{ii'}) \times (1 - y_{23}^{jj'})$$
$$+ \sum_{i \in I} \sum_{i' \in I} \sum_{j \in J} \sum_{j' \in J} h_4^{ii'} \times (1 - y_{12}^{ii'}) \times (1 - y_{24}^{jj'}) \tag{5}$$

subject to:

$$\sum_{j \in J} x_{12}^{ij} = 1, \quad i \in I, \tag{6}$$

which means that each B_i must be assigned to only one RNC_j.

$$\sum_{k \in K} x_{23}^{jk} = 1, \quad j \in J, \tag{7}$$

$$\sum_{l \in L} x_{24}^{jl} = 1, \quad l \in L, \tag{8}$$

which means that each RNC_j must be assigned to only one MSC_k and only one $SGSN_l$, respectively.

$$\sum_{i \in I} f_{12}^{vi} . x_{12}^{ij} \leq w_2^{vj} \quad j \in J, \tag{9}$$

$$\sum_{i \in I} f_{12}^{di} . x_{12}^{ij} \leq w_2^{dj} \quad j \in J, \tag{10}$$

which means that the traffic generated by all Nodes Bs connected with RNC_j cannot exceed the RNC capacities in terms of voice and data traffic.

$$\sum_{j \in J} f_{23}^{vj} . x_{23}^{jk} \leq w_3^{vk} \quad k \in K, \tag{11}$$

$$\sum_{j \in J} f_{24}^{dj} . x_{24}^{jl} \leq w_4^{dl} \quad l \in L, \tag{12}$$

which means that voice traffic from the $RNCs$ to MSC_k and data traffic from the $RNCs$ to $SGSN_l$ cannot exceed the MSC and the $SGSN$ capacities, respectively.

According to [1], among others, the global problem consists in minimizing the objective function $f_1 + f_2$ subject to the constraints (6), (7), (8), (9), (10), (11) and (12).

2.2   Improvement of Mathematical Modeling

As we saw in the previous section, to minimize f_1 and minimize f_2, the authors in [1] choose to oversimplify the problem by minimizing $f_1 + f_2$.

In our view, this simplification is not always reasonable. Indeed, minimizing f_1 and minimizing f_2 generate a multi-objective problem. A reasonable solution to a multi-objective problem is to determine an entire Pareto optimal solution set, or to transform this multi-objective problem into an appropriate mono-objective one. In this section, we will show the drawback of the existing model, then we present our improved mathematical modeling.

Assume that f_1 is much greater than f_2. When applying genetic algorithm (GA) to minimize the objective function $f_1 + f_2$, there is a great risk that the GA selection procedure chooses only solutions which improve f_1 by neglecting f_2, since the function f_1 dominates f_2. Now, we present our mathematical modeling of the global assignment problem.

Consider the two sub-problems (4) and (5) subject to the constraints (6), (7), (8), (9), (10), (11) and (12). Since we wish to minimize f_1 and minimize f_2 simultaneously, then the global assignment problem can be expressed as a multi-objective problem. In our approach, we transform this multi-objective problem into a mono-objective one as follows:

$$\text{Minimize } w_1 f_1 + w_2 f_2, \tag{13}$$

subject to the constraints (6), (7), (8), (9), (10), (11) and (12), where the weights w_1 and w_2 are positive values satisfying $w_1 + w_2 = 1$.

In the literature, the weights are usually taken as constants. In [10], authors show that, when using genetic algorithm (GA) to solve problem (13), it is not always appropriate to take w_1 and w_2 as constants. Instead, they introduce dynamic weights. Therefore, our problem (13) becomes:

$$\begin{cases} \text{Minimize } w_1(t)f_1 + w_2(t)f_2 \\ |w_1(t)f_1 - w_2(t)f_2| \prec \varepsilon, \end{cases} \tag{14}$$

subject to the constraints (6), (7), (8), (9), (10), (11) and (12), where ε is a positif number in the vicinity of 0, t is a time-step (in this paper it is an iteration step of the genetic algorithm), and $w_i(t)$, $i = 1, 2$, are dynamic weights satisfying $w_1(t) + w_2(t) = 1$.

Since the global assignment problem is NP-hard (see for instance [1,11]), then it is more appropriate to use metaheuristics method in order to find good solutions in reasonable computing time. In this paper, we use genetic algorithm (GA) method. In the next section, we describe how to use GA method and we present a dynamic approach to choose the weights w_1 and w_2.

3 Dynamic Genetic Algorithm Approach

Genetic algorithm (GA) is a search and optimization technique that mimics natural evolution. GA has already a relatively old history since the first work of John Holland on the adaptive systems goes back to 1962 [12]. The work of David Goldberg [13] largely contributed to popularize the GA. GA is inspired by the evolutionist theory explaining the origin of species. In GA terminology, a solution x is called an individual or a chromosome. Chromosomes are made of discrete units called genes. The main components of a GA are: selection, crossover and mutation.

3.1 Proposed Solution Method Using Genetic Algorithms

Consider the problem presented in Sect. 2.2 and described by Eq. (14).

Chromosome Representation

To code the chromosome we use integer coding as follows. If we have n nodes Bs, r radio network controllers (RNCs), m Mobile Switching Centers (MSCs) and s Serving GPRS Support Nodes (SGSNs), then the chromosome will have $(n + 2 \times r)$ genes, where the first n genes present the assignment of Bs to RNCs, the second r genes present the assignment of RNCs to MSCs and the remanning r genes present the assignment of RNCs to SGSNs. For example, if we have $n = 6$, $r = 3$, $m = 2$ and $s = 2$, then the chromosome 213121122112 means that the B_1 is assigned to RNC_2, $\cdots$, B_6 to RNC_1, RNC_1 to MSC_1, $\cdots$, RNC_3 to MSC_2 and RNC_1 to $SGSN_1, \cdots$, RNC_3 to $SGSN_2$.

Initial Population

Suppose we have n nodes Bs, r RNCs, m MSCs and s SGSNs. To define each chromosome of the population we generate $(n + 2 \times r)$ random genes; the first n genes are integers in the set $\{1, \ldots, r\}$, the second r genes are integers in the set $\{1, \ldots, m\}$ and the remaining r genes are integers in the set $\{1, \ldots, s\}$.

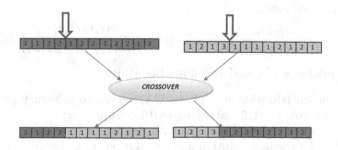

Fig. 2. Illustration of crossover operator

Crossover and Mutation

For crossover operator, a single crossover point on both parents' chromosomes is selected. All data beyond that point in either chromosome is swapped between the two parent chromosomes. The resulting organisms are the new chromosomes (children). Figure 2 illustrates this operator.

For mutation, we choose a random position. If the gene to mutate is a Bs, we replace it by an integer chosen randomly from the set $\{1, 2, \ldots, r\}$. If the mutation position is between $(n + 1)$ and $(n + r)$, we replace the selected gene by an integer chosen randomly from the set $\{1, 2, \ldots, m\}$. Finally, if the mutation position is between $(n + r + 1)$ and $(n + 2 \times r)$, we replace the selected gene by an integer chosen randomly from the set $\{1, 2, \ldots, s\}$. Figure 3 illustrates this operator.

Fig. 3. Illustration of mutation operator

3.2 Genetic Algorithm and Dynamic Weights

In this section we present a GA approach using dynamic weights, as proposed by Gabli et al. in [10]. Let $g(x, t) = w_1(t)f_1(x) + w_2(t)f_2(x)$, be the fitness function of the GA. In each iteration t of the GA we take:

$$w_1(t) = \frac{|f_2(x_{t-1})|}{|f_1(x_{t-1})| + |f_2(x_{t-1})|} \quad \text{and} \quad w_2(t) = \frac{|f_1(x_{t-1})|}{|f_1(x_{t-1})| + |f_2(x_{t-1})|},$$

where x_{t-1} is the best solution of the iteration $(t - 1)$ of the GA; if $f_1(x_{t-1}) = f_2(x_{t-1}) = 0$, then we take $w_1(t) := w_1(t - 1)$ and $w_2(t) := w_2(t - 1)$. It is easy to see that $0 \le w_i(t) < 1$, $i = 1, 2$, and $w_1(t) + w_2(t) = 1$. In this case, the fitness function becomes

$$g(x, t) = \frac{|f_2(x_{t-1})|}{|f_1(x_{t-1})| + |f_2(x_{t-1})|} f_1(x) + \frac{|f_1(x_{t-1})|}{|f_1(x_{t-1})| + |f_2(x_{t-1})|} f_2(x).$$

Then the algorithm is outlined as follows (see [10]):

Step 0. At the initialization step of the GA, we assign arbitrary positive real numbers to $w_i(0)$, $i = 1, 2$, satisfying $w_1(0) + w_2(0) = 1$;

Step 1. Run an iteration t of the GA, with the fitness function g;

Step 2. Let x_t be the best solution among solutions of the current population;

Step 3. Calculate $f_i(x_t)$, $i = 1, 2$;

Step 4. If $|f_1(x_t)| + |f_2(x_t)| \neq 0$ then take

$$w_1(t + 1) := \frac{|f_2(x_t)|}{|f_1(x_t)| + |f_2(x_t)|}, \quad w_2(t + 1) := \frac{|f_1(x_t)|}{|f_1(x_t)| + |f_2(x_t)|};$$

Step 5. $t := t + 1$;

Step 6. Repeat steps 1 through 5 until a stopping criterion is satisfied.

This algorithm has two immediate advantages:

- It automates the choice of the weights.
- It ensures an equitable treatment of each objective function, so we have an equitable chance to minimize both functions f_1, and f_2. For more detail, see [10].

4 Application

4.1 Data Description

To evaluate the performance of the proposed algorithm, we consider three instances of the problem. For each instance, four discrete parameters are specified: the number of Nodes Bs, the number of RNCs, the number of MSCs and the number of SGSNs. Using a pseudorandom number generator, each parameter is assigned a position in the service area. The simulation instances are presented in Table 2.

Table 2. Number of Bs, RNCs, MSCs and SGSNs for each instance of problem.

	Number of Bs	Number of RNCs	Number of MSCs	Number of SGSNs
First instance	6	3	2	2
Second instance	15	8	3	3
Third instance	100	20	4	4

For each instance of problem, we consider the following simulation data:

- Node B to RNC connection cost;
- RNC to MSC connection cost;
- RNC to SGSN connection cost;
- Handoff costs (involving MSCs) between each pair of Nodes Bs;
- Handoff costs (involving SGSNs) between each pair of Nodes Bs;
- Voice traffic from each Node B;
- Data traffic from each Node B;
- Capacity of each equipment.

Throughout this application, input costs are taken randomly.

4.2   Computational Results

The algorithms were coded in JAVA programming language and implemented on a machine of *CPU Intel Core2Duo-2GHz* and memory *RAM 2Go*. In the GA approaches we have used three selection methods; roulette, scaling and sharing. After several experiments, we decided to take the parameters of GA as follows: crossover probability $p_c = 0.5$, mutation probability $p_m = 0.01$, population size $ps = 10$, $ps = 15$ and $ps = 20$ for first, second and third instance, respectively, and maximum number of generations is respectively 50, 300 and 1000. In the sharing selection method, the threshold of dissimilarity between two parents is taken as $\sigma_s = ps/2$, and $\alpha = 1$. Each experiment were conducted on ten times. Tables 3, 4 and 5 show average and best cost with the simple method $(f_1 + f_2)$ and with our dynamic method for the three instances of problem, respectively.

Table 3. First instance of assignment problem: comparison between $f_1 + f_2$ and $w_1 f_1 + w_2 f_2$ with dynamic weights.

Method of selection	Average cost $(f_1 + f_2)$	Average cost (dynamic weights)	Best cost $(f_1 + f_2)$	Best cost (dynamic weights)	Time in second
Roulette	85.35	**70.62**	59.66	**55.3**	1.49
Scaling	65.06	**62.38**	56.41	**52.23**	1.52
Sharing	67.96	**59.2**	50.25	**48.5**	1.52

Table 4. Second instance of assignment problem: comparison between $f_1 + f_2$ and $w_1 f_1 + w_2 f_2$ with dynamic weights.

Method of selection	Average cost $(f_1 + f_2)$	Average cost (dynamic weights)	Best cost $(f_1 + f_2)$	Best cost (dynamic weights)	Time in second
Roulette	775.85	**774.07**	720.32	**660.59**	2.83
Scaling	844.88	**812.62**	754.37	**710.88**	2.92
Sharing	861.65	**830.73**	761.52	**712.89**	2.93

Table 5. Third instance of assignment problem: comparison between $f_1 + f_2$ and $w_1 f_1 + w_2 f_2$ with dynamic weights.

Method of selection	Average cost $(f_1 + f_2)$	Average cost (dynamic weights)	Best cost $(f_1 + f_2)$	Best cost (dynamic weights)	Time in second
Roulette	61166.25	**60648.88**	57933.70	**56314.04**	9.8
Scaling	60208.42	**60176.74**	57173.52	**55997.48**	10.5
Sharing	61236.90	**60896.4**	58698.95	**57598.68**	10.6

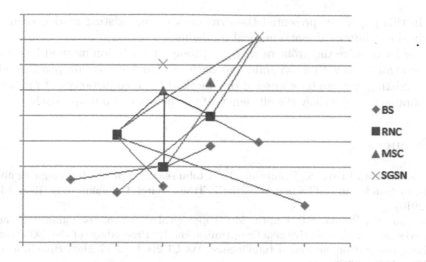

Fig. 4. Presentation of a solution to the first instance of problem.

When we compare the average costs and the best costs with our method and with the simple method, we find that our method gives the best solutions in the three instances of problem. In the details, the best solution in the first instance is given by the sharing selection method with a cost equal to 48.5 (see the third line in Table 3), the best solution in the second instance is given by the roulette selection method with a cost equal to 660.59 (see the first line in Table 4) and the best solution in the third instance is given by the scaling selection method with a cost equal to 55997.48 (see the second line in Table 5). Figure 4 presents the best assignment solution to the first instance of problem, using roulette method which is *231231111222*.

5   Conclusion

In this paper we have considered the problem of the universal mobile telecommunication system (UMTS) network assignment. In this context, the total cost function will be divided into two parts: the cost of assigning a set of Nodes Bs to a set of radio network controllers (RNCs), which is denoted f_1, and the cost of assigning those RNC concurrently to a set of Mobile Switching Centers (MSCs) and a set of Serving GPRS Support Nodes (SGSNs), which is denoted f_2. The objective is to find an assignment that minimizes the cost of such implementation, i.e. that minimizes f_1 and minimizes f_2.

In the literature, authors choose to oversimplify the problem by minimizing $f_1 + f_2$. In our view, this simplification is not always reasonable. Indeed, minimize f_1 and minimize f_2 generate a multi-objective problem. A reasonable solution to a multi-objective problem is to determine an entire Pareto optimal solution set, or to transform this multi-objective problem into an appropriate mono-objective one. In this paper, we presented the drawback of the existing model, then we described our improved mathematical modeling.

In order to solve the problem we have proposed a solution method based on genetic algorithms with a dynamic approach. To compare our proposed model to the existing one, we have applied our method to three instances of problem. The obtained results show the efficiency of our model and our approach.

References

1. Diallo, M.M., Pierre, S., Beaubrun, R.: A tabu search approach for assigning node Bs to switches in UMTS networks. IEEE Trans. Wirel. Commun. **9**(4), 1350–1359 (2010)
2. Kumar, R., Parida, P.P, Gupta, M.: Topological design of communication networks using multiobjective genetic optimization. In: Proceedings of the 2002 World Congress on Computational Intelligence, WCCI 2002, 12–17 May, Honolulu, HI, USA. IEEE (2002)
3. Juttner, A., Orban, A., Fiala, Z.: Two new algorithms for UMTS access network topology design. Eur. J. Oper. Res. **164**, 456–474 (2005)
4. Hashemi, S.M., Moradi, A., Rezapour, M.: An ACO algorithm to design UMTS access network using divided and conquer technique. Eng. Appl. Artif. Intell. **21**, 931–940 (2008)
5. Amaldi, E., Capone, A., Malucelli, F.: Planning UMTS base station location: optimization models with power control and algorithms. IEEE Trans. Wirel. Commun. **2**, 939–952 (2003)
6. St-Hilaire, M., Chamberland, S., Pierre, S.: Uplink UMTS network design-an integrated approach. Comput. Netw. **50**, 2747–2761 (2006)
7. Gabli, M., Jaara, E.M., Mermri, E.B.: Planning UMTS base station location using genetic algorithm with a dynamic trade-off parameter. In: Gramoli, V., Guerraoui, R. (eds.) NETYS 2013. LNCS, vol. 7853, pp. 120–134. Springer, Heidelberg (2013). doi:10.1007/978-3-642-40148-0_9
8. Gabli, M., Jaara, E.M., Mermri, E.B.: UMTS base-station location problem for uplink direction using genetic algorithms and fuzzy logic. In: Noubir, G., Raynal, M. (eds.) NETYS 2014. LNCS, vol. 8593, pp. 257–269. Springer, Cham (2014). doi:10.1007/978-3-319-09581-3_18
9. Gabli, M., Jaara, E.M., Mermri, E.B.: A possibilistic approach to UMTS base-station location problem. Soft. Comput. **20**(7), 2565–2575 (2016)
10. Gabli, M., Jaara, E.M., Mermri, E.B.: A genetic algorithm approach for an equitable treatment of objective functions in multi-objective optimization problems. IAENG Int. J. Comput. Sci. **41**(2), 102–111 (2014)
11. Merchant, A., Sengupta, B.: Assignment of cells to switches in PCS networks. IEEE-ACM Trans. Netw. **3**(5), 521–526 (1995)
12. Holland, J.: Outline for a logical theory of adaptive systems. J. Assoc. Comput. Mach. **9**(3), 297–314 (1962)
13. Goldberg, D.E.: Genetic Algorithms in Search, Optimization, and Machine Learning. Addison-Wesley, Boston (1989)

Improving Network Lifetime of Ad Hoc Network Using Energy Aodv (E-AODV) Routing Protocol in Real Radio Environments

Hassan Faouzi[1](✉), Mohamed Er-rouidi[1], Houda Moudni[1],
Hicham Mouncif[2], and Mohamed Lamsaadi[2]

[1] Sultan Moulay Slimane University, FST,
Beni Mellal, Morocco
faouzi.hassan.mi@gmail.com,
{m.errouidi,h.moudni}@usms.ma
[2] Sultan Moulay Slimane University, FP,
Beni Mellal, Morocco
{hmouncif,lamsaadima}@yahoo.fr

Abstract. One of the very serious problems facing a MANET (Mobile Ad hoc Network) is very limited life of its mobile nodes. Most MANET routing protocols use hop count as the cost metric, so the nodes along shortest paths may be used more often and exhaust their batteries faster, these protocols do not consider the energy problem because there is no exchange of information on the state of mobile nodes between the MAC protocol (Medium Access Control) and the routing protocols in order to support the power saving mechanisms. In this paper we propose the improvements of one of the most important routing protocols that is AODV (Ad hoc On demand Distance Vector). These improvements take into account a metric based on energy consumption during route discovery, thereby increasing the network lifetime, packet delivery ratio and decreasing load of control packets. Most researches in this domain are based on an ideal radio channel, in which a successful transmission is guaranteed if the distance between nodes is less than a certain threshold. However, wireless communication links normally suffer from the characteristics of realistic physical layer. So in order to give credibility to our work we use a realistic physical layer by modeling transmission errors by the Gilbert-Elliot model.

Keywords: Mobile Ad-hoc Network · Routing protocols · AODV · Energy consumption · NS2(Simulator) · Radio channel · Control overhead · Quality of Service (QoS) · Markov chain · Gilbert-Elliot model

1 Introduction

Ad-hoc network is a collection of mobile nodes forming a network topology, operating without alternative base station and without centralized administration. For MANET the most important is probably to establish optimization criteria for energy conservation because the energy depletion of a node does not only affect its ability to communicate

© Springer International Publishing AG 2017
A. El Abbadi and B. Garbinato (Eds.): NETYS 2017, LNCS 10299, pp. 27–39, 2017.
DOI: 10.1007/978-3-319-59647-1_3

but could actually cause network partitioning. MANET routing protocols use in general the same metric (number of hops) so the choice of a route can deplete some nodes because they do not take into consideration the energy consumption in the choice of route. Our work is a part of the study of the routing problem in mobile ad hoc networks in which we propose an improvement of AODV [1] protocol using a metric based on the energy in order to prolong the nodes lifetime and thus the network lifetime. Our proposition will be implemented and simulated in NS2 [2] to show the impact on QoS including the consumption of energy in the network.

The rest of this paper is organized as follows: Sect. 2 gives a brief description of the AODV protocol. Section 3 presents a discussion on the related works in this area, Sect. 4 the details working of the proposed E-AODV, Sect. 5 shows the simulation environment, Experimental Results and Discussions. Conclusion and future work are given in Sect. 6.

2 AODV Protocol

AODV is essentially an improved proactive DSDV [3] algorithm. It is an on demand algorithm, meaning that it builds routes between nodes only as desired by source nodes. The AODV protocol reduces the number of broadcasts of messages. A node broadcasts a route request (RREQ) if it would need to know a route to a destination and that this route is not available. It can happen in one of three cases: if the destination is not known beforehand, it became defective or if the existing path to the destination has expired its lifetime. After the broadcast of RREQ, the source waits for the route reply packet (RREP) if it is not received after some time (called RREP_WAIT_TIME), the source can resume the process of looking for destination by a new request RREQ. A node receiving the RREQ may send a route reply (RREP) if it is either the destination or if it has a matching route in its routing table. In this last case the RREQ is not forwarded but a RREP is sent to make the discovery more efficient less delay and less overhead. To maintain consistent route, periodic transmission of the message "HELLO" (which is a RREP with TTL (Time To Live) 1) is performed. If three messages "HELLO" are not consecutively received from a neighboring node, the link in question is considered failed. The process of execution the RREQ, RREP and HELLO message of AODV protocol is presented in Fig. 1.

When choosing a route, AODV routing protocol only considers the path that is the shortest without considering the energy of the nodes. So when AODV routing protocol chooses the routes, it is very necessary to consider the residual energy of nodes, so it is necessary to improve this protocol to solve the problem of energy consumption in MANET routing nodes.

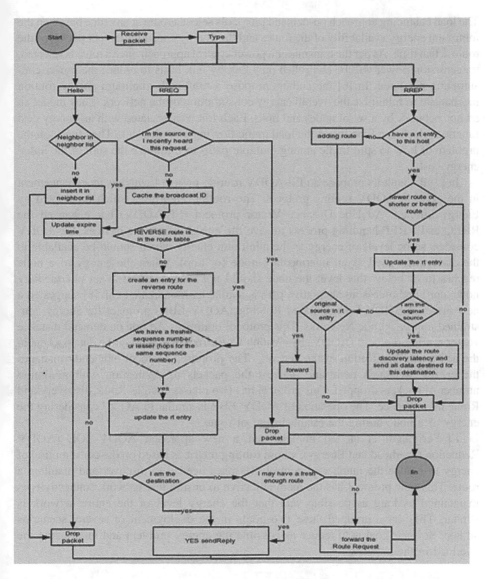

Fig. 1. The process of execution the RREQ, RREP and HELLO messages of AODV protocol

3 Related Works

This section delivers some of the many energy efficient schemes based on AODV developed by researchers in the field, in [4] the authors propose an improvement for the AODV protocol to maximize the networks lifetime by applying an Energy Mean Value algorithm which considerate node energy-aware.

In [5] a mechanism involving the integration of load balancing approach and transmission power control approach is introduced to maximize the lifetime of MANETs.

The load balancing approach on-demand protocols select a route at any time based on the minimum energy availability of the routes and the energy consumption per packet of the route at that time. As per the transmission power control approach once a route is selected, transmission power will be controlled on a link by link basis to reduce the power consumption per node. In [6] the authors propose a multipath minimum energy routing mechanism to minimize the overall energy consumption of the network. They model an ad hoc network by a set of nodes and links. Each link is associated with an energy cost function which is a function of the total traffic flowing over this link. They focus on the problem of how to split traffic among multiple paths to minimize the sum of the links' energy cost.

In [7] the authors propose an EE-AODV routing protocol which is an enhancement in the existing AODV routing protocol. The routing algorithm which is adopted by Energy Efficient Ad Hoc Distance Vector protocol (EE-AODV) has enhanced the RREQ and RREP handling process to save the energy in mobile devices. EE-AODV considers some levels of energy as the minimum energy which should be available in the node to be used as an intermediary node (or hop). When the energy of a node reaches to or below that level the node should not be considered as an intermediary node, until and unless no alternative path is available. Manickam et al. [8] suggested a new protocol AODV Energy Based Routing (AODV-EBR) protocol for energy constrained mobile ad hoc Networks. This protocol optimizes Ad hoc on demand distance vector routing protocol (AODV) by creating a new route for routing the data packets in the active communication of the network. The proposed protocol efficiently manages the energy weakness node and delivers the packets to destination with minimum number of packets dropped. This protocol has two phases such as Route discovery and Route maintenance. The operation of AODV-EBR is similar to AODV considering the energy of a node during the establishment of route.

El Fergougui et al. [9] implemented a new approach AODV-ROE (AODV Reduction Overhead and Energy), whose routing metric is based on the consumption of energy to reduce the number of control messages needed to discover and maintain a route. This new protocol has the main objective to ensure that network connectivity is maintained as long as possible, and that the energy level of the entire network is similar. They have grouped these two goals in the deployment of several scenarios ad-hoc. So their goal is to reduce as possible the energy problem and minimizing the overload in the network.

4   Proposed Work: Algorithm for Energy Efficient AODV

In order to implement residual energy in AODV protocol, two new vectors, called Residual Energy vector (RE) and node label vector (LB) are added to the RREQ and RREP messages. To find a route to a destination node, a source node floods a RREQ packet over the network. When neighbors nodes receive the RREQ packet, they update the RE and LB by adding their residual energy, their index and it triggers the data collection timer in order to receive all RREQ messages forwarded through other routes, after this process each node has a complete database of energy of all links connecting the nodes which are inserted in the LB vector, when time expires each node finds the shortest paths between it and all other nodes in LB vector using Dijkstra algorithm and rebroadcast the packet to the next nodes until the packet arrives at a destination node.

NB: we fix the threshold value (Th) for the nodes on the network when the energy (Ei) of the node is less than the threshold value (Th) that node does not forward the RREQ, but drops it.

4.1   Graph Construction

The graph G(V, E) is represented by an N × N (N is the number of nodes in LB vector) the weights of the edges are calculated by:

$$w_{ij} = \begin{cases} 0 & if\ i = j \\ \frac{H}{means\ (EN_i, EN_j)} & if\ i \neq j\ and\ (i, j) \in E \\ \infty & if\ i \neq j\ and\ (i, j) \notin E \end{cases} \tag{1}$$

where:
ENi is the current remaining energy of the node i
ENj is the current remaining energy of the node j
H: The number of hops from the current node to the node that transmits the request.

Figure 2 shows the processes of constructing the weighted graph during a broadcasting RREQ packet from the source node (s) to the destination node (d).

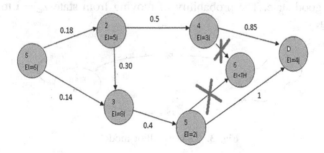

Fig. 2. Processes of constructing the weighted graph

4.2   Running Dijkstra Algorithm

Using the Dijkstra algorithm, the nodes can determine the shortest distance between them and any other node in LB vector. The idea of the algorithm is to continuously calculate the shortest distance beginning from a starting point, and to exclude longer distances when making an update. So here is the pseudo code of function for this algorithm:

```
function Dijkstra(Graph, source):
  for each vertex v in Graph: // Initialization
dist[v] := infinity // initial distance from source //to
//vertex v is set to infinite
previous[v] := undefined // Previous node in optimal
//path from source
dist[source] := 0// Distance from source to source
Q := the set of all nodes in Graph
while Q is not empty:
  u := node in Q with smallest dist[ ]
  remove u from Q
for each neighbor v of u:  // where v has not yet been
//removed from Q.
  alt := dist[u] + dist_between(u, v)
  if alt < dist[v] // Relax (u,v)
  dist[v] := alt
  previous[v] := u
return previous[ ]
```

4.3   Media Transmission Error

We consider the 2-state Markov approach as introduced by Gilbert and Elliott [10, 11], which is widely used for describing error patterns in transmission channels. This model is shown below in Fig. 3, where at time k, $z_k = 1$ represents the bad state and $z_k = 0$ represents the good state. The probability of moving from state $z_k = i$ to $z_{k+1} = j$ is denoted by pig.

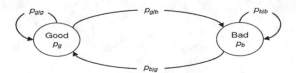

Fig. 3. Gilbert-Elliot model

Let t_g and t_b the mean duration in good state and in bad state, respectively.
The steady state probability for being in good state can be obtained as follows:

$$p_{g/g} = \frac{t_g}{t_g + t_b} \tag{2}$$

In same way, the steady state probability for being in bad state can be obtained as follows:

$$p_{b/b} = \frac{t_b}{t_g + t_b} \tag{3}$$

The probability of a transition occurs from good to bad state is computed as:

$$p_{b/g} = 1 - p_{g/g} \qquad (4)$$

The probability of a transition occurs from bad to good state is computed as:

$$p_{g/b} = 1 - p_{b/b} \qquad (5)$$

The parameters p and q can be derived from experimental observations measurements of errors on the wireless link, given in [12], show $p_{b/g} = 0.3820$ and $p_{g/b} = 0.0060$.

5 Simulation and Results

5.1 Simulation Environment

We have created several scenarios to evaluate E-AODV protocol. The topology of simulation varies with the number of nodes (35, 40, 45, 50, 55, 60) which are placed uniformly and forming a Mobile Ad-hoc Network with nodes over a 1000 × 1000 m area for 600 s of simulated time in NS2. Using this simulator (NS2) the complex scenarios can be easily tested and results can be quickly obtained. For network traffic we create a CBR connection pattern between nodes, having random of connections, with a seed value of 1.0 and a rate of 5.0 pkts/s. The Table 1 show the parameters used in the simulation:

Table 1. Parameters settings for the simulation

Simulator	NS2 Version 2.35	
	Simulator network size	500 m × 500 m
	Number of nodes	35, 40, 45, 50, 55, 60
	Duration	600 s
Physical layer	Signal propagation	Two-ray ground
	Antenna model Omni antenna	Omni antenna
Mac layer	MAC protocol	802.11
	Mac layer link bandwidth	1 MB (by default)
Traffic model	Traffic type	CBR
Queue	Queue type	DropTail/PriQueue
	Size	50
Error model	Uniform, Two state (Markov)	

5.2   Performance Metric

We use four different quantitative metrics to compare the performance of the original AODV and the improvement AODV(E-AODV):

- Normalized Routing Load: This is the number of routing packets per data packets delivered at the destination.
- Packet delivery ratio: The ratio of the data packets delivered to the destinations to those generated by the CBR sources.
- Total Energy Consumption: This metric gives the energy consumption in the network at the end of simulation.
- Number of Alive Nodes (AN): This efficiency metric gives the number of nodes have a non-zero energy at the end of the simulation.

5.3   Results

For each performance metric two experiments were carried out. In the first experiment, the impact of network density on the performance of AODV and E-AODV was tested by varying the number of nodes. In the second experiment, the effect of the pause times on the performance of the protocol was studied.

- Normalized Routing Load.

Figures 4 and 5 show the simulation results of Normalized Routing Load of E-AODV and AODV in the different number of nodes and different Pause time. We can observe that E-AODV demonstrates significantly lower routing load than AODV due to the nodes of the more residual energy are selected on the route in E-AODV, so the route will not quickly come into force, thus it reduces the number of routing discovery.

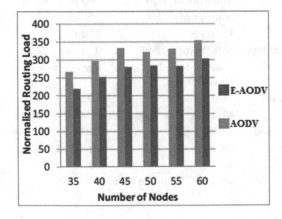

Fig. 4. Comparison of normalized routing load with number of nodes

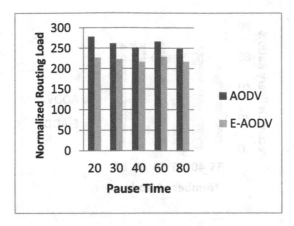

Fig. 5. Comparison of normalized routing load with pause time

We can also see that the value of Normalized Routing Load is increasing when we raise the number of nodes because adding nodes will automatically increase the number of periodic messages (HELLO messages) and the broadcast messages like RREQ. Less pause time indicate high mobility scenario which leads to frequent link failures and more pause time indicates less mobility scenario, so the number of route discoveries is directly proportional to the number of link failures.

- Packet Delivery Ratio.

When looking at the packet delivery ratio in Fig. 6 and 7, it can be seen that E-AODV perform much better than AODV. The reason is that the nodes of the less residual energy can be selected on the route in AODV so if these packets are sent, and the route chosen is not satisfying the requirements energy, packets have more probability to be dropped at the intermediate nodes. In other words, the E-AODV decreases the probability for dropping packets by selecting the paths which have more energy. It helps to save the data rate as well.

From the Fig. 7 it is observed that as the pause time increases the PDR increases too. The reason for this is, since the network is static there is more probability of the source and destination nodes staying in transmission range of each other, the source node doesn't need the intermediate nodes to transfer the data packets, so the probability for dropping packets decreases.

- Total Energy Consumed.

The consumed energy for E-AODV is lesser than AODV is clearly illustrated in Figs. 8 and 9 due to AODV considers the hop count as the metric for choosing the best route, while our protocol considers a metric based on residual energy in the best route selection. When we only consider the hop count in route selection, a lot of data packets will share the same path simultaneously and will result in a quick diminution of the battery power of the nodes along this path.

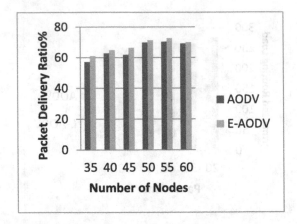

Fig. 6. Comparison of packet delivery ratio with number of nodes

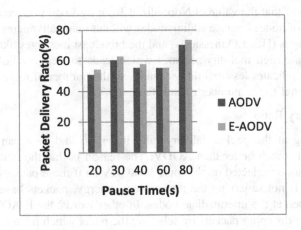

Fig. 7. Comparison of packet delivery ratio with pause time

- Number of Alive Nodes.

Figures 10 and 11 show the comparison between the number of nodes have a non-zero energy after the end of the simulation versus the number of the nodes in the network and in different pause time for the original AODV and E-AODV. As seen in Fig. 10, the number of alive nodes decreases with the number of nodes in the network because the network load is increased.

Figure 11 gives the number of alive nodes with varying pause time, with increase in pause time the network is less mobile and the packets control become fewer. That's why there is an increasing number of alive nodes.

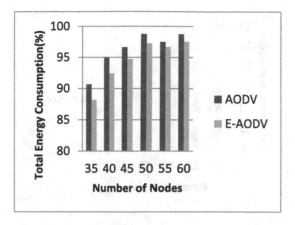

Fig. 8. Comparison of total energy consumed with number of nodes

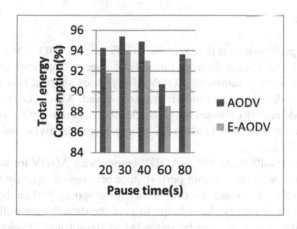

Fig. 9. Comparison of total energy consumed with pause time

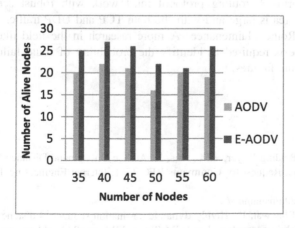

Fig. 10. Comparison of number of alive nodes with number of nodes

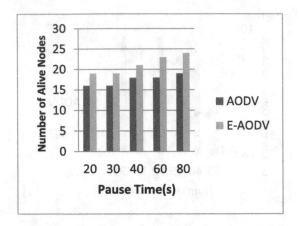

Fig. 11. Comparison of number of alive nodes with pause time

6 Conclusion

We examine the performance differences of AODV and E-AODV. We measure Normalized Routing Load, Packet delivery ratio, Total Energy Consumption and Number of Alive Nodes as QoS parameters. AODV always uses shortest hop route, so congestion occurs and distribution of load is not considered. Also, AODV does not consider available node energy of nodes for path selection and communication purposes. In this paper, algorithm with the addition of energy metric is given and simulation is performed using NS2.

Our simulation results show that E-AODV outperforms AODV for number of alive nodes by 25 to 30% with considering performance parameters as pause time and node density. The E-AODV decreases the probability for dropping packets by selecting the paths which have more energy. So it helps to save the data rate as well.

The present research work can be extended to design and develop new routing protocols to meet the following additional desirable features.

Robust Scenario- A routing protocol must work with robust scenarios where mobility is high, area is large and with the both TCP and UDP traffic.

Probabilistic Route Maintenance- A more research in the field like probabilistic route maintenance is required to identify the probability of route failure before the occurrences of route failures.

References

1. Perkins, C.E., Belding-Royer, E.M., Das, S.: Ad hoc On-Demand Distance Vector (AODV) Routing. Internet Request for Comments RFC 3561, Internet Engineering Task Force, July 2003
2. http://www.isi.edu/nsnam/ns/
3. Perkins, C.E., Bhagwat, P.: Highly dynamic destination sequenced distance-vector routing (DSDV) for mobile computers. In: ACM SIGCOMM, pp. 234–244, August 1994

4. Kim, J.-M., Jang, J.-W.: AODV based energy efficient routing protocol for maximum lifetime in MANET. IEEE (2006)
5. Tamilarasi, M., Palanivelu, T.G.: Integrated energy-aware mechanism for MANETs using on demand routing. Int. J. Comput. Inf. Eng. **2**, 212–216 (2008)
6. Yin, S., Lin, X.: Multipath minimum energy routing in ad hoc network. In: Proceedings of the International Conference on Communications (ICC), pp. 3182–3186. IEEE (2005)
7. Singh, R., Gupta, S.: EE-AODV: energy efficient AODV routing protocol by optimizing route selection process. Int. J. Res. Comput. Commun. Technol. **3**(1), 158–163 (2014)
8. Manickam, P., Manimegalai, D.: A highly adaptive fault tolerant routing protocol for energy constrained mobile ad hoc networks. J. Theor. Appl. Inf. Technol. **57**(3), 388–397 (2013)
9. El Fergougui, A., Jamali, A., Naja, N., El Ouadghiri, D., Zyane, A.: Improved aodv routing protocol based on the energy model. J. Theor. Appl. Inf. Technol. **76**(3), 366–372 (2015)
10. Elliott, E.O.: Estimates of error rates for codes on burst-error channels. Bell Syst. Tech. J. **42**, 1977–1997 (1963)
11. Gilbert, E.: Capacity of a burst-noise channel. Bell Syst. Tech. J. **39**, 1253–1266 (1960)
12. Janevski, T.: Book Traffic Analysis and Design of Wireless IP. Artech House, Boston (2003)

A Fuzzy-Based Routing Strategy to Improve Route Stability in MANET Based on AODV

Mohamed Er-rouidi[1]([⊠]), Houda Moudni[1], Hassan Faouzi[1], Hicham Mouncif[2], and Abdelkrim Merbouha[1]

[1] Faculty of Sciences and Technology,
Sultan Moulay Slimane University, Beni Mellal, Morocco
{m.errouidi,h.moudni,h.faouzi,merbouha}@usms.ma
[2] Faculty Polydisciplinary, Sultan Moulay Slimane University Beni Mellal,
Beni Mellal, Morocco
hmouncif@yahoo.fr

Abstract. In recent years, mobile ad hoc network (MANET) is becoming more and more useful in many domains. While MANETs still suffer from several problems. Among these problems, the energy conservation. Where the energy presents one of the greatest restriction, and has a massive effect on others metrics like packet delivery ratio, overhead, end-to-end delay and the lifetime of the network. As most of mobile ad hoc stations based on a limited battery in their mission. For these reasons, we propose in this paper a fuzzy logic system (FLS) to enhance the performance of one of the reactive routing protocols Ad hoc On-demand Distance Vector (AODV) by avoiding nodes with low amount of energy and select the more stable path. Our fuzzy system uses three input parameters that have a large impact on the stability of the links: energy drain rate, mobility of the node and the distance between two communicating nodes. Simulation results show that our protocol gives good result by reducing significantly the energy dissipation, also certain parameters affected by the energy issue.

Keywords: MANET · AODV · Routing protocol · Fuzzy logic system · Energy

1 Introduction

With the increase of using wireless terminals, mobile ad-hoc networks receive significant attention in recent years as a technique to offer the communications between these terminals without the existing of any fixed infrastructure or centralized administration. Each node in this network operates as a host and also as a router, by forwarding packets of other nodes whose destinations are not in their direct transmission range. Based on a routing protocol nodes can select the next node and forward the packets. Various routing protocols have been submitted to the Internet Engineering Task Force Mobile Ad Hoc Networking group [1], based on different assumptions, such as AODV [2], Dynamic Source Routing

© Springer International Publishing AG 2017
A. El Abbadi and B. Garbinato (Eds.): NETYS 2017, LNCS 10299, pp. 40–48, 2017.
DOI: 10.1007/978-3-319-59647-1_4

(DSR) [3], Destination Sequenced Distance-Vector (DSDV) [4] and Temporally Ordered Routing Algorithm (TORA) [5]. Most of these protocols take the shortest path as the main metric in building routes. While this selection method presents several effects on the network. Among this effects traffic, concentration on certain part of nodes, which results in the consumption of large amount of resource of selected nodes. Energy is one of valuable resource in mobile ad-hoc networks, since most nodes in such network are powered by battery which cannot be recharged in most cases. In order to keep the network functional as long as possible, energy-efficient routing algorithms should be developed. In this paper, we propose an enhancement of the routing protocol AODV by introducing a fuzzy logic system that use as inputs parameters three important metrics that have a large impact on the stability of the routs which are the average energy of the route, mobility of the node and the distance between two communicating nodes in order to select routs with more stability. The rest of the paper is organized as follows. In Sect. 2, we address the related work Sect. 3 gives a brief description of AODV routing protocol and the fuzzy logic theory. Section 4 describe the proposed solution. The performance of the proposed protocol evaluated in Sect. 5. Finally, Sect. 6 concludes the paper.

2 Related Work

To face these problems, many improvements to these protocols are proposed. In [6] the authors propose a fuzzy inference system as an adaptive computational approach to compute a node's trust value based on the residual energy level and speed of node. Also, introduce an efficient routing scheme by selecting the most trustworthy nodes to establish a stable route. In order to decreases the probability of route breaks during the data relay period. During this process, intermediate node initiates a timer if the RREQ packet has not been previously received, in purpose of waiting another RREQ from node with best trust value. But this technique leads to a higher latency. In other hand authors of [7] propose the same technique. However, only the destination node who apply the fuzzy logic system and wait for the best route. As well, authors in [8] Propose a dynamic fuzzy energy state based AODV (DFES-AODV) routing protocol for MANETs, based on fuzzy logic and reinforcement learning [9]. In route discovery phase of this protocol, each node uses a Mamdani [10] fuzzy logic system (FLS) and use like inputs the residual battery level and energy drain rate of mobile node to decide its Route REQuests (RREQs) forwarding probability.

3 Applied Methods and Routing Protocol

3.1 Fuzzy Logic

We use Fuzzy Logic theory [11] to combine some metrics in order to make good routing decisions. In general, Fuzzy Logic can be seen as a generalization of classical set theory. By introducing the notion of degree in the verification of a condition, thus enabling a condition to be in a real value in $[0, 1]$ other than true or false. Let U be a nonempty set and x an element in U, A is a set in U characterized by the membership function μ_A, In classical set theory, the membership function of x in A is evaluated by 1 or 0 (1). But in fuzzy set, the membership function of x in A will be a real value in $[0, 1]$ (2). Fuzziness is a language concept; its main strength is its valuable flexibility for reasoning, which makes it possible to take into account inaccuracies and uncertainties.

$$\forall x \in U, \mu_A(x) = \begin{cases} 1 & x \in A \\ 0 & x \notin A \end{cases} \tag{1}$$

$$\mu_A(x) : U \to [0, 1] \tag{2}$$

3.2 Ad Hoc On-Demand Distance Vector (AODV) Routing Protocol

AODV [2] routing protocol is an adaptation of the Destination Sequenced Distance-Vector (DSDV) [4] and Dynamic Source Routing (DSR) [3] algorithms. It is belonging to on-demand protocol family: only the node that requires a route toward a given destination launch the route discovery process, if it has no fresher route in its routing table. During the construction of the routes AODV protocol take the shortest path as the main metric, and does not take into consideration the capabilities of intermediate nodes, which play an important role in achieving the quality of service.

4 Fuzzy AODV

To deal with the problem of route selection in AODV protocol, in our proposed solution we are introduce three new parameters in the selection criteria of AODV. These parameters have a large impact on the stability of the links, which are residual energy, the mobility of the node and the distance between two communicating nodes. In [12,13] authors show that the distance between two communicating nodes and their mobility can affect the link stability between these nodes. The packet transmission error rate becomes higher if the distance of the link is longer, as it approaches the transmission range of mobile nodes. In this case, a small movement of one of the involved nodes can result in packet loss due to a link failure. As the link has a high probability of being broken, if one of the intermediate nodes have a low amount of energy [14]. Furthermore, packets are more likely to be lost due to external environmental factors like white noise and wireless interference if the signal strength is not very strong. For this reason, in our approach we try to investigate these parameters to enhance the performance of the network. We propose a system that contains two fuzzy logic system. The first FLS1 has three inputs: harmonic mean of the energy of the traversed nodes by the route request message, the distance between the two communicating nodes and the variation of the distance between nodes. This FLS1 executed at each intermediate node, does not have the route to the destination. And it is executed when the intermediate node receives the route request message. FLS1 calculates and makes a suitable adaptation decisions of a stability values that measure the quality of the links between source and the intermediate node. The second FLS2 take two inputs parameters: stability (the output of FLS1) and the hope count number of the route. FLS2 executed at each intermediate node knows the route to the destination node or the destination node itself. The output of FLS2 give us the weight of the route, based on the stability and the length of the route. According to this value intermediate and destination node, select the right route between available routes (Fig. 1). The process of the fuzzy logic system is composed of three parts (Fig. 2): firstly, the crisp set of input data are gathered and converted to a fuzzy set using fuzzy linguistic variables and membership functions as shown in (Fig. 3); this part is known as **Fuzzification**; afterwards, an **inference** engine is made based on a set of IF-THEN rules as shown in Table 1; finally, the fuzzy output is mapped to a crisp output using the membership functions, in the **Defuzzification** part (Fig. 3). The main advantages of using the fuzzy logic system are ease to model our reasoning, the ability to deal with uncertainty and non-linearity, the ease of implementation, the use of linguistic variables and it requiring less computing power [15, 16].

The estimated remaining energy is computed periodically as follows in each node:

$$RE_i(t) = \max \left\{ CE_t - \Sigma_{j=1}^{j=Nbr-pkts} E_t(j), 0 \right\} \tag{3}$$

where EC_t is the current energy value of the node. For more accurate estimation of this residual energy, we reduce the value of the power that will be consumed to transmit the remaining packets in the buffer noted by Nbr-pkts. The parameter $EC_t(j)$ represents the energy needed for transmitting the packet number j. Our fuzzy system take as input the harmonic mean of the energy of traversed nodes by the route request message and is computed as follows:

$$H_{mean} = \frac{Nbr\ of\ Hops}{\Sigma_{i=1}^{Nbr\_Hops} \dfrac{1}{RE_i}} \tag{4}$$

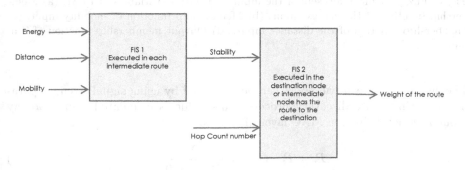

Fig. 1. Proposed fuzzy logic system

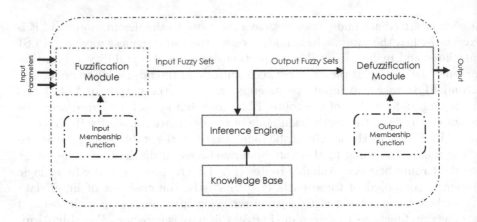

Fig. 2. Module of Fuzzy logic system

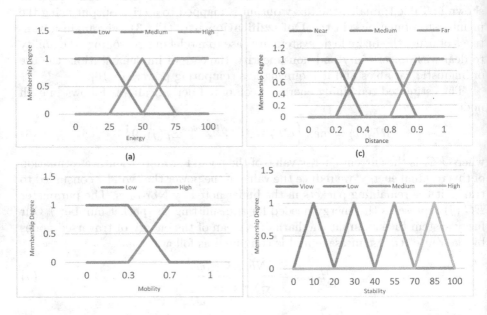

Fig. 3. Fuzzy membership sets of the input and output variables of FLS1. (a) Membership function of the energy input. (b) Membership function of mobility input. (c) Membership function of the distance input. (d) Output membership function of Stability

The distance between two nodes can be predicted by using signal strength parameter during route discovery process. This value is calculated using two ray ground model defined in MAC layer of ns-2.35.

$$P_r = P_t * G_t * G_r \frac{\lambda^2}{(4 * \pi * d)^2} \tag{5}$$

Table 1. The Fuzzy inference rules of FLS1.

Energy	Distance	Mobility	Stability	Energy	Distance	Mobility	Stability
Low	Near	Low	VLow	Medium	Medium	High	Medium
Low	Near	High	VLow	Medium	Far	Low	High
Low	Medium	Low	VLow	Medium	Far	High	VLow
Low	Medium	High	VLow	High	Near	Low	Medium
Low	Far	Low	Low	High	Near	High	Low
Low	Far	High	VLow	High	Medium	Low	High
Medium	Near	Low	Medium	High	Medium	High	Low
Medium	Near	High	Low	High	Far	Low	High
Medium	Medium	Low	Medium	High	Far	High	VLow

where Pr = received power, Pt = transmitted power, Gt = antenna gain of the transmitter, Gr = antenna gain of the receiver, λ = wavelength, and d = distance. For the third input parameter of our fuzzy system. We measure the variation of the distance between nodes over time in order to estimate the relative mobility of two nodes. To calculate this value, we compute the difference of the distance at time t and the distance at time $t-1$. Relative mobility at node X with respect to node Y at t is calculated as follows:

$$RM_{XY} = D_{XY}^t - D_{XY}^{t-1} \qquad (6)$$

Then the variation of the distance is defined as the changes of estimated distances between node. Each node in the network has a series of estimated distance values from its neighbors, measured at certain time interval for n times where $n \leq 10$ [17].

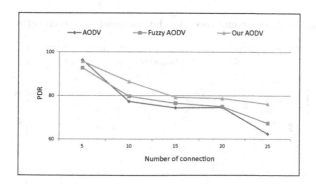

Fig. 4. Packet Delivery Ratio vs number of connection

5   Simulation and Results

The performance of our proposed protocol is evaluated and compared with the basic AODV and the Fuzzy AODV protocol proposed in [6]. Simulator NS-2 was used during these simulations. In these simulations, we consider 100 mobile nodes move within a square field of 1000 m × 1000 m in size. Nodes max moving is 10.0 m/s and the pause time between movements is 5 s with 200 s of simulated time. Every plot is taken as the average of twenty different runs. Each run is executed with a random sources and destinations pairs, and a random destination mobility. Our protocol is evaluated using four metrics Packet delivery ratio, Normalized routing load, End-to-End delay and energy consumption. Figure 4 present the variation of packet delivery ratio with the modification of the connection number. As we can see our approach perform better especially when the number of connection increases. Also, the normalized routing load that represent the ratio of control message per the packet received. We observe that the NRL generated by the Enhanced AODV is less than Fuzzy-AODV by 1% and 4% than AODV protocol, and that with 25 connections. These improvements are due to the decrease in the number of retransmissions of control packets (RREP

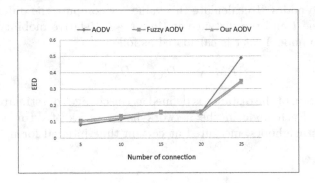

Fig. 5. Average end to end delay vs number of connection

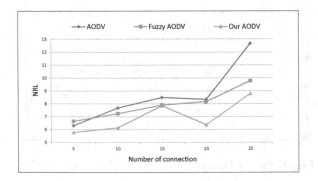

Fig. 6. Normalized Routing Load Vs Number of connection

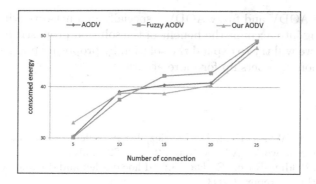

Fig. 7. Energy consumption vs number of connection

and RREQ) to construct a new route after link breakage, which engendered by the bad selection of intermediate nodes that have a low remaining energy Fig. 5. Figure 6 depicts the average end-to-end delay. All protocols have higher end-to-end delay with high number of connections. Mostly because frequent route breaks due to the dead of intermediate nodes and mobility. Our protocol reduces this problem and still perform better than AODV and Fuzzy-AODV, Even if the traffic load increases. This is due to our protocol decrease the number of link failure, as the time lost during the reconstruction of the route after link failure are eliminated. The average of energy consumption of the three protocols are presented in Fig. 7. Energy consumption increases respectively with the increase of the number of connection. However, our protocol performs better than others with more 15 connections. This is because the our modified AODV tends to avoid intermediate nodes with low remaining energy in its construction of the route. As our protocol leads to decrease the number of link failure, the energy lost during the broadcast of the route request packet are minimized. Consequently, the lifetime is significantly improved.

6   Conclusion

Given the problems that face mobile ad-hoc network, especially that use reactive routing protocols. As the stability of the route is very important. In this paper, we are proposed an enhancement protocol of the reactive routing protocol AODV. In our solution, we added three parameters among the selection criteria of AODV. These parameters have an important impact on the stability of the route, which are energy, the mobility of the node and distance between two communicating nodes. We are used fuzzy logic theory that combines these parameters, in order to produce a value that represent the stability of the route. Our enhanced protocol take this value in consideration with the number of hope during the selection of the route, to select a route with more stability. Our protocol show significant performance improvements in terms of packet delivery ratio, normalized routing load, end-to-end delay and average of energy consumption compared with AODV and fuzzy AODV, especially in a network with more connections. Taking into account the benefit of the solution proposed in this paper, in future work we will try to expand the solution by proposing fuzzy system with dynamic function membership for more accuracy.

References

1. Abolhasan, M., Wysocki, T., Dutkiewicz, E.: A review of routing protocols for mobile ad hoc networks. Ad hoc Netw. **2**(1), 1–22 (2004)
2. Perkins, C., Belding-Royer, E., Das, S.: Ad hoc on-demand distance vector (aodv) routing. Technical report (2003)
3. Johnson, D.B., Maltz, D.A.: Dynamic source routing in ad hoc wireless networks. In: Imielinski, T., Korth, H.F. (eds.) Mobile computing, pp. 153–181. Springer, New York (1996)
4. Perkins, C.E., Bhagwat, P.: Highly dynamic destination-sequenced distance-vector routing (dsdv) for mobile computers. In: ACM SIGCOMM Computer Communication Review, vol. 24, pp. 234–244. ACM (1994)
5. Park, V., Corson, M.S.: Temporally-ordered routing algorithm (tora) version 1 functional specification. Technical report, Internet-Draft (1997). draft-ietf-manet-tora-spec-00.txt
6. Abbas, N.I., Ilkan, M., Ozen, E.: Fuzzy approach to improving route stability of the aodv routing protocol. EURASIP J. Wirel. Commun. Netw. **2015**(1), 235 (2015)
7. Torshiz, M.N., Amintoosi, H., Movaghar, A.: A fuzzy energy-based extension to aodv routing. In: International Symposium on Telecommunications 2008, IST 2008, pp. 371–375. IEEE (2008)
8. Chettibi, S., Chikhi, S.: Dynamic fuzzy logic and reinforcement learning for adaptive energy efficient routing in mobile ad-hoc networks. Appl. Soft Comput. **38**, 321–328 (2016)
9. Al-Rawi, H.A.A., Ng, M.A., Alvin Yau, K.-L.: Application of reinforcement learning to routing in distributed wireless networks: a review. Artif. Intell. Rev. **43**(3), 381–416 (2015)
10. Mamdani, E.H.: Application of fuzzy logic to approximate reasoning using linguistic synthesis. In: Proceedings of the Sixth International Symposium on Multiple-Valued Logic, pp. 196–202. IEEE Computer Society Press (1976)
11. Zadeh, L.A.: Fuzzy sets. Inf. Control **8**(3), 338–353 (1965)
12. Sarma, N., Nandi, S.: Route stability based qos routing in mobile ad hoc networks. Wirel. Pers. Commun. **54**(1), 203–224 (2010)
13. Youssef, M., Ibrahim, M., Latif, M.A., Chen, L., Vasilakos, A.V.: Routing metrics of cognitive radio networks: a survey. IEEE Commun. Surv. Tutorials **16**(1), 92–109 (2014)
14. Fotino, M., De Rango, F.: Energy issues and energy aware routing in wireless ad hoc networks. INTECH Open Access Publisher (2011)
15. De Reus, N.M.: Assessment of benefits and drawbacks of using fuzzy logic, especially in fire control systems. Technical report, DTIC Document (1994)
16. Driankov, D., Saffiotti, A.: Fuzzy logic techniques for autonomous vehicle navigation. Physica **61**, 392 (2013)
17. Er, I.I., Seah, W.K.G.: Mobility-based d-hop clustering algorithm for mobile ad hoc networks. In: Wireless Communications and Networking Conference 2004, WCNC 2004, vol. 4, pp. 2359–2364. IEEE (2004)

Distributed Algorithms

Self-stabilizing Reconfiguration

Shlomi Dolev[1], Chryssis Georgiou[2], Ioannis Marcoullis[2(✉)],
and Elad M. Schiller[3]

[1] Department of Computer Science,
Ben-Gurion University of the Negev, Be'er Sheva, Israel
[2] Department of Computer Science, University of Cyprus, Nicosia, Cyprus
`imarcoullis@cs.ucy.ac.cy`
[3] Department of Computer Science and Engineering,
Chalmers University of Technology, Gothenburg, Sweden

Abstract. Current reconfiguration techniques depend on starting the
system in a consistent configuration, in which all participating entities
are in a predefined state. Starting from that state, the system must preserve consistency as long as a predefined churn rate of processors joins
and leaves is not violated, and unbounded storage is available. Many systems cannot control this churn rate and lack access to unbounded storage.
System designers that neglect the outcome of violating the above assumptions may doom the system to exhibit illegal behaviors. We present the
first automatically recovering reconfiguration scheme that recovers from
transient faults, such as temporal violations of the above assumptions.
Our self-stabilizing solutions regain safety automatically by assuming
temporal access to reliable failure detectors (FDs). Once safety is established, the FD reliability is no longer needed. Still, liveness is conditioned
by the FD's unreliable signals. Our self-stabilizing reconfiguration techniques can serve as the basis for the implementation of several dynamic
services over message passing systems. Examples include self-stabilizing
reconfigurable virtual synchrony, extendable to a self-stabilizing reconfigurable state machine replication.

1 Introduction

Motivation. We consider distributed systems working in dynamic asynchronous
environments, such as a shared storage system [17]. Quorum configurations [19],
i.e., sets of active processors (servers or replicas), are typically used to provide

A full version of this paper can be found in [8].

S. Dolev—The research was partially supported by the Rita Altura Trust Chair in
Computer Sciences; Frankel center for computer science, grant of the Ministry of
Science, Technology and Space, Israel, and the National Science Council (NSC) of
Taiwan; the Ministry of Foreign Affairs, Italy; the Ministry of Science, Technology
and Space, Infrastructure Research in the Field of Advanced Computing and Cyber
Security and the Israel National Cyber Bureau.

I. Marcoullis—Partially supported by a Doctoral Scholarship program of the
University of Cyprus.

A. El Abbadi and B. Garbinato (Eds.): NETYS 2017, LNCS 10299, pp. 51–68, 2017.
DOI: 10.1007/978-3-319-59647-1_5

service to the system's participants. A configuration may gradually lose active participants due to voluntary leaves or stop failures, rendering service provision poor or impossible. It is important to instate a new configuration, i.e., to *reconfigure*, on time, based on a more recent participation set. In recent years, several reconfiguration techniques were proposed, mainly for state machine replication and atomic memory emulation (e.g., [1–4,13–16,18]). Such reconfiguration techniques depend on initiating the system in a consistent configuration, with all processors in a predefined state. Continuing from this state, the system must preserve consistency assuming a predefined churn rate is not violated and unbounded storage availability. Also, they do not claim to tolerate *transient faults* that may arbitrarily alter the system's variables.

Many working systems cannot control their churn rate and do not have access to unbounded storage. System designers that neglect the outcome of violating the above assumptions may doom the system to forever exhibit a behavior that does not satisfy the system requirements. Furthermore, the dynamic and difficult-to-predict nature of distributed systems gives rise to many fault-tolerance issues and requires efficient solutions. Large-scale message passing networks are asynchronous and they are subject to transient faults due to hardware or software temporal malfunctions, short-lived violations of the assumed failure rates or violation of correctness invariants, such as the uniform agreement among all current participants about the current configuration. Fault tolerant systems that are *self-stabilizing* [6] can recover after the occurrence of transient faults as long as the program's code is still intact.

Contributions and Approach. We present the first automatically recovering reconfiguration scheme that recovers from transient faults, such as temporal violations of the predefined churn rate or the unexpected activities of processors and communication channels. Our blueprint for self-stabilizing reconfigurable distributed systems can withstand a temporal violation of such assumptions, and recover once conditions are resumed, using a bounded amount of local storage and message size. Our self-stabilizing solutions regain safety automatically by assuming temporal access to reliable failure detectors[1] (FDs). Once safety is established, the FDs' reliability is no longer needed; liveness is conditioned by the FDs' unreliable signals. We now overview our approach.

Reconfiguration scheme. Our scheme comprises of two layers that appear as a single "black-box" module to any application that uses the reconfiguration service. The objective is to provide the application with a *conflict-free* configuration, such that no two alive processors consider different configurations.

The first layer, called *Reconfiguration Stability Assurance* (*recSA*) and detailed in Sect. 3.1, is mainly responsible for detecting configuration conflicts (possibly the result of transient faults). It deploys a *brute-force* technique for converging to a conflict-free new configuration. It also employs a *delicate* configuration replacement technique when a processor notifies that it wishes to replace

---

[1] Transient faults pose challenges in managing dynamic membership that justify the use of FDs; see discussion in Related work.

the current configuration with a new set of participants. For both techniques, processors use an implementable FD (cf. Section 2) to obtain membership information. Configuration convergence is reached when the FDs have temporal reliability. Once a uniform configuration is installed, the FDs' reliability is no longer needed. Liveness conditions thereafter consider unreliable FDs.

The decision for requesting a delicate reconfiguration is controlled by the other layer, called *Reconfiguration Management* or *recMA* for short (detailed in Sect. 3.2). Specifically, if a processor suspects that the dependability of the current configuration is under jeopardy, it seeks to obtain a majority approval from the alive *members* of the current configuration, and requests a (delicate) reconfiguration from *recSA*. Moreover, in the absence of such a majority (e.g., configuration replacement was not activated "on time" or the churn assumptions were violated), the *recMA* can aim to control the recovery via a *recSA* reconfiguration request. The current participant set can, over time, become different than the configuration member set. As new members arrive and others go, changing the configuration based on system membership would imply a high frequency of (delicate) reconfigurations, especially in the presence of high churn. Note that we avoid unnecessary reconfiguration requests by requiring a weak liveness condition: if a majority of the configuration set has not collapsed, then there exists at least one processor that is known to trust this majority in the FD of each alive processor. Such active configuration members can aim to replace the current configuration with a newer one (that would provide an approving majority for prospective reconfigurations) without the use of the brute-force stabilization technique.

Joining mechanism. We complement our reconfiguration scheme with a self-stabilizing joining mechanism *JoinMec* (detailed in Sect. 3.3) that manages and controls the introduction of new processors into the system. It is crucial to ensure that newly joining processors do not carry stale information (due to arbitrary faults) into the system state. To this end, we employ several techniques along with a snap-stabilizing data link protocol (see Sect. 2). We have designed *JoinMec* to grant the application the control on whether to allow new processors to join the system or not. In this way, the churn (regarding new arrivals) can be "fine-tuned" based on the application requirements; we have modeled this by having joining processors obtaining approval from a majority of the current configuration's members given no reconfiguration is taking place. These, in turn, provide such approval if the application's (among other) criteria are met. We note that in the event of transient faults, such as unavailable approving majority, *recSA* assures recovery via brute-force stabilization that includes *all* alive processors.

Applications. The presented reconfiguration scheme is modular and can be used to extend the capabilities of algorithms designed for more static environments, i.e., for environments where processors are aware of a single set of processors that can fail by crashing. The reconfiguration scheme allows for this set to be renewed and thus service can continue. We have used our reconfiguration scheme to obtain dynamic versions of a multipurpose counter increment algorithm and a self-stabilizing virtual synchrony algorithm that also leads to a self-stabilizing replicated state machine (cf., Sect. 4).

Related Work. Existing solutions for providing reconfiguration in dynamic systems, such as [1,14], do not consider transient faults and self-stabilization, as their correctness proofs (implicitly) depend on a coherent start [17] and also assume that fail-stops can never prevent the (quorum) configuration to facilitate configuration updates. They also often use unbounded counters for ordering consensus messages (or for shared memory emulation) and by that facilitate configuration updates, e.g., [14]. Our self-stabilizing solution recovers after the occurrence of transient faults, which we model as an arbitrary starting state, and guarantees a consistent configuration that provides (quorum) services, e.g., allowing reading from and writing to distributed shared memory, and at the same time managing the configuration that provides these services.

In existing non self-stabilizing solutions, dynamic membership is usually maintained by the exchange of "membership sets" (e.g., the set *World* in [14]). But when dealing with transient faults, it is possible that local membership sets may change arbitrarily resulting in sets with large numbers of identifiers of processors that are not present in the system. Given the asynchronous environment, this would result in a deadlock if the processors wait for some majority (or quorum) of these non-existing processors to respond while they have no means for detecting their non-existence. To this respect, our self-stabilizing solution makes use of failure detectors (cf. Sect. 2).

There exists a significant amount of research to characterize the fault-tolerance guarantees that different quorum system designs can provided; see [19] for an in depth discussion. In this paper we use majorities, generally regarded as the simplest quorum system (each set composed of a majority of the processors is a quorum). One can modify our reconfiguration scheme to support more complex, quorum systems, as long as processors have access to a mechanism (that is a function) that, given a set of processors, can generate the specific quorum system. The *when* a reconfiguration (delicate in our case) should take place is another important design decision; see related discussion in [17]. A simple approach is to reconfigure when a fraction (e.g., 1/4th) of the members of a configuration appear to have failed. More complex decisions use prediction mechanisms (possibly based on statistics). This issue is beyond the scope of this work; however, we have designed our reconfiguration scheme (specifically the *recMA* layer) to use any decision mechanism imposed by the application (via an application interface).

2   System Settings

Processing Entities. We consider an asynchronous message-passing system of processors. Each processor p_i has a unique identifier, i, taken from a totally-ordered set of identifiers P. The number of live and connected processors at any time of the computation is bounded by some integer N such that $N \ll |P|$. We refer to such processors as *active*. We assume that processors have knowledge of the upper bound N, but not of the actual number of active processors. Processors may stop-fail by crashing at any point without warning. A crashed processor takes no further steps and never rejoins the computation. (For readability's sake, we model rejoins as transient faults rather than considering them explicitly. Self-stabilization inherently deals with rejoins by regarding the past join information as possibly corrupted.) New processors may join the system (using a joining procedure) at any point in time with an identifier drawn from P, such that this identifier is only used by this processor forever. A *participant* is an active processor that has joined the computation and sends configuration-related messages. Note that N accounts for all active processors, both the participants and those still joining.

Communication. The network topology is that of a fully connected graph, and links have a bounded capacity *cap*. Processors exchange low-level messages called *packets* to enable a reliable delivery of high level *messages*. Packets sent may be lost, reordered, or duplicated but not arbitrarily created, although the channels may initially (after transient faults) contain stale packets, which due to the boundedness of the channels are also bounded in a number that is in $O(N^2 cap)$. We assume the availability of self-stabilizing protocols for reliable FIFO end-to-end message delivery (over unreliable channels with bounded capacity), e.g., [9], and that channels provide *fair communication*, i.e., a packet sent infinitely often is received infinitely often.

Using the underlying packet exchange protocol described, a processor p_i that has received a packet from some processor p_j which did not belong to p_i's FD, engages in a two phase protocol with p_j in order to clean their intermediate link. This is done before any messages are delivered to the reconfiguration and joining services or the applications. We follow the snap-stabilizing data link protocol of [12]. A *snap-stabilizing* protocol allows the system (after faults cease) to behave according to its specification upon its first invocation. We require that every data-link between any two processors is initialized and cleaned straight after it is established. In contrast to [12] where the protocol runs on a tree we require that each pair of processors takes the responsibility of cleaning their intermediate link. Snap-stabilizing data links do not ignore signals indicating the existence of new connections (such as physical carrier signal from the port). In fact, when such a connection signal is received by the newly connected parties, they start a communication procedure that uses the bound on the packet in transit (possibly in buffers too) to clean all unknown packets in transit, possibly repeatedly sending the same packet until more than the round trip capacity acknowledgments arrive.

(N, Θ)-**Failure Detector.** It extends the Θ-FD used in [5]. It allows each processor p_i to order other processors according to how recently they have communicated. To achieve this, p_i maintains an ordered vector *nonCrashed* where every other communicating processor p_k is ranked according to the message exchanges that it has performed with p_i and relative to the communication it has with some other processor p_j. Specifically, when p_i receives a message from p_j, it sets p_j's corresponding counter to 0, and increments the counters of any other processor p_k by one. Since there are at most N processors in the computation at any given time, we can ignore any processors that rank below the Nth vector entry. Each processor p_i uses the *nonCrashed* vector to get an estimate on the number of processors n_i that p_i believes to be active in the system; $n_i \leq N$. Processor p_i

will find that between the last processor that is still communicating with, and the first processor that has not communicated for some time, there is a significant difference in their counter. Thus, the last processor is the $n_i{}^{th}$ processor and provides an estimate on the number of active processors. If, for example, the first 30 processors in the vector have corresponding counters of up to 30, then the 31st will have a counter much greater than that, say 100; so n_i will be estimated at 30. This estimation mechanism is suggested in [10] and in [11]. (For implementation details see [8].)

The Interleaving Model and Self-stabilization. A program is a sequence of *(atomic) steps*. Each atomic step starts with local computations and ends with a communication operation, i.e., packet *send* or *receive*. We assume the standard interleaving model where at most one step is executed in every given moment. An input event can either be the arrival of a packet or a periodic timer triggering p_i to (re)send. Note that the system is asynchronous and the rate of the timer is totally unknown. The *state*, c_i, consists of p_i's variable values and the content of p_i's incoming communication channels. A step executed by p_i can change p_i's state. The tuple of the form $(c_1, c_2, \cdots, c_n)$ is used to denote the *system state*. An *execution (or run)* $R = c_0, a_0, c_1, a_1, \ldots$ is an alternating sequence of system states c_x and steps a_x, such that each c_{x+1}, except the initial system state c_0, is obtained from c_x by the execution of a_x. A practically infinite execution is an execution with many steps, where many is defined to be proportional to the time it takes to execute a step and the life-span time of a system. The system's task is a set of executions called *legal executions* (LE) in which the task's requirements hold. An algorithm is *self-stabilizing* with respect to LE when every (unbounded) execution of the algorithm has a suffix that is in LE.

3   Self-stabilizing Reconfiguration Scheme

We now describe the reconfiguration scheme and joining mechanism. Figure 1 depicts the interaction between the modules and the application. The Reconfiguration Stability Assurance $(recSA)$ layer ensures that participants eventually have a common configuration. It provides information on the current configuration and on whether a reconfiguration is not taking place using interfaces $getConfig()$ and $noReco()$ respectively. This is based on local informa-

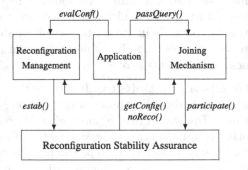

Fig. 1. Module Interaction.

tion. The Reconfiguration Management $(recMA)$ layer uses the (application-based) prediction mechanism $evalConf()$ to evaluate if a reconfiguration is required. If a reconfiguration is necessary, $recMA$ initiates it with $estab()$. Joining only proceeds if no reconfiguration is taking place. A joiner becomes a participant via $participate()$ only if $passQuery()$ of a majority of configuration members is reported as True. Arrows directed from module A to B show the transfer of specified information from A to B. We proceed with details.

3.1 The Reconfiguration Stability Assurance Layer

This layer uses Algorithm 1 for assuring correct configuration while allowing updates from the $recMA$ layer (next section). Algorithm 1 guarantees that (1) all active processors have eventually identical copies of a single configuration, (2) when participants notify the system that they wish to replace the current configuration with another, the algorithm selects one proposal and replaces the current configuration with it, and (3) joining processors can become participants eventually.

The Algorithm Structure. The algorithm combines two techniques: one for *brute force stabilization* that recovers from stale information and a complementary technique for *delicate (configuration) replacement*, where participants jointly select a single new configuration that replaces the current one.

Combining the two techniques. As long as a given processor is not aware of ongoing configuration replacements, Algorithm 1 merely monitors the system for stale information, e.g., that the config fields hold the same non-$\perp$ value. During these periods the algorithm allows the invocation of configuration replacement processes (via the $estab(set)$ interface) as well as the acceptance of joining processors as participants (via the $participate()$ interface). During the process of configuration replacement, the algorithm selects a single configuration proposal and replaces the current one with that proposal before returning to monitor for configuration disagreements.

Blocking joins to the participants' set during reconfiguration periods. While the system reconfigures, there is no immediate need to allow joining processors to become participants. By temporarily disabling this functionality, the algorithm can focus on completing the configuration replacement using the current participant set. To that end, only participants broadcast their state when finishing the do forever loop (line 17) and only their messages arrive to the other active processors (line 18). Moreover, we assume that the only way for a joining processor to start executing Algorithm 1 is by responding to an interrupt call (line 19), where the assignment of $\sharp$ to config nullifies the configuration. Thus, joining processors cannot broadcast (line 17) before their safe entry to participant set via the function $participate()$ (line 2), which enables broadcasting. Note that non-participants monitor the intersection between the current configuration and the set of active participants (line 8). In case it is empty, the processors (participants or not) call $configSet(\perp)$ and start a *reset process* that ends with a brute-force stabilization, which we explain below. Thus, the $\sharp$ values are removed from config and there is no more blocking of joining processors to become participants.

Algorithm 1. Stabilizing Reconfiguration Stability Assurance; p_i's code

---

1 **Variables:** Each field is held in an array that stores p_i's own values and p_j's most recently received ones. For example, in the case of the config[] field, config[i] is p_i's view on the current configuration and config[j] stores the most recently received one. Note that p_i assigns $\perp$ (the *empty configuration*) after receiving a conflicting (different) non-empty configuration value. FD[i] and FD[i].*part* represent p_i's failure detector, and respectively, an alias to $\{p_j \in \text{FD}[i] : \text{config}[j] \neq \sharp\}$. Note that we consider only the *trusted* (unsuspected) processors. Namely, crashed processors are eventually suspected and the FD field of every message encodes also this participation info. The field prp[i] = $\langle phase \in \{0, 1, 2\}, set \subseteq P\rangle$, where prp[$i$] refers to p_i's configuration replacement proposal. The case of no proposal is denoted by $\langle 0, \perp\rangle$. The field all[i] is true when p_i observes that all trusted nodes notice its current (max) proposal and they hold the same value. The variable allSeen stores the set of nodes p_k for which p_i received the all = *true* indication.

2 **Interfaces:** function *participate*() replaces p_i's configuration (possibly set to $\sharp$) with *chsConfig*(). Only allowed when no reconfiguration is taking place.

3 **function** *chsConfig*() is the current config value, or $\perp$ when there is no single non-$\sharp$ value.

4 **function** *getConfig*() {**if** *noReco*() **then** **return**(*chsConfig*()) **else** **return**(config[i])};

5 **function** *noReco*() test (locally) whether p_i runs a reconfiguration process.

6 **function** *estab*(set) = {**if** (*noReco*() $\wedge$ (*set* $\notin$ {config[i], $\emptyset$})) **then** prp[i] $\leftarrow$ $\langle 1, set\rangle$};

7 **do forever begin**

8   **if** *stale info present, e.g., different (non-$\perp$ or-$\sharp$) config values or empty intersection between config and participant set* **then** reset, i.e., call *configSet*($\perp$);

9   **if** *there is no proposal for configuration replacement* **then**

10   **if** $|\{\text{config}[k]\}_{p_k \in FD[i]} \setminus \{\perp, \sharp\}| > 1$ **then** *configSet*($\perp$) // once a trusted processor has sent a different (non-$\perp$ or $\sharp$) configuration, $\perp$-nullify the stored one – i.e., nullify the configuration upon conflict;

11   **if** (config[i] = $\perp \wedge |\{FD[j] : p_j \in FD[i]\}| = 1$) **then** *configSet*(FD[i]) // once all trusted nodes trust the same nodes, use this node set as the new configuration;

12   **else**

13   **if** *all trusted participants report the same proposals and participation sets and they echo back the sent values of these fields* **then** all[i] $\leftarrow$ *true*;

14   **else if** *trusted participant p_k reports* all[i] = *true* **then**

15   add p_k to allSeen;

16   **if** *allSeen includes all trusted participants* **then** run the automaton (Fig. 2) and empty allSeen $\leftarrow$ $\emptyset$;

17   **if** config[i] $\neq \sharp$ **then** send to p_j the state of p_i (including p_j's recently received info.);

18 **upon receive** m from p_j **do** store m's fields as the recently received values from p_j;

19 **upon interrupt** p_i's booting **do foreach** p_k **do** (config[k], prp[k], all[k]) $\leftarrow$ ($\sharp$, $\langle 0, \perp\rangle$, *false*) // during boot, nullify the stored fields and disable message transmissions;

Brute-force Stabilization. The proposed algorithm detects the presence of stale information and recovers from these transient faults. *Configuration conflicts* are one of several kinds of such stale information and they refer to differences in the field config, which stores the configuration values. Processor p_i can signal to all processors that it has detected stale information by assigning $\perp$ to config$_i$ and by that starts a *reset process* that nullifies all config fields in the system (lines 8 and 10). Algorithm 1 uses the brute-force technique for letting processor p_i to

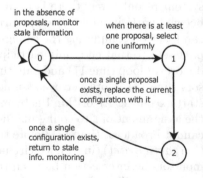

Fig. 2. The automaton

assign to config$_i$ its set of trusted processors (line 11), which the failure detector FD$_i$ provides. Note that brute-force stabilization removes any $\sharp$ value from config and allows all processors (joining or participants) to become a participant at the end of the brute-force process. Theorem 1 together with Lemma 2 show that eventually all active processors share identical (non-$\bot$) config values.

Delicate (configuration) Replacement. Participants can propose to replace the current configuration with a new set, via the *estab*(set) interface. This replacement uses the *configuration replacement* automaton (Fig. 2) that a self-stabilizing mechanism for *(phase transition) coordination* emulates.

The configuration replacement automaton. When the system is free from stale information, the configuration uniformity invariant (of the config field values) holds. Then, any number of calls to the *estab*(set) interface starts the automaton, which controls the configuration replacement using the following three phases: (1) selecting uniformly a single proposal (while verifying the eventual absence of "unselected" proposals), (2) replacing uniformly all config fields with the jointly selected proposal, and (3) bringing the system back to a state where it merely tests for stale information.

A self-stabilizing mechanism for phase transition coordination. The configuration replacement automaton, requires coordinated phase transition. Algorithm 1 lets processor p_i represent proposals as $prp_i[j] = (phase, set)$, where p_j is the processor from which p_i received the proposal, *phase* $\in \{0, 1, 2\}$ and *set* is a processor set or the null value, $\bot$. The *default proposal*, $\langle 0, \bot \rangle$, refers to the case in which prp encodes "no proposal" (line 1). When p_i calls the function *estab*(set), it changes prp to $\langle 1, set \rangle$ (line 6) as long as p_i is not aware of an ongoing configuration replacement process, i.e., *noReco*() returns *true*. Upon this change, the algorithm disseminates $prp_i[i]$ and by that guarantees that eventually *noReco*() returns *false* for any processor that calls it. Once this happens, no call to *estab*(set) adds a new proposal for configuration replacement and no call to *participate*() lets a joining processor to become a participant (line 2). Algorithm 1 can then use the lexical value of the $prp_i[]$'s tuples to deterministically select one of them (Fig. 2). To that end, each participant ensures that all other participants report the same tuples by waiting until they "echo" back the same values as the ones it had sent them. After this, participant p_i makes sure that the communication channels do not include other "unselected" proposals, by raising a flag $all_i = true$ (line 13) and waiting for the echoed values of these three fields, i.e., participant set, $prp_i[i]$ and all_i. This waiting continues until the echoed values match the values of any other active participant in the system (while monitoring their well-being). Before this participant proceeds, it makes sure that all active participants have noticed its phase completion (line 15). Each processor maintains the allSeen variable; a set of participants that have noticed its phase completion and has thus added them to the set allSeen.

The above self-stabilizing mechanism for phase transition coordination allows progression in a unison fashion. Namely, no processor starts a new phase before it has seen that all other active participants have completed the current phase and have noticed that all others have done so (because they have identical participant set, prp and all values). This is the basis for emulating every step of the configuration replacement automaton (line 16) and making sure that the phase 2 replacement occurs correctly before returning to phase 0, in which the system simply tests for stale information. Since the FDs monitor the participants' well-being, this process terminates.

Correctness. We here highlight the main steps of the proof, starting with some key definitions. An execution R is *admissible* when throughout R the FD values of active processors are identical, do not change and consist of only themselves (the set of active processors). I.e., $\forall c \in R$, $p_i, p_j \in P$ that are active in R, we have $\mathrm{FD}_i[i] = \mathrm{FD}_j[j]$ and $p_k \in \mathrm{FD}_i[i] \iff p_k$ is active. Furthermore, we say that system state c has *no stale information* when (1) all (quorum) configuration proposals are valid, e.g., the proposal $\langle 0, set \rangle$ is not valid when $set \neq \bot$, (2) all config values are non-$\bot$ and the same, (3) the phase information (including *allSeen*) is in synch, and (4) the config set includes active participants. The correctness proof shows that eventually there is no stale information (Theorem 1), because they are all detected and cleaned eventually (lines 8 and 10), as processors run configuration *reset processes* (by calling $configSet(\bot)$). To guarantee the success of such reset processes (Lemma 2), we assume that the system reaches eventually an admissible execution until the reset process terminates.

Failure Detector Usage: The above assumption implies that Algorithm 1 completes the reset process by having a temporal access to reliable FDs. However, once it completes this process, safety holds forever thereafter because, as Theorem 1 shows, the system cannot introduce stale information (or start another reset process) after the process terminates. In other words, once the reset process establishes safety, the FD reliability is no longer needed, because the success of Algorithm 1 to achieve its task does not require that the system reaches admissible executions, and liveness is conditioned by the FD's unreliable signals. Since Theorem 1 shows that no stale information eventually exists, all the processors p_i for which the field $\mathrm{config}_i[i] \notin \{\bot, \sharp\}$ store the same value in that field. We now give the main result and a proof sketch. (For the full proof see [8]).

Theorem 1 (Convergence). *Let R be an admissible execution of Algorithm 1. R has no stale information eventually.*

Proof Sketch. Lines 8 and 10 detect stale information and start the configuration reset, which by Lemma 2 terminates. The proof uses Claim 5 and Lemma 6 to imply the theorem's correctness, the first assuming that R does not include (notifications about) replacement proposals, and the second that it does.

Lemma 2. *During admissible executions R, reset processes terminate, eventually leading to no configuration conflicts.*

Proof Sketch. Suppose that R's starting system state does include a detection (line 8), does not include a conflict, i.e., $\exists p_i, p_j \in P : (\mathrm{config}_i[i] = \bot) \lor (\mathrm{config}_i[i] \neq \mathrm{config}_i[j]) \lor (\mathrm{config}_i[i] \neq \mathrm{config}_j[j])$ or there is a message, $m_{i,j}$, in the communication channel from p_i to p_j, such that the field

$(m_{i,j}.\text{config}[k] = \bot) : p_k \in FD_i[i] \lor (m_{i,j}.\text{config} \neq \text{config}_i[i])$, where both p_i and p_j are active processors. We use Claims 3 and 4 to show that in all of these cases, eventually $\forall p_i \in P : \text{config}_i[i] \in \{\bot, FD_i[i]\}$ before using Claim 5 to show that eventually there are no configuration conflicts. Claims 3 and 4 consider the values in the field config that are either held by an active processor $p_i \in P$ or in its outgoing communication channel to another active processor $p_j \in P$. We define the set $S = \{S_i \cup S\_out_i\}_{p_i \in P}$ to be the set of all these values, where $S_i = \{\text{config}_i[j]\}_{p_j \in FD_i[i]}$ and $S\_out_i = \{m_{i,j}.\text{config}\}_{p_j \in FD_i[i]}$.

Claim 3. *Suppose that in R's starting system state, there are processors $p_i, p_j \in P$ that are active in R, for which $|S \setminus \{\bot, \natural\}| > 1$. (1) $\exists S' \subseteq S : S' \in \{\{\text{config}_i[i], \text{config}_i[j]\}, \{\text{config}_i[i], m_{i,j}.\text{config}\}\}$ implies that eventually the system reaches a state in which $\text{config}_i[i] \in \{\bot, FD_i[i]\}$ holds. (2) $\exists S' \subseteq S : S' \in \{\{\text{config}_i[i], \text{config}_j[j]\}\}$ implies that eventually the system reaches a state in which $\text{config}_i[i] \in \{\bot, FD_i[i]\}$ or $\text{config}_j[j] \in \{\bot, FD_i[i]\}$ holds.*

Claim 4. *Suppose that $\text{config}_i[i] \in \{\bot, FD_i[i]\} : p_i \in P$ in R's starting system state. (1) For any system state $c \in R : \text{config}_i[i] \in \{\bot, FD_i[i]\}$, and (2) $R = R' \circ R''$ has a suffix, R'', such that $\forall c'' \in R'', \forall p_i, p_j$ that are active in R : $(\{m_{i,j}.\text{config}, \text{config}_j[i], \text{config}_j[j]\} \setminus \{\bot, FD_i[i]\}) = \emptyset$.*

Claim 5. *Suppose for any two active $p_i, p_j \in P$, we have that $(\{\text{config}_i[i], \text{config}_j[i], m_{i,j}.\text{config}\} \setminus \{\bot, FD_i[i]\}) = \emptyset$. Eventually $\text{config}_i[i] = FD_i[i]$.*

Lemma 6. *Let R be an admissible execution (wrt the participant sets) of Algorithm 1. Let n be a configuration replacement notification in R. Eventually n leaves the system.*

Proof Sketch. We assume, towards a contradiction, that notification n never leaves the system and it has a maximal lexical value among all the notifications in R. We begin by assuming that all of R's notifications appear in its starting state before removing this assumption. We use the fact that only lines 15 to 16 change the notifications and by that we show the non-decrease property of their lexical values. A contradiction is achieved by showing that the following invariants hold. suppose that $\text{prp}_i[i] = n$ holds in every system state $c' \in R$. Eventually the system reaches a state $c'' \in R$, such that for any $p_j \in P$ that is an active participant in R, it holds that: (1) $\text{prp}_j[i] = n$ and $FD_j[i] = FD_i$. Moreover, $\text{prp}_j[j] = n$ and $FD_j[j] = FD_i$ in c'' eventually, (2) $\text{echo}_i[j].\text{prp} = n$, $\text{echo}_i[j].\text{part} = FD_i[i].\text{part}$ and $\text{prp}_i[j] = n$ in c'', (3) $\text{all}_i[i] = true$ in c''. (4) $\text{all}_j[i] = true$ in c''. (5) $\text{echo}_i[j] = (FD_i[i].\text{part}, \text{prp}_i[i], \text{all}_i[i])$ in c''. (6) $p_i \in allSeen_j$ in c''. (7) the if-statement condition of line 16 holds in c''. Note that there exists a system state $c_{\exists n} \in R$ in which there are no notifications, because of invariant (7) there is a step a_i that immediately follows c'' and in which p_i for any n.*phase* value contradicts the assumption that n is of maximal value or that it never leave the system. We complete the proof by showing that even in executions in which not all of R's notifications appear in its starting state, the above eventually holds. To that end, the proof considers all notifications that appeared in R's starting state and shows that they must leave the system eventually because their (continuous) presence causes $noReco()$ to return false and by that disable the effect of the function $estab$(set) (line 6). Once this is true for every active processor in the system, the conditions for invariants (1) to (7) hold and all notifications leave the system eventually.

3.2   Reconfiguration Management

The Reconfiguration Management ($recMA$) layer (Algorithm 2), bears the weight of initiating (or "triggering") a reconfiguration when either the majority has been lost, or when the prediction function $evalConf()$ indicates to a majority of processors that a reconfiguration is needed to preserve the majority. To achieve this, it uses the $estab()$ interface of Algorithm 1. In spite of using majorities, the algorithm is generalizable to other (more complex) quorum systems, while the prediction function $evalConf()$ (used as a black box) can be either very simple, e.g., asking for reconfiguration once $1/4^{th}$ of the members appear to have failed, or more complex, based on application criteria or network considerations. More elaborate methods may also be used to define the set of processors that Algorithm 2 proposes as the new configuration. Our current implementation, aiming at simplicity of presentation, defines the set of trusted participants of the proposer as the proposed set for the new configuration.

Algorithm Description. Each processor executing the algorithm maintains two variables, $noMaj$ and $needReconf$. The first stores True/False on whether p_i's FD considers a majority of the configuration members as alive. $needReconf$ stores the outcome of the last call to the prediction function $evalConf()$. These two variables are sent to all participating processors in every iteration of the algorithm and the received variables are stored for every participating processor. All decisions on whether a reconfiguration should take place or not, is based on the received values for the two flags.

Algorithm 2 persistently refrains from triggering a reconfiguration if one is already taking place, by the check of line 9. If a reconfiguration is not taking place, two cases can force the algorithm to reconfigure.

(i) Processor p_i sees that a majority of members suggests a reconfiguration. If a majority of active configuration members exists and locally they see that $evalConfig()$ = True, each propagates $needReconf$ = True. Any such processor, that locally sees a majority of $needReconf$ = True (lines 14–15), will proceed to propose $FD_i[i]$ as the new configuration (line 15). We note that this will be a delicate reconfiguration.

(ii) Processor p_i sees a loss of majority also seen by p_i's core. If a processor p_i suspects that the majority has collapsed, it propagates $noMaj$ = True. Given that FDs are not required to be always perfect (this is only required by Algorithm 1 to converge to a new configuration), local information may inaccurately at times present a loss of majority. In order to prevent unnecessary reconfigurations, we require that a processor considers a "core" of information from the

---

Algorithm 2. Self-stabilizing Reconfiguration Management; code for processor p_i

---

1 **Interfaces:** $evalConf()$ returns True/False on whether a reconfiguration is required or not by based on a user-defined prediction function. The rest of the interfaces are specified in Algorithm 1. $noReco()$ returns True if a reconfiguration is not taking place, else False. $estab(set)$ initiates the creation of a new configuration based on the processor set provided. $getConfig()$ returns the current local configuration.

2 **Variables:** $needReconf[]$ is an array of size at most N, composed of booleans {True, False}, where $needReconf_i[j]$ holds the last value of $needReconf_j[j]$ that p_i received from p_j as a result of exchange (lines 16 and 17) and $needReconf$ is an alias to $needReconf_i[i]$ i.e., of p_i's last reading of $evalConf()$. Similarly, $noMaj_i[]$ is an array of booleans of size at most N on whether a trusted processor of p_i detects a majority of members that are active per the reading of line 11. $noMaj_i[j]$ (for $i \neq j$) holds the last value of $noMaj_j[j]$ that p_i received from p_j. $prevConfig$ holds p_i's believed previous $config$.

3 **Macros:** $core() = \bigcap_{p_j \in FD_i[i].part} FD[j].part$;

4 $flushFlags()$: **foreach** $p_j \in FD[i]$ **do** $needReconf[j] \leftarrow (noMaj[j] \leftarrow$ False$)$;

5 **Do forever begin**

6   **if** $p_i \in FD[i].part$ **then**

7         $curConf = getConfig()$; $needReconf[i] \leftarrow (noMaj[i] \leftarrow$ False$)$;

8   **if** $prevConfig \notin \{curConf, \bot\}$ **then** $flushFlags()$;

9   **if** $noReco() =$ True **then**

10             $prevConfig \leftarrow curConf$;

11   **if** $|\{p_j \notin curConf \cap FD[i]\}| < (\frac{\lfloor curConf \rfloor}{2} + 1)$ **then** $noMaj[i] \leftarrow$ True;

12   **if** $(noMaj[i] =$ True$) \wedge (|core()| > 1) \wedge (\forall p_k \in core() : noMaj[k] =$ True$)$ **then**

13                 $estab(FD[i].part)$; $flushFlags()$;

14   **else if** $(needReconf[i] \leftarrow evalConf(curConf)) \wedge$ $|\{p_j \subseteq curConf \cap FD[i] : needReconf[j] =$ True$\}| > \frac{\lfloor curConf \rfloor}{2}$ **then**

15                 $estab(FD[i].part)$; $flushFlags()$;

16   **foreach** $p_j \in FD[i].part$ **do** $send(\langle noMaj[i], needReconf[i]\rangle)$;

17 **Upon receive** m **from** p_j **do if** $p_i \in FD[i].part$ **then** $\langle noMaj[j], needReconf[j]\rangle \leftarrow m$;

---

processors that seem to be regarded active by all the processors. We thus introduce the notion of the local *core* as the intersection of the FDs of participating processors in p_i's FD (line 3). If every processor in p_i's core appears to have $noMaj =$ True based on p_i's local information (collected via the exchange of line 17) then a reconfiguration is triggered by p_i with $FD_i[i]$ as the new configuration (lines 12–13). The core is required to have size greater than 1 to prevent p_i from triggering if it is the only processor of its core. Using the notion of the core, we also place the following *liveness* assumption on the FDs.

Majority-supportive core assumption. If a majority (of the configuration) has not collapsed, then in the core of every participant p_i, there exists at least one processor that is known (by p_i) to trust this majority in its FD.

In triggering a reconfiguration, Algorithm 2 uses the $estab(set)$ interface with Algorithm 1. In this perspective the two algorithms display modularity as to their workings. Several processors may trigger reconfiguration simultaneously, but by the correctness of Algorithm 1 this does not affect the delicate reconfiguration, and by the correctness of Algorithm 2, a processor can only trigger once when this is needed.

Correctness. Algorithm 2 achieves correctness based on the ability of delicate reconfiguration in Algorithm 1 to converge to a single configuration even if many proposals are given. We use the term *steady config state* to indicate a system state were $recSA$ has imposed a conflict-free state at least once. We refer to a system state c_{safe} during an execution R_{safe} of Algorithm 2, as one which contains no stale information. We first show that the algorithm eventually cleans stale information from an initial arbitrary state (in variables and program counters) after a bounded number of reconfiguration triggerings that may be the result of this arbitrary state. We then proceed to prove that $recMA$ prevents processors that are already reconfiguring to trigger a new reconfiguration.

Lemma 7. *Starting from an arbitrary initial state in an execution R, where stale information exists, Algorithm 2 eventually converges to a steady config state, where local stale information is removed.*

Lemma 8. *Starting from an R_{safe} execution, any call to estab() (lines 13 and 15) related to a specific event (majority collapse or agreement of majority to change config), can only cause a one per participant trigger. After the config has been established, no triggering that relates to this event takes place.*

A *legal execution R'* of Algorithm 2, refers to an execution composed of conflict-free states and delicate configurations triggered due to loss of majority of members, or due to the need of a majority of the members to reconfigure. Given the above lemmas, the proof concludes that a reconfiguration will take place when required and only when it is necessary, if the majority-supportive core assumption holds. This provides liveness to the application and leads to the following theorem.

Theorem 9. *Let R be an execution of Algorithm 2 starting from an arbitrary system state. R has an execution suffix R' which is a legal execution.*

3.3   Joining Mechanism (*JoinMec*)

Every processor that wants to become a participant, uses the snap-stabilizing data-link protocol (cf. Sect. 2) so as to avoid introducing stale information before establishing a connection with the system's processors. Algorithm 1 enables a joiner to obtain the agreed *config* when no reconfiguration is taking place. In spite of eventually acquiring knowledge of this *config* via $recSA$, a processor should only be able to participate in the computation if the application allows it. In order to sustain the self-stabilization property, it is also important that a new processor initializes its application-related local variables to either default values or to the latest values that a majority of the configuration members suggest. The joining protocol, Algorithm 3, illustrates the above and introduces joiners to the system as *participants* and not as *config members*.

Algorithm Description. Both non-participants and participants execute the algorithm.

Algorithm 3. Self-stabilizing Joining Mechanism (*JoinMec*); code for processor p_i

---

1 **Interfaces.** The algorithm uses following interfaces from Algorithm 1. *noReco()* returns True if a reconfiguration is not taking place. *participate()* makes p_i a participant. *getConfig()* returns the agreed configuration from Algorithm 1 or $\perp$ if reconfiguration is taking place. The *passQuery()* interface to the application, returns a True/False in response to granting a permission to a joining processor.

2 **Variables.** $FD[]$ as defined in Algorithm 1. *state[]* an array of application states, where *state[i]* represents p_i's local variables and *state[j]* the state that p_i most recently received from p_j. *pass[]* a boolean array of passes that p_i receives from configuration members.

3 **Functions.** *resetVars()* initializes all variables related to the application based on default values. *initVars()* initializes all variables related to the application based on states exchanged with the configuration members.

4 **procedure** *join()* **begin**
5   **foreach** $p_j \notin FD$ **do** $pass[j] \leftarrow$ False;
6   **do forever begin**
7   **if** $p_i \in FD[i].part$ **then**
8   *resetVars()*;
9   **repeat**
10   **let** $conf = getConfig()$;
11   **if** $noReco() \wedge (|\{p_j : p_j \in conf \cap FD[i] \wedge pass[j] = \text{True}\}| > \frac{|conf|}{2})$ **then** $initVars()$; *participate()*;
12   **foreach** $p_j \subset FD[i]$ **do** send("Join");
13   **until** $p_i \in FD[i].part$;

14 **upon receive** ("Join") **from** $p_j \in FD \setminus FD[i].part$ **do begin**
15   **if** $p_i \in config \wedge noReco() = \text{True}$ **then** send($\langle passQuery(), state_i \rangle$);
16 **upon receive** $m = \langle pass, state \rangle$ **from** $p_j \subset FD$ **do if** $p_i \notin FD[i].part$ **then** $\langle pass[j], state[j] \rangle \leftarrow m$;

The joiner's side. Upon a call to the *join()* procedure, a joiner sets all the entries of its *pass[]* array to False (line 5) and resets application-related variables to default values, (lines 8). The processor then enters a do-forever loop, the contents of which it executes only while it is not a participant (line 7). Joiners enter an inner loop in which they try to gather enough support from a majority of configuration members in order to become participants. In every iteration, the joiner sends a "Join" request (line 12) and stores the responses by any configuration member p_j in $pass[j]$, along with the latest application *state* that p_j had. If a majority of active members has granted a *pass* = True and there is no reconfiguration taking place, then application-related variables are initialized and *participate()* is called to allow the joining processor to become a participant (line 11).

The participant's side. A participant only executes the do–forever loop (line 6) but none of its contents since it always fails the condition of line 7. Participants however respond to join requests, by checking whether a joining processor has the correct configuration, and whether a reconfiguration is not taking place, as well as if the application can accept a new processor (line 15). If the above are satisfied, then the participant sends a *pass* = True and its application *state*, otherwise it responds with False.

Correctness. The proof first considers safety, by establishing that a processor becomes a participant through *JoinMec* only while a reconfiguration is not taking place. In the case of a pending delicate reconfiguration, joining processors running Algorithm 3 can only wait. In case of brute force reconfiguration, *recSA* was shown to bypass the *JoinMec* in order to introduce more processors to the configuration. The proof proceeds to show that eventually a processor will become a participant if the application permits it, unless it crashes. Theorem 10 summarizes the correctness.

Theorem 10. *Given an execution R of Algorithm 3 with an arbitrary initial state, R has a suffix in which every joining processor p eventually becomes a participant if the application grants permission. Moreover, p respects the installed configuration and does not affect a LE as defined by Theorem 9.*

4   Applications of the Reconfiguration Scheme

Our self-stabilizing reconfiguration scheme allows applications built for static crash-prone systems to endure more adverse system dynamics. When a configuration exists and no reconfiguration is running, applications work in the same way as in their static version, since they run their service on the configuration set as in the original static setting. A main consideration, however, is functionality *during* and *after* reconfiguration.

A general framework for adapting the static algorithm to form a reconfigurable one, involves developing an interface between the application and the reconfiguration scheme to adapt the applications structures and data to the new configuration set. We note that using this framework, the algorithms are *suspending*, i.e., they do not provide service *during* reconfiguration, albeit we believe that it is possible with more elaborate frameworks and under certain conditions to sustain service even during reconfiguration. It is an interesting open question whether this is achievable, but in the meanwhile we refer the reader to [4] for tradeoffs between suspending and non-suspending services.

Due to space limitations (and to focus on presenting the reconfiguration mechanism) we omit details of how this adaptation is performed and refer the reader to [8]. There, we show how the self-stabilizing algorithms of [7] can be adapted to be reconfigurable and prove that the algorithms remain correct and extend their capabilities after this adaptation. Specifically, we present a *self-stabilizing counter* algorithm that is multipurpose (e.g., for Paxos ballot numbers, or view identifiers in group communication services). This forms the basis for *virtually synchronous state machine replication* (SMR).

5   Conclusion

We presented the first self-stabilizing reconfiguration scheme that recovers automatically from transient faults, such as temporal violations of the predefined churn rate or the unexpected activities of processors and communication channels, using a bounded amount of local storage and message size. We use a number of bootstrapping techniques for allowing the system to always recover from arbitrary transient faults, even in cases where the current configuration includes no active processors. We believe that the presented techniques provide a generic blueprint for different solutions that are needed in the area of self-stabilizing high-level communication and synchronization primitives, which need to deal with processor joins and leaves as well as transient faults.

References

1. Aguilera, M.K., Keidar, I., Malkhi, D., Shraer, A.: Dynamic atomic storage without consensus. J. ACM **58**(2), 7 (2011)
2. Alon, N., Attiya, H., Dolev, S., Dubois, S., Potop-Butucaru, M., Tixeuil, S.: Practically stabilizing SWMR atomic memory in message-passing systems. J. Comp. Syst. Sci. **81**(4), 692–701 (2015)
3. Attiya, H., Chung, H.C., Ellen, F., Kumar, S., Welch, J.L.: Simulating a shared register in an asynchronous system that never stops changing. In: Moses, Y. (ed.) DISC 2015. LNCS, vol. 9363, pp. 75–91. Springer, Heidelberg (2015). doi:10.1007/978-3-662-48653-5_6
4. Birman, K., Malkhi, D., van Renesse, R.: Virtually synchronous methodology for dynamic service replication. Technical report MSR-TR-2010-151, Microsoft Research (2010)
5. Blanchard, P., Dolev, S., Beauquier, J., Delaët, S.: Practically self-stabilizing paxos replicated state machine. In: Noubir, G., Raynal, M. (eds.) NETYS 2014. LNCS, vol. 8593, pp. 99–121. Springer, Cham (2014). doi:10.1007/978-3-319-09581-3_8
6. Dolev, S.: Self-Stabilization. The MIT press, Cambridge (2000)
7. Dolev, S., Georgiou, C., Marcoullis, I., Schiller, E.M.: Self-stabilizing virtual synchrony. In: Pelc, A., Schwarzmann, A.A. (eds.) SSS 2015. LNCS, vol. 9212, pp. 248–264. Springer, Cham (2015). doi:10.1007/978-3-319-21741-3_17
8. Dolev, S., Georgiou, C., Marcoullis, I., Schiller, E.M.: Self-stabilizing reconfiguration. CoRR, abs/1606.00195 (2016)
9. Dolev, S., Hanemann, A., Schiller, E.M., Sharma, S.: Self-stabilizing end-to-end communication in (bounded capacity, omitting, duplicating and non-FIFO) dynamic networks. In: Richa, A.W., Scheideler, C. (eds.) SSS 2012. LNCS, vol. 7596, pp. 133–147. Springer, Heidelberg (2012). doi:10.1007/978-3-642-33536-5_14
10. Dolev, S., Herman, T.: Superstabilizing protocols for dynamic distributed systems. Chicago J. Theor. Comput. Sci. (1997)
11. Dolev, S., Schiller, E., Welch, J.L.: Random walk for self-stabilizing group communication in ad hoc networks. IEEE Trans. Mob. Comput. **5**(7), 893–905 (2006)
12. Dolev, S., Tzachar, N.: Empire of colonies: self-stabilizing and self-organizing distributed algorithm. Theor. Comput. Sci. **410**(6–7), 514–532 (2009)
13. Gafni, E., Malkhi, D.: Elastic configuration maintenance via a parsimonious speculating snapshot solution. In: Moses, Y. (ed.) DISC 2015. LNCS, vol. 9363, pp. 140–153. Springer, Heidelberg (2015). doi:10.1007/978-3-662-48653-5_10
14. Gilbert, S., Lynch, N.A., Shvartsman, A.A.: Rambo: a robust, reconfigurable atomic memory service for dynamic networks. Distrib. Comput. **23**(4), 225–272 (2010)
15. Jehl, L., Vitenberg, R., Meling, H.: SmartMerge: a new approach to reconfiguration for atomic storage. In: Moses, Y. (ed.) DISC 2015. LNCS, vol. 9363, pp. 154–169. Springer, Heidelberg (2015). doi:10.1007/978-3-662-48653-5_11

16. Lamport, L., Malkhi, D., Zhou, L.: Reconfiguring a state machine. SIGACT News **41**(1), 63–73 (2010)
17. Musial, P.M., Nicolaou, N.C., Shvartsman, A.A.: Implementing distributed shared memory for dynamic networks. Commun. ACM **57**(6), 88–98 (2014)
18. Spiegelman, A., Keidar, I., Malkhi, D.: Dynamic reconfiguration: a tutorial. In: OPODIS (2015)
19. Vukolic, M.: Quorum Systems: With Applications to Storage and Consensus. Synthesis Lectures on Distributed Computing Theory. Morgan & Claypool Publishers, San Rafael (2012)

Convergence of Even Simpler Robots without Position Information

Debasish Pattanayak[1], Kaushik Mondal[1], Partha Sarathi Mandal[1(✉)],
and Stefan Schmid[2,3]

[1] Indian Institute of Technology Guwahati, Guwahati, India
psm@iitg.ernet.in
[2] Aalborg University, Aalborg, Denmark
[3] TU Berlin, Berlin, Germany

Abstract. The design of distributed gathering and convergence algorithms for tiny robots has recently received much attention. In particular, it has been shown that the convergence problem, that is, the problem of moving robots close to each other (i.e., inside an area of some maximum size, where the position of the area is not fixed beforehand), can even be solved for very weak, *oblivious* robots: robots which cannot maintain state from one round to the next. The oblivious robot model is hence attractive from a self-stabilization perspective, where the state is subject to adversarial manipulation. However, to the best of our knowledge, all existing robot convergence protocols rely on the assumption that robots, despite being "weak", can measure distances.

We in this paper initiate the study of convergence protocols for even simpler robots, called *monoculus robots*: robots which cannot measure distances. In particular, we introduce two natural models which relax the assumptions on the robots' cognitive capabilities: (1) a Locality Detection ($\mathscr{LD}$) model in which a robot can only detect whether another robot is closer than a given constant distance or not, (2) an Orthogonal Line Agreement ($\mathscr{OLA}$) model in which robots only agree on a pair of orthogonal lines (say North-South and West-East, but without knowing which is which).

The problem turns out to be non-trivial, as simple strategies like median and angle bisection can easily increase the distances among robots (e.g., the area of the enclosing convex hull) over time. Our main contribution is deterministic self-stabilizing convergence algorithms for these two models. We also show that in some sense, the assumptions made in our models are minimal: by relaxing the assumptions on the *monoculus robots* further, we run into impossibility results.

Keywords: Convergence · Weak robots · Oblivious mobile robots · Asynchronous · Distributed algorithm

S. Schmid—Trip to IIT Guwahati and research funded by the Global Initiative of Academic Networks (GIAN), an initiative by the Govt. of India for Higher Education.

A. El Abbadi and B. Garbinato (Eds.): NETYS 2017, LNCS 10299, pp. 69–85, 2017.
DOI: 10.1007/978-3-319-59647-1_6

1   Introduction

1.1   The Context: Tiny Robots

In the recent years, there has been a wide interest in the cooperative behavior of tiny robots. In particular, many distributed coordination protocols have been devised for a wide range of models and a wide range of problems, like convergence, gathering, pattern formation, flocking, etc. At the same time, researchers have also started characterizing the scenarios in which such problems cannot be solved, deriving impossibility results.

1.2   Our Motivation: Even Simpler Robots

An interesting question regards the minimal cognitive capabilities that such tiny robots need to have for completing a particular task. In particular, researchers have initiated the study of "weak robots" [6]. Weak robots are *anonymous* (they do not have any identifier), *autonomous* (they work independently), *homogeneous* (they behave the same in the same situation), and *silent* (they also do not communicate with each other). Weak robots are usually assumed to have their own local view, represented as a Cartesian coordinate system with origin and unit length and axes. The orientation of axes, or the *chirality* (relative order of the orientation of axes or handedness), is not common among the robots. The robots move in a sequence of three consecutive actions, *Look-Compute-Move*: they observe the positions of other robots in their local coordinate system and the observation step returns a set of points to the observing robot. The robots cannot distinguish if there are multiple robots at the same position, i.e., they do not have the capability of *multiplicity detection*. Importantly, the robots are *oblivious* and cannot maintain state between rounds (essentially moving steps). The computation they perform are always based on the data they have collected in the *current* observation step; in the next round they again collect the data. Such weak robots are therefore interesting from a self-stabilizing perspective: as robots do not rely on memory, an adversary cannot manipulate the memory either. Indeed, researchers have demonstrated that weak robots are sufficient to solve a wide range of problems.

We in this paper aim to relax the assumptions on the tiny robots further. In particular, to the best of our knowledge, all prior literature assumes that robots can observe the positions of other robots in their local view. This enables them to calculate the distance between any pair of robots. This seems to be a very strong assumption, and accordingly, we in this paper initiate the study of even weaker robots which cannot locate other robots positions in their local view, preventing them from measuring distances. We define these kinds of robots as *monoculus robots*.

In particular, we explore two natural, weaker models for monoculus robots with less cognitive capabilities, those are *Locality Detection* and *Orthogonal Line Agreement*. The locality detection model is motivated by, e.g., capacitive sensing or sensing differences in temperature or vibration. The orthogonal line model is practically motivated by robots having a simple compass align for orthogonal line agreement.

1.3   The Challenge: Convergence

We focus on the fundamental convergence problem for monoculus robots and show that the problem is already non-trivial in this setting.

In particular, many naive strategies lead to non-monotonic behaviors. For example, strategies where boundary robots (robots located on the convex hull) move toward the "median" robot (i.e., the median in the local ordering of the robots) they see, may actually *increase* the area of the convex hull in the next round, counteracting convergence as shown in Fig. 1(a). A similar counterexample exists for a strategy where robots move in the direction of the angle bisector as shown in Fig. 1(b).

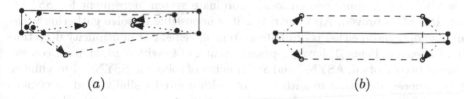

$$(a) \hspace{6cm} (b)$$

Fig. 1. The 4 boundary robots are moving (a) towards the median robot (b) along the angle bisector. The discs are the old positions and circles are the new positions. The old convex hull is drawn in solid line, the new convex hull is dashed. The arrows denote the direction of moving.

But not only enforcing convex hull invariants is challenging, also the fact that visibility is restricted and we cannot detect multiplicity: We in this paper assume that robots are not transparent, and accordingly, a robot does not see whether and how many robots may be hidden behind a visible robot. As robots are also not able to perform multiplicity detection (i.e., determine how many robots are collocated at a certain point), strategies such as "move toward the center of gravity" (the direction in which most robots are located), are not possible.

1.4   Our Contributions

This paper studies distributed convergence problems for anonymous, autonomous, oblivious, non-transparent, monoculus, point robots under a most general asynchronous scheduling model and makes the following contributions.

1. We initiate the study of a new kind of robot, the *monoculus robot* which cannot measure distances. The robot comes in two natural flavors, and we introduce the Locality Detection ($\mathscr{LD}$) and the Orthogonal Line Agreement ($\mathscr{OLA}$) model accordingly.

2. We present and formally analyze deterministic and self-stabilizing distributed convergence algorithms for both $\mathscr{LD}$ and $\mathscr{OLA}$.
3. We show our assumptions in $\mathscr{LD}$ and $\mathscr{OLA}$ are minimal in the sense that robot convergence is not possible for monoculus robots.
4. We report on the performance of our algorithms through simulation.
5. We show that our approach can be generalized to higher dimensions and, with a small extension, supports termination.

1.5 Related Work

The problems of gathering [13], where all the robots gather at a single point, convergence [2], where robots come very close to each other and pattern formation [5,13] have been studied intensively in the literature.

Flocchini et al. [6] introduced the CORDA or Asynchronous (ASYNC) scheduling model for weak robots. Suzuki et al. [12] have introduced the ATOM or Semi-synchronous (SSYNC) model. In [13], the impossibility of gathering for $n = 2$ without assumptions on local coordinate system agreement for $SSYNC$ and $ASYNC$ is proved. Also, for $n > 2$ it is impossible to solve gathering without assumptions on either coordinate system agreement or multiplicity detection [10]. Cohen and Peleg [1] have proposed a center of gravity algorithm for convergence of two robots in ASYNC and any number of robots in SSYNC. Flocchini et al. [7] propose algorithm to gather robots with limited visibility and agreement in coordinate system in $ASYNC$ model. Souissi et al. have proposed an algorithm to gather robots with limited visibility if the compass achieves stability eventually in $SSYNC$ in [11]. For two robots with unreliable compass Izumi et al. [9] investigate the necessary conditions required to gather them under $SSYNC$ and $ASYNC$ setting.

In many of the previous works, the mathematical models assume that the robots can find out the location of other robots in their local coordinate system in the Look step. This in turn implies that the robots can measure the distance between any pair of robots albeit in their local coordinates. All the algorithms exploit this location information to create an invariant point or a robot where all the other robots gather. But in this paper, we deprive the robots of the capability to determine the location of other robots. This leads to robots incapable of finding any kind of distance or angles. Note that any kind of pattern formation requires these robots to move to a particular point of the pattern. Since the monoculus robots cannot figure out locations, they cannot stop at a particular point. Hence any kind of pattern formation algorithm described in the previous works which require location information as input are obsolete. Gathering problem is nothing but the point formation problem [13]. Hence gathering is also not possible for the monoculus robots.

1.6 Paper Organization

The rest of this paper is organized as follows. Section 2 introduces the necessary background and preliminaries. Section 3 introduces two algorithms for convergence. Section 4 presents an impossibility result which shows the minimality of our assumptions. We report on simulation results in Sect. 5 and discuss extensions in Sect. 6. We finally conclude in Sect. 7.

2   Preliminaries

2.1   Model

We are given a system of n robots, $R = \{r_1, r_2, \cdots, r_n\}$, which are located in the Euclidean plane. We consider anonymous, autonomous, homogeneous, oblivious point robots with unlimited visibility. The robots are non-transparent, so any robot can see at most one robot in any direction. The robots have their local coordinate system, which may not be the same for all the robots. The robots in each round execute a sequence of *Look-Compute-Move* steps: First, each robot $r \in R$ observes other robots and obtains a set of directions $LC = \{\theta_1, \theta_2, \cdots, \theta_k\}$ where $k \leq n - 1$ (*Look* step). Each $\theta \in LC$ is the angle of a robot in the local coordinate system of robot r with respect to the positive direction of the x-axis with the robot itself as the origin. Second, on the basis of the observed information, it executes an algorithm which computes a direction (*Compute* step); the robot then moves in this direction (*Move* step), for a fixed distance b (the step size). The robots are silent, cannot detect multiplicity points, and can pass over each other. We ignore the collisions during movement. We name this kind of robots as **monoculus robots**. We also consider the following two additional capability of the monoculus robots.

Locality Detection ($\mathscr{LD}$): Locality detection is the ability of a robot to determine whether its distance from any visible robot is greater than a predefined value c or not.

A robot with *locality detection* capability can divide the visible robots into two sets based on the distance from itself. So a monoculus robot with locality detection can partition the set LC to two disjoint sets LC_{local} and $LC_{non-local}$, where LC_{local} and $LC_{non-local}$ are the set of directions of robots with distances less than equal to c and more than c respectively.

Orthogonal Line Agreement ($\mathscr{OLA}$): The robots agree on a pair of orthogonal lines, but can neither distinguish the two lines in a consistent way nor have a common sense of direction.

Robots with *orthogonal line agreement capability* agree on the direction of two perpendicular lines, but the lines themselves are indistinguishable: the robots neither agree on a direction (e.g., North) nor can they mark a line as, e.g., the North-South or East-West line. In other words, any two robots agreeing on the pair of orthogonal lines, either have their x-axis parallel or perpendicular to the other. In case of parallel orientation, the plus/minus direction of the x-axis may point to the same or the opposite direction, and in the case of a perpendicular orientation, the rotation of the axis can be clockwise or counter-clockwise.

We consider the most general CORDA or ASYNC scheduling model known from weak robots [6] as well as the ATOM or Semi-Synchronous (SSYNC) model [12]. These models define the activation schedule of the robots: the SSYNC model considers instantaneous computation and movement, i.e., the robots cannot observe other robots in motion, while in the ASYNC model any robot can look at any time. In SSYNC the time is divided into global rounds and a subset of the robots are activated in each round which finish their *Look-Compute-Move* within that round. In case of ASYNC, there is no global notion of time. The Fully-synchronous (FSYNC) model is a special case of SSYNC, in which all the robots are activated in each round. The algorithms presented in this paper, work in both the ASYNC and the SSYNC setting. For the sake of generality, we present our proofs in terms of the ASYNC model.

2.2 Notation and Terminology

A *Configuration* (C) is a set containing all the robot positions in 2D. At any time t the configuration (the mapping of robots in the plane) is denoted by C_t. The convex hull of configuration C_t is denoted as CH_t. We define *Augmented Configuration* at time t (AC_t) as C_t augmented with the destinations of each robot from the most recent look state on or before t. If all the robots are idle at time t, then AC_t is the same as C_t. The convex hull of AC_t is denoted as ACH_t as shown in Fig. 2. *Convergence* is achieved when the distance between any pair of robots is less than a predefined value ζ (and subsequently does not violate this). Our multi-robot system is vulnerable to adversarial manipulation, however, the algorithms presented in this paper are self-stabilizing [4] and robust to state manipulations. Since the robots are oblivious, they only depend on the *current state*: if the state is perturbed, the algorithms are still able to converge in a self-stabilizing manner [8].

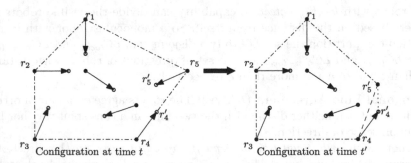

Fig. 2. r_4' is the destination of robot r_4 from the most recent look state on or before time t, and analogously for r_5. At t, $\bigcirc r_1 r_2 r_3 r_4 r_5$ is both the CH_t and ACH_t. At t' $(> t)$, $\bigcirc r_1 r_2 r_3 r_4 r_5'$ is $CH_{t'}$, while $\bigcirc r_1 r_2 r_3 r_4 r_4' r_5'$ is $ACH_{t'}$. ACH_t contains both r_4 and r_4' because r_4 has not moved. $ACH_{t'}$ contains r_4' as a corner which is outside $CH_{t'}$, because r_5 moved to r_5'.

3   Convergence Algorithms

The robot convergence is the problem of moving all the robots inside a sufficiently small non-predefined area. In this section, we present distributed robot
convergence algorithms for both our models, $\mathscr{LD}$ and $\mathscr{OLA}$. We converge the
robots inside a disc and a square, respectively, for the two models.

3.1   Convergence for $\mathscr{LD}$

In this section, we consider the convergence problem for the monoculus robots
in the $\mathscr{LD}$ model. Our claims hold for any $c \geq 2b$, where c is the predefined
distance of locality detection and b is the step size a robot moves each time it
is activated. The step size b and locality detection distance c is common for all
the robots. Algorithm 1 distinguishes between two cases: (1) If the robot only
sees one other robot, it infers that the current configuration must be a line (of 2
or more robots), and that this robot must be on the border of this line; in this
case, the boundary robots always move inside (usual step size b). (2) Otherwise,
a robot moves towards any visible, non-local robot (distance at least c), for a b
distance (the step size). The algorithm works independent of n, the number of
robots present, but depends on D, the diameter of smallest enclosing circle in
the initial configuration.

Our proof unfolds in a number of lemmas followed by a theorem. First,
Lemma 1 shows that it is impossible to have a pair of robots with distance
larger than $2c$ in the converged situation. Lemma 2 shows that our algorithm
ensures a monotonically decreasing convex hull size. Lemma 3 then proves that
the decrement in perimeter for each movement is greater than a constant (the
convex hull decrement is strictly monotonic). Combining all the three lemmas,
we obtain the correctness proof of the algorithm. In the following, we call two
robots *neighboring* if they see each other (line of sight is not obstructed by
another robot).

Algorithm 1. CONVERGELOCALITY

    Input   : Any arbitrary configuration LC
    Output: A direction θ towards the robot moves

1 **if** $|LC| = 1$ **then**
2 | Move distance b in the direction θ, where $\theta \in LC$
3 **else**
4 | **if** $|LC_{non-local}| \geq 1$ **then**
5 | | Move distance b towards any θ, where $\theta \in LC_{non-local}$
6 | **else**
7 | | Do not move   // All neighbor robots are within a distance c

---

Lemma 1. *If there exists a pair of robots at distance more than $2c$ in a non-linear configuration, then there exists a pair of neighboring robots at distance more than c.*

Proof. Proof by contradiction. If there is a pair of robots with distance more than $2c$, then they themselves are the neighboring pair with more than c distance. To prevent them from being a neighboring pair with more than c distance, there should be at least two robots on the line joining them positioned such that each neighboring pair has a distance less than c. Since the robots are non-transparent, the end robots cannot look beyond their neighbors to find another robot at a distance more than c. In Fig. 3, r_1 and r_4 are $2c$ apart. So r_2 and r_3 block the view such that $\overline{r_1 r_2} < c$, $\overline{r_2 r_3} < c$ and $\overline{r_3 r_4} < c$. Since it is a non-linear configuration, say robot r_5 is not on the line joining r_1 and r_4. l is the perpendicular bisector of $\overline{r_1 r_4}$. If r_5 is on the left side of l, then it is more than c distance away from r_4 and if it is on the right side of l then it is more than c distance away from r_1. If there is another robot on $\overline{r_4 r_5}$, then consider that as the new robot in a non-linear position, and we can argue similarly considering that robot to be r_5. If r_5 is on l, then $\overline{r_1 r_5} = \overline{r_4 r_5} > c$. Hence there would at least be a single robot similar to r_5 in a non-linear configuration for which the distance is more than c. □

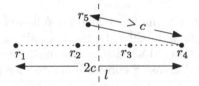

Fig. 3. A non-linear configuration with a pair of robots at a distance $2c$

Lemma 2. *For any time $t' > t$ before convergence, $ACH_{t'} \subseteq ACH_t$.*

Proof. The proof follows from a simple observation. Consider any robot r_i. If r_i decides to move towards some robot, say r_j, then it moves on the line joining two robots. There are two cases.

Case 1: If all the robots are on a straight line, then the boundary robots move monotonically closer in each step. The distance between the end robots is a monotonically decreasing sequence until it reaches c.

Case 2: For a non-linear configuration the robot moves when the distance between r_i and r_j is more than c and it moves only a distance b, where $c \geq 2b$. The movement path at the time when it looks, is always contained inside the CH_t, and $CH_t \subseteq ACH_t$. So the ACH_t contains its entire movement path and it continues to do so until the robot has reached its destination. For any $t' > t$, parts of the path traversed by the robot and outside $CH_{t'}$ are removed from ACH_t.

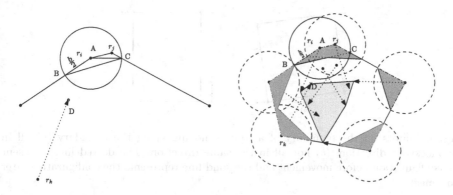

Fig. 4. On activation, r_i and r_j will move outside the solid circle inside the convex hull. The radius of the solid circle is $b/2$. The robot r_k moves a distance b towards r_i because the distance between them is more than $2b$ and stops at D. In the second figure the shadowed area is the decrement considered for each corner and the central convex hull inside solid lines is the new convex hull after every robot moves.

Hence $ACH_{t'} \subseteq ACH_t$. □

Lemma 3. *After each robot is activated at least once, the decrement in the perimeter of the convex hull is at least $b\left(1 - \sqrt{\frac{1}{2}\left(1 + \cos\left(\frac{2\pi}{n}\right)\right)}\right)$, where b is the step size and n is the total number of robots.*

Proof. Suppose the n robots form a k ($k \leq n$) sided convex hull. The sum of internal angles of a k-sided convex polygon is $(k-2)\pi$. So there exists a robot r at a corner A (ref. Fig. 4) of the convex hull such that the internal angle is less than $\left(1 - \frac{2}{n}\right)\pi$, where n is the total number of robots. Let B and C be the points where the circle centered at A with radius $b/2$ intersects the convex hull. Any robot lying outside the circle will not move inside the circle according to Algorithm 1, because the maximum distance between any two points in the circle is b and all the robots move towards a robot which is more than c distance apart, and $c \geqslant 2b$. All the robots inside the circle will eventually move out once they are activated, because the robot which is activated will have to move at least b distance, and since the distance between any two points in the $b/2$ radius circle is less than or equal to b, the robot will find itself outside the $b/2$ radius circle inside the convex hull. After all the robots are activated at least once, the decrement in the perimeter is at least $AB + AC - BC$. From cosine rule,

$$AB + AC - BC = \frac{b}{2} + \frac{b}{2} - \sqrt{\left(\frac{b}{2}\right)^2 + \left(\frac{b}{2}\right)^2 - 2\frac{b}{2}\frac{b}{2}\cos\left(\pi - \frac{2\pi}{n}\right)}$$

$$= b\left(1 - \sqrt{\frac{1}{2}\left(1 + \cos\left(\frac{2\pi}{n}\right)\right)}\right)$$

□

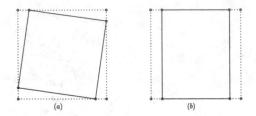

Fig. 5. Robots on the boundary of a square moving along the boundary (a) all in the clockwise direction, (b) not all in the same direction. The dotted line represent the configuration before movement and the solid line represents the configuration after movement.

Remark 1. Let us consider a special case of the execution of the algorithm. Here all n robots are on the boundary of the convex hull with side length more than c and move only on the boundary of the convex hull. Then the n-sided polygon will again become an n-sided polygon, but the perimeter will decrease overall as a consequence of Lemma 3 as shown in Fig. 5.

Theorem 1 *(Correctness). Algorithm 1 always terminates after at most $\Theta\left(\frac{D}{b}\right)$ fair scheduling rounds and for any arbitrary but fixed n, where D is the diameter of smallest enclosing circle in initial configuration and b is the step size. After termination all the robots converge within a c radius disc.*

Proof. If a corner robot on the boundary of convex hull is activated, then the perimeter of the convex hull decreases from Lemma 3. If non-corner robots are activated, then the perimeter of the convex hull remains the same. If we have a fair scheduler, the idle time for robots are unpredictable but finite. Consequently, the time between successive activations is also finite. So we can always assume a time step which is large enough for each robot to activate at least once. The total number of robots n is finite and invariant throughout the execution, so $1 - \sqrt{\frac{1}{2}\left(1 + \cos\left(\frac{2\pi}{n}\right)\right)} = \delta$ is constant. Hence the decrement of perimeter is at least $b\delta$ according to Lemma 3. Notice that the perimeter of convex hull is always smaller than the perimeter of the smallest enclosing circle. According to Lemma 1, eventually there will not be a pair of robots with more than $2c$ distance. Note that the distance between any two points in a disc of radius c is less than or equal to $2c$. In other words, $\zeta = 2c$. Hence the robots will converge within a disc of radius c. So the perimeter of the circle at termination is $2\pi c$. Now the decrement in the perimeter is $\pi D - 2\pi c$. Total time required is $\frac{\pi(D-2c)}{\delta b} = \Theta\left(\frac{D}{b}\right)$. $\qquad\square$

3.2   Convergence for $\mathcal{OLA}$

In this section, we consider monoculus robots in the $\mathcal{OLA}$ model. Our algorithm will distinguish between *boundary-*, *corner-* and *inner-robots*, defined in the canonical way. We note that robots can determine their type: From the Fig. 6, we can observe that for r_2, all the robots lie below the horizontal line. That means, one side of the horizontal line is empty and therefore r_2 can figure out that it is a boundary robot. Similarly all r_i, $i \in \{3, 4, 5, 6, 7, 8\}$ are boundary robots. Whereas, for r_1, both horizontal and vertical lines have one of the sides empty, hence r_1 is a corner robot. Other robots are all inner robots. Consequently, we define *boundary robots* to be those, which have exactly one side of one of the orthogonal lines empty.

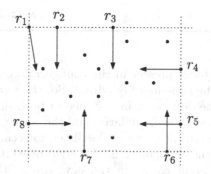

Fig. 6. Movement direction of the boundary robots

Algorithm 2 (CONVERGEQUADRANT) can be described as follows. A rectangle can be constructed with lines parallel to the orthogonal lines passing through boundary robots such that, all the robots are inside this rectangle. In Fig. 6, each boundary robot always moves inside the rectangle perpendicular to the boundary and the inside robots do not move. Note that the corner robot r_1 has two possible directions to move. So it moves toward any robot in that common quadrant. Gradually the distance between opposite boundaries becomes smaller and smaller and the robots converge. In case all the robots are on a line which is parallel to either of the orthogonal lines, then the robots will find that both sides of the line are empty. In that case, they should not move. But the robots on either end of the line would only see one robot. So they would move along the line towards that robot.

Theorem 2 *(Correctness).* *Algorithm 2 moves all the robots inside some $2b$-sided square in finite time, where b is the step size.*

Proof. Consider the distance between the robots on the left and right boundary. The horizontal distance between them decreases each time either of them gets activated. The rightmost robot will move towards the left and the leftmost will move towards the right. The internal robots do not move. So in at most n activation rounds of the boundary robot, the distance between two of the boundary nodes will decrease by at least b. Hence the distance is monotonically decreasing until $2b$. Afterward, the total distance will never exceed $2b$ anymore.

Algorithm 2. CONVERGEQUADRANT

 Input : Any arbitrary configuration and robot r
 Output: All robots are inside a square with side $2b$
1 **if** *only one robot is visible* **then**
2 | Move towards that robot
3 **else if** *r is a boundary robot* **then**
4 | Move perpendicular to the boundary to the side with robots
5 **else if** *r is a corner robot* **then**
6 | Move towards any robot in the non-empty quadrant
7 **else**
8 | Do not move   `// It is an inside robot`

If there is a corner robot present in the configuration, that robot will move towards any robot in the non-empty quadrant. So, the movement of the corner robot contributes to the decrement in distance in both directions. If an inside robot is very close to one of the boundaries and the corner robot moves towards that robot, then the decrement in one of the dimensions can be small (an $\epsilon > 0$). Consider for example the configuration of a strip of width b, then the corner robot becomes the adjacent corner in the next round; this can happen only finitely many times. Each dimension converges within a distance $2b$, so in the converged state the shape of the converged area would be $2b$-sided square, i.e., $\zeta = 2\sqrt{2}b$.   □

Remark 2. If the robots have some sense of angular knowledge, the corner robots can always move in a $\pi/4$ angle, so the decrement in both dimension is significant, hence convergence time is less on average.

4   Impossibility and Optimality

Given these positive results, we now show that the assumptions we made on the capability of monoculus robots are minimal for achieving convergeability: the following theorem shows that monoculus robots by themselves cannot converge deterministically.

Theorem 3. *There is no deterministic convergence algorithm for monoculus robots.*

Proof. We prove the theorem using a symmetry argument. Consider the two configurations C_1 and C_2 in Fig. 7. In C_1, all the robots are equidistant from robot r, while in C_2, the robots are at different distances, however, the relative angle of the robots is the same at r. Now considering the local view of robot r, it cannot distinguish between C_1 and C_2. Say a deterministic algorithm ϕ decides a direction of movement for robot r in configuration C_1. Since both C_1 and C_2 are the same from robot r's perspective, the deterministic algorithm outputs the same direction of movement for both cases.

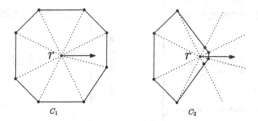

Fig. 7. Locally indistinguishable configurations with respect to r

Now consider the convex hull CH_1 and CH_2 of C_1 and C_2 respectively. The robot r moves a distance b in one round. The distance from any point inside CH_1 is more than b but we can skew the convex hull in the direction of movement, so to make it like CH_2, where if the robot r moves a distance b it exits CH_2. Therefore there exists a situation for any algorithm ϕ such that the area of the convex hull increases. Hence it is impossible for the robots to converge.   □

5 Simulation

We now complement our formal analysis with simulations, studying the average case. We assume that robots are distributed uniformly at random in a square initially, that $b = 1$ and $c = 2$, and we consider fully synchronous (FSYNC) scheduling [13]. As a baseline to evaluate performance, we consider the optimal convergence distance and time if the robots had the capability to observe positions, i.e., they are *not* monoculus. Moreover, as a lower bound, we compare to an algorithm which converges all robots to the centroid, defined as follows: $\{\bar{x}, \bar{y}\} = \left\{ \frac{\sum_{i=1}^{n} x_i}{n}, \frac{\sum_{i=1}^{n} y_i}{n} \right\}$ where $\{x_i, y_i\} \forall i \in \{1, 2, \cdots, n\}$ are the robots' coordinates. We calculate the distance d_i from each robot to the centroid in the initial configuration. The optimal distance we have use as convergence distance is the sum of distances from each robot to the unit disc centered at the centroid. So the sum of the optimal convergence distances d_{opt} is given by $d_{opt} = \sum_{i=1}^{n}(d_i - 1)$, if $d_i > 1$.

In the simulation of Algorithm 1, we define d_{CL} as the cumulative number of steps taken by all the robots to converge (sometimes also known as the *work*). Now we define the performance ratio, ρ_{CL} as $\rho_{CL} = \frac{d_{CL}}{d_{opt}}$. Similarly for Algorithm 2 we define d_{CQ} and ρ_{CQ}.

We have used BoxWhiskerChart [3] to plot the distributions. The BoxWhiskerChart in the Figs. 8 and 9 show four quartiles of the distribution notched at the median taken from 100 executions of the algorithms. Figures 8, and 9 show the comparison between the performance ratio (PR) for distance. We can observe that the distance traveled compared to optimal distance increases for same size region as the number of robots increase for Algorithm 1 but it

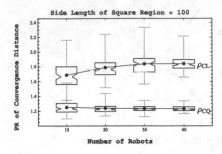

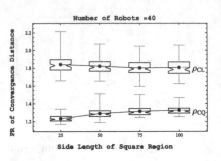

Fig. 8. ρ_{CL} vs ρ_{CQ} for the same size of region

Fig. 9. ρ_{CL} vs ρ_{CQ} for the same number of robots

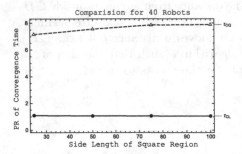

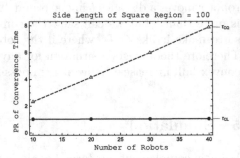

Fig. 10. τ_{CL} vs τ_{CQ} for the same number of robots

Fig. 11. τ_{CL} vs τ_{CQ} for the same size of region

remains almost the same for Algorithm 2. We can observe that Algorithm 2 performs better. This is due to the fact that, in Algorithm 2 only boundary robots move.

Let d_{max} be the distance of farthest robot from the centroid and t_{CL} be the number of synchronous rounds taken by Algorithm 1 for convergence. We define τ_{CL} as follows $\tau_{CL} = \frac{t_{CL}}{d_{max}}$. Similarly for Algorithm 2, we define t_{CQ} and τ_{CQ}. τ_{CL} and τ_{CQ} show performance ratio for convergence time of Algorithms 1 and 2 respectively. In Figs. 10 and 11, we can observe that τ_{CL} is very close to 1, so Algorithm 1 converges in almost the same number of synchronous rounds (proportional to distance covered, since step size $b = 1$) as the maximum distance from the centroid of the initial configuration. We can observe that Algorithm 2 takes more time as the number of robots and the side length of square region increases. Since Algorithm 2 only boundary robots move, the internal robots wait to move until they are on the boundary. As expected, this creates a chain of dependence which in turn increases the convergence time.

6   Discussion

This section shows that our approach supports some interesting extensions.

6.1   Termination for $\mathcal{OLA}$ Model

While we only focused on convergence and not termination so far, we can show that with a small amount of memory, termination is also possible in the $\mathcal{OLA}$ model.

Algorithm 3. CONVERGEQUADRANTTERMINATION

Input   : Any arbitrary configuration and robot r with 4-bit memory
Output: All robots are inside a square with side $2b$

1 **if** *the robot is on a boundary(ies)* **then**
2 $\quad$| $\quad$ set the corresponding bit(s) to 1
3 **else**
4 $\quad$⌊ Do nothing $\hfill$ // r **is an inside robot**

5 **if** r *is a boundary robot and the bits corresponding to that dimension are not 1*
$\quad$**then**
6 $\quad$| $\quad$ Move perpendicular to the boundary to the side with robots
7 **else if** r *is a corner robot* **then**
8 $\quad$| $\quad$ **if** *Both bits corresponding to a dimension is 1* **then**
9 $\quad$| $\quad$| $\quad$ Move in other dimension to the side with robots
10 $\quad$| $\quad$ **else**
11 $\quad$| $\quad$⌊ Move towards any robot in the non-empty quadrant

12 **else**
13 $\quad$⌊ Do not move $\hfill$ // r **is not on boundary OR all four bits are 1**

To see this, assume that each robot has a 2-bit persistent memory in the $\mathcal{OLA}$ model for each dimension, total 4-bits for two dimensions. Algorithm 2 has been modified to Algorithm 3 such that it can accommodate termination. All the bits are initially set to 0. Each robot has its local coordinate system, which remains consistent over the execution of the algorithm. The four bits correspond to four boundaries in two dimensions, i.e., left, right, top and bottom. If a robot finds itself on one of the boundaries according to its local coordinate system, then it sets the corresponding bit of that boundary to 1. Once both bits corresponding to a dimension become 1, the robot stops moving in that dimension. Consider a robot r. Initially, it was on the left boundary in its local coordinate system. Then it sets the first bit of the pair of bits corresponding to x-axis. It moves towards right. Once it reaches the right boundary, then it sets the second bit corresponding to x-axis to 1. Once both the bits are set to 1, it stops moving along the x-axis. Similar movement termination happens on the y-axis also. Once all the 4-bits are set to 1, the robot stops moving.

6.2   Extension to d-Dimensions

Both our algorithms can easily be extended to d-dimensions. For the $\mathcal{LD}$ model, the algorithm remains exactly the same. For the proof of convergence, similar arguments as Lemma 3 can be used in d dimensions. We can consider the convex hull in d-dimensions and the boundary robots of the convex hull always move inside. The size of convex hull reduces gradually and the robots converge.

Analogously for the $\mathcal{OLA}$ model, the distance between two robots in the boundary of any dimension gradually decreases and the corner robots always move inside the d-dimensional cuboid. Hence it converges. Here the robot would require $2d$ number of bits for termination.

7   Conclusion

This paper introduced the notion of *monoculus robots* which cannot measure distance: a practically relevant generalization of existing robot models. We have proved that the two basic models still allow for convergence (and with a small memory, even termination), but with less capabilities, this becomes impossible.

The $\mathcal{LD}$ model converges in an almost optimal number of rounds, while the $\mathcal{OLA}$ model takes more time. But the cumulative number of steps is less for the $\mathcal{OLA}$ model compared to the $\mathcal{LD}$ model since only boundary robots move. Although we found in our simulations that the median and angle bisector strategies successfully converge, finding a proof accordingly remains an open question. We see our work as a first step, and believe that the study of weaker robots opens an interesting field for future research.

References

1. Cohen, R., Peleg, D.: Convergence properties of the gravitational algorithm in asynchronous robot systems. SIAM J. Comput. **34**(6), 1516–1528 (2005)
2. Cohen, R., Peleg, D.: Convergence of autonomous mobile robots with inaccurate sensors and movements. SIAM J. Comput. **38**(1), 276–302 (2008)
3. Wolfram Mathematica Documentation: BoxWhiskerChart (2010). http://reference.wolfram.com/language/ref/BoxWhiskerChart.html
4. Dolev, S.: Self-stabilization. MIT press, Cambridge (2000)
5. Flocchini, P., Prencipe, G., Santoro, N., Widmayer, P.: Distributed coordination of a set of autonomous mobile robots. In: Proceedings of the IEEE Intelligent Vehicles Symposium, pp. 480–485 (2000)
6. Flocchini, P., Prencipe, G., Santoro, N., Widmayer, P.: Hard tasks for weak robots: the role of common knowledge in pattern formation by autonomous mobile robots. ISAAC 1999. LNCS, vol. 1741, pp. 93–102. Springer, Heidelberg (1999). doi:10.1007/3-540-46632-0_10
7. Flocchini, P., Prencipe, G., Santoro, N., Widmayer, P.: Gathering of asynchronous robots with limited visibility. Theor. Comput. Sci. **337**(1–3), 147–168 (2005)
8. Gilbert, S., Lynch, N., Mitra, S., Nolte, T.: Self-stabilizing robot formations over unreliable networks. ACM Trans. Auton. Adapt. Syst. **4**(3), 17:1–17:29 (2009)
9. Izumi, T., Souissi, S., Katayama, Y., Inuzuka, N., Défago, X., Wada, K., Yamashita, M.: The gathering problem for two oblivious robots with unreliable compasses. SIAM J. Comput. **41**(1), 26–46 (2012)
10. Prencipe, G.: Impossibility of gathering by a set of autonomous mobile robots. Theor. Comput. Sci. **384**(2–3), 222–231 (2007)

11. Souissi, S., Défago, X., Yamashita, M.: Using eventually consistent compasses to gather memory-less mobile robots with limited visibility. TAAS **4**(1), 9:1–9:27 (2009)
12. Sugihara, K., Suzuki, I.: Distributed algorithms for formation of geometric patterns with many mobile robots. J. Rob. Syst. **13**(3), 127–139 (1996)
13. Suzuki, I., Yamashita, M.: Distributed anonymous mobile robots: formation of geometric patterns. SIAM J. Comput. **28**(4), 1347–1363 (1999)

ABAC Rule Reduction via Similarity Computation

Maryem Ait El Hadj[1]([✉]), Yahya Benkaouz[2], Bernd Freisleben[3],
and Mohammed Erradi[1]

[1] Networking and Distributed Systems Research Group, TIES,
SIME Lab, ENSIAS, Mohammed V University in Rabat, Rabat, Morocco
maryem_aitelhadj@um5.ac.ma, mohamed.erradi@gmail.com
[2] Conception and Systems Laboratory, FSR,
Mohammed V University in Rabat, Rabat, Morocco
y.benkaouz@um5s.net.ma
[3] Department of Mathematics and Computer Science,
Philipps-Universität Marburg, Marburg, Germany
freisleb@informatik.uni-marburg.de

Abstract. Attribute-based access control (ABAC) represents a generic
model of access control that provides a high level of flexibility and pro-
motes information and security sharing. Since ABAC considers a large
set of attributes for access decisions, using it might get very complicated
for large systems. Hence, it is interesting to offer techniques to reduce
the number of rules in ABAC policies without affecting the final decision. In this paper, we present an approach based on K-nearest neighbors
algorithms for clustering ABAC policies. To the best of our knowledge,
it is the first approach that aims to reduce the number of policy rules
based on similarity computations. Our evaluation results demonstrate
the efficiency of the suggested approach. For instance, the reduction rate
can reach up to 10% for an ABAC policy with more than 9000 rules.

Keywords: Clustering · K-nearest neighbors · Access control · ABAC

1 Introduction

Collaborative computing environments (i.e., cloud computing) bring numerous
benefits, such as flexibility, scalability and reliability. While benefiting from these
advantages, such systems entail multiple security risks, by exercising limited
control to make information accessible to only those who are allowed to access it.
In this direction, access control models represent a key component for providing
security features.

Access control is concerned with determining the allowed activities of legitimate users, mediating every attempt by a user to access a resource in the system
[10]. Traditionally, access control was based on user identities (Access Control
Lists - ACL), or through predefined roles or groups assigned to that user (Role-
based Access Control - RBAC) [18]. In the ACL model, a user is allowed to

© Springer International Publishing AG 2017
A. El Abbadi and B. Garbinato (Eds.): NETYS 2017, LNCS 10299, pp. 86–100, 2017.
DOI: 10.1007/978-3-319-59647-1_7

perform an access depending on whether that user appears in the list of authorized users or not. In the RBAC model, the access decision is based on the role of the requestor (i.e., the roles associated with a hospital can include doctor, nurse, clinician, etc.). One of the advantages of the RBAC model is the fact that a given user might have multiple roles. Therefore, such a user might have different permissions according to the selected role.

Several variants of access control models have been proposed as extended version of the RBAC model. For instance, Rule-based RBAC [1] provides a mechanism to dynamically assign users to roles based on a finite set of authorization rules. The Task-Role-based Access Control (T-RBAC) model [16] is based on the concept of classification of tasks, where a task is a fundamental unit of business activity. Another variant of RBAC is the context-aware access control model [6], where the access control takes into account the context-sensitive requirements (such as time, location, or environmental state). Besides these works, the Attribute-based Access Control (ABAC) model has been suggested as a generic access control model [25]. ABAC considers a set of attributes, based on which the access decision will be taken. An attribute is assigned to a subject (e.g., user, application or process), resource (e.g., data structure, web service or system component) and environment (e.g., current time, location). These attributes may be considered as characteristics of anything that may be defined and to which a value may be assigned.

ABAC policy representation is more expressive and fine-grained, because it might consider any combination of subject, resource and environment attributes. However, in distributed environments such as cloud computing, deploying and managing an ABAC model to ensure access control might become more complex and hard to manage. This is due to the massive amount of information that should be considered as attributes. For example, considering an e-health use case, each piece of data related to the patients' medical records should be taken into account as an attribute to help deciding the types of person (determined by their attributes) having access to each individual piece of data in a given environment (location, time, etc.). In fact, an ABAC policy in distributed applications may be aggregated from multiple parties and can be managed by more than one administrator. Therefore, it may contain several redundant rules, which may lead to high implementation complexity. Hence, reducing the number of rules in ABAC policies without affecting the final decision in large sets of complex policies is primordial.

Following the idea of using K-nearest neighbors (KNN) algorithms to reduce the number of ABAC policy rules to enhance the policy analysis [4], in this paper we propose a new approach referred to as ABAC-PC (ABAC Policy Clustering). ABAC-PC works as follows: (1) First, the policy rules are grouped according to their decision effects (i.e., permit rules, deny rules), and for each group, the similarity scores of each pair of rules are computed; (2) clusters of rules are created based on the similarity scores; (3) finally, given the set of clusters, ABAC-PC produces the minimum set of rules that represent each cluster. Regarding the algorithmic complexity, the computation time is in $O(n^2)$ where n is the number of rules. ABAC-PC has been tested on a synthetic dataset of up to 9000 rules, and the obtained results show that ABAC-PC can successfully reduce the number of policy rules up to 10% for a policy with more than 9000 rules. In a nutshell, given an ABAC policy, ABAC-PC produces a reduced policy and guarantees the policy's conformity. Furthermore, our approach can be extended and integrated with other policy analysis tools in order to enhance managing authorization policies, such as detecting and resolving anomalies among XACML (eXtensible Access Control Markup Language) policies (since XACML is the most convenient way to express ABAC policies).

The paper is organized as follows. Section 2 presents related work. Section 3 presents the ABAC model. Section 4 gives an overview on the KNN algorithms. ABAC-PC is described in Sect. 5. Section 6 reports experimental results. Section 7 concludes the paper and outlines areas for future work.

2   Related Work

To the best of our knowledge, this paper presents the first approach specifically designed to reduce the number of ABAC policy rules. ABAC-PC is based on KNN, which has been often used in data mining. In the following, we present existing work that considers data mining techniques to resolve some of the access control related issues.

In the literature, several works have considered the usage of data mining for role mining to discover roles from existing system configuration data [7,13,19]. Role mining refers to the process of mining data about the actual user-to-resource permission assignments to extract role definitions. Molloy et al. [14] consider the problem of migrating a non-RBAC system to an RBAC system. Then, a role mining algorithm constructs an RBAC state with low cost and complexity, while maintaining the semantic meaning of roles.

Ni et al. [15] have investigated the role adjustment problem. It consists of how to automate the process that provisions existing roles with entitlements from newly deployed applications. In this direction, the authors have suggested the use of supervised machine learning algorithms to automate the process of providing users with access to data and resources.

Xu and Stoller [20] attempt to produce small RBAC policies (i.e., with low weighted structural complexity) with meaningful roles. The same authors [22] present a parameterized RBAC (PRBAC) framework, in which users and permissions have attributes, i.e., implicit parameters of the roles that can be used in role definitions.

An ABAC policy mining algorithm has been suggested by Xu and Stoller [21,24]. This algorithm aims to reduce the cost of migration to an ABAC policy from an ACL or from an RBAC policy with accompanying attributes. Another variant of the ABAC policy mining algorithm has been presented by Xu and Stoller [23], where the authors consider the logs as attribute data. These works might be considered to detect either roles or attributes during RBAC and ABAC policies construction, whereas in our work, we consider the optimization of the ABAC policies themselves.

3 Attribute-Based Access Control

In this section, we briefly present the ABAC model [25]. An ABAC policy defines permissions based on predefined attributes. Attributes describe any character-istics that should be taken into account for the authorization decisions. These attributes are associated to three different entities: *Subject* (i.e., the user or the process that takes an action on a resource), *Resource* (i.e., the entity that is acted upon by a subject) and *Environment* (i.e., the operational, technical or situational context in which the information access occurs). Thus, the attributes are Subject attributes, Resource attributes and Environment attributes.

Regarding the ABAC policy formulation, we consider the following notation:

- S: Set of subjects.
- RS: Set of resources.
- E: Set of environments.
- For a given subject with M attributes: SA_m is a subject attribute with $1 \leq m < M$.
- For a given resource with N attributes: RSA_n is a resource attribute with $1 \leq n \leq N$.
- For a given environment with O attributes: EA_o is a environment attribute with $1 < o \leq O$.
- $ATTR(s) \subseteq SA_1 \times ... \times SA_m$: Attribute assignment relations for a subject s.
- $ATTR(rs) \subseteq RSA_1 \times ... \times RSA_n$: Attribute assignment relations for a resource rs.
- $ATTR(e) \subseteq EA_1 \times ... \times EA_o$: Attribute assignment relations for an environment e.

A policy $P = \{r_1, r_2, ..., r_n\}$ is made up of a set of rules. A rule r decides whether a subject s can access a resource rs in an environment e. To this end, a Boolean function is evaluated based on the values of all the attributes of s, rs and e. Thus, the *Policy rule* that regulates this access is expressed as follows:

$$Rule : can\_access(s, rs, e) \leftarrow f(ATTR(s), ATTR(rs), ATTR(e))$$

The next section gives an overview of the KNN algorithm that will be used in ABAC-PC.

4 K-Nearest Neighbors

The K-nearest neighbor algorithm (KNN) is widely used in pattern recognition, text categorization, ranking models, and so on. The KNN algorithm classifies objects based on closest training examples in the feature space [5]. Given a sys-tem with N objects, where each object has a specific profile, a KNN algorithm provides each object with its K most similar objects, based on a given similar-ity metric. This results in a KNN graph where there is an edge between each object and its K most similar objects (based on the comparison of profiles).

Such a graph can be useful in the context of many applications such as similarity search [2], data mining [17] and machine learning [8]. To illustrate the use of the KNN algorithm, assume that a web-based platform is visited by multiple users to listen to different kinds of music. It would be interesting to provide a given user with items matching its interest. One approach is to look for K different users sharing similar profiles (i.e., users with the same music tastes). Then, recommend the most popular songs among the music liked by the K selected users.

The most straightforward way to construct the KNN graph is to rely on a brute-force solution computing the similarity between each pair of nodes. The similarity between nodes can be computed by several metrics, such as the cosine similarity metric or Jaccard similarity. These similarities are computed as follows:

- The cosine similarity: It is represented using the dot product and the magnitude of two vectors:

$$Cosine(v_1, v_2) = \frac{v_1.v_2}{\parallel v_1 \parallel . \parallel v_2 \parallel}$$

- The Jaccard similarity: Given two sets of attributes, this measure is defined as the cardinality of the intersection divided by the size of the union of the two sets:

$$Jaccard(s_1, s_2) = |\frac{s_1 \cap s_2}{s_1 s_2}|$$

After the presentation of the basic idea of the KNN algorithm, the next section shows how such algorithms are useful for ABAC policy optimization. Therefore, we present the suggested ABAC Policy Clustering Approach (ABAC-PC).

5   ABAC-PC: ABAC Policy Clustering

Let us recall that the aim of the suggested approach is to reduce the number of rules in ABAC policies. To achieve this goal, we create clusters of rules that share similar characteristics based on similarity scores. Then, for each cluster, we compute the minimum set of rules that represent each cluster. The ABAC-PC process is depicted in Fig. 1. In this section, we will first present the steps of ABAC-PC and then prove its correctness.

5.1   Rule Profiling

Without loss of generality, we consider that an ABAC policy consists of two categories of decision effects (permit and deny rules). Therefore, the policy base is split into two categories. Rules from each category are extracted and expressed as profiles. The general format of a profile is as follows:

$Decision\_effect(attr\_name_1 = attr\_value_1, ..., attr\_name_n = attr\_value_n)$

The profile represents the combination of the whole sets of subject, resource and environment attributes (ATTR(s), ATTR(rs) and ATTR(e)). For instance,

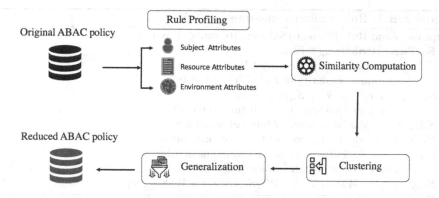

Fig. 1. ABAC-PC steps

the profile of a given rule with permit access between 12:00 and 16:00 to an MRI scan for a female nurse belonging to the oncology team, the nursing department and the Steatl organization might be expressed as:

permit_access (position = {nurse}, team = {oncology}, gender = {female}, department = {Nursing}; type = {MRI}, formatType = {TXT}; Organization = {Steatl}, time in {{12–16}}).

5.2   Similarity Computation

The similarity measures adopted in ABAC-PC are inspired by Lin et al. [11]. The rule similarity measure assigns a similarity score S_{rule} for any two given rules, which reflects how similar these rules are with respect to subject, resource and environment attributes values. The formal definition of the rule similarity measure is given in Eq. (1), the score for each rule pair is the sum of the similarity scores of all the subject, resource and environment attributes of these rules.

$$S_{rule}(r_i, r_j) = W_s S_s(r_i, r_j) + W_{rs} S_{rs}(r_i, r_j) + W_e S_e(r_i, r_j) \qquad (1)$$

where S_s, S_{rs} and S_e are functions to compute similarity scores based on the Subject, Resource, and Environment attributes respectively. W_s, W_{rs} and W_e are weights that can be chosen to reflect the relative importance to be given to the similarity computation. The weight values should satisfy the constraint: $W_s + W_{rs} + W_e = 1$.

The similarity score is a value between 0 and 1. Two equivalent rules are expected to obtain a similarity score that equals 1. The rule similarity measure algorithm is shown in Algorithm 1. Given two rules, the algorithm, first computes the similarity score regarding the same rule elements (subject, resource and environment). Then, the obtained scores for the different rule elements are combined according to the weights chosen in order to produce an overall similarity score.

Algorithm 1. Rule similarity measure algorithm

Require: *Elm*: Rule Element (Subject, Resource, Environment)
1: **ForEach** attribute $a_i \in Elm_{r_i}$
2:          **ForEach** attribute $a_j \in Elm_{r_j}$
      //Compute similarity of Rule Element ¡*Elm*¿
3: $S_{<Elm>}(r_i, r_j) + = w_{Elm}S_{<Elm>}(a_i, a_j)$
      //Compute similarity for each rule elements
4: $S_s(r_i, r_j) \leftarrow$ similarity score of Subject attributes
5: $S_{rs}(r_i, r_j) \leftarrow$ similarity score of Resource attributes
6: $S_e(r_i, r_j) \leftarrow$ similarity score of Environment attributes
      //Compute the overall similarity score
7: $S_{rule}(r_i, r_j) = W_s S_s(r_i, r_j) + W_{rs}S_{rs}(r_i, r_j) + W_e S_e(r_i, r_j)$

Similarity Score of Rule Elements: Each rule element *Subject*, *Resource*, and *Environment* are represented as a set of predicates in the form of:

$$(attr\_name_1 = attr\_value_1, attr\_name_2 = attr\_value_2, ...)$$

The similarity score between two rules and regarding the same element is denoted as $S_{<Elm>}(r_i, r_j)$, where $<Elm>$ refers to *Subject, Resource*, or *Environment*. The $S_{<Elm>}$ is computed as the sum of the similarity scores of attribute elements (Eq. (2)).

$$S_{<Elm>}(r_i, r_j) = \sum_{k=1}^{|ATTR(Elm)|} w_{k,Elm}S_{Elm}(a_i, a_j) \qquad (2)$$

where $w_{k,Elm}$ is the weight assigned to each attribute element. a_i, a_j are attributes for r_i, r_j, respectively, regarding the same element, and $|ATTR(Elm)|$ is the number of attribute elements being computed.

Similarity Score of Attribute Elements: The similarity score of attribute elements for two rules is computed only for sets of attribute elements having the same attribute names (Eq. (3)).

$$S_{<Elm>}(a_i, a_j) = \frac{|AN_i \cap AN_j|}{|AN_i \cup AN_j|} \sum_{AN_i = AN_j} S_{<att\_typ>}(v_i, v_j) \qquad (3)$$

where AN_i and AN_j denote the attribute names for a_i, a_j respectively. $|AN_i \cap AN_j|$ denote the common number of attribute names and $|AN_i \cup AN_j|$ the total number of attribute names. $S_{<att\_typ>}(v_i, v_j)$ denotes the similarity score of attribute values, where v_i, v_j are the attribute values for a_i, a_j respectively. The condition $AN_i = AN_j$ ensures that the similarity score is only computed for sets of attribute elements having the same attribute names for both rules (i.e. $\frac{|AN_i \cap AN_j|}{|AN_i \cup AN_j|} \neq 0$).

The similarity score of attribute elements algorithm is presented in Algorithm 2. Given two attribute elements, we compute the similarity score of attribute values for attribute elements having the same attribute names.

Algorithm 2. Attribute Elements Similarity Algorithm

Require: AN_i, AN_j: set of attribute names for r_i, r_j respectively, $AttrElm$: Attribute
　　element
1: **ForEach** attribute value $v_i \in AttrElm_{a_i}$
2: 　　　　**ForEach** attribute value $v_j \in AttrElm_{a_j}$
3: **if** $AN_i = AN_j$ **then**
　　　　//Compute similarity of Attribute Element
4: 　　$S_{<Elm>}(a_i, a_j) += S_{att\_typ}(v_i, v_j)$
5: **end if**
6: **return** $\frac{|AN_i \cap AN_j|}{|AN_i \cup AN_j|} \times S_{<Elm>}(a_i, a_j)$

Algorithm 3. Attribute Values Similarity Algorithm

1: **if** v_1 and v_2 are single values **then**
2: 　　**if** $v_1 = v_2$ **then**
3: 　　　　return 1
4: 　　**else**
5: 　　　　return 0
6: 　　**end if**
7: **else if** v_1 and v_2 are bounded intervals **then**
8: 　　**return** $\frac{len|v_i \cap v_j|}{len|v_i \cup v_j|}$
9: **else** v_1 and v_2 are Categorical values
10: 　　**return** $\frac{|v_i \cap v_j|}{|v_i \cup v_j|}$
11: **end if**

The similarity score between attribute values differs, depending on whether
their type is categorical (i.e., the string data type) or numerical (i.e., integer,
real, or date/time data types). For the categorical values, we only consider the
exact match of two values. The similarity is computed based on Jaccard measure
(Algorithm 3).

5.3 Clustering

The results obtained in the similarity measures are used to classify rules into
clusters, where similar rules are grouped together, while different rules belong
to different groups.

Two rules r_i and r_j are similar if their similarity score is no less than a
predefined threshold: $S_{rule}(r_i, r_j) \geq threshold$. The value of the threshold is set
to 0.8, based on previous works regarding recommender systems and a similarity
measure for security policies [9,11]. Lowe [12] has proposed to use the value 0.8
reporting that this threshold allows to eliminate 90% of the false matches while
discarding less than 5% of the correct matches.

Given a policy with n rules, the clustering method constructs k sets of rules
with $k \leq n$. Rules are classified into k clusters, which satisfy the following requirements:

- Each cluster contains at least one rule.
- Each rule must belong to exactly one cluster.

Formally, a policy P is represented as a set of clusters, where $P = \bigcup_{i=1}^{k} C_i$, such that $C_i \cap C_j = \emptyset$ for $i \neq j$.

5.4   Generalization

After constructing clusters of rules, the purpose of this step is to compute the minimum set of rules that represent each cluster. To this end, a generalization function is applied in each cluster. This function attempts to reduce the number of policy rules, by **removing redundant rules** and **merging pairs of rules**. Let $Rules_c$ denotes the rules in a cluster c.

Redundancy Removal: A rule $r_i \in Rules_c$ is redundant if $Rules_c$ contains another rule r_j such that:

- $r_i = r_j$ (i.e. $S_{rule}(r_i, r_j) = 1$): for all the shared attribute elements of subject, resource and environment are identical. In this case, the generalization function will remove one of these two rules, or
- $r_i \subseteq r_j$: Some of the shared attribute elements of subject, resource and environment are identical, i.e. $r_i \cup r_j = r_j$. In this case, the subset rule is removed (i.e. r_i is removed).

For instance, let us consider the following rules r_1 and r_2:

- r_1: permit_access (Designation = {Professor, Student}; FileType = {Source, Documentation}; time = [8:00, 18:00])
- r_2: permit_access (Designation = {Professor}; FileType = {Source, Documentation}; time = [8:00, 18:00])

In this case, r_2 will be removed because r_2 represents the subset rule of r_1 (i.e. $r_2 \subseteq r_1$).

Rule Merging: For the merging process, two policy rules r_i and r_j are mergeable if one of their shared attribute elements of subject, resource and environment do not intersect, while the rest of the attribute elements are identical:

$$ATTR(s_{r_i}) \cap ATTR(s_{r_j}) = \emptyset \text{ or } ATTR(rs_{r_i}) \cap ATTR(rs_{r_j}) = \emptyset \text{ or}$$
$$ATTR(e_{r_i}) \cap ATTR(e_{r_j}) = \emptyset$$

Given two rules r_i and r_j, the merging process consists of the union of the subject, resource and environment attributes.

$$ATTR(s_{r_{merge}}) = ATTR(s_{r_i}) \cup ATTR(s_{r_j})$$
$$ATTR(rs_{r_{merge}}) = ATTR(rs_{r_i}) \cup ATTR(rs_{r_j})$$
$$ATTR(e_{r_{merge}}) = ATTR(e_{r_i}) \cup ATTR(e_{r_j})$$

Algorithm 4. Generalization Algorithm

1: **ForEach** rule $r_i \in cluster_i$
2: // Remove subset of rules
3: subRules$= \{r_i \in cluster_i | \exists r_j \in cluster_i \setminus r_i.r_i \subseteq r_j\}$
4: $cluster_i$.**removeAll**(subRules)
5: // merge of rules
6: subRules$= \{(r_i, r_j) | r_i \in cluster_i \wedge r_j \in cluster_i\}$
7: **if** $(S_s(r_i, r_j) = 1 \wedge S_{rs}(r_i, r_j) = 1) \vee (S_s(r_i, r_j) = 1 \wedge S_e(r_i, r_j) = 1) \vee (S_{rs}(r_i, r_j) = 1 \wedge S_e(r_i, r_j) = 1)$ **then**
8: $\quad r_{merge} = (ATTR(s_{r_1}) \cup ATTR(s_{r_2}), ATTR(rs_{r_1}) \cup ATTR(rs_{r_2}), ATTR(e_{r_1}) \cup ATTR(e_{r_2}))$
$\quad$ // Add the merged rule to $cluster_i$
9: $\quad cluster_i$.**add**(r_{merge})
$\quad$ // remove rules that become subset of r_{merge}
10: $\quad$ subRules$= \{r_k \in cluster_i | r_k \subseteq r_{merge}\}$
11: $\quad cluster_i$.**removeAll**(subRules)
12: **end if**
13: **return** $cluster_i$

---

r_{merge}, which is the merging rule, is added to $Rules_c$, while rules being merged (i.e., r_i and r_j) are removed from $Rules_c$.

For instance, let us consider the following rules r_1 and r_2:

- r_1: permit_access (Designation = {Professor, Student}; FileType = {Source, Documentation};time = [8:00, 12:00])
- r_2: permit_access (Designation = {Professor, Student}; FileType = {Source, Documentation};time = [12:00, 18:00])
- r_{merge}: permit_access (Designation = {Professor, Student}; FileType = {Source, Documentation}; time = [8:00, 12:00]∪[12:00, 18:00])

Given a cluster of rules $cluster_i$, the generalization function in Algorithm 4 attempts to update rules in $cluster_i$. It eliminates redundant rules and merges pairs of rules. If there is a valid generalization, the algorithm outputs an updated cluster with minimum rules. Otherwise, the algorithm outputs the same cluster.

5.5 Correctness

The aim of this subsection is to prove the correctness of the suggested approach. Given an original policy base OP where $OP = \bigcup_{i=1}^{n} r_i$, we want to find a reduced policy base $RP = \bigcup_{j=1}^{m} r_j$ which is conform to OP with $n \geq m$. In order to prove the correctness of the suggested approach, first, we define the concepts of *Conformity* and *Access Domain*.

Definition 1 *(Conformity)*.
An original policy OP conforms to a reduced policy RP if OP's access domain is equivalent to RP's access domain: $AD_{OP} \equiv AD_{RP}$.

Definition 2 *(Access Domain)*.
Given a rule $r(s, rs, e) \leftarrow f$ *(ATTR(s), ATTR(rs), ATTR(e)), the access domain of* r *denoted* AD_r *is defined as the set of all possible combinations of ATTR(s), ATTR(rs) and ATTR(e). Therefore, the access domain of the global policy* P *is* AD_P, *defined by the union of the access domains of the individual rules of* P.

Theorem 1. *Consider an original policy base OP with n rules. ABAC-PC produces a reduced policy base RP with m rules conforming to OP with* $n \geq m$.

Proof. ABAC-PC is composed of four steps (i.e., rules profiling, similarity computation, clustering and generalization). During the first three steps, the policy conformity holds, since no change is performed on attribute values. In the fourth step, two actions are performed: (1) redundancy removal and (2) rule merging.

Let r_i and r_j be two rules in OP. Thus, the union of their access domains belong to OP's access domain.

$$(r_i, r_j) \subseteq OP \implies AD_{r_i} \cup AD_{r_j} \subseteq AD_{OP}$$

(1) Redundancy removal
In case $r_i = r_j$ (i.e. $AD_{r_i} = AD_{r_j}$), either r_i or r_j is removed. Let r_j be the removed one.

$$r_i \subseteq RP \implies AD_{r_i} \subseteq AD_{RP}$$

While $AD_{r_i} = AD_{r_j}$, the access domain represented by the reduced policy RP is the same as OP's access domain.

In case $r_i \subseteq r_j$ (i.e. $AD_{r_i} \subseteq AD_{r_j}$), r_i represents the subset of r_j. Thus, r_i is the removed rule.

$$r_j \subseteq RP \implies AD_{r_j} \subseteq AD_{RP}$$

Since our function keeps the superset of rules (i.e., r_j), the access domain selected is the general one. Therefore, the access domain represented by the reduced policy RP is the same as OP's access domain.

(2) Rule merging
Let r_i and r_j are good candidates for the merging process (i.e., two of their attribute elements are matched) and r_{merge} be the merging rule. r_{merge} represents the union of the subject, resource and environment attributes of r_i and r_j:

$$ATTR(s_{r_{merge}}) = ATTR(s_{r_i}) \cup ATTR(s_{r_j})$$
$$ATTR(rs_{r_{merge}}) = ATTR(rs_{r_i}) \cup ATTR(r_{r_j})$$
$$ATTR(e_{r_{merge}}) = ATTR(e_{r_i}) \cup ATTR(e_{r_j})$$

While $r_{merge} = r_i \cup r_j$, the access domain specified by r_{merge} is the union of the access domains of r_i and r_j (i.e., $AD_{r_{merge}} = AD_{r_i} \cup AD_{r_j}$). r_i and r_j are removed from the resulting policy. Thus, the access domain represented by the reduced policy RP is the same as OP's access domain.

$$r_{merge} \subseteq RP \implies AD_{r_{merge}} \subseteq AD_{RP}$$

Therefore, for all performed actions we guarantee that the access domain specified by the OP is the same specified by RP, Thus, the policy RP conforms to OP.

Complexity analysis: Let n be the number of rules of a policy, K the number of clusters and n_k the number of rules in a cluster k. The running time of the rule profiling step is in $O(n)$. During the similarity computation step, we use brute force approach to compute to the rules similarities. Thus, the complexity is $O(n^2)$. The running time of the clustering step is in $O(C_n^2)$ since every pair of n rules is explored to construct clusters. The running time of the last step (generalization) in the worst is $O(K \times n_k^2)$. Therefore, the overall time complexity for constructing a reduced policy is in $O(n^2)$.

6 Experimental Results

To evaluate ABAC-PC, we consider a synthetic dataset composed of the combination of eight subject attributes, four resource attributes and two environment attributes. Evaluation on policies from real organization would be perfect. Unfortunately, no benchmarks have been published in this area and real medical data are hard to obtain because of confidentiality constraints.

The number of rules varies between 1000 and 10000. ABAC-PC has been implemented in Java and the experiments were made using a laptop with a 2.7 GHz Intel Core i5 CPU, 8 Gb RAM.

As comparison metrics, we mainly consider the running time, the size of the resulted policy and the reduction rate. Figure 2 shows the running time as a function of policy size. The graph explicitly shows that the running time increases with the number of policy rules in a quadratic way. This is related to the number of the combinations generated and being treated for policy rules during the ABAC-PC steps, especially in the similarity computation.

Figure 3 shows the size of reduced policy based on the similarity threshold. The obtained results represent the evaluation of the ABAC-PC on three bases with different number of policy rules (1000, 3000 and 5000 rules). As depicted in this figure, the lowest threshold (i.e., 0.6) returns a very reduced policy. The threshold effect is negligible from the value 0.8, where the reduced policy size is close to the original policy size. Therefore, the default value of the threshold selected for our experiments is 0.8.

Figures 4 and 5 show the reduction rate for five policy bases with different number of rules. The reduction rate increases significantly for large policies. The obtained results can be explained by the fact that the probability of having redundant and mergeable rules increases.

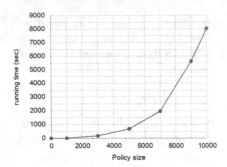

Fig. 2. Running time

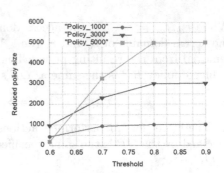

Fig. 3. Reduced policy size vs. threshold

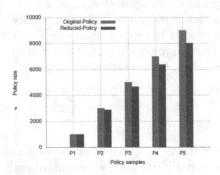

Fig. 4. Original and reduced policy sizes

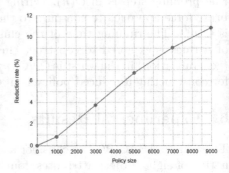

Fig. 5. Reduction rate

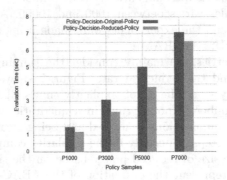

Fig. 6. Policy decision evaluation time

In order to evaluate the impact of the reduced policy on the functionality of ABAC, we consider the policy decision time (i.e., the time required for sending the final decision regarding a given request). The policy decision time is directly related to the size of the overall policy. Hence, reducing the number of rules will be beneficial for the policy decision performance.

The policy decision evaluation is depicted in Fig. 6. The obtained results represent the time evaluation for a request on four policies (original and reduced policies). The experiments were made on *Balana* [3] as the Open source XACML 3.0 implementation. As depicted in this figure, the time required for the decision on original policies is higher than the one on reduced policies. The difference can be explained by the fact that our approach reduces the policy size by eliminating redundant rules and merging pairs of rules. Therefore, the PDP takes more time to evaluate the request in a policy that contains more rules.

7 Conclusion

Since an ABAC policy is based on combination of subject, resource and environment attributes for access decisions, its policy representation is rich and expressive. However, using the ABAC model for large systems might generate a large number of security policy rules. In this direction, we have presented an approach that reduces the number of the ABAC policy rules. The suggested approach is mainly based on the K-nearest neighbors algorithm. The evaluation results demonstrate the efficiency of the proposed approach. Directions for future work include the integration of the suggested ABAC-PC in a real world policy analysis project.

References

1. Al-Kahtani, M.A., Sandhu, R.: Induced role hierarchies with attribute-based RBAC. In: Proceedings of the Eighth ACM Symposium on Access Control Models and Technologies, pp. 142–148. ACM (2003)
2. Amato, G., Falchi, F.: kNN based image classification relying on local feature similarity. In: Proceedings of the Third International Conference on SImilarity Search and APplications, pp. 101–108. ACM (2010)
3. Balana: Open source xacml 3.0 implementation (2012). http://xacmlinfo.org/2012/08/16/balana-the-open-source-xacml-3-0-implementation/
4. Benkaouz, Y., Erradi, M., Freisleben, B.: Work in progress: K-nearest neighbors techniques for ABAC policies clustering. In: Proceedings of the 2016 ACM International Workshop on Attribute Based Access Control, pp. 72–75. ACM (2016)
5. Bhatia, N., et al.: Survey of nearest neighbor techniques. arXiv preprint arXiv:1007.0085 (2010)
6. Bhatti, R., Bertino, E., Ghafoor, A.: A trust-based context-aware access control model for web-services. Distrib. Parallel Databases 18(1), 83–105 (2005)
7. Ene, A., Horne, W., Milosavljevic, N., Rao, P., Schreiber, R., Tarjan, R.E.: Fast exact and heuristic methods for role minimization problems. In: Proceedings of the 13th ACM Symposium on Access Control Models and Technologies, pp. 1–10. ACM (2008)
8. Guo, G., Wang, H., Bell, D., Bi, Y., Greer, K.: KNN model-based approach in classification. In: Meersman, R., Tari, Z., Schmidt, D.C. (eds.) OTM 2003. LNCS, vol. 2888, pp. 986–996. Springer, Heidelberg (2003). doi:10.1007/978-3-540-39964-3_62
9. Guo, S.: Analysis and evaluation of similarity metrics in collaborative filtering recommender system. Master's thesis. Lapland University of Applied Sciences (2014)

10. Hu, V.C., Ferraiolo, D., Kuhn, D.R.: Assessment of access control systems. US Department of Commerce, National Institute of Standards and Technology (2006)
11. Lin, D., Rao, P., Ferrini, R., Bertino, E., Lobo, J.: A similarity measure for comparing XACML policies. IEEE Trans. Knowl. Data Eng. **25**(9), 1946–1959 (2013)
12. Lowe, D.G.: Distinctive image features from scale-invariant keypoints. Int. J. Comput. Vis. **60**(2), 91–110 (2004)
13. Molloy, I., Chen, H., Li, T., Wang, Q., Li, N., Bertino, E., Calo, S., Lobo, J.: Mining roles with semantic meanings. In: Proceedings of the 13th ACM Symposium on Access Control Models and Technologies, pp. 21–30. ACM (2008)
14. Molloy, I., Chen, H., Li, T., Wang, Q., Li, N., Bertino, E., Calo, S., Lobo, J.: Mining roles with multiple objectives. ACM Trans. Inf. Syst. Secur. (TISSEC) **13**(4), 36 (2010)
15. Ni, Q., Lobo, J., Calo, S., Rohatgi, P., Bertino, E.: Automating role-based provisioning by learning from examples. In: Proceedings of the 14th ACM Symposium on Access Control Models and Technologies, pp. 75–84. ACM (2009)
16. Oh, S., Park, S.: Task-role-based access control model. Inf. Syst. **28**(6), 533–562 (2003)
17. Pan, R., Dolog, P., Xu, G.: KNN-based clustering for improving social recommender systems. In: Cao, L., Zeng, Y., Symeonidis, A.L., Gorodetsky, V.I., Yu, P.S., Singh, M.P. (eds.) ADMI 2012. LNCS, vol. 7607, pp. 115–125. Springer, Heidelberg (2013). doi:10.1007/978-3-642-36288-0_11
18. Sandhu, R.S., Coynek, E.J., Feinsteink, H.L., Youmank, C.E.: Role-based access control models yz. IEEE Comput. **29**(2), 38–47 (1996)
19. Vaidya, J., Atluri, V., Guo, Q., Adam, N.: Migrating to optimal RBAC with minimal perturbation. In: Proceedings of the 13th ACM Symposium on Access Control Models and Technologies, pp. 11–20. ACM (2008)
20. Xu, Z., Stoller, S.D.: Algorithms for mining meaningful roles. In: Proceedings of the 17th ACM Symposium on Access Control Models and Technologies, pp. 57–66. ACM (2012)
21. Xu, Z., Stoller, S.D.: Mining attribute-based access control policies from RBAC policies. In: 2013 10th International Conference and Expo on Emerging Technologies for a Smarter World (CEWIT 2013), pp. 1–6. IEEE (2013)
22. Xu, Z., Stoller, S.D.: Mining parameterized role-based policies. In: Proceedings of the Third ACM Conference on Data and Application Security and Privacy, pp. 255–266. ACM (2013)
23. Xu, Z., Stoller, S.D.: Mining attribute-based access control policies from logs. In: Atluri, V., Pernul, G. (eds.) DBSec 2014. LNCS, vol. 8566, pp. 276–291. Springer, Heidelberg (2014). doi:10.1007/978-3-662-43936-4_18
24. Xu, Z., Stoller, S.D.: Mining attribute-based access control policies. IEEE Trans. Dependable Secure Comput. **12**(5), 533–545 (2015)
25. Yuan, E., Tong, J.: Attributed based access control (ABAC) for web services. In: IEEE International Conference on Web Services (ICWS 2005). IEEE (2005)

A Distributed Recommender System Based on Graded Multi-label Classification

Khalil Laghmari[1,2]([⊠]), Christophe Marsala[2], and Mohammed Ramdani[1]

[1] Laboratoire Informatique de Mohammedia, FSTM,
Hassan II University of Casablanca, BP 146, 20650 Mohammedia, Morocco
laghmari.khalil@gmail.com, ramdani@fstm.ac.ma
[2] Sorbonne Universités, UPMC Univ Paris 06, CNRS, LIP6 UMR 7606,
4 Place Jussieu, 75005 Paris, France
christophe.marsala@lip6.fr

Abstract. Recommender systems are designed to find items in which each user has most likely the highest interest. Items can be of any type such as commercial products, e-learning resources, movies, songs, and jokes. Successful web and mobile applications can collect easily thousands of users, thousands of items, and millions of item ratings in only few months. A solution to store and to process these continuously growing data is to build distributed recommender systems. The challenging task is to find the appropriate distribution strategy allowing an efficient retrieval of needed information. Considering the similarity between the task of predicting a rating, and the task of predicting a membership grade in graded multi-label classification (GMLC), we propose an adapted distribution strategy to efficiently build a decentralized recommender system based on GMLC.

Keywords: Recommender system · Graded multi-label classification

1 Introduction

A recommender system collect available users' item-ratings, along with users and items informations to predict ratings for unrated items, and then recommends to each active user the items with the highest predicted ratings. Indeed, there are three main strategies for making item recommendation that may be combined together [19]: the first strategy is content-based filtering which is based on item descriptive attributes such as the weight and the price. The second is collaborative filtering which is based on item ratings made by users similar to the active user [23]. The third is demographic filtering which is based on user descriptive attributes such as age and gender.

Recommender systems can be memory-based or model-based. Memory-based methods [3] act directly on collected data and rely on similarity measures to find the k-nearest neighbours of the active user. Model-based methods [26] avoid querying the entire database by building a model to predict item ratings and output recommendations.

A. El Abbadi and B. Garbinato (Eds.): NETYS 2017, LNCS 10299, pp. 101–108, 2017.
DOI: 10.1007/978-3-319-59647-1_8

A recommender system is designed to work in an infinite streaming context where new users, new items, and new ratings can be added at any time. Considering the fact that continuously growing data may affect the recommender system performance, the actual tend in recommender systems is to use decentralized and distributed architectures [1,6].

In fuzzy classification each data can be associated to multiple labels with membership degrees ranging from 0 to 1 [2]. However, it is easier for users to rate items using discrete ordered values such as the one-to-five star ranking. Graded multi-label classification (GMLC) [5,13,15] is the task of assigning to each data a set of labels with corresponding membership grades. Predicting the membership grade associated to a label is similar to predicting the rating value for an item.

The main idea of this paper is to build a distributed recommender system based on GMLC. The underlying advantage is that GMLC can be easily decomposed into a set of parallel binary classification tasks.

The paper is organized as follows: in Sect. 2, a review of main approaches for distributed recommender systems and GMLC is done. In Sect. 3, we describe our proposed distributed recommender system. Experiment results are discussed in Sect. 4. Conclusions and perspectives are presented in Sect. 5.

2   State of the Art

One way of tackling the problem of big data is to use a decentralized architecture [14]. Hadoop framework based on the concept of map reduce facilitates the task of building distributed recommender systems [6,16]. Peer to peer (P2P) recommender systems [10] are less easier to implement since they are based on communication between servers (peers). Each peer stores a subset of the data and a routing table to find the location of the data needed by the recommender algorithm. One drawback of the first recommender systems is that some peers may be under-used while others may be over-used. Multi-agent systems can be combined with P2P strategies to reduce the impact of cooperative peer false assumption [24].

Another way of answering the challenge of big data in recommender systems is to use a predictive model instead of computing neighbours over the entire database. GMLC is a predictive model which can be decomposed into a set of ordinal classification (OC) models [9], that can be decomposed into a set of binary classification models. GMLC models are usually used in static data contexts. Recommender systems can be built based on GMLC if the binary classifiers forming the GMLC model are incremental classifiers [8,18] that handle data streams.

Decision tree models are intuitive and fast at making predictions, but they are slower at the learning step and can not handle data streams. Very fast decision trees (VFDT) [7] where introduced to tackle those limitations. The idea is to update leaf statistics for each received data, and to grow the tree by splitting a leaf when its statistics meet some conditions [12]. Some stopping criteria should be fixed to avoid growing the tree indefinitely. The tree may become inefficient for prediction if the underlying distribution of data changes over time. This problem is known as concept-drift and can be answered using different strategies. The simplest strategy is to use a sliding window to rebuild the tree using only the last N received instances [25]. Another strategy is to rank instances according to a reward or a loss measure, and to rebuild the tree using the N highest ranked instances [17].

Some applications generate only ratings as data for recommender systems. Other applications also provide users and items attributes. Other applications start with collecting only ratings and, afterwards, incorporate users and items attributes. Hence, learning data for recommender systems depends on the associated application. In the next section, we introduce a distributed recommender system that can handle the fact that new items, new users, and new attributes may be added at any time.

3   Proposed Distributed Recommender System

Data integration: Users and items are identified by positive ids. Users' attributes and items' attributes are also identified by positive ids. Usually, to prevent overlaps between ids, the matrix of ratings is separated from attributes' values. The drawback of this separation approach is that it is difficult to build a classifier that combines attributes' values and ratings to make predictions.

The idea of our proposed recommender system is to consider user attributes as items with negative ids, and item attributes as users with negative ids. Attributes' values are then considered as ratings (Fig. 1). The reason of using negative ids is to allow new collected attributes to be added in the negative region, while new users and new items are to be added in the positive region so that attributes, users and items never overlap. This data integration step handles new added attributes, users, and items. It results in a set of entries where for each entry (u, i, r): r can be either a rating or an attribute value for the user u or for the item i.

Predictive meta-model: There are two straightforward approaches to build a predictive model for ratings using the integrated data. The first approach is to consider each set of ratings with the same user id as one sparse instance. The prediction is then based on user attributes and ratings. The second approach is to build a predictive model considering each set of ratings with the same item id as one sparse instance. The prediction is then based on item attributes and ratings. We propose to combine both the first and the second method by predicting the average rating. The underlying advantage is to combine demographic, content-based, and collaborative filtering strategies.

Distributed architecture: The distributed architecture of our approach works as follows: the main server S is both a database and an aggregation server that keeps all sparse user instances and item instances. Each other server s is a smart

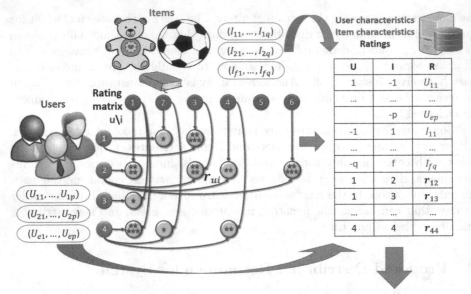

User sparse instance $1\{\{-1, U_{11}\}, ... \{-p, U_{1p}\}, \{2, r_{12}\}, \{3, r_{13}\}\}$

Item sparse instance $1\{\{-1, I_{11}\}, ... \{-q, I_{1q}\}, \{2, r_{21}\}, \{3, r_{11}\}, \{4, r_{41}\}\}$

Fig. 1. Mapping user attributes, item attributes, and ratings

server that handles data and predictive models for a range of users' ids and a range of items' ids (Fig. 2). The main server receives continuously a new rating tuple (u, i, r) where u is the user id, i is the item id, and r is the rating value. After receiving each rating, the main server should communicate with the smart servers and aggregate their answers to output the next recommendations.

Main server role (Database part): For each tuple (u, i, r), the main server finds the corresponding user sparse instance a_u and item sparse instance b_i. The main server updates the user instance a_u by adding the rating of the ith item, and do the same with the item instance b_i. The main server determines the corresponding servers to all items rated by the instance user a_u, and then sends a_u to them so that the corresponding classifier to each item rated by a_u can be updated. The main server does the same with the instance item b_i so that the corresponding classifier to each user who rated the item b_i can be updated.

Smart server role: For each received instance a_u, the smart server updates the corresponding classifiers. A classifier is a binary decision tree that predicts whether the rating for an item i is greater or equals to a specific rating value R. Updating a classifier consists of giving the received instance a_u a weight 1, and letting a_u fell down to the bottom of the decision tree. Since a_u is a sparse instance, it may not have a value for the attribute at a specific node. When such case occurs data fells down to all child nodes but with different weights as in the C4.5 decision tree [21]. When a_u reaches a leaf node, either the number of positive instances or the number of negative instances is increased by the weight of a_u depending on whether the rating of the item i is greater or equals to R or not. A threshold is used to determine the number of instances a leaf should receive before trying to split data using the entropy measure. Another threshold is used to determine the number of instances the tree should receive before it is rebuilt using only the last received instances.

Complexity of the smart server role: A smart server handles a range of users' ids and items' id, and for each id there is an ordinal classifier [20] which consists of as much decision trees as the number of possible ratings minus one. Actually there is no need to build a decision tree for the lowest rating because if no decision trees predicts the positive class (the rating is greater or equals to some value) then the ordinal classifier predicts the lowest rating. Let E be the number of rated items by a received user instance a_u that are in the items' ids range of the smart server. Let F be the number of possible ratings minus one. The number of classifiers that are updated after receiving a_u is $E \times F$. The update can concern just statistics, a node split in a worst case, and a tree rebuild in the most worst case, but in practice trees are very rarely or never rebuilt at the same time.

Main server role (Aggregation part): For the main server to predict the rating for an item i by a user u, it collects both the prediction of the ordinal classifier responsible of predicting ratings for the item i, and the prediction of the one responsible of predicting ratings for the user u. Then the main server predicts the average of those two ratings. Other aggregations may be used such as discarding the predicted rating with the lowest confidence, or a weighted average according to the uncertainty of each prediction.

4 Experiments

In our experiment we used a subset of the MovieLens dataset[1] [11]. It is composed of three files: the first one contains attribute values (gender, age, occupation, and zip-code) for 6040 users, the second one contains attribute values (title, year, and a set of categories like 'action', 'drama', 'comedy', ... etc.) for 3883 movies, and the third one contains 391384 'one to five' star ratings.

We used our implementation of incremental binary decision trees in order to implement easily the wanted decision tree behaviour. Each decision tree receives instances one by one and updates leaf statistics. After each 100 instances The decision tree can grow by splitting nodes according to the minimum description length pre-pruning strategy [22], and after each new 500 instances the tree is rebuilt using only the last 1000 received data [25].

The centralized approach has been stopped after 104549 ratings due to memory insufficiency. The proposed distributed architecture with five servers having a memory capacity of $4Go$ has completed successfully the experiment in about 5 h.

---

[1] http://grouplens.org/datasets/movielens/.

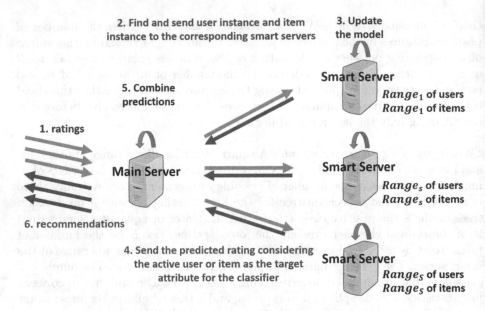

Fig. 2. The distributed architecture

The average of maximal memory use has been maintained under $1.1Go$. The prediction is evaluated using Hamming-loss measure [4]. It is defined for an instance x as the mean of absolute error to the maximum absolute error:

$$HammingLoss(x) = \frac{1}{k} \sum_{l=0}^{k} \frac{|y_l - z_l|}{|maximumRating - minimumRating|} \quad \text{where } y_l$$

and z_l are the actual and the predicted values of the lth attribute for the instance x, and k is the number of target attributes. Table 1 illustrates collected results averaged over all instances for each rating value.

Hamming-loss evaluation is higher for the ratings 1 because the rating value 1 is predicted only if binary decision trees predicting whether the rating is greater than $2, 3, 4, 5$ give negative predictions. Hamming-loss is also higher for the rating

Table 1. Experiment results using Movielens dataset

Rating	Count	Hamming-loss average	Hamming-loss standard deviation
1	23864	0.4336	0.2404
2	46244	0.2462	0.2617
3	108280	0.1451	0.2023
4	135574	0.2147	0.2645
5	77422	0.4437	0.2799
All	391384	0.2578	0.2749

5 due to the class imbalance because the majority class is the negative one (77422 positive examples and 313962 negative examples).

5   Conclusion and Future Work

In this paper, a distributed architecture is proposed for recommender systems based on graded multi-label classification. The proposed approach combines demographic, content-based, and collaborative filtering to output recommendations. The experiment on MovieLens dataset gives promising results that can be enhanced by handling the class imbalance problem. For future work we plan to answer this issue and to validate our approach using different datasets.

References

1. Bhatia, L., Prasad, S.S.: Building a distributed generic recommender using scalable data mining library. In: 2015 IEEE International Conference on Computational Intelligence Communication Technology, pp. 98–102 (2015)
2. Bouchon-Meunier, B., Marsala, C., Ramdani, M.: Learning from Imperfect Data. John Wiley & Sons, New York (1997)
3. Breese, J.S., Heckerman, D., Kadie, C.: Empirical analysis of predictive algorithms for collaborative filtering. In: Proceedings of the Fourteenth Conference on Uncertainty in Artificial Intelligence, UAI 1998, pp. 43–52. Morgan Kaufmann Publishers Inc., San Francisco (1998)
4. Brinker, C., Menca, E.L., Frnkranz, J.: Graded multilabel classification by pairwise comparisons. In: 2014 IEEE International Conference on Data Mining, pp. 731–736 (2014)
5. Cheng, W., Dembczynski, K., Hllermeier, E.: Graded multilabel classification: the ordinal case. In: Atzmller, M., Benz, D., Hotho, A., Stumme, G. (eds.) Proceedings of LWA 2010 - Workshop-Woche: Lernen, Wissen & Adaptivitaet, Kassel, Germany (2010)
6. Chiky, R., Ghisloti, R., Kazi-Aoul, Z.: Development of a distributed recommender system using the hadoop framework. In: Lechevallier, Y., Melanon, G., Pinaud, B. (eds.) EGC. Revue des Nouvelles Technologies de l'Information, vol. RNTI-E-23, pp. 495–500. Hermann-Éditions (2012)
7. Domingos, P., Hulten, G.: Mining high-speed data streams. In: Proceedings of the Sixth ACM SIGKDD International Conference on Knowledge Discovery and Data Mining, KDD 2000, pp. 71–80. ACM, New York (2000)
8. Duda, P., Jaworski, M., Pietruczuk, L., Rutkowski, L.: A novel application of hoeffding's inequality to decision trees construction for data streams. In: 2014 International Joint Conference on Neural Networks (IJCNN), pp. 3324–3330 (2014)
9. Frank, E., Hall, M.: A simple approach to ordinal classification. In: Raedt, L., Flach, P. (eds.) ECML 2001. LNCS, vol. 2167, pp. 145–156. Springer, Heidelberg (2001). doi:10.1007/3-540-44795-4_13
10. Han, P., Xie, B., Yang, F., Shen, R.: A scalable P2P recommender system based on distributed collaborative filtering. Expert Syst. Appl. **27**(2), 203–210 (2004)
11. Harper, F.M., Konstan, J.A.: The movielens datasets: history and context. ACM Trans. Interact. Intell. Syst. **5**(4), 19:1–19:19 (2015)

12. Hoeffding, W.: Probability inequalities for sums of bounded random variables. J. Am. Stat. Assoc. **58**, 13–30 (1963)

13. Laghmari, K., Marsala, C., Ramdani, M.: Graded multi-label classification: compromise between handling label relations and limiting error propagation. In: 2016 11th International Conference on Intelligent Systems: Theories and Applications (SITA), pp. 1–6 (2016)

14. Laghmari, K., Ramdani, M., Marsala, C.: A distributed graph based approach for rough classifications considering dominance relations between overlapping classes. In: 2015 10th International Conference on Intelligent Systems: Theories and Applications (SITA), pp. 1–6 (2015)

15. Laghmari, K., Marsala, C., Ramdani, M.: Classification multi-labels gradue: apprendre les relations entre les labels ou limiter la propagation derreur? Revue des Nouvelles Technologies de l'Information Extraction et Gestion des Connaissances, RNTI-E-33, pp. 381–386 (2017)

16. Lin, K., Wang, J., Wang, M.: A hybrid recommendation algorithm based on hadoop. In: 2014 9th International Conference on Computer Science Education, pp. 540–543 (2014)

17. Loeffel, P.X., Marsala, C., Detyniecki, M.: Memory management for data streams subject to concept drift. In: European Symposium on Artificial Neural Networks, Computational Intelligence and Machine Learning (2016)

18. Marsala, C.: Incremental tuning of fuzzy decision trees. In: 2012 Joint 6th International Conference on Soft Computing and Intelligent Systems (SCIS) and 13th International Symposium on Advanced Intelligent Systems (ISIS), pp. 2061–2064 (2012)

19. Pazzani, M.J.: A framework for collaborative, content-based and demographic filtering. Artif. Intell. Rev. **13**(5), 393–408 (1999)

20. Qiao, X.: Learning ordinal data. Wiley Interdisc. Rev. Comput. Stat. **7**(5), 341–346 (2015)

21. Quinlan, J.R.: C4.5: Programs for Machine Learning. Morgan Kaufmann, San Mateo (1988)

22. Quinlan, J.: The minimum description length principle and categorical theories. In: Hirsh, W.W.C. (ed.) Machine Learning Proceedings 1994, pp. 233–241. Morgan Kaufmann, San Francisco (1994)

23. Su, X., Khoshgoftaar, T.M.: A survey of collaborative filtering techniques. Adv. Artif. Intell. **2009**, 4:2–4:2 (2009)

24. Vidal, J.M.: A protocol for a distributed recommender system. In: Falcone, R., Barber, S., Sabater-Mir, J., Singh, M.P. (eds.) Trusting Agents. LNCS(LNAI), vol. 3577, pp. 200–217. Springer, Heidelberg (2005). doi:10.1007/11532095_12

25. Xioufis, E.S., Spiliopoulou, M., Tsoumakas, G., Vlahavas, I.: Dealing with concept drift and class imbalance in multi-label stream classification. In: Proceedings of the Twenty-Second International Joint Conference on Artificial Intelligence, IJCAI 2011, vol. 2, pp. 1583–1588. AAAI Press (2011)

26. Zhang, Y., Liu, X., Liu, W., Zhu, C.: Hybrid recommender system using semi-supervised clustering based on gaussian mixture model. In: 2016 International Conference on Cyberworlds (CW), pp. 155–158 (2016)

Multithreading Approach to Process Real-Time Updates in KNN Algorithms

Anne-Marie Kermarrec, Nupur Mittal, and Javier Olivares[(⊠)]

Inria Rennes, Rennes, France
{anne-marie.kermarrec,nupur.mittal,javier.olivares}@inria.fr

Abstract. K-Nearest Neighbors algorithm (KNN) is the core of a considerable amount of online services and applications, like recommendation engines, content-classifiers, information retrieval systems, etc. The users of these services change their preferences over time, aggravating the computational challenges of KNN. In this work, we present *UpKNN*: an efficient *thread-based* out-of-core approach to take the updates of users preferences into account while it computes the KNN efficiently.

1 Introduction

K-Nearest Neighbors (KNN) has been one of the most important classification techniques, specially used on recommender systems [1,2], and information retrieval applications.

KNN is a process of finding the most similar neighbors of a node/entity from a dataset. Each node of the dataset is represented for some data, commonly known as *profile*. We consider two data entities as neighbors if their profiles are similar based on a similarity metric as cosine or Jaccard.

Unfortunately, the main bottleneck of KNN is its huge memory requirements. Besides, some of the KNN applications witness high rate of changes in profiles over time, making very difficult to take these changes into account. These updates only increase the computation time considerably, making the algorithm less and less scalable. Due to this cost, many current approaches [2–4] simplify the processing assuming the dataset remains static throughout the computation. Consequently, the computation of KNN on static datasets does not consider data's dynamism, relying on content that is always outdated. Unfortunately, nowadays data changes continuously [7,8] at unimaginable rates, specially on those web-based, or recommendation systems' applications [5,6].

Hence, we propose *UpKNN*, a multithreading approach for processing real-time profile updates in KNN algorithms. *UpKNN* is designed to perform well on a single commodity PC, through an efficient *out-of-core* approach that leverages disk and main memory efficiently. The use of a single commodity PC, instead of a more complex computing platform, is motivated by its lower cost and ease of access for a vast majority of potential users, compared to a distributed system.

© Springer International Publishing AG 2017
A. El Abbadi and B. Garbinato (Eds.): NETYS 2017, LNCS 10299, pp. 109–114, 2017.
DOI: 10.1007/978-3-319-59647-1_9

2   Background

Given N entities with their profiles in a D-dimensional space, the K-Nearest Neighbors (KNN) algorithm finds the K closest neighbors for each entity. The distance between two entities is computed based on a well-defined metric that takes into account their profiles. To compute KNN efficiently we adopt an approximate approach as proposed in [1].

Let us consider a set of entities U ($|U| = N$), associated with a set of items denoted by I. Each entity u has a profile UP_u, composed of items in I. UpKNN assumes that the N entities are randomly partitioned into M partitions, in such a way that at least one partition can be processed in memory at a time.

Corresponding to each of the M partitions there is a partition file PF_j in disk, storing the profiles UP of all the entities belonging to partition j.

To update the profiles, UpKNN receives an unsorted set of updates S consisting of entity-item tuples: $S = \{< u, i > \mid u \in U, i \in I\}$.

3   UpKNN Algorithm

3.1   Classify

UpKNN classifies each update of the set S per its entity's partition, such that all updates for the entities of a partition are applied at once, avoiding further IO operations. For a fast classification, we use a set of in-memory buffers, which are read and written in parallel. UpKNN performs the expensive read operations from S (on disk) in parallel with the classification, achieving a higher throughput.

Figure 1 depicts the *classify* phase. The classification separates the updates and stores them into M update files, UF_m. To do so, we have pairs of *reader-classifier* threads (T_{ri} and T_{ci}). Each pair shares a unique communication channel C_i.

Each reader thread T_{ri} reads one of the equal-sized slices of S at a time. Once the T_{ri} has read a slice from S, it puts that slice in the communication channel C_i and notifies the corresponding T_{ci}. When T_{ci} receives the notification, it reads data from C_i, freeing it for new data (from T_{ri}).

To classify the updates into the update files UF_m, each classifier thread T_{ci} has access to its M partitioned local buffer LB_i of size $M \times 4[mb]$.

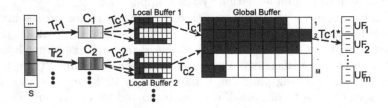

Fig. 1. Classify. *Reader* threads in continuous lines, *classifier* threads in dashed lines

Keeping the large size of updates in mind, we implement a second level of buffer called *Global buffer*, mostly to reduce synchronizations and IO operations. This buffer of size $M \times 8 [mb]$ is common to all the classifier threads, consequently is protected by a *mutex*, preventing multiple classifiers to access the same partition concurrently. The size of the buffer is experimentally selected to achieve the best performance.

Each thread T_{ci} classifies the updates and stores them into their corresponding local buffer partitions: LB_{ij}. As soon as a partition j of the local buffer LB_i becomes full, its data is put into the corresponding partition of the global buffer by T_{ci}. Once the global buffer partition is full, the data of that particular partition j is written into the update profile file UF_j. The thread $T_{ci}*$, who made j's partition in the global buffer full, writes the update profile file UF_j. As only one thread has access to the global buffer of some partition j, when this is full, there is no need of synchronization to write UF_j file.

In *UpKNN* a key factor to achieve high performance is the overlap of computations and IO operations. While a reader thread obtains data from S (IO request), a classifier thread classifies updates in partitions, preliminarily stored on in-memory buffers and later written into the corresponding update files.

3.2   Merge

The phase merges the updates from these UF_m files with the already existing M profile files PF_m in disk. We use a set of M threads T_{me} to process the updates from these files in parallel. We have enough threads T_{me} so that each file is read and merged in parallel, leveraging IO parallelism observed on modern SSDs.

To merge, each thread T_{me} loads the updates from the corresponding update profile file UF_i into memory. These updates are inserted sequentially into a *heap* to sort them by entities' id. The purpose of sorting the updates by entities' id is to have all the occurrences of a particular user continuously. Now that the updates are sorted by id, T_{me} proceeds to read sequentially from disk the profile file PF_i (obtained from the underlying KNN approach) and to merge them with the updates from the heap. The process of merging old profiles with new items is performed in-memory. Finally, T_{me} writes the updated profiles back to PF_i. Using the same thread for reading and writing, avoids synchronization operations and related costs, and hence, achieves full parallelism in IO operations.

4   Evaluation

UpKNN is implement in C++, clang-omp++ 3.5.0, $-O2$ optimization. *Openmp* and *Pthreads* enable multithreading computation. We ran our experiments on a MacBook Pro laptop, Intel Core i7 4 cores, 16 GB RAM and a 500 GB SSD.

Although *UpKNN* is independent of the underlying KNN algorithm, we show a particular instance of its implementation on *Pons* [3]. *UpKNN* is evaluated on *Movielens*, which provides the movie-rating data from the Movielens website. Users' profiles are composed of their affinities for some movies. Additionally, we

Table 1. Datasets

Dataset	Users	Items	#Up (80% items)	M
Movielens (MOV)	138,493	20,000,263	16,000,210	2
Mediego (MED)	4,130,101	7,954,018	6,363,214	2

use *Mediego (MED)*'s dataset, which consists of users and the webpages they visit from various websites. In both cases, each user activity has a timestamp, which is used to divide the profiles into initial profiles (20% of the items) and the update set S (80% of the items) (Table 1).

Baseline. To the best of our knowledge, there are no out-of-core algorithms updating profiles while computing the KNN. To overcome this, we choose a natural baseline, which also uses a multithreading approach, where several threads read the updates from the update set and add them to the respective profiles.

4.1   *UpKNN*'s Performance

Runtime. Table 2 shows *UpKNN*'s and baseline's wall-time and speedup for computing the corresponding #Up (20/80% division, 10 M and 100 M randomly generated updates).

UpKNN considerably outperforms the baseline on both the datasets. *UpKNN* achieves a speedup of 49.5X on *Movielens*, taking only 3.687 s for about 16 million updates. We obtain a speedup of 47X on Mediego's dataset.

We notice from Table 3, that *UpKNN* processes more than 4 million [updates/second], for both the datasets, being consistent with the motivation of our work. *UpKNN* not only performs the computation on a single commodity PC, but also does it in real-time, making it a novel approach in itself.

In Fig. 2, we verify *UpKNN*'s scalability in terms of updates processed. Even after increasing the number of updates from 10 M to 100 M, the execution time increases only by a factor of 10.

Number of Threads. Figure 3 presents the wall-time of executing 100 M updates, varying the numbers of threads. We observe near-linear decrease in

Table 2. *UpKNN*'s performance

Data	#Up	UpKNN[s]	Base.[s]	Speedup
MOV	10 M	3.635	105.747	29.08X
MOV	20/80	3.687	184.513	**49.5X**
MOV	100 M	39.662	1055.804	26.61X
MED	20/80	1.543	72.576	**47X**
MED	10 M	17.665	198.658	11.24X
MED	100 M	47.329	1931.154	40.80X

Table 3. #Up/second

Dataset and #Up	Time[s]	#Up/sec
MOV 20/80 (16 M)	3.678	4.33 M
MED 20/80 (6.3 M)	1.543	4.12 M
MOV 100 M	39.662	2.52 M
MED 100 M	46.329	2.11 M

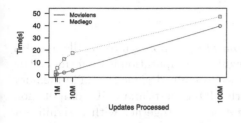

Fig. 2. Updates Scalability

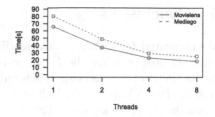

Fig. 3. Threads Scalability

the runtime when the number of threads increases. This small difference is due to the increase in threads synchronization, and to some small pieces of sequential code.

Disk Operations. As evident from Table 4, *UpKNN* reduces considerably the number of disk operations performed throughout the process. In the case of ordering the updates in time, we obtain better results than the case where the updates are randomly put in the set. In the former case, *UpKNN* takes only 0.0006% of the seeks performed by the baseline. The bytes written in our approach are reduced to only 1.98% of those of the baseline, and the bytes read are reduced to 3.88% of those of the baseline. These differences are explained by *UpKNN*'s capability to apply all the updates for a profile at once. Conversely, the baseline reads/writes the whole profile each time there is an update for it.

UpKNN's performance relies on its capacity to reduce disk operations throughout each phase of the computation. For instance, the updates (read from disk) are accessed only once on the classification. In addition, the *heap* reduces the need of multiple profile readings/writings.

Table 4. Disk Operations

MOV 20/80				MED 20/80		
	UpKNN	Baseline	%	*UpKNN*	Baseline	%
Disk seeks	29	48 M	0.0006	27	19 M	0.0001
Written [bytes]	128 M	6400 M	1.98	50 M	2570 M	1.98
Write op. [#]	12	16 M	0.0001	10	6 M	0.0001
Read [bytes]	256 M	6592 M	3.88	101 M	2621 M	3.88
Read op. [#]	127	32 M	0.0004	55	12 M	0.0004
MOV 100 M				MED 100 M		
Disk seeks	277 K	300 M	0.092	8 M	300 M	2.753
Written [bytes]	856 M	40 KM	2.118	2468 M	40 KM	6.110
Write op. [#]	138 K	100 M	0.138	4.1 M	100 M	4.130
Read [bytes]	1656 M	41 KM	4.019	3268 M	41 KM	7.933
Read op. [#]	139 K	200 M	0.069	4.1 M	200 M	2.065

5   Conclusions

We presented *UpKNN*, a multithreading *out-of-core* approach to handle updates on users-profiles, while the K-Nearest Neighbors computation is performed. The performance of our novel approach relies on a carefully designed set of in-memory buffers. *UpKNN* uses these buffers to overlap IO requests and CPU computation throughout the processing. This optimization goes together with a significant reduction in IO operations, the main bottleneck on out-of-core algorithms.

Acknowledgments. This work was partially funded by Conicyt/Beca Doctorado en el Extranjero Folio 72140173 and Google Focused Award Web Alter-Ego.

References

1. Boutet, A., Frey, D., Guerraoui, R., Kermarrec, A.M., Patra, R.: Hyrec: leveraging browsers for scalable recommenders. In: Middleware (2014)
2. Boutet, A., Kermarrec, A.M., Mittal, N., Taïani, F.: Being prepared in a sparse world: the case of knn graph construction. In: ICDE (2016)
3. Chiluka, N., Kermarrec, A.-M., Olivares, J.: The out-of-core KNN awakens: the light side of computation force on large datasets. In: Abdulla, P.A., Delporte-Gallet, C. (eds.) NETYS 2016. LNCS, vol. 9944, pp. 295–310. Springer, Cham (2016). doi:10. 1007/978-3-319-46140-3_24
4. Dong, W., Moses, C., Li, K.: Efficient k-nearest neighbor graph construction for generic similarity measures. In: WWW (2011)
5. Lathia, N., Hailes, S., Capra, L., Amatriain, X.: Temporal diversity in recommender systems. In: SIGIR (2010)
6. Rana, C., Jain, S.: A study of dynamic features of recommender systems. Artif. Intell. Rev. **43**, 141–153 (2012)
7. Yang, C., Yu, X., Liu, Y.: Continuous knn join processing for real-time recommendation. In: ICDM (2014)
8. Yu, C., Zhang, R., Huang, Y., Xiong, H.: High-dimensional knn joins with incremental updates. Geoinformatica **14**(1), 55–82 (2010)

Atomicity

Oh-RAM! One and a Half Round Atomic Memory

Theophanis Hadjistasi[1]([⊠]), Nicolas Nicolaou[2],
and Alexander A. Schwarzmann[1]

[1] University of Connecticut, Storrs, CT, USA
{theo,aas}@uconn.edu
[2] IMDEA Networks Institute, Madrid, Spain
nicolas.nicolaou@imdea.org

Abstract. Implementing atomic read/write shared objects in a message-passing system is an important problem in distributed computing. Considering that communication is the most expensive resource, efficiency of read and write operations is assessed primarily in terms of the needed communication and the associated latency. Attiya, Bar-Noy, and Dolev established that two communication round-trip phases involving in total *four* message exchanges are sufficient to implement atomic operations when a majority of processors are correct. Subsequently Dutta et al. showed that one round involving *two* communication exchanges is sufficient as long as the system adheres to certain constraints with respect to crashes on the number of readers and writers in the system. It was also observed that three exchanges are sufficient in some settings.

This extended abstract presents work that explores algorithms where operations are able to complete in *three* message exchanges without imposing constraints on the number of participants, i.e., the aim is *One and half Round Atomic Memory*, hence the name Oh-RAM! Recently Hadjistasi et al. showed that three-exchange implementations are *impossible* in the MWMR (multi-writer/multi-reader) setting. This paper shows that this is achievable in the SWMR (single-writer/multi-reader) setting, and also achievable for read operations in the MWMR setting by "sacrificing" the performance of write operations. In particular, a SWMR implementation is presented, where reads complete in *three* and writes complete in *two* exchanges. Next, a MWMR implementation is given, where reads involve *three* and writes involve *four* exchanges. In light of the impossibility result these algorithms are optimal in terms of the number of communication exchanges. Both algorithms are then refined to allow some reads to complete in just *two* exchanges. These algorithms are evaluated and compared using the NS3 simulator with different topologies and operation loads.

1 Introduction

Emulating atomic [9] (or linearizable [8]) read/write objects in message-passing environments is an important problem in distributed computing. Atomicity is

Supported in part by FP7-PEOPLE-2013-IEF grant ATOMICDFS No: 629088.

A. El Abbadi and B. Garbinato (Eds.): NETYS 2017, LNCS 10299, pp. 117–132, 2017.
DOI: 10.1007/978-3-319-59647-1_10

the most intuitive consistency semantic as it provides the illusion of a single-copy object that serializes all accesses such that each read operation returns the value of the latest preceding write operation. Solutions to this problem are complicated when the processors are failure-prone and when the environment is asynchronous. To cope with processor failures, distributed object implementations use *redundancy* by replicating the object at multiple network locations. Replication introduces the problem of consistency because operations may access different object replicas possibly containing obsolete values.

The seminal work of Attiya, Bar-Noy, and Dolev [2] provided an algorithm, colloquially referred to as ABD, that implements single-writer/multiple-reader (SWMR) atomic objects in message-passing crash-prone asynchronous environments. The operations are ordered with the help of logical *timestamps* associated with each value. Here each operation is guaranteed to terminate as long as some majority of replica servers do not crash. Each write operation takes one communication round-trip phase, or round, involving *two* message exchanges and each read operation takes two rounds involving in total *four* message exchanges. Subsequently, [11] showed how to implement multi-writer/multiple-reader (MWMR) atomic memory where both read and write operations involve two communication round trips involving in total four message exchanges.

The work by Dutta et al. [3] introduced a SWMR implementation where both reads and writes involve a single round consisting of *two* communication exchanges. Such an implementation is called *fast*, and it was shown that this is possible only when the number of readers r is bounded with respect to the number of servers s and the number of server failures f, viz. $r < \frac{s}{f} - 2$. An observation made in [3] suggests that atomic memory may be implemented (using a max/min technique) so that each read and write operation complete in *three* communication exchanges. The authors did not elaborate on the inherent limitations that such a technique may impose on the distributed system.

Subsequent works, e.g., [4,5], focused in relaxing the bound on the number of readers and writers in the service by proposing hybrid approaches where some operations complete in *one* and others in *two* rounds. Tight bounds were provided in [4] on the number of rounds that read and write operations require in the MWMR model.

A natural question arises whether one can devise implementations where all operations complete in at most *three* communication exchanges without imposing any restrictions on the numbers of participants in the service. A recent work by Hadjistasi, Nicolaou, and Schwarzmann [7] showed that such implementations are impossible in the MWMR setting. It is not known whether there is an SWMR implementation and whether there exists some trade off that allows operations to complete in three communication exchanges in the MWMR setting.

Contributions. We focus on the gap between one-round and two-round algorithms by presenting atomic memory algorithms where read operations can take "one and a half rounds," i.e., complete in *three* message exchanges. We also provide SWMR and MWMR algorithms where read operations complete in either *two* or *three* communication exchanges. We rigorously reason about the correct-

Table 1. Summary of communication exchanges and communication complexities.

Model	Algorithm	Read Exch.	Write Exch.	Read Comm.	Write Comm.
SWMR	ABD [2]	4	2	$4|\mathcal{S}|$	$2|\mathcal{S}|$
SWMR	Oh-SAM	3	2	$|\mathcal{S}|^2 + 2|\mathcal{S}|$	$2|\mathcal{S}|$
SWMR	Oh-SAM'	2 or 3	2	$|\mathcal{S}|^2 + 3|\mathcal{S}|$	$2|\mathcal{S}|$
MWMR	ABD [2,11]	4	4	$4|\mathcal{S}|$	$4|\mathcal{S}|$
MWMR	Oh-MAM	3	4	$|\mathcal{S}|^2 + 2|\mathcal{S}|$	$4|\mathcal{S}|$
MWMR	Oh-MAM'	2 or 3	4	$|\mathcal{S}|^2 + 3|\mathcal{S}|$	$4|\mathcal{S}|$

ness of the algorithms. To assess the practicality of these implementations we simulate them and compare their performance. Additional details are as follows.

1. We present a new SWMR algorithm (Oh-SAM) for atomic objects in the asynchronous message-passing model with processor crashes. Write operations take *two* communication exchanges and are similar to the write operations of ABD. Read operations take *three* communication exchanges: (1) the reader sends a message to servers, (2) the servers share this information, and (3) once this is "sufficiently" done, servers reply to the reader. A key idea of the algorithm is that the reader returns the value that is associated with the *minimum* timestamp (cf. the observation in [3]). The read operations are optimal in terms of communication exchanges in light of [7] (Sect. 3).
2. We extend the SWMR algorithm to yield a MWMR algorithm (Oh-MAM). In the new algorithm the write operations are more complicated, taking *four* communication exchanges (cf. [11]). Read operations complete as before in *three* communication exchanges (Sect. 4).
3. We then present a revised SWMR algorithm (Oh-SAM') and a revised MWMR algorithm (Oh-MAM'), where read operations complete in either *two* or *three* communication exchanges. The original and the revised versions of each algorithm are presented for pedagogical reasons: for ease of understanding and reasoning about the algorithms (Sect. 5).
4. We simulate our algorithms using the NS3 simulator and assess their performance under practical considerations. We note that the relative performance of our algorithms depends on the simulation topologies and object server placement; this is another reason for presenting both versions of each algorithm (Sect. 6).

Table 1 summarizes the results. Improvements in the latency (in terms of the number of exchanges) are obtained in a trade-off with communication complexity. We note that increases in the communication complexity need not necessarily have negative consequences in some practical settings, such as data centers, where servers communicate over high-bandwidth links.

2   Models and Definitions

The system consists of a collection of crash-prone, asynchronous processors with unique identifiers from a totally-ordered set $\mathcal{I}$ partitioned into: set $\mathcal{W}$ of writer identifiers, set $\mathcal{R}$ of reader identifiers, and set $\mathcal{S}$ of replica server identifiers with each *server* maintaining a copy of the object. Any subset of writers and readers, and up to f servers, $f < \frac{|\mathcal{S}|}{2}$, may crash at any time. Processors communicate by exchanging messages via asynchronous point-to-point reliable channels; messages may be reordered. For convenience we use the term *broadcast* as a shorthand denoting sending point-to-point messages to multiple destinations.

Executions. An algorithm A is a collection of processes, where process A_p is assigned to processor $p \in \mathcal{I}$. The *state* of processor p is determined over a set of state variables, and the state of A is a vector that contains the state of each process. Algorithm A performs a *step*, when some process p (i) receives a message, (ii) performs local computation, (iii) sends a message. Each such action causes the state at p to change. An *execution* is an alternating sequence of states and actions of A starting with the initial state and ending in a state. A process p *crashes* in an execution if it stops taking steps; otherwise p is *correct*.

Atomicity. An implementation of a read or a write operation contains an *invocation* action (such as a call to a procedure) and a *response* action (such as a return from the procedure). An operation π is *complete* in an execution ξ, if ξ contains both the invocation and the *matching* response actions for π; otherwise π is *incomplete*. An execution is *well formed* if any process invokes one operation at a time. We say that an operation π *precedes* an operation π' in an execution ξ, denoted by $\pi \to \pi'$, if the response step of π appears before the invocation step in π' in ξ. Two operations are *concurrent* if neither precedes the other. The correctness of an atomic read/write object implementation is defined in terms of *atomicity* (safety) and *termination* (liveness) properties. Termination requires that any operation invoked by a correct process eventually completes. Atomicity is defined following [10]. For any execution ξ, if all invoked read and write operations are complete, then the operations can be partially ordered by an ordering $\prec$, so that the following properties are satisfied:

P1. The partial order $\prec$ is consistent with the external order of invocation and responses, that is, there do not exist operations π and π', such that π completes before π' starts, yet $\pi' \prec \pi$.

P2. All write operations are totally ordered and every read operation is ordered with respect to all writes.

P3. Every read operation returns the value of the last write preceding it in the partial order, and any read operation ordered before all writes returns the initial value of the object.

Efficiency and Message Exchanges. Efficiency of implementations is assessed in terms of *operation latency* and *message complexity*. *Latency* of each operation is determined by the *computation time* and the *communication delays*. Computation time accounts for the computation steps that the algorithm performs in each operation. Communication delays are measured in terms of *communication exchanges*. The protocol implementing each operation involves sends (or broadcasts) of typed messages and the corresponding receives. *Communication exchange* within an execution of an operation is the set of sends and receives for the specific message type within the protocol. With this definition, traditional implementations in the style of ABD are structured in terms of *rounds*, cf. [2,5], where each round consists of two message exchanges, the first, a broadcast, is initiated by the process executing an operation, and the second consists of responses to the initiator. The number of messages that a process expects during a convergecast depends on the implementation. *Message complexity* measures the worst-case total number of messages exchanged during an operation.

3   SWMR Algorithm Oh-SAM

We now present our SWMR algorithm Oh-SAM: *One* and a *half Round Single-writer Atomic Memory*. The write operation takes *two* communication exchanges (similarly to ABD). Read operations take *three* communication exchanges: (1) the reader sends message to servers, (2) each server that receives the request *relays* the request to all servers, and (3) once a server receives the relay for a particular read from a majority of servers, it replies to the reader. The read completes once it collects a majority of these replies. A key idea of the algorithm is that the reader returns the value that is associated with the *minimum* timestamp. The code is given in Algorithm 1. Now we give additional details.

Counter variables *read_op*, *operations* and *relays* are used to help processes identify "new" read and write operations, and distinguish "fresh" from "stale" messages (since messages can be reordered). The value of the object and its associated timestamp, as known by each process, are stored in variables v and ts respectively. Variable $minTS$ holds the minimum timestamp discovered in the received messages.

Writer Protocol. Writer w increments its local timestamp ts and broadcasts request *writeReq* to servers S (lines 19–20). It terminates when at least $|S|/2+1$ replies are collected (lines 21–22).

Reader Protocol. Reader r creates request *readReq*, with its id r and its local operation counter *read_op*, and broadcasts it to servers S (line 7). It then awaits at least $|S|/2 + 1$ messages from servers. When "fresh" messages are collected from a majority of servers, the reader returns the value v associated with the *minimum* ts among the received messages (lines 11–14).

Server Protocol. (1) Upon receiving message $\langle readReq, r, op \rangle$, the server broadcasts a *readRelay* message, containing its ts and v, to servers S (lines 28–29).

(2) Upon receiving message $\langle readRelay, ts', v', r, op \rangle$, if $ts < ts'$, then s updates its local timestamp and value. (lines 36–37). Next, s checks if the received *readRelay* indicates a new read operation by r, i.e., $op > operations(r)$ (line 38). If so, then it a) sets its local counter for r to the received counter, i.e., $operations(r) = op$; and b) initializes the relay counter for r to zero, i.e.,

Algorithm 1. Reader, Writer, and Server Protocols for SWMR algorithm Oh-SAM

1: At each reader r in $\mathcal{R}$	24: At server s in $\mathcal{S}$
2: **Variables:**	25: **Variables:**
3: $ts \in \mathbb{N}$ init 0, $minTS \in \mathbb{N}$ init 0	26: $ts \in \mathbb{N}$ init 0, $v \in V$ init $\perp$
4: $read\_op \in \mathbb{N}$ init 0, $v \in V$	27: $operations, relays : \mathcal{R} \rightarrow \mathbb{N}$, init $\{0\}^{|\mathcal{R}|}$
5: **function** READ	28: **Upon receive**($\langle readReq, r, op \rangle$)
6: $read\_op \leftarrow read\_op + 1$	29: **bcast**($\langle readRelay, ts, v, r, op \rangle$) to $\mathcal{S}$
7: **bcast**($\langle readReq, r, read\_op \rangle$) to $\mathcal{S}$	30: **Upon receive**($\langle writeReq, ts', v', w \rangle$)
8: **await** $|\mathcal{S}|/2 + 1$ server messages m	31: **if** $(ts < ts')$ **then**
9: with $(m.read\_op = read\_op)$	32: $(ts, v) \leftarrow (ts', v')$
10: Let $Q = \{\langle s, m \rangle | m$ received from $s\}$	33: **send**($\langle writeAck, ts, v \rangle$) to w
11: $minTS \leftarrow min\{m.ts' | m \in Q\}$	34: **Upon**
12: $v = m.val$ such that	35: **receive**($\langle readRelay, ts', v', r, op \rangle$)
13: $m \in Q \wedge m.ts' = minTS$	36: **if** $(ts < ts')$ **then**
14: **return**(v)	37: $(ts, v) \leftarrow (ts', v')$
	38: **if** $(operations(r) < op)$ **then**
15: At writer w	39: $operations(r) \leftarrow op$
16: **Variables:**	40: $relays(r) \leftarrow 0$
17: $ts \in \mathbb{N}^+$ init 0, $v \in V$	41: **if** $(operations(r) = op)$ **then**
18: **function** WRITE($val : input$)	42: $relays(r) \leftarrow relays(r) + 1$
19: $(ts, v) \leftarrow (ts + 1, val)$	43: **if** $(relays(r) = |\mathcal{S}|/2 + 1)$ **then**
20: **bcast** ($\langle writeReq, ts, v, w \rangle$) to $\mathcal{S}$	44: **send**($\langle readAck, ts, v, op \rangle$) to r
21: **await** $|\mathcal{S}|/2 + 1$ $writeAck$ messages	
22: m with $(m.ts = ts)$	
23: **return**	

$relays(r) = 0$ (lines 38–40). Server s also updates the number of collected *read-Relay* messages regarding the read request created by reader r (lines 41–42). When s receives $\langle readRelay, ts, v, read\_op \rangle$ from a majority of servers, it sends message $\langle readAck, ts, v, read\_op \rangle$ to reader r (lines 43–44).

(3) Upon receiving message $\langle writeReq, ts', v', w \rangle$, if $ts < ts'$, then the server updates its local timestamp and value (lines 31–32). In any other case, no update takes place. Finally, the server sends an acknowledgment to writer w.

Correctness. To prove correctness of algorithm Oh-SAM (Algorithm 1) we reason about its *liveness* (termination) and *atomicity* (safety). Termination holds with respect to our failure model: up to f servers may fail, where $f < |\mathcal{S}|/2$ and each operation waits for messages from some majority of servers. We now outline the proof (the details appear in the full paper).

To prove the atomicity we order operations by means of the timestamps used by each operation, expressing the required (to be proved) partial order as follows.

A1. If a *read* ρ succeeds a *write* ω, where ω writes value with timestamp ts and ρ returns the value for timestamp ts', then $ts' \geq ts$.

A2. If a write operation ω_1 that writes the value with timestamp ts_1 precedes a write operation ω_2 that writes the value with timestamp ts_2, i.e., $\omega_1 \rightarrow \omega_2$, then $ts_2 > ts_1$.

A3. If ρ_1 and ρ_2 are two read operations such that $\rho_1 \to \rho_2$ and ρ_1 returns the value with timestamp ts_1 and ρ_2 returns the value with timestamp ts_2, then ρ_2 returns $ts_2 \geq ts_1$.

Property A2 follows from *well-formedness* of the sole writer in the system and the fact that the writer always increments the timestamp. It is easy to see that the ts variable in each server s is monotonically increasing. This leads to the following lemma.

Lemma 1. *In any execution ξ of the algorithm, the variable ts maintained by any server s in the system is non-negative and monotonically increasing.*

Proof. When a server s receives a timestamp ts then s updates its local timestamp ts_s if and only if $ts > ts_s$ (lines 31–32 and 36–37). Thus the local timestamp of the server monotonically increases and the lemma follows.   □

As a next step we show how atomicity Property A3 is satisfied.

Lemma 2 (Property A3). *In any execution ξ of the algorithm, if ρ_1 and ρ_2 are two read operations such that ρ_1 precedes ρ_2, i.e., $\rho_1 \to \rho_2$, and ρ_1 returns the value for timestamp ts_1, then ρ_2 returns the value for timestamp $ts_2 \geq ts_1$.*

Proof. Let the two operations ρ_1 and ρ_2 be invoked by processes with identifiers r_1 and r_2 respectively (not necessarily different). Also, let $RSet_1$ and $RSet_2$ be the sets of servers that sent a *readAck* message to r_1 and r_2 during ρ_1 and ρ_2.

Assume by contradiction that read operations ρ_1 and ρ_2 exist such that ρ_2 succeeds ρ_1, i.e., $\rho_1 \to \rho_2$, and the operation ρ_2 returns a timestamp ts_2 that is smaller than the ts_1 returned by ρ_1, i.e., $ts_2 < ts_1$. According to our algorithm, ρ_2 returns a timestamp ts_2 that is smaller than the minimum timestamp received by ρ_1, i.e., ts_1, if ρ_2 obtains ts_2 and v in the *readAck* message of some server $s_x \in RSet_2$, and ts_2 is the minimum timestamp received by ρ_2.

Let us examine if s_x replies with ts' and v' to ρ_1, i.e., $s_x \in RSet_1$. By Lemma 1, and since $\rho_1 \to \rho_2$, then it must be the case that $ts' \leq ts_2$. According to our assumption $ts_1 > ts_2$, and since ts_1 is the smallest timestamp sent to ρ_1 by any server in $RSet_1$, then it follows that r_1 does not receive the *readAck* message from s_x, and hence $s_x \notin RSet_1$.

Now let us examine the actions of the server s_x. From the algorithm, server s_x collects *readRelay* messages from a majority of servers in S before sending a *readAck* message to ρ_2 (lines 43–44). Let $RRSet_{s_x}$ denote the set of servers that sent *readRelay* to s_x. Since, both $RRSet_{s_x}$ and $RSet_1$ contain some majority of the servers then it follows that $RRSet_{s_x} \cap RSet_1 \neq \emptyset$.

Thus there exists a server $s_i \in RRSet_{s_x} \cap RSet_1$, which sent (i) a *readAck* to r_1 for ρ_1, and (ii) a *readRelay* to s_x during ρ_2. Note that s_i sends a *readRelay* for ρ_2 only after it receives a read request from ρ_2 (lines 28–29). Since $\rho_1 \to \rho_2$, then it follows that s_i sent the *readAck* to ρ_1 before sending the *readRelay* to s_x. By Lemma 1, if s_i attaches a timestamp ts_{s_i} in the *readAck* to ρ_1, then s_i attaches a timestamp ts'_{s_i} in the *readRelay* message to s_x, such that $ts'_{s_i} \geq ts_{s_i}$. Since ts_1 is the minimum timestamp received by ρ_1, then $ts_{s_i} \geq ts_1$, and hence

$ts'_{s_i} \geq ts_1$ as well. By Lemma 1, and since s_x receives the *readRelay* message from s_i before sending a *readAck* to ρ_2, it follows that s_x sends a timestamp $ts_2 \geq ts'_{s_i}$. Thus, $ts_2 \geq ts_1$ and this contradicts our initial assumption.   □

Using standard arguments about the non-empty intersections of majority sets of processor identifiers in any execution we show in the full paper [6] that any read operation following a write operation receives *readAck* messages from servers where each timestamp is at least as large as one returned by any complete write operation. Likewise, we show that if a read operation succeeds a write operation, then it returns a value at least as recent as the one that was written, proving Property A1. Having shown liveness and atomicity of algorithm Oh-SAM the result follows.

Theorem 1. *Algorithm* Oh-SAM *implements an atomic SWMR object.*

Performance. In algorithm Oh-SAM write operations take 2 exchanges and read operations take 3 exchanges. The (worst case) message complexity of read operations is $|\mathcal{S}|^2 + 2|\mathcal{S}|$ and the (worst case) message complexity of write operations is $2|\mathcal{S}|$. This follows directly from the structure of the algorithm.

4   MWMR Algorithm Oh-MAM

Given the impossibility result [7], we seek a solution that involves three or four communications exchanges per operation, and we present our MWMR algorithm Oh-MAM: O*ne* and a h*alf* R*ound* M*ulti-writer* A*tomic* M*emory*. To impose an ordering on the values written by the writers we associate each value with a *tag* defined as the pair $\langle ts, id \rangle$, where ts is a timestamp and id is the identifier of a writer. Tags are ordered lexicographically (cf. [11]). The read protocol is identical to the SWMR setting (except that tags are used instead of timestamps), thus in Algorithm 2 we give only the code for writer and server processes.

Writer Protocol. This protocol is similar to [11]. When a write operation is invoked, writer w broadcasts a *discover* message to all servers (line 55), and awaits $|\mathcal{S}|/2 + 1$ *discAck* acknowledgments. When these messages are collected, writer w determines the maximum timestamp $maxTS$ from the tags (line 59) and sets its local *tag* to $\langle maxTS + 1, w \rangle$ (line 60). The writer then broadcasts request *writeReq* that includes this tag, the value to be written, and its write operation counter *write_op* to all servers (line 62). It then awaits $|\mathcal{S}|/2 + 1$ *writeAck* messages (line 63) and terminates.

Server Protocol. Servers react to messages from the readers exactly as in Algorithm 1. Here we describe server actions for *discover* and *writeReq* messages.

(1) Upon receiving message $\langle discover, write\_op, w \rangle$, server s sends message *discAck* that includes its local tag and local value to writer w.

(2) Upon receiving a *writeReq* request, if the message is not stale and $tag_s < tag'$, the server updates its local timestamp and local value to those

Algorithm 2. Writer and Server Protocols for MWMR algorithm Oh-MAM

49: At each writer w in $\mathcal{W}$
50: **Variables:**
51: $tag \in \langle \mathbb{N}, \mathcal{I} \rangle$ init $\langle 0, w \rangle$, $v \in V$ init $\perp$
52: $write\_op, maxTS \in \mathbb{N}^+$ init 0
53: **function** WRITE($val : input$)
54:     $write\_op \leftarrow write\_op + 1$
55:     **bcast**($\langle discover, write\_op, w \rangle$) to $\mathcal{S}$
56:     **await** $|\mathcal{S}|/2 + 1$ $discAck$ messages
57:         m with ($write\_op = m.write\_op$)
58:     Let $Q = \{\langle s, m \rangle | m$ received from $s\}$
59:     $maxTS \leftarrow \max\{m.tag.ts' | m \in Q\}$
60:     $(tag, v) \leftarrow (\langle maxTS + 1, w \rangle, val)$
61:     $write\_op \leftarrow write\_op + 1$
62:     **bcast**($\langle writeReq, tag, v, write\_op, w \rangle$)
        to $\mathcal{S}$
63:     **await** $|\mathcal{S}|/2 + 1$ $writeAck$ messages
64:         m with ($write\_op = m.write\_op$)
65:     **return**

66: At each server s in $\mathcal{S}$
67: **Variables:**
68: $tag \in \langle \mathbb{N}, \mathcal{I} \rangle$ init $\langle 0, s \rangle$, $v \in V$ init $\perp$
69: $write\_ops : \mathcal{W} \rightarrow \mathbb{N}$ init $\{0\}^{|\mathcal{W}|}$
70: **Upon receive**($\langle discover, write\_op, w \rangle$)
71: **send**($\langle discAck, tag, v, write\_op, s \rangle$)
        to w
72: **Upon**
73: **receive**($\langle writeReq, tag', v', write\_op, w \rangle$)
74: **if** (($tag < tag'$)
75:     $\wedge (write\_op(w) < write\_op)$) **then**
76:     $(tag, v) \leftarrow (tag', v')$
77:     $write\_ops(w) \leftarrow write\_op$
78: **send**($\langle writeAck, tag, v, write\_op \rangle$)
        to w

received (lines 75–77). Otherwise, no update takes place. The server then sends acknowledgment $writeAck$ to writer w. (line 78).

Correctness. *Termination* of Algorithm 2 is satisfied with respect to our failure model as in Sect. 3. *Atomicity* is reasoned about on the basis of the lexicographical order on the *tags* (instead of timestamps) in properties A1, A2, and A3 given in Sect. 3. Properties A1 and A3 are proved following the approach in Sect. 3 (the complete development is found in the full paper). It is easy to see that the *tag* variable in each server s is monotonically increasing. This leads to the following lemma.

Lemma 3. *In any execution ξ of the algorithm, the variable tag maintained by any server s in the system is non-negative and monotonically increasing.*

Proof. When server s receives a tag tag then s updates its local tag tag_s iff $tag > tag_s$ (Algorithm 1 in lines 36–37 and Algorithm 2 in lines 75–77). Thus the local tag of the server monotonically increases and the lemma follows.   □

Lemma 4 (Property A2). *In any execution ξ of the algorithm, if a write operation ω_1 writes a value with tag tag_1 then for any succeeding write operation ω_2 that writes a value with tag tag_2 we have $tag_2 > tag_1$.*

Proof. Let $WSet_1$ be the set of servers that send a $writeAck$ message within write operation ω_1. Let $Disc_2$ be the set of servers that send a $discoverAck$ message within write operation ω_2.

Based on the assumption, write operation ω_1 is complete. By Lemma 3, we know that if a server s receives a tag tag from a process p, then s includes tag tag' s.t. $tag' \geq tag$ in any subsequently message. Thus the servers in $WSet_1$

send a *writeAck* message within ω_1 with tag at least tag tag_1. Hence, every server $s_x \in WSet$ obtains tag $tags_{s_x} \geq tag_1$.

When write operation ω_2 is invoked, it obtains the maximum tag, max_tag, from the tags stored in at least a majority of servers. This is achieved by sending *discover* messages to all servers and collecting *discAck* replies from a majority of servers forming set $Disc_2$ (lines 55–59 and 70–71).

Sets $WSet_1$ and $Disc_2$ contain a majority of servers, and so $WSet_1 \cap Disc_2 \neq \emptyset$. Thus, by Lemma 3, any server $s_k \in WSet \cap Disc_2$ has a tag $tags_{s_k}$ s.t. $tags_{s_k} \geq tags_{s_x} \geq tag_1$. Furthermore, the invoker of ω_2 discovers a max_tag s.t. $max\_tag \geq tags_{s_k} \geq tags_{s_x} \geq tag_1$. The invoker updates its local tag by increasing the maximum tag it discovered, i.e., $tag_2 = \langle max\_tag + 1, v \rangle$ (line 60), and associating tag_2 with the value to be written. We know that, $tag_2 > max\_tag \geq tag_1$, hence $local\_tag > tag_1$.

Now the invoker of ω_2 includes its tag $local\_tag$ with *writeRequest* message to all servers, and terminates upon receiving *writeAck* messages from a majority of servers. By Lemma 3, ω_2 receives *writeAck* messages with a tag tag_2 s.t. $tag_2 \geq local\_tag > tag_1$ hence $tag_2 > tag_1$, and the lemma follows.   □

Having shown liveness and atomicity of algorithm Oh-MAM the result follows.

Theorem 2. *Algorithm* Oh-MAM *implements an atomic MWMR object.*

Performance. In algorithm Oh-MAM write operations take 4 exchanges and read operations take 3 exchanges. The (worst case) message complexity of read operations is $|\mathcal{S}|^2 + 2|\mathcal{S}|$ and the (worst case) message complexity of write operations is $4|\mathcal{S}|$. This follows directly from the structure of the algorithm (the complete development is given in the full paper).

5   Reducing the Latency of Read Operations

We next revise the protocol implementing read operations of algorithms Oh-SAM and Oh-MAM to yield protocols that implement read operations that terminate in either *two* or *three* communication exchanges. The key idea here is to let the reader determine "quickly" that a majority of servers hold the same timestamp (or tag) and its associated value. This is done by having the servers send relay messages to each other as well as to the readers. While a reader collects the relays and the read acknowledgment messages, if it observes in the set of the received relay messages that a majority of servers holds the same timestamp (or tag), then it safely returns the associated value and the read operation terminates in *two* communication exchanges. If that is not the case, then the reader proceeds similarly to algorithm Oh-SAM and terminates in *three* communication exchanges. We name the revised algorithms Oh-SAM' and Oh-MAM'. The code for the changes to algorithm Oh-SAM is given in Algorithm 3.

The code in lines 81–83 replaces the code in lines 8–9 of the original algorithm, and the code in lines 84–85 replaces the code in lines 28–29.

Algorithm 3. Read Protocol Changes for SWMR algorithm Oh-SAM'

81: **await** ($|\mathcal{S}|/2{+}1$ *readAck* messages m)   84: **Upon receive**($\langle readReq, r, op \rangle$)
       OR ($|\mathcal{S}|/2{+}1$ *readRelay* messages m 85:   **bcast**($\langle readRelay, ts, v, r, op \rangle$)
       with same timestamp ts)   to $\mathcal{S}$ and r
       with ($m.read\_op = read\_op$)
82: **if** $|\mathcal{S}|/2{+}1$ *readRelay* messages received
       with same timestamp ts **then**
83:      **return**(v associated with ts)

Revised Server Protocol. The server sends a *readRelay* message to all servers *and* to the invoker of the read operation (line 85).

Revised Reader Protocol. Here the reader awaits either (*a*) *readAck* messages from a majority of servers, or (*b*) *readRelay* messages from a majority of servers that include the same timestamp ts (line 81). In either case we check the enclosed *read_op* values to ensure "freshness" as before. For case (*b*) the reader returns the value v associated with the timestamp ts from the *readRelay* messages (lines 82–83). Otherwise case (*a*) holds and the reader proceeds as in Oh-SAM. Algorithm Oh-MAM' is obtained similarly by using tags instead of timestamps.

Liveness and *atomicity* of the revised algorithms Oh-SAM' and Oh-MAM' is shown similarly to algorithms Oh-SAM and Oh-MAM (the complete development is in the full paper).

Theorem 3. *Algorithm* Oh-SAM' *implements an atomic SWMR object.*

Proof sketch. The modifications do not affect the update of timestamp ts, thus ts grows monotonically at any server s and process p. Since only the writer increments the value of timestamp ts, Property A2 follows from the *well-formedness* of the sole writer.

In Oh-SAM all read operations terminate in 3 communication exchanges. Thus from Lemma 2 we know that any two non-concurrent 3-exchange read operations satisfy Property A3. Additionally for algorithm Oh-SAM' we show that Property A3 holds for the cases where (*i*) a 2-exchange read operation ρ_1 precedes a 2-exchange read operation ρ_2; (*ii*) a 2-exchange read operation ρ_1 precedes a 3-exchange read operation ρ_2; and (*iii*) a 3-exchange read operation ρ_1 precedes a 2-exchange read operation ρ_2.

Using the same approach we can prove Property A1. In particular, borrowing from the analysis of algorithm Oh-SAM we know that Property A1 is satisfied if a 2-exchange read operation succeeds a write operation. Thus for Oh-SAM' we show that the same holds for 2-exchange read operations.   □

We show the following for algorithm Oh-MAM' (similarly to Theorem 3).

Theorem 4. *Algorithm* Oh-MAM' *implements an atomic MWMR object.*

Performance. In algorithm Oh-SAM' write operations take 2 exchanges and read operations take 2 or 3 exchanges. The (worst case) message complexity of read operations is $|S|^2 + 3|S|$ and the (worst case) message complexity of write operations is $2|S|$.

In algorithm Oh-MAM' write operations take 4 exchanges and read operations take 2 or 3 exchanges. The (worst case) message complexity of read operations is $|S|^2 + 3|S|$ and the (worst case) message complexity of write operations is $4|S|$.

These results follows directly from the structure of the algorithms.

6   Empirical Evaluations

Here we present a comparative study if our algorithms by simulating them using the NS3 discrete event simulator [1]. We implemented the following three SWMR algorithms: ABD [2], Oh-SAM, and Oh-SAM'. We also implemented the corresponding three MWMR algorithms: ABD-MW (following the multi-writer extension [11]), Oh-MAM, and Oh-MAM'. For comparison we also implemented two algorithms, SW and MW, that mimic the minimum message requirements for the SWMR and MWMR settings respectively, but without performing any computation or ensuring consistency. SW performs two communication exchanges for read and write operations and MW performs three exchanges for read and write operations, thus providing a lower bound on performance in simulated scenarios.

Experimentation Setup. The experimental configuration consists of a single (SWMR) or multiple (MWMR) writers, a set of readers, and a set of servers. We assume that at most one server may fail. This is done to subject the system to a high communication burden. Communication among the nodes is established via point-to-point bidirectional links implemented with a DropTail queue.

For our evaluation, we use simulations representing two different topologies, *Series* and *Star*, that include the same array of routers

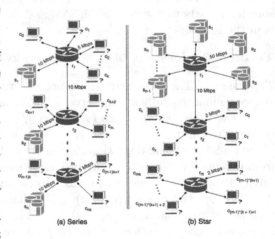

(a) Series   (b) Star

Fig. 1. Simulated topologies.

but differ in the deployment of server nodes. In both topologies clients are connected to routers over 5 Mbps links with 2 ms delay, the routers are connected over 10 Mpbs links with 4 ms delay. In the *Series* topology in Fig. 1(a), a server is connected to each router over 10 Mbps bandwidth with 2ms delay. This topology models a network where servers are separated and appear to be in different networks. In the *Star* topology in Fig. 1(b) all servers are connected to a single router over 50 Mbps links with 2 ms delay, modeling a network where servers are in a close proximity and are well-connected, e.g., as in a datacenter. In both topologies readers and writer(s) are located uniformly with respect to the

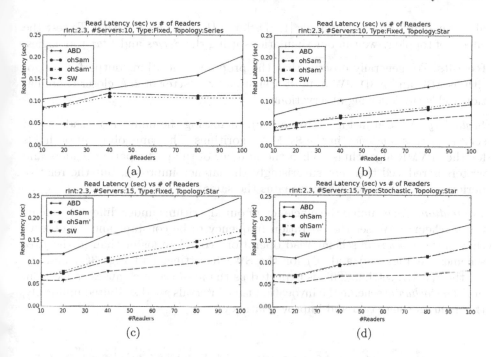

Fig. 2. SWMR simulation results.

routers. We ran NS3 on a Mac OS X with 2.5 Ghz Intel Core i7 processor. The results are compiled as averages over five samples per each scenario.

Performance. We assess algorithms in terms of *operation latency* that depends on communication delays and local computation delays. NS3 supports simulated time events, but does not measure delays due to local computation. In order to measure operation latency we combine two clocks: the simulation clock to measure communication delays, and a real time clock to measure computation delays. The sum of the two times yields operation latency.

Scenarios. To measure performance we define several scenarios. The scenarios are designed to test (i) the scalability of the algorithms as the number of readers, writers, and servers increases; (ii) the contention effect on efficiency, by running different concurrency scenarios; and (iii) the effects of chosen topologies on the efficiency. For scalability we test with the number of readers $|\mathcal{R}|$ from the set $\{10, 20, 40, 80, 100\}$ and the number of servers $|\mathcal{S}|$ from the set $\{10, 15, 20, 25, 30\}$. For the MWMR setting we use at most 80 readers and we range the number of writers $|\mathcal{W}|$ over the set $\{10, 20, 40\}$. To test contention we set the frequency of each read and write operation to be constant and we define two different invocation schemes. We issue reads every $rInt = 2.3$ s and write operations every $wInt = 4$ s. We define two invocation schemes: *fixed* and *stochastic*. In the *fixed* scheme all operations are scheduled periodically at a constant interval. In the *stochastic* scheme read and write operations are scheduled randomly from the intervals $[1, rInt]$ and $[1, wInt]$ respectively. To test the effects of topology we run our simulations using the *Series* and *Star* topologies.

Results. We generally observe that the proposed algorithms outperform algorithms ABD and ABD-MW in most scenarios by a factor of 2. A closer examination yields the following observations.

Scalability: As seen in Figs. 2(b) and (c), increasing the number of readers and servers increases latency in the SWMR algorithms. The same observation holds for the MWMR algorithms. When the number of the participating readers and writers is reduced then not surprisingly the latency improves, but the relative performance of the algorithms remains the same.

Contention: We examine the efficiency of our algorithms under different concurrency schemes. We set the operation frequency to be constant and we observe that in the *stochastic* scheme read operations complete faster than in the *fixed* scheme; see Figs. 2(c) and (d) for the SWMR setting, and Figs. 3(c) and (d) for the MWMR setting. This is expected as the *fixed* scheme causes congestion. For the *stochastic* scheme the invocation time intervals are distributed uniformly, this reduces congestion and improves latency.

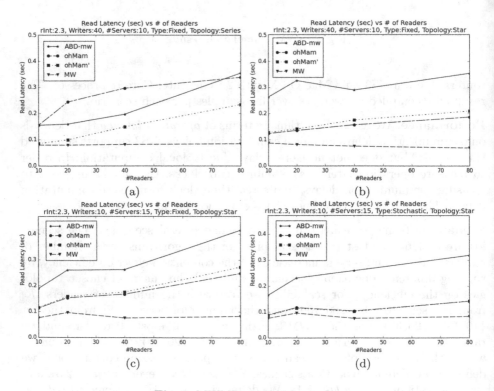

Fig. 3. MWMR simulation results.

Topology: Figs. 2(a) and (b) for the SWMR setting, and Figs. 3(a) and (b) for the MWMR setting show that topology substantially impacts performance. For both the SWMR and MWMR settings our algorithms outperform algorithms ABD and ABD-MW by a factor of at least 2 in *Star* topology where servers are well-connected. Our SWMR algorithms perform much better than ABD also in the *Series* topology. For the MWMR setting and *Series* topology, we note that ABD-MW generally outperforms algorithm Oh-MAM, however the revised algorithm Oh-MAM' noticeably outperforms ABD-MW.

Lastly we compare the performance of algorithms Oh-SAM and Oh-MAM with revised versions Oh-SAM' and Oh-MAM'. We note that Oh-SAM' and Oh-MAM' outperform all other algorithms in *Series* topologies. However, and perhaps not surprisingly, Oh-SAM and Oh-MAM outperform Oh-SAM' and Oh-MAM' in *Star* topology. This is explained as follows. In *Star* topology *readRelay* and *readAck* messages are exchanged quickly at the servers and thus delivered quickly to the clients. On the other hand, the bookkeeping mechanism used in the revised algorithms incur additional computational latency, resulting in worse latency.

An important observation is that while algorithms Oh-SAM' and Oh-MAM' improve the latencies of some operations (allowing some reads to complete in two exchanges), their performance relative to algorithms Oh-SAM and Oh-MAM depends on the deployment setting. Simulations show that Oh-SAM and Oh-MAM are more suitable for datacenter-like deployment, while in the "looser" settings algorithms Oh-SAM' and Oh-MAM' perform better.

7   Conclusions

We focused on the problem of emulating atomic read/write shared objects in message-passing settings with the goal of using three communication exchanges (to the extent allowed by the impossibility result [7]). We presented algorithms for the SWMR and MWMR models. The algorithms do not impose any constrains on the number of readers (SWMR and MWMR) and on the number of the writers for the MWMR model. Finally we performed an empirical study of the performance of algorithms using simulations.

References

1. NS3 network simulator. https://www.nsnam.org/
2. Attiya, H., Bar-Noy, A., Dolev, D.: Sharing memory robustly in message passing systems. J. ACM **42**(1), 124–142 (1996)
3. Dutta, P., Guerraoui, R., Levy, R.R., Chakraborty, A.: How fast can a distributed atomic read be? In: Proceedings of the 23rd ACM Symposium on Principles of Distributed Computing (PODC), pp. 236–245 (2004)
4. Englert, B., Georgiou, C., Musial, P.M., Nicolaou, N., Shvartsman, A.A.: On the efficiency of atomic multi-reader, multi-writer distributed memory. In: Abdelzaher, T., Raynal, M., Santoro, N. (eds.) OPODIS 2009. LNCS, vol. 5923, pp. 240–254. Springer, Heidelberg (2009). doi:10.1007/978-3-642-10877-8_20

5. Georgiou, C., Nicolaou, N.C., Shvartsman, A.A.: Fault-tolerant semifast implementations of atomic read/write registers. J. Parallel Distrib. Comput. **69**(1), 62–79 (2009)
6. Hadjistasi, T., Nicolaou, N., Schwarzmann, A.A.: Oh-Ram! one and a half round atomic memory (2016). arXiv:1610.08373
7. Hadjistasi, T., Nicolaou, N., Schwarzmann, A.A.: On the impossibility of one-and-a-half round atomic memory (2016). www.arXiv.com
8. Herlihy, M.P., Wing, J.M.: Linearizability: a correctness condition for concurrent objects. ACM Trans. Program. Lang. Syst. (TOPLAS) **12**(3), 463–492 (1990)
9. Lamport, L.: How to make a multiprocessor computer that correctly executes multiprocess program. IEEE Trans. Comput. **28**(9), 690–691 (1979)
10. Lynch, N.: Distributed Algorithms. Morgan Kaufmann Publishers, San Francisco (1996)
11. Lynch, N.A., Shvartsman, A.A.: Robust emulation of shared memory using dynamic quorum-acknowledged broadcasts. In: Proceedings of Symposium on Fault-Tolerant Computing, pp. 272–281 (1997)

Locality and Singularity for Store-Atomic Memory Models

Egor Derevenetc[1,3], Roland Meyer[2], and Sebastian Schweizer[3]([✉])

[1] Fraunhofer ITWM, Kaiserslautern, Germany
[2] TU Braunschweig, Braunschweig, Germany
`roland.meyer@tu-braunschweig.de`
[3] TU Kaiserslautern, Kaiserslautern, Germany
`{derevenetc,schweizer}@cs.uni-kl.de`

Abstract. Robustness is a correctness notion for concurrent programs running under relaxed consistency models. The task is to check that the relaxed behavior coincides (up to traces) with sequential consistency (SC). Although computationally simple on paper (robustness has been shown to be PSPACE-complete for TSO, PGAS, and Power), building a practical robustness checker remains a challenge. The problem is that the various relaxations lead to a dramatic number of computations, only few of which violate robustness.

In the present paper, we set out to reduce the search space for robustness checkers. We focus on store-atomic consistency models and establish two completeness results. The first result, called locality, states that a non-robust program always contains a violating computation where only one thread delays commands. The second result, called singularity, is even stronger but restricted to programs without lightweight fences. It states that there is a violating computation where a single store is delayed.

As an application of the results, we derive a linear-size source-to-source translation of robustness to SC-reachability. It applies to general programs, regardless of the data domain and potentially with an unbounded number of threads and with unbounded buffers. We have implemented the translation and verified, for the first time, PGAS algorithms in a fully automated fashion. For TSO, our analysis outperforms existing tools.

1 Introduction

Performance drives the design of computer architectures. The computation time of a task depends on the time it takes to access the memory. To reduce the access time, the idea is to place the data close to the compute unit. This idea is applied on virtually all design layers, from multiprocessors to high-performance computing clusters. Yet, the realization is different. Multiprocessors like Intel's x86 [39] and Sparc's PSO [43] implement thread-local instruction buffers that allow to

---

This work was supported by the DFG project *R2M2: Robustness against Relaxed Memory Models*.

A. El Abbadi and B. Garbinato (Eds.): NETYS 2017, LNCS 10299, pp. 133–148, 2017.
DOI: 10.1007/978-3-319-59647-1_11

execute store commands without waiting for the memory. The effect of buffered stores will be visible to other threads only when the multiprocessor decides to batch process the buffer, thus leading to a reordering of instructions. Clusters often implement a programming model called partitioned global address space (PGAS), either in terms of APIs like SHMEM [20], ARMCI [36], GASNET [11], GPI [33], and GASPI [26], or by HPC languages like UPC [21], Titanium [27], and Co-Array Fortran [37]. The PGAS model joins the partitioned memories of the cluster nodes into one (virtual) global memory. The selling point of PGAS is one-sided communication: A thread can modify a part of the global memory that resides in another node, without having to synchronize with that node. The drawback is the network delay. Although already computed, it may take a moment to install a value in the memory of another node.

Moving the data to the computation is delicate. When the data is shared, it has to be split into copies, one copy for each thread holding the datum. But then, in the interest of performance, updates to one copy cannot be propagated immediately to the other copies. This means the computations have to *relax* the guarantees given by an atomic memory and captured by the notion of sequential consistency (SC) [32]. The commands no longer take effect on the global memory in program order but may be reordered by the architecture. An important guarantee of SC, however, remains true in all the above models: *Store atomicity.* Once a store command arrives at the global memory, it is visible to all threads.

Programming a shared memory is difficult. Having to take into account the reorderings of the architecture makes programming in the presence of relaxed consistency close to impossible. SC-preserving compilers have been proposed as an approach to the problem and receive considerable attention [6,14,25,34,40,41]. The idea is to let the developer implement for SC, and make it the task of the compiler to insert synchronization primitives that justify the SC-assumption for the targeted architecture. Algorithmically, justifying the SC-assumption amounts to checking a problem known as *robustness* (against the architecture of interest): For every relaxed computation there has to be an SC-computation with the same behavior. The notion of behavior to be preserved typically (and also in this work) is the happens-before traces [31]. When developing an SC-preserving compiler, checking robustness is the main task. Inferring synchronization primitives from indications of non-robustness is better understood [1–3,5,7,13,28,30,35,42].

An SC-preserving compiler needs an over-approximate robustness analysis that should be as precise as possible. Under-approximations like bounded model checking [5,15,16], simulation [8], or monitoring [17,18] may miss non-robust computations and insert too few fences. Over-approximations, if too coarse, lead to over-fencing. Although decision procedures for robustness exist [14,19,23], building an efficient and yet precise robustness checker remains a challenge. The problem is the immense degree of non-determinism brought by the instruction reorderings that is hard to reflect in the analysis. This non-determinism forces over-approximations into explicitly modeling architectural details like instruction buffers [1,4,22,29] (operational approaches) or right-away operating on the code (axiomatic approaches) [3,6,40].

In this paper, we contribute two semantical results about robustness that limit the degree of non-determinism that has to be taken into account by algorithmic analyses. Both results state that robustness violations can be detected — in a complete way — with a restricted form of reorderings. The first result, called locality, states that only one thread needs to make use of instruction reorderings. The other threads operate as if they were running under SC: *A program is not robust if and only if there is a violating computation where exactly one thread delays stores.* The second result, called singularity, is even stronger: *A program without lightweight fence instructions is not-robust if and only if there is a violating computation with exactly one delayed store.* Note that a program without delays is robust. This means the result is an optimal characterization of non-robustness. Singularity only holds in the absence of lightweight fences. We do not consider this a severe limitation. Robustness is meant as a subroutine for fence inference inside an SC-preserving compiler. In that setting, programs naturally come without fences.

Our third contribution shows that the development of specialized robustness analyses can be avoided. Utilizing locality and singularity, we give an instrumentation that reduces robustness to reachability *under SC*. By instrumentation, we mean a source-to-source translation of a given program $\mathcal{P}$ into a program $\mathcal{P}'$ so that the former is robust if and only if the latter does not reach under SC a designated state. This allows us to employ for the analysis of robustness all techniques and tools that have been developed for SC-reachability. As a side-effect, we obtain the decidability of robustness for parameterized programs over a finite data domain. The restriction to finite data domains is not necessary for the instrumentation itself, but for the back-end SC-reachability analysis.

Concerning the model, we show that locality holds for virtually all store-atomic consistency models (singularity holds in the absence of dependencies). Inspired by [9], we introduce a programming language for concurrent programs that is meant to act as a programming framework for store-atomic models. The syntax of our language is an assembly dialect enriched with a variety of fence commands. The semantics is defined weak enough to support the relaxations found in the models discussed above. What makes our programming language a programming framework is that, given a program, we can add appropriate fences to obtain the behavior under SC, TSO, PSO, and PGAS. The motivation for having a programming framework is that we can show locality and singularity once for this model, and it will then hold for all instances of the framework.

Due to space constraints, this paper contains only a high-level explanation of our techniques. Further details and examples can be found in [24].

2   Related Work

Robustness checks that the relaxed behavior of a program is the same as the behavior under SC. The definition is relative to a notion of behavior, and there are various proposals in the literature [1,2,40]. To make the most of the consistency model in terms of performance, the notion of behavior should be

Memory Model	Ordered	Locality	Singularity	Cost Function
TSO	(√)	(√) [14]	X	Delays
PGAS − fence	(√)	(√)	√	DRL (Sec. 4.1)
PGAS + fence	(√) [19]	√	X	DRL (Sec. 4.1)
Power	√ [23]	?	X	Length

√ : holds   X : fails   ? : open

(−) : implied from right or below   shaded : this paper

Fig. 1. Normal-form results for violating computations under relaxed consistency.

liberal enough to equate quite distinct computations. On the other hand, it should be strong enough to be easy to check algorithmically. Equivalence of the happens-before traces [40] appears to be a good compromise between expressiveness and algorithmics, and is the favored notion in the literature on robustness [6,13,14,17–19]. Abdulla et al. recently proposed an alternative that is incomparable with the happens-before traces [2]. The idea is to preserve the total ordering of all stores and drop the relations for loads. This equivalence leads to efficient algorithmics for TSO but does not seem to fit well with consistency models beyond TSO. State-space equivalence from [1] leads to non-primitive recursive lower bounds for robustness, and will therefore also not be our choice.

In our earlier work on TSO [13], PGAS [19], and Power [23], we established normal form results similar to locality and singularity and also made use of the combinatorial proof principle. We elaborate on why the reasoning in this paper is substantially different from our earlier efforts. Figure 1 summarizes the comparison. The results about PGAS [19] and Power [23] rely on a normal form (Ordered in Fig. 1) for violating computations where all threads delay commands. As the normal form gives weak guarantees, it can be established with a cost function that simply measures the length of violating computations. The value of these earlier results is in that they apply to all consistency models which forbid out-of-thin-air values, while giving the precise complexity (but no useful algorithms). For TSO, we proved locality in [14]. As TSO architectures have one buffer per thread, we were able to apply a cost function that only measures delays, i.e., the number of commands that are processed while a store is being buffered (Fig. 1). In this paper, we also have to account for overtakes of stores in different buffers. Another aspect is that, for TSO, we managed to leave the happens-before trace unchanged. We tried to lift this strategy to PGAS but failed. Instead, we show how to construct a different computation that still is a violation. Taking apart the computation was a big step.

The instrumentation we present in Sect. 7 is related to our work on TSO [13]. To be precise, we adapt the instrumentation of the attacker (that delays commands) to the assumption of singularity and to the more relaxed consistency model. The instrumentation of the helper threads (that close the happens-before cycle) is the one from ESOP'13. Since our earlier work assumes locality, the new instrumentation (for singularity) is more compact (we save a linear number of auxiliary addresses). An alternative instrumentation-based robustness analysis is presented in [4]. The instrumentation precomputes an optimized cycle and then checks robustness wrt. that cycle. The idea can be understood as trading one complex verification task (robustness) for a number of tasks (robustness wrt. a cycle) that can be solved more efficiently. A strong point is that the approach is general enough to apply to non-store-atomic consistency models, including Power. For TSO, PSO, and PGAS, also that instrumentation will benefit (in terms of size) from locality and singularity. Related is also the instrumentation in [2]. Atig et al. only have to add two variables to the program, which means the instrumentation is more compact than ours. But, as explained above, the approach does not seem to be generalizable beyond TSO.

Instrumentations that mimic the effect of instruction buffers can also be found in reachability analyses for relaxed consistency models. Bouajjani et al. apply the idea of bounded context switching to TSO [10]. Vechev et al. [22] precompute the utilization of the instruction buffers in TSO and PSO, and show how to mimic them under SC without having to shift content between variables. Common to both works is that they eagerly simulate the effect of buffers. In [12], we show how to introduce store buffering lazily, and only where needed to satisfy a TSO reachability query: The idea is to guide the store buffering by non-robust computations. Hence, also reachability analyses benefit from the improvements for robustness presented here.

In this paper, we focus on store-atomic memory models. Although store atomicity feels like a natural requirement, important multiprocessors like Power [8,23,38] or ARM [8] are known to be non-store atomic. There, stores to independent variables may arrive in independent threads in a different order. What remains true is coherence. All threads see the stores to each variable in the same order. A major challenge for future work is to understand whether a locality result can be established for Power, potentially under mild assumptions on the programs. With the results in this paper, singularity can be shown not to hold, Fig. 1.

3   Concurrent Programs

Syntax. The syntax of our programming language is defined below. A concurrent program is identified by a name and consists of a finite set of named threads. The threads share a global memory. Moreover, each thread defines a finite set of local registers. The code is given as a finite set of labelled instructions. Each instruction includes a command and the label of the instruction to be executed next. To model non-deterministic choices, several instructions can have the same label. The instruction set includes loads from memory, stores to memory, local assignments, asserts, and two kinds of fences. SC-fences forbid relaxations altogether. The second fence command is parameterized by a set of addresses. To be more precise, the program comes with a domain DOM the elements of which model the data values as well as the addresses in the global memory. We assume the domain contains a distinguished value $0 \in$ DOM that will be used for initialization purposes. Besides DOM, there is also a function domain FUN that contains elements from DOM* → DOM. All functions that are used in expressions have to stem from FUN.

$\langle prog \rangle ::= \textbf{program } \langle pid \rangle \langle thrd \rangle^*$
$\langle thrd \rangle ::= \textbf{thread } \langle tid \rangle$
     $\textbf{regs } \langle reg \rangle^*$
     $\textbf{init } \langle label \rangle$
     $\textbf{begin } \langle linst \rangle^* \textbf{ end}$
$\langle linst \rangle ::= \langle label \rangle : \langle inst \rangle ; \textbf{goto } \langle label \rangle ;$

$\langle inst \rangle ::= \langle reg \rangle \leftarrow \textbf{mem} [\langle expr \rangle]$
     $| \quad \textbf{mem} [\langle expr \rangle] \leftarrow \langle expr \rangle$
     $| \quad \langle reg \rangle \leftarrow \langle expr \rangle$
     $| \quad \textbf{assert } \langle expr \rangle$
     $| \quad \textbf{scfence}$
     $| \quad \textbf{fence } \langle expr \rangle^*$
$\langle expr \rangle ::= \langle fun \rangle (\langle reg \rangle^*)$

Semantics. Under SC, a store command takes immediate effect on the global memory. We consider consistency models that relax the program order but preserve store atomicity. This means the effect of a store command may not become visible immediately (to the other threads), but later commands may overtake the store and hit the memory earlier than the store. What is guaranteed, however, is that once the store is visible it is visible to all threads.

The semantics specifies $C(\mathcal{P})$, i.e., the set of computations for program $\mathcal{P}$. We define the relaxed semantics of our assembly language in an operational style, in terms of a hardware architecture that processes instructions. In this model, out-of-program-order computations result from the use of instruction buffers inside the architecture. To provide an umbrella for different store-atomic models, the architecture has two types of buffers. Buffers of the first type are per thread and per address FIFO buffers that only hold stores of one thread to one address. Buffers of the second type are per thread FIFO buffers that hold stores of one thread to potentially different addresses. The per-address buffers emulate PGAS. An all-addresses buffer mimics TSO.

When a thread issues a store, the instruction is put into the corresponding per-address buffer. From the per-address buffers, the store non-deterministically advances to the all-addresses buffer of that thread. From the all-addresses buffer, the store eventually arrives at the global memory. Due to the per-address buffers, stores of the same thread to different addresses may enter the memory in an order different from the order in which they were issued.

When doing a load, a thread checks whether there is a store to the address of interest kept in one of the store buffers. If not, the thread loads the current value from the main memory. If so, the thread loads the value of the most recent store in the buffers (where stores in the per-address buffers are more recent than stores in the all-addresses buffer). The definition ensures that the thread sees its own stores in issue order. Even more, for a sequential program the architecture appears to implement SC.

To synchronize different threads, the language offers two fence instructions. The scfence instruction can only be executed if all buffers of the executing thread are empty. Additionally, we have the fence instruction that carries a list of addresses. It can be executed if the buffers for the given addresses in the executing thread are empty.

We show that the framework encompasses the consistency models we aim at.

Sequential consistency. Lamport's SC [32] is the intuitive consistency model that reflects an atomic shared memory. Formally, the SC-computations are the valid interleavings of the computations of all threads. We can mimic SC in our framework by letting stores directly go to memory. To enforce this, one can insert an scfence after each store. We avoid this modification and just write $C_{SC}(\mathcal{P})$ to mean the set of SC-computations of program $\mathcal{P}$.

Total Store Ordering. TSO implements the store-to-load relaxation. Each thread has a single buffer for stores, and loads may overtake buffered stores when early reads fail. Notably, the thread-local total order of stores is preserved. Intel's x86 architecture implements TSO [39].

The all-addresses buffers in our framework are meant to mimic TSO. To preserve the total order of stores, the per-address buffers must not be used. We can insert fence instructions after each store command to enforce TSO.

Partial Store Ordering. For PSO [43], there are two kinds of relaxation, the store-to-load relaxations of TSO and the store-to-store relaxation. The latter means that stores of the same thread to different addresses can be reflected in the global memory in an order that is different from the program order.

The per-address-buffers enable the additional store-to-store relaxation. As long as a store resides in its per-address buffer, stores to other addresses can be executed faster and the buffered store gets delayed. A program that is executed unmodified (without further fences) in our framework will run with PSO semantics. The benefit of PSO is that it approximates well the behavior of PGAS.

Partitioned Global Address Space. In a PGAS clusters, the cluster nodes create FIFO buffers to transfer data to and request data from neighboring nodes. The transfer itself is handled by the network infrastructure. PGAS APIs allow the user to specify the buffer that should be used for a transfer. A comparison and precise model of PGAS APIs can be found in [19]. The model presented here is designed as an approximation of PGAS that is less complex and hence easier to handle wrt. the theory we develop. Rather than assigning stores to buffers, we give each store a separate buffer, like in PSO. The user defined sharing of buffers is mimicked by the parameterized fences. The approximation is a bit weak as it forces different buffers into a total ordering.

4   Robustness

We first define the happens-before relation and, based on this, the notion of robustness. As a first step towards locality and singularity, we then work out properties of computations that violate robustness.

Given $\tau \in C(\mathcal{P})$, the happens-before relation highlights the crucial control and data-flow dependencies in the computation. Crucial means that an alternative computation with the same relations and valid delays is guaranteed to be executable in the program. In particular, all asserts will receive the same values. Technically, the happens-before relation $\to_{hb} = \to_{po} \cup \to_{st} \cup \to_{src} \cup \to_{cf}$ is the union of different dependencies between two actions. The program order

$\rightarrow_{po}$ denotes the control flow between actions of the same thread. The remaining orders can be summarized as follows. Whenever two actions x and y operate on the same address in the shared memory, follow each other in τ, and at least one of them is a store, then we have $x \rightarrow_{hb} y$. It is common to distinguish the relations according to the commands. The store order $\rightarrow_{st}$ denotes the order in which two stores to the same address reach the memory. The source relation $\rightarrow_{src}$ goes from a store action to a load action of the same address and denotes the fact that the load reads the value written by that store. The conflict relation $\rightarrow_{cf}$ is a derived relation and says that a load has to happen before a store that potentially overwrites the value to be read.

The *happens-before trace* $\mathrm{Tr}(\tau)$ associated with computation $\tau \in C(\mathcal{P})$ is the directed graph where the nodes are the actions from τ. To be precise, isu_x and store or fence x are represented by the same node x. The edges are given by the four happens-before relations. Note that each computation induces a trace but several computations can have the same trace.

The *robustness problem* is to check, given a concurrent program, whether the traces obtained from the computations in the model from the previous section are included in the traces of the SC computations:

Given program $\mathcal{P}$, does $\mathrm{Tr}(C(\mathcal{P})) \subseteq \mathrm{Tr}(C_{SC}(\mathcal{P}))$ hold?

Algorithmically, the task is to look for *violations* of robustness, computations $\tau \in C(\mathcal{P})$ with $\mathrm{Tr}(\tau) \notin \mathrm{Tr}(C_{SC}(\mathcal{P}))$. Shasha and Snir observed that violating computations are precisely those with a cyclic happens-before relation.

Lemma 1 ([40]). *Consider $\tau \in C(\mathcal{P})$. Then $\mathrm{Tr}(\tau) \in \mathrm{Tr}(C_{SC}(\mathcal{P}))$ if and only if $\mathrm{Tr}(\tau)$ is acyclic.*

To see this, consider an acyclic trace. It will have a linearization that forms an SC computation. In turn, every SC computation will have an acyclic trace. Under SC, all commands execute atomically and there is no chance for delays. The following development can be understood as strengthening the insight of Shasha and Snir.

4.1   Minimal Violations

To deepen our understanding of violating computations, we will concentrate on violations that are minimal in a carefully chosen order. The main finding is the following. In a minimal violation, *every delay is due to a cycle*. To derive this fact, we employ an interesting proof strategy that establishes properties by contradiction and that will occur in variants throughout the paper. Starting from a minimal violation, we assume the property of interest would not hold and from this deduce the existence of a smaller violation.

Technically, we define minimal violations with the help of a cost function $\$(-)$ mapping computations to a well-founded domain. Intuitively, the cost of a computation reflects its degree of relaxation. A minimal violation is then a violation that is as little relaxed as possible (while being a violation).

Phrased differently, the computation is as close to SC as possible. Hence, the cost can also be understood as a penalty for deviating from SC.

The thing to note about the definition of cost is that we define it on the per-thread computations. This means that two computations $\tau_1, \tau_2 \in C(\mathcal{P})$ with the same per-thread computations, $\tau_1 \downarrow t = \tau_2 \downarrow t$ for all threads t, will have the same cost, $\$(\tau_1) = \$(\tau_2)$. Like the proof strategy, this equality will be applied over and over again. It allows us to choose between different interleavings while preserving minimality.

Technically, the *cost* of a computation is a triple of natural numbers:

$$\$(\tau) := (\text{delays}(\tau), \text{reorders}(\tau), \text{length}(\tau)) \in \mathbb{N}^3.$$

We refer to the three auxiliary functions as penalty functions and define them below. Cost triples in $\mathbb{N}^3$ are compared lexicographically, so $(4, 0, 6) < (4, 1, 5)$. When we refer to a *minimal violation*, we mean a violation τ where the cost $\$(\tau)$ is minimal in the set of violating computations.

The intuitive meaning of the penalty functions is as follows. The function delays($-$) increases when actions happen between an issue and the corresponding store or fence action in memory. Such intermediary actions indicate a delay of the store. Since delays are impossible under SC, there is a penalty for them. To be precise, we only consider intermediary actions from the thread that executed the store or fence. The function reorders($-$) gives a penalty to reordering delayed stores. It increases when stores reach the memory in an order different from the order in which they were issued. Keeping this function value small forces stores of the same thread to different variables to respect the program order. Finally, function length($-$) gives the computation's length as we would like to focus on violations that do not contain unnecessary actions. We turn to the formalization.

The *length* of a computation τ, denoted by length(τ), is the number of actions in τ. The special case ε is defined to have length zero.

To define the *number of delays*, consider the computation $\tau = \tau_1 \cdot \text{isu}_a \cdot \tau_2 \cdot a \cdot \tau_3$ where a is a delayed store or fence action. Let thread(a) := t. We say that a *overtakes* every action in τ_2 projected to t. Hence, for this one store or fence the number of delays is delays(a) := length($\tau_2 \downarrow t$). The number of delays in τ is the sum of the delays of all stores and fences:

$$\text{delays}(\tau) := \sum_{\text{all stores and fences } a \text{ in } \tau} \text{delays}(a).$$

A store or fence a is said to be *reordered* if it overtakes another issue isu_b together with the corresponding store or fence b. Here, a and b are supposed to have the same thread thread(a) = t = thread(b). So we have

$$\tau = \tau_1 \cdot \text{isu}_a \cdot \tau_2 \cdot a \cdot \tau_3 \quad \text{with} \quad \tau_2 = \tau_{2a} \cdot \text{isu}_b \cdot \tau_{2b} \cdot b \cdot \tau_{2c}.$$

The *number of reorders* for the store a, denoted by reorders(a), is the number of such stores or fences b in $\tau_2 \downarrow t$. The number of reorders in a computation τ, reorders(τ), is again the sum of the reorders of all stores and fences in τ.

4.2 Cycles

Our goal is to establish the following result about minimal violations. Whenever we have an action a that has been overtaken by another action b, then we already find a cycle involving the two. To be more precise, either the cycle is via the intermediary actions between a and b (Proposition 1(i)), or the cycle is via a dependency from isu_b to a (Proposition 1(ii)). For the precise statement, we need a stronger variant of the happens-before relation.

We will often argue that some of the intermediary actions are sufficient to establish the existence of a happens-before path between two actions. To make this dependence on the intermediary actions explicit, we recall the happens-before-through relation from [14]. It can be understood as embedding the happens-before relation, or more generally the trace, into the underlying computation, which is a linear structure. Consider the computation $\tau = \tau_1 \cdot a \cdot \tau_2 \cdot b \cdot \tau_3 \in C(\mathcal{P})$. We say that *action a happens before action b through τ_2*, if there is a subsequence $a_1 \ldots a_n$ of τ_2 so that one of

$$a_i \xrightarrow{+}_{po} a_{i+1}, \quad a_i \to_{src} a_{i+1}, \quad a_i \to_{st} a_{i+1}, \quad \text{or} \quad a_i \to_{cf} a_{i+1}$$

holds for all $0 \le i \le n$ with $a_0 := a$ and $a_{n+1} := b$. We also refer to $a_0 \cdot \ldots \cdot a_{n+1}$ as a *happens-before-through chain*.

Proposition 1 (Cycles). *Let $\tau = \tau_1 \cdot a \cdot \tau_2 \cdot b \cdot \tau_3 \in C(\mathcal{P})$ be a minimal violation where a has been overtaken by b. One of the following holds:*

(i) $b \xrightarrow{+}_{po} a$ *and* $a \xrightarrow{+}_{hb} b$ *through* τ_2
(ii) $a \xrightarrow{+}_{po} b$ *and* $\tau_1 = \tau_{1a} \cdot \text{isu}_b \cdot \tau_{1b}$ *and* $\text{isu}_b \xrightarrow{+}_{hb} a$ *through* τ_{1b}.

Remark: Both cases lead to a happens-before cycle with actions in $\tau_1 \cdot a \cdot \tau_2 \cdot b$.

The proof of Proposition 1 is non-trivial and relies on a strong dichotomy result, Lemma 2. The lemma is a disjunction (i) or (ii) and should be read as two implications. If we read it as $\neg(i)$ implies (ii), it states that given a minimal violation two actions can be swapped as long as they are not separated by a happens-before-through chain. This will allow us to modify a given computation. If we read the dichotomy as $\neg(ii)$ implies (i), it states that given a minimal violation whenever we see two actions of the same thread we are already sure to have a happens-before-through chain between them.

Lemma 2 (Dichotomy [14]). *In a minimal violation $\tau = \tau_1 \cdot a \cdot \tau_2 \cdot b \cdot \tau_3 \in C(\mathcal{P})$*

(i) $a \xrightarrow{+}_{hb} b$ *through τ_2 or*
(ii) *there is $\tau' = \tau_1 \cdot \tau_{21} \cdot b \cdot a \cdot \tau_{22} \cdot \tau_3 \in C(\mathcal{P})$ with $\text{Tr}(\tau) = \text{Tr}(\tau')$, $\tau \downarrow t = \tau' \downarrow t$ for every thread t, and τ_{22} a subsequence of τ_2.*

We note that a similar result has been shown to hold for TSO [14]. The current setting requires a more subtle cost function on computations.

Corollary 1. *In a minimal violation $\tau = \tau_1 \cdot a \cdot \tau_2 \cdot b \cdot \tau_3 \in C(\mathcal{P})$ with $\text{thread}(a) = \text{thread}(b)$ we have $a \xrightarrow{+}_{hb} b$ through τ_2.*

The corollary is particularly interesting in the setting where action b has overtaken action a. In this case, it states that the overtake was actually required to execute the actions in the following sense. The intermediary actions form a happens-before-through chain that prevents b from being executed before a. The existence of this chain renders formally the intuition that minimal violations do not contain unnecessary delays.

To see the corollary, assume there was no happens-before-through chain. Lemma 2 would allow us to swap the actions a and b while preserving the per-thread computations — in contradiction to the fact that the actions stem from the same thread.

Proof (of Proposition 1). Since b overtakes a, they are from the same thread and thus program-order dependent. Furthermore, b is a store or a fence. If $b \rightarrow^+_{po} a$, it is immediate to complete the cycle stated in (i): Corollary 1 yields $a \rightarrow^+_{hb} b$ through τ_2. If $a \rightarrow^+_{po} b$, we find the issue action isu_b in τ_1, say $\tau_1 = \tau_{1a} \cdot isu_b \cdot \tau_{1b}$. From Corollary 1, $isu_b \rightarrow^+_{hb} a$ through τ_{1b}, as required in (ii). □

5 Locality

Theorem 1 (Locality). *A concurrent program is not robust if and only if there is a violating computation where exactly one thread delays actions.*

The difficult task is to show completeness. We can show that we only need to consider minimal violations of the form $\tau = \tau_1 \cdot x \cdot \tau_2 \cdot y \cdot \tau_3 \cdot st_y \cdot \tau_4 \cdot st_x \cdot \tau_5$ where x is overtaken by st_x and y is overtaken by st_y with x and y being from different threads. There are two happens-before cycles: one between x and st_x, the other between y and st_y. The goal is to move st_y back over y to save one delay while preserving the computation's trace, or at least get another valid computation with a slightly different trace that also contains a happens-before cycle. This will be the cycle between x and st_x. Therefore, we get a violation with less delays than the original one. This contradicts the initial assumption that the chosen computation was a minimal violation.

With locality at hand, we can constrain the shape of minimal violations. A similar normal form was presented for TSO in [13], and we can adapt it to the current setting with minimal changes.

Proposition 2 (Witnesses [13]). *Program $\mathcal{P}$ is robust if and only if there is no minimal violation $\tau = \tau_1 \cdot isu_{st} \cdot \tau_2 \cdot a \cdot \tau_3 \cdot st \cdot \tau_4 \in C(\mathcal{P})$, called* witness *computation, that satisfies the following requirements.*

(W1) Only $t_A := \text{thread}(st) = \text{thread}(a)$ delays actions.
(W2) $\tau_3 \downarrow t_A = \varepsilon$.
(W3) τ_1 and $\tau_2 \cdot a \cdot \tau_3$ do not contain delayed actions.
(W4) For every b in $\tau_3 \cdot st$ we have $a \rightarrow^+_{hb} b$ through the intermediary actions.
(W5) τ_4 only contains delayed stores and fences of t_A.

Following [13], thread t_A is referred to as the *attacker*, the remaining threads are called *helpers*.

6 Singularity

Our second main result shows that it is sufficient to delay only a single store action. The theorem only holds in the absence of lightweight fence commands, scfence is still allowed. We stress that the theorem is optimal in the sense that it characterizes the least relaxation required to violate sequential consistency. A program without delayed stores is always robust.

Theorem 2 (Singularity). *Consider a program without* fence*. It is not robust if and only if there is a violation with exactly one delayed store.*

The proof is short and derives a contradiction to a strong combinatorial property. The reasoning is as follows. If the program has a violation with one delayed store, it is not robust. If the program is not robust, by Proposition 2 there is a minimal violation that is a witness computation as defined in the previous section. In this computation, τ_4 only consists of delayed stores and fences of the attacker thread. We assume the program does not contain fence commands. This means τ_4 only consists of delayed stores of the attacker. Now, if more than one store was delayed, we would have a contradiction to the following Proposition 3 that came as a surprise to us. A minimal violation will never place two delayed stores next to each other. This already concludes the argumentation.

Proposition 3 (Two Stores). *In the absence of* fence*, there is no minimal violation* $\tau_1 \cdot \text{st}_1 \cdot \text{st}_2 \cdot \tau_2$ *with* $\text{thread}(\text{st}_1) = \text{thread}(\text{st}_2)$.

7 Instrumentation

To check robustness, we have to look for minimal violations. Proposition 2 reduces the search space as we only have to consider minimal violations in witness form. If the program does not use the fence instruction, then also singularity holds and τ_4 will be empty in all witness computations. Our instrumentation is an adaptation of [13].

Attacks. An *attack* is a triple $A = (t_A, \text{stinst}, \text{lastinst})$, where t_A is a thread, stinst is a store instruction of t_A, and lastinst is a store or load instruction of t_A. Note that attacks are syntactic objects and there is a quadratic number of them. An attack A is *feasible* if there is a witness computation where t_A plays the role of the attacker, st is an instance of stinst, and a is an instance of lastinst. With Proposition 2, the program is robust if and only if no attack is feasible. Given an attack, we now develop an instrumentation that finds a witness for it.

The witness computation of interest has four phases:

1. In τ_1, all issued stores are immediately written to the memory. Eventually, the attacker decides to delay a store.
2. In τ_2, further actions of the attacker happen either without delay or they are delayed until τ_4. The helpers execute arbitrary actions. At some point, the attacker does its last normal action a, which is a load or non-delayed store.

3. In τ_3, the helpers execute only actions that are happens-before-dependent on a while the attacker pauses.
4. In τ_4, only the attacker's delayed actions get executed.

We use an observation from [13] that limits the information we have to track about the delayed stores. The argumentation is as follows. If there are delayed stores to an address, the attacker will load the last value that was put into the corresponding buffer. The helpers will load the last value that was stored in memory. Combined with Property (W3) of witness computations — $\tau_2 \cdot a \cdot \tau_3$ does not contain delayed actions — the content of the buffers is not needed. All we have to track is two values per address: The current value in memory and the value of the last buffered store, if any. When the attacker executes a store that is delayed, it will set the buffered value. When the attacker executes a store without delay or the helpers execute a store, it updates the current value in memory. Loads from helpers will always read the current value from memory while loads from the attacker will prefer the buffered one, if it is set.

Recall that the values in DOM act as addresses. We extend DOM as follows: For each $x \in$ DOM we add auxiliary addresses (x, d) and (x, hb). The addresses (x, d) hold the values of the last buffered stores. The addresses (x, hb) are used to track the happens-before-dependencies required by (W4). Here, we rely on the mechanism from [13]. Furthermore, we add the auxiliary addresses hb and suc. Flag hb will tell the helpers that Phase 3 has started and they must execute hb-dependent actions. Flag suc indicates a feasible attack.

Instrumentation of the Attacker for Locality. The attacker operates in three modes. Initially, instructions are executed under SC (Phase 1). Upon execution of stinst, the attacker can decide to delay that store. If the store is to address x, we save the stored value to (x, d) and the address x to an auxiliary register $r_{\mathsf{st_A}}$. The control flow changes to a modified copy of the code for Phase 2.

During Phase 2, when the attacker has to load from address y, it will first check whether (y, d) is set. If so, it reads that value, otherwise it reads the value of y. A store to address y can either directly go to memory location y or it is delayed and stored to (y, d). If there already is a buffered value, then the store cannot be done on memory and has to update the buffered value — due to the FIFO property of buffers. Additionally, we have to delay all stores if there was a fence that had to be delayed. A fence has to be delayed if there is a buffered value for at least one of its addresses. We use an additional register r_{fence} as a flag indicating that a fence has been delayed. An scfence action is not permitted in Phase 2 and will lead to a deadlock.

Upon execution of lastinst, the attacker can decide that this is its last action. If it is a load, we make sure that there is no buffered value for that address. Otherwise, there is no possibility for hb-dependent actions in τ_3. We set the hb flag and go to a special wait label. If lastinst is a store, then we have to make sure that it can be stored directly, i.e., there is no delayed fence and no delayed store for that address. We execute the store, set the hb flag, and go to the wait label.

The third mode is in the wait label. The attacker waits until a helper thread has completed the happens-before chain, in which case it sets the success flag.

Compared to [13] for TSO, what is new is the handling of non-delayed stores and fences, and the optimized detection of violations by the attacker.

Optimized Instrumentation of the Attacker for Singularity. When the program does not make use of the `fence` instruction, then singularity holds. We can simplify the above instrumentation as follows. As only one store is delayed, we can use a single register $r_{delayval}$ instead of the auxiliary addresses (x, d) to save the corresponding value. Recall that the address is kept in r_{st_A}.

References

1. Abdulla, P.A., Atig, M.F., Chen, Y.-F., Leonardsson, C., Rezine, A.: Counter-example guided fence insertion under TSO. In: Flanagan, C., König, B. (eds.) TACAS 2012. LNCS, vol. 7214, pp. 204–219. Springer, Heidelberg (2012). doi:10.1007/978-3-642-28756-5_15
2. Abdulla, P.A., Atig, M.F., Ngo, T.-P.: The best of both worlds: trading efficiency and optimality in fence insertion for TSO. In: Vitek, J. (ed.) ESOP 2015. LNCS, vol. 9032, pp. 308–332. Springer, Heidelberg (2015). doi:10.1007/978-3-662-46669-8_13
3. Alglave, J., Kroening, D., Nimal, V., Poetzl, D.: Don't sit on the fence – a static analysis approach to automatic fence insertion. In: Biere, A., Bloem, R. (eds.) CAV 2014. LNCS, vol. 8559, pp. 508–524. Springer, Cham (2014). doi:10.1007/978-3-319-08867-9_33
4. Alglave, J., Kroening, D., Nimal, V., Tautschnig, M.: Software verification for weak memory via program transformation. In: Felleisen, M., Gardner, P. (eds.) ESOP 2013. LNCS, vol. 7792, pp. 512–532. Springer, Heidelberg (2013). doi:10.1007/978-3-642-37036-6_28
5. Alglave, J., Kroening, D., Tautschnig, M.: Partial orders for efficient bounded model checking of concurrent software. In: Sharygina, N., Veith, H. (eds.) CAV 2013. LNCS, vol. 8044, pp. 141–157. Springer, Heidelberg (2013). doi:10.1007/978-3-642-39799-8_9
6. Alglave, J., Maranget, L.: Stability in weak memory models. In: Gopalakrishnan, G., Qadeer, S. (eds.) CAV 2011. LNCS, vol. 6806, pp. 50–66. Springer, Heidelberg (2011). doi:10.1007/978-3-642-22110-1_6
7. Alglave, J., Maranget, L., Sarkar, S., Sewell, P.: Fences in weak memory models. In: Touili, T., Cook, B., Jackson, P. (eds.) CAV 2010. LNCS, vol. 6174, pp. 258–272. Springer, Heidelberg (2010). doi:10.1007/978-3-642-14295-6_25
8. Alglave, J., Maranget, L., Tautschnig, M.: Herding cats: modelling, simulation, testing, and data mining for weak memory. ACM TOPLAS **36**(2), 7:1–7:74 (2014)
9. Atig, M.F., Bouajjani, A., Burckhardt, S., Musuvathi, M.: What's Decidable about Weak Memory Models? In: Seidl, H. (ed.) ESOP 2012. LNCS, vol. 7211, pp. 26–46. Springer, Heidelberg (2012). doi:10.1007/978-3-642-28869-2_2
10. Atig, M.F., Bouajjani, A., Parlato, G.: Getting rid of store-buffers in TSO analysis. In: Gopalakrishnan, G., Qadeer, S. (eds.) CAV 2011. LNCS, vol. 6806, pp. 99–115. Springer, Heidelberg (2011). doi:10.1007/978-3-642-22110-1_9
11. Bonachea, D.: GASNet specification, v1.1. Technical report UCB/CSD-02-1207, University of California, Berkeley (2002)

12. Bouajjani, A., Calin, G., Derevenetc, E., Meyer, R.: Lazy TSO reachability. In: Egyed, A., Schaefer, I. (eds.) FASE 2015. LNCS, vol. 9033, pp. 267–282. Springer, Heidelberg (2015). doi:10.1007/978-3-662-46675-9_18

13. Bouajjani, A., Derevenetc, E., Meyer, R.: Checking and enforcing robustness against TSO. In: Felleisen, M., Gardner, P. (eds.) ESOP 2013. LNCS, vol. 7792, pp. 533–553. Springer, Heidelberg (2013). doi:10.1007/978-3-642-37036-6_29

14. Bouajjani, A., Meyer, R., Möhlmann, E.: Deciding robustness against total store ordering. In: Aceto, L., Henzinger, M., Sgall, J. (eds.) ICALP 2011. LNCS, vol. 6756, pp. 428–440. Springer, Heidelberg (2011). doi:10.1007/978-3-642-22012-8_34

15. Burckhardt, S., Alur, R., Martin, M.M.K.: Bounded model checking of concurrent data types on relaxed memory models: a case study. In: Ball, T., Jones, R.B. (eds.) CAV 2006. LNCS, vol. 4144, pp. 489–502. Springer, Heidelberg (2006). doi:10.1007/11817963_45

16. Burckhardt, S., Alur, R., Martin, M.: Checkfence: checking consistency of concurrent data types on relaxed memory models. In: PLDI, pp. 12–21. ACM (2007)

17. Burckhardt, S., Musuvathi, M.: Effective program verification for relaxed memory models. In: Gupta, A., Malik, S. (eds.) CAV 2008. LNCS, vol. 5123, pp. 107–120. Springer, Heidelberg (2008). doi:10.1007/978-3-540-70545-1_12

18. Burnim, J., Sen, K., Stergiou, C.: Sound and complete monitoring of sequential consistency for relaxed memory models. In: Abdulla, P.A., Leino, K.R.M. (eds.) TACAS 2011. LNCS, vol. 6605, pp. 11–25. Springer, Heidelberg (2011). doi:10.1007/978-3-642-19835-9_3

19. Calin, G., Derevenetc, E., Majumdar, R., Meyer, R.: A theory of partitioned global address spaces. In: FSTTCS, pp. 127–139 (2013)

20. Chapman, B., Curtis, T., Pophale, S., Poole, S., Kuehn, J., Koelbel, C., Smith, L.: Introducing OpenSHMEM: SHMEM for the PGAS community. In: PGAS, p. 2. ACM (2010)

21. UPC Consortium. UPC language specification v1.2. Technical report (2005)

22. Dan, A., Meshman, Y., Vechev, M., Yahav, E.: Effective abstractions for verification under relaxed memory models. In: D'Souza, D., Lal, A., Larsen, K.G. (eds.) VMCAI 2015. LNCS, vol. 8931, pp. 449–466. Springer, Heidelberg (2015). doi:10.1007/978-3-662-46081-8_25

23. Derevenetc, E., Meyer, R.: Robustness against power is PSPACE-complete. In: Esparza, J., Fraigniaud, P., Husfeldt, T., Koutsoupias, E. (eds.) ICALP 2014. LNCS, vol. 8573, pp. 158–170. Springer, Heidelberg (2014). doi:10.1007/978-3-662-43951-7_14

24. Derevenetc, E., Meyer, R., Schweizer, S.: Locality and singularity for store-atomic memory models (2017). arXiv:1703.04603

25. Fang, X., Lee, J., Midkiff, S.: Automatic fence insertion for shared memory multiprocessing. In: SC, pp. 285–294. ACM (2003)

26. Global address space programming interface. http://www.gaspi.de/

27. Hilfinger, P.N., Bonachea, D.O., Datta, K., Gay, D., Graham, S.L., Liblit, B.R., Pike, G., Su, J.Zh., Yelick, K.A.: Titanium language reference manual, version 2.19. Technical report UCB/EECS-2005-15, UC Berkeley (2005)

28. Kuperstein, M., Vechev, M., Yahav, E.: Automatic inference of memory fences. In: FMCAD, pp. 111–119. IEEE (2010)

29. Kuperstein, M., Vechev, M.T., Yahav, E.: Partial-coherence abstractions for relaxed memory models. In: PLDI, pp. 187–198. ACM (2011)

30. Kuperstein, M., Vechev, M.T., Yahav, E.: Automatic inference of memory fences. SIGACT News **43**(2), 108–123 (2012)

31. Lamport, L.: Time, clocks, and the ordering of events in a distributed system. CACM **21**(7), 558–565 (1978)
32. Lamport, L.: How to make a multiprocessor computer that correctly executes multiprocess programs. IEEE Trans. Comput. **28**(9), 690–691 (1979)
33. Machado, R., Lojewski, C.: The Fraunhofer virtual machine: a communication library and runtime system based on the RDMA model. Comput. Sci. Res. Dev. **23**(3–4), 125–132 (2009)
34. Marino, D., Singh, A., Millstein, T., Musuvathi, M., Narayanasamy, S.: A case for an SC-preserving compiler. In: PLDI, pp. 199–210. ACM (2011)
35. Meshman, Y., Dan, A., Vechev, M., Yahav, E.: Synthesis of memory fences via refinement propagation. In: Müller-Olm, M., Seidl, H. (eds.) SAS 2014. LNCS, vol. 8723, pp. 237–252. Springer, Cham (2014). doi:10.1007/978-3-319-10936-7_15
36. Nieplocha, J., Carpenter, B.: ARMCI: a portable remote memory copy library for distributed array libraries and compiler run-time systems. In: Rolim, J., et al. (eds.) IPPS 1999. LNCS, vol. 1586, pp. 533–546. Springer, Heidelberg (1999). doi:10.1007/BFb0097937
37. Numrich, R.W., Reid, J.: Co-array Fortran for parallel programming. In: ACM Sigplan Fortran Forum, vol. 17, pp. 1–31. ACM (1998)
38. Sarkar, S., Sewell, P., Alglave, J., Maranget, L., Williams, D.: Understanding POWER multiprocessors. In: PLDI, pp. 175–186. ACM (2011)
39. Sewell, P., Sarkar, S., Owens, S., Nardelli, F.Z., Myreen, M.O.: x86-TSO: a rigorous and usable programmer's model for x86 multiprocessors. CACM **53**, 89–97 (2010)
40. Shasha, D., Snir, M.: Efficient and correct execution of parallel programs that share memory. ACM TOPLAS **10**(2), 282–312 (1988)
41. Singh, A., Narayanasamy, S., Marino, D., Millstein, T., Musuvathi, M.: End-to-end sequential consistency. In: ISCA, pp. 524–535. IEEE (2012)
42. Vafeiadis, V., Zappa Nardelli, F.: Verifying fence elimination optimisations. In: Yahav, E. (ed.) SAS 2011. LNCS, vol. 6887, pp. 146–162. Springer, Heidelberg (2011). doi:10.1007/978-3-642-23702-7_14
43. Weaver, D., Germond, T. (eds.): The SPARC Architecture Manual Version 9. PTR Prentice Hall, Upper Saddle River (1994)

Policies

Policy Expressions and the Bottom-Up Design of Computing Policies

Rezwana Reaz[1(✉)], H.B. Acharya[1], Ehab S. Elmallah[2],
Jorge A. Cobb[3], and Mohamed G. Gouda[1]

[1] University of Texas at Austin, Austin, USA
{rezwana,acharya,gouda}@cs.utexas.edu
[2] University of Alberta, Edmonton, Canada
elmallah@ualberta.ca
[3] University of Texas at Dallas, Richardson, USA
cobb@utdallas.edu

Abstract. A policy is a sequence of rules, where each rule consists of a predicate and a decision, and where each decision is either "accept" or "reject". A policy P is said to accept (or reject, respectively) a request iff the decision of the first rule in P, that matches the request is "accept" (or "reject", respectively). Examples of computing policies are firewalls, routing policies and software-defined networks in the Internet, and access control policies. In this paper, we present a generalization of policies called policy expressions. A policy expression is specified using one or more policies and the three policy operators: "not", "and", and "or". We show that policy expressions can be utilized to support bottom-up methods for designing policies. We also show that each policy expression can be represented by a set of special types of policies, called slices. Finally, we present several algorithms that use the slice representation of given policy expressions to verify whether the given policy expressions satisfy logical properties such as adequacy, implication, and equivalence.

Keywords: Policies · Firewalls · Access control · Routing policies

1 Introduction

A computing policy is a filter that is placed at the entry point of some resource. Each request to access the resource needs to be first examined against the policy to determine whether to accept or reject the request. The decision of a policy to accept or reject a request depends on two factors:

1. The values of some attributes that are specified in the request and
2. The sequence of rules in the policy that are specified by the policy designer.

Examples of computing policies are firewalls in the Internet, routing policies and software-defined networks in the Internet, and access control policies [12]. Early methods for the logical analysis of computing policies have been reported in [6,7,15].

© Springer International Publishing AG 2017
A. El Abbadi and B. Garbinato (Eds.): NETYS 2017, LNCS 10299, pp. 151–165, 2017.
DOI: 10.1007/978-3-319-59647-1_12

A rule in a policy consists of a predicate and a decision, which is either "accept" or "reject". To examine a request against a policy, the rules in the policy are considered one by one until the first rule, whose predicate satisfies the values of the attributes in the request, is identified. Then the decision of the identified rule, whether "accept" or "reject", is applied to the request.

Note that there are three sets of requests that are associated with each policy P: (1) the set of requests that are accepted by P, (2) the set of requests that are rejected by P, and (3) the set of requests that are ignored by P (i.e. neither accepted nor rejected by P). This third set is usually, but not always, empty.

Next, we present two policy examples P and Q and use these examples to introduce the concept of "policy expressions", the subject matter of the current paper.

Let u and v be two attributes whose integer values are taken from the interval $[1, 9]$. A policy P over these two attributes can be defined as follows:

$$((u \in [1, 4]) \wedge (v \in [8, 9])) \rightarrow \text{reject}$$
$$((u \in [2, 4]) \wedge (v \in [7, 9])) \rightarrow \text{accept}$$
$$((u \in [1, 9]) \wedge (v \in [1, 9])) \rightarrow \text{reject}$$

Policy P consists of three rules. The first rule states that each request (u, v), where the value of u is an integer in the interval $[1, 4]$ and where the value of v is an integer in the interval $[8, 9]$, is to be rejected. The second rule states that each request (u, v), that does not match the first rule and where the value of u is an integer in the interval $[2, 4]$ and where the value of v is an integer in the interval $[7, 9]$, is to be accepted. The third rule states that each request (u, v) that does not match the first two rules is to be rejected. Thus, the set of requests that are accepted by policy P is $\{(2, 7), (3, 7), (4, 7)\}$. Notice that because the third rule rejects all requests that do not match the first two rules, we conclude policy P ignores no requests.

A second policy Q over attributes u and v can be defined as follows:

$$((u \in [2, 3]) \wedge (v \in [7, 7])) \rightarrow \text{accept}$$
$$((u \in [2, 4]) \wedge (v \in [7, 8])) \rightarrow \text{accept}$$
$$((u \in [1, 9]) \wedge (v \in [1, 9])) \rightarrow \text{reject}$$

The set of requests that are accepted by Q is $\{(2, 7), (3, 7), (4, 7), (2, 8), (3, 8), (4, 8)\}$ and all other requests are rejected.

Now assume that we need to use the two given policies P and Q to design a policy expression $(P \text{ or } Q)$. This policy expression accepts every request that is accepted by policy P or accepted by policy Q. Thus, the set of requests that is accepted by $(P \text{ or } Q)$ is $\{(2, 7), (3, 7), (4, 7), (2, 8), (3, 8), (4, 8)\}$.

In this paper, we show that every policy expression that is specified using one or more policies and the three policy operators "not", "and", and "or" can be represented by a set $\{S_1, S_2, \cdots, S_k\}$ of a special class of policies called slices such that the following condition holds. A request is accepted by a policy expression iff this request is accepted by at least one slice in the set of slices that represents the policy expression.

As an example, let P and Q refer to the two policies defined above. As discussed in Algorithm 4 below, the policy expression (P or Q) can be represented by the set of three slices $\{S_1, S_2, S_3\}$:

Slice S_1 is defined as follows:

$$((u \in [1,4]) \wedge (v \in [8,9])) \rightarrow \text{reject}$$
$$((u \in [2,4]) \wedge (v \in [7,9])) \rightarrow \text{accept}$$

Slice S_2 is defined as follows:

$$((u \in [2,3]) \wedge (v \in [7,7])) \rightarrow \text{accept}$$

Slice S_3 is defined as follows:

$$((u \in [2,4]) \wedge (v \in [7,8])) \rightarrow \text{accept}$$

(Notice that, as discussed below, each slice is a policy that consists of zero or more reject rules followed by exactly one accept rule.)

Similarly, as discussed below, the policy expression (P and Q) accepts any request r iff both policies P and Q accept r. As discussed in Algorithm 3 below, the policy expression (P and Q) can be represented by the set of two slices $\{S_4, S_5\}$:

Slice S_4 is defined as follows:

$$((u \in [1,4]) \wedge (v \in [8,9])) \rightarrow \text{reject}$$
$$((u \in [2,3]) \wedge (v \in [7,7])) \rightarrow \text{accept}$$

Slice S_5 is defined as follows:

$$((u \in [1,4]) \wedge (v \in [8,9])) \rightarrow \text{reject}$$
$$((u \in [2,4]) \wedge (v \in [7,8])) \rightarrow \text{accept}$$

This paper suggests a novel bottom-up design method that can be followed by a designer in designing a computing policy. This design method proceeds as follows. First, the designer designs several simple elementary policies. Second, the designer combines these elementary policies using the three policy operators "not", "and", and "or" into a single policy expression PE. Finally, the designer uses the algorithms in Sect. 6 below to verify that designed policy expression PE satisfies desired adequacy, implication, and equivalence properties.

As an example, a designer can start by designing two policies P and Q, then use these two policies to design the policy expression (P and not(Q)). This policy expression accepts every request that is accepted by policy P and rejected by policy Q. Then the designer can use Algorithm 7 in Sect. 6 below to prove that this policy expression implies both policy P and policy not(Q).

The rest of this paper is organized as follows. In Sect. 2, we present our formal definition of policies. Then in Sect. 3, we present our formal definition of policy expressions and discuss three theorems that state fundamental properties of policy expressions. In Sect. 4, we discuss an algorithm that can be used to enforce a given policy expression over any input stream of requests. In Sect. 5, we introduce the concept of a base of a policy expression as a set of slices that satisfies the following condition. For every request r, the policy expression accepts r iff at least one slice in the base of the policy expression accepts r. Also in Sect. 5, we present algorithms for constructing a base for every policy expression. In Sect. 6, we show that the bases of given policy expressions can be used to determine whether the given policy expressions satisfy some logical properties such as adequacy, implication, and equivalence. Finally, we discuss related work in Sect. 7, and present our concluding remarks in Sect. 8.

2   Preliminaries About Policies

In this section, we formally introduce the main concepts related to computing policies. These concepts are: Intervals, Attributes, Requests, Predicates, Decisions, Rules, Policies, and Complete Policies.

2.1   Intervals

An interval is a finite and nonempty set of consecutive integers. An interval X can be denoted by a pair of integers $[y, z]$, where y is the smallest integer in X, and z is the largest integer in X. Note that an interval $[y, y]$ has only one integer y. Note also that any pair $[y, z]$, where $y > z$, is not an interval.

2.2   Attributes

An attribute is a "variable" that has a "name" and a "value". Throughout this paper, we assume that there are t attributes whose names are $u_1, u_2, \ldots,$ and u_t. The value of each attribute u_i is taken from an interval that is called the domain of attribute u_i and is denoted $D(u_i)$.

2.3   Requests

A request is a tuple $(b_1, \ldots, b_t)$ of t integers, where t is the number of attributes and each integer b_i is taken from the domain $D(u_i)$ of attribute u_i. We adopt R to denote the set of all requests. Notice that set R is finite.

2.4   Predicates

A predicate is of the form $((u_1 \in X_1) \wedge \cdots \wedge (u_t \in X_t))$, where each u_i is an attribute, each X_i is an interval that is contained in the domain $D(u_i)$ of attribute u_i, and $\wedge$ is the logical AND or conjunction operator.

The value of each conjunct $(u_i \in X_i)$ in a predicate is true iff the value of attribute u_i is an integer in interval X_i.

The value of a predicate is true iff the value of every conjunct $(u_i \in X_i)$ in this predicate is true.

A predicate $((u_1 \in X_1) \wedge \cdots \wedge (u_t \in X_t))$, where each interval X_i is the whole domain of the corresponding attribute u_i, is called the ALL predicate.

A request $(b_1, \ldots, b_t)$ is said to match a predicate $((u_1 \in X_1) \wedge \cdots \wedge (u_t \in X_t))$ iff each integer b_i in the request is an element in the corresponding interval X_i in the predicate.

2.5   Decisions

We assume that there are two distinct decisions: "accept" and "reject". Henceforth, we write "accept" and "reject" with quotation marks to indicate the "accept" and "reject" decisions, respectively. We also write accept and reject without quotation marks to indicate the English words accept and reject, respectively.

2.6   Rules

A rule (in a policy) is defined as a pair, one predicate and one decision, written as follows:

$$\langle \text{predicate} \rangle \rightarrow \langle \text{decision} \rangle$$

A rule whose decision is "accept" is called an accept rule, and a rule whose decision is "reject" is called a reject rule. An accept rule whose predicate is the ALL predicate is called an accept-ALL rule, and a reject rule whose predicate is the ALL predicate is called the reject-ALL predicate.

A request is said to match a rule iff the request matches the predicate of the rule. (Note that each request matches every ALL rule.)

2.7   Policies

A policy is a (possibly empty) sequence of rules. A policy P is said to accept (or reject, respectively) a request rq iff P has an accept (or reject, respectively) rule r such that request rq matches rule r and does not match any rule that precedes rule r in policy P.

2.8   Complete Policies

A policy P is complete iff every request is either accepted by P or rejected by P.

Let P be a policy. We adopt the notation $\text{not}(P)$ to denote the policy that is obtained from policy P by (1) replacing each "accept" decision in P by a "reject" decision in $\text{not}(P)$ and (2) replacing each "reject" decision in $\text{not}(P)$ by an "accept" decision in $\text{not}(P)$.

Note that a policy P is complete iff the policy $\text{not}(P)$ is complete.

3   Definition of Policy Expressions

In this section, we present a generalization of policies called policy expressions. Informally, a policy expression is specified using one or more policies and three policy operators: "not", "and", and "or". Each one of these policy operators can be applied to one or two policy expressions to produce a policy expression.

Formally, a ⟨policy expression PE⟩ is defined recursively as one of the following four options:

> A complete policy P
> A complete policy not(P)
> ⟨policy expression PE_1⟩ and ⟨policy expression PE_2⟩
> ⟨policy expression PE_1⟩ or ⟨policy expression PE_2⟩

An example of a policy expression is as follows:

$$(P \text{ and } \text{not}(Q)) \text{ or } (\text{not}(P) \text{ and } Q)$$

In this example, P and Q are complete policies, "not", "and", and "or" are called policy operators.

Associated with each policy expression PE is a request set RS defined as follows:

- If PE is a complete policy P,
  then RS is the set of all requests accepted by P
- If PE is a complete policy not(P),
  then RS is the set of all requests accepted by not(P)
- If PE is a policy expression (PE_1 and PE_2),
  then RS is the intersection of two request sets RS_1 and RS_2 where RS_1 is the request set associated with PE_1 and RS_2 is the request set associated with PE_2
- If PE is a policy expression (PE_1 or PE_2),
  then RS is the union of two request sets RS_1 and RS_2 where RS_1 is the request set associated with PE_1 and RS_2 is the request set associated with PE_2

As an example, the request set associated with the policy expression (P and not(Q)) is the intersection of the two request sets RS_1 and RS_2, where RS_1 is the set of all requests accepted by policy P and RS_2 is the set of all requests accepted by policy not(Q).

Two policy expressions PE_1 and PE_2 are said to be *equivalent* iff the two request sets associated with PE_1 and PE_2 are identical.

For example, the policy expression (P and not(Q)) and the policy expression (not(Q) and P) are equivalent.

Let PE be a policy expression. We adopt the notation not(PE) to denote the policy expression that is recursively obtained from PE as follows:

- If PE is a complete policy P,
  then not(PE) denotes the policy expression not(P)

- If PE is a complete policy not(P),
  then not(PE) denotes the policy expression P
- If PE is a policy expression $(PE_1$ and $PE_2)$,
  then not(PE) denotes the policy expression $($not(PE_1) or not$(PE_2))$
- If PE is a policy expression $(PE_1$ or $PE_2)$,
  then not(PE) denotes the policy expression $($not(PE_1) and $(PE_2))$

As an example, not$\big((P$ and not$(Q))$ or $($not(P) and $Q)\big)$ denotes the policy expression $\big(($not(P) or $Q)$ and $(P$ or not$(Q))\big)$.

The following three theorems state fundamental properties of policy expressions.

Theorem 1. *For every policy expression PE, (1) the request set associated with the policy expression $(PE$ and not$(PE))$ is the empty set, and (2) the request set associated with the policy expression $(PE$ or not$(PE))$ is the set R of all requests.*

Proof. Our proof of this theorem makes use of the following definition of the "rank" of a policy expression PE.

The rank k of a policy expression PE is a non-negative integer defined recursively as follows:

- If PE is a complete policy P or is a complete policy not(P), then $k = 0$
- If PE is of the form $(PE_1$ and $PE_2)$ or is of the form $(PE_1$ or $PE_2)$,
  then $k = (1 + \max(k_1, k_2))$, where k_1 is the rank of PE_1 and k_2 is the rank of PE_2

Our proof of this theorem is by induction on the rank k of the policy expression PE. Details of this proof are presented in [13].

Theorem 2. *For every policy expression PE, the request set associated with the policy expression not(PE) is $(R - RS)$, where R is the set of all requests, RS is the request set associated with PE, and "$-$" is the set difference operator.*

Proof. Let NS denote the request set associated with not(PE). Thus, the request set associated with the policy expression $(PE$ and not$(PE))$ is $(RS \cap NS)$, and the request set associated with the policy expression $(PE$ or not$(PE))$ is $(RS \cup NS)$. Hence, from Theorem 1, the set $(RS \cap NS)$ is empty and the set $(RS \cup NS)$ is the set R of all requests. Therefore, set NS is $(R - RS)$.

A policy expression PE is said to be *complete* iff for every request r either PE accepts r or PE rejects r.

Theorem 3. *Every policy expression is complete.*

Proof. Proof by contradiction: Assume that there is a policy expression PE that is not complete. Thus, there is a request r such that PE neither accepts r nor rejects r. Hence, from Theorem 2, request r is neither in the request set RS associated with PE nor in the request set $(R - RS)$ associated with not(PE). Therefore, request r is not in the union of the two sets RS and $(R - RS)$, which constitutes the set R of all requests. This contradicts the fact that r is a request in the set R of all requests.

4   Enforcement of Policy Expressions

In this section, we discuss an algorithm that takes as input any given policy expression PE and any given request r and produces as output a determination of whether or not PE accepts r. This algorithm can be used to enforce the given policy expression PE over any input stream of requests.

The main idea of this algorithm is to represent the given PE and r by a Boolean expression BE, that involves the two Boolean values "T" (which denotes true) and "F" (which denotes false), and the three Boolean operators "$\neg$", "$\wedge$", and "$\vee$".

The Boolean expression BE, that represents the given policy expression PE and the given request r, is required to satisfy the following two conditions:

- $(PE$ accepts $r)$ iff $(BE$ is T$)$
- $(PE$ rejects $r)$ iff $(BE$ is F$)$

Next, we discuss an example for constructing the Boolean expression BE that represents a policy expression PE and a request r. Let,

$$PE = (P \text{ and } (Q \text{ or } R)) \text{ or } \text{not}(Q)$$

where P, Q, and R are complete policies and assume that P accepts r, Q rejects r, and R rejects r.

Therefore, the Boolean expression BE that represents PE and r can be constructed as follows:

- Because P accepts r, replace policy P in PE by the Boolean value T in BE
- Because Q rejects r, replace policy Q in PE by the Boolean value F in BE
- Because R rejects r, replace policy R in PE by the Boolean value F in BE
- Replace the policy operator "not" in PE by the Boolean operator "$\neg$" in BE
- Replace the policy operator "and" in PE by the Boolean operator "$\wedge$" in BE
- Replace the policy operator "or" in PE by the Boolean operator "$\vee$" in BE
- The Boolean expression BE can now be computed as follows:

$$BE = (\text{T} \wedge (\text{F} \vee \text{F})) \vee \neg \text{F} = \text{F} \vee \text{T} = \text{T}$$

Because BE is T, we conclude that the given policy expression PE accepts the given request r.

Next, we discuss the time complexity for computing the Boolean expression BE that represents a given policy expression PE and a given request r. Assume that the given policy expression PE has m distinct policies and k policy operators. Also assume that each distinct policy has t attributes and at most n rules. Therefore, the time complexity to determine whether each distinct policy in PE accepts the given request r is $\mathcal{O}(n \times t)$. Also the time complexity to construct the Boolean expression is $\mathcal{O}(n \times t \times m)$. The "length" of the constructed Boolean expression BE is $\mathcal{O}(k)$. Thus, the time complexity of computing the Boolean value of BE is $\mathcal{O}(k^2)$. Therefore the time complexity for constructing the Boolean expression BE and computing its Boolean value is $\mathcal{O}((n \times t \times m) + k^2)$.

5   Bases of Policy Expressions

In the next section, Sect. 6, we discuss several properties of policy expressions and present algorithms to determine whether given policy expressions satisfy these properties. For example, we discuss in Sect. 6, what does it mean for two policy expressions to be equivalent and present algorithm to determine whether any given two policy expressions are equivalent.

Our discussion in Sect. 6 is based on two concepts, namely "slices" and "bases of policy expressions" that we introduce in the current section.

A *slice* is a policy that consists of zero or more reject rules followed by exactly one accept rule.

Let SS be a set of slices and let PE be a policy expression. Set SS is said to be a *base* of the policy expression PE iff the following condition holds. Each request that is accepted by at least one slice in set SS is in the request set associated with the policy expression PE, and vice versa.

The following five algorithms can be applied to any policy expression PE to construct a slice set SS that is a base of PE.

Algorithm 1
Input: A complete policy P
Output: A slice set SS that is a base of P
Steps: For each accept rule ar in P, construct a slice sl in SS as follows. All the reject rules that precede rule ar in P are added to slice sl. Then rule ar is added at the end of slice sl.
Time Complexity: The time complexity of Algorithm 1 is of $\mathcal{O}(n^2 \times t)$ where n is the number of rules and t is the number of attributes in the input policy P.
End

Algorithm 2
Input: A complete policy not(P)
Output: A slice set SS that is a base of not(P)
Steps: For each accept rule ar in not(P), construct a slice sl in SS as follows. All the reject rules that precede rule ar in not(P) are added to slice sl. Then rule ar is added at the end of slice sl.
Time Complexity: The time complexity of Algorithm 2 is of $\mathcal{O}(n^2 \times t)$ where n is the number of rules and t is the number of attributes in the input policy not(P).
End

Algorithm 3
Input: A policy expression PE of the form (PE_1 and PE_2)
          A slice set SS_1 that is a base of PE_1
          A slice set SS_2 that is a base of PE_2
Output: A slice set SS that is a base of PE
Steps: For every slice sl_1 in SS_1 and every slice sl_2 in SS_2, construct a slice sl in SS as follows:

1. The reject rules of slice sl is constructed by merging the reject rules of sl_1 with the reject rules of sl_2 in any order
2. The accept rule of slice sl is constructed by taking the intersection of the predicates of the two accept rules of slices sl_1 and sl_2. If this intersection is empty, then discard slice sl from the base SS of the policy expression PE.

Time Complexity: The time complexity of Algorithm 3 is of $\mathcal{O}((m_1 \times m_2) \times (n_1 \times t + n_2 \times t))$ where m_1 is the number of slices in SS_1, m_2 is the number of slices in SS_2, n_1 is the number of rules in the largest slice in SS_1, n_2 is the number of rules in the largest slice in SS_2, and t is the number of attributes.
End

Algorithm 4
Input: A policy expression PE of the form $(PE_1$ or $PE_2)$
        A slice set SS_1 that is a base of PE_1
        A slice set SS_2 that is a base of PE_2
Output: A slice set SS that is a base of PE
Steps: The slice set SS is constructed as the union of the two slice sets SS_1 and SS_2.
Time Complexity: The time complexity of Algorithm 4 is of $\mathcal{O}((m_1 \times n_1 \times t) + (m_2 \times n_2 \times t))$ where m_1 is the number of slices in SS_1, m_2 is the number of slices in SS_2, n_1 is the number of rules in the largest slice in SS_1, n_2 is the number of rules in the largest slice in SS_2, and t is the number of attributes.
End

Algorithm 5
Input: A policy expression PE
Output: A slice set SS that is a base of PE
Steps: SS is constructed by recursively applying the following four steps:

1. If PE is a complete policy P then use Algorithm 1 to construct SS as a base of P
2. If PE is a complete policy not(P) then use Algorithm 2 to construct SS as a base of not(P)
3. If PE is $(PE_1$ and $PE_2)$ and SS_1 is a base of PE_1 and SS_2 is a base of PE_2 then use Algorithm 3 to construct SS as a base of PE from the two slice sets SS_1 and SS_2
4. If PE is $(PE_1$ or $PE_2)$ and SS_1 is a base of PE_1 and SS_2 is a base of PE_2 then use Algorithm 4 to construct SS as a base of policy expression PE from the two slice sets SS_1 and SS_2

Time Complexity: The time complexity of Algorithm 5 depends on the number and type of operators in the input policy expression PE.
End

6   Properties of Policy Expressions

In this section, we present several important properties of policy expressions (namely adequacy, implication, and equivalence) and present algorithms that can be used to determine whether any given policy expression satisfies these properties.

A policy expression PE is said to be *adequate* iff PE accepts at least one request. The following algorithm can be used to determine whether any given policy expression is adequate.

Algorithm 6
Input: A policy expression PE
Output: A determination of whether PE accepts a request.
Steps: Construct a base SS of the policy expression PE using Algorithm 5. For each slice in the constructed base SS, determine whether this slice accepts a request using the PSP method described in [1, 14]. If one or more slices in SS accepts a request, then PE accepts a request. Otherwise, PE does not accept any request.
Time Complexity: Let T denote the time complexity of Algorithm 5 when applied to the input policy expression to construct its base SS. Also let m be the number of slices in the constructed base SS and n be the number of rules in the largest slice in SS. As discussed in [1, 14], the time complexity of using the PSP method to determine whether a slice of n rules and t attributes accepts a request is of $\mathcal{O}(n^{t+1} \times t)$. Therefore, the time complexity of Algorithm 6 is of $\mathcal{O}(T + (m \times (n^{t+1} \times t)))$.
End

A policy expression PE_1 is said to *imply* a policy expression PE_2 iff the request set associated with the policy expression $(PE_1$ and $\text{not}(PE_2))$ is empty.

Theorem 4. PE_1 *implies* PE_2 *iff the request set* RS_1 *associated with* PE_1 *is a subset of the request set* RS_2 *associated with* PE_2.

Proof. Proof of the If-Part: Assume that PE_1 implies PE_2. Thus, the request set associated with the policy expression $(PE_1$ and $\text{not}(PE_2))$ is empty. From Theorem 2, the request set associated with $\text{not}(PE_2)$ is the set $(R - RS_2)$, where R is the set of all requests. Therefore, the set $(RS_1 \cap (R - RS_2))$ is empty and RS_1 is a subset of RS_2.

Proof of the Only-If-Part: Assume that the request set RS_1 associated with PE_1 is a subset of the request set RS_2 associated with PE_2. Thus, the set $(RS_1 \cap (R - RS_2))$, where R is the set of all requests, is empty. From Theorem 2, the request set associated with $\text{not}(PE_2)$ is the set $(R - RS_2)$. Therefore, the request set associated with the policy expression $(PE_1$ and $\text{not}(PE_2))$ is empty and PE_1 implies PE_2.

Algorithm 7
Input: Two policy expressions PE_1 and PE_2
Output: A determination of whether PE_1 implies PE_2
Steps: First, construct a policy expression PE from the policy expression (PE_1 and not(PE_2)) by pushing the "not" (which is applied to PE_2) deeper into PE_2 until every "not" is applied to a policy. Second, use Algorithm 6 to determine whether the constructed policy expression PE accepts a request. From the definition of "implies", if PE accepts no request then PE_1 implies PE_2. Otherwise, PE_1 does not imply PE_2.
Time Complexity: The time complexity of Algorithm 7 is of $\mathcal{O}(T + (m \times n^{t+1} \times t))$, where T is the time complexity for constructing the policy expression PE and its base SS, m is the number of slices in the constructed base SS, n is number of rules in the largest slice in SS, and t is the number of attributes in each slice in SS.
End

Theorem 5. *Two policy expressions PE_1 and PE_2 are equivalent iff PE_1 implies PE_2 and PE_2 implies PE_1.*

Proof. Proof of the If-Part: Assume that PE_1 and PE_2 are equivalent. Thus, the request set RS_1 associated with PE_1 and the request set RS_2 associated with PE_2 are identical. Therefore, RS_1 is a subset of RS_2 and RS_2 is a subset of RS_1. From Theorem 2, PE_1 implies PE_2 and PE_2 implies PE_1.

Proof of the Only-If-Part: Assume that PE_1 implies PE_2 and PE_2 implies PE_1. Thus, from Theorem 2, RS_1 is a subset of RS_2 and RS_2 is a subset of RS_1. Therefore, the request set RS_1 associated with PE_1 and the request set RS_2 associated with PE_2 are identical and the two policy expressions PE_1 and PE_2 are equivalent.

Algorithm 8
Input: Two policy expressions PE_1 and PE_2
Output: A determination of whether PE_1 and PE_2 are equivalent
Steps: Use Algorithm 7 twice to determine: (1) whether PE_1 implies PE_2 and (2) whether PE_2 implies PE_1. From Theorem 5, if PE_1 implies PE_2 and PE_2 implies PE_1, then PE_1 and PE_2 are equivalent. Otherwise, also from Theorem 5, PE_1 and PE_2 are not equivalent.
Time Complexity: The time complexity of Algorithm 8 is twice the time complexity of Algorithm 7.
End

7   Related Work

As mentioned earlier, this paper suggests the following bottom-up design method that can be followed by a designer in designing a desired computing policy.

First, the designer designs several simple elementary policies. Second, the designer combines these elementary policies using the three policy operators "not", "and", and "or" into a single policy expression PE that specifies the desired policy. Third, the designer uses Algorithm 5 to construct a base for the policy expression PE. Fourth, the designer uses the constructed base and Algorithms 6, 7, and 8 to verify that the policy expression PE satisfies desired adequacy, implication, and equivalence properties.

Other methods that can be used in designing policies are reported in [2, 5, 11, 14]. A brief survey of these methods is in order.

The method for designing policies in [5] consists of two steps. In the first step, the designer designs the desired policy using a large conflict-free decision diagram instead of a compact sequence of often conflicting rules. In the second step, the designer uses several algorithms to convert the large decision diagram into a compact, yet functionally equivalent, sequence of rules. This design method can be referred to as "simplifying policies by introducing conflicts".

The method for designing policies in [11] consists of three steps. In the first step, the same specification of the desired policy is given to multiple teams who proceed independently to design different versions of the policy. In the second step, the resulting multiple versions of the policy are compared with one another to detect all functional discrepancies between them. In the third step, all discrepancies between the multiple policy versions are resolved, and a final policy that is agreed upon by all teams is generated. This design method can be referred to as "diverse policy design".

The method for designing policies in [2] consists of three steps. In the first step, the set of all expected requests is partitioned into non-overlapping subsets $S_1, S_2, \cdots, S_k$. In the second step, for each subset S_i (obtained in the first step), design a policy P_i that accepts some of the requests in the subset S_i. In the third step, identify policies $P_1, P_2, \cdots, P_k$ generated in the second step as the desired policy. This design methods can be referred to as "divide-and-conquer".

The method for designing policies in [14] consists of k steps. In the first step, the designer starts with a simple policy P_1 that accepts more requests than the designer wishes. In the second step, the designer designs a second policy P_2 such that if any request is accepted by P_2 then the same request is also accepted by P_1. (In other words, P_2 implies P_1.) This process is repeated k times until the designer reaches a policy P_k that accepts those requests and only those requests that the designer wishes to be accepted. This design method can be referred to as "step-wise refinement".

These design methods, along with the bottom-up method in the current paper can constitute a library of policy design methods. When designing a policy, it is up to the designer to decide which design method in this library will the designer follow to generate the desired policy.

8   Concluding Remarks

The main contribution in this paper is to present a generalization of policies called policy expressions. Each policy expression is specified using one or more policies and the three policy operators "not", "and", and "or". We showed that each policy expression can be represented by a set of slices called a base of the policy expression. We also showed that the bases of given policy expressions can be used to determine whether the given policy expressions satisfy some desired properties of adequacy, implication, and equivalence. Finally, we showed that policy expressions can be utilized to support bottom-up methods for designing policies.

The authors in [9,10] investigated a novel representation of policies as finite automata rather than as sequences of rules. They show later in [8], how to use the automata representation of a given policy to determine whether the given policy satisfies some desired properties of adequacy, implication, and equivalence. The question of whether a policy expression can be represented as a finite automaton rather than as a set of slices remains open.

It has been shown in [4] that the problems of determining whether given policies satisfy some desired properties of adequacy, implication, and equivalence are all NP-hard. From this fact and the fact that each (complete) policy is also a policy expression, it follows that the problems of determining whether given policy expressions satisfy some desired properties of adequacy, implication, and equivalence are also NP-hard. Indeed, the time complexities of Algorithms 6, 7, and 8 that can be used to determine whether given policy expressions satisfy some desired properties of adequacy, implication, and equivalence are all exponential.

There are two main approaches to face the NP-hardness of determining whether given policy expressions satisfy some desired properties of adequacy, implication, and equivalence. The first approach is to use SAT solvers, for example as discussed in [3,16], to determine whether given policy expressions satisfy some desired properties of adequacy, implication, and equivalence. Note that the time complexity of using SAT solvers is polynomial in most practical situations.

The second approach is to use probabilistic algorithms. Note that the time complexities of probabilistic algorithms are always polynomial but unfortunately these algorithms can yield wrong determinations in rare cases.

References

1. Acharya, H.B., Gouda, M.G.: Projection and division: linear-space verification of firewalls. In: Proceedings of the 30th IEEE International Conference on Distributed Computing Systems (ICDCS), pp. 736–743. IEEE (2010)
2. Acharya, H.B., Joshi, A., Gouda, M.G.: Firewall modules and modular firewalls. In: Proceedings of the 18th IEEE International Conference on Network Protocols (ICNP), pp. 174–182. IEEE (2010)
3. Acharya, H.B., Kumar, S., Wadhwa, M., Shah, A.: Rules in play: on the complexity of routing tables and firewalls. In: Proceedings of the 24th IEEE International Conference on Network Protocols (ICNP). IEEE (2016)
4. Elmallah, E.S., Gouda, M.G.: Hardness of firewall analysis. In: Noubir, G., Raynal, M. (eds.) NETYS 2014. LNCS, vol. 8593, pp. 153–168. Springer, Cham (2014). doi:10.1007/978-3-319-09581-3_11

5. Gouda, M.G., Liu, A.X.: Structured firewall design. Comput. Netw. **51**(4), 1106–1120 (2007)
6. Hoffman, D., Yoo, K.: Blowtorch: a framework for firewall test automation. In: Proceedings of the 20th IEEE/ACM International Conference on Automated Software Engineering (ASE), pp. 96–103. ACM (2005)
7. Kamara, S., Fahmy, S., Schultz, E., Kerschbaum, F., Frantzen, M.: Analysis of vulnerabilities in internet firewalls. Comput. Secur. **22**(3), 214–232 (2003)
8. Khoumsi, A., Erradi, M., Ayache, M., Krombi, W.: An approach to resolve NP-hard problems of firewalls. In: Abdulla, P.A., Delporte-Gallet, C. (eds.) NETYS 2016. LNCS, vol. 9944, pp. 229–243. Springer, Cham (2016). doi:10.1007/978-3-319-46140-3_19
9. Khoumsi, A., Krombi, W., Erradi, M.: A formal approach to verify completeness and detect anomalies in firewall security policies. In: Cuppens, F., Garcia-Alfaro, J., Zincir Heywood, N., Fong, P.W.L. (eds.) FPS 2014. LNCS, vol. 8930, pp. 221–236. Springer, Cham (2015). doi:10.1007/978-3-319-17040-4_14
10. Krombi, W., Erradi, M., Khoumsi, A.: Automata-based approach to design and analyze security policies. In: Proceedings of the 12th Annual International Conference on Privacy, Security and Trust (PST), pp. 306–313. IEEE (2014)
11. Liu, A.X., Gouda, M.G.: Diverse firewall design. IEEE Trans. Parallel Distrib. Syst. (TPDS) **19**(9), 1237–1251 (2008)
12. Mayer, A., Wool, A., Ziskind, E.: Fang: a firewall analysis engine. In: Proceedings of IEEE Symposium on Security and Privacy, pp. 177–187. IEEE (2000)
13. Reaz, R., Acharya, H.B., Elmallah, E.S., Cobb, J.A., Gouda, M.G.: Policy expressions and the bottom-up design of computing policies. Technical report No. TR-17-01, Department of Computer Science, The Universisty of Texas at Austin (2017). https://apps.cs.utexas.edu/apps/tech-reports
14. Reaz, R., Ali, M., Gouda, M.G., Heule, M.J.H., Elmallah, E.S.: The Implication Problem of Computing Policies. In: Pelc, A., Schwarzmann, A.A. (eds.) SSS 2015. LNCS, vol. 9212, pp. 109–123. Springer, Cham (2015). doi:10.1007/978-3-319-21741-3_8
15. Wool, A.: A quantitative study of firewall configuration errors. Computer **37**(6), 62–67 (2004)
16. Zhang, S., Mahmoud, A., Malik, S., Narain, S.: Verification and synthesis of firewalls using SAT and QBF. In: Proceedings of the 20th IEEE International Conference on Network Protocols (ICNP), pp. 1–6. IEEE (2012)

Aspect-Oriented State Machines for Resolving Conflicts in XACML Policies

Meryeme Ayache[1]([✉]), Mohammed Erradi[1], Bernd Freisleben[2],
and Ahmed Khoumsi[3]

[1] ENSIAS, Mohammed V University, Rabat, Morocco
meryemeayache@gmail.com, mohamed.erradi@gmail.com
[2] Department of Mathematics and Computer Science,
Philipps-Universität Marburg, Marburg, Germany
freisleb@informatik.uni-marburg.de
[3] Department of Electrical and Computer Engineering,
University of Sherbrooke, Sherbrooke, Canada
ahmed.khoumsi@usherbrooke.ca

Abstract. Authorization in collaborative systems is defined by a *global policy* that represents the combination of the collaborators' access policies. However, the enforcement of such a global policy may create conflicting authorization decisions. In this paper, we categorize two types of conflicts that may occur in such policies. Furthermore, to resolve these conflicts and to reach a unique decision for an access request, we present an approach that uses XACML policy combining algorithms and considers the category of the detected conflicts. The approach is implemented using aspect-oriented finite state machines.

1 Introduction

XACML (eXtensible Access Control Markup Language) [7] is one of the access control policy languages that support the combination of multiple sub-policies. This combination may create several conflicting decisions. Therefore, XACML proposes four policy combining algorithms (PCAs) [4] to avoid conflicts between multiple policies, namely: *deny-overrides, permit-overrides, first applicable*, and *only one applicable*. These algorithms take, as input, the authorization decision from each policy matching the request and apply some standard logic to come up with a final decision.

The PCAs are currently chosen in advance by the policy administrator and hence they are static and remain available for all kinds of requests. However, in dynamic environments such as hospitals, there is a need to select the PCAs dynamically depending on the context of the request [5]: emergencies, normal interventions, etc. For emergencies, for example, we usually need to adopt *permit-overrides* in order to grant access to different doctors to save lives. In this paper, we propose a strategy to dynamically choose the adequate PCA based on the type of the detected conflicts and the request's context.

© Springer International Publishing AG 2017
A. El Abbadi and B. Garbinato (Eds.): NETYS 2017, LNCS 10299, pp. 166–171, 2017.
DOI: 10.1007/978-3-319-59647-1_13

The paper is organized as follows. Section 2 presents the conflicts' categorization. In Sect. 3, we present our conflict resolution strategy. Section 4 discusses some aspects of the implementation using aspect-oriented finite state machines. Section 5 concludes the work and outlines future work.

2   Conflict Categorization

A security policy consists of a set of filtering rules, where each rule is specified as a triplet (S, O, a_A), S is a set of subjects (human resources: e.g., doctors), O is a set of objects (physical resources: e.g., patient records), $a \in \{p, d\}$ denotes a permission (if $a = p$) or prohibition (if $a = d$, for deny), and A contains the permitted/prohibited actions among read (r), write (w), create (c) and delete (del). Consider, for example, the rule (S, O, p_r), where S represents the generalist doctor of a hospital H_1, and O represents the medical record of a given patient of another hospital H_2. This rule means that S is permitted to read O.

The composition of many security policies may produce a set of conflicts. A conflict occurs when two policies with different decisions are applicable to the same request. We identify two types of conflicts: conflict of modalities, and conflict of fraction permissions [2]. The first type occurs when two different rules assign contradictory authorizations to the same subject to perform an action over a given object. For example, a conflict of modalities occurs between the following two rules: "The generalist doctor of hospital H_1 is permitted to read the medical records (MR) of the patient x in hospital H_2" and "The generalist doctor of hospital H_1 is forbidden to read the medical record (MR) of all the patients of hospital H_2". The second type represents an ambiguity to make a decision. This ambiguity occurs if two rules with different permitted actions (e.g., read and write) match the same request. For instance, "The radiologists can read the electroencephalogram (EEG) of all the patients" and at the same time "The radiologists can write into the EEG of all the patients". In this case, we have a conflict of fraction permissions, because we do not know which policy to apply since the *write* permission overlaps with the *read* permission. The overlap means if the *write* permission is granted, then obviously the *read* permission is granted, too.

3   Conflict Resolution Strategy

In distributed environments, each organization has its own Policy Decision Point (PDP) that decides which permission is granted to a given subject to perform a specific action on a given object. In collaborative systems, a *master PDP* combining the collaborative policies is used. Our proposed conflict resolution strategy is associated to the *master PDP*. The approach consists of three main steps: (a) select the match policies (policies that match the request), (b) combine the policies into one global policy, and (c) detect and resolve the conflicts. If a conflict of fraction permissions is detected, we resolve it by a prioritization of permissions approach (see Sect. 3.1). If a conflict of modality is detected, we

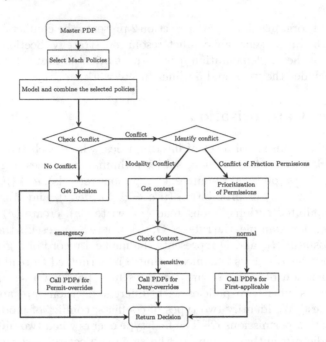

Fig. 1. Workflow representing the conflict resolution strategy

resolve it by a context-based approach (see Sect. 3.2). A workflow representing the conflict resolution strategy is presented in Fig. 1.

3.1 Prioritization of Permissions Approach

In this approach, the access permissions have distinct priorities. Therefore, for each policy decision associated to several access permissions, we select the one with the highest priority. Table 1 presents two ways of prioritizing permissions, where > denotes *has higher priority than*. The most secure approach is restrictive prioritization. For instance, to resolve the conflict detected in a policy with two different permissions $(p_{r,w}; p_r)$ using restrictive prioritization, we eliminate $p_{r,w}$ and keep p_r. If, on the other hand, we use the permissive conflict prioritization, we eliminate p_r and keep $p_{r,w}$.

Table 1. Prioritization of permissions.

Restrictive prioritization	$p_\emptyset > p_r > p_{r,w} > p_{r,w,c,del}$
Permissive prioritization	$p_{r,w,c,del} > p_{r,w} > p_r > p_\emptyset$

3.2   Context-Based Approach

In the case of a *conflict of modality*, we need to check the request's context. According to the most frequent cases of healthcare, we propose three types of context: *"emergency"*, *"sensitive"* and *"normal"*. The first context corresponds to the case of emergencies where the patient needs a quick intervention of the doctors to save his life. The *sensitive* context corresponds to patients with sensitive political positions who need to keep their health state secret and there are no emergencies. The *normal* context corresponds to general health cases.

In the case of *emergency*, the *master PDP* chooses *Permit-Overrides* as the appropriate PCA: if one of the policies returns the permit decision, then the *master PDP* permits the access to the required object. If the context is *sensitive*, the chosen PCA is *Deny-Overrides*. Finally, if the context is evaluated to *normal*, the PCA is *First-Applicable*, the master PDP always evaluates the first policy that matches the request.

4   Implementation

To represent security policies, we adopt the automata-based approach that we proposed in our previous work [1]. The approach consists of modeling each security policy by a finite state automaton (or briefly: automaton). We model each rule (S, O, a_A) of a policy by a simple automaton with 3 or 4 states that has two types of transitions: an S-transition is labeled by a set of subjects, and an O-transition is labeled by a set of objects. The authorization a_A is associated with the final state of the automaton. We combine simple automata using the *synchronous product*. The resulting automaton models the security policy.

In this paper, we use aspect-oriented finite state machines (AO-FSM) defined in our previous work [3] to implement our dynamic conflict resolution strategy. An AO-FSM defines a set of states and transition patterns where pointcuts and advices are used to adopt domain-specific language (DSL) [6] state machine artifacts. The pointcuts define matching state (final states) patterns that correspond to the conflicts that may occur in a security policy. For instance, the example of a pointcut in Fig. 2 represents a final state with a fraction permission conflict. As for the advice in Fig. 2, it implements the adequate resolution strategy that consists of removing one of the permissions to avoid the conflict.

Basically, pointcut sub-classes match the current state parameters with the context of a corresponding point of execution in the base code (joinpoint).

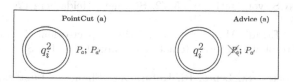

Fig. 2. Examples of aspect artifacts: pointcut and advice

It returns "true" if the pointcut matches, and "false" if not. For instance, the pointcut *FinalState2PermPC*, shown in Listing 1.1, checks if the current state in the pointcut pattern is final. If it is the case, it compares its name with the labels passed in the context. If they are equal, the pointcut matches and returns "true", otherwise it returns "false".

The advice language deals with making changes to FSMs to which pointcuts have been matched. The advices implement the resolution strategies of Sect. 3.

Listing 1.1. Excerpt of FinalState2PermPC to define final states with two permissions (pointcut (a) in Fig. 2)

```
public class FinalState2PermPC extends Pointcut {
    ...
    public FinalState2PermPC(String Label1, String Label2) {
    super("pFinalState");
        ...
    @Override
    public boolean match(JoinPoint jp) {
        return ((jp instanceof FinalStateMachineJoinPoint)&&
                (((FinalStateMachineJoinPoint) jp).getFinalStateNames().contains(Label1) &&
                ((FinalStateMachineJoinPoint) jp).getFinalStateNames().contains(Label2)));}}
```

5   Conclusion

In this paper, we have presented two categories of conflicts: fraction of permissions and conflict of modality. We have also presented a conflict resolution strategy that consists of two different approaches: prioritization of permissions and a context-based approach. The selection of the appropriate strategy depends on the type of the detected conflict. The approach uses aspect-oriented finite state machines to intercept, prevent, and dynamically manipulate rules that cause conflicts.

As future work, we intend to integrate the proposed resolution strategy in a cloud environment to evaluate its performance in detecting and resolving conflicts within a large set of policies.

References

1. Ayache, M., Erradi, M., Khoumsi, A., Freisleben, B.: Analysis and verification of XACML policies in a medical cloud environment. Scalable Comput. Pract. Experience **17**(3), 189–206 (2016)
2. Boyland, J.: Checking interference with fractional permissions. In: Cousot, R. (ed.) SAS 2003. LNCS, vol. 2694, pp. 55–72. Springer, Heidelberg (2003). doi:10.1007/3-540-44898-5_4
3. Dinkelaker, T., Erradi, M., Ayache, M.: Using aspect-oriented state machines for detecting and resolving feature interactions. Comput. Sci. Inf. Syst. **9**(3), 1045–1074 (2012)
4. Lorch, M., Proctor, S., Lepro, R., Kafura, D., Shah, S.: First experiences using XACML for access control in distributed systems. In: Proceedings of the 2003 ACM Workshop on XML Security, pp. 25–37. ACM (2003)

5. Matteucci, I., Mori, P., Petrocchi, M.: Prioritized execution of privacy policies. In: Pietro, R., Herranz, J., Damiani, E., State, R. (eds.) DPM/SETOP 2012. LNCS, vol. 7731, pp. 133–145. Springer, Heidelberg (2013). doi:10.1007/978-3-642-35890-6_10
6. Mernik, M., Heering, J., Sloane, A.M.: When and how to develop domain-specific languages. ACM Comput. Surv. (CSUR) 37(4), 316–344 (2005)
7. Moses, T., et al.: Extensible access control markup language XACML version 2.0. Oasis Standard (2005)

Agreement and Consensus

Agreement Functions for Distributed Computing Models

Petr Kuznetsov$^{(\boxtimes)}$ and Thibault Rieutord

LTCI, Télécom ParisTech, Université Paris Saclay, Paris, France
petr.kuznetsov@telecom-paristech.fr

Abstract. The paper proposes a surprisingly simple characterization of a large class of models of distributed computing, via an *agreement function*: for each set of processes, the function determines the best level of set consensus these processes can reach. We show that the task computability of a large class of *fair* adversaries that includes, in particular *superset-closed* and *symmetric* one, is precisely captured by agreement functions.

1 Introduction

In general, a model of distributed computing is a set of *runs*, i.e., all allowed interleavings of *steps* of concurrent processes. There are multiple ways to define these sets of runs in a tractable way.

A natural one is based on *failure models* that describe the assumptions on where and when failures might occur. By the conventional assumption of *uniform* failures, processes fail with equal and independent probabilities, giving rise to the classical model of *t-resilience*, where at most t processes may fail in a given run. The extreme case of $t = n - 1$, where n is the number of processes in the system, corresponds to the *wait-free* model.

The notion of *adversaries* [6] generalizes uniform failure models by defining a set of process subsets, called *live sets*, and assuming that in every model run, the set of *correct*, i.e., taking infinitely many steps, processes must be a live set. In this paper, we consider adversarial read-write shared memory models, i.e., sets of runs in which processes communicate via reading and writing in the shared memory and live sets define which sets of processes can be correct.

A conventional way to capture the power of a model is to determine its *task computability*, i.e., the set of distributed tasks that can be solved in it. For example, consider the 0-*resilient* adversary $\mathcal{A}_{0\text{-}res}$ defined through a single live set $\{p_1, \ldots, p_n\}$: the adversary says that no process is allowed to fail (by taking only finitely many steps). It is easy to see that the model is strong enough to solve *consensus*, and, thus, any task [14].[1]

T. Rieutord—Supported by ANR project DISCMAT, grant agreement ANR-14-CE35-0010-01.

[1] In the "universal" task of consensus, every process has a private *input* value, and is expected to produce an *output* value, so that (validity) every output is an input of some process, (agreement) no two processes produce different output values, and (termination) every process taking sufficiently many steps returns.

A. El Abbadi and B. Garbinato (Eds.): NETYS 2017, LNCS 10299, pp. 175–190, 2017.
DOI: 10.1007/978-3-319-59647-1_14

In this paper, we propose a surprisingly simple characterization of the task computability of a large class of adversarial models through *agreement functions*.

An agreement function α maps subsets of processes $\{p_1, \ldots, p_n\}$ to positive integers in $\{0, 1, \ldots, n\}$. For each subset P, $\alpha(P)$ determines, intuitively, the level of *set consensus* that processes in P can reach when no other process is active, i.e., the smallest number of distinct input values they can decide on.

For example, the agreement function of the wait-free shared-memory model is $\alpha_{wf} : P \mapsto |P|$ and the t-resilient model, where at most t processes may fail or not participate, has $\alpha_{t,res} : P \mapsto \max(0, |P| - n + t + 1)$.

The agreement function of an adversary $\mathcal{A}$ can be computed using the notion of *set consensus power* of an adversary introduced in [13]: $\alpha_{\mathcal{A}}(P) = setcon(\mathcal{A}|_P)$. Here $\mathcal{A}|_P$ is the *restriction of $\mathcal{A}$ to P*, i.e., the adversary defined through the live sets of $\mathcal{A}$ that are subsets of P.

To each agreement function α, corresponding to an existing model, we associate a particular model, the α-*model*. The α-model is defined as the set of runs satisfying the following property: the set P of *participating* (taking at least one step) processes in a run is such that $\alpha(P) \geq 1$ and is such that at most $\alpha(P) - 1$ processes take only finitely many steps in it. An algorithm solves a task T in the α-model if processes taking infinitely many steps produces an output in any run.

We show that, for the class of *fair* adversaries, agreement functions "tell it all" about task computability: a task is solvable in a fair adversarial model with agreement function α *if and only if* it is solvable in the α-model. Fair adversaries include notably the class of superset-closed [16, 19] and the class of symmetric [23] adversaries. Intuitively, superset-closed adversaries do not anticipate failures of processes: if $S \in \mathcal{A}$ and $S \subseteq S'$, then $S' \in \mathcal{A}$. Symmetric adversaries do not depend on processes identifiers: if $S \in \mathcal{A}$, then for every set of processes S' such that $|S'| = |S|$, we have $S' \in \mathcal{A}$.

A corollary of our result is a characterization of the k-concurrency model [9, 10]. Here we use the fact that the k-concurrency model is equivalent, with respect to task solvability, to the k-*obstruction-freedom* [13], a symmetric adversary consisting of live sets of sizes from 1 to k. Thus, the agreement function $\alpha_{k\text{-}conc} : P \mapsto \min(|P|, k)$ captures the k-concurrent task computability. An alternative characterization of k-concurrency via a compact *affine* task was recently suggested in [11].

There are, however, models that are not captured by their agreement functions. We give an example of a *non-fair* adversary that solves strictly more tasks than its α-*model*. Characterizing the class of models that can be captured through their agreement function is an intriguing open question.

The rest of the paper is organized as follows. Section 2 gives model definitions. In Sect. 3, we formally define the notion of an agreement function. In Sect. 4, we prove a few useful properties of α-models. In Sect. 5, we present the class of fair adversary, show that superset-closed and symmetric adversaries are fair and that fair adversaries are captured by their agreement functions. In Sect. 6, we give examples of models that are *not* captured by agreement functions. Section 7 reviews related work, and Sect. 8 concludes the paper.

2 Preliminaries

Processes, Runs, Models. Let Π be a system of n asynchronous processes, $p_1, \ldots, p_n$ that communicate via a shared atomic-snapshot memory [1]. The atomic-snapshot (AS) memory is represented as a vector of n shared variables, where each process is associated with a distinct position in this vector, and exports two operations: *update* and *snapshot*. An *update* operation performed by p_i replaces position i with a new value and a *snapshot* operation returns the current state of the vector.

We assume that processes run the *full-information* protocol: the first value each process writes is its *input value*. A process alternates between taking snapshots of the memory and writing back the result of its latest snapshot. A *run* is thus a sequence of process identifiers stipulating the order in which the processes take operations: each odd appearance of i in the sequence corresponds to an *update* and each even appearance corresponds to a *snapshot*. A *model* is a set of runs.

Failures and Participation. A process that takes only finitely many steps of the full-information protocol in a given run is called *faulty*, otherwise it is called *correct*. A process that took at least one step in a given run is called *participating* in it. The set of participating processes in a given run is called its *participating set*. Note that, since every process writes its input value in its first step, the inputs of participating processes are eventually known to every process that takes sufficiently many steps.

Tasks. In this paper, we focus on distributed *tasks* [18]. A process invokes a task with an input value and the task returns an output value, so that the inputs and the outputs across the processes which invoked the task respect the task specification. Formally, a *task* is defined through a set $\mathcal{I}$ of input vectors (one input value for each process), a set $\mathcal{O}$ of output vectors (one output value for each process), and a total relation $\Delta : \mathcal{I} \mapsto 2^{\mathcal{O}}$ that associates each input vector with a set of possible output vectors. An input $\bot$ denote a *not participating* process and an output value $\bot$ denote an *undecided* process. Check [15] for more details.

In the task of *k-set consensus*, input values are in a set of values V ($|V| \geq k + 1$), output values are in V, and for each input vector I and output vector O, $(I, O) \in \Delta$ if the set of non-$\bot$ values in O is a subset of values in I of size at most k. The special case of 1-set consensus is called *consensus* [7].

Solving a Task. We say that an algorithm A solves a task $T = (\mathcal{I}, \mathcal{O}, \Delta)$ in a model M if A ensures that (1) in every run in which processes start with an input vector $I \in \mathcal{I}$, all decided values form a vector $O \in \mathcal{O}$ such that $(I, O) \in \Delta$, and (2) if the run is in M, then every correct process decides.

This gives rise to the notion of task solvability, i.e., a task T is solvable in a model M if and only if there exists an algorithm A which solves T in M.

BGG Simulation. The principal technical tool in this paper is a simulation technique that we call the *BGG simulation*, after Borowski, Gafni, Guerraoui, collecting algorithmic ideas presented in [3, 8–10]. The technique allows a system of n processes that communicate via read-write shared memory and k-set consensus objects to *simulate* a k-process system running an arbitrary read-write algorithm. In particular, we can use this technique to run an extended BG simulation [8] on top of these k simulated processes, which gives a simulation of an arbitrary k-concurrent algorithm. An important feature of the simulation is that it adapts to the number of currently active simulated processes a: if it goes below k (after some simulated processes complete their computations), the number of used simulators also becomes a. We refer to [11] for a detailed description of this simulation algorithm.

3   Agreement Functions

Definition 1 (Agreement function). *The* agreement function *of a model M is a function* $\alpha : 2^{\Pi} \to \{0, \ldots, n\}$, *such that for each* $P \in 2^{\Pi}$, *in the set of runs of M in which no process in $\Pi \setminus P$ participates, iterative $\alpha(P)$-set consensus can be solved, but $(\alpha(P) - 1)$-set consensus cannot. By convention, if M contains no (infinite) runs with participating set P, then $\alpha(P) = 0$.*

Intuitively, for each P, we consider a model consisting of runs of M in which only processes in P participate and determine the best level of set consensus that can be reached in this model, with 0 corresponding to a model that consists of *finite* runs only.

Note the agreement function α of a model M is *monotonic*: $P \subseteq P' \Rightarrow \alpha(P) \leq \alpha(P')$. Indeed, the set of runs of M where the processes in $\Pi \setminus P$ do not take any step is a subset of the set of runs of M where the processes in $\Pi \setminus P'$ do not take any step. In this paper, we only consider monotonic functions α.

Definition 2 (α-model). *Given a monotonic agreement function α, the α-model is the set of runs in which, the participating set P satisfies: (1) $\alpha(P) \geq 1$; and, (2) at most $\alpha(P) - 1$ participating processes take only finitely many steps.*

We say that a model is *characterized by its agreement function α* if and only if it solves the same set of task as the α-model.

Definition 3 (α-adaptive set consensus). *The α-adaptive set consensus task satisfies the* **validity** *and* **termination** *properties of consensus and the α-* **agreement** *property: if at some time τ, k distinct values have been returned, then the current participating set P_{τ} is such that $\alpha(P_{\tau}) \geq k$.*

We can easily show that any model with agreement function α can solve the α-adaptive set consensus task, i.e., to achieve the best level of set consensus without this an priori knowledge of the set of processes that are allowed to participate [20].

4   Properties of the α-model

We now relate task solvability in the α-model and in M. More precisely, we show that (1) the agreement function of the α-model is α and (2) any task T solvable in the α-model is also solvable in every model with agreement function α.

Theorem 1. *The agreement function of the α-model is α.*

Proof. Take P such that $\alpha(P) > 1$ and consider the set of runs of the α-model in which no process in $\Pi \setminus P$ participates and, thus, according to the monotonicity property, at most $\alpha(P) - 1$ processes are faulty. To solve $\alpha(P)$-set consensus, we use the *safe-agreement* protocol [2], the crucial element of BG simulation. Safe agreement solves consensus if every process that participates in it takes enough steps. The failure of a process then may *block* the safe-agreement protocol. In our case as at most $\alpha(P) - 1$ processes in P can fail, so we can simply run $\alpha(P)$ safe agreement protocols: every process goes through the protocols one by one using its input as a proposed value, if the protocol blocks, it proceeds to the next one in the round-robin manner. The first protocol that returns gives the output value. Since at most $\alpha(P) - 1$ processes are faulty, at least one safe agreement eventually terminates, and there are at most $\alpha(P)$ distinct outputs. To see that $(\alpha(P) - 1)$ cannot be solved in this set of runs, recall that one cannot solve $(\alpha(P) - 1)$-set consensus $(\alpha(P) - 1)$-resiliently [2,18,22].

The following result is instrumental in our characterizations of *fair* adversaries:

Theorem 2. *For any task T solvable in an α-model, T is solvable in any read-write shared memory model which solves the α-adaptive set consensus task.*

Proof. Using α-adaptive set consensus and read-write shared memory, we can run *BGG*-simulation so that, when the participating set is P, at most $\alpha(P)$ *BG simulators* are activated and at least one is live (i.e., takes part in infinitely many simulation steps). Moreover, we make a process provided with a (simulated) task output to stop proposing simulated steps to BGG simulation. Hence, the number of active simulators is also bounded by the number of participating processes without an output, with at least one live BG simulator if there is a correct process without a task output.

These BG simulators are used to simulate an execution of a protocol solving T in the α-model. And so, since any finite run can be extended to a valid run of the α-model, the protocol can only provide valid outputs.

We make BG simulators execute the *breadth-first* simulation: every BG simulator executes an infinite loop consisting of (1) updating the estimated participating set P, then (2) try to execute a simulation step of every process in P, one by one.

Now assume that there exist $k \geq 1$ correct processes that are never provided with a task output. BGG simulation ensure that we eventually have at most $min(k, \alpha(P))$ active simulators, with at least one live among them. Let s be such a live simulator. After every process in P have taken their first steps, s tries to simulate steps for every process of P infinitely often. A process simulation step can be blocked forever only due to an active but not live BG simulator[2], thus there are at most $min(k, \alpha(P)) - 1$ simulated processes in P taking only finitely many steps.

As at most $\alpha(P) - 1$ processes have a finite number of simulated steps, the simulated run is a valid run of the α-model. Moreover, as at most $k - 1$ processes have a finite number of simulated steps, there is one process never provided with a task output simulated as a correct process. But, a protocol solving a task eventually provides task outputs to every correct process — a contradiction.

Any model can solve its associated α-adaptive set consensus task [20]. Along with Theorem 2, we derive that:

Corollary 1. *Let M be any model, α_M be its agreement function, and T be any task that is solvable in the α_M-model. Then M solves T.*

5   Characterizing Fair Adversaries

An *adversary* $\mathcal{A}$ is a set of subsets of Π, called *live sets*, $\mathcal{A} \subseteq 2^\Pi$. An infinite run is $\mathcal{A}$-*compliant* if the set of processes that are correct in that run belongs to $\mathcal{A}$. An adversarial $\mathcal{A}$-model is thus defined as the set of $\mathcal{A}$-compliant runs.

An adversary is *superset-closed* [19] if each superset of a live set of $\mathcal{A}$ is also an element of $\mathcal{A}$, i.e., if $\forall S \in \mathcal{A}, \forall S' \subseteq \Pi, S \subseteq S' \implies S' \in \mathcal{A}$. Superset-closed adversaries provide a non-uniform generalization of the classical t-*resilient* adversary consisting of sets of $n - t$ or more processes.

An adversary $\mathcal{A}$ is a *symmetric* adversary if it does not depend on process identifiers: $\forall S \in \mathcal{A}, \forall S' \subseteq \Pi, |S'| = |S| \implies S' \in \mathcal{A}$. Symmetric adversaries provides another interesting generalization of the classical t-resilience condition and k-obstruction-free progress condition [9] which was previously formalized by Taubenfeld as its symmetric progress conditions [23].

5.1   Set Consensus Power

The notion of the *set consensus power* [12] was originally proposed to capture the power of adversaries in solving *colorless* tasks [3,4], i.e., tasks that can be defined by relating *sets* of inputs and outputs, independently of process identifiers.

Definition 4. *The* set consensus power *of $\mathcal{A}$, denoted by $setcon(\mathcal{A})$, is defined as follows:*

- *If $\mathcal{A} = \emptyset$, then $setcon(\mathcal{A}) = 0$*
- *Otherwise, $setcon(\mathcal{A}) = \max_{S \in \mathcal{A}} \min_{a \in S} setcon(\mathcal{A}|_{S \setminus \{a\}}) + 1$.[3]*

---

[2] Note that the extended BG-simulation provides a mechanism which ensures that a simulation step is not blocked forever by a no longer active BG simulator.

[3] $\mathcal{A}|_P$ is the adversary consisting of all live sets of $\mathcal{A}$ that are subsets of P.

Thus, for a non-empty adversary $\mathcal{A}$, $setcon(\mathcal{A})$ is determined as $setcon(\mathcal{A}|_{S\setminus\{a\}})$ $+\,1$ where S is an element of $\mathcal{A}$ and a is a process in S that "max-minimize" $setcon(\mathcal{A}|_{S\setminus\{a\}})$. Note that for $\mathcal{A} \neq \emptyset$, $setcon(\mathcal{A}) \geq 1$.

It is shown in [12] that $setcon(\mathcal{A})$ is the smallest k such that $\mathcal{A}$ can solve k-set consensus.

It was previously shown in [13] that for a superset-closed adversary $\mathcal{A}$, the set consensus power of $\mathcal{A}$ is equal to $csize(\mathcal{A})$, where $csize(\mathcal{A})$ denote the minimal hitting set size of $\mathcal{A}$, i.e., a minimal subset of Π that intersects with each live set of $\mathcal{A}$. Therefore if $\mathcal{A}$ is superset-closed, then $setcon(\mathcal{A}) = csize(\mathcal{A})$. For a symmetric adversary $\mathcal{A}$, it can be easily derived from the definition of $setcon$ that $setcon(\mathcal{A}) = |\{k \in \{1,\ldots,n\} : \exists S \in \mathcal{A}, |S| = k\}|$.

Theorem 3. *The agreement function of adversary $\mathcal{A}$ is $\alpha_{\mathcal{A}}(P) = setcon(\mathcal{A}|_P)$.*

Proof. An algorithm A_P that solves $\alpha_{\mathcal{A}}(P)$-set consensus, assuming that the participating set is a subset of P, is a straightforward generalization of the result of [12]. It is shown in [12] that $setcon(\mathcal{A})$-set consensus can be solved in $\mathcal{A}$. But if we restrict the runs to assume that the processes in $\Pi \setminus P$ do not take a single step, then the set of possible live sets reduces to $\mathcal{A}|_P$. Thus using the agreement algorithm of [12] for the adversary $\mathcal{A}|_P$, we obtain a $setcon(\mathcal{A}|_P)$-set consensus algorithm, or equivalently, an $\alpha_{\mathcal{A}}(P)$-set consensus algorithm.

It is immediate from Theorem 3 that $\mathcal{A} \subseteq \mathcal{A}'$ implies $setcon(\mathcal{A}) \leq setcon(\mathcal{A}')$.

5.2 Fair adversaries

In this paper we propose a class of adversaries which encompasses both classical classes of super-set closed and symmetric adversaries. Informally, an adversary is *fair* if its set consensus power does not change if only a subset of the processes are participating in an agreement protocol.

More precisely, consider $\mathcal{A}$-compliant runs with participating set P and assume that processes in $Q \subseteq P$ want to reach agreement *among themselves*: only these processes propose inputs and are expected to produce outputs. We can only guarantee outputs to processes in Q when the set of correct processes include some process in Q, i.e., when the current live set intersect with Q. Thus, the best level of set consensus reachable by Q is defined the set consensus power of adversary $\mathcal{A}|_{P,Q} = \{S \in \mathcal{A}|_P, S \cap Q \neq \emptyset\}$, unless $|Q| < setcon(\mathcal{A}|_P)$.

Definition 5 (Fair adversary). *An adversary $\mathcal{A}$ is fair if and only if:*

$$\forall P \subseteq \Pi, \forall Q \subseteq P, setcon(\mathcal{A}|_{P,Q}) = min(|Q|, setcon(\mathcal{A}|_P)).$$

Property 1.

$$setcon(\mathcal{A}|_{P,Q}) \leq min(|Q|, setcon(\mathcal{A}|_P))$$

Proof. For any $P \subseteq \Pi$ and $Q \subseteq P$, $\mathcal{A}|_{P,Q} = \{S \in \mathcal{A}|_P, S \cap Q \neq \emptyset\}$ is a subset of $\mathcal{A}|_P$ and, thus, $setcon(\mathcal{A}|_{P,Q}) \leq setcon(\mathcal{A}|_P)$. Moreover, $setcon(\mathcal{A}|_{P,Q}) \leq |Q|$, as $|Q|$-set consensus can be solved in $\{S \in \mathcal{A}|_P, S \cap Q \neq \emptyset\}$ as follows: every process waits until some process in Q writes its input and decides on it.

Theorem 4. *Any superset-closed adversary is fair.*

Proof. Suppose that there exists a superset-closed adversary $\mathcal{A}$ that is not fair, i.e., by Property 1, $\exists P \subseteq \Pi, \exists Q \subseteq P, setcon(\{S \in \mathcal{A}|_P, S \cap Q \neq \emptyset\}) < min(|Q|, setcon(\mathcal{A}|_P))$. Clearly $\mathcal{A}|_P$ and $\mathcal{A}|_{P,Q}$ are also superset-closed and, thus, $setcon(\mathcal{A}|_P) = csize(\mathcal{A}|_P)$ and $setcon(\mathcal{A}|_{P,Q}) = csize(\mathcal{A}|_{P,Q})$.

Since $setcon(\mathcal{A}|_{P,Q}) < |Q|$, a minimal hitting set H' of $\mathcal{A}|_{P,Q}$ is such that $|H'| < |Q|$, and therefore there exists a process $q \in Q$, $q \notin H'$. Also, since $setcon(\mathcal{A}|_{P,Q}) < setcon(\mathcal{A}|_P)$, H' is not a hitting set of $\mathcal{A}|_P$. Thus, there exists $S \in \mathcal{A}|_P$ such that $S \cap H' = \emptyset$. Hence, $(S \cup \{q\}) \cap H' = \emptyset$. Since $\mathcal{A}|_P$ is superset closed, we have $S \cup \{q\} \in \mathcal{A}|_P$ and, since $q \in Q$, $S \cup \{q\} \in \mathcal{A}|_{P,Q}$. But $(S \cup \{q\}) \cap H' = \emptyset$—a contradiction with H' being a hitting set of $\mathcal{A}|_{P,Q}$.

Theorem 5. *Any symmetric adversary is fair.*

Proof. The set consensus power of a generic adversary $\mathcal{A}$ is defined recursively through finding $S \in \mathcal{A}$ and $p \in S$ which max-minimize the set consensus power of $\mathcal{A}|_{S \setminus \{p\}}$. Let us recall that if $\mathcal{A} \subseteq \mathcal{A}'$ then $setcon(\mathcal{A}) \leq setcon(\mathcal{A}')$. Therefore, S can always be selected to be *locally maximal*, i.e., such that there is no live set in $S' \in \mathcal{A}$ with $S \subsetneq S'$.

Suppose by contradiction that $\mathcal{A}$ is symmetric but not fair, i.e., by Property 1, for some $P \subseteq \Pi$ and $Q \subseteq P$, $setcon(\mathcal{A}|_{P,Q}) < min(|Q|, setcon(\mathcal{A}|_P))$. We show that if the property holds for P and Q such that $\mathcal{A}|_{P,Q} \neq \emptyset$ then it also holds for some $P' \subsetneq P$ and $Q' \subseteq Q$.

First, we observe that $|Q| > 1$, otherwise $setcon(\mathcal{A}|_{P,Q}) = 0$ and, thus, we have $\mathcal{A}|_{P,Q} = \emptyset$.

Since $\mathcal{A}$ is symmetric, $\mathcal{A}|_P$ is also symmetric. Thus, for every $S \in \mathcal{A}|_P$ and $p \in S$ such that $setcon(\mathcal{A}|_P) = 1 + setcon(\mathcal{A}|_{S \setminus \{p\}})$, any S' such that $|S'| = |S|$ and for any $p' \in S'$, we also have $setcon(\mathcal{A}|_P) = 1 + setcon(\mathcal{A}|_{S' \setminus \{p'\}})$. Since we can always choose S to be a maximal set, we derive that the equality holds for every maximal set S in $\mathcal{A}|_P$ and every $p \in S$.

Let us recall that, by the definition of $setcon$, there exists $L \in \mathcal{A}|_{P,Q}$ and $a \in L$ such that $setcon(\mathcal{A}|_{P,Q}) = 1 + setcon((\mathcal{A}|_{P,Q})|_{L \setminus \{a\}}) = setcon(\mathcal{A}|_{L,Q})$. Since $\mathcal{A}|_P$ is symmetric, for all L', $|L'| = |L|$ and $L \cap Q \subseteq L' \cap Q$, we have $setcon(\mathcal{A}|_{L',Q}) \geq setcon(\mathcal{A}|_{L,Q})$. Indeed, modulo a permutation of process identifiers, $\mathcal{A}|_{L',Q}$ contains all the live sets of $\mathcal{A}|_{L,Q}$ plus live sets in $\mathcal{A}|_{L'}$ that overlap with $(L' \cap Q) \setminus (L \cap Q)$. Since $setcon(\mathcal{A}|_{L,Q}) = setcon(\mathcal{A}|_{P,Q})$ and $L' \in \mathcal{A}|_{P,Q}$, we have $setcon(\mathcal{A}|_{L',Q}) = setcon(\mathcal{A}|_{L,Q})$. Therefore, for any $a \in L'$, $setcon(\mathcal{A}|_{L' \setminus \{a\},Q}) < setcon(\mathcal{A}|_{L' \setminus \{a\}})$.

In particular, for L' with $L' \cap Q \in \{L', Q\}$, $setcon(\mathcal{A}|_{L',Q}) = setcon(\mathcal{A}|_{L,Q})$. Note that $L' \not\subseteq Q$, otherwise, $\mathcal{A}|_{L',Q} = \mathcal{A}|_{L'}$ and, thus, $setcon(\mathcal{A}|_{L',Q}) = setcon(\mathcal{A}|_{L'}) = setcon(\mathcal{A}|_P)$, contradicting our assumption.

Thus, let us assume that $Q \subsetneq L'$. Note that $Q' = Q \setminus \{a\} \subsetneq L' \setminus \{a\}$, and since $|Q| \geq 2$, $Q' \neq \emptyset$, we have $setcon(\mathcal{A}|_{P',Q'}) < setcon(\mathcal{A}|_{P'})$ for $P' = L' \setminus \{a\}$ and $Q' \subseteq P'$, $Q' \neq \emptyset$. Furthermore, since $setcon(\mathcal{A}|_{P,Q}) < |Q|$, we have $setcon(\mathcal{A}|_{P',Q'}) < |Q'|$.

By applying this argument inductively, we end up with a live set P and $Q \subseteq P$ such that $setcon(\mathcal{A}|_P) \geq 1$, $Q \neq \emptyset$ and $setcon(\mathcal{A}|_{P,Q}) = 0$. By the definition of $setcon$, $\mathcal{A}|_P \neq \emptyset$ and $\mathcal{A}|_{P,Q} = \emptyset$. But $\mathcal{A}|_P$ is symmetric and $Q \neq \emptyset$, so for every $S \in \mathcal{A}|_P$, there exists $S' \in \mathcal{A}|_P$ such that $|S| = |S'|$ and $S' \cap Q \neq \emptyset$, i.e., $\mathcal{A}|_{P,Q} \neq \emptyset$—a contradiction.

Note that not all adversaries are fair. For example, the adversary $\mathcal{A} = \{\{p_1\}, \{p_2, p_3\}, \{p_1, p_2, p_3\}\}$ is not fair. On the other hand, not all fair adversaries are either super-set closed or symmetric. For example, the adversary $\mathcal{A} = 2^{\{p_1, p_2, p_3\}} \setminus \{p_1, p_2\}$ is fair but is neither symmetric not super-set closed. Understanding what makes an adversary fair is an interesting challenge.

5.3   Task Computability in Fair Adversarial Models

In this section, we show that the task computability of a fair adversarial $\mathcal{A}$-model is fully grasped by its associated agreement function $\alpha_{\mathcal{A}}$.

Algorithm 1. Code for BG simulator s_i to simulate adversary $\mathcal{A}$.

---

1 **Shared variables:** $R[1, \ldots, \alpha_{\mathcal{A}}(\Pi)] \leftarrow (\bot, \emptyset)$, $P_{MEM}[p_1, \ldots, p_n] \leftarrow \bot$;
2 **Local variables:** $S_{cur}, S_{tmp}, P, A, W \in 2^{\Pi}$, $p_{cur}, p_{tmp} \in \mathbb{N}$, $S_{cur} \leftarrow \emptyset$;

3 **Repeat**
4 | $P = \{p \in \Pi, P_{MEM}[p] \neq \bot\}$;
5 | $A = \{p \in P, P_{MEM}[p] \neq \top\}$;
6 | **if** $i \geq min(|A|, \alpha_{\mathcal{A}}(P))$ **then**
7 | $W = P$;
8 | **for** $j = \alpha_{\mathcal{A}}(\Pi)$ **down to** $i + 1$ **do**
9 | $(p_{tmp}, S_{tmp}) \leftarrow R[j]$;
10 | **if** $(p_{tmp} \neq \bot) \wedge (S_{tmp} \subseteq W) \wedge ((setcon(\mathcal{A}|_{S_{tmp},A}) \geq j))$ **then**
11 | | $W \leftarrow S_{tmp} \setminus \{p_{tmp}\}$;

12 | **if** $(S_{cur} \not\subseteq W) \vee (setcon(\mathcal{A}|_{S_{cur},A}) < i)$ **then**
13 | **if** $\exists S \in \mathcal{A}|_W, setcon(\mathcal{A}|_{S,A}) \geq i$ **then**
14 | | $S_{cur} = S \in \mathcal{A}|_W$ such that $setcon(\mathcal{A}|_{S,A}) \geq i$;
15 | **else** $S_{cur} = S \in \mathcal{A}|_P$;
16 | $p_{cur} = S_{cur}.first()$;
17 | $R[i] \leftarrow (p_{cur}, S_{cur})$;

18 | **if** (**SimulateStep**$(p_{cur}) = SUCCESS$) **then**
19 | **if** **Outputed**(p_{cur}) **then** $P_{MEM}[p_{cur}] = \top$;
20 | $p_{cur} = S_{cur}.next(p_{cur})$;
21 | **else** **AbortStep**(p_{cur}) ;
22 **Forever**;

Using BGG simulation, we show that the $\alpha_{\mathcal{A}}$-model can be used to solve any task T solvable in the $\mathcal{A}$-model. In the simulation, up to $\alpha(P)$ BG simulators execute the given algorithm solving T, where P is the participating set of the current run. We adapt the currently simulated live set to include processes not yet provided with a task output, and ensure that the chosen live set is simulated sufficiently long until some active processes are provided with outputs of T. The simulation terminates as soon as all correct processes are provided with outputs.

The code for BG simulator $b_i \in \{b_1, \ldots, b_{\alpha_{\mathcal{A}}(\Pi)}\}$ is given in Algorithm 1. It consists of two parts: (1) selecting a live set to simulate (lines 7–17), and (2) simulating processes in the selected live set (lines 18–21).

Selecting a Live Set. This is the most involved part. The idea is to select a participating live set $L \subseteq P$ such that: (1) the set consensus power of $\mathcal{A}|_{L,A} = \{S \in \mathcal{A}|_L, S \cap A \neq \emptyset\}$, with A the set of participating processes not yet provided with a task output, is greater than or equal to the BG simulator identifier i; (2) L is a subset of the live sets currently selected by live BG simulators with greater identifiers; (3) L does not contain the processes currently simulated by live BG simulators with greater identifiers.

The live set selection in Algorithm 1 consists in two phases. First, BG simulators determine a *selection window* W, $W \subseteq P$, i.e., the largest set of processes which is a subset of the live sets selected by live BG simulators with greater identifiers, and which excludes the processes currently selected by live BG simulators with greater identifiers (lines 7–11). This is done iteratively on all BG simulators with greater identifiers, from the greatest to the lowest. At each iteration, if the targeted BG simulator b_k *appears live*, the current window is restricted to the live set selected by b_k, but excluding the process selected by b_k. Determining if b_k appears live is simply done by checking whether, with the current simulation status observed, the live set selected by b_k is *valid*, i.e., satisfies conditions (1), (2) and (3) above.

The second phase (lines 12–17), consists in checking if the currently selected live set is valid (line 12). If not, the BG simulator tries to select a live set L which belongs to the selection window W, and hence satisfies (2) and (3), but also such that the set consensus power of $\mathcal{A}_{L,A}$ is greater than i, the BG simulator identifier (line 14). If the simulator does not find such a live set, it simply selects any available live set (line 15).

Simulating a Live Set. The idea is that, if the selected live set does not change, the BG simulator simulates steps of every process in its selected live set infinitely often. Unlike conventional variations of BG simulations, a BG simulator here does not skip a blocked process simulation, instead it aborts and re-tries the same simulation step until it is successful.

Intuitively, this does not obstruct progress because, in case of a conflict, there are two live BG simulators blocked on the same simulation step, but the BG simulator with the smaller identifier will eventually change its selected live set and release the corresponding process.

Pseudocode. The protocol executed by processes in the $\alpha_{\mathcal{A}}$-model is the following: Processes first update their status in P_{MEM} by replacing $\perp$ with their initial state. Then, processes participate in an $\alpha_{\mathcal{A}}$-adaptive BGG simulation (i.e., BGG simulation runs on top of an $\alpha_{\mathcal{A}}$-adaptive set consensus protocol), where BG simulators use Algorithm 1 to simulate an algorithm solving a given task T in the adversarial $\mathcal{A}$-model. When a process p observes that $P_{MEM}[p]$ has been set to $\top$ ("termination state"), it stops to propose simulation steps.

Proof of Correctness. Let P_f be the participating set of the $\alpha_{\mathcal{A}}$-model run, and let A_f be the set of processes $p \in P_f$ such that $P_{MEM}[p]$ is never set to $\top$.

Lemma 1. *There is a time after which variables P and A in Algorithm 1 become constant and equal to A_f and P_f for all live BG simulators.*

Proof. Since Π is finite, the set of processes p such that $P_{MEM}[p] \neq \perp$ eventually corresponds to P_f as the first step of p is to set $P_{MEM}[p]$ to its initial state and $P_{MEM}[p]$ can only be updated to $\top$ afterwards. As after $P_{MEM}[p]$ is set to $\top$, it cannot be set to another value, eventually, the set of processes from P_f such that $P_{MEM}[p] \neq \top$ is equal to A_f. Live BG simulators update P and A infinitely often, so eventually their values of P and A are equal to P_f and A_f respectively.

Lemma 2. *If A_f contains a correct process, then there is a correct BG simulator with an identifier smaller or equal to $min(|A_f|, \alpha_{\mathcal{A}}(P_f))$.*

Proof. In our protocol, eventually only correct processes in A_f are proposing BGG simulation steps. Thus eventually, at most $|A_f|$ distinct simulations steps are proposed. The $\alpha_{\mathcal{A}}$-adaptive set consensus protocol used for BGG simulation ensures that at most $\alpha_{\mathcal{A}}(P_f)$ distinct proposed values are decided. But as there is a time after which only processes in A_f propose values, eventually, $min(|A_f|, \alpha_{\mathcal{A}}(P_f))$-set consensus is solved. Thus BGG simulation ensures that, when this is the case, there is a live BG simulator with an identifier smaller or equal to $min(|A_f|, \alpha_{\mathcal{A}}(P_f))$.

   Suppose that A_f contains a correct process, and let b_m be the greatest live BG simulator such that $m \leq min(|A_f|, \alpha_{\mathcal{A}}(P_f))$ (by Lemma 2). Let $S_i(t)$ denote the value of S_{cur} and let $p_i(t)$ denote the value of p_{cur} at simulator b_i at time t. Let also τ_f be the time after which every active but not live BG simulators have taken all their steps, and after which A and P have become constant and equal to A_f and P_f for every live BG simulator (by Lemma 1).

Lemma 3. *For every live BG simulator b_s, with $s \leq min(|A_f|, \alpha_{\mathcal{A}}(P_f))$, eventually, b_s cannot fail the test on line 13.*

Proof. Consider a correct BG simulator b_s starting a round after time τ_f. Let W_s be the value of W at the end of line 11. Two cases may arise:

– If $W_s = P_f$, as $\mathcal{A}$ is fair, then $setcon(\mathcal{A}|_{W_s, A_f}) = min(|A_f|, setcon(\mathcal{A}|_{P_f}))$. Thus, $setcon(\mathcal{A}|_{W_s, A_f}) \geq s$.

– Otherwise, W_s is set on line 11 to some $S_{target} \setminus \{p_{target}\}$ at some itera-
tion l, with $setcon(\mathcal{A}|_{S_{target},A_f}) \geq l$ for $l > s$. We have $setcon(\mathcal{A}|_{W_s,A_f}) = setcon((\mathcal{A}|_{S_{target},A})|_{S_{target}\setminus\{p_{target}\}})$ which, by the definition of $setcon$, is
greater or equal to $setcon(\mathcal{A}|_{S_{target},A}) - 1 \geq l - 1 \geq s$, so we have
$setcon(\mathcal{A}|_{W_s,A_f}) \geq s$.

By the definition of $setcon$, as $setcon(\mathcal{A}|_{W_s,A_f}) \geq s$, there exists $S \subseteq W_s$ such
that $setcon(\mathcal{A}|_{S,A_f}) \geq s$. So, eventually b_s will always succeed the test on line 13.

Lemma 4. *For every live BG simulator b_s, with $s \leq min(|A_f|, \alpha_{\mathcal{A}}(P_f))$, even-
tually, the value of W computed at the end of iteration $m + 1$ (at lines 8–11) is
equal to some constant value $W_{m,f}$.*

Proof. No BG simulator b_l, with $l > m$, executes lines 7–21 after time τ_f. Therefore $R[l]$ is constant after time τ_f, $\forall l > m$. As the computation of W, on lines 7–
11, only depends on the value of A, P and $R[l]$, for $\alpha_{\mathcal{A}}(\Pi) \geq l > m$, all constant
after time τ_f, then the value of W computed at the end of line 11 for iteration
$m+1$ is the same at every round initiated after time τ_f for any live BG simulator
b_s, with $s \leq min(|A_f|, \alpha_{\mathcal{A}}(P_f))$.

Lemma 5. *If A_f contains a correct process, then the set of processes with an
infinite number of simulated steps is a live set of $\mathcal{A}$ containing a process of A_f.*

Proof. As b_m is live, it proceeds to an infinite number of rounds. By Lemma 4,
eventually b_m computes the same window in every round. By Lemma 3, if b_m
does not have a valid live set selected, then it eventually selects a valid one
for $W_{m,f}$. Thus, eventually b_m never changes its selected live set. Let $S_{m,f}$ be
this live set. Afterwards, in each round, b_m tries to complete a simulation step
of $p_m(t)$ and, if successfully completed, changes $p_m(t)$ in a round robin manner
among $S_{m,f}$. Two cases may arise:

– If $p_m(t)$ never stabilizes, then the set of processes with an infinite number of
simulated steps includes $S_{m,f}$. By Lemma 4, every other live BG simulator
with a smaller identifier computes the same value of W at the end of round
$m+1$ (of the loop at lines 8–11). Thus, after the $S_{m,f}$ is selected by b_m, as $S_{m,f}$
is valid, every BG simulator will select a subset of $S_{m,f}$ for its window value
in every round. Moreover, by Lemma 3, these BG simulators will always find
valid live sets to select, and so they will eventually simulate only processes in
$S_{m,f}$. Thus, the set of processes with infinitely many simulated steps is equal
to $S_{m,f}$, a live set intersecting with A_f.
– Otherwise, $p_m(t)$ eventually stabilizes on some $p_{m,f}$. Therefore, b_m attempts
to complete a simulation step of $p_{m,f}$ infinitely often. Two sub-cases may
arise:
  – Either $|S_{m,f}| = 1$ and, therefore, b_m is the only one live BG simulator per-
    forming simulation steps, and thus, the set of processes with an infinite
    number of simulated steps is equal to $S_{m,f}$, a live set intersecting with A_f.

- Otherwise, by Lemma 4, every live BG simulator with a smaller identifier eventually selects a window, and thus a live set (Lemma 3), which is a subset of $S_{m,f} \setminus \{p_{m,f}\}$. Thus every live BG simulator with a smaller identifier eventually selects processes to simulate distinct from $p_{m,f}$ and, thus, cannot block b_m infinitely often—a contradiction.

Lemma 6. *If $\mathcal{A}$ is fair, then any task T solvable in the $\mathcal{A}$-model is solvable in the $\alpha_{\mathcal{A}}$-model.*

Proof. Let us assume that it is not the case: there exists a task T and a fair adversary $\mathcal{A}$ such that T is solvable in the adversarial $\mathcal{A}$-model but not in the $\alpha_{\mathcal{A}}$-model. As every finite run of the $\mathcal{A}$-model can be extended to and $\mathcal{A}$-compliant run, the simulated algorithm can only provide valid outputs to the simulated processes. Thus, it can only be the case that a correct process is not provided with a task output, i.e., belongs to A_f.

Therefore, by Lemma 5, the simulation provides an $\mathcal{A}$-compliant run, i.e., the set of processes with an infinite number of simulated steps is a live set. As the run is $\mathcal{A}$-compliant then each process p with an infinite number of simulated steps is eventually provided with a task output and thus $p_{MEM}[p]$ is set to $\top$. Thus, they cannot belong to A_f — a contradiction.

Combining Corollary 1 and Lemma 6 we obtain the following result:

Theorem 6. *For any fair adversary $\mathcal{A}$, the adversarial $\mathcal{A}$-model and the $\alpha_{\mathcal{A}}$-model are equivalent regarding task solvability.*

6   Agreement Functions Do not Always Tell it All

We observe that agreement functions are not able to characterize the task computability power of *all* models. In particular there are non-fair adversaries not captured by their agreement functions.

Consider for example the adversary $\mathcal{A} = \{\{p_1\}, \{p_2, p_3\}, \{p_1, p_2, p_3\}\}$. It is easy to see that $setcon(\mathcal{A}) = 2$, but that $setcon(\mathcal{A}|_{\Pi, \{p_2, p_3\}}) = 1$ which is strictly smaller than $\min(|\{p_2, p_3\}|, setcon(\mathcal{A})) = 2$. Therefore, $\mathcal{A}$ is non-fair.

Consider the task $Cons_{2,3}$ consisting in consensus among p_2 and p_3: every process in $\{p_2, p_3\}$ proposes a value and every correct process in $\{p_2, p_3\}$ decides a proposed value, so that p_2 and p_3 cannot decide different values. $Cons_{2,3}$ is solvable in the adversarial $\mathcal{A}$-model: every process in $\{p_2, p_3\}$ simply waits until p_2 writes its proposed value and decides on it. Indeed, this protocol solves $Cons_{2,3}$ in the $\mathcal{A}$-model as if p_3 is correct, p_2 is also correct.

The agreement function of $\mathcal{A}$, $\alpha_{\mathcal{A}}$, is equal to 0 for $\{p_2\}$ or $\{p_3\}$, to 2 for $\{p_1, p_2, p_3\}$, and to 1 for all other values. It is easy to see that $\alpha_{\mathcal{A}}$ only differs from α_{1-res}, the agreement function of the 1-resilient adversary, for $\{p_1\}$ where $\alpha_{\mathcal{A}}(\{p_1\}) = 1 > \alpha_{1-res}(\{p_1\}) = 0$. Therefore, $\forall P \subseteq \Pi, \alpha_{\mathcal{A}}(P) \geq \alpha_{1-res}(P)$, and thus any task solvable in the $\mathcal{A}$-model is solvable in the 1-resilient model.

The impossibility of solving such a task 1-resiliently can be directly derived from the characterization of task solvable t-resiliently from [8]. Indeed, let p_1

wait for some process to output in order to decide the same value. Processes p_2 and p_3 use the ability to solve consensus among themselves to output a unique value. As there are two correct processes in the system, p_2 or p_3 will eventually terminate and thus p_1 will not wait indefinitely. This gives a 3-process 1-resilient consensus algorithm—a contradiction [7,21]. Thus, the $\mathcal{A}$-model is not equivalent with the $\alpha_{\mathcal{A}}$-model, even though they have the same agreement function.

7   Related Work

Adversarial models were introduced by Delporte et al. in [6]. With respect to colorless tasks, Herlihy and Rajsbaum [17] characterized a class *superset-closed* [19] adversaries (closed under the superset operation) via their minimal core sizes. Still with respect to colorless tasks, Gafni and Kuznetsov [12] derived a characterization of general adversary using its *consensus power* function *setcon*. A side result of this present paper is an extension of the characterization in [12] to any (not necessarily colorless) tasks.

Taubenfeld [23] introduced the notion of symmetric progress conditions, equivalent to our symmetric adversaries.

The BG simulation establishes equivalence between t-resilience and wait-freedom with respect to task solvability [3,4,8]. Gafni and Guerraoui [10] showed that if a model allows for solving k-set consensus, then it can be used to simulate a k-*concurrent* system in which at most k processes are concurrently invoking a task. In our simulation, we use the fact that a model M associated to an agreement function α_M allows to solve an α-adaptive set consensus, using the technique proposed in [5], which enables a composition of the ideas in [3,4,8] and [10]. Running BG simulation on top of a k-concurrent system, we are able to derive the equivalence between fair adversaries and their corresponding α-models.

8   Concluding Remarks

By Theorem 6, task computability of a fair adversary $\mathcal{A}$ is *characterized* by its agreement function α: a task is solvable with $\mathcal{A}$ if and only if it is solvable in the α-model. The result implies characterizations of superset-closed [16,19] and symmetric [23] adversaries and, via the equivalence result established in [9], the model of k-concurrency.

As a corollary, for all models M and M' characterized by their agreements functions, such that $\forall P \in \Pi, \alpha_{M'}(P) \geq \alpha_M(P)$, we have that M is *stronger* than M', i.e., the set of tasks solvable in M contains the set of tasks solvable in M'. In particular, if the two agreement functions are equal, then M and M' solve exactly the same sets of tasks. Note that if a model M is characterized by its agreement function α, then it belongs to the weakest equivalence class among the models whose agreement function is α.

An intriguing open question is therefore how to precisely determine the scope of the approach based on agreement functions and if it can be extended to capture larger classes of models.

References

1. Afek, Y., Attiya, H., Dolev, D., Gafni, E., Merritt, M., Shavit, N.: Atomic snapshots of shared memory. J. ACM **40**(4), 873–890 (1993)
2. Borowsky, E., Gafni, E.: Generalized FLP impossibility result for t-resilient asynchronous computations. In: STOC, pp. 91–100. ACM Press, May 1993
3. Borowsky, E., Gafni, E.: Immediate atomic snapshots and fast renaming. In: PODC, pp. 41–51. ACM Press, New York (1993)
4. Borowsky, E., Gafni, E., Lynch, N.A., Rajsbaum, S.: The BG distributed simulation algorithm. Distrib. Comput. **14**(3), 127–146 (2001)
5. Delporte-Gallet, C., Fauconnier, H., Gafni, E., Kuznetsov, P.: Wait-freedom with advice. Distrib. Comput. **28**(1), 3–19 (2015)
6. Delporte-Gallet, C., Fauconnier, H., Guerraoui, R., Tielmann, A.: The disagreement power of an adversary. Distrib. Comput. **24**(3–4), 137–147 (2011)
7. Fischer, M.J., Lynch, N.A., Paterson, M.S.: Impossibility of distributed consensus with one faulty process. J. ACM **32**(2), 374–382 (1985)
8. Gafni, E.: The extended BG simulation and the characterization of t-resiliency. In: STOC, pp. 85–92 (2009)
9. Gafni, E., Guerraoui, R.: Simulating few by many: limited concurrency = set consensus. Technical report (2009). http://web.cs.ucla.edu/eli/eli/kconc.pdf
10. Gafni, E., Guerraoui, R.: Generalized universality. In: Katoen, J.-P., König, B. (eds.) CONCUR 2011. LNCS, vol. 6901, pp. 17–27. Springer, Heidelberg (2011). doi:10.1007/978-3-642-23217-6_2
11. Gafni, E., He, Y., Kuznetsov, P., Rieutord, T.: Read-write memory and k-set consensus as an affine task. In: OPODIS (2016). Technical report. https://arxiv.org/abs/1610.01423
12. Gafni, E., Kuznetsov, P.: Turning adversaries into friends: simplified, made constructive, and extended. In: Lu, C., Masuzawa, T., Mosbah, M. (eds.) OPODIS 2010. LNCS, vol. 6490, pp. 380–394. Springer, Heidelberg (2010). doi:10.1007/978-3-642-17653-1_28
13. Gafni, E., Kuznetsov, P.: Relating L-resilience and wait-freedom via hitting sets. In: ICDCN, pp. 191–202 (2011)
14. Herlihy, M.: Wait-free synchronization. ACM Trans. Prog. Lang. Syst. **13**(1), 123–149 (1991)
15. Herlihy, M., Kozlov, D.N., Rajsbaum, S.: Distributed Computing Through Combinatorial Topology. Morgan Kaufmann, Burlington (2014)
16. Herlihy, M., Rajsbaum, S.: The topology of shared-memory adversaries. In: PODC, pp. 105–113 (2010)
17. Herlihy, M., Rajsbaum, S.: Simulations and reductions for colorless tasks. In: PODC, pp. 253–260 (2012)
18. Herlihy, M., Shavit, N.: The topological structure of asynchronous computability. J. ACM **46**(2), 858–923 (1999)
19. Kuznetsov, P.: Understanding non-uniform failure models. Bull. EATCS **106**, 53–77 (2012)

20. Kuznetsov, P., Rieutord, T.: Agreement functions for distributed computing models. CoRR, abs/1004.4701 (2017)
21. Loui, M.C., Abu-Amara, H.H.: Memory requirements for agreement among unreliable asynchronous processes. Adv. Comput. Res. **4**, 163–183 (1987)
22. Saks, M., Zaharoglou, F.: Wait-free k-set agreement is impossible: The topology of public knowledge. SIAM J. Comput. **29**, 1449–1483 (2000)
23. Taubenfeld, G.: The computational structure of progress conditions. In: Lynch, N.A., Shvartsman, A.A. (eds.) DISC 2010. LNCS, vol. 6343, pp. 221–235. Springer, Heidelberg (2010). doi:10.1007/978-3-642-15763-9_23

Anomalies and Similarities Among Consensus Numbers of Variously-Relaxed Queues

Edward Talmage$^{(\boxtimes)}$ and Jennifer L. Welch

Texas A&M University, College Station, TX, USA
etalmage@tamu.edu, welch@cse.tamu.edu

Abstract. Shared data structures are a basic building block in distributed computing, but can be expensive to implement. One way to circumvent the high implementation cost of linearizability is to relax the sequential specification of the data type. This gives up some guarantees, for instance on the ordering of data elements, as a tradeoff against performance. We want to explore the effects of this tradeoff on the computational power of the shared data structures.

In this paper, we characterize the effects of three different types of relaxation, chosen from the literature, on the computational power of FIFO queues. By parametrically relaxing each of the three operations on a queue (*Enqueue*, *Dequeue*, *Peek*), we obtain an infinite 3-dimensional space for each type of relaxation. We find the *consensus number*, a standard measure of the computational power of shared data types, of each point in these spaces, completely describing the effect of these three types of relaxation on the computational power of queues.

Keywords: Distributed data types · Relaxed data types · Consensus numbers

1 Introduction

Shared data structures are a critical abstraction making real-world message-passing systems appear to a programmer as shared memory systems. These abstractions can hide much of the complexity of programming on a distributed system. To be practically useful, though, we need high-performance implementations of shared data structures.

Past work has shown that to satisfy strong, intuitive conditions on the concurrent behavior of shared data structure implementations, those implementations have a high time cost spent in communication [2, 7, 8, 14]. One approach to circumvent these lower bounds is to use weaker conditions on concurrent behavior. This can, in fact, increase performance [2], but tends to lead to less intuitive behavior, making distributed programming confusing and difficult to guarantee correct.

Another approach some researchers have proposed is to introduce some non-determinism into the sequential specifications of the data types of shared structures [1, 5], while keeping the consistency condition strong. By doing this in a

© Springer International Publishing AG 2017
A. El Abbadi and B. Garbinato (Eds.): NETYS 2017, LNCS 10299, pp. 191–205, 2017.
DOI: 10.1007/978-3-319-59647-1_15

controlled fashion, one can reduce contention in distributed implementations of the data type and achieve improved performance. By changing the sequential specification, it is easier to intuitively understand the changes in allowable behavior of the shared data type under concurrent access by multiple processes. Past work has shown that these relaxed data types can be implemented more efficiently, in an amortized sense, than their unrelaxed counterparts [12].

Given these relaxed data type specifications, we wish to formally analyze their computational power. In this paper, we explore the ability of relaxed data types, exemplified by queues, to solve the asynchronous consensus problem among several processes which may crash. Solving consensus allows us to implement any other data type among those processes. Thus, the largest number of processes which can solve consensus using a given data type, called the *consensus number* of the type, is a measure of the data type's computational strength [6].

We consider the space of possible parameters for three different relaxations of queues. We extend the classical method of bivalency arguments to handle the non-determinism in relaxed data types. Using this expanded method, we prove consensus numbers directly for several base classes, and show how these imply useful bounds on the consensus numbers of other parameter values.

To generalize our results, we show how parameterization of the relaxation of the three operations on a queue gives a 3-dimensional space. In this space, we give lemmas based on those in [10,11] which allow us to extend bounds proved for certain points across infinite areas. This allows us to totally cover the space of possible relaxations with only a handful of results.

Due to space constraints, while we have complete proofs of all theorems, we omit most proofs in this paper.

1.1 Related Work

The first explorations of relaxed data types came when Afek et al. [1] proposed a weak consistency condition, Quasi-Linearizability, which requires each concurrent execution to have a permutation of operation instances which is a bounded "distance" from a legal execution of the operation type. This can equivalently be viewed as a relaxation of the sequential specification of an object, allowing operations to return slightly out-of-date values.

Henzinger et al. [5] generalized the notion of relaxing the sequential specification of a data type. They used a state machine model to abstractly define several relaxations and gave shared memory implementations of several relaxed data types to provide empirical evidence that a distributed system using such relaxed types could out-perform one using unrelaxed types.

Talmage and Welch [12] re-formulated the relaxations of [5] specifically for operations on Queues and considered performance in a message-passing system with bounded delays. They gave upper and lower bounds showing that relaxing Queues cannot improve the worst-case time per operation, but may greatly reduce the amortized time per operation.

Consensus numbers were defined by Herlihy in [6] and are the standard measure of the computational strength of a shared data type. He showed that in an asynchronous system, a consensus object among a certain number of processes can wait-free implement any other shared data type among those processes. Thus, if a shared object can implement consensus among n processes, it is "universal" among n processes and can implement any data type in that system.

Lo and Hadzilacos [9] showed that consensus numbers do not form a robust wait-free hierarchy, in that multiple types of low consensus number can combine to implement types of high consensus number, if non-deterministic types are allowed. It remains an open question whether this is true for any amount or type of non-determinism, or what is the minimum amount of non-determinism which causes the hierarchy to collapse. For implementations using objects of a single type to solve consensus, though, consensus numbers are still useful, even for non-deterministic types, such as relaxed Queues. [9] also set up the mechanisms for proving upper bounds on consensus numbers of non-deterministic types, which we use in this paper.

Shavit and Taubenfeld [10,11] began exploring the computational power of relaxed data types by proving consensus numbers for some relaxed queues. Specifically, they proved a selection of results for Out-of-Order relaxed Queues, one of the relaxations specified in [5] and used in [12]. We extend their work to include all possible Out-of-Order Queues and prove results for Lateness and Restricted Out-of-Order relaxed Queues, as well. An attentive reader may notice that some of our results for Out-of-Order relaxed Queues do not agree with those in [10,11]. This is because our definition of the relaxation differs from theirs. For example, if there are only 3 elements in the Queue, and *Dequeue* can return any of the top 5, our definition allows the *Dequeue* instance to return $\perp$, indicating an empty Queue, while that of [10,11] requires the *Dequeue* to return one of the elements currently in the Queue. Their extra requirement can be viewed as allowing less relaxation when the Queue is almost empty. There are good practical reasons to do this, but from a theoretical perspective, the relaxation parameter is changing based on the object's state. This means that their results do not fully apply to k-relaxed Queues, as defined in the literature [5].

Chen et al. [3] explored the edge-condition behavior of several shared objects, with respect to their consensus numbers. They showed that the consensus power of Queues is different if a *Dequeue* on an empty Queue returns a unique $\perp$ value or breaks and can never be used again, and several other examples. While we do not explore different edge-condition behaviors in depth, we note that the results we obtain do depend on our assumptions about when a *Dequeue* or *Peek* can see an empty Queue.

2   Model, Definitions, and Background

We consider an asynchronous, shared-memory model of computation among n processes, up to $n-1$ of which may fail by *crashing*. A crashed process performs no further actions of any kind. Processes communicate by invoking operations on shared objects and receiving responses to those operation invocations. Each shared object is linearizable (or atomic) and thus operations on each object appear to happen instantaneously. A *data type* specifies the behavior of an object. A data type provides (1) a set of possible operation invocations and (2) a set of *legal* sequences of *instances* of those operations, where an instance of operation OP, denoted $OP(arg, ret)$ is an invocation, with argument(s) arg, and return value ret. We assume that every data type satisfies the following properties:

- *Prefix Closure*: If a sequence ρ is legal, every prefix of ρ is legal
- *Completeness*: If a sequence ρ is legal, then for every operation OP in the data type and every argument arg to OP, there exists a response ret such that $\rho.OP(arg, ret)$ is legal

We use *state* of an object to refer to the equivalence class of operation sequences which allow the same set of extending sequences. We will express state by the sequence of instances which have been executed on the object. Every operation on a shared object must be either an *accessor*, which returns some information dependent on the state of the object, a *mutator*, which changes the state of the object, or both, which we call a *mixed* operation. Operations which are neither accessors nor mutators would be constants or no-ops, and are thus not useful operations on a shared object.

2.1   Relaxed Data Types

Intuitively, a relaxed data type is the result of relaxing the ordering constraints on some "classic" data type. We introduce some non-determinism, allowing multiple possible return values and changes the object's state. This can reduce the contention of operations such as *Dequeue* on a Queue and *Pop* on a stack, if we allow them to return elements near the head or top, instead of always exactly the head or top element.

We will consider three different types of relaxation introduced in [5] and reformulated for relaxing *Dequeue* on Queues in [12]. Each one has a parameter specifying the maximum amount of relaxation allowed, either for each operation instance or bounding the number of consecutive operation instances which can behave differently than the unrelaxed type. The Out-of-Order k-relaxation allows each operation instance to take effect up to k places out of order. For example, a *Dequeue* can return any of the first k elements at the head of a Queue, instead of only the first. The Lateness k-relaxation merely requires that at least one in every k instances must behave as the unrelaxed version, while the other instances may disregard ordering. The Restricted Out-of-Order k-relaxation is the intersection of the previous two relaxations, requiring that consecutive instances which behave in an out-of-order fashion are increasingly near to the correct order.

Each relaxation can be pictured as ideal for different applications. Consider a job queue, where tasks are inserted in order, but may be claimed and completed by different actors. The owner of the queue may not require that jobs are completed exactly in order, but may want to maintain different guarantees on the ordering. An Out-of-Order relaxed queue is good when we want to guarantee that every job completed is one of the oldest jobs in the queue. Lateness relaxed queues provide a guarantee on the maximum number of jobs added after a particular job which may be completed before that job. Restricted Out-of-Order relaxed queues provide both of these guarantees, requiring that every job performed is one of the oldest in the queue, and no job is left undone for too long.

We will next formally define these three relaxations by giving their sequential specifications. First, we must note that each type will have three different relaxation parameters, one for each operation on a Queue. Each of these parameters may be in the set $\mathbb{Z}^+ \cup \{*, \emptyset\}^1$, which we will denote as $\mathbb{Z}^*$. A $\emptyset$ parameter, equivalent to a 0 in [10,11], means that the operation is not supported, while we consider that $* > x, \forall x \in \mathbb{Z}$. That is, $*$-relaxed is infinitely relaxed, and such operations have no ordering constraints, since at any particular point in time, there will be a finite number of elements in the Queue. For technical reasons, we will define $\emptyset > * > x, \forall x \in \mathbb{Z}^+$.

We assume that all arguments to Queue operations are unique (accomplishable by logical timestamps). Represent the state of a relaxed Queue by a sequence, denoting one end as the *head* and the other as the *tail*. In an unrelaxed Queue, *Enqueue(val)* appends *val* to the tail of the Queue, while *Dequeue* and *Peek* return the value at the head of the Queue, with *Dequeue* also removing that element from the Queue. *Peek* and *Dequeue* may return a special symbol $\perp$ if the Queue appears to contain no elements (relaxation may allow the Queue to appear empty even when it is not).

Definition 1. *An* Out-of-Order *relaxed Queue with parameters $a, b, c \in \mathbb{Z}^*$, denoted OQueue[a, b, c], provides three operations, as follows:*

- *Enqueue[a](val) adds val to the OQueue such that at most $a - 1$ elements already in the OQueue are nearer the tail than val*
- *Dequeue[b]() removes and returns one of the first b elements at the head end of the OQueue; Dequeue[b]() may return $\perp$ if there are fewer than b elements in the OQueue,*
- *Peek[c]() returns, without removing, one of the first c elements at the head end of the OQueue; if there are fewer than c elements in the OQueue, Peek[c]() may return $\perp$*

Enqueue[$\emptyset$], Dequeue[$\emptyset$] and Peek[$\emptyset$] are no-ops.

For the next two relaxations, we need the concept of *lateness*, which is a measure of how many consecutive operations of a specific type have been out of order. Define *lateness(OP[k])* for a finite sequence ρ of operations instances on a relaxed Queue as the number of instances of *OP[k]* appearing in ρ after the latest instance of *OP[k]* that behaved as the unrelaxed version, *OP[1]*, would. That is, the number of *Enqueue[a]* instances since the last one which put an element at the tail, the number of *Dequeue[b]* instances since the last which removed the head, or the number of *Peek[c]* instances since the last which returned the head.

---

[1] We use $*$, not ∞, to maintain consistency with the literature, e.g. [11]. We also use $\emptyset$ where [11] used 0. This maintains visual consistency, while avoiding the problem that $0 < x, \forall x \in \mathbb{Z}^+$, while we want $\emptyset > x, \forall x \in \mathbb{Z}^+$.

Definition 2. *A* Lateness *relaxed Queue with parameters* $a, b, c \in \mathbb{Z}^*$, *denoted* $LQueue[a, b, c]$, *provides three operations, as follows:*

- *Enqueue[a](val) adds val to an arbitrary location in the LQueue while main-taining lateness(Enqueue[a]) < a*
- *Dequeue[b]() removes and returns any element in the LQueue, or ⊥, while maintaining lateness(Dequeue[b]) < b*
- *Peek[c]() returns, without removing, any element in the LQueue or ⊥, while maintaining lateness(Peek[c]) < c*

Enqueue[∅], Dequeue[∅] and Peek[∅] are no-ops.

In effect, $OP[k]$ operations on an LQueue ignore all ordering, as long as at least one in every k consecutive instances of $OP[k]$ exhibits the behavior of an unrelaxed OP, acting on the appropriate end of the LQueue, which resets that operation's *lateness*.

An RQueue keeps the requirement of an LQueue that at least a fixed fraction $(1/k)$ of $OP[k]$ instances must behave as if unrelaxed, but also requires every operation instance to approximately respect the ordering of an unrelaxed Queue. Thus, it can be seen as the intersection of the last two definitions.

Definition 3. *A* Restricted Out-of-Order *relaxed Queue with parameters* $a, b, c \in \mathbb{Z}^*$, *denoted* $RQueue[a, b, c]$, *provides three operations, as follows:*

- *Enqueue[a](val) adds val to the Queue such that at most* $(a - 1) - lateness(Enqueue[a])$ *elements already in the RQueue are nearer the tail than val*
- *Dequeue[b]() removes and returns one of the first* $b - lateness(Dequeue[b])$ *elements at the head end of the RQueue; Dequeue[b]() may return ⊥ if there are fewer than* $b - lateness(Dequeue[b])$ *elements in the RQueue*
- *Peek[c]() returns, without removing, one of the first* $c - lateness(Peek[c])$ *elements at the head end of the RQueue; if there are fewer than* $c - lateness(Peek[c])$ *elements in the RQueue, Peek[c]() may return ⊥*

Enqueue[∅], Dequeue[∅] and Peek[∅] are no-ops.

We will use natural reductions of notation to increase readability, such as denoting $Enqueue[1]$ as $Enqueue$, etc., since this is an unrelaxed operation. To specify an $Enqueue[a]$ instance, we will also use the notation $Enqueue_i^t(x)$ to denote an $Enqueue$ instance executed by process p_i which places x immediately head-ward of the tail-most t elements.

2.2   Consensus Numbers

To classify the computational power of shared data types, we use the *consensus* problem. The consensus problem is for each of n processes, starting with an input value in $\{0, 1\}$, to either crash or in a finite amount of time agree on (*decide*) and return the same output value as all other deciding processes, such that the decided value was some process' input. We say that a data type T can wait-free implement consensus if there is an algorithm which uses one or more objects of type T, plus *Read/Write* registers, to solve consensus. The *consensus number* of T, which we denote as $CN(T)$, is the maximum number of processes for which such an algorithm exists. If there is no such maximum number, we say $CN(T) = \infty$.

To prove a lower bound on a type's consensus number, we merely exhibit an algorithm which uses objects of that type to solve consensus among some number of processes. For an upper bound, we use the technique of *valency*, as in [6], and its extensions to non-deterministic types from [9]. We here re-state several concepts and lemmas from these papers, as well as [4,13], which allow us to streamline our proofs.

A *configuration* of an algorithm consists of the local states of all processes and the states of all shared objects. An *initial configuration* is one where every process is in an initial local state and every shared object has an initial state, as specified by the algorithm. We say that two configurations C and D are *indistinguishable* to a process p_i if p_i has the same local state and all shared objects have the same state in C and D.

Process p_i takes *step* (C, op_i, C'), where C and C' are configurations we call the old and new configurations of the step, if it executes an atomic operation instance op_i on a shared variable V. V and op_i's operation and argument are specified by p_i's state in C. This is said to be an *enabled* step. The resulting configuration C' differs from C only in the local state of p_i, according to the algorithm, and V's state, according to its type. We call C' a *child configuration* of C and use the notation $C.op_i$ to denote the child configuration C'. Note that for each configuration C, there is at least one enabled step for each process. There may be more than one enabled step for a single process if the algorithm executes a nondeterministic operation. For example, a relaxed *Enqueue* may lead to one of several different child configurations depending on where the argument is placed in the Queue.

An *execution* of an algorithm A is an infinite sequence of steps, starting from an initial configuration, with the new configuration of each step equal to the old configuration of the next step. Processes that take only a finite number of steps are said to be crashed. We assume that executions are infinite, as this implies that at least one process does not crash. If a process terminates the stated algorithm without crashing, we say that it triggers an infinite series of no-op steps. A *reachable configuration* is one that appears in some execution.

Let C be a configuration reachable by some prefix E of an execution of a consensus algorithm A. Consider all executions E' which are extensions of E. A must terminate, so in each E', some value is decided. Let $vals(C)$ be the set of values decided in all E's. We call C *bivalent* if $vals(C) = \{0, 1\}$, *1-valent* if $vals(C) = \{1\}$, and 0-valent if $vals(C) = \{0\}$. We call C *critical* if it is bivalent, but every child configuration of C is univalent.

Lemma 1 ([6,9,13]). *Every critical configuration has child configurations with different valencies which are reached by different processes acting on the same* *shared object, which is not a register. Further, every enabled step in a critical configuration must be a mutator.*

Lemma 1's claim that steps leading to different valencies must exist at different processes is trivial for deterministic types, since each process can have only one enabled step. With non-deterministic types, a single process may have multiple enabled steps from a single configuration. Here, the lemma follows from the fact that there must be at least one 0-valent child configuration and at least one 1-valent child configuration. If these are not at different processes but both at the same process, then the valency of a step by some other process can be neither 0 nor 1, contradicting the definitions of valency and critical configurations.

Lemma 2 (Extended from [4]**).** *A consensus algorithm (1) always has an initial bivalent configuration and (2) must have a critical configuration in every execution.*

Lemma 3 (Univalency Lemma, implicit in [6]**).** *If two univalent configurations are indistinguishable to a process, they have the same valency.*

3   Characterizing the Space of Relaxed Queues

Since we are considering relaxations of Queues with three operations, and the relaxation parameter for each is taken from $\mathbb{Z}^*$, an extension of the positive integers, we can visualize the space of possible relaxed Queues, for a given relaxation, as a 3-dimensional lattice. We can thus state the following general version of two lemmas from [10,11] and then reason about the space of consensus numbers of relaxed Queues.

Lemma 4. *For $t \in \{O, L, R\}$ and $a, b, c, a', b', c' \in \mathbb{Z}^*$ such that $a \leq a', b \leq b'$, and $c \leq c'$, $CN(tQueue[a, b, c]) \geq CN(tQueue[a', b', c'])$.*

Lemma 4 states that relaxing an unrelaxed operation, increasing the relaxation of an operation, or disabling an operation will not increase a type's consensus number. The less-relaxed version of the operation satisfies the definition of the more-relaxed version, so any consensus algorithm using the more-relaxed version will also work with the less-relaxed version of the operation. Similarly, any algorithm which does not use a particular operation will work if its underlying data type is replaced by a type which differs only in that it provides additional operations.

Lemma 4 allows us to prove consensus number bounds for a finite number of points in the relaxation space and immediately have either an upper or lower bound on the consensus strength of many more relaxations. In the rest of the paper, we will fill in the consensus numbers of all relaxations of the three types defined above. We will use standard techniques, with a few novel twists, to show the consensus numbers of a handful of specific relaxations and apply Lemma 4, as well as the next two lemmas relating the spaces of different relaxation types, to achieve results for all relaxation values.

Since we are considering different types of relaxation, we state the next lemma to show the points where the 3-dimensional spaces of consensus numbers for each relaxation type are the same. Disabled operations are no different in different types of relaxation and a relaxation parameter of 1 means that the operation is not relaxed. Finally, recall that all relaxation types are equivalent with parameter $*$, imposing no ordering constraints on the operation.

Lemma 5. *For $a, b, c \in \{1, *, \emptyset\}$,*
$CN(OQueue[a, b, c]) = CN(LQueue[a, b, c]) = CN(RQueue[a, b, c])$.

Similarly, since an $RQueue[a, b, c]$ satisfies both the definition both of an $OQueue[a, b, c]$ and that of an $LQueue[a, b, c]$, any algorithm using one of these relaxed Queues will be correct if all of its relaxed Queues are replaced with $RQueue[a, b, c]$s. We thus have the following lemma:

Lemma 6. *For $a, b, c \in \mathbb{Z}^*$,*
$CN(RQueue[a, b, c]) \geq \max\{CN(OQueue[a, b, c]), CN(LQueue[a, b, c])\}$.

We end this section with the results for unrelaxed Queues from [6]. The results stated in [6] are for $Queue[1, 1, 1]$ and $Queue[1, 1, \emptyset]$, respectively, but the algorithms apply exactly as stated to the below versions, which are more useful for determining the values of relaxed Queues.

Theorem 1.

- $CN(Queue[1, \emptyset, 1]) = \infty$, *and thus* $CN(Queue[1, b, 1]) = \infty, \forall b \in \mathbb{Z}^*$
- $CN(Queue[\emptyset, 1, \emptyset]) \geq 2$, *so* $CN(Queue[a, 1, c]) \geq 2, \forall a, c \in \mathbb{Z}^*$.

These theorems imply that any relaxation which provides a $Dequeue[1]$ operation will have consensus number at least 2 and any relaxation which provides $Enqueue[1]$ and $Peek[1]$ will have infinite consensus number. In the rest of the paper, we will show where the boundaries between infinite and finite consensus number are, and those between consensus number 1 and 2. This allows us to understand which relaxations have maximum computational power and which have no more power than a register.

4   Two Example Results

Before we get into the details of exploring every possible relaxation, we draw attention to two particular interesting results. This also allows us to showcase the extended techniques we use for proving consensus numbers that are necessary for non-deterministic data types.

A large part of the motivation for determining the consensus number of relaxed Queues is to ease the choice of data type to use in solving a particular problem. However, if the consensus numbers of relaxed Queues were easily predictable, or always the same for every type of relaxation, it would hardly be worth proving them all. The first result we highlight shows that different types of relaxation do, in fact, have different consensus numbers for the same relaxation parameters. This seems an intuitive result, but is not entirely obvious to verify.

We also observe that it is important to be completely familiar with the consensus numbers because they change suddenly. In this result, the choice of relaxation type determines whether the consensus number is 2 or ∞. We will shortly see that even increasing a single parameter by as little as 1 can have a similarly disastrous effect on the computational strength of a data type. This leads to the conclusion that it is imperative to fully understand the space of consensus numbers of relaxed Queues.

Our proof of Theorem 2 must handle the extra detail required for proving impossibility for non-deterministic data types. The number of cases which we must consider increases, handling different possible choices for the non-determinism. At the same time we also have extra leverage from non-determinism. If one branch of a non-deterministic possibility is enabled, we can argue that another is as well, and use that to show the desired result. A small case of this technique is included in the proof of Lemma 7, below.

Theorem 2. For $a > 1 \in \mathbb{Z}^+$, $CN(RQueue[a, 1, 1]) = CN(OQueue[a, 1, 1]) = \infty$, but $CN(LQueue[a, 1, 1]) = 2$.

The second result we highlight shows that even a very slight relaxation, moving from a $Peek[1]$ to a $Peek[2]$, drops the consensus number of every type of relaxed Queue we consider from ∞ to 1. This illustrates the ease with which a developer could use the wrong relaxation and lose all guarantees on computational power, unless all relaxations' consensus numbers are known.

The proof of Theorem 3 uses another major technique by which we prove upper bounds on consensus numbers in this paper. We exploit the non-determinism of the relaxed data type to force certain return values at each process. If each process only sees its own actions after a critical configuration, then it must conclude that it is running alone. Since different processes' steps have different valencies, this leads to erroneous decision values, proving the impossibility result. This "hiding" technique was introduced in [13] and is a formal and general version of a technique used to prove bounds for Queues with relaxed $Peeks$ in [10,11].

Theorem 3. $CN(RQueue[1, \emptyset, c]) = 1, \forall 1 < c \in \mathbb{Z}^*$.

We can then extend this result, to cover another column in the relaxation space for each type of relaxation, by the following lemma. Note that this lemma is not part of Lemma 4, since $\emptyset > *$ in $\mathbb{Z}^*$, so the inequality is in the other direction.

Lemma 7. $\forall t \in \{O, L, R\}, CN(tQueue[a, *, c]) \leq CN(tQueue[a, \emptyset, c]), \forall a, c \in \mathbb{Z}^*$

Proof. Suppose there exists a consensus algorithm A, for some relaxed Queue $tQueue[a, *, c], t \in \{O, L, R\}, a, c \in \mathbb{Z}^*$ among some number n of processes such that $CN(tQueue[a, \emptyset, c]) < n$. Then A must invoke $Dequeue[*]$, or it would also solve consensus using objects of type $tQueue[a, \emptyset, c]$, contradicting the assumption on $tQueue[a, \emptyset, c]$'s consensus number. But with a $Dequeue[*]$, every instance can return $\perp$ in each type of relaxation. Thus, from any initial configuration, there is an execution of A in which $Dequeue[*]$ is a no-op. If A can successfully solve consensus in this execution, then we can replace each instance of $Dequeue[*]$ with a constant function to generate an algorithm A' which can solve consensus using $tQueue[a, \emptyset, c]$ from the same initial state, a contradiction.

Applying Lemma 7 to Theorem 3 gives us the following more general formulation:

Theorem 4. $\forall t \in \{O, L, R\}, CN(tQueue[a, *, c]) = 1, \forall a \in \mathbb{Z}^*, 1 < c \in \mathbb{Z}^*$

5   Filling the Space

All we have left to do is to prove upper and lower bounds on boundary cases. These are the cases where adjusting relaxation parameters changes the consensus number of the relaxed Queue. Most upper bounds we need only to prove for RQueues, since by Lemma 6 an upper bound for RQueues applies to both LQueues and OQueues. On the other hand, algorithms for either LQueues or OQueues give lower bounds for RQueues as well.

We present consensus algorithms for lower bounds, but omit the proofs since they are completely standard. At the end of the section, we present Fig. 1, a graphical representation of the relaxation spaces for each relaxation type.

For RQueues, we show that any relaxation of $Peek$ results in consensus number at most 2. This upper bound applies to the entire relaxation space of $RQueue[a, b, c]$s, except where $c = 1$. For that part of the space, we show that when a reaches $*$, then any further relaxation has consensus number at most 2, and if both a and b reach $*$, then the RQueue is no stronger for consensus than a register.

The result in Theorem 3 shows that when we have relaxed $Peek$s ($c > 1$), we drop from consensus number 2 to 1 when the relaxation of $Dequeue[b]$ reaches $b = *$. The following theorems, along with the result we will show next for $OQueue[\emptyset, b, \emptyset]$, completely and precisely give the consensus numbers of any $RQueue[a, b, c]$ with $a, b, c \in \mathbb{Z}^*$.

Theorem 5. $CN(RQueue[1, 1, c]) \leq 2, \forall c > 1 \in \mathbb{Z}^*$.

This theorem is proved with a hiding proof, similar to the proof of Theorem 3. In constructing the indistinguishable executions, we need only be careful of when the elements $Enqueue$d immediately after a critical configuration are $Dequeue$d.

The two bounds in Theorem 6 both have proofs in the style of Theorem 2. Both proofs involve arguing that if one $Enqueue[*]$ is enabled, then $Enqueue[*]$s to other locations in the RQueue must also be enabled, and showing that a contradiction arises. To prove the second, we show that $CN(RQueue[*, \emptyset, 1]) = 1$ and use Lemma 7. The third bound in Theorem 6 is implied by an algorithm for $LQueue[\emptyset, b, \emptyset]$, which we will describe when we discuss LQueues.

Theorem 6. $CN(RQueue[*, 1, 1]) \leq 2$, $CN(RQueue[*, *, 1]) = 1$ and $CN(RQueue[\emptyset, b, \emptyset]) \geq 2, 1 < b < * \in \mathbb{Z}^*$.

By Lemma 6, upper bounds for RQueues also apply to LQueues, so we immediately have that $CN(LQueue[1, 1, c]) \leq 2, 1 < c \in \mathbb{Z}^*$ and $CN(LQueue[1, *, c]) = 1, 1 < c \in \mathbb{Z}^*$.

To determine the consensus numbers of all other $LQueue[a, b, c]$s, we also need the following two bounds in Theorem 7. The proof of the first bound shows that $CN(LQueue[a, \emptyset, 1]) = 1$, using the techniques of Theorem 2, then expands the result with Lemma 7.

To prove the second, there is a consensus algorithm for 2 processes. We initialize the $LQueue[\emptyset, b, \emptyset]$ to contain one special element. Each process writes its input to a register, then invokes $Dequeue[b]$ b times. If it returns the initial element, the process decides its own input, otherwise it decides the other process'. Intuitively, we can see that the algorithm is correct since the definition of $Dequeue[b]$ on an LQueue requires that at least one in every b consecutive $Dequeue[b]$ instances returns the element at the head of the LQueue. Thus, one of the $Dequeue[b]$ instances will return the initial element, and the process which does not $Dequeue[b]$ that element will know the other process must have.

Theorem 7. $CN(LQueue[a, *, 1]) = 1, \forall a > 1 \in \mathbb{Z}^*$ and $CN(LQueue[\emptyset, b, \emptyset]) \geq 2, \forall b > 1 \in \mathbb{Z}^+$.

From the results for RQueues and since an upper bound on the consensus number of an $RQueue[a, b, c]$ implies the same upper bound on $OQueue[a, b, c]$, we immediately have the following results for OQueues: $CN(OQueue[1, 1, c]) \leq 2, 1 < c \in \mathbb{Z}^*$, $CN(OQueue[1, *, c]) = 1, 1 < c \in \mathbb{Z}^*$, $CN(OQueue[*, 1, 1]) \leq 2$, and $CN(OQueue[*, *, 1]) = 1$.

The following theorem determines the last of the consensus numbers of relaxed OQueues. The two bounds have very similar proofs, using the techniques of Theorem 2 applied to both $Enqueue[a]$ and $Dequeue[b]$, taking advantage of the non-determinism implying that multiple steps by a single process may be enabled in a single configuration.

Theorem 8. $CN(OQueue[1, b, c]) = 1, \forall 1 < b, c \in \mathbb{Z}^*$ and $CN(OQueue[*, b, 1]) = 1, \forall 1 < b \in \mathbb{Z}^*$.

Finally, we give a graphical presentation of our results. Recall that for each relaxation type, we have a 3-dimensional lattice. In the charts, we use a, b, c to indicate integers greater than 1, since it happens that within that range, consensus numbers do not change. Moving right in a grid increases the relaxation of $Dequeue$, moving down increases the relaxation of $Peek$, and moving back from one grid to the next increases the relaxation of $Enqueue$.

We mark cells with "(imp)" or "(alg)" to indicate an impossibility result or algorithm proved or restated in this paper. Lemma 4 implies that consensus numbers must decrease while moving to the right or down within a single grid or moving back from one grid to the next. An algorithm, giving a lower bound

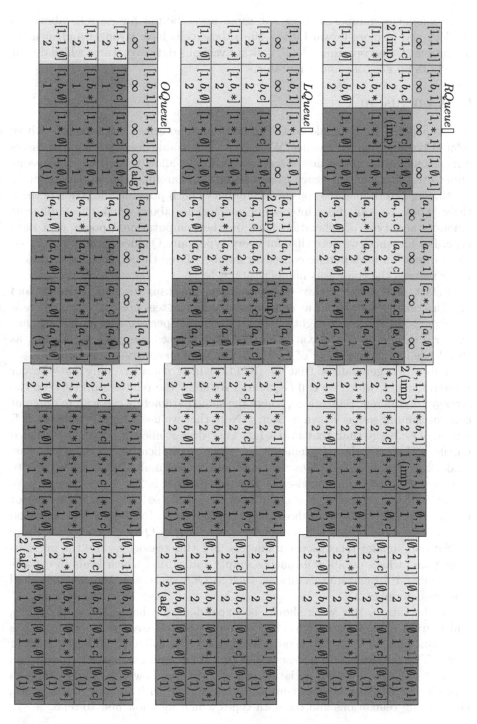

Fig. 1. Graphical representation of relaxation space for different relaxation types

on a consensus number, implies the same lower bound for all cells above, to the left, and in more-forward grids, since those cells have stronger and/or more operations. Cells containing "(1)" indicate vacuous data structures which do not have both an accessor and a mutator.

6   Conclusion

In this paper, we have explored the space of parameterized relaxations for three related types of relaxed Queues. We used a visualizable description of the three-dimensional parameter space of each relaxation to allow us to draw conclusions about every point in the space from a handful of carefully-chosen parameters.

Having determined the consensus number of each possible relaxation of these three types, we can draw interesting conclusions about what effect different amounts and type of relaxation have on the computational power of a data type. For instance, we note that for every type, only Queues with an unrelaxed *Peek* operation have infinite consensus number. Even the slightest relaxation of *Peek* reduces the consensus number to 2 or less.

In fact, none of these relaxation types have consensus numbers between 2 and ∞. This means that, as far as computational guarantees are concerned, there is little purpose in using a slightly-relaxed Queue. If performance is the primary concern, the degree of relaxation should be increased as much as possible, as that leads to the possibility of more efficient implementations [12].

This work generalizes that in [10,11], which considers only out-of-order relaxed Queues, which we call *OQueues*. We show the relationship between the strength of different relaxations, where the same parameters can lead to different consensus numbers, as shown in Sect. 4. Note that we use a slightly different definition of *OQueue* than that in [10,11]. They do not allow a non-empty relaxed Queue with fewer than k elements to return $\bot$, indicating an empty Queue. Under this definition, an *OQueue*[$*, *, \emptyset$] is simply a multiset, allowing them to use the known fact that multiset's consensus number is 2.

This does not match the definitions in [5,12], so the conclusions about increased performance from those papers do not hold. Intuitively, the definition in [10,11] restricts the relaxation of an almost-empty Queue, making it behave as if it had smaller relaxation parameters. For this reason, we use the previous definitions, which do allow erroneous empty indicators, which leads to consensus number 1 for certain relaxations, such as *OQueue*[$*, *, \emptyset$], where [10,11] had consensus number 2.

In the future, this work should be expanded to other data types. Stacks, which are a natural extension, are less interesting, as even a *Stack*[1, 1, 1] has consensus number 2, so all relaxations of these types will have consensus number 1 or 2. The generalization of relaxations is still not well understood. [5] gives an abstract specification, but it is not always obvious how this applies to data types beyond Stacks, Queues, and a few others. We wish to explore this space, generalizing relaxations and the data types which we know how to relax.

Acknowledgement. This work was supported in part by NSF grant 1526725.

References

1. Afek, Y., Korland, G., Yanovsky, E.: Quasi-linearizability: relaxed consistency for improved concurrency. In: Lu, C., Masuzawa, T., Mosbah, M. (eds.) OPODIS 2010. LNCS, vol. 6490, pp. 395–410. Springer, Heidelberg (2010). doi:10.1007/978-3-642-17653-1_29
2. Attiya, H., Welch, J.L.: Sequential consistency versus linearizability. ACM Trans. Comput. Syst. **12**(2), 91–122 (1994)
3. Chen, W., Guangda, H., Zhang, J.: On the power of breakable objects. Theor. Comput. Sci. **503**, 89–108 (2013)
4. Fischer, M.J., Lynch, N.A., Paterson, M.: Impossibility of distributed consensus with one faulty process. J. ACM **32**(2), 374–382 (1985)
5. Henzinger, T.A., Kirsch, C.M., Payer, H., Sezgin, A., Sokolova, A.: Quantitative relaxation of concurrent data structures. In: Giacobazzi, R., Cousot, R. (eds.) The 40th Annual ACM SIGPLAN-SIGACT Symposium on Principles of Programming Languages, POPL 2013, Rome, Italy, 23–25 January 2013, pp. 317–328. ACM (2013)
6. Herlihy, M.: Wait-free synchronization. ACM Trans. Program. Lang. Syst. **13**(1), 124–149 (1991)
7. Kosa, M.J.: Time bounds for strong and hybrid consistency for arbitrary abstract data types. Chicago J. Theor. Comput. Sci. (1999)
8. Lipton, R.J., Sandberg, J.S.: PRAM: a scalable shared memory. Technical report CS-TR 180-88, Princeton University, Department of Computer Science, September 1988
9. Lo, W.-K., Hadzilacos, V.: All of us are smarter than any of us: nondeterministic wait-free hierarchies are not robust. SIAM J. Comput. **30**(3), 689–728 (2000)
10. Shavit, N., Taubenfeld, G.: The computability of relaxed data structures: queues and stacks as examples. In: Scheideler, C. (ed.) Structural Information and Communication Complexity. LNCS, vol. 9439, pp. 414–428. Springer, Cham (2015). doi:10.1007/978-3-319-25258-2_29
11. Shavit, N., Taubenfeld, G.: The computability of relaxed data structures: queues and stacks as examples. Distrib. Comput. **29**(5), 395–407 (2016)
12. Talmage, E., Welch, J.L.: Improving average performance by relaxing distributed data structures. In: Kuhn, F. (ed.) DISC 2014. LNCS, vol. 8784, pp. 421–438. Springer, Heidelberg (2014). doi:10.1007/978-3-662-45174-8_29
13. Talmage, E., Welch, J.L.: Generic proofs of consensus numbers for abstract data types. In: Anceaume, E., Cachin, C., Potop-Butucaru, M.G. (eds.) 19th International Conference on Principles of Distributed Systems, OPODIS 2015, 14–17 December 2015, Rennes, France. LIPIcs, vol. 46, pp. 32:1–32:16. Schloss Dagstuhl - Leibniz-Zentrum fuer Informatik (2015)
14. Wang, J., Talmage, E., Lee, H., Welch, J.L.: Improved time bounds for linearizable implementations of abstract data types. In: 2014 IEEE 28th International Parallel and Distributed Processing Symposium, Phoenix, AZ, USA, 19–23 May 2014, pp. 691–701. IEEE Computer Society (2014)

Early Decision and Stopping in Synchronous Consensus: A Predicate-Based Guided Tour

Armando Castañeda[1], Yoram Moses[2], Michel Raynal[3,4], and Matthieu Roy[5(✉)]

[1] Instituto de Matemáticas, UNAM, Mexico City, Mexico
[2] Technion, Haifa, Israel
[3] Institut Universitaire de France, Paris, France
[4] IRISA, Université de Rennes, Rennes, France
[5] LAAS, CNRS, Université de Toulouse, Toulouse, France
roy@laas.fr

Abstract. Consensus is the most basic agreement problem encountered in fault-tolerant distributed computing: each process proposes a value and non-faulty processes must agree on the same value, which has to be one of the proposed values. While this problem is impossible to solve in asynchronous systems prone to process crash failures, it can be solved in synchronous (round-based) systems where all but one process might crash in any execution. It is well-known that $(t+1)$ rounds are necessary and sufficient in the worst case execution scenario for the processes to decide and stop executing, where $t < n$ is a system parameter denoting the maximum number of allowed process crashes and n denotes the number of processes in the system.

Early decision and stopping considers the case where $f < t$ processes actually crash, f not being known by processes. It has been shown that the number of rounds that have to be executed in the worst case is then $\min(f+2, t+1)$. Following Castañeda, Gonczarowski and Moses (DISC 2014), the paper shows that this value is an upper bound attained only in worst execution scenarios. To this end, it investigates a sequence of three early deciding/stopping predicates $P_1 = P_{\text{count}}$, $P_2 = P_{\text{dif}}$ and $P_3 = P_{\text{pref0}}$, of increasing power, which differ in the information obtained by the processes from the actual failure, communication and data pattern. It is shown that each predicate P_i is better than the previous one P_{i-1}, $i \in \{2, 3\}$, in the sense that there are executions where P_i allows processes to reach a decision earlier than P_{i-1}, while P_{i-1} never allows a process to decide earlier than P_i. Moreover, $P_3 = P_{\text{pref0}}$ is an *unbeatable* predicate in the sense that it cannot be strictly improved: if there is an early deciding/stopping predicate P' that improves the decision time of a process with respect to P_{pref0} in a given execution, then there is at least one execution in which a process decides with P' strictly later than with P_{pref0}.

Keywords: Agreement · Consensus · Early decision · Early stopping · Process crash · Round-based algorithm · Synchronous message-passing system · t-Resilience

© Springer International Publishing AG 2017
A. El Abbadi and B. Garbinato (Eds.): NETYS 2017, LNCS 10299, pp. 206–221, 2017.
DOI: 10.1007/978-3-319-59647-1_16

1   Introduction

1.1 t-Resilient Crash-Prone Synchronous System

This paper considers a distributed system with n processes, among which at most t may crash, $1 \leq t < n$. Hence, n and t are two system model parameters that are statically defined and known when designing an algorithm. A crash is a premature halt: a process behaves correctly, executing the algorithm assigned to it, until it possibly crashes. After a crash, a process executes no more actions. A process that does not crash in a given execution is said to be *correct* or *non-faulty* there, otherwise it is *faulty*. Moreover, given an execution, let f, with $0 \leq f \leq t$, denote the number of processes that actually crash in this execution. Notice that while n and t are two parameters (of the system model) that can be used in an algorithm executed by processes, f is specific to each execution and cannot be known in advance, and consequently no process knows its value.

The processes communicate by broadcasting and receiving messages. If a process does not crash while executing a broadcast, the message is received by all processes, including itself. If it crashes while executing a broadcast, an arbitrary subset of processes (not predetermined and possibly empty) receive the message (without alteration). Hence, a broadcast operation is not atomic.

The processes execute collectively a sequence of synchronous rounds. In each *round* a process first broadcasts a message, then receives messages, and finally executes a local computation whose inputs are its current local state and the messages it has received during the current round. The *synchrony* model assumption states that a message is received in the very same round as the round in which it is sent. Hence, synchrony means that the processes progress in a lock-step manner.

An *distributed algorithm* (or *protocol*) is made of a collection of local algorithms, one per process. Each local algorithm indicates messages to be sent by the corresponding process at each round. Sometimes it is convenient to consider *full-information* algorithms where in every round, each process broadcasts all it knows so far. Full-information algorithms are not meant to be efficient — messages may contain unnecessary information— but are easy to describe and useful to prove lower bounds on step complexity: any information transfer scheme used by another algorithm is contained in the full information transfer scheme.

1.2   The Consensus Problem

The *consensus* problem was introduced in the Eighties by Lamport, Shostack, and Pease in the context of synchronous message-passing systems prone to Byzantine (arbitrary) failures [14,16]. Here we consider the case of process crash failures [11].

Each process is assumed to propose a value, and the processes have to agree on the same value. Of course, a process may crash before proposing a value, or before deciding a value. For the problem to be meaningful, the decided value must be related to the proposed values. This is captured by the following properties, which constitute a specification of the consensus problem (hence, any algorithm that claims to solve the problem must satisfy these properties).

- Termination. Every correct process decides on a value.
- Validity. A decided value is a proposed value.
- Agreement. No two (correct or faulty) processes decide different values.

1.3 Bounds on the Number of Rounds

The bound $(t + 1)$. It is shown in [1,10] that $(t + 1)$ rounds are necessary and sufficient to solve consensus in a synchronous system prone to up to $t < n$ process crash failures. An intuition that underlies this bound is the following. A "worst case" scenario is when there is a crash per round, which prevents processes from knowing the state of the system at the beginning of the round. But if $(t + 1)$ rounds are executed, there is a failure-free round (a.k.a. *clean* round [7]) during which all the correct processes can exchange and obtain proposed values, from which a value can be deterministically extracted to be decided.

The bound $\min(f + 2, t + 1)$. As t is known by the processes while $f \leq n$ is not, an interesting question is the following: is it possible to solve the consensus problem in crash-prone synchronous systems in fewer than $(t + 1)$ rounds when the number of actual crashes f is smaller than t? This question is known as the *early deciding/stopping*, problem [6]. In early stopping, a process stops executing when it decides; In early deciding, a process can continue executing rounds after it has decided. Here, we consider early deciding/stopping algorithms, i.e., algorithms were a process stops executing in the same round as the one in which it decides.

In other words, can we adapt the efficiency of a consensus algorithm to the actual value of f, instead of always having the "$(t + 1)$ rounds" cost? Thus, the main target in early deciding/stopping algorithms is to allow at least one process to detect as soon as possible a predicate on the execution, e.g., a failure-free round, which will allow it to safely decide and stop.

It is shown in [2,6,13,18,22] that $\min(f + 2, t + 1)$ is a necessary and sufficient condition for early deciding/stopping consensus. Interestingly, this bound is independent of the failure model, be it crash failure, omission failure, or Byzantine failure. An intuition for the $(f + 2)$ bound is the following. As there are only f failures in the considered execution, after $(f + 1)$ rounds there is at least one process that executed a round in which it saw no failures. Thereby, this process knows which value can be decided, but, as $f \neq t$, it does not know if the other processes are aware of it. Hence, it needs an additional round to inform the other processes of this knowledge before deciding.

1.4 Content of the Paper

In the following we are interested in predicates that, not only match the lower bound of $\min(f + 2, t + 1)$ rounds for reaching consensus in worst case scenarios, but allow processes to reach a decision in much fewer rounds in a lot of frequent cases, such as when there are initial crashes, or when several processes crash during the very same round.

These predicates are denoted P_{count}, P_{dif}, and P_{prefo}. We investigate their respective power to solve early deciding/stopping binary consensus[1] and consider those predicates in sequence $P_1 = P_{count}$, $P_2 = P_{dif}$ and $P_3 = P_{prefo}$. We show that each predicate in the sequence P_i ($i \in \{2, 3\}$) is better than the previous one P_{i-1}: there are executions in which P_i allows processes to reach a decision earlier than P_{i-1}, while P_{i-1} never allows processes to reach a decision earlier than P_i.

To go further, we consider the notion of *unbeatability* [12] (initially called *optimality*), that has been introduced to formally compare the decision-time performance of algorithms. For binary consensus, P_{prefo} is an *unbeatable* predicate in the sense that it cannot be strictly improved: if there is an early deciding/stopping predicate that improves the decision time of a process for binary consensus in a given execution, then there is an execution in which a process decides strictly later than by P_{prefo}. Thus, in principle, there are predicates that can improve the decision time of a process in an execution at the cost of deciding/stopping strictly later in another case.

2   The Three Early Deciding/Stopping Predicates

2.1 P_{count} (P_1): a Predicate Based on the Counting of Crashed Processes

Let us observe that "to be crashed" is a stable property, i.e., after it crashed, a process never recovers. A crash is a premature halt. This observation can be used to detect process crashes, by requiring each process to broadcast a message at every round, until it decides or crashes. Hence, if r is the first round during which p_i does not receive a message from p_j, and p_i has not yet received a decision message from p_j, then p_i can safely conclude that p_j crashed.

Let $faulty_i[r]$ be the number of processes that p_i considers faulty after the reception of messages during round r, i.e., the number of processes from which it did not receive a message during r. A simple early decision predicate used by p_i at round r is $P_1 = P_{count}$:

$$P_{count}[i, r] \equiv \left(faulty_i[r] < r\right).$$

This predicate (used in [17]) specifically targets the worst case scenario: it allows a process p_i to detect the first round in which, from its point of view, there is no crash. Let r be the first round such that $P_{count}[i, r]$ is true. This means that (a) for any round $r' < r$ we have $faulty_i[r'] \geq r'$, and (b) r is a failure-free round from p_i point of view. Those properties will be exploited to obtain a P_{count}-based early stopping consensus algorithm, that we describe in Sect. 3.3.

---

[1] While P_{prefo} is specific to binary consensus, P_{count} and P_{dif} can be used for multivalued consensus (where the size of the proposed value is not restricted to be only one bit). However, the predicate can be modified to handle multivalued consensus.

2.2 P_{Dif} (P_2): a Round-based Differential Predicate

A second early stopping predicate, introduced in [19], is a differential predicate, in the sense that it is based on each pair of consecutive rounds (the current and the previous rounds). It requires that each process broadcasts a message until it decides or crashes, and each message m indicates if its sender is about to decide after having broadcast m.

Let $UP[r]$ be the set of processes that start round r, i.e., the set of alive processes when round r starts. Let $rec_i[r]$ be the set of processes from which p_i receives messages during round $r > 0$, and $rec_i[0]$ be the set of n processes. Let us notice that, while it executes round r, no process knows the value of $UP[r]$, but each p_i can easily compute the value of $rec_i[r-1]$ and $rec_i[r]$. Moreover, as crashes are "stable", p_i knows that $rec_i[r-1] \subseteq UP[r] \subseteq rec_i[r]$. The early deciding/stopping predicate $P_2 = P_{\text{dif}}$ is then

$$P_{\text{dif}}[i,r] \equiv (rec_i[r-1] = rec_i[r]).$$

As shown in Fig. 1, the fact that $P_{\text{dif}}[i,r]$ holds does not mean that there is no crash during round r. A cross means that the corresponding process crashed during its broadcast phase, sending a message to a single process only.

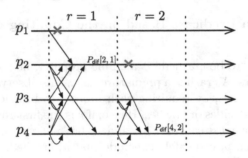

Fig. 1. An execution illustrating P_{dif}. Crosses denote crashes, $P_{\text{dif}}[i,j]$ indicates when P_{dif} holds.

When $P_{\text{dif}}[i,r]$ becomes satisfied, p_i received a message from all the processes that were alive at the beginning of round r. Due to the message exchange pattern, it can know all values known by these processes from the first round until the previous round $(r-1)$. Consequently, it will never know new values in the future. It follows that it can deterministically decide value among all values it know (smallest or greatest one, for example).

It is possible that $rec_i[r-1] = rec_i[r]$ while there is a process p_j such that $rec_j[r-1] \neq rec_j[r]$. As a simple example, let us consider again Fig. 1 and assume that $v_1 < \min(v_2, v_3, v_4)$ (v_i being the value proposed by p_i). During round 1, p_1 sent v_1 to p_2 only before crashing, and then, during round 2, p_2 sent v_1 to p_4 only before crashing. It follows that, while p_4 can decide v_1, no other (not crashed) process knows v_1. This issue is solved as follows: when $P_{dif}[4, r]$ becomes satisfied, p_4 does not decide and stop during round r, but proceeds to round $(r + 1)$ during which it broadcasts v_1 plus a flag indicating it is about to decide and stop, which it does only after the broadcast is completed.

2.3 P_{Pref0} (P_3): A Knowledge-Based Unbeatable Predicate

The predicate P_{pref0}, introduced in [3], allows processes to decide as soon as possible on a preferred value, 0 in this case, while the other value 1 is decided only when the process is sure that no process decides on the preferred value 0. The predicate is expressed in the knowledge-based approach in distributed computing, in the spirit of [9]. This approach leads us to understand, in a precise sense, the information needed for a process to decide as fast as possible.

Roughly speaking, a process p_i *knows* a statement A if in every execution which is *indistinguishable* from the point of view of p_i (i.e., in which p_i has the same local view), A is true. For example, if p_i receives a message with an input 0, it knows the statement "there is a 0 in the system".

Assuming that processes want to decide as soon as possible, preferring value 0, there are two cases:

- When is it safe for a process to decide on 0? As soon as the process knows that every correct process knows that there is a 0 in the system, i.e., each correct process has received in some round a message communicating that someone started with input 0.
- When is it safe for a process to decide on 1? Since processes decide 0 as soon as possible, the process can safely decide on 1 as soon as the process knows that there is no 0 in the system, namely, no active process got a message containing a 0. Thus, no process will ever know there is a 0.

This is formalized as follows. In an execution, we say that p_j is *revealed* to p_i in round r if either p_i knows the information p_j has at the beginning of round r or it knows that p_j is crashed before that round. As a consequence, p_j cannot carry information in round r that is hidden to p_i because, in the first case, p_i knows the information p_j knows, while in the second case, p_j crashed before (hence it is not active in round r). A round r is *revealed* to p_i if every process p_j is revealed to p_i in round r. Therefore, when r is revealed to p_i, the process knows all the information than went through the system from round $r - 1$ to r.

The predicate P_{pref0} is based on the following sub-predicates. Let $\exists$ correct_0(i, r) denote the predicate: "p_i knows that at least one correct process knows in round r that there is a 0" and let $\exists$ revealed(i, r) denote the predicate: "a round $r' \leq r$ has been revealed to p_i". The early deciding/stopping predicate $P_3 = P_{pref0}$ is defined as [3]:

$$P_{pref0}[i, r] \equiv \exists \text{ correct\_0}(i, r) \vee \exists \text{ revealed}(i, r).$$

We stress that if $\exists$ correct_0(i, r) holds, then, at the end of round $r + 1$, *every* correct process will know that there is a 0: the correct process knowing a 0 (whose existence is guaranteed by $\exists\,\mathsf{correct\_0}(i, r)$) will have communicated this value to every correct process.

The way each sub-predicate of $P_{\mathsf{prefo}}[i, r]$ is made operational will be detailed in Sect. 3.3, where a P_{prefo}-based algorithm is presented. To give a flavor of it, we consider below two executions, each one satisfying one sub-predicate of P_{prefo}.

- The simplest case is when a process p_i starts with input 0, then broadcasts this value to every process in round 1, and finally receives the messages sent to it in this round. At the end of the round, since p_i succinctly communicates 0 to every process, the predicate $\exists\,\mathsf{correct\_0}(i, 1)$ is satisfied. Hence, using P_{prefo}, a process can decide on 0 at the end of round 1, even in presence of failures. In the execution there might be another process p_j such that $P_{\mathsf{prefo}}[j, 1]$ is not true. This can happen if p_j starts the execution with input 1 and sees failures in round 1, and hence it does not decide in this round. However, p_j is prevented from deciding 1 because it knows there is a 0 in the system (as it gets the message from p_i in round 1 containing a 0). While our example involved round 1, the same holds for an arbitrary round r: if a process broadcasts a 0 in round r and does not crash in this round, the condition $\exists\,\mathsf{correct\_0}(i, r)$ holds at the end of round r.
- A second example is shown in Fig. 2 where every process starts with input 1. In round 1, process p_4 gets messages from every process but p_1, hence, by the end of the round, p_4 has uncertainty on the input of p_1 and the fact that this input may be known by some other process. In the example, before crashing, p_1 sends its message to p_3, and in round 2, p_4 gets a message from p_3 but not from p_2. Although p_4 sees a failure in round 2, it knows all inputs from all processes since p_4 gets indirectly the input of p_1 from the message of p_3 in round 2 (assuming full-information algorithms). Thus, round 1 is revealed to p_4 during round 2, namely, the sub-predicate $\exists\,\mathsf{revealed}(4, 2)$ is satisfied, and thus p_4 can safely decide on 1, regardless of the fact that it sees failures in both rounds.

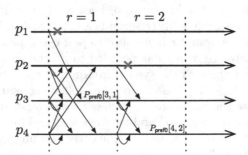

Fig. 2. An illustration of P_{prefo}. Crosses denote crashes, $P_{\mathsf{prefo}}[i, j]$ indicates when P_{prefo} holds.

3 Consensus Algorithms Based on the Predicates

For ease of exposition, an algorithm based on $P_2 = P_{\mathsf{dif}}$ is first presented, and only then it is shown that a simple replacement of the predicate $P_2 = P_{\mathsf{dif}}$ by $P_1 = P_{\mathsf{count}}$ produces an algorithm based on $P_1 = P_{\mathsf{count}}$. The algorithm based on $P_3 = P_{\mathsf{pref0}}$ is described at the end of the section.

3.1 An Algorithm Based on P_{Dif} (P_2)

An early deciding/stopping consensus algorithm based on P_{dif} is described in Fig. 3. The variable r denotes the current round number, whose progress is automatically ensured by the underlying system (synchrony assumption of the distributed computing model). When the consensus algorithm starts (round 1), each process locally invokes the operation propose(v_i) where v_i is the value it proposes to the consensus instance. If it does not crash before, it terminates when it executes the statement return(v) where v is the value it decides.

Local variables. A process p_i manages three local variables.

- est_i is p_i's current estimate of the decided value. It is initialized to v_i.
- $nb_i[r]$ is the number of processes from which p_i received messages during round r. By assumption $nb_i[0] = n$. As crashes are stable, rec_i can only decrease. It follows that the predicate $rec_i[r-1] = rec_i[r]$ can be replaced by $nb_i[r-1] = nb_i[r]$.
- $early_i$ is a Boolean initialized to false. It is set to true when p_i discovers that it can early decide at the next round.

Local algorithm. During a round r, a process p_i first broadcasts a message carrying its current estimate est_i and the Boolean $early_i$ (line 4). If $early_i =$ true, p_i early decides by executing the statement return(est_i) which stops its execution (line 4). Let us notice that if p_i decides at round r, at each round $r' \leq r$, it broadcasts the smallest value it has seen up to round r'.

If p_i does not decide, it checks if another process early decides (line 5) during this round, and updates est_i according to the estimates received during the current round (line 6). Then, if its early deciding/stopping predicate is true, or if it learns another process early decides, it sets $early_i$ to true (line 8). Finally, if $r < t + 1$, p_i proceeds to the next round. Otherwise, it returns its current estimate value.

The proof of the Termination property follows directly from the synchrony assumption provided by the computing model. The proof of the Validity property follows from the observation that the est_i local variables can only contain proposed values (lines 1 and 6). The proof of the Agreement property is given in [19]. Let us notice that, in the executions where no process decides at line 4, the algorithm boils down to the very classical synchronous consensus algorithm described and proved in several textbooks (e.g., [17,19,20]). We prove in the following only the early decision property.

```
operation propose(v_i) is
(1)    est_i ← v_i; nb_i[0] ← n; early_i ← false;
(2)    when r = 1, 2, ..., t + 1 do
       begin synchronous round
(3)        broadcast EST(est_i, early_i);
(4)        if (early_i) then return(est_i) end if;
(5)        let decide_i ← ⋁(early_j values received during current round r);
(6)        est_i ← min({est_j values received during current round r});
(7)        let nb_i[r] = number of messages received by p_i during r;
(8)        if ((nb_i[r − 1] = nb_i[r]) ∨ decide_i) then early_i ← true end if;
(9)        if (r = t + 1) then return(est_i) end if
       end synchronous round
end operation.
```

Fig. 3. P_{dif}-based early deciding/stopping synchronous consensus (code for p_i, $t < n$)

Theorem 1. *When considering the P_{dif}-based early deciding/stopping synchronous consensus algorithm, no process executes more than* $\min(f+2, t+1)$ *rounds.*

Proof. The $(t+1)$ bound follows directly from the predicate of line 9. So let us assume that a process p_i decides at line 4 of a round d. There are two cases.

- There is a process p_i that decides at line 4 of round $d \le f + 1$. Hence, it previously broadcast the message $\text{EST}(est_i, early_i)$ at line 3, and all non-crashed processes receive this message during round d. Let p_j be any of them. If p_j does not early decide during round d, it sets $early_j$ to true during round d (lines 5 and 8). It follows that, if it does not crash, it will decide during the next round $d + 1 \le f + 2$.
- No process decides at line 4 of a round $d \le f + 1$. Let p_i be any process that executes round $f + 1$. As it did not decide by the end of the round $f + 1$, we have $nb_i[r − 1] \ne nb_i[r]$ at any round r, $1 \le r \le f$. As there are exactly f crashes, this means that we necessarily have $nb_i[0] = n$, $nb_i[1] = n − 1$, ..., $nb_i[f − 1] = n − (f − 1)$, and $nb_i[f] = n − f$ (there is one crash per round and the process that crashed did not send a message to p_i). Moreover, as there are f crashes, we have $nb_i[f + 1] = n − f$. It follows that $nb_i[f] = nb_i[f + 1]$ at round $f + 1$, and p_i sets $early_i$ to true at line 8. Hence, p_i (which is any process that executes the rounds $f + 1$ and $f + 2$) early decides at line 4 of round $d \le f + 2$, which concludes the proof.

$\square_{Theorem\ 1}$

3.2 An Algorithm Based on P_{Count} (P_1)

Let us remark that $faulty_i[r] = n − nb_i[r]$. An algorithm based on P_{count} can be easily obtained from Fig. 3 by replacing at line 8 the predicate $(nb_i[r−1] = nb_i[r])$ by the predicate $P_{\text{count}}[i, r] \equiv (n − nb_i[r] < r)$. The correctness proof and the bounds on the decision times of process can be proven similarly as before.

Theorem 2. *When considering the P_{count}-based early deciding/stopping synchronous consensus algorithm, no process executes more than $\min(f + 2, t + 1)$ rounds.*

3.3   An Algorithm Based on P_{Pref0} (P_3)

Figure 3 contains the early deciding/stopping consensus algorithm based on P_{prefo}, introduced in [3]. The processes proceed in a sequence of synchronous rounds (the variable r denotes the current round). As before, when the consensus starts, all processes simultaneously invoke the operation **propose** with the values they propose to the consensus instance.

Local variables. Each process p_i uses the following local variables.

- $vals_i$: set of values p_i is aware of. The set it is initialized to $\{v_i\}$ as, at the beginning of the execution, p_i knows its input only.
- G_i: directed graph containing p_i's *view* in the current round, namely, the chain of messages that has been sent to p_i so far. Initially, it has a single node $\langle i, 0 \rangle$ denoting that p_i is not aware of any message before round 1. This graph is formally defined below. $V(G_i)$ denotes the vertices of G_i, and $E(G_i)$ denotes its edges.
- $knew\_0_i$. Boolean indicating if p_i knows there was a zero in the previous round, namely, $vals_i$ contained a zero by the end of the previous round.
- $correct\_0_i$: Boolean indicating if the predicate $\exists \, correct\_0(i, r)$ is satisfied in the current round r.
- $revealed_i$: Boolean indicating if the predicate $\exists \, revealed\_0(i, r)$ is satisfied in the current round r.
- $early_i$: Boolean indicating if p_i discovers that it can decide at the next round.

Local algorithm. At the beginning of every round, p_i first broadcasts its set of known values, $vals_i$, together with its view graph, G_i (i.e. it communicates all it knows so far) and then checks if it can decide early, namely, $early_i = \text{true}$. If so, it simply decides 0, otherwise, it updates its local variables, lines 5–9, in order to test the predicate $P_{prefo}[i, r] \equiv \exists \, correct\_0(i, r) \lor \exists \, revealed(i, r)$, lines 10–14.

Before receiving the messages sent to it in the current round, p_i sets $knew\_0_i$ to **true** if, at the end of the previous round, p_i was aware that there was a zero in the system, line 5. Then, p_i updates its set of known values $vals_i$, line 6, and records in n_0_i and n_f_i the number of messages from the current round containing a zero and the number of processes it does not receive a message from in the current round, lines 7 and 8.

To explain how p_i updates its view graph G_i, let us consider the *communication graph* G_c of an execution of a full-information algorithm. Intuitively, the communication graph G_c is the directed graph that represents how communication and failures occur in a given execution. Formally, each vertex of the graph has the form $\langle i, r \rangle$, representing p_i at the beginning of round $r + 1$ (hence the vertex also represents p_i at the end of round r), and there is a directed edge

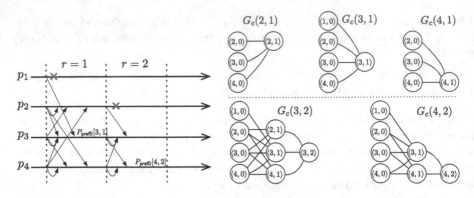

Fig. 4. Local views of the communication graph of the execution from Fig. 2

$(\langle j,r\rangle, \langle i,r+1\rangle)$ if process p_j sends a message to p_i in round $r+1$. The *view* of p_i at the end of round r, denoted $G_c(i,r)$, is the subgraph of G_c containing every directed path that ends at $\langle i,r\rangle$. Notice that $G_c(i,r)$ contains all Lamport message chains from all processes in previous rounds to p_i at round r. Roughly speaking, $G_c(i,r)$ contains the maximal amount of information p_i has (directly or indirectly heard of up to round r. Figure 4 provides, as an illustration, the views of processes of the communication graph, computed for the execution of Fig. 2.

In the algorithm, p_i computes its view graph inductively as rounds go by. The main invariant in this construction is that at the beginning of round r, the local variable G_i is equal to $G_c(i,r-1)$ (which holds for $r=1$ by the initialization of G_i). Then, at the end of round r, G_i is equal to $G_c(i,r)$ because, in line 9, p_i adds to G_i the edges due to (a) the messages it receives in round r, and (b) the view graphs of round $r-1$ carried by those messages.

Once p_i handles all messages and updates its local variables, it verifies if $P_{\mathsf{prefo}}[i,r]$ is satisfied by separately testing the sub-predicates $\exists\,\mathsf{correct\_0}(i,r)$ and $\exists\,\mathsf{revealed\_0}(i,r)$, lines 10 and 11.

If the condition in line 10 is true, there are two not necessarily mutually exclusive subcases. If $knew\_0_i = \mathtt{true}$, then p_i knew there was a zero at the end of the previous round, hence, in the current round, it broadcasts that zero to all correct processes. And if $t - n\_f_i \le n\_0_i$, then at least $t - n\_f_i + 1$ processes know there is a zero at the current round (where the $+1$ is because p_i itself knows there is a zero), from which follows that at least one correct process knows there is a zero, since at most another $t - n\_f_i$ processes can crash. In both cases, $\exists\,\mathsf{correct\_0}(i,r)$ is satisfied, hence $correct\_0_i$ is set accordingly.

To test if $\exists\,\mathsf{revealed\_0}(i,r)$ is satisfied, line 11, p_i directly verifies on G_i if a round is revealed to p_i: for some $r' \le r$, for each p_j, either (a) there is a chain of messages from $\langle j,r'\rangle$ (p_j at the beginning of round $r'+1$) to $\langle i,r\rangle$ (p_i at the end of round r), i.e. $\langle j,r'\rangle \in V(G_i)$, or (b) there is a $\langle \ell,r'\rangle \in V(G_i)$ with $(\langle j,r'-1\rangle, \langle \ell,r'\rangle) \notin E(G_i)$ (i.e. p_ℓ did not receive a message from p_j in round r'). If so, the round $r'+1$ is revealed to p_i, and thus $\exists\,\mathsf{revealed\_0}(i,r)$ is satisfied.

```
operation propose(v_i) is
(1)  vals_i ← {v_i}; G_i ← ({⟨i, 0⟩}, ∅);
     early_i, knew_0_i, correct_0_i, revealed_i ← false;
(2)  when r = 1, 2, ..., t + 1 do
     begin synchronous round
(3)    broadcast MSG_CONS(vals_i, G_i);
(4)    if (early_i) then return(0) end if;
(5)    if (0 ∈ vals_i) then knew_0_i ← true end if;
(6)    vals_i ← ⋃(vals_j values received during round r);
(7)    let n_0_i = number of messages received in round r with 0 ∈ vals_j;
(8)    let n_f_i = number of processes from which no message was received in round r;
(9)    G_i ← ⋃(G_j graphs received during round r and directed edges (⟨j, r⟩, ⟨i, r + 1⟩));
       %% Testing ∃ correct_0(i, r)
(10)   if (0 ∈ vals_i ∧ (knew_0_i ∨ (t − n_f_i ≤ n_0_i)))
           then correct_0_i ← true end if;
       %% Testing ∃ revealed(i, r)
(11)   if (∃r' ≤ r, ∀p_j, ((⟨j, r'⟩ ∈ V(G_i)) ∨ (∃⟨ℓ, r'⟩ ∈ V(G_i), (⟨j, r' − 1⟩, ⟨ℓ, r'⟩) ∉ E(G_i))))
           then revealed_i ← true end if;
       %% Testing P_prefo[i, r]
(12)   if (correct_0_i) then return(0) end if;
(13)   if (revealed_i ∧ 0 ∉ vals_i) then return(1) end if;
(14)   if (revealed_i ∧ 0 ∈ vals_i) then early_i ← true end if
     end synchronous round
end operation.
```

Fig. 5. P_{prefo}-based early deciding/stopping synchronous consensus (code for p_i, $t < n$)

Finally, p_i verifies if it can decide. If $correct\_0_i = \text{true}$, then all correct processes know there is a zero and hence p_i can safely decide 0, line 12. If $revealed_i = \text{true} \land 0 \notin vals_i$, then a round has been revealed to p_i and there is no zero in the system (as $0 \notin vals_i$), hence it is safe for p_i to decide 1, line 13. However, if $revealed_i = \text{true} \land 0 \in vals_i$, then there might be a correct process that knows a zero (but p_i does not know that fact as $correct\_0_i = \text{false}$), hence it cannot decide 1 but sets $early_i$ to true, indicating that it can decide at the very next round. Observe that after p_i broadcasts its message in the next round, $\exists correct\_0(i, r)$ is satisfied as it knew there was a zero and consequently sent its message to everyone, and thus it decides 0 in line 4.

The correctness proof of the algorithm is shown in [3]. The validity and termination properties are easy to prove. For agreement, the main observation is that the only way a process decides on 1 is if it is sure that no process ever will know there is a 0 (as it knows there is no 0 and a round has been revealed to it), hence no process will ever decide 0.

The decision time bound in the following theorem follows directly from Theorem 1 above and Theorem 4 in the next section comparing the predicates and showing that at any time that $P_{\text{dif}}[i, r]$ is satisfied, $P_{\text{prefo}}[i, r]$ is satisfied as well.

Theorem 3. *When considering the P_{prefo}-based early deciding/stopping synchronous consensus algorithm, no process executes more than $\min(f+2, t+1)$ rounds.*

4 Comparing the Predicates

While the three predicates presented above ensure that the processes decide in at most $\min(f+2, t+1)$ rounds in the worst cases, is one predicate better than the other?

We show here that, in a precise sense, $P_3 = P_{\mathrm{prefo}}$ is the strongest predicate for early deciding/stopping binary consensus, and $P_2 = P_{\mathrm{dif}}$ is strictly stronger than $P_1 = P_{\mathrm{count}}$, resulting in the above mentioned strict hierarchy in the sequence P_1, P_2, P_3.

Theorem 4. *Consider the predicates $P_{\mathrm{count}}[i, r]$, $P_{\mathrm{dif}}[i, r]$ and $P_{\mathrm{prefo}}[i, r]$.*

(a) *Given an execution, let r be the first round at which $P_{\mathrm{dif}}[i, r]$ is satisfied. We have $P_{\mathrm{count}}[i, r] \Rightarrow P_{\mathrm{dif}}[i, r]$.*

(b) *Given an execution, let r be the first round at which $P_{\mathrm{prefo}}[i, r]$ is satisfied. We have $P_{\mathrm{dif}}[i, r] \Rightarrow P_{\mathrm{predo}}[i, r]$.*

(c) *There are executions in which $\neg(P_{\mathrm{dif}}[i, r] \Rightarrow P_{\mathrm{count}}[i, r])$, where r is the first round at which $P_{\mathrm{dif}}[i, r]$ is satisfied.*

(d) *There are executions in which $\neg(P_{\mathrm{prefo}}[i, r] \Rightarrow P_{\mathrm{dif}}[i, r])$, where r is the first round at which $P_{\mathrm{prefo}}[i, r]$ is satisfied.*

Proof. Each case is handled separately.

Proof of item (a). As r is the first round during which $P_{\mathrm{count}}[i, r] \equiv (n - nb_i[r] < r)$ is satisfied, $P_{\mathrm{count}}[i, r-1]$ is false, i.e., $n - nb_i[r-1] \geq r-1$. It follows from these inequalities that $(n - nb_i[r]) - (n - nb_i[r-1]) < r - (r-1) = 1$. Combined with the fact that $nb_i[r] \geq nb_i[r]$, we obtain $nb_i[r] - nb_i[r-1] = 0$ which concludes the proof of item (a).

Proof of item (b). Since $P_{\mathrm{dif}}[i, r]$ is satisfied, we have that $nb_i[r-1] = nb_i[r]$. Therefore, in round r, p_i receives a message from any process p_j that sends a message to p_i in round $r-1$. Moreover, p_i knows for sure that all other processes crash before round r simply because it does not get any message from them in round $r-1$. We conclude that round r is revealed to p_i, from which follows that $P_{\mathrm{prefo}}[i, r]$ is satisfied (as $\exists\,\mathrm{revealed}(i, r)$ is true).

Proof of item (c). The proof follows from a counter-example. Consider a run in which $2 \leq x \leq t$ processes have crashed before taking any step, and then no other process crashes. The predicate $P_{\mathrm{count}}[i, r] \equiv (n - nb_i[r] < r)$ becomes true for the first time at round $x + 1$. Let us now look at the predicate $P_{\mathrm{dif}}[i, r] \equiv (nb_i[r-1] = nb_i[r])$. We have, $nb_i[1] = nb_i[2] = n - x$. Consequently, $P_{\mathrm{dif}}[i, 2]$ is satisfied. As $x \geq 2$, it follows that $\neg P_{\mathrm{count}}[i, 2] \wedge P_{\mathrm{dif}}[i, 2]$, which concludes the proof.

Proof of item (d). Consider any execution in which (1) all processes start with input 0, (2) p_n crashes without communicating its input to any process, and (3) all other processes are correct. Then, for every process p_i, $1 \leq i \leq n - 1$, $\exists$ revealed$(i, 1)$ is true, as p_i starts with 0 and communicates it to every one. Thus, $P_{\mathsf{prefo}}[i, 1]$ is satisfied. In contrast, $P_{\mathsf{dif}}[i, r]$ is not satisfied because p_i does not receive a message from p_n, and hence $nb_i[0] = n \wedge nb_i[1] = n - 1$. $\square_{Theorem\ 4}$

Operational view. The fact that $P_{\mathsf{dif}}[i, r]$ is better than $P_{\mathsf{count}}[i, r]$ comes from the following. The predicate $P_{\mathsf{count}}[i, r] \equiv (n - nb_i[r] < r)$ considers the number of crashes since the beginning, while $P_{\mathsf{dif}}[i, r]$ considers the failure pattern in a finer way: it is a differential predicate based on the number of crashes perceived by a process p_i between each pair of consecutive rounds. Similarly, $P_{\mathsf{prefo}}[i, r]$ is better than $P_{\mathsf{dif}}[i, r]$ because of the following two things: (a) each process decides on 0 as soon as possible without considering failures (as in the execution explained in the proof of Theorem 4(d)); and (b) processes detect rounds in which no information is hidden by looking at "how information flowed in the past" (like in the execution described in Sect. 2.3) and not only looking at the current round.

It is interesting to notice that with $P_{\mathsf{dif}}[i, r]$ (a) if no process crashes, the processes decide in two rounds, and (b) if the crashes occur before the execution, the correct processes decide in three rounds. In the failure pattern (b), $P_{\mathsf{count}}[i, r]$ does not allow to decide before round $(f+2)$. Similarly, with $P_{\mathsf{prefo}}[i, r]$, any correct process starting with 0 decides at the end of round 1, while there are executions in which such a process would decide in round $f + 2$ (or, in the worst case, in round $t + 1$) with $P_{\mathsf{dif}}[i, r]$.

On the unbeatability of P_{prefo}. As already mentioned, P_{prefo} is unbeatable in the sense that it cannot be *strictly* improved. Thus, there might be predicates that improve the decision time of a process in a given execution but the decision time of a (possibly different) process in a (possibly different) execution is strictly worse. An example of such a predicate is P_{pref1} where the roles of 0 and 1 are exchanged. Thus, the aim of the predicate is to decide on 1 as soon as possible (to adapt the algorithm in Fig. 5 to P_{pref1}, 0's and 1's are exchanged). Observe that in executions in which all processes start with 0, P_{prefo} is fast, regardless of the failure pattern, while P_{pref1} might need up to $t + 1$ rounds, and vice versa, in executions in which all processes start with 1, P_{pref1} is fast while P_{prefo} might be slow.

Interestingly, it is shown in [15] that there is no *all case optimal* predicate P for consensus that is at least as fast as any predicate that allows to solve consensus.

A similar result was observed for the *non-blocking atomic commit* problem in synchronous systems ([8], see also Chap. 10 in [19]). According to its local computation, each process votes yes or no. If all processes vote yes and there is no failure, they all must commit their local computations. If one of them votes no, they must abort their local computations. It is shown in [8] that there is no algorithm that, whatever the decision (abort or commit), is fast in all executions: a fast algorithm for commit cannot be fast for abort, and vice versa.

5   Conclusion

This article explored the notion of early deciding/stopping for consensus, trying to better understand the relationship between static and dynamic decisions. Indeed, it turns out that dynamicity in early deciding/stopping can be based on several properties of actual execution, namely, failure pattern, flow of information, and input pattern. To compare existing solutions, we presented three early deciding/stopping strategies as a sequence of predicates, respectively based on (i) counting crashed processes, (ii) consecutive rounds message pattern, and (iii) a finer analysis of the information flow in the execution.

On the pedagogical side, we advocate that having all algorithms presented in the same framework eases understanding and comparison of early deciding/stopping consensus algorithms, and pinpoints the subtle differences between those strategies.

The question whether such an approach can be conducted on the k-set agreement problem, the most natural extension of consensus where up to k different values can be decided [5,21], remains an open question. The predicate given in [4] is strictly better than any other predicate found in the literature but the question of its unbeatability is still an open problem.

Acknowledgements. Armando Castañeda is supported by UNAM-PAPIIT project IA102417. Yoram Moses is the Israel Pollak chair at the Technion. Michel Raynal is supported by the French ANR project DESCARTES devoted to distributed software engineering.

References

1. Aguilera, M.K., Toueg, S.: A simple bi-valency proof that t-resilient consensus requires $t + 1$ rounds. Inf. Process. Lett. **71**, 155–158 (1999)
2. Berman, P., Garay, J.A., Perry, K.J.: Optimal early stopping in distributed consensus. In: Segall, A., Zaks, S. (eds.) WDAG 1992. LNCS, vol. 647, pp. 221–237. Springer, Heidelberg (1992). doi:10.1007/3-540-56188-9_15
3. Castañeda, A., Gonczarowski, Y.A., Moses, Y.: Unbeatable consensus. In: Kuhn, F. (ed.) DISC 2014. LNCS, vol. 8784, pp. 91–106. Springer, Heidelberg (2014). doi:10.1007/978-3-662-45174-8_7
4. Castañeda A., Gonczarowski Y.A., Moses, Y.: Unbeatable set consensus via topological and combinatorial reasoning. In: Proceedings of the 35th ACM Symposium on Principles of Distributed Computing (PODC 2016), pp. 107–116. ACM Press (2016)
5. Chaudhuri, S.: More choices allow more faults: set consensus problems in totally asynchronous systems. Inf. Comput. **105**, 132–158 (1993)
6. Dolev, D., Reischuk, R., Strong, H.R.: Early stopping in Byzantine agreement. J. ACM **37**(4), 720–741 (1990)

7. Dwork, C., Moses, Y.: Knowledge and common knowledge in a Byzantine environment: crash failure. Inf. Comput. **88**(2), 156–186 (1990)
8. Dutta, P., Guerraoui, R., Pochon, B.: Fast non-blocking atomic commit: an inherent tradeoff. Inf. Process. Lett. **91**(4), 195–200 (2004)
9. Fagin, R., Halpern, J.Y., Moses, Y., Vardi, M.Y.: Reasoning about Knowledge. MIT Press, Cambridge (2003)
10. Fischer, M., Lynch, N.: A lower bound for the time to ensure interactive consistency. Inf. Process. Lett. **14**, 183–186 (1982)
11. Fischer, M., Lynch, N.A., Paterson, M.S.: Impossibility of distributed consensus with one faulty process. J. ACM **32**(2), 374–382 (1985)
12. Halpern, J.Y., Moses, Y., Waarts, O.: A characterization of eventual Byzantine agreement. SIAM J. Comput. **31**(3), 838–865 (2001)
13. Keidar, I., Rajsbaum, S.: A simple proof of the uniform consensus synchronous lower bound. Inf. Process. Lett. **85**(1), 47–52 (2003)
14. Lamport, L., Shostack, R., Pease, M.: The Byzantine generals problem. ACM Trans. Prog. Lang. Syst. **4**(3), 382–401 (1982)
15. Moses, Y., Tuttle, M.R.: Programming simultaneous actions using common knowledge. Algorithmica **3**, 121–169 (1988)
16. Pease, M., Shostak, R.R., Lamport, L.: Reaching agreement in the presence of faults. J. ACM **27**, 228–234 (1980)
17. Lynch, N.A.: Distributed algorithms, 872 p. Morgan Kaufmann Publishers, San Francisco (1996). ISBN 1-55860-384-4
18. Raïpin Parvédy, Ph., Raynal, M.: Optimal early stopping uniform consensus in synchronous systems with process omission failures. In: Proceedings of the 16th ACM Symposium on Parallel Algorithms and Architectures (SPAA 2004), pp. 302–310. ACM Press (2004)
19. Raynal, M.: Fault-tolerant agreement in synchronous message-passing systems, 189 p. Morgan & Claypool Publishers (2010). ISBN 978-1-60845-525-6
20. Raynal, M.: Concurrent Programming: Algorithms, Principles and Foundations, 515 p. Springer, Heidelberg (2013). ISBN 978-3-642-32026-2
21. Raynal, M.: Set Agreement, 2nd edn. Encyclopedia of Algorithms, pp. 1956–1959. Springer, New York (2016)
22. Wang, X., Teo, Y.M., Cao, J.: A bivalency proof of the lower bound for uniform consensus. Inf. Process. Lett. **96**, 167–174 (2005)

The Disclosure Power of Shared Objects

Peva Blanchard, Rachid Guerraoui, Julien Stainer, and Igor Zablotchi[(✉)]

EPFL, Lausanne, Switzerland
{peva.blanchard,rachid.guerraoui,julien.stainer,igor.zablotchi}@epfl.ch

Abstract. Shared objects are the means by which processes gather and exchange information about the state of a distributed system. Objects that disclose more information about the system are therefore more desirable. In this paper, we propose the schedule reconstruction (SR) problem as a new metric for the disclosure power of shared memory objects. In schedule reconstruction, processes take steps which are interleaved to form a schedule; each process needs to be able to reconstruct the schedule up to its last step. We show that objects can be ranked in a hierarchy according to their ability to solve SR. In this hierarchy, stronger objects can implement weaker objects via a SR-based universal construction. We identify a connection between SR and consensus and prove that SR is at least as hard as consensus. Perhaps surprisingly, we show that objects that are powerful in solving consensus—such as compare-and-swap—are not always powerful in their ability to solve SR.

1 Introduction

Programming a computing system in a centralized way is significantly more powerful than doing so in a distributed way. The main difficulty of distributed programming comes from the lack of knowledge that a process has about the state of the other processes and the overall state of the system. The more information a process has about the state of the system, the easier it is to write an algorithm for that process to achieve a task in coordination with the other processes. In a distributed system, this information can only be obtained by processes from shared objects. So, intuitively, the more information an object discloses about the rest of the system, the more appealing it is.

In this paper, we propose the schedule reconstruction (SR) problem as a new metric for the disclosure power of shared objects. In order to solve SR, processes in a shared memory system need to be able to accurately identify the interleaving of steps (shared memory accesses) taken by all processes (the schedule). It is easy to see why objects that can identify the schedule are desirable. Knowing the schedule basically equates knowing the full system state and thus overcoming the main difficulty of distributed programming, as mentioned above.

We associate a SR number with each object A, representing the maximum number of processes of a system in which A can solve SR. Objects can thus be organized in a hierarchy, with each level corresponding to a different SR number.

This work has been supported in part by the European ERC Grant 339539 (AOC).

A. El Abbadi and B. Garbinato (Eds.): NETYS 2017, LNCS 10299, pp. 222–227, 2017.
DOI: 10.1007/978-3-319-59647-1_17

There is a natural connection between disclosure power as measured by the SR number and synchronization power as measured by the consensus number [2]. Intuitively, synchronization is a means of restricting the very large space of executions of a concurrent algorithm, whereas SR is a way of identifying which one of these possible executions actually occurred. At first glance, one would expect that objects with a high reconstruction power (high SR number) should also have a high synchronization power (high consensus number). We confirm this intuition by showing that SR is at least as hard as consensus: the SR number of an object is at most its consensus number.

Due to this connection between SR and consensus, intuition might also predict the inverse relationship to hold true: that objects with a high consensus number should also possess a high SR number. Surprisingly, this is not always the case, as we show in this paper. We prove that compare-and-swap, a very powerful, even universal [2], synchronization primitive, is no more powerful than simple read-write registers in terms of schedule reconstruction.

An object A's position in the SR hierarchy also determines A's power to implement other objects. We show that in the SR hierarchy a stronger object A is always able to implement a weaker object B, by providing a universal construction based on SR objects. We also show that B is unable to implement A in such a way that the implementation maintains the same disclosure power as A. In other words, implementing a stronger object from a weaker one always entails losing disclosure power.

2   Model and Problem Statement

2.1   Processes

We consider a set of n processes $P = \{P_1, ..., P_n\}$ that communicate through shared memory using a set of memory access primitives. The processes are executing an algorithm A, which consists of a sequence of shared memory accesses and local steps. We assume local steps to be instantaneous and shared memory steps to be atomic.

An execution of algorithm A by a set of processes P is modeled by a *schedule*—a finite or infinite sequence of process identifiers which represents the interleaving of steps taken by the processes. When describing a schedule, we ignore local steps, so a schedule defines a global total order on the shared memory accesses done by all processes participating in the execution.

2.2   Schedule Reconstruction Object

A *schedule reconstruction object* (or *SR object*) provides two methods, step and reconstruct, neither of which takes any arguments. Basically, a call to reconstruct by a process p returns the schedule up to the last step call by p. The two methods need to satisfy the following conditions:

- the execution of each call to step performs exactly one primitive shared memory access and any number of local steps.
- reconstruct may only be implemented using local steps and shared memory accesses *that do not modify the state of shared memory* (such as reads).
- a call to reconstruct by process p returns the schedule as a mapping from step numbers to process ids or an empty mapping if there are no step calls by p preceding the reconstruct call.

We are interested in wait-free implementations of SR objects that correctly reconstruct *any possible schedule* (any interleaving of step calls). We call any such implementation a *SR algorithm*. A class C of objects solves n-process schedule reconstruction if there exists an SR algorithm $\mathcal{A}$ that solves n-process schedule reconstruction using any number of objects of class C and any number of atomic registers. We define the *schedule reconstruction number* (or *SR number*) of a class C to be the largest n for which C solves n-process schedule reconstruction. If no largest n exists, we say that the SR number of the class is *infinite*.

3   SR and Consensus

In this section, we establish a connection between SR and consensus: SR is at least as hard as consensus.

Theorem 1. *Any class C of objects that solves n-process SR also solves n-process consensus.*

Proof. Let $\mathcal{A}$ be an algorithm solving n-process SR using only objects of class C and atomic registers. We use $\mathcal{A}$ to solve consensus. Each process writes its proposed value in a single-writer, multi-reader register. Then, each processes calls step once and then calls reconstruct. Thus, every process knows the schedule and is able to decide on the value proposed by the process which was scheduled first.

Corollary 1. *The SR number of a class C is at most equal to its consensus number.*

4   The SR Hierarchy

We examine specific classes of objects according to their ability to solve SR. Due to space limitations, we omit full proofs throughout this section and refer the reader to the full version of the paper [1]. Proof sketches are provided.

4.1   Fetch-and-Increment

Fetch-and-increment objects have consensus number 2 [3] and thus have SR number at most 2 (Corollary 1). We now show that they have SR number exactly 2.

Theorem 2. *Fetch-and-increment has SR number 2.*

Proof. Consider the following protocol for 2-process SR. The two processes share a fetch-and-increment object which initially has value 0. A `step` call simply invokes `getAndIncrement` and receives a (unique) ticket number, which it appends the result to a local list of observations. A `reconstruct` call by p simply assigns to p the steps corresponding to the tickets in p's local observation list and assigns to the other process the steps corresponding to the gaps in p's observation list.

4.2 Compare-and-Swap: A Surprising Result

In this section, we show that the SR number of compare-and-swap (CAS) is 1. We know that it is (trivially) at least 1, by the same argument used for atomic registers. It remains to show that it is also at most 1.

Theorem 3. *CAS has SR number at most 1.*

Proof. We assume towards a contradiction that there exists some algorithm $\mathcal{A}$ for 2-process SR using only CAS objects and registers and examine the first step of $\mathcal{A}$ by each process. This first step cannot be a read, since reads do not modify the observable state of the system and thus cannot be reconstructed. The first step of a process p cannot be a register write either, because immediately after a write p cannot establish whether its write was performed before or after the other process's step. Thus, the first step of both processes must be a CAS. Both CAS's must succeed, because a failed CAS does not modify the observable system state. Moreover, both CAS's must be executed on the same memory location, otherwise they would commute. However, if two CAS's succeed in some schedule S, at least one of them will fail in a schedule S' in which the order of the CAS's is reversed—making S' not reconstructible by $\mathcal{A}$, a contradiction.

4.3 Multiple Atomic Append: Every Level Is Populated

An *append register* is similar to a regular register, except that every write appends its value to the current value of the register, instead of overwriting it. A k-writer append register is an append register from which any number of processes can read but to which only k processes can append. Interestingly, append registers have been studied in a Byzantine setting as well [4].

Theorem 4. *k-writer append registers have SR number $s = k$.*

Proof. First, we show that $s \geq k$. A SR algorithm for k processes using a shared k-writer append register r is as follows. A `step` call appends the invoking process's id to r. A `reconstruct` call reads r and assigns step numbers to processes according to the order of id's in r. It remains to show that $s < k + 1$. Assume towards a contradiction that there exists a SR algorithm for $k + 1$ processes using only k-writer append registers and atomic read-write registers. We consider the first step of the algorithm for each process. Similarly to the proof of Theorem 3, all processes must access append registers during their first step. Because there are $k + 1$ processes but the append registers only support k writers, there must exist two processes which do not write to the same append register for their first step. Thus, their appends commute and are not reconstructible.

4.4 SWAP3: the Hierarchy is Infinite

We define a new primitive called SWAP3. SWAP3 takes three arguments a, b and c. It atomically writes the value of b into c and the value of a into b.

Theorem 5. *SWAP3 has SR number* ∞.

Proof. We describe an algorithm that solves SR for any number of processes. The processes maintain a shared linked list which encodes the schedule. A step call prepares a new node with the invoking process's id and appends it to the head of the list (a single global step using SWAP3: atomically assign the head of the list to point to the new node and the new node's next field to the old value of the head). Reconstructing the schedule is done by traversing the linked list and assigning step numbers to processes in reverse order.

5 A SR-Based Universal Construction

In this section, we examine the relationships between the levels in the SR hierarchy. We give two main results: a positive one—stronger objects can implement weaker objects—and a negative one—weaker objects cannot implement stronger objects in a way that preserves reconstructibility.

We begin with the positive result: in a system of n processes, given any object A with SR number $\geq n$ and any deterministic object B, A implements B. By definition of SR number, A can be used to implement SR objects in a system of n processes. Furthermore, B can be implemented from SR objects in the following way (full details in our paper [1]). The processes use an SR object to determine the order in which their invocations take effect and then use this information to simulate the execution on local copies of B.

We have just shown that in the SR hierarchy, as in the consensus hierarchy, there exist objects that are *universal*. Given sufficiently many of them, any object with a sequential specification can be implemented in a wait-free linearizable way.

We now turn to the negative result: in a system of n processes, given any object A with SR number $\geq n$ and any object B with SR number $< n$, B cannot 1-implement A. We say that A 1-implements B if A implements B and the implementation performs at most one shared memory accesses per call to B's methods. Towards a contradiction, assume that B can 1-implement A in a system of n processes. Since A has SR number $\geq n$, there exists an implementation of a SR object from A and atomic registers. By replacing A in this implementation with its 1-implementation from B, we obtain a valid implementation of an SR object from B, a contradiction of the fact that B's SR number is less than n.

Note that this negative result does not contradict the universality of objects in the sense of consensus, which states that an object with consensus number at least n can implement any object in a system of n or less processes. Our negative result states that objects with lower SR number cannot *1-implement* objects with higher SR number. So, for instance, CAS has infinite consensus number, so it can implement any object, but it has SR number 1, so it cannot *implement in a single step* any object with SR number larger than 1 (e.g., fetch-and-increment) in a system of 2 or more processes. In other words, no such object can be implemented from CAS in such a way that the implementation has the same SR number as the abstract object.

6   Conclusion

In this paper, we propose the schedule reconstruction problem and the SR number as a new measure for the disclosure power of objects in shared memory systems. Objects can be organized in a dense hierarchy where strong objects implement weaker objects via a universal construction based on SR. Furthermore, we identify a link between SR and consensus and show that SR is at least as hard as consensus. Finally, we evaluate the SR number of well known objects and show that universal consensus objects are not always universal SR objects.

References

1. Blanchard, P., Guerraoui, R., Stainer, J., Zablotchi, I.: The disclosure power of shared objects. Technical report, EPFL (2017)
2. Herlihy, M.: Wait-free synchronization. TOPLAS **13**(1), 124–149 (1991)
3. Herlihy, M., Shavit, N.: The Art of Multiprocessor Programming, Revised Reprint, 1st edn. Morgan Kaufmann Publishers Inc., San Francisco (2012)
4. Imbs, D., Rajsbaum, S., Raynal, M., Stainer, J.: Read/write shared memory abstraction on top of asynchronous byzantine message-passing systems. JPDC **93**, 1–9 (2016)

Clustering-Based Techniques

Competitive Clustering of Stochastic Communication Patterns on a Ring

Chen Avin[1], Louis Cohen[2], and Stefan Schmid[3,4(✉)]

[1] Ben-Gurion University of the Negev, Beersheba, Israel
[2] Ecole Normale Superieure Paris Saclay, Cachan, France
[3] Aalborg University, Aalborg, Denmark
schmiste@gmail.com
[4] TU Berlin, Berlin, Germany

Abstract. This paper studies a fundamental dynamic clustering problem. The input is an online sequence of pairwise communication requests between n nodes (e.g., tasks or virtual machines). Our goal is to minimize the communication cost by partitioning the communicating nodes into ℓ clusters (e.g., physical servers) of size k (e.g., number of virtual machine slots). We assume that if the communicating nodes are located in the same cluster, the communication request costs 0; if the nodes are located in different clusters, the request is served remotely using inter-cluster communication, at cost 1. Additionally, we can migrate: a node from one cluster to another at cost $\alpha \geq 1$.

We initiate the study of a stochastic problem variant where the communication pattern follows a fixed distribution, set by an adversary. Thus, the online algorithm needs to find a good tradeoff between benefitting from quickly moving to a seemingly good configuration (of low inter-cluster communication costs), and the risk of prematurely ending up in a configuration which later turns out to be bad, entailing high migration costs.

Our main technical contribution is a deterministic online algorithm which is $O(\log n)$-competitive with high probability (w.h.p.), for a specific but fundamental class of problems: namely on ring graphs.

1 Introduction

Modern distributed systems are often highly virtualized and feature unprecedented resource allocation flexibilities. For example, these flexibilities can be exploited to improve resource utilization, making it possible to multiplex more applications over the same shared physical infrastructure, reducing operational costs and increasing profits. However, exploiting these resource allocation flexibilities is non-trivial, especially since workloads and resource requirements are time-varying.

Research supported by the German-Israeli Foundation for Scientific Research and Development, (G.I.F. No I-1245-407.6/2014). Part of the research was done while the second author was visiting Ben Gurion University and TU Berlin.

© Springer International Publishing AG 2017
A. El Abbadi and B. Garbinato (Eds.): NETYS 2017, LNCS 10299, pp. 231–247, 2017.
DOI: 10.1007/978-3-319-59647-1_18

This paper studies a fundamental dynamic resource allocation problem underlying many network-intensive distributed applications, e.g., batch processing or streaming applications, or scale-out databases. To minimize the resource footprint (in terms of bandwidth) of such applications as well as latency, we want to collocate frequently communicating tasks or virtual machines on the same physical server, saving communication across the network. The underlying problem can be seen as a clustering problem [3]: nodes (the tasks or virtual machines) need to be partitioned into different clusters (the physical servers), minimizing inter-cluster communications.

The clustering problem is challenging as the detailed communication patterns are often stochastic and the specific distribution unknown ahead of time. In other words, a clustering algorithm must *deal with uncertainties*: although two nodes may have communicated frequently in the past, it can turn out later that it is better to collocate different node pairs. Accordingly, clustering decisions may have to be reconsidered, which entails migrations.

Our Contributions. This paper initiates the study of a natural dynamic clustering problem where communication patterns follow an unknown distribution, chosen by an adversary: the distribution represents the worst-case for the given online algorithm, and communication requests are drawn i.i.d. from this distribution. Our goal is to devise online algorithms which perform well against an optimal offline algorithm which has perfect knowledge of the distribution. Our main technical contribution is a deterministic online algorithm which, for a special but fundamental request pattern family, namely the ring, achieves a competitive ratio of $O(\log n)$, with high probability (w.h.p.), i.e., with probability at least $1 - 1/n^c$, where n is the total number of nodes and c is a constant.

Novelty and Challenges. Our work presents an interesting new perspective on several classic problems. For example, our problem is related to the fundamental statistical problem of guessing the most likely distribution (and its parameters) from which a small set of samples is drawn. Indeed, one natural strategy of the online algorithm could be to first simply sample requests, and once a good estimation of the actual distribution emerges, directly move to the optimal clustering configuration. However, as we will show in this paper, the competitive ratio of this strategy can be very bad: the communication cost paid by the online algorithm during sampling can be high. Accordingly, the online algorithm is forced to eliminate distributions early on, i.e., it needs to migrate to seemingly low-cost configurations. And here lies another difference to classic distribution learning problems: in our model, an online algorithm needs to pay for changing configurations, i.e., when revising the "guessed distribution". In other words, our problem features an interesting *combination of distribution learning and efficient searching*. It turns out that amortizing the migration costs with the expected benefits (i.e., the reduced communication costs) at the new configuration however is not easy. For example, if the request distribution is uniform, i.e., if all clustering configurations have the same probability, the best

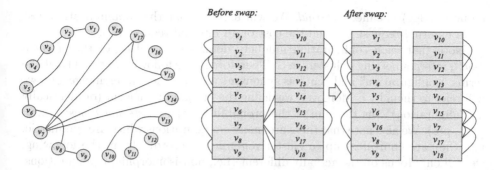

Fig. 1. Example: Communication patterns drawn from a certain distribution (*on the left*, represented as a communication graph) need to be learned and clustered. In this example, we have $\ell = 2$ clusters of size $k = 9$. In the middle, a bad clustering is shown: there are four inter-cluster edges ("before swap"). However, by swapping nodes v_7 and v_{16}, all inter-cluster edges can be removed (*on the right* in the figure). Note that different edges can have different frequencies, which however are not depicted in this example.

strategy is not to move: the migration costs cannot be amortized. However, if the distribution is "almost uniform", migrations are required and "pay off". Clearly, distinguishing between uniform and almost uniform distributions is difficult from an online perspective.

Organization. The remainder of this paper is organized as follows. In Sect. 2, we introduce our formal model. In Sect. 3, we provide intuition about our problem and highlight the challenges. In Sect. 4, we present our deterministic online algorithm, and we analyze it formally in Sect. 5. After reviewing related work in Sect. 6, we conclude our contribution in Sect. 7.

2   Model

We consider the problem of partitioning n nodes $V = \{v_1, v_2, \ldots, v_n\}$ into ℓ clusters of capacity k each. We assume that $n = \ell \cdot k$, i.e., nodes perfectly fit into the available clusters, and there is no slack. We call a specific node-cluster assignment a *configuration* c. We assume that the communication request is generated from a fixed distribution $\mathscr{D}$, chosen in a worst-case manner by the adversary. The sequence of actual requests $\sigma(\mathscr{D}) = (\sigma_1, \sigma_2, ..., \sigma_T)$, is sampled i.i.d. from this distribution: the communication event at time t is a (directed) node pair $\sigma_t = (v_i, v_j)$. Alternatively, we represent the distribution $\mathscr{D}$ as a weighted graph $G = (V, E)$. For an edge $(v_i, v_j) \in E(G)$, let the weight of the edge $p(v_i, v_j)$ denote the probability of a communication request from between v_i and v_j: each edge $e \in E$ has a certain probability $p(e)$ and $\sum_{e \in E} p(e) = 1$. A request (i.e., edge in G) $\sigma_t = (v_i, v_j)$ is called *internal* if v_i and v_j belong to the same cluster at the current configuration (i.e., at the time of the request); otherwise, the request (edge) is called *external*. We will assume that the communication cost of an external request is 1 and the cost of an internal request is 0.

Note that each configuration uniquely defines external edges that form a "*cut*", interconnecting ℓ clusters in G. Therefore in the following, we will treat the terms "configuration" and "cut" as synonyms and use them interchangeably; we will refer to them by c. Moreover, we define the probability of a cut (or identically a configuration) c as the sum of the probabilities of its *external edges*: $p(c) = \sum_{e \in c} p(e)$. We also note that there are many configurations which are symmetric, i.e., they are equivalent up to cluster renaming. Accordingly, in the following, we will only focus on the actually different (i.e., non-isomorphic) configurations.

To reduce external communication costs, an algorithm can change the current configuration by using *node swaps*. Swapping a node pair costs 2α (two node migrations of cost α each). Since the request probability of different configurations/cuts differs, the goal of the algorithm will be to quickly guess and move toward a good cut, a configuration that reduces its future cost. Figure 1 shows an example.

In particular, we are interested in the *online problem variant*: we assume that the distribution $\mathscr{D}$ of the communication pattern (and hence the σ we observe is generated from) is initially *unknown* to the online algorithm. Nevertheless, we want the performance of an online clustering algorithm, ON, to be similar to the one of a hypothetical offline algorithm, OFF, which knows the request distribution as well as the number of requests σ, henceforth denoted by $|\sigma|$, ahead of time. In particular, OFF can move before any request occurs or σ is generated.

We aim to minimize the competitive ratio, the worst ratio of the online algorithm cost divided by the offline algorithm cost (for a given distribution $\mathscr{D}$ and the same starting configuration c_o):

$$\rho = \max_{\sigma(\mathscr{D})} \frac{ON(\sigma(\mathscr{D}))}{OFF(\sigma(\mathscr{D}))}$$

Here, the cost $ON(\sigma(\mathscr{D}))$ of any algorithm ON for a sequence $\sigma(\mathscr{D})$ is the sum of the overall communication costs and the migration costs. We consider bounds on ρ with high probability.

As a first step, we focus on partitioning problems where $\ell = 2$ and consider fundamental ring communication patterns. That is, the communication graph G is the cycle graph and the event space is defined over the edges $E = \{(v_1, v_2), (v_2, v_3), \dots, (v_{n-1}, v_k), (v_n, v_1)\}$. Moreover, we assume configurations that minimize the cut, that is nodes are partitioned according to contiguous subsequences of the identifier space. Each cluster is (up to modulo) of the form, $\{(v_i, v_{i+1}, \dots, v_{i+k-1}\}$. This communication pattern is not only fundamental but also captures the aspects and inherent tradeoffs rendering the problem non-trivial. In this model, an algorithm changes configurations using *rotations* (either clockwise or counter-clockwise). See Fig. 2.

3   The Challenge of Dynamic Clustering

In order to acquaint ourselves with the problem and understand the fundamental challenges involved in dynamic clustering, we first provide some examples and discuss naive strategies. Let us consider an example with $n = 2k$ nodes divided into $\ell = 2$ clusters of size k. There are k possible configurations/cuts: $\{c_0, c_1, \ldots, c_{k-1}\}$. At one end of the algorithmic spectrum lies a lazy algorithm which never moves, let's call it *LAZY*. At the other end of the spectrum lies a very proactive algorithm which greedily moves to the configuration which so far received the least external requests, let's call it *GREEDY*. Both *LAZY* and *GREEDY* are doomed to fail, i.e., they have a large competitive ratio: *LAZY* fails under a request distribution where the initial external cut has probability 1, i.e., $p(c_0) = 1$ and for any $i > 0$, $p(c_i) = 0$: *LAZY* pays for all requests, while after a simple node swap all communication costs would be 0. *GREEDY* fails in uniform distributions, i.e., if $p(c_i) = 1/k$ for all i: the best configuration is continuously changing, and in particular, the best cut is likely to be at distance $\Omega(k)$ from the initial configuration c_0: *GREEDY* quickly occurs migration costs in the order of $\Omega(\alpha \cdot k)$, while staying at the same location would cost $1/k$ per request. Thus, the competitive ratios grow super-linearly in the number of requests and in the number of nodes.

Another intuitive strategy could be to wait in the initial configuration c_0 for some time, simply observing and sampling the actual distribution, until a "sufficiently accurate" estimation of the distribution is obtained. Then, we move directly to the (hopefully) optimal configuration. Thus, the problem boils down to the classic statistical problem of estimating the distribution (and its parameters) from samples. However, it is easy to see that waiting for the optimal distribution to emerge is costly. Imagine for example a scenario where the initial configuration/cut c_0 has a high probability, and there are two additional cuts c_1 and c_2 which have almost the same low probability (for example polynomially low probability). Clearly, waiting at c_0 to learn whether c_1 or c_2 is better is not only very costly, but it may also be pointless: even if the online algorithm ended up at c_1 although c_2 was a little bit better, the resulting competitive ratio could be still small.

Thus, the key challenge of our problem lies in its required joint optimization of *learning and searching*: while learning the distribution, an efficient search algorithm must be employed to minimize reconfiguration costs. In particular, the following criteria need to be met:

1. *Migrate early...:* An online algorithm should migrate away from a suboptimal configuration early, possibly long before the optimal configuration can be guessed.
2. *... but not too early...:* An online algorithm should avoid frequent migrations, e.g., due to a wrong or poor estimate of the actual request distribution.
3. *... and locally:* Especially if the length of σ is small (small number of requests), it may not make sense to migrate to an optimal but faraway location, even if the distribution is known: even *OFF* would not move there.

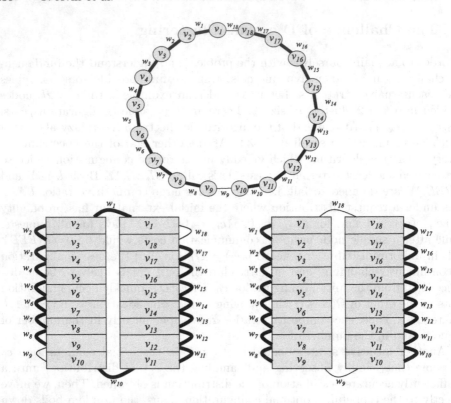

Fig. 2. Weighted ring communication pattern: frequently used edges (in *bold*) should not be part of the cut. The cut can be changed using rotations: in the figure, a counter-clockwise rotation leads from the middle to the right configuration.

4   Deterministic and Competitive Clustering

With these intuitions and challenges in mind, we present our solution. Let us first start with the offline algorithm. It is easy to see that *OFF*, knowing the distribution as well as the number of requests, only moves *once* in time (i.e., one move consisting of multiple migrations or node swaps): namely *in the beginning* and *to the configuration providing an optimal cost-benefit tradeoff*. Concretely, *OFF* computes for each configuration c_i, its expected cost-benefit tradeoff: the communication cost of configuration c_i is $|\sigma| \cdot p(c_i)$ and the cost of moving there is $2\alpha \cdot d(c_0, c_i)$, where $d(\cdot, \cdot)$ is the rotation distance between the two configurations (the smallest number of rotation moves to reach the other configuration). Thus, *OFF* will move to $c_{OFF} := \arg\min_{c_i} p(c_i) + (2\alpha \cdot d(c_0, c_i))/|\sigma|$ (note that this configuration is not necessarily unique). In the following, we will use the short form $d_i = d(c_0, c_i)$ to denote distances relative to c_0, the initial configuration.

The online algorithm is more interesting. The competitive and deterministic online algorithm presented in this paper relies on three key ideas:

- *Eliminating bad configurations:* We define conditions for configurations which, if met, allow us to eliminate the corresponding configurations once and for all. In particular, we will guarantee (w.h.p.) that an online algorithm be competitive (even) if it never moves back to such a configuration anymore in the future. In other words, our online algorithm will only move between configurations for which this condition is not true yet.
- *Local migrations and growing-radius search strategy:* In order to avoid high migration costs, our online algorithm is local in the sense that it only moves to nearby cuts/configurations once the condition of the current configuration is met and it needs to be eliminated. Concretely, our online algorithm is based on a growing-radius search strategy: we only migrate to valid configurations lying within the given radius. Only if no such configurations exist, the search radius is increased.
- *Amortization:* The radius growth strategy alone is not sufficient to provide the necessary amortization for being competitive. Two additions are required:
  1. *Directed search:* An online algorithm may still incur a high migration cost when frequently moving back-and-forth within a given radius, chasing the next best configuration. Therefore, our proposed online algorithm first moves in one direction only (clockwise), and then in the other direction, bounding the number of times the c_0 configuration is crossed.
  2. *Lazy expansion:* Even once all configurations within this radius have been eliminated, the online algorithm should not immediately move to configurations in the next larger interval. Rather, the algorithm waits until a certain amount of requests have been accumulated, allowing to amortize the migrations (an "insurance").

With these high-level ideas in mind, we now describe the algorithm in detail (cf. Algorithm 1). We consider a time t, and assume that the online algorithm is at configuration c_t. The algorithm maintains an array $r[]$ where it counts, for each possible configuration $c_0, \ldots c_{k-1}$, the number of samples that hit an external edge of the corresponding cut; in other words, $r[]$ is used to estimate the distribution of the communication pattern. Let $\mathscr{E}$ be the set of the eliminated configurations, and let $\overline{\mathscr{E}}$ be the complement of $\mathscr{E}$: the set of configurations not eliminated yet. R is the search radius, initially $R = 1$. Upon each request, σ_t, we first increment the value of the corresponding configuration in the sampling array $r[]$ (only one configuration is affected by a given external request). We then compare all configurations not eliminated yet to the "seemingly best configuration": the configuration which received the least (external) requests so far (i.e., $\arg\min_{c_i} r[c_i]$). Let $r_{\min} := \min_{c_i} r[c_i]$ be the minimum value. We now eliminate any configuration c_j for which the condition $\mathrm{Cond}(r[c_j], r_{\min})$ is fulfilled: c_j is too far from the optimum. Concretely, w.l.o.g. assume that $r[c_j] > r[c_i]$ and let $\gamma = r[c_i]/r[c_j] < 1$. Then for $\epsilon > 0$ (a parameter for the error probability), we use the following condition:

$$\mathrm{Cond}(j, i) := \begin{cases} \texttt{True} & r[c_j] \geq \frac{\ln(\frac{1}{\epsilon})}{\ln(\frac{2}{1+\gamma}) - (\frac{1-\gamma}{2})} \\ \texttt{False} & \text{otherwise} \end{cases} \tag{1}$$

If on this occasion, we eliminated our own current configuration $c(t)$, we then have to decide where we want to move next, using the function $next(\overline{\mathscr{E}})$ (unless all configurations have been eliminated). The distance from the suggested next configuration c_{next} to c_0 (the initial configuration) may be greater than the current radius R, in which case we double R until $R \geq d_{next}$. However, before moving, we also test whether $\min_{\{d_{c_{next}} < R\}}(r[c_{next}]) \geq \alpha \cdot R$. Only if this is fulfilled, we can move to the new configuration c_{next}; otherwise, we lazily stay on the current configuration.

Algorithm 1. Online Algorithm ON (upon receiving request $\sigma(t)$ and current configuration $c(t)$)

Initialize: $r := [0; ..; 0]$, $\mathscr{E} := \{\}$, $\overline{\mathscr{E}} := [-\frac{k}{2}, \frac{k}{2}]$, $R := 1$ $\epsilon := \frac{1}{n^2}$
1: $c_j = c(\sigma(t))$ (* configuration to which $\sigma(t)$ is external *)
2: $r[c_j]++$
3: $r_{min} := \min\{r[i] \mid i \in [|1, k|]\}$
4: **if** $c_j \in \overline{\mathscr{E}}$ **then**
5:      **if** $\mathrm{Cond}(r[c_j], r_{min})$ **then**
6:          remove c_j from $\overline{\mathscr{E}}$
7:          add c_j to $\mathscr{E}$
8:      **end if**
9: **end if**
10: **if** $c(t) \in \mathscr{E}$ **then**
11:     $c_{next} :=$ The next configuration $c_i \in \overline{\mathscr{E}}$ on the *searching path*
12:     **while** $d_{next} > R$ **do**
13:         $R = 2R$
14:     **end while**
15:     **if** $r[c(t)] \geq \alpha \cdot d_{next}$ **then**
16:         move from $c(t)$ to c_{next}
17:         $c(t) := c_{next}$
18:     **end if**
19: **end if**

Let us now elaborate more on the moving strategy. Before going into the details however, let us note that for ease of presentation, we will use two different but equivalent numbering schemes to refer to configurations: depending on what is more useful in the current context. In particular, while when talking about the number of requests, $r[]$, we often enumerate configurations globally, $0, 1, 2, \ldots, k$. When discussing moving strategies, we often enumerate configurations relative to c_0, i.e., $-1, 1, -2, 2, \ldots, c_{k/2}$, depending on whether they are located clock- or counter-clock wise from c_0.

Given this remark, let us consider a simple migration strategy: we could always move to the closest not eliminated configuration next. However, we can show that this strategy is flawed. To see this, consider the following distribution:

$$\forall i \in [1; \frac{k}{2}] \quad : \quad p(c_i) = \frac{1}{k^i}, \quad p(c_0) = \left(1 - \sum_{i \in [1;\frac{k}{2}]} p(c_i)\right),$$

$$\forall i \in [-\frac{k}{2}, -1] \quad : \quad p(c_i) = 0$$

In such a situation, we have to move away from the configuration c_0 as soon as possible: we pay a cost close to 1 on this configuration, for each request. In particular, we cannot wait until we even observe the first request on c_1: we would incur high communication costs. Now, however, the algorithm may move in the wrong direction: e.g., to c_1, and then to the closer configuration not eliminated, c_2. Thus, eventually all configurations in $[c_0, c_{k/2}]$ may be visited before reaching the minimal configurations.

This is reminiscent of classic line searching [12] type problems like "the goat searches the hole in the fence"-escape problems: moving in one direction only, the goat may risk missing a nearby hole in the other direction. That is, moving greedily in one direction is $\Omega(F)$ competitive only, where F is the circumference of the fence, which in our case means that the competitive ratio is $\Omega(k)$. Accordingly, some combination of search-left and search-right is required. Our search radius R is centered around c_0 at any time during the execution of the algorithm, and we always first explore all remaining non-eliminated configurations in one direction, and then explore the remaining configurations in the other direction. In other words, starting from c_0, we alternate the search between the positive and negative configurations following the sequence: $(1, -1, 2, 3, -2, -3, \ldots, 2^{2i-2} + 1, \ldots, 2^{2i}, -2^{2i-1} - 1, \ldots, -2^{2i+1}, \ldots)$. Thus, configuration c_0 is crossed only a constant number of times per given radius R. We call this sequence the *searching path*.

Given a moving strategy, we next note that we should not move too fast: we introduce a second condition for when it is safe to move. When in a configuration 2^{2i} and before we want to explore configurations in $[-2^{2i+1}, -2^{2i-1}]$, we wait in the configuration $c_{\min}$ between configurations -2^{2i-1} and 2^{2i}, until this configuration fulfills $r[c_{\min}] \geq \alpha \cdot 2^{2i+1}$. Similarly, when moving from the configuration -2^{2i+1} to explore the configurations in $[2^{2i}, 2^{2i+2}]$, we will wait at $c_{\min}$ between $[-2^{2i+1}, 2^{2i}]$, until $r[c_{\min}] \geq \alpha \cdot 2^{2i+2}$.

5   Analysis

We first make some general observations on our elimination condition. Subsequently, we will present a cost-breakdown which will be helpful to analyze the competitive ratio of ON: we will show that each cost component is competitive with respect to the optimal offline algorithm.

The following lemma provides an intuition of our algorithm and its condition.

Lemma 1. *Let $\epsilon > 0$, then if $\texttt{Cond}(j, i) = \textit{True}$,*

$$\Pr\left(p(c_j) > p(c_i)\right) \geq 1 - \epsilon$$

Proof. We first prove the following helper claim.

Claim. Assume c_i and c_j occur with the same (unknown) probability, let $b > a$ and assume w.l.o.g. that $r[c_j] > r[c_i]$, then,

$$\Pr\Big(r[c_i] \leq a \ \text{ and } \ r[c_j] \geq b \mid p(c_i) = p(c_j)\Big) \leq \Pr\Big(r[c_j] \geq (1+\delta)X\Big) \leq \left(\frac{e^{\delta}}{(1+\delta)^{1+\delta}}\right)^X$$

where $\delta = \frac{b-a}{b+a}$ and $X = \frac{b}{1+\delta} = \frac{b+a}{2}$

Proof. The proof idea is to consider two probabilities using known Chernoff Bounds [16]:

$$P_1[\delta_i] := \Pr(r[c_i] \leq (1 - \delta_i)E[r[c_i]]) \leq \left(\frac{e^{-\delta_i}}{(1 - \delta_i)^{1-\delta_i}}\right)^{E[r[c_i]]} \tag{2}$$

and

$$P_2[\delta_j] := \Pr(r[c_j] \geq (1 + \delta_j)E[r[c_j]]) \leq \left(\frac{e^{\delta_j}}{(1 + \delta_j)^{1+\delta_j}}\right)^{E[r[c_j]]} \tag{3}$$

The two events are not independent, but we can bound the probability that both events occur by the maximum of the two probabilities when we assume $p(c_j) = p(c_i)$ and $E[r[c_j]] = E[r[c_i]] = (a + b)/2 = X$. In this case, we have that $\delta = (b - a)/(b + a)$. We now want to bound the maximum of these two probabilities. Towards this objective, we study which one of our bounds is greater and bound the maximum of the probability by the maximum of the bounds. Let $B_1[\delta]$ (resp $B_2[\delta]$) the bound on $P_1[\delta]$ (resp. $P_2[\delta]$).

$$B_1[\delta] = \left(\frac{e^{-\delta}}{(1 - \delta)^{1-\delta}}\right)^X \qquad B_2[\delta] = \left(\frac{e^{\delta}}{(1 + \delta)^{1+\delta}}\right)^X$$

To determine which one is greater than the other, we now study the function:

$$F(\delta) = \frac{B_1[\delta]}{B_2[\delta]} = \left(e^{-2\delta}\frac{(1 + \delta)^{1+\delta}}{(1 - \delta)^{1-\delta}}\right)^X$$

We obtain that $\forall \delta \geq 0 \ \ F(\delta) \leq 1$, so $\Pr\Big(r[c_i] = a \ \text{ and } \ r[c_j] = b \mid p(c_i) = p(c_j)\Big) \leq B_2[\delta] = \left(\frac{e^{\delta}}{(1+\delta)^{1+\delta}}\right)^X$.

We can now prove Lemma 1. Specifically, we want to prove that $\Pr(\mathrm{Cond}(j, i) \mid p(c_j) \leq p(c_i)) \leq \epsilon$. First note that for $x \leq y$:

$$\Pr(\mathrm{Cond}(j, i) \mid p(c_j) = x, p(c_i) = y) \leq \Pr(\mathrm{Cond}(j, i) \mid p(c_j) = y, p(c_i) = y)$$

Next we bound $\Pr\left(\text{Cond}(j,i) \mid p(c_j) = p(c_i)\right)$ using Claim 5.

$$\Pr\left(\text{Cond}(j,i) \mid p(c_j) = p(c_i)\right) \leq \Pr\left(r[c_j] \geq (1+\delta)X\right) = P_2$$

$$P_2 \leq \left(\frac{e^\delta}{(1+\delta)^{1+\delta}}\right)^{\frac{r[c_j]}{1+\delta}}$$

We want that $P_2 \leq \epsilon$:

$$\left(\frac{e^\delta}{(1+\delta)^{1+\delta}}\right)^{\frac{r[c_j]}{1+\delta}} \leq \epsilon \Longleftrightarrow \left(\frac{e^{\frac{\delta}{1+\delta}}}{(1+\delta)}\right)^{r[c_j]} \leq \epsilon$$

$$\leq \epsilon \Longleftrightarrow \left(\frac{\delta}{1+\delta} - \ln(1+\delta)\right)r[c_j] \leq \ln(\epsilon) \Longleftrightarrow$$

$$r[c_j] \geq \frac{\ln(\epsilon)}{\left(\frac{\delta}{1+\delta} - \ln(1+\delta)\right)} \Longleftrightarrow r[c_j] \geq \frac{\ln(\frac{1}{\epsilon})}{\ln(1+\delta) - \left(\frac{\delta}{1+\delta}\right)}$$

Now let $\gamma = \frac{r[c_i]}{r[c_j]} < 1$, so $\delta = \frac{1-\gamma}{1+\gamma}$, and we have:

$$r[c_j] \geq \frac{\ln(\frac{1}{\epsilon})}{\ln\left(1 + \frac{1-\gamma}{1+\gamma}\right) - \left(\frac{\frac{1-\gamma}{1+\gamma}}{1+\frac{1-\gamma}{1+\gamma}}\right)} \Longleftrightarrow r[c_j] \geq \frac{\ln(\frac{1}{\epsilon})}{\ln\left(\frac{2}{1+\gamma}\right) - \left(\frac{\frac{1-\gamma}{1+\gamma}}{\frac{2}{1+\gamma}}\right)}$$

$$\Longleftrightarrow r[c_j] \geq \frac{\ln(\frac{1}{\epsilon})}{\ln\left(\frac{2}{1+\gamma}\right) - \left(\frac{1-\gamma}{2}\right)}$$

which concludes the proof of the lemma.   □

5.1   A Cost Breakdown

It is convenient to break down the algorithm costs into different components. In case of *OFF*, the situation is fairly easy: *OFF* simply incurs a migration cost, henceforth denoted by OFF_{mig}, of $\text{OFF}_{mig} = 2\alpha \cdot d_{OFF}$ to move to the optimal location c_{OFF}, where d_{OFF} is the rotation distance between c_0 and c_{OFF}, plus an expected communication cost OFF_{comm} of $|\sigma| \cdot p(c_{OFF})$.

In case of *ON*, the situation is more complicated. In particular, while we do not distinguish between different migration costs for *ON* either, we consider three types of communication costs for *ON*: ON_{elim} is the elimination cost, i.e., the total communication cost incurred while *ON* is waiting on every configuration that has not been eliminated yet, until the condition $\text{Cond}(j,i)$ is fulfilled for the current configuration. ON_{ins} is the "insurance" cost paid by *ON* when waiting in an already eliminated configuration, until being allowed to actually move beyond the current radius to a non-eliminated configuration. Finally, ON_{final} is the communication cost paid by *ON* once it reached its final configuration and all other configurations have been eliminated. (Note that the cost incurred at the final configuration while there are still other, non-eliminated configurations, is counted toward elimination costs).

The total communication cost ON_{comm} is the sum of these three costs. In the following, we will prove that all these cost components are competitive compared to OFF's overall costs, from which the bound on the competitive ratio is obtained.

5.2   Competitive Ratio

We now prove that our online algorithm ON performs well with high probability (w.h.p.). That is, we derive a competitive ratio of $O(\log k)$ which holds with probability at least $1 - 1/n^c$ for some constant c.

Theorem 1. *The competitive ratio achieved by* ON *is* $\rho \in O(\log n)$ *with high probability.*

The remainder of this section is devoted to the proof of this theorem. In particular, we will use our cost breakdown, and express the competitive ratio as (where $\sigma = \sigma(\mathscr{D})$):

$$\rho = \max_{\sigma}(\frac{\text{ON}(\sigma)}{\text{OFF}(\sigma)}) = \max_{\sigma} \left(\frac{\text{ON}_{mig}(\sigma) + \text{ON}_{elim}(\sigma) + \text{ON}_{ins}(\sigma) + \text{ON}_{final}(\sigma)}{\text{OFF}_{comm}(\sigma) + \text{OFF}_{mig}(\sigma)} \right)$$

We will prove that each cost component in ON is competitive to OFF's overall cost, therefore resulting in an $O(\log n \cdot \text{OFF}(\sigma))$ bound.

Elimination Costs. To calculate the elimination cost (the total cost resulting from waiting at different configurations until Cond() holds for the current configuration), we divide all configurations into two sets: configurations c for which $p(c) \le 20p_{\min}$ and configurations c' for which $p(c') > 20p_{\min}$. We consider the elimination cost for these two sets in turn.

– All configurations c for which $p(c) \le 20p_{\min}$. We will consider again two cases. Let $e[c]$ the cost of elimination on a position c (number of requests served until the condition of elimination of c is fulfilled). Either $e[c] \le 20 \log n$ or $e[c] > 20 \log n$. In the first case we can just say that the number of configuration we have to eliminate is in $O(\text{ON}_{migr})$ and so $\sum_{e(c_i) \le \log n} e(c_i) \le O(\log n \cdot \text{ON}_{migr}) = O(\log n \cdot \text{OFF})$.

  For the other case, where $e(c_i) > 20 \cdot \log n$, we use the following claim:

Claim. Let $\Delta = [t_1, t_2]$ be a time interval. We note $r[c](\Delta) = r[c](t_2) - r[c](t_1)$, where $r[c](t)$ is the number of requests on the configuration c at the time t. Then: If $p(c_j) \le 20p(c_i)$ and $r[c_j](\Delta) \ge 20 \log n$ then w.h.p. $r[c_j](\Delta) \le 40r[c_i](\Delta)$.

Proof. First note that from the bound of Eq. (3) w.h.p. $r[c_j](\Delta) \le 2E[r[c_j](\Delta)]$. Similarly since $E[r[c_i]] \ge \frac{1}{20}E[r[c_j]]$ we have that w.h.p. $r[c_i](\Delta) \ge \frac{1}{2}E[r[c_i](\Delta)] \ge \frac{1}{40}E[r[c_j](\Delta)]$. So w.h.p. $r[c_j](\Delta) \le 40r[c_i](\Delta)$. □

From the above lemma and union bound over at most n states we get that w.h.p. $r[c_j](\Delta_j) \leq 40 r_{c_{\min}}(\Delta_j)$ for all such configurations, with Δ_j denoting the time interval where we stayed on the configuration c_j, and c_j was not eliminated.

So

$$\sum_{e(c_i) \leq \log n} e(c_i) = \sum_{e(c_i) \leq \log n} r[c_i](\Delta_i) \leq \sum_{e(c_i) \leq \log n} 20 r[c_{min}](\Delta_i)$$

$$\leq 20 r[c_{min}]([0, |\sigma|]) = 20 r[c_{min}] \leq O(OFF_{comm})$$

In conclusion as $ON_{elim \leq 20} = \sum_{e(c_i) \leq \log n} e(c_i) + \sum_{e(c_i) > \log n} e(c_i)$ we have w.h.p.:

$$\frac{ON_{elim \leq 20}(\sigma)}{OFF(\sigma)} = O(1)$$

– All configurations c' for which $p(c') > 20 p_{\min}$. For this we claim:

Claim. If $p(c_j) \geq 20 p(c_i)$ and $r[c_j] \geq 20 \log n$ then w.h.p. $r[c_j] > 5 r[c_i]$ and Cond(j, i) is **True** for $\epsilon = \frac{1}{n^2}$.

Proof. Since $r[c_j] \geq 20 \log n$ w.h.p. $E[r[c_j]] \leq 2 r[c_j]$. If $r[c_i] > \frac{1}{5} r[c_j]$ then w.h.p. $E[r[c_i]] > \frac{1}{10} [c_j]$, but this contradicts the assumption that $E[r[c_i]] \leq \frac{1}{20} E[r[c_j]]$. So we have $\frac{r[c_i]}{r[c_j]} \leq \frac{1}{5}$ and Cond(j, i) holds for $\epsilon = \frac{1}{n^2}$.   □

Now since the number of configurations ON needs to eliminate is lower than $ON_{mig}/\alpha \leq ON_{mig}$, the total cost ON paid is $O(ON_{mig} \cdot \log n)$. But since $\frac{ON_{mig}(\sigma)}{OFF(\sigma)} = O(1)$ (as we show next) we have:

$$\frac{ON_{elim > 20}(\sigma)}{OFF(\sigma)} = O(\log n)$$

To conclude $ON_{elim} = ON_{elim \leq 20} + ON_{elim > 20}$, and: $ON_{elim}(\sigma)/OFF(\sigma) = O(\log n)$.

Migration Cost. We distinguish two cases. Let c_{far} be the farthest configuration reached by our online algorithm. Either d_{far} (the distance between c_{far} and c_0) is lower than d_{OFF}, or it is greater than d_{OFF}.

– In the first case, $d_{OFF} \geq d_{far}$, we can prove

Lemma 2. *if $d_{OFF} \geq d_{far}$ then $ON_{mig} \leq 6 \cdot OFF_{mig}(\sigma)$.*

Proof. $\exists x \in \mathbb{N}$ $2^{2x} \leq d_{far} < 2^{2x+2}$. Then, in the worst case, we have to go to 2^{2x+2}. So

$$ON_{mig}(\sigma) \leq \sum_{i=0}^{2x+1} 3 \cdot 2^i \cdot \alpha \leq 6 \cdot 2^{2x+1} \cdot \alpha \leq 6 d_{far} \alpha \leq 6 \cdot d_{OFF} \cdot \alpha \leq 6 \cdot OFF_{mig}(\sigma)$$

□

- If $d_{OFF} < d_{far}$, then from Claim 5.2 with $\Delta = [0, |\sigma|]$ it follows that w.h.p. $r[c_{OFF}] \geq \Omega(\alpha \cdot d_{far})$: Recall that in our algorithm (line 15) we only move beyond the current radius if the corresponding costs have been amortized. Hence $\text{ON}_{mig} \leq \text{OFF}_{comm}$.

In conclusion, in both cases: $\text{ON}_{mig}(\sigma)/\text{OFF}(\sigma) = O(1)$.

Insurance Costs. For the insurance cost we also consider several cases. Let c_{far} be the farthest configuration reached by our online algorithm. Let c_{OFF} denote the location of the offline algorithm. We split ON_{ins} into two parts: $\text{ON}_{ins<far}$ and $\text{ON}_{ins=far}$. $\text{ON}_{ins<far}$ is the insurance cost up to (not including) c_{far} while $\text{ON}_{ins=far}$ is the insurance cost paid on c_{far}. The last insurance cost, paid before the last migration to c_{far}, is αd_{far}, so we have $\text{ON}_{ins<far} \leq O(\text{ON}_{mig}) = O(\text{OFF})$ (see the migration cost analysis).

The only possible problem is therefore $\text{ON}_{ins=far}$. Now we consider two cases:

- c_{OFF} is in $\mathscr{E}$ (eliminated configuration). Since c_{OFF} was eliminated before c_{far} if follows from Claim 5.2 that w.h.p. $r[c_{OFF}] > \Omega(r[c_{far}])$ so $\text{ON}_{ins=far} \leq O(\text{OFF}_{comm})$.
- c_{OFF} is in $\overline{\mathscr{E}}$. In this case because of our *searching path* and the selection of c_{next}, we have $d_{OFF} \geq d_{next}/2$. Therefore $\text{ON}_{ins=far} \leq O(\text{OFF}_{mig})$.

Overall we have: $\text{ON}_{ins}(\sigma)/\text{OFF}(\sigma) = O(1)$.

Final Costs. By definition, in the final configuration, all other configurations have been eliminated. Thus, our condition, $\text{Cond}(j, i)$, has been fulfilled at some point for any c_j, with respect to some c_i. The probability that we eliminate a minimum configuration and end up at a suboptimal configuration is small. This follows from Lemma 1, when setting $\epsilon := \frac{1}{n^2}$: once we stopped in a configuration, it is, with high probability, a (not necessarily unique) minimal configuration. Since OFF directly moves to a minimum configuration (which may not be unique), ON cannot incur a higher cost than OFF on a specific minimum configuration, i.e., not more than $r[c_{\min}]$. As the offline algorithm moved from the start to a configuration c_{OFF} and $r[c_{\min}]$ is the configuration with the lowest number of requests, $r[c_{OFF}] \geq r[c_{\min}]$. Thus, $\text{ON}_{final}(\sigma) \leq \text{OFF}(\sigma)$, and also $\text{ON}_{final}(\sigma)/\text{OFF}(\sigma) = O(1)$.

Overall Costs. In conclusion, with high probability:

$$\rho \leq \max_{\sigma} \left(\frac{\text{ON}_{mig}(\sigma) + \text{ON}_{elim}(\sigma) + \text{ON}_{ins}(\sigma) + \text{ON}_{final}(\sigma)}{\text{OFF}_{comm}(\sigma) + \text{OFF}_{mig}(\sigma)} \right) = O(\log n)$$

6   Related Work

Our paper takes a novel perspective on a range of classic problems. First, clustering and graph partitioning problems as well as repartitioning problems [21] have been studied for many years and in many contexts. These problems are usually NP-complete and even hard to approximate [2]. Especially partitioning problems for two clusters ($\ell = 2$ in our case), known as minimum bisection problems [9], have been studied intensively. Minimum bisection problems are known to allow for good, $O(\log^{1.5} n)$-factor approximations [13]. Problem variants with $k = 2$ correspond to maximum matching problems, which are polynomial-time solvable. In contrast to our work however, these models assume an offline perspective where the problem input is given ahead of time. In the online world, our problem is related to page (resp. file) migration [4,6] and server migration [5] problems: in these problems, a server needs to be migrated close to requests occurring on a graph, trading off access and migration costs. In the former problem variant, migration costs relate to distance; in the latter, migration costs relate to the available bandwidth along migration paths. Moreover, in our problem, a ski-rental resp. rent-or-buy like tradeoff between migration and communication costs needs to be found. However, migrations do not occur along a graph but between clusters, and multiple nodes can be migrated simultaneously. The large configuration space also renders solutions based on metrical task system approaches [7] inefficient. Another interesting connection exists to k-server problems [11], where multiple servers can "collaboratively" serve requests. In some sense, our problem can be seen as the opposite problem, where rather than aiming to move servers to the locations where the requests occur, we aim to move away and *avoid* configurations (i.e., cuts) where requests occur. More importantly, compared to classic online migration problems where requests define a unique optimal location from which they can be served at minimal cost (namely at the corresponding graph vertex), in our case, a request only reveals very limited information about the optimal (minimal cost) configuration. In other words, a single request only contains very limited information about how good a current clustering is, and how far (in terms of migrations) we are from an optimal offline location.

Our model can be seen as a generalization of online paging [10,14,15,20,22], and especially its variants *with bypassing* [1,8]. However, in general, in our model, the "cache" is *distributed*: requests occur *between* nodes and *not to* nodes, and costs can be saved by collocation.

Our problem also has connections to online packing problems, where items of different sizes arriving over time need to be packed into a minimal number of bins [18,19]. In contrast to these problems, however, in our case the objective is not to minimize the number of bins but rather the number of "links" between bins, given a fixed number of bins.

The paper closest to ours is [3] which studies online partitioning problems from a deterministic perspective, i.e., σ is generated in a deterministic manner. In this setting, it has been shown that the competitive ratio is inherently high, at least linear in k, and even if the online algorithm is allowed to user larger clusters than the offline algorithm (scenario with augmentation). We in this paper initiate the study of stochastic models where request patterns are drawn from an unknown but fixed distribution, and show that polylogarithmic bounds can be achieved under ring patterns, even without augmentation.

In general, we believe that a key conceptual contribution of our model itself regards the underlying combination of learning and searching. Indeed, while the fundamental problem of how to efficiently learn a distribution has been explored for many decades [17], our perspective comes with an additional locality requirement, namely that searching induces costs (i.e., migrations).

7   Conclusion

This paper initiated the study of a natural cluster learning problem where the search procedure entails costs: communication costs occur in "suboptimal" clustering configurations and migration costs occur when switching between configurations. In particular, we presented an efficient online clustering algorithm which performs well even if compared to an offline algorithm which knows the distribution of the communication pattern ahead of time. Indeed, the $O(\log k)$ competitive ratio is interesting as k is likely to be small in the applications considered in this paper: k corresponds to the number of virtual machines that can be hosted on the same server, e.g., the number of cores. Moreover, we believe that our online approach is interesting in practice as it does not rely on any assumptions on the communication distribution, which may turn out to be wrong.

We believe that our work sheds an interesting new light on multiple classic problems, and opens an interesting field for future research. In particular, it would be interesting to know whether similar competitive ratios can be achieved even for more general communication patterns. Moreover, so far we have only focused on deterministic algorithms, and the exploration of randomized algorithms constitutes another interesting avenue for future research.

References

1. Adamaszek, A., Czumaj, A., Englert, M., Räcke, H.: An O(log k)-competitive algorithm for generalized caching. In: Proceedings of the 23rd SODA, pp. 1681–1689 (2012)
2. Andreev, K., Räcke, H.: Balanced graph partitioning. Theor. Comput. Syst. **39**(6), 929–939 (2006)
3. Avin, C., Loukas, A., Pacut, M., Schmid, S.: Online balanced repartitioning. In: proceedings of the 30th International Symposium on Distributed Computing (DISC) (2016)
4. Bartal, Y., Charikar, M., Indyk, P.: On page migration and other relaxed task systems. Theoret. Comput. Sci. **268**(1), 43–66 (2001). Also appeared in Proceedings of the 8th SODA, pp. 43–52 (1997)
5. Bienkowski, M., Feldmann, A., Grassler, J., Schaffrath, G., Schmid, S.: The wide-area virtual service migration problem: a competitive analysis approach. IEEE/ACM Trans. Netw. (ToN) **22**, 165–178 (2014)
6. Black, D.L., Sleator, D.D.: Competitive algorithms for replication and migration problems (1989)

7. Borodin, A., Linial, N., Saks, M.E.: An optimal on-line algorithm for metrical task system. J. ACM **39**(4), 745–763 (1992). Also appeared in Proceedings of the 19th STOC, pp. 373–382 (1987)
8. Epstein, L., Imreh, C., Levin, A., Nagy-György, J.: Online file caching with rejection penalties. Algorithmica **71**(2), 279–306 (2015)
9. Feige, U., Krauthgamer, R.: A polylogarithmic approximation of the minimum bisection. SIAM J. Comput. **31**(4), 1090–1118 (2002)
10. Fiat, A., Karp, R.M., Luby, M., McGeoch, L.A., Sleator, D.D., Young, N.E.: Competitive paging algorithms. J. Algorithms **12**(4), 685–699 (1991)
11. Fiat, A., Rabani, Y., Ravid, Y.: Competitive k-server algorithms. J. Comput. Syst. Sci. **48**(3), 410–428 (1994)
12. Franck, W.: An optimal search problem. SIAM Rev. **7**(4), 503–512 (1965)
13. Krauthgamer, R., Feige, U.: A polylogarithmic approximation of the minimum bisection. SIAM Rev. **48**(1), 99–130 (2006)
14. McGeoch, L.A., Sleator, D.D.: A strongly competitive randomized paging algorithm. Algorithmica **6**(6), 816–825 (1991)
15. Mendel, M., Seiden, S.S.: Online companion caching. Theoret. Comput. Sci. **324** (2–3), 183–200 (2004)
16. Mitzenmacher, M., Upfal, E.: Probability and Computing: Randomized Algorithms and Probabilistic Analysis. Cambridge University Press, New York (2005)
17. Pöschel, T., Ebeling, W., Rosé, H.: Guessing probability distributions from small samples. J. Stat. Phys. **80**(5–6), 1443–1452 (1995)
18. Ramanan, P.V., Brown, D.J., Lee, C.C., Lee, D.T.: On-line bin packing in linear time. J. Algorithms **10**(3), 305–326 (1989)
19. Seiden, S.S.: On the online bin packing problem. J. ACM **49**(5), 640–671 (2002)
20. Sleator, D.D., Tarjan, R.E.: Amortized efficiency of list update and paging rules. Commun. ACM **28**(2), 202–208 (1985)
21. Vaquero, L., Cuadrado, F., Logothetis, D., Martella, C.: Adaptive partitioning for large-scale dynamic graphs. In: Proceedings of the 4th Annual Symposium on Cloud Computing (SOCC), pp. 35:1–35:2 (2013)
22. Young, N.E.: On-line caching as cache size varies. In: Proceedings of the 2nd ACM-SIAM Symposium on Discrete Algorithms (SODA), pp. 241–250 (1991)

Toward a Resource Availability Measurement in Peer to Peer Systems

Moufida Rahmani$^{(\boxtimes)}$ and Mahfoud Benchaïba

LSI Laboratory, Department of Computer Science,
University of Science and Technology Houari Boumediene, Algiers, Algeria
{morahmani,mbenchaiba}@usthb.dz

Abstract. A fundamental challenge in unstructured peer-to-peer systems is how to identify rare resources. Actual solutions only base on local information of peers or from their direct neighbors, which is not enough to know if resources are rare or not. We propose a Resource Availability Measurement for mobile P2P systems which considers knowledge from all peers of the system. Preliminary simulation results show that our estimation of availability is close to the real one.

Keywords: Mobile peer-to-peer · Availability · Rare resource · Replication · Clustering

1 Introduction

Peer-to-peer (P2P) systems are an alternative to traditional client/server systems: every peer acts as both a client and a server for respectively asking and sharing resources. P2P applications consist mainly of file-sharing like Gnutella [4], distributed computing and streaming. Mobile P2P systems, that consist of P2P systems deployed over the devices composing a MANET, constitute an interesting environment for sharing files in public spaces like airport lounges or temporary events like music concerts. An object has a measurement of its availability in the P2P system. It can be rare if it is less available compared to number of the peers in the system. Identifying rare resources in P2P system is a fundamental challenge because a peer is neither aware of the number of peers in the whole system nor of their shared resources. The resource availability assessment can be efficiently used in object search and in replication strategies to improve the network performances. Some works on the replication [1] and hybrid search [2] have proposed different methods to identify rare files but they only base on information local to peers or from their direct neighbors, which is not enough to know if file are rare or not. This paper proposes a Resource Availability Measurement for mobile P2P systems, which considers knowledge from all peers of the system. Our estimated availability is close to the real one. The remainder of the paper is organized as follows. Section 2 describes our contribution. In the Sect. 3, we present our experimental evaluation. Finally, Sect. 4 concludes the paper.

© Springer International Publishing AG 2017
A. El Abbadi and B. Garbinato (Eds.): NETYS 2017, LNCS 10299, pp. 248–252, 2017.
DOI: 10.1007/978-3-319-59647-1_19

2   Resource Availability Measurement

The file's availability is the ratio of its total number of copies in the network and the total number of peers in the network. We use a clustering method as we need information from all peers of the network and there is no central entity to keep information of all peers. Clustering is used to efficiently retrieve global information. Each clusterhead (CH) has global knowledge about its cluster and keeps counters of the number of all cluster file copies and the number of peers in the cluster which helps to give a more realistic estimation. We can use any clustering method proposed in the literature as proposed in [3] to apply resource availability calculation. We consider an unstructured MP2P system, each peer indexes its own files and has no knowledge about the other shared files in the network and their locations. Each joining peer must establish connections with some neighbors and join a cluster.

2.1   Calculation of Resource Availability

In this section, we explain the collaboration between the CHs through *hello* messages to calculate the global availability of a file. Each CH communicates the information of its members to neighboring CHs. A CH aggregates its own information with the received one to compute global-like availability but also propagates the information to other CHs to cover the entire network. All the calculations are done locally at each CH. Two main measurements, local file availability (LA) and Global file availability (GA), are estimated; they are updated continuously based on local knowledge and received global knowledge.

Based on Local Knowledge: Each CH calculates for each file in the cluster its LA based on the number of file copies (NC) and the number of peers including $CH(NP)$ in the cluster as follows:

$$LA = NC/NP \tag{1}$$

The total number of file copies in the network (TNC) is set to NC and is updated each time the number of file copies in the cluster is updated. Additionally, the total number of peers of the network (TNP) is set to NP and updated when NP is updated. Therefore, the global availability (GA) is set to local availability and updated when LA is updated. If member peer shares a new file or deletes one, it informs its clusterhead by piggybacking the *file_key* of this file to the periodic *hello* message. This leads the CH to update locally *file_key list* of this member peer, NC and TNC.

Based on Global Knowledge: Before any contact with other CHs, the global availability is equal to the local availability because at this step, the computation is only based on local information. However, since it is not enough to reflect the real value, we consider information (files list and peers number) of other CHs.

All the necessary information is piggybacked in *hello* messages. *CH* executes two phases: initial phase and update phase. In the initial phase, Each new *CH* sends to its neighbors *NC* of its local *file_key* and *NP*. After that, the update phase consists only to send the update information (add new file, delete file, etc.) to avoid redundancy. Between two *hello* messages, a member peer may share new file or delete file and a new peer may join a cluster or member peer may discon-nect. A *CH* takes into consideration all these changes locally as explained above, but also needs to inform its neighbors. All these changes are in cache and *CH* sends them with a *timestamp* (i.e. *Seq_Num* variable) in the next *hello* message. *Timestamp* is used to determine the freshness of the information contained in the *hello* message. When a *CH* receives a *hello* message from one of its *CH* neighbors, it extracts the necessary information $(Info_1,..., Info_j,..., Info_m)$. Each $Info_j$ contains:

- $IPaddress_j$: is the IP address of the source *CH*.
- $Timestamp_j$: is used to show the freshness of this information.
- $Peer\_number_j$: is equal to *NP* if the sender is in the initial phase. During the update phase, $Peer\_number_j$ may take a positive value, meaning that new peer member has joined the cluster or a negative value, meaning that a peer member is disconnected.
- $(file\_key_{1j} = val_{1j},..., file\_key_{ij} = val_{ij},..., file\_key_{nj} = val_{nj})$: if a *CH* is in initial phase, $file\_key_{ij}$ is key of a cluster local file and val_{ij} equals its *NC*. During the update phase, $file\_key_{ij}$ may be the key of a new shared file or of a deleted file and val_{ij} can take a positive value if a new file is shared and a negative value if a file is deleted.

The *CH* checks the freshness of each $Info_j$ by comparing its *timestamp* to the last *timestamp*. If the information is not up-to-date, the *CH* ignores it. Otherwise, the *CH* applies the following modifications:

$$TNP = TNP + \sum_{j=1}^{m} Peer\_number_j \qquad (2)$$

For each $file\_key_i$:

$$TNC = \begin{cases} TNC + \sum_{j=1}^{m} val_{ij} & \text{if } file\_key_i \text{ exists in } Index2 \\ \sum_{j=1}^{m} val_{ij} & \text{else} \end{cases} \qquad (3)$$

Where *Index2* is structure that contains file_key, *NC*, *TNC*, *LA*, *GA* of each file. Then, *GA* is updated as follows :

$$GA = TNC/TNP \qquad (4)$$

Figure 1 shows a simple example of file availability estimation. Before any contact between *CH*s, the global availability in each cluster equals the local availability (Fig. 1(A)). After the exchange of *hello* messages between *CH*s, the availabilities of all files in each cluster equal the real ones (Fig. 1(B)).

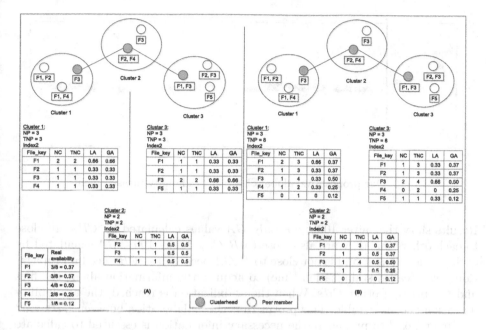

Fig. 1. The global file availability estimation

3   Simulation

We used OMNeT++ [5], a discrete event simulation environment which provides both P2P model and ad-hoc 802.11 model, to study the performance of proposal with number of mobile nodes equals to 300. Simulations area is $1500\,\text{m}* 1500\,\text{m}$ and transmission range is 120 m. Random Way Point mobility is used with maximum speed of 2 m/s. We compared the global file availability measurement (GA) with the real availability value denoted R_GA, since we are not aware of another global resource availability measurement in the literature. We used the global observer algorithm implemented in OMNeT++. The global observer has a global view of the P2P network and is able to calculate R_GA with Eq. (4) for a given file F_1. We considered in this paper that there are one hop between CH and its member peers (1-hop clustering approach) and maximum number of members is 10. The average neighbor per CH is 5. Each peer has a random number of local files limited to 50. For our simulations, we chose one file denoted F_1 and observed its GA evolution compared to its R_GA. Initially, 60% of the peers possess F_1 and we do not apply any replication strategy; consequently, if a number of peers equals 180 then the copies number of F_1 is equal to 108 and R_GA is equal to 0.58 ($= 108/180$).

Figure 2 presents the availability measurement of the file F_1 during a simulation time of 600 s. The *hello* delay is the time interval between two *hello* messages and is set to 20 s. The thin lines represent GA measurements of F_1 at some participating CHs in the network and thick line represents R_GA of F_1.

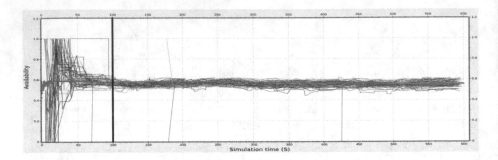

Fig. 2. Our proposal vs. global observer availability measurement

Results show that after 100 s, not only GA values calculated by CHs are close to each others but they are also close to R_GA. Before 100 s, GA calculated by each CH is different and is not close to R_GA because the CHs need a propagation delay (called stabilization time) to acquire the information about the files and the peers of other CHs. When the stabilization is reached, the availability deviation becomes stable. This proves that the collaboration between CHs used in our proposal to propagate the necessary information is essential to calculate the global-like file availability.

4   Conclusion

In this paper, we have proposed a simple and efficient resource availability algorithm for MP2P. We benefited from a clustering method and collaboration between clusters to gain a global-like knowledge. Preliminary experimental results showed that our proposal is close to real measurement. More details and simulation tests will be added in our future contributions.

References

1. Gao, G., Li, R., Wen, K., Gu, X.: Proactive replication for rare objects in unstructured peer-to-peer networks. Netw. Comput. Appl. **35**, 85–96 (2012)
2. Loo, B.T., Huebsch, R., Stoica, I., Hellerstein, J.M.: The case for a hybrid P2P search infrastructure. In: Voelker, G.M., Shenker, S. (eds.) IPTPS 2004. LNCS, vol. 3279, pp. 141–150. Springer, Heidelberg (2005). doi:10.1007/978-3-540-30183-7_14
3. Rahmani, M., Benchaïba, M.: Cross-layer design of clustering scheme for peer to peer over manet. In: Proceedings of the 1st International Conference on Advanced Networking Distributed Systems and Applications, INDS 2014, pp. 5–10 (2014)
4. Ripeanu, M., Iamnitchi, A., Foster, I.T.: Mapping the Gnutella network. IEEE Internet Comput. **6**(1), 50–57 (2002). http://dx.doi.org/10.1109/4236.978369
5. Varga, A., Hornig, R.: An overview of the OMNeT++ simulation environment. In: Proceedings of the 1st International Conference on Simulation Tools and Techniques for Communications, Networks and Systems & Workshops (2008)

Verification

Concurrent Program Verification with Lazy Sequentialization and Interval Analysis

Truc L. Nguyen[1]([✉]), Bernd Fischer[2], Salvatore La Torre[3],
and Gennaro Parlato[1]

[1] Electronics and Computer Science, University of Southampton, Southampton, UK
tnl2g10@soton.ac.uk
[2] Division of Computer Science, Stellenbosch University, Stellenbosch, South Africa
[3] Dipartimento di Informatica, Università degli Studi di Salerno, Fisciano, Italy

Abstract. Lazy sequentialization has proven to be one of the most effective techniques for concurrent program verification. The Lazy-CSeq sequentialization tool performs a "lazy" code-to-code translation from a concurrent program into an equivalent non-deterministic sequential program, i.e., it preserves the valuations of the program variables along its executions. The obtained program is then analyzed using sequential bounded model checking tools. However, the sizes of the individual states still pose problems for further scaling. We therefore use abstract interpretation to minimize the representation of the concurrent program's (shared global and thread-local) state variables. More specifically, we run the Frama-C abstract interpretation tool over the programs constructed by Lazy-CSeq to compute overapproximating intervals for all (original) state variables and then exploit CBMC's bitvector support to reduce the number of bits required to represent these in the sequentialized program. We have implemented this approach in the last release of Lazy-CSeq and demonstrate the effectiveness of this approach; in particular, we show that it leads to large performance gains for very hard verification problems.

1 Introduction

Concurrent programming is becoming more important as concurrent computer architectures such as multi-core processors are becoming more common. However, concurrent program verification remains a stubbornly hard problem, due to the large number of interleavings that a verifier must analyze. Techniques such as testing that analyze interleavings individually struggle to find "rare" concurrency bugs, i.e., bugs that manifest themselves only in a few of the interleavings. Techniques that use symbolic representations to analyze all interleavings collectively typically fare better, especially for rare concurrency bugs.

Sequentialization has proven to be one of the most effective symbolic techniques for concurrent program verification, shown for example by the fact that

---

Partially supported by EPSRC EP/M008991/1, INDAM-GNCS 2016, and MIUR-FARB 2014–2016 grants.

A. El Abbadi and B. Garbinato (Eds.): NETYS 2017, LNCS 10299, pp. 255–271, 2017.
DOI: 10.1007/978-3-319-59647-1_20

most concurrency medals in the recent SV-COMP program verification competitions were won by various sequentialization-based tools [17,31,32,35]. It is based on the idea of translating concurrent programs into non-deterministic sequential programs that (under certain assumptions) behave equivalently, so that the different interleavings do not need to be treated explicitly during verification and, consequently, sequential program verification methods can be reused. Eager sequentialization approaches [10,24,33] guess the different values of the shared memory before the verification and then simulate (under this guess) each thread in turn. They can thus explore infeasible computations that need to be pruned away afterwards, which requires a second copy of the shared memory, and so increases the state space. Lazy sequentialization approaches [20] instead guess the context switch points and (re-) compute the memory contents, and thus explore only feasible computations. They also preserve the sequential ordering of the interleaved thread executions and thus the local invariants of the original program. Lazy approaches, such as Lazy-CSeq, are thus typically more efficient than eager approaches.

Lazy-CSeq [15,17] is implemented as a source-to-source transformation in the CSeq framework [9]: it reads a multi-threaded C program that uses the Pthreads API [18], applies the translation sketched in Sect. 2 and described in more detail in [16], and outputs the resulting non-deterministic sequential C program. This allows us to use any off-the-shelf sequential verification tool for C as backend, although we have achieved the best results with CBMC [6].

Lazy-CSeq's translation is carefully designed to introduce very small memory overheads and very few sources of nondeterminism, so that it produces simple formulas. It also aggressively exploits the structure of bounded programs and works well with backends based on bounded model checking (BMC). It is very effective in practice, and scales well to larger and harder problems. Currently, Lazy-CSeq is the only tool able to find bugs in the two hardest known concurrency benchmarks, safestack [37] and eliminationstack [12]. However, for such hard benchmarks the computational effort remains high, and for eliminationstack Lazy-CSeq requires close to six hours on a standard machine.

A detailed analysis of these benchmarks shows that a large fraction of the overall effort is not spent on finding the right interleavings that expose the bugs, but on finding the right values of the original (concurrent) programs' shared global and individual thread-local variables. We found that this is caused by the unnecessarily large number of propositional variables (reflecting the default bit-widths of the variables in C) that CBMC uses. In an experiment, we manually reduced this to the minimum required to find the bug (three bits in the case of safestack), which leads to a 20x speed-up. This clearly indicates the potential benefits of such a reduction.

In this paper, we describe an automated method based on abstract interpretation to reduce the size of the concurrent programs' shared global and thread-local state variables. More specifically, we run the Frama-C abstract interpretation tool [2] over the sequentialized programs constructed by Lazy-CSeq to compute overapproximating intervals for these variables. We use the intervals to minimize the representation of the (original) state variables, exploiting CBMC's bitvector support to reduce the number of bits required to represent these in the sequentialized program, and, hence, ultimately in the formula fed into the SAT solver. Note that this approach relies on two crucial aspects of Lazy-CSeq's design. On the theoretical side, we rely on the fact that lazy sequentializations only explore feasibly computations to infer "useful" invariants that actually speed up the verification; our approach would not work with eager sequentializations because they leave the original state variables unconstrained, leading to invariants that are too weak. On the practical side, we rely on the source-to-source approach implemented in Lazy-CSeq, in order to re-use an existing abstract interpretation tool.

We have implemented this approach in the last release of Lazy-CSeq and demonstrate its effectiveness. We show that the effort for the abstract interpretation phase is relatively small, and that the inferred intervals are tight enough to be useful in practice and lead to large performance gains for very hard verification problems. In particular, we demonstrate a 5x speed-up for eliminationstack.

2 Verification Approach

In this section we illustrate the verification approach we propose in this paper. We recall multi-threaded programs and context-bounded analysis before we give some details on the two pillars of our approach: the lazy sequentialization performed by the tool Lazy-CSeq [16] and the value analysis performed by the tool Frama-C [2].

2.1 The General Scheme

Verification by sequentialization is based on a translation of the input multi-threaded program into a corresponding sequential program which is then analysed by an off-the-shelf backend verification tool for sequential programs. We improve on this by applying value analysis to the sequentialized program to derive overapproximating intervals for the original program variables and using these intervals to reduce the number of bits used to represent each variable in the backend verification tool. In particular, our approach works in four steps:

1. We compute a sequential program that preserves the reachable states of the input program up to a given number of thread context-switches (*sequentialization*).
2. We compute the bounds on the values that the variables can store along any computation of the sequential program (*value analysis*).
3. We transform the sequentialized program by changing the program variables of numerical type (i.e., integer and double) to bitvector types of sizes determined by the results of the value analysis (*model refinement*).
4. We verify the resulting sequential program (*verification*).

In sequentializations the control nondeterminism of the original program is replaced by data nondeterminism and thread invocations are replaced by function calls. Lazy sequentialization methods also preserve the sequential ordering of the interleaved thread executions, and thus also the local invariants of the original program. This property ensures that the value analysis can produce good overapproximations of the variable ranges (i.e., tight intervals). We instantiate our approach with the lazy sequentialization implemented in Lazy-CSeq, and the value analysis given by Frama-C.

2.2 Multithreaded Programs

We consider standard multi-threaded programs with shared variables, dynamic thread creation, thread join, and mutex locking and unlocking operations for thread synchronization. We omit the formal definition of the syntax and the semantics of multi-threaded programs which is standard [16]. We adopt a C-like syntax in our examples.

We assume that each multi-threaded program contains a function main, which is the starting function of the only thread that exists in the beginning. We call this the *main thread*. As usual, there are no calls to main and that no other thread can be created that uses main as starting function.

We assume a sequentially consistent semantics by interleaving, thus only one of the *executable* threads can be *active* (i.e., running) at any given time. Initially, only the *main thread* is active; new threads can be spawned from any thread by invoking create. Once created, a thread is added to the pool of the executable threads. At a *context switch* the currently active thread is suspended (but remains executable), and one of the executable threads is resumed and becomes the active thread. When a thread becomes active it resumes from the point where it was suspended (or from the beginning, if it becomes active for the first time). For ease of presentation, we assume that each statement is executed atomically.

Each *thread configuration* is a triple $\langle locals, pc, stack \rangle$, where *locals* is a valuation of the local variables, *pc* is the *program counter* that tracks the currently executing statement, and *stack* is a stack of function calls that works as usual. A *configuration* of a multithreaded program is a tuple of thread configurations along with valuation of the global variables that are shared by all threads.

A *context* is a possibly empty sequence of statements that consecutively executed by a thread in a computation. We underapproximate the behavior of a concurrent program by allowing computations up to a given round of a round-robin schedule (*bounded round-robin computations*). In such computations, each executable thread executes exactly one context for each round and in all considered rounds threads are always scheduled according to a same schedule (note that this is not a real restriction since a thread can execute zero statements in a round).

As an example consider the multithreaded program in Fig. 1. It encodes a producer/consumer system. The program has two shared variables: a mutex m and an integer c that stores the number of items that have been produced but not yet consumed. The main function initializes the mutex and spawns two threads executing P (*Producer*) and two threads executing C (*Consumer*). Each producer acquires m, increments c, and terminates by releasing m. Each consumer first checks whether there are still elements not yet consumed; if so (i.e., the assume-statement on $c > 0$ holds), it decrements c, checks the assertion $c \geq 0$ and terminates. Otherwise it terminates immediately.

Note that the mutex ensures that at any point of the computation at most one producer is operating. However, the assertion can still be violated since there are two consumer threads, whose behaviors can be freely interleaved: with $c = 1$, both consumers can pass the assumption, so that both decrement c and one of them will write the value -1 back to c, and thus violate the assertion.

2.3 Lazy Sequentialization Schema

In this section, we briefly recall the lazy sequentialization encoding that we use in our approach. This is implemented in our Lazy-CSeq tool [15,16]. We assume that a concurrent program P consists of $n + 1$ functions $f_0, \ldots, f_n$, where f_0 denotes the main function, and that P creates at most n threads, with the respective start functions $f_1, \ldots, f_n$. Moreover, no function f_i contains loops. Note that these assumptions can easily be enforced by bounding the programs in BMC fashion and cloning the start functions, if necessary (*bounded multi-threaded program*). Since each start function is thus associated with at most one thread, we can identify threads and (start) functions.

Consider a bounded multithreaded program P as described above. In our analysis of bounded round-robin computations, we fix a number of rounds K and an arbitrary schedule ρ by permuting the functions $f_0, \ldots, f_n$ that form the starting program. Thus, the lazy sequentialization of P yields a sequential program P' such that P fails an assertion in K rounds if and only if P' fails the same assertion. P' is composed of a new function main and a thread simulation function T_i for each thread f_i in P. The lazy sequentialization of the

```
mutex m; int c=0;                    void C() {
                                       assume(c>0);
                                       c--;
void P(void *b) {                      assert(c>=0);
  int tmp=(*b);                      }
  lock(&m);
  if(c>0)                            int main(void) {
    c++;                               int x=1,y=5;
  else {                              thread p0,p1,c0,c1;
    c=0;                               mutex_init(&m);
    while(tmp>0) {                     create(&p0,P,&x);
      c++; tmp--;                      create(&p1,P,&y);
    }                                  create(&c0,C,0);
  }                                    create(&c1,C,0);
  unlock(&m);                          return 0;
}                                    }
```

Fig. 1. Producer/Consumer program.

```
bool active[T]={1,0,0,0,0};
int cs,ct,pc[T],size[T]={5,8,8,2,2};
#define G(L) assume(cs>=L);
#define J(A,B) if(pc[ct]>A||A>=cs) goto B;
mutex m; bitvector[4] c=0;

void P1(void *b) {                    int Tmain() {
  0:J(0,1) static bitvector[4] tmp;            static bitvector[2] x=1;
           tmp=(*b);                           static bitvector[4] y=5;
  1:J(1,2) lock(&m);                           static thread p0,p1,c0,c1;
  2:J(2,3) if(c>0)                    0:J(0,1) mutex_init(&m);
  3:J(3,4)   c++;                     1:J(1,2) create(&p0,P0,&x,1);
           else { G(4)               1:J(2,3) create(&p1,P1,&y,2);
  4:J(4,5)   c=0;                     2:J(3,4) create(&c0,C0,0,3);
           if(!(tmp>0)) goto _l1;     3:J(4,5) create(&c1,C1,0,4);
  5:J(5,6)   c++; tmp--;                       goto _main; _main: G(4)
           if(!(tmp>0)) goto _l1;     5:       return 0;
  6:J(6,7)   c++; tmp--;              }
           assume(!(tmp>0));
           _l1: G(7);                 int main() {
           } G(7)                       for(r=1; r<=K; r++) {
  7:J(7,8) unlock(&m);                   ct=0;
           goto _P0; _P0: G(8)          if(active[ct]) {           //thread active?
  8:       return;                       cs=pc[ct]+nd_uint(); //next ctx. switch
  }                                      assume(cs<=size[ct]);//value in range?
                                         Tmain();                  //thread simulation
  void P2(void *b) {...}                 pc[ct]=cs;                //store ctx. switch
                                         }
  void C1() {                         .........
  0:J(0,1) assume(c>0);                 ct=2;
  1:J(1,2) c--;                         if(active[ct]) {
           assert(c>=0);                  .........
           goto _C0; _C0: G(2)         }
  2:       return;                      }
  }                                   }

  void C2() {...}
```

Fig. 2. Lazy-CSeq sequentialized code of the Consumer/Producer program modified according to the value analysis by Frama-C.

Producer/Consumer program given in Fig. 1 generated by Lazy-CSeq (with two loop unwindings) is the code shown in Fig. 2 with the bitvector type in bold replaced by the integer type. In the figure, we emphasize the code injected by Lazy-CSeq showing in black the original code and in gray the injected code.

Note that the sequential verification of P' relies on stubs provided by Lazy-CSeq. P' thus uses a slightly modified version of the Pthreads API. For example, the create stub takes an additional argument for the (statically known) id of the calling thread; see [16] for details.

The new main of P' is a driver that calls, in the order given by ρ, the functions T_i for K complete rounds. For each thread it maintains the label at which the context switch was simulated in the previous round and where the computation must thus resume in the current round. Moreover, before each call of T_i, the label at which the control will context-switch out is nondeterministically guessed.

Each T_i is essentially f_i with few lines of injected control code and with labels to denote the relevant context-switch points in the original code.

When executed, each T_i jumps (in multiple hops) to the saved position in the code and then restarts its execution until the label of the next context switch is reached. This is achieved by the J-macro. Context-switching at branching statements requires some extra care; see [16] for details. We also make the local variables persistent (i.e., `static`) such that we do not need to re-compute them when resuming suspended executions.

We use some additional data structures and variables to control the context-switching in and out of threads as described above. The data structures are parameterized over T $\leq n$ which denotes the maximal number of threads activated in P's executions. We keep track of the active threads (`active`), the arguments passed in each thread creation (we omitted it in our example since the considered thread functions have no arguments), the largest label used in each T_i (`size`), the current label of each T_i (`pc`), and for the currently executed thread its index (`ct`) and the context-switch point guessed in the main driver before calling the thread (`cs`).

Note that the control code that is injected in the translation is designed such that each T_i reads but does not write any of the additional data structures. These are updated only in the main driver and in the portions of code simulating the API functions concerning thread creation and termination. This introduces fewer dependencies between the injected code and the original code, which typically leads to a better performance of the backend tool (e.g., for BMC backends this results in smaller formulas).

2.4   Value Analysis

The value analysis of programs aims at computing supersets of possible values for all the variables at each statement of the analyzed program. All executions of the instruction that are possible starting from the function chosen as the entry-point of the analysis are taken into account.

The value analysis of Frama-C [2] is a plug-in based on abstract interpretation and is capable of handling C programs with pointers, arrays, structs, and type casts. Abstract interpretation links the set of all possible executions of a program (*concrete semantics*) to a more coarse-grained semantics (*abstract semantics*). Frama-C explores symbolic execution of the program, translating all operations into the abstract semantics. For the soundness of the approach, any transformation in the concrete semantics must have an abstract counterpart that captures all possible outcomes of the concrete operation. Thus, when several execution paths are possible, e.g., when analyzing an if-statement, all branches need to be explored and then at the point where the branches join together, e.g., after the if statement, the lattice-theoretic join of the results along each branch is taken. In Frama-C this is implemented as the smallest interval that encloses all intervals computed along the individual branches. For-loops require additional care, since value analysis is not guaranteed to terminate. However, this aspect is not relevant to our approach as the output of Lazy-CSeq does not contain loops but only bounded programs.

As an example, consider the sequentialization of the Producer/Consumer program generated by Lazy-CSeq. On this program, Frama-C computes for the integer shared variable c and the integer local variable tmp of producer threads the interval of values $[-2, 5]$. Thus, in the verification analysis we can safely reduce the size of these integer variables to 4 bits (one bit is for the sign) instead of the standard 32 bits used for the type int. Therefore, we can transform the sequentialized program accordingly by replacing the type int in the declaration of these variables with the bitvector type. The resulting sequentialized code is shown in Fig. 2.

3 Implementation

We have implemented our approach in a relatively straightforward way within the CSeq framework, as an extension (Lazy-CSeq+ABS) to the existing Lazy-CSeq implementation. CSeq consists of a number of independent Python modules that provide different program transformations (e.g., function inlining, loop unrolling) as well as parsing and unparsing [15]. These modules can be configured and composed easily to implement different sequentializations as source-to-source transformation tools.

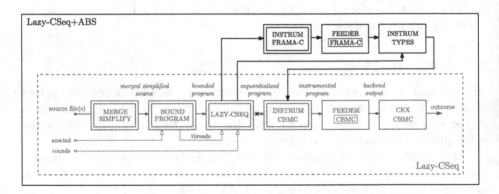

Fig. 3. Lazy-CSeq+ABS Architecture (Color figure online)

The architecture of Lazy-CSeq+ABS is shown in Fig. 3. We now briefly illustrate the architecture of Lazy-CSeq (shown in Fig. 3 in blue), and then incrementally describe how we have extended it. Lazy-CSeq consists of a chain of modules:

- a module that preprocesses the source files merging them into a single file;
- a module that simplifies the syntax;
- a module for unrolling loops and inlining functions to produce a bounded program;
- a module that implements the Lazy-CSeq sequentialization [16] which produces a backend-independent sequentialized file;

- a module to instrument the sequentialized file for a specific backend (in our case, CBMC);
- This module then replaces two wrappers, one for backend invocation (FEEDER), and another one that generates counterexamples (CEX).

We reuse all these module as follows. The output of the LAZY-CSEQ module, which produces a backend-independent sequentialized file, is now instrumented for Frama-C by replacing the nondeterministic choice, assert, and assume statements with the equivalent Frama-C primitives. The next module consists of a wrapper that invokes Frama-C on the instrumented code. The result of this analysis, which reports for each variable a lower and upper bound on the value that the variable can take along any execution of the bounded program, is used by the INSTRUM TYPES module to compute the minimal number of bits required for each program variable. This module then replaces the original scalar type of each variable, say x, in the sequentialized file produced by the LAZY-CSEQ module with the CBMC type __CPROVER_bitvector[i] where i is the number of bits computed for x. The resulting program is then passed to the INSTRUM module and the remaining process is the same as Lazy-CSeq. The additional modules of Lazy-CSeq+ABS are implemented in Python as well.

Lazy-CSeq+ABS is publicly available at: http://users.ecs.soton.ac.uk/gp4/cseq/cseq.html.

4   Experimental Evaluation

In this section we report on a large number of experiments where we compare Lazy-CSeq v1.0 and Lazy-CSeq+ABS with the aim of demonstrating the effectiveness of the approach proposed in this paper. The results of this empirical study show that Lazy-CSeq+ABS is substantially more efficient on complex benchmarks, i.e., larger programs that contain rare bugs. Furthermore, for simple benchmarks, which Lazy-CSeq v1.0 already solves quickly, the overhead of running Frama-C on is often negligible.

In our experiments we use CBMC[1] v5.6 as sequential backend for both Lazy-CSeq v1.0 and Lazy-CSeq+ABS. CBMC encodes symbolically the executions of the bounded program into a CNF formula that is then checked by the SAT solver MINISAT v2.2.1. Furthermore, we use Frama-C[2] v13-Aluminium for Lazy-CSeq+ABS. In the remainder of the paper we denote Lazy-CSeq v1.0 simply as Lazy-CSeq.

We have performed the experiments on an otherwise idle machine with a Xeon W3520 2.6 GHz processor and 12 GB of memory, running a Linux operating system with 64-bit kernel 2.6.32.

Since we use a BMC tool as a backend, we individually set the parameters for the analysis (i.e., loop unwinding, function inlining and rounds of computations) for each unsafe benchmark (i.e., program with a reachable error location) to the minimum values required to expose the corresponding error.

---

[1] CBMC: http://www.cprover.org/cbmc/.
[2] Frama-C: http://frama-c.com.

SV-COMP'16 Benchmarks

The first series of experiments is conducted on the benchmark set from the Concurrency category of the Software Verification Competition (SV-COMP'16) held at TACAS. This set consists of 1005 concurrent C files using the Pthread library, with a total size of about 277,000 lines of code. 784 of the files contain a reachable error location. We use this benchmark set because it is widely used and many state-of-the-art analysis tools have been trained on it. Moreover, it offers a good coverage of the core features of the C programming language as well as of the basic concurrency mechanisms.

Table 1 reports on the experiments for the unsafe benchmarks and Table 2 on those for the safe ones. Each row of these two tables summarizes the experiments by grouping them into sub-categories. For each sub-category, we report the number of files and the total number of lines of code in that sub-category. The tables also gather the results of the experiments performed using Lazy-CSeq v1.0 and Lazy-CSeq+ABS on these benchmarks. For the CBMC backend analysis, we indicate with *time* the average time in seconds, *mem* the average memory peak usage expressed in MB, and with *#vars* and *#clauses* the average number of variables and clauses of the CNF formula produced by CBMC. Furthermore, only for Lazy-CSeq+ABS, the column *Frama-C* denotes the average time in seconds taken by Frama-C for the value analysis.

Table 1. Experiments on SV-COMP unsafe benchmarks

			Lazy-CSeq				Lazy-CSeq+Abs					
			CBMC				CBMC				Frama-C	Total
Subcategory	#files	LOC	sec.	GB	#vars	#clauses	sec.	GB	#vars	#clauses	sec.	sec.
pthread	17	4085	34.7	84.9	89317.7	336250.1	18.0	66.8	47961.4	184287.8	5.5	23.5
pthread-atomic	2	204	1.7	33.3	9131.0	29186.0	1.8	46.2	6259.5	17936.0	0.9	2.7
pthread-ext	8	780	6.5	358.4	647840.1	2654905.9	4.5	83.1	89718.9	423391.8	1.1	5.5
pthread-lit	3	123	1.9	38.3	9993.0	31206.7	1.9	49.3	5882.0	16421.0	1.2	3.1
pthread-wmm	754	236496	2.0	31.4	2427.1	5668.3	2.2	46.1	2402.2	5578.8	0.9	3.1

The two tables paint a relatively clear picture in terms of runtimes. For the larger and more complex benchmark categories pthread (both safe and unsafe instances) and pthread-ext (only safe instances), where Lazy-CSeq takes on average more than 30 s, the effort for the abstract interpretation is relatively small (approx. 5%–20% of the original CBMC runtimes) and is easily recouped, so that we see overall performance gains of approx. 25%–40%. For the simpler benchmarks, Frama-C takes almost as much time as Lazy-CSeq on its own, without substantially reducing the size or complexity of the problems. In most cases we thus see some slow-downs, but in absolute terms these are small (approx. 2 s) and outweighed by the larger gains on the more complex benchmarks.

A very similar picture emerges for peak memory consumption—reductions of approx. 15%–75% for the larger benchmarks that outweigh the relatively large but absolutely small increases for the smaller benchmarks.

Table 2. Experiments on SV-COMP safe benchmarks

Subcategory	#files	LOC	Lazy-CSeq				Lazy-CSeq+Abs				Frama-C	Total
			CBMC				CBMC					
			sec.	GB	#vars	#clauses	sec.	GB	#vars	#clauses	sec.	sec.
pthread	15	1285	172.4	1124.4	1732068.1	7270420.0	98.6	945.3	1424912.1	6004425.3	8.4	107.0
pthread-atomic	9	1136	2.7	37.9	18947.4	67709.0	2.9	47.7	16611.9	58334.0	2.0	4.9
pthread-ext	45	3683	71.7	876.8	1660452.6	6949976.3	49.4	552.6	937205.0	4036919.5	2.2	51.6
pthread-lit	8	432	5.8	43.7	15207.3	57356.2	4.9	51.6	11094.2	42161.0	1.0	5.9
pthread-wmm	144	29282	1.6	31.5	3154.7	9420.2	1.6	45.7	3065.4	9084.0	0.9	2.5

If we look at the number of variables and clauses, we can see how effective our approach is in reducing the size of the induced SAT problems. In most case we see a reduction of approx. 30% to 50%. These reductions are not necessarily correlated to reductions in either the SAT solver's runtime or peak memory consumption, but this is expected, as the size of a SAT problem is generally not a reliable predictor for its difficulty. However, there are two notable exceptions. For the unsafe pthread-ext benchmarks we see a much larger reduction of approx. 85%, but this is skewed by two benchmarks that involve large arrays that allow these large reductions. Conversely, for the pthread-wmm benchmarks we see almost no reduction in size. This is a consequence of the very simple structure of these benchmarks—they are typically loop-free, which means that the unwound programs only contain a (relatively) small number of assignments. Hence, there is little scope to optimize the representation of the program variables.

Complex Benchmarks

We now report on the experiments for three unsafe benchmarks that present a non-trivial challenge for bug-finding tools. These benchmarks consist of non-blocking algorithms for shared data-structures. It is hardly surprising that lock-free programming is an important source of benchmarks whose complexity truly stems from the system's concurrent interactions, not its computations. In fact, the focus there is to minimize the amount of synchronization for performance optimization, thus generating a large amount of nondeterminism due to inter-leaving. Here we demonstrate that Lazy-CSeq is very effective in spotting rare bugs in these programs, and that Lazy-CSeq+Abs allows to amplify its effectiveness both in terms of verification time and memory peak usage.

safestack. This is a real world benchmark implementing a lock-free stack
designed for weak memory models. It
was posted to the CHESS forum by
Dmitry Vyukov.[3] It is unique in the
sense that it contains a very rare bug
that requires at least three threads
and five context-switches to be exposed
when running under the SC seman-
tics. In the verification literature, it was
shown that real-world bugs require at
most three context-switches to manifest themselves [30]. safestack, for

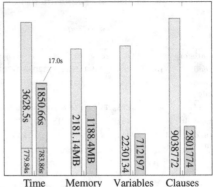

this reason, presents a non-trivial challenge for concurrency testing and symbolic tools. Lazy-CSeq is the only tool we are aware of that can automatically find such concurrency bugs in safestack. It requires about 1 h:13 m:28 s
(of which about one hour is spent in the SAT solver) to find a bug and
has a memory peak of 2.18 GB (by setting the minimal parameters to
expose the bug to 4 rounds of computation and 3 loop-unwinding). Lazy-
CSeq+ABS, with the same parameters, requires 44 m:11 s time, where the
same time is spend in the symbolic execution, and 17 s is the time required
for the value analysis by Frama-C, which leads to a 1.7x speed-up. Also, it
uses only 1.19 GB of memory, i.e., roughly half of the memory required by
Lazy-CSeq. All this is illustrated in the figure on the right where we also
report on the number of variables and clauses of the produced CNF formulas.

eliminationstack. This is a C
implementation of Hendler et al.'s Elimination Stack [12] that follows the original pseudocode presentation. It aug-
ments Treiber's stack with a "collision
array", used when an optimistic push or
pop detects a conflicting operation; the
collision array pairs together concurrent
push and pop operations to "eliminate"
them without affecting the underlying
data structure. This implementation is
incorrect if memory is freed in pop operations. In particular, if memory is freed
only during the "elimination" phase,

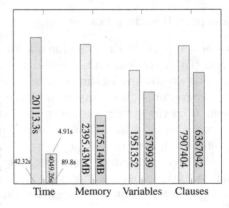

then exhibiting a violation (an instance of the infamous ABA problem) requires
a seven thread client where three push operations are concurrently executed
with four pops. To witness the violation, the implementation is annotated with
several assertions that manipulate counters as described in [4]. Lazy-CSeq is the
only tool we are aware of that can automatically find bugs in this benchmark

---

[3] https://social.msdn.microsoft.com/Forums/.

and requires 5 h:35 m:13 s time and 2.39 GB of memory to find a bug. Lazy-CSeq+ABS, with the same parameters, requires 1 h:07 m:29 s time, where 4.9 s is the time required for the value analysis by Frama-C, which leads to a 5x speed-up. As for the memory usage, it uses only half of the memory required by Lazy-CSeq, namely 1.17 GB. All this is illustrated in the figure on the right where we also report on the number of variables and clauses of the produced CNF formulas.

DCAS. This is a non-blocking algorithm for two-sided queues presented in [1]. This algorithm has a subtle bug that was discovered in an attempt to prove its correctness with the help of the PVS theorem prover. The discovery of the bug took several months of human effort. Although the bug has been automatically discovered using the model checker SPIN (see [13] and http://spinroot.com/dcas/), a generalized version of the benchmark remains a challenge for explicit exploration approach.

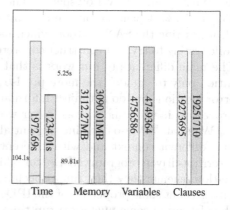

In fact, after 138 h of CPU-time (using 1000 cores), and an exploration of 10^{11} states the error was still undetected [14]. Here, we have translated this benchmark from Promela to C99 with Pthread library considering a more complex version that has 10 threads while the version of [14] only considers 8 threads. Lazy-CSeq can detect the bug within 32 m:52 s and with a memory peak usage of 3.11 GB. Instead, Lazy-CSeq+Abs takes only 20 m:34 s with a memory peak of 3.09 GB. All this is illustrated in the figure on the right where we also report on the number of variables and clauses of the produced CNF formulas.

5   Related Work

The idea of sequentialization was originally proposed by Qadeer and Wu [29]. The first scheme for an arbitrary but bounded number of context switches was given in [24]. Since then, several algorithms and implementations have been developed (see [3,9,19,20,23,33]). *Lazy* sequentialization schemes have played an important role in the development of efficient tools. The first such sequentialization was given in [20] for bounded context switching and extended to unboundedly many threads in [21,22]. These schemes require frequent recomputations and are not suitable for use in combination with bounded model-checking (see [11]). Lazy-CSeq [16] avoids such recomputations and achieves efficiency by handling context-switches with a very lightweight and decentralized control code. Lazy-CSeq has been recently extended to handle relaxed memory models [34] and to prove correctness [25].

Abstract interpretation [7] is a widely used static analysis technique which has been scaled up to large industrial systems [8]. However, since the abstraction functions typically overapproximate the values a program variable can take on, abstract interpretation is prone to false alarms, and considerable effort went into designing suitable abstractions (e.g., [27, 36]).

An alternative approach combines abstract interpretation with a post-processing phase based on a more precise analysis to either confirm or filter out warnings. Post et al. [28] describe a semi-automatic process in which they use CBMC repeatedly on larger and larger code slices around potential error locations identified by Polyspace.[4] They report a reduction of false alarms by 25% to 75%, depending on the amount of manual intervention. Chebaro et al. [4,5] describe the SANTE tool, which uses dynamic symbolic execution or concolic testing to try and construct concrete test inputs that confirm the warnings. The main difference to our work is that such approaches use abstract interpretation only to "guide" the more precise post-processing phase towards possible error locations but do not inject information from the abstractions into the post-processing in the same way as in our work.

Wu et al. [38] also combine sequentialization and abstract interpretation, but in a different context and with different goals. More specifically, they consider interrupt-driven programs (IPDs) for which they devise a specific lazy sequentialization schema; they then run a specialized abstract interpretation, which takes into account some properties of the IPDs such as schedulability, in order to prove the absence of some numerical run-time errors. In contrast, we consider general C programs over the more general Pthreads API, and use a generic sequentialization schema but a simpler abstract interpretation. However, the main difference is that we use the abstract interpretation only to produce hints for a more precise analysis (i.e., BMC), and not to produce the ultimate analysis result.

6 Conclusions and Future Work

Concurrent program verification remains a stubbornly hard problem, but lazy sequentialization has proven to be one of the most effective techniques, and has, in combination with a SAT-based BMC tool as sequential verification backend, been used successfully to find errors in hard benchmarks on which all other tools failed. However, the sizes of the individual states (which are determined by concurrent program's shared global and thread-local variables) still pose problems for further scaling. We have therefore proposed an approach where we use abstract interpretation to minimize the representation of these variables. More specifically, we run the Frama-C abstract interpretation tool over the programs constructed by Lazy-CSeq to compute overapproximating intervals for all (original) program variables and then exploit CBMC's bitvector support to reduce the number of bits required to represent these in the sequentialized program. We have implemented this approach on top of Lazy-CSeq and have demonstrated the effectiveness of this approach; it has performed very well in SV-COMP'17 competition, where it solved all tasks [26]. In this paper, in particular, we have further shown that it leads to large performance gains for very hard verification problems.

---

[4] https://www.mathworks.com/products/polyspace.html.

Our approach is easy to implement and effective because of the confluence of four different strands. First, we use a source-to-source transformation tool for the sequentialization. This makes it easy to re-use an off-the-shelf tool (i.e., Frama-C) for the interval analysis. Second, we use a backend verification tool (i.e., CBMC) that can effectively exploit the information provided by Frama-C, by means of a specialized bitvector type. Third, we are using a lazy sequentialization, which ensures that the interval analysis can compute tight intervals; our approach would not work with an eager sequentialization where the state variables remain unconstrained. Fourth, the interval analysis strikes the right balance between analysis efforts and results—that is, it runs fast enough, and the computed intervals are tight enough, so that the overheads are easily recouped, and we actually improve the overall performance. Other, more elaborate, abstract interpretations have in fact proven to be counter-productive.

In this paper, we have demonstrated our approach for sequentially consistent concurrent programs that use the Pthreads API. However, all specific aspects of the concurrency model are actually encapsulated in the sequentialization. Our approach is therefore also applicable to other concurrency models, as long as we have (or can design) a corresponding lazy sequentialization, and we plan to extend our work to weak memory models, based on our previous work [34].

Another avenue for future work is to investigate other "cheap" analyses that can be run over sequentialized program; specifically, we plan to use a points-to analysis to reduce the amount of possible sharing that the BMC backend needs to encode into the SAT formula.

References

1. Agesen, O., Detlefs, D., Flood, C.H., Garthwaite, A., Martin, P.A., Shavit, N., Steele Jr., G.L.: Dcas-based concurrent deques. In: SPAA, pp. 137–146 (2000)
2. Canet, G., Cuoq, P., Monate, B.: A value analysis for C programs. In: SPAA, pp. 123–124 (2009)
3. Chaki, S., Gurfinkel, A., Strichman, O.: Time-bounded analysis of real-time systems. In: FMCAD, pp. 72–80 (2011)
4. Chebaro, O., Cuoq, P., Kosmatov, N., Marre, B., Pacalet, A., Williams, N., Yakobowski, B.: Behind the scenes in SANTE: a combination of static and dynamic analyses. Autom. Softw. Eng. 21(1), 107–143 (2014)
5. Chebaro, O., Kosmatov, N., Giorgetti, A., Julliand, J.: The SANTE tool: value analysis, program slicing and test generation for C program debugging. In: Gogolla, M., Wolff, B. (eds.) TAP 2011. LNCS, vol. 6706, pp. 78–83. Springer, Heidelberg (2011). doi:10.1007/978-3-642-21768-5_7
6. Clarke, E., Kroening, D., Lerda, F.: A tool for checking ANSI-C programs. In: Jensen, K., Podelski, A. (eds.) TACAS 2004. LNCS, vol. 2988, pp. 168–176. Springer, Heidelberg (2004). doi:10.1007/978-3-540-24730-2_15
7. Cousot, P., Cousot, R.: Abstract interpretation: a unified lattice model for static analysis of programs by construction or approximation of fixpoints. In: POPL, pp. 238–252 (1977)
8. Cousot, P., Cousot, R., Feret, J., Mauborgne, L., Miné, A., Rival, X.: Why does astrée scale up? Formal Methods Syst. Des. 35(3), 229–264 (2009)

9. Fischer, B., Inverso, O., Parlato, G.: CSeq: a concurrency pre-processor for sequential C verification tools. In: ASE, pp. 710–713 (2013)
10. Fischer, B., Inverso, O., Parlato, G.: CSeq: a sequentialization tool for C. In: Piterman, N., Smolka, S.A. (eds.) TACAS 2013. LNCS, vol. 7795, pp. 616–618. Springer, Heidelberg (2013). doi:10.1007/978-3-642-36742-7_46
11. Ghafari, N., Hu, A.J., Rakamarić, Z.: Context-bounded translations for concurrent software: an empirical evaluation. In: Pol, J., Weber, M. (eds.) SPIN 2010. LNCS, vol. 6349, pp. 227–244. Springer, Heidelberg (2010). doi:10.1007/978-3-642-16164-3_17
12. Hendler, D., Shavit, N., Yerushalmi, L.: A scalable lock-free stack algorithm. In: SPAA, pp. 206–215. ACM (2004)
13. Holzmann, G.J.: Mars code. Commun. ACM 57(2), 64–73 (2014)
14. Holzmann, G.J.: Cloud-based verification of concurrent software. In: Jobstmann, B., Leino, K.R.M. (eds.) VMCAI 2016. LNCS, vol. 9583, pp. 311–327. Springer, Heidelberg (2016). doi:10.1007/978-3-662-49122-5_15
15. Inverso, O., Nguyen, T.L., Fischer, B., La Torre, S., Parlato, G.: Lazy-cseq: a context-bounded model checking tool for multi-threaded c-programs. In: ASE, pp. 807–812 (2015)
16. Inverso, O., Tomasco, E., Fischer, B., La Torre, S., Parlato, G.: Bounded model checking of multi-threaded C programs via lazy sequentialization. In: Biere, A., Bloem, R. (eds.) CAV 2014. LNCS, vol. 8559, pp. 585–602. Springer, Cham (2014). doi:10.1007/978-3-319-08867-9_39
17. Inverso, O., Tomasco, E., Fischer, B., La Torre, S., Parlato, G.: Lazy-CSeq: a lazy sequentialization tool for C. In: Ábrahám, E., Havelund, K. (eds.) TACAS 2014. LNCS, vol. 8413, pp. 398–401. Springer, Heidelberg (2014). doi:10.1007/978-3-642-54862-8_29
18. ISO/IEC: Information technology–portable operating system interface (POSIX) base specifications, Issue 7. ISO/IEC/IEEE 9945:2009 (2009)
19. La Torre, S., Madhusudan, P., Parlato, G.: Analyzing recursive programs using a fixed-point calculus. In: PLDI, pp. 211–222 (2009)
20. La Torre, S., Madhusudan, P., Parlato, G.: Reducing context-bounded concurrent reachability to sequential reachability. In: Bouajjani, A., Maler, O. (eds.) CAV 2009. LNCS, vol. 5643, pp. 477–492. Springer, Heidelberg (2009). doi:10.1007/978-3-642-02658-4_36
21. La Torre, S., Madhusudan, P., Parlato, G.: Model-checking parameterized concurrent programs using linear interfaces. In: Touili, T., Cook, B., Jackson, P. (eds.) CAV 2010. LNCS, vol. 6174, pp. 629–644. Springer, Heidelberg (2010). doi:10.1007/978-3-642-14295-6_54
22. La Torre, S., Madhusudan, P., Parlato, G.: Sequentializing parameterized programs. In: FIT, pp. 34–47 (2012)
23. Lal, A., Qadeer, S., Lahiri, S.K.: A solver for reachability modulo theories. In: Madhusudan, P., Seshia, S.A. (eds.) CAV 2012. LNCS, vol. 7358, pp. 427–443. Springer, Heidelberg (2012). doi:10.1007/978-3-642-31424-7_32
24. Lal, A., Reps, T.W.: Reducing concurrent analysis under a context bound to sequential analysis. Formal Methods Syst. Des. 1, 73–97 (2009)
25. Nguyen, T.L., Fischer, B., La Torre, S., Parlato, G.: Lazy sequentialization for the safety verification of unbounded concurrent programs. In: Artho, C., Legay, A., Peled, D. (eds.) ATVA 2016. LNCS, vol. 9938, pp. 174–191. Springer, Cham (2016). doi:10.1007/978-3-319-46520-3_12

26. Nguyen, T.L., Inverso, O., Fischer, B., La Torre, S., Parlato, G.: Lazy-CSeq 2.0: combining lazy sequentialization with abstract interpretation. In: Legay, A., Margaria, T. (eds.) TACAS 2017. LNCS, vol. 10206, pp. 375–379. Springer, Heidelberg (2017). doi:10.1007/978-3-662-54580-5_26

27. Oulamara, M., Venet, A.J.: Abstract interpretation with higher-dimensional ellipsoids and conic extrapolation. In: Kroening, D., Păsăreanu, C.S. (eds.) CAV 2015. LNCS, vol. 9206, pp. 415–430. Springer, Cham (2015). doi:10.1007/978-3-319-21690-4_24

28. Post, H., Sinz, C., Kaiser, A., Gorges, T.: Reducing false positives by combining abstract interpretation and bounded model checking. In: ASE, pp. 188–197 (2008)

29. Qadeer, S., Wu, D.: KISS: keep it simple and sequential. In: PLDI, pp. 14–24 (2004)

30. Thomson, P., Donaldson, A.F., Betts, A.: Concurrency testing using schedule bounding: an empirical study. In: PPoPP, pp. 15–28 (2014)

31. Tomasco, E., Inverso, O., Fischer, B., La Torre, S., Parlato, G.: MU-CSeq: sequentialization of C programs by shared memory unwindings. In: Ábrahám, E., Havelund, K. (eds.) TACAS 2014. LNCS, vol. 8413, pp. 402–404. Springer, Heidelberg (2014). doi:10.1007/978-3-642-54862-8_30

32. Tomasco, E., Inverso, O., Fischer, B., La Torre, S., Parlato, G.: MU-CSeq 0.3: sequentialization by read-implicit and coarse-grained memory unwindings. In: Baier, C., Tinelli, C. (eds.) TACAS 2015. LNCS, vol. 9035, pp. 436–438. Springer, Heidelberg (2015). doi:10.1007/978-3-662-46681-0_38

33. Tomasco, E., Inverso, O., Fischer, B., La Torre, S., Parlato, G.: Verifying concurrent programs by memory unwinding. In: Baier, C., Tinelli, C. (eds.) TACAS 2015. LNCS, vol. 9035, pp. 551–565. Springer, Heidelberg (2015). doi:10.1007/978-3-662-46681-0_52

34. Tomasco, E., Nguyen, T.L., Inverso, O., Fischer, B., La Torre, S., Parlato, G.: Lazy sequentialization for TSO and PSO via shared memory abstractions. In: FMCAD, pp. 193–200 (2016)

35. Tomasco, E., Nguyen, T.L., Inverso, O., Fischer, B., La Torre, S., Parlato, G.: MU-CSeq 0.4: individual memory location unwindings. In: Chechik, M., Raskin, J.-F. (eds.) TACAS 2016. LNCS, vol. 9636, pp. 938–941. Springer, Heidelberg (2016). doi:10.1007/978-3-662-49674-9_65

36. Venet, A.J.: The gauge domain: scalable analysis of linear inequality invariants. In: Madhusudan, P., Seshia, S.A. (eds.) CAV 2012. LNCS, vol. 7358, pp. 139–154. Springer, Heidelberg (2012). doi:10.1007/978-3-642-31424-7_15

37. Vyukov, D.: Bug with a context switch bound 5 (2010)

38. Wu, X., Chen, L., Miné, A., Dong, W., Wang, J.: Numerical static analysis of interrupt-driven programs via sequentialization. In: EMSOFT, pp. 55–64 (2015)

Parity Games on Bounded Phase Multi-pushdown Systems

Mohamed Faouzi Atig[1], Ahmed Bouajjani[2], K. Narayan Kumar[3], and Prakash Saivasan[4(✉)]

[1] Uppsala University, Uppsala, Sweden
mohamed_faouzi.atig@it.uu.se
[2] IRIF, Université Paris Diderot, Paris, France
abou@irif.fr
[3] Chennai Mathematical Institute, Chennai, India
kumar@cmi.ac.in
[4] TU Braunschweig, Braunschweig, Germany
p.saivasan@tu-bs.de

Abstract. In this paper we address the problem of solving parity games over the configuration graphs of bounded phase multi-pushdown systems. A non-elementary decision procedure was proposed for this problem by A. Seth. In this paper, we provide a simple and inductive construction to solve this problem. We also prove a non-elementary lower-bound, answering a question posed by A. Seth.

1 Introduction

Multithreaded programs are widely used in computer systems. They are notoriously complex and hard to get right. Therefore methods and tools for checking systematically their correctness are of paramount importance. Model checking is a well established algorithmic verification approach that allows to check automatically if a formal (automata-based) model of a program/system satisfies a property expressed in some specification logic, typically a temporal logic or a fixpoint calculus. The most expressive of these logics, when only regular properties are considered, is the propositional mu-calculus. It has been shown that the model checking problem of a given model against the proposition mu-calculus is tightly related to the problem of solving 2-player parity games on the state graph of the model. Solving games means to determine if one of the player has a winning strategy. This problem is decidable for finite-state systems, and even for classes of infinite-state models such as pushdown systems [12]. The latter are known to be natural formal models for sequential programs with recursive procedure calls. In this paper, we investigate the extension of the game-theoretic verification framework to the case of multi-threaded programs.

The authors acknowledge partial support by Indo-French Project AVeCSo, TCS-Fellowship, Indo-Swedish DST-VR Project P-02/2014, Infosys Foundation.

A. El Abbadi and B. Garbinato (Eds.): NETYS 2017, LNCS 10299, pp. 272–287, 2017.
DOI: 10.1007/978-3-319-59647-1_21

Natural models for multi-threaded (shared memory concurrent) programs are multi pushdown systems, i.e., several pushdown systems that can access to a shared (finite) memory. However, this model is clearly Turing powerful, and therefore, any nontrivial problem stated on this model is obviously undecidable. Then, one possibility to obtain decidability is to consider restrictions on the kind of behaviours for which the decision problem is stated. This can be useful in the context of finding errors. Indeed, good under-approximations of the set of behaviours are useful to orient the search toward some special classes of computations where most of the errors are visible. To this aim, parameterized under-approximation schema have been proposed and shown to be useful and efficient for the analysis of muti-threaded programs such as context-bounding in [5] and phase-bounding in [10]. Context-bounding consists in bounding the number of context-switches between threads, while phase-bounding is a more liberal concept where each phase corresponds to a sequence of operations where all pops are from one fixed stack, while pushes are non restricted and allowed to be on any stack. In fact, phase-bounding is more general than context-bounding in the sense that sets of behaviours explored under phase-bounding, for some fixed bound on the number of phases, would require an unbounded number of context-switches to be explored. Then, the issue we address in this paper is exploring the limits of the decidability of the problem of solving parity games on muti-pushdown systems under phase bounding, and establishing its complexity.

Anil Seth provides in [8] a decision procedure for solving the parity games on phase bounded muti-pushdown systems for a fixed initial state. The procedure has a non-elementary complexity (i.e., a tower of exponentials with a height depending on the number of phases). His result is based on an extension of Walukiewicz's proof for solving this problem in the case of pushdown systems [12]. This is proof is very difficult, based on reducing the problem of solving a parity game on a phase bounded muti-pushdown system to the problem of solving the parity game on a complex finite state graph. An important question is whether it is possible to provide a conceptually simpler proof allowing to have a better understanding of the structure of the problem. Also, a natural question is whether the high, non-elementary complexity is unavoidable.

The first contribution of this paper is to provide a proof that is based on a simple inductive argument on the number of phases by effectively reducing a $(k + 1)$-phase game to a k-phase game, for any $k \geq 1$. Our proof exploits the global approach used in, e.g., [1,3,7] to construct the set of winning states in a parity game on pushdown systems. Roughly, the latter construction is used to construct the winning states in last phase, and the obtained set is plugged in the system to get a new one with one less phase, and so on.

The second contribution of the paper is to establish a non-elementary lower bound for the parity games on bounded-phase multi-pushdown systems, showing that this problem is inherently hard and that our construction is optimal for computing the set of winning states. The proof is based on a reduction of the satisfiability problem of first-order logic over natural numbers with ordering. The details missing in the paper can be found in [6].

2   Bounded Phase Multi Pushdown Systems

Multi pushdown systems (MPDS) are generalizations of pushdown systems with multiple stacks. The kinds of transitions performed by an MPDS are (i) pushing a symbol into one of the stacks (ii) popping a symbol from one of the stacks and (iii) an internal move that changes the state but leaves the stacks unchanged.

Definition 1 (MPDS). *A* Multi-PushDown System *(MPDS) is a tuple* M = $(n, Q, \Gamma, \Delta, q_0)$ *where* $n \geq 1$ *is the number of stacks,* Q *is the non-empty set of states,* Γ *is the finite set of stack symbols, containing a special symbol* $\perp$, $q_0 \in Q$ *is the initial state and* $\Delta \subseteq Q \times \mathbf{Op} \times Q$ *is the transition relation, where* $\mathbf{Op} = \bigcup_{i \in [1..n]} \mathbf{Op}_i \cup \{\mathbf{Int}\}$ *and* $\mathbf{Op}_i = \{\mathbf{Push}_i(a), \mathbf{Pop}_i(a) \mid a \in \Gamma \setminus \{\perp\}\} \cup \{\mathbf{Zero}_i\}$.

A configuration of the MPDS M is a $(n+1)$ tuple $(q, \gamma_1, \gamma_2, \cdots, \gamma_n)$ with $q \in Q$, and $\gamma_1, \gamma_2, \ldots, \gamma_n \in (\Gamma \setminus \perp)^* \perp$. The set of all configurations of the MPDS M is denoted by $\mathcal{C}(M)$. The initial configuration c_M^{init} of the MPDS M is $(q_0, \perp, \ldots, \perp, \perp)$. Given $\tau = (q, op, q') \in \Delta$ and two configurations $c = (q, \gamma_1, \cdots, \gamma_n) \in \mathcal{C}(M)$ and $c' = (q', \gamma_1', \cdots, \gamma_n') \in \mathcal{C}(M)$, we say $c \xrightarrow{\tau} c'$ iff one of the following holds.

- $\tau = (q, \mathbf{Push}_i(a), q')$, $\gamma_i' = a.\gamma_i$ and $\forall j \in [1..n] \setminus \{i\}$, $\gamma_j' = \gamma_j$
- $\tau = (q, \mathbf{Pop}_i(a), q')$, $\gamma_i = a.\gamma_i'$ and $\forall j \in [1..n] \setminus \{i\}$, $\gamma_j' = \gamma_j$
- $\tau = (q, \mathbf{Zero}_i, q')$, $\gamma_i' = \gamma_i = \perp$ and $\forall j \in [1..n] \setminus \{i\}$, $\gamma_j' = \gamma_j$
- $\tau = (q, \mathbf{Int}, q')$ and $\forall j \in [1..n]$, $\gamma_j' = \gamma_j$

A *computation* π of M starting from a configuration c is a (possibly infinite) sequence of the form $c_0 \xrightarrow{\tau_1} c_1 \xrightarrow{\tau_2} \cdots$ such that $c_0 = c$ and $c_{i-1} \xrightarrow{\tau_i} c_i$ for all $1 \leq i \leq |\tau_1 \tau_2 \cdots|$. Given a finite computation $\pi_1 = c_0 \xrightarrow{\tau_1} c_1 \xrightarrow{\tau_2} c_2 \cdots \xrightarrow{\tau_m} c_m$ and a (possibly infinite) computation $\pi_2 = c_{m+1} \xrightarrow{\tau_{m+2}} c_{m+2} \xrightarrow{\tau_{m+3}} \cdots$, π_1 and π_2 are said to be *compatible* if $c_m = c_{m+1}$. Then, we write $\pi_1 \bullet \pi_2$ to denote the computation $\pi \overset{def}{=} c_0 \xrightarrow{\tau_1} c_1 \xrightarrow{\tau_2} c_2 \cdots \xrightarrow{\tau_m} c_m \xrightarrow{\tau_{m+2}} c_{m+2} \xrightarrow{\tau_{m+3}} \cdots$. Given a configuration $c = (q, w_1, w_2, \cdots, w_n)$, we will use $Stack_i(c)$ to denote the stack-i content i.e. w_i and $State(c)$ to denote the state q.

It is easy to see that a multi-pushdown system with just one stack is a pushdown system. When refering to pushdown systems, we will omit any references to the stack number.

2.1   Bounded Phase

The bounded phase restriction on an MPDS was introduced in [11]. Informally a phase is a sequence of operations in which the **Pop** and **Zero** operations are performed on only one stack. In a *bounded-phase* computation, there is an a-priori bound on the number of phases that it can involve.

Definition 2. Phase: *A* Phase *of a stack* $i \in [1..n]$ *is a computation involving pops and zero tests only from stack-i i.e. it is a computation of the form*

$\pi = c_0 \xrightarrow{\tau_1} c_1 \xrightarrow{\tau_2} \cdots$ in which $\tau_1, \tau_2, \ldots \in \Delta^{\downarrow i}$, where $\Delta^{\downarrow i} = \Delta \cap (Q \times (\mathbf{Op} \setminus \bigcup_{j \neq i} \bigcup_{a \in \Gamma} \{\mathbf{Pop}_j(a)\} \cup \{\mathbf{Zero}_j\}) \times Q)$.

Bounded Phase computation: *Given $k \in \mathbb{N}$, a computation $\pi = c_0 \xrightarrow{\tau_1}$ $c_1 \xrightarrow{\tau_2} \cdots$ is said to be k phase-bounded if it can be seen as a concatenation of at most k-phases i.e. $\pi = \pi_1 \bullet \pi_2 \bullet \ldots \bullet \pi_l$ such that $\pi_1, \cdots, \pi_l$ are phases and $l \leq k$.*

3 Parity Games

Parity game is a two player game that is played on a directed graph (possibly infinite). Informally the game can be thought of as one that starts from a designated node in which a token is placed. Each of the nodes in the graph are owned by one of the two players. Further every node in the graph is assigned a number from a predetermined finite set of natural numbers, we will refer to this number as the rank of the node. The game proceeds in rounds. In each round, the player who owns the node in which token is placed makes a move. We will assume that the graph has no dead ends and that a player can always make a move. During a move, a player removes the token from a node and places it on one of the adjacent nodes. The winner of the game is determined by the minimum rank visited infinitely often in the play. The game is formalised below.

Definition 3. *Parity game is defined over game graph $\mathcal{G} = (V, E, \tau, \sigma)$ where V is (possibly infinite) set of nodes, $E \subseteq V \times V$ is set of edges, $\tau : V \mapsto [0, 1]$ is a function that defines ownership of the node and $\sigma : V \mapsto [1..m]$ for some $m \in \mathbb{N}$ is a ranking function that assigns a rank to each node.*

For any node $s \in V$, we define $E(s) = \{s' \mid (s, s') \in E\}$. We say a π is a finite play of $\mathcal{G}$ iff $\pi = s_1 s_2 \cdots s_n$ such that for all $i \in [1 \ldots n - 1]$, $(s_i, s_{i+1}) \in E$ and $E(s_n) = \emptyset$. π is said to be infinite play of $\mathcal{G}$ iff $\pi = s_1 s_1 s_2 \cdots$ such that for all $i \in \mathbb{N}$, we have $(s_i, s_{i+1}) \in E$. We will assume w.l.o.g. that graphs we deal with do not have any dead end nodes and hence assume that all our plays are infinite. For any infinite play $\pi = s_0 s_1 s_2 \cdots$, we let S_π^∞ to be the set of all nodes that appear infinitely often in the play π. We define $Parity(\pi) = min(inf(\pi)) mod\ 2$, where $inf(\pi) = \{\sigma(s) \mid s \in S_\pi^\infty\}$ i.e. it is the parity of the minimum rank that is seen infinitely often along the run. An infinite play π is winning for player-0 iff $Parity(\pi)$ is 0, otherwise it is winning for player-1.

For any $i \in [0, 1]$, we will let $V_i = \{s \mid s \in V \wedge \tau(s) = i\}$ i.e. it is the set of positions owned by player-i. A strategy function f for player-0 is defined as $f : V^* V_0 \mapsto 2^V \setminus \emptyset$. An infinite play $\pi = v_0 v_1 v_2 \cdots$ is said to be confirming to a strategy function f iff for any prefix of the play $\pi' = v_0 \cdots v_i \in V^* V_0$, $v_{i+1} \in f(\pi')$. A strategy function f is said to be winning for player-0 from any node s, if the set of all possible plays π which start from the node s and confirms to the strategy function f are winning for player-0. The strategy function for player-1 is defined analogously. We say a node s is winning for player-0 (or player-1) iff there is a strategy function that is winning for player-0 (or player-1) from that position. A strategy function f of player-i is called memory less strategy or positional strategy if it is of the form $f : V_i \mapsto 2^V \setminus \emptyset$, i.e. it only depends on a single node. Any given play $\pi = v_0 v_1 \cdots$ is said to be confirming to the memoryless strategy function f of player-i, if for all nodes $v_j \in V_i$ ($j \in \mathbb{N}$), we have $v_{j+1} \in f(v_j)$.

A natural question in this setting is whether for any position s, one of the two players has a winning strategy (determinacy) from that position and if so whether the strategy is memoryless (memoryless determinacy). The determinacy of parity games follows from a very general result due to Martin's determinacy theorem [4] which establishes the determinacy for a much wider class of games. Memory less determinacy theorem (Theorem 1) for parity games [2] establishes that we not only have determinacy, we also have that the winning player has a memoryless winning strategy.

Theorem 1 [2]. *Given a parity game $G = (V, E, \tau, \sigma)$, there is a partition of nodes V, $V = W_0 \uplus W_1$ and memoryless strategy functions σ_0 and σ_1 such that σ_i is winning for player-i from each positions in W_i.*

Determining the winning sets and strategies in such games is an interesting problem, which is easy to solve for finite games and not so for infinite games.

4   Bounded Phase Parity Games on MPDS

In this paper, we are interested in parity games played over the configuration graphs of a MPDS with bounded-phase restriction (also refered to as the *bounded phase parity games*). For purpose of defining the bounded-phase parity games, we will first enhance the configurations of a multi-pushdown system with the information about the number of phases remaining and the identity of the currently active stack.

Definition 4 (Bounded-phase parity games). *Given a multi-pushdown system $M = (n, Q, \Gamma, \Delta, q_0)$ and a constant k, we define the set of enhanced configurations of M, $\mathcal{E}^k(M)$ as $\mathcal{C} \times [0..n] \times [1..k]$. Such an enhanced configuration, apart from containing the configuration of multi-pushdown system, also records the currently active stack and number of remaining phases. We will omit the k and simply refer to it as $\mathcal{E}(M)$ when ever k is clear from the context. At the beginning of any computation, we let the current stack component (the penultimate component) of $\mathcal{E}(M)$ to be 0, indicating that none of the stacks are active. From such a position, a stack gets active on the very first pop or zero test. Given any two configurations $(c, i, j), (c', i', j') \in \mathcal{E}(M)$, we say $(c, i, j) \rightsquigarrow (c', i', j')$ iff $c \xrightarrow{\tau} c'$ and one of the following holds.*

- *If $\tau = (q, \mathbf{Pop}_l, q')$ or $\tau = (q, \mathbf{Zero}_l, q')$ for some $l \in [1..n]$ and $i = 0$ then $j = j' = k$ and $i' = l$.*
- *if $\tau = (q, \mathbf{Push}_k(a), q')$ for some $k \in [1 \ldots n]$ or $\tau = (q, \mathbf{Int}, q')$ or $\tau = (q, \mathbf{Pop}_i, q')$ or $\tau = (q, \mathbf{Zero}_i, q')$ then $i' = i, j' = j$*

– if $\tau = (q, \mathbf{Pop}_l(a), q')$ or $\tau = (q, \mathbf{Zero}_l, q')$ for some $l \neq i$ and $j > 1$ then $i' = l, j' = j - 1$

Let $\tau : Q \mapsto [0, 1]$ be a map that designates each of the states to a player, let $\sigma : Q \mapsto [1..m]$ be a map that assigns a rank to each of the states and let k be any natural number, then a k-bounded-phase parity game is the parity game played on the game graph $\mathcal{G} = (\mathcal{E}(M), \leadsto, \tau, \sigma)$, where τ, σ are extended to configurations as follows. For any $(c, i, j) \in \mathcal{E}(M)$, we let $\tau((c, i, j)) = \tau(\text{State}(c))$ and $\sigma((c, i, j)) = \sigma(\text{State}(c))$. We will refer to such games as $\mathcal{G} = (k, M, \tau, \sigma)$.

Given a bounded phase parity game $\mathcal{G} = (k, M, \tau, \sigma)$ and a node $s \in \mathcal{E}(M)$, in this paper we are interested in the problem of determining whether there is a strategy function g that is winning for player-0 from the node s.

5   Some Results on Parity Games

In this section, we will prove/recall some lemmas that we will use later. The following lemma states that if there is a mapping from one game graph to another such that any move in the former can be simulated in the latter, and if such a simulation preserves the player and the rank at each position of the play, then the winning positions are also preserved by the mapping.

Lemma 1. Let $G = (V_G, E_G, \tau_G, \sigma_G)$ and $H = (V_H, E_H, \tau_H, \sigma_H)$ be games graphs and let $\mathbf{F} : V_G \longrightarrow V_H$ be any function such that for any position $x \in V_G$

1. $\sigma_G(x) = \sigma_H(\mathbf{F}(x))$, the function is rank preserving.
2. $\tau_G(x) = \tau_H(\mathbf{F}(x))$ i.e. x and $\mathbf{F}(x)$ belongs to the same player i.
3. If $x \to x'$ then $\mathbf{F}(x) \to \mathbf{F}(x')$.
4. If $\mathbf{F}(x) \to y$ then there exists x' such that $x \to x'$ and $\mathbf{F}(x') = y$.

Then, any position x is winning for player 0 (player-1) in G if and only if $\mathbf{F}(x)$ is winning for player 0 (resp player-1) in H.

Given a game graph $\mathcal{G} = (V, E, \tau, \sigma)$, $U \subseteq V$ is said to be a trap of $\mathcal{G}$ iff $E \cap U \times (V \setminus U) = \emptyset$. i.e. once the game enters U, there is no way for it to exit. The following Lemma states that given any parity game graph, the game graph obtained by fusing all the winning positions of player-0 (and that of player-1), into one node, preserves the winning positions.

Lemma 2. Let $G = (V_G, E_G, \tau_G, \sigma_G)$ be a parity game and let $V_H \subseteq V_G$ be a trap of G. Suppose V_{H0} and V_{H1} are the winning positions for the players 0 and 1 respectively, in the subgame V_H. Then, consider the game graph $G' = (V_{G'}, E_{G'}, \tau_{G'}, \sigma_{G'})$ constructed as follows:

1. Delete the subgame V_H, add two new positions q_w and q_l and add edges from q_w to q_w and q_l to q_l.
2. For $s \to t$ in E with $s \notin V_H$ and $t \in V_{H0}$, add an edge from s to q_w.
3. For $s \to t$ in E with $s \notin V_H$ and $t \in V_{H1}$, add an edge from s to q_l.

4. For all $v \in V_G \setminus V_H$, we let $\tau_{G'}(v) = \tau_G(v)$, $\tau_{G'}(q_w) = 0$, $\tau_{G'}(q_l) = 1$.
5. For all $v \in V_G \setminus V_H$, $\sigma_{G'}(v) = \sigma(v)$ and $\sigma_{G'}(q_w) = 0$, $\sigma_{G'}(q_l) = 1$.

Then, any position in V_G that is not in V_H is winning for any player in G if and only if it is winning for that player in the game G'.

In [1,7], T. Cachat and O. Serre independently proved that the set of all winning positions of a particular player in a parity game played on a pushdown system is effectively regular. This can also be obtained using tree automata techniques as shown in [3].

Definition 5 (Parity game on PDS). Given a pushdown system $P = (Q, \Gamma, \Delta, q_0)$ and mappings $\tau : Q \mapsto [0,1]$ and $\sigma : Q \mapsto [1..m]$, parity game on PDS is simply a parity game played on the game graph $\mathcal{G} = (\mathcal{C}(P), \to, \tau, \sigma)$, where τ and σ are extended to configurations as follows. For any configuration of the form $c = (q, \gamma)$, $\tau(c) = \tau(q)$ and $\sigma(c) = \sigma(q)$.

Theorem 2 [1,7]. The set of all winning positions of player 0 (or player 1) in a pushdown game can be effectively characterised by an exponential sized finite state automaton over the alphabet $\Gamma \cup Q$. Such an automaton accepts a word $wq \in \Gamma^* Q$ if and only if the configuration (q, w) is winning for player 0 (or player 1).

6   Decidability of Bounded Phase Parity Games

Theorem 3. Given a k bounded phase parity game, deciding whether player 0 can win from the initial configuration can be done in time which is NON-ELEMENTARY in the number of phases.

In this section we prove the Theorem 3 which states that the winner of a bounded phase parity game can be decided in non-elementary time. The proof of the theorem is obtained by inductively solving the k bounded-phase parity game. The intuitive idea is to first show that if the game is a single phase game, then the game graph of such a game actually corresponds to just the positions of a pushdown game and by Theorem 2 we know the set of winning positions are recognisable. Secondly observe that the positions in the game graph are stratified in the following sense – if (c', i', k') is reachable from (c, i, k) then $k' \leq k$. From this, we know that if the game were to enter the last phase, it will continue to remain in that phase. Hence any position in the last phase corresponds to a position of a pushdown game, which is known to be recognisable. Using this information, we will go onto show how to reduce the k bounded-phase game to a $k - 1$ bounded-phase game.

6.1   Decidability of a 1-Phase Game

In an 1-phase game, the configurations can be of the form $(c, i, 1)$ with $i \neq 0$ or of the form $(c, 0, 1)$. We will show in each of the cases that the set of positions winning for player-0 is a recognisable set (i.e. it can be effectively determined). For the sub-game involving only configurations of the form $(c, i, 1)$, we will show that such positions correspond to positions of a pushdown game. Now using the fact that the set of all positions winning for player-0 in a pushdown game is a recognisable set, we will show that the nodes that are winning for player-0 in sub-game involving configurations of the form $(c, i, 1)$ is also a recognisable set. For the case involving configurations of the form $(c, 0, 1)$, we will reduce such a sub-game to a parity game involving only finitely many states.

Lemma 3. *Let $\mathcal{G} = (1, M, \tau, \sigma)$ be a bounded-phase parity game, with $M = (n, Q, \Gamma, \Delta, q_0)$. We can effectively determine the set of all positions of the form $\mathcal{E}^1(M)$, that are winning for player 0. Further the size of such an automaton that recognises the winning positions is at most exponential.*

Proof. The nodes in $\mathcal{E}^1(M)$ are either of the form $(c, 0, 1)$ or of the form $(c, i, 1)$ for some $i \neq 0$. We will first consider the nodes of the form $(c, i, 1)$ and show that the winner can be determined. The general idea of the proof is to first construct a pushdown system for each $i \in [1..n]$, from the given multi-pushdown system M. Such a pushdown system will simulate the moves of stack-i by using its own stack for any operations on stack i, and ignoring the pushes on other stacks. The pushdown system (corresponding to stack-i) is defined as, $P_i = (Q, \Gamma, \delta_i, q_0)$, where δ_i is defined as

- For every $\tau = (q, \mathbf{Pop}_i(a), q') \in \Delta$, we add $\tau' = (q, \mathbf{Pop}(a), q') \subset \delta_i$. We add similar transitions for $\tau = (q, \mathbf{Zero}_i(a), q') \in \Delta$, $\tau = (q, \mathbf{Push}_i(b), q') \in \Delta$ and $\tau = (q, \mathbf{Int}, q') \in \Delta$.
- For $j \neq i$ and for every $\tau = (q, \mathbf{Push}_j(b), q') \in \Delta$, we add $\tau' = (q, \mathbf{Int}, q') \in \delta_i$.

The winning positions of each player of the sub-game with configurations of the form $(c, i, 1)$ with $i \neq 0$, can be captured using the pushdown game $\mathcal{H} = (\mathcal{C}(P_i), \to, \tau, \sigma)$. Let the function $\mathbf{F} : \mathcal{E}^1(M) \mapsto \mathcal{C}(P_i)$ be given by $\mathbf{F}(((q, \gamma_1, \gamma_2, \cdots, \gamma_n), i, 1)) = ((q, \gamma_i))$. The function $\mathbf{F}$ simply disregards content of stacks other than i and keeps stack i intact. Following lemma shows that such a mapping will preserve the properties required by Lemma 1.

Lemma 4. *The mapping $\mathbf{F}$ preserves the following properties. For any $v \in \mathcal{E}^1(M)$, we have $\tau(v) = \tau(\mathbf{F}(v))$ and $\sigma(v) = \sigma(\mathbf{F}(v))$. For any $u = (c, i, 1), v = (c', i, 1) \in \mathcal{E}(M)$, if $(u \rightsquigarrow v)$ then we have $\mathbf{F}(u) \to \mathbf{F}(v)$. Suppose for some $v \in \mathcal{E}(M)$, we have $\mathbf{F}(v) \to d$, then there is an $u \in \mathcal{E}(M)$ such that $\mathbf{F}(u) = d$ and $v \rightsquigarrow u$.*

Thus using Lemma 1, the position $(c, i, 1)$ in our subgame is winning for a player-i if and only if $\mathbf{F}((c, i, 1))$ is winning for player-i in the pushdown game $(\mathcal{C}(P_i), \to, \tau, \sigma)$. Thus, the set of all winning positions of a 1-phase game involving stack-i is given by $\mathcal{S} = \{(c, i, 1) \mid \mathbf{F}((c, i, 1)) \in \mathcal{R}_{P_i}\}$ where $\mathcal{R}_{P_i}$ is the set of winning positions in the game $(\mathcal{C}(P_i), \to, \tau, \sigma)$. It is easy to see that $\mathcal{S}$ is recognisable set since $\mathcal{R}_{P_i}$ is recognisable by Theorem 2.

Finally we consider the positions of the form $(c, 0, 1)$. Any configuration (c', i, k') reached from configuration $(c, 0, 1)$ must necessarily have $k' = 1$. Further, if the game ever enters a position with $i \neq 0$, we may immediately determine the winner of the game from thereon (Since we already know how to compute the set of all winning positions of a 1-phase game involving stack-i). This allows us to formulate a finite state game whose solution determines the winning positions of the form $(c, 0, 1)$. Note that the game can remain in a position of the form $(c, 0, 1)$ iff the transitions involve only push moves or internal moves. The moment a pop move is made, the stack is fixed and the game enters a configuration of the form $(c, i, 1)$, for some $i \in [1..n]$.

Let $B_i = (Q_{B_i}, \Gamma \cup Q, s_i, \delta^{B_i}, F_i)$ be the deterministic finite state automaton that accepts a word of the form $\perp w^R q$ (where $(q, w\perp)$ is a configuration of the pushdown system P_i) iff it belongs to the winning positions of the game $(\mathcal{C}(P_i), \rightarrow, \tau, \sigma)$. Such an automata is guaranteed by Theorem 2, we note that the size of such an automata is exponential in the size of the pushdown system. The finite state game we have in mind is one which instead of keeping track of the contents of each stack i, only keeps track of the top of stack symbol and the state reached by B_i on reading the contents of that stack. We plan to do this only for the push and the internal moves and hence it is indeed feasible. Any pop or zero test moves would commit to a stack. In this case we may immediately determine the winner using the state of B_i.

The state space of the finite state game H is $(Q \times \Gamma^n \times Q_{B_1} \times Q_{B_2} \cdots Q_{B_n}) \cup \{q_w, q_l\}$, we will refer to this as $V(H)$. The state q_w is entered on determining that the game will be won by player 0 and q_l if it is determined that the game will be lost by player 0. The edges $\rightarrow_H$ of the game graph are given as follows:

1. $q_w \rightarrow q_w$ and $q_l \rightarrow q_l$
2. For all $i \in [1..n]$, we have if $(q, \mathbf{Push}_i(b), q') \in \Delta$, then we have $(q, a_1, \cdots, a_n, p_1, \cdots p_n) \rightarrow (q', a_1, \cdots, b, \cdots, a_n, p_1, \cdots, \delta^{B_i}(p_i, a_i), \cdots, p_n)$, for all $a_1, a_2, \cdots, a_n \in \Gamma$ and for all $j \in [1..n], p_j \in Q_{B_j}$.
3. If $(q, \mathbf{Int}, q') \in \Delta$ then we have $(q, a_1, \cdots, a_n, p_1, \cdots p_n) \rightarrow (q', a_1, \cdots, a_n, p_1, \cdots, p_n)$. This handles the case of internal moves.
4. If $(q, \mathbf{Pop}_i(a_i), q') \in \Delta$ then if $\delta^{B_i}(p_i, q') \in F_i$, we have $(q, a_1, \cdots, a_n, p_1, \cdots, p_n) \rightarrow q_w$ else if $\delta^{B_i}(p_i, q') \notin F_i$, we have $(q, a_1, \cdots, a_n, p_1, \cdots, p_n) \rightarrow q_l$
5. If $(q, \mathbf{Zero}_i, q') \in \Delta$ then, if $\delta^{B_i}(s_i, \perp.q') \in F_i$, we have $(q, a_1, \cdots, a_{i-1}, \perp, a_{i+1} \cdots, a_n, p_1, \cdots, p_{i-1}, s_i, p_{i+1}, p_n) \rightarrow q_w$ else if $\delta^{B_i}(s_i, \perp.q') \notin F_i$, we have $(q, a_1, \cdots, a_{i-1}, \perp, a_{i+1} \cdots, a_n, p_1, \cdots, p_{i-1}, s_i, p_{i+1}, \cdots, p_n) \rightarrow q_l$

Now consider the ranking function σ' that assigns 0 to q_w, 1 to q_l, i.e. $\sigma(q_w) = 1$ and $\sigma(q_l) = 0$ and for all other positions of the form $c = (q, a_1, \cdots, a_n, p_1, \cdots, p_n)$, we let $\sigma'(c) = \sigma(q)$. Similarly, consider τ' that assigns $\tau'(q_w) = 0$ and $\tau'(q_l) = 1$. Further we let $\tau'(c) = \tau(q)$ for any $c = (q, a_1, \cdots, a_n, p_1, \cdots, p_n)$. We claim that nodes in the subgame involving configurations of the form $(c, 0, 1)$ can be reduced to the finite state parity game given by $H = (V(H), \rightarrow_H, \sigma', \tau')$.

The idea now is to provide a mapping from positions of the form $(c, 0, 1)$ in G to positions in H. For this, we wish to first eliminate from G, using Lemma 2, any positions of the form $(c, i, 1)$ for $i \neq 0$. Note that, the set of all position

$S = \{(c,i,1) \mid (c,i,1) \in \mathcal{E}(M), i \neq 0\}$ is a trap in G. Let $W_i \subseteq S$ be the set of winning positions for player-i. Now consider the game graph G' obtained by deleting S from G, adding two new vertices p_{win}, p_{lose} replacing all the edges to W_0 by edges to p_{win} and the edges to W_1 by edges to p_{lose}. Then by application of Lemma 2, a position in $\mathcal{E}(M) \setminus S$ is winning for any player iff it is winning in G'. Observe that the set $\mathcal{E}(M) \setminus S$ is exactly $\{(c,0,1) \mid c \in \mathcal{C}(M)\}$. Now consider the mapping $\mathbf{F}$ from positions of G' to positions in H defined as $\mathbf{F}((q, a_1\gamma_1, a_2\gamma_2, \cdots, a_n\gamma_n), 0, 1)) = ((q, a_1, \cdots, a_l, \delta_1^P(x_1, \gamma_1^R), \delta_2^P(x_2, \gamma_2^R), \cdots, \delta_n^P(x_n, \gamma_n^R))$ and $\mathbf{F}(p_{\text{win}}) = q_w$ and $\mathbf{F}(p_{\text{lose}}) = q_l$. Notice that such a mapping preserves the properties required by Lemma 1. As a result, we get the following lemma.

Lemma 5. *A position $(c,0,1)$ is winning for player-i in G' if and only if $\mathbf{F}((c,0,1))$ is winning for player-i in H.*

In addition note that the set of positions of the form $(c,0,1)$ that are winning for player-0 are precisely those in $S_{\text{Win}} = \{w \mid f(w) \text{ is winning for player-0}\}$ and this clearly is a recognizable set. This completes the proof of Lemma 3.

6.2   Decidability of a k Phase Game

The idea is to use the fact that the 1-phase sub-game of a k-phase game is determined. Notice that after execution of $k-1$ phases, what remains is a 1-phase sub-game. In this 1-phase sub-game, the stack contents of all other stacks (excluding the currently active stack) are irrelevant and hence it can easily be simulated by a pushdown automata.

Let $\mathcal{K} = \{(c,i,1) \mid (c,i,1) \in \mathcal{E}^k \wedge i \in [1..n]\}$. Recall the pushdown automata P_i constructed in Lemma 3. As in the case of Lemma 3, we can provide a mapping $\mathbf{F}$ from the sub-game involving positions from $\mathcal{K}$ to positions in the game $\mathcal{H} = (\mathcal{C}(P_i), \rightarrow, \tau, \sigma)$, such that $\mathbf{F}$ satisfies the properties of Lemma 1 (as a matter of fact, the game graph $\mathcal{H}$ is isomorphic to the trap consisting of positions of the form $(c,i,1), i \neq 0$ in the game graph of a 1-phase parity game). From this, we get the following Lemma which states that the set of winning positions of a 1-phase sub-game can be effectively determined using the set of winning positions of the pushdown system P_i.

Lemma 6. *$s \in \mathcal{K}$ is winning for player-0 iff $\mathbf{F}(s)$ is winning for player-0 in the pushdown game $\mathcal{H} = (\mathcal{C}(P_i), \rightarrow, \tau, \sigma)$*

Now to handle the case of k-phase game, we first invoke Theorem 2 to obtain $B_i = (Q_{B_i}, \Gamma \cup Q, s_i, \delta^{B_i}, F_i)$ that recognises the winning positions of the pushdown system P_i. Suppose at the end of $k-1$ phase, we know the state that the automata B_i reaches on reading stack i, then, at the beginning of phase k, we can determine whether player-0 is winning from that position or not. The case for 1-phase game was easy since we had only pushes to contend with (and hence it was possible to simulate B_i using only the state space). However, in case of a $k-1$ phase game, we need to also handle pop operations. Hence it is not possible to simulate B_i automata by just keeping it in the state space. The informal idea is to keep the B_i automata as part of the state space and simulate it on each push onto the stack-i. In addition, on each push, along with the stack symbol we also store in the stack the state of B_i that was reached before the current push. Now each time a pop operation is performed, we can retrieve the correct state of the B_i automata and delegate it to the state space. The details are formalised below.

Let (k, M, τ, σ) be a k-bounded-phase game with $M = (n, Q, \Gamma, \Delta, q_0)$ and $k > 1$. We define a new MPDS as $M(k) = (n, Q_{M(k)}, \Gamma_{M(k)}, \Delta', q_0^{M(k)})$, where $Q_{M(k)} = Q \times Q_{B_1} \times \cdots \times Q_{B_n} \times \Gamma^n \times [0..n] \times [2..k] \cup \{q_w, q_l\}$, $\Gamma_{M(k)} = \bigcup_{i \in [1..n]} (\Gamma \times Q_{B_i}) \cup \{\bot\}$, $q_0^{M(k)} = (q_0, s_1, \cdots, s_n, \bot^n, 0, k)$ and the transition relation Δ' is defined as follows

1. if $(q, \mathbf{Push}_i(b), q') \in \Delta$ then we have for all $i \in [1..n]$, $p_i \in Q_{B_i}$, $m \in [0..n]$, $l \in [2..k]$ and $a_i \in \Gamma$, $((q, p_1, \cdots, p_n, a_1, \cdots, a_n, m, l), \mathbf{Push}_i(a_i, p_i), (q', p_1, \cdots, p_{i-1}, \delta_i^P(p_i, a_i), \cdots, p_n, a_1, \cdots, a_{i-1}, b, a_{i+1}, \cdots, a_n, m, l)) \in \Delta'$. We always store the top of stack and current state of B_i in the state space. Every time we push, the previously stored top of stack in the state (a_i) and the previously stored state of B_i (p_i) is pushed into the actual stack.

2. if $(q, \mathbf{Int}, q') \in \Delta$ then we have for all $i \in [1..n]$, $p_i \in Q_{B_i}$ and $a_i \in \Gamma$, $((q, p_1, \cdots, p_n, a_1, \cdots, a_n, m, l), \mathbf{Int}_i, (q', p_1, \cdots, p_n, a_1, \cdots, a_n, m, l)) \in \Delta'$.

3. For each $(q, \mathbf{Pop}_j(a_j), q') \in \Delta$ we add the following transitions.
   - $((q, p_1, \cdots, p_n, a_1, \cdots, a_n, 0, k), \mathbf{Pop}_j(b_j, p'_j), (q', p_1, \cdots, p_{j-1}, p'_j, p_{j+1}, \cdots, p_n, a_1, \cdots, a_{j-1}, b_j, a_{j+1}, \cdots, a_n, j, k)) \in \Delta'$, for all $b_j \in \Gamma$. This transition corresponds to the case where no pop or zero test operation were performed previously.
   - $((q, p_1, \cdots, p_n, a_1, \cdots, a_n, j, l), \mathbf{Pop}_j(b_j, p'_j), (q', p_1, \cdots, p_{j-1}, p'_j, p_{j+1}, \cdots, p_n, a_1, \cdots, a_{j-1}, b_j, a_{j+1}, \cdots, a_n, j, l)) \in \Delta'$. This transition corresponds to poping from the currently active stack.
   - For any $l > 2, i \neq j$, $((q, p_1, \cdots, p_n, a_1, \cdots, a_n, i, l), \mathbf{Pop}_j(b_j, p'_j), (q', p_1, \cdots, p_{j-1}, p'_j, p_{j+1}, \cdots, p_n, a_1, \cdots, a_{j-1}, b_j, a_{j+1}, \cdots, a_n, j, l - 1)) \in \Delta'$. This transition corresponding to a pop from stack-j when the currently active stack is i.
   - For any $i \neq j$ and $\delta(p'_j, q') \in F_j$, $((q, p_1, \cdots, p_n, a_1, \cdots, a_n, i, 2), \mathbf{Int}, q_w) \in \Delta'$.
   - For any $i \neq j$ and $\delta(p'_j, q') \notin F_j$, $((q, p_1, \cdots, p_n, a_1, \cdots, a_n, i, 2), \mathbf{Int}, q_l) \in \Delta'$.

4. For each $(q, \mathbf{Zero}_j, q') \in \Delta$ we add the following transitions.
   - $((q, p_1, \cdots, p_n, a_1, \cdots, a_{j-1}, \bot, \cdots, a_n, 0, k), \mathbf{Zero}_j, (q', p_1, \cdots, p_{j-1}, \cdots, p_n, a_1, \cdots, a_{j-1}, \bot, \cdots, a_n, j, k)) \in \Delta'$.
   - $((q, p_1, \cdots, p_n, a_1, \cdots, a_{j-1}, \bot, \cdots, a_n, j, l), \mathbf{Zero}_j, (q', p_1, \cdots, p_{j-1}, \cdots, p_n, a_1, \cdots, a_{j-1}, \bot, \cdots, a_n, j, l)) \in \Delta'$, for all $l \in [2..k]$.
   - For all $l > 2$ and $i \neq j$, $((q, p_1, \cdots, p_n, a_1, \cdots, \bot, a_{j-1}, \cdots, a_n, i, l), \mathbf{Zero}_j, (q', p_1, \cdots, p_{j-1}, \cdots, p_n, a_1, \cdots, a_{j-1}, \bot, \cdots, a_n, j, l - 1)) \in \Delta'$.

- For any $i \neq j$ and $\delta(s_j, q') \in F_j$, $((q, p_1, \cdots, p_n, a_1, \cdots, a_{j-1}, \perp, \cdots, a_n, i, 2), \textbf{Int}, q_w) \in \Delta'$.
- For any $i \neq j$ and $\delta(s_j, q') \in F_j$, $((q, p_1, \cdots, p_n, a_1, \cdots, a_{j-1}, \perp, \cdots, a_n, i, 2), \textbf{Int}, q_w) \in \Delta'$.

5. We further add $(q_l, \textbf{Int}, q_l)$ and $(q_w, \textbf{Int}, q_w)$ to the transitions

Observe that any run of such a system may involve at most $k - 1$ phases, as every change of phase results in a reduction in the last component. After $k - 1$ reductions, we end up in one of the states q_w or q_l. For correctness of the construction, we first define a ranking function σ' as follows. $\sigma'(q_w) = 0$, $\sigma'(q_l) = 1$ and for all other states $s = (q, p_1, \cdots, p_n, a_1, \cdots, a_n) \in Q_{M(k)}$, we let $\sigma'(s) = \sigma(q)$. Similarly we define τ' as $\tau'(q_w) = 0$, $\tau'(q_l) = 1$ and for all other states $s = (q, p_1, \cdots, p_n, a_1, \cdots, a_n) \in Q_{M(k)}$, we let $\tau'(s) = \tau(q)$ and we show that we may associate positions of the form (c, i, k) in the bounded-phase game on (k, M, τ, σ) with positions of the form $(d, i, k-1)$ in the bounded-phase game on $(k - 1, M(k), \tau', \sigma')$ that preserves the winner.

For a sequence $w = a_n a_{n-1} \ldots a_1 a_0 \in (\Gamma \setminus \{\perp\})^+ \perp$ and $1 \leq j \leq l$, let $\rho_j(w) = (a_{n-1}, p_{n-1}) \ldots (a_2, p_2)(a_1, p_1)(a_0, p_0) \perp$ (we let $\rho_j(\perp) = \perp$) where $p_0 = s_j$ and for all $i \in [1..n]$, $p_i = \delta^{B_j}(p_{i-1}, a_{i-1})$. Further, let $\delta_j(w) = \delta^{B_j}(p_{n-1}, a_{n-1})$ (we let $\delta_j(\perp) = p_0$). We now define the map $\textbf{F}$ from the k-bounded-phase parity game on (k, A, τ, σ) to the $k - 1$-bounded-phase parity game on the game $(k - 1, A(k), \tau, \sigma)$ as $\textbf{F}((q, \gamma_1, \cdots, \gamma_n), i, j) = (((q, \delta_1(\gamma_1), \cdots, \delta_n(\gamma_n), \text{Top}(\gamma_1), \cdots, \text{Top}(\gamma_l), i, j), \rho_1(\gamma_1), \cdots, \rho_l(\gamma_n)), i, j)$, if $j > 1$ (where Top is a function that returns top of the stack), $\textbf{F}((q, \gamma_1, \cdots, \gamma_n), i, 1) = q_w$ if $(q, \gamma_1, \cdots, \gamma_n)$ is winning for player-0 and $\textbf{F}((q, \gamma_1, \cdots, \gamma_n), i, 1) = q_l$ if $(q, \gamma_1, \cdots, \gamma_n)$ is losing for player-0. Now using arguments similar to Lemma 3, we get the following.

Lemma 7. *The map $\textbf{F}$ satisfies the following properties*
(1) *The ownership and the rank of all positions (c, i, j) with $j > 1$ are preserved.* (2) *For any configuration (c, i, j) if $(c, i, j) \rightarrow (c', i', j')$ with $j' > 1$ then $\textbf{F}((c, i, j)) \rightarrow \textbf{F}((c', i', j'))$.* (3) *For any configuration (c, i, j) if $\textbf{F}(c, i, j) \rightarrow d$ for any $d \notin \{q_w, q_l\}$ then there is (c', i', j') with $(c, i, j) \rightarrow (c', i', j')$, $j' > 1$ such that $\textbf{F}(c', i', j') = d$.* (4) *If $(c, i, 2) \rightarrow (c', i', 1)$, then $\textbf{F}(c, i, 2) \rightarrow q_w$ iff $(c', i', 1)$ is a winning position and $\textbf{F}(c, i, 2) \rightarrow q_l$ iff $(c', i', 1)$ is a losing position for player-0.*

Hence we can effectively determine the set of all positions that are winning for player 0, in the bounded-phase parity game (k, M, τ, σ).

We have shown how to reduce a k-bounded-phase game to a $k - 1$-bounded-phase game. However note that each such a reduction is exponential in the size of the system. Since we do as many such reductions as the number of phases, the overall complexity will be a tower of exponents. Hence the overall reduction is NON-ELEMENTARY in nature. This completes the proof of theorem 3. Next we show that such a blow up cannot be avoided.

7 Lower Bounds for Bounded Phase Parity Game

We show that the satisfiability of a first order formula with ordering relation over natural numbers, can be reformulated as a bounded-phase parity game over *MPDS*. We first briefly recall the first order theory of natural numbers with ordering relation $(FO(<))$.

Let $\mathcal{V}$ be countably infinite set of variables, we will use $x, y, z, x_1, x_2 \cdots$ to refer to the variables in $\mathcal{V}$. The set of terms in $FO(<)$ is defined as $t := x \mid t < t \mid t = t$. The set of formulas is defined to be $\Psi := t \mid \neg t \mid \Psi \vee \Psi \mid \Psi \wedge \Psi \mid \forall x \Psi \mid \exists x \Psi$. The notion of free, bound (quantified) variable are defined as usual. We write $Var(\Psi) \subseteq \mathcal{V}$ to denote the set of all free variables (unquantified variables) of Ψ.

Given any formula Ψ over variables $\mathcal{V}$, we define a valuation function as $\mu : \mathcal{V} \mapsto \mathbb{N}$ in the usual way. Given any formula Ψ and a valuation function μ, we call μ a model of Ψ, iff $\mu \models \Psi$. A formula with no free variables is called a sentence. A sentence is said to be satisfied iff there is some valuation function that satisfies it. Note that the negation is defined only on the atomic formulas. However, given any formula Ψ, we can easily obtain another formula $\text{Duel}(\Psi)$ such that for any model μ of Ψ, $\mu \models \Psi$ iff $\mu \not\models \text{Duel}(\Psi)$. w.l.o.g we will assume that formulas that we deal henceforth with will be in prenix normal form.

Given a formula Ψ and its model μ we define the linearisation of μ w.r.t. Ψ to be a word of the form $x_1 a^{j_1} x_2 a^{j_2} \cdots x_n a^{j_n} \perp$, where $\{x_1, \cdots, x_n\} = Var(\Psi)$ and for each $k \in [1..n]$, $\mu(x_{i_k}) = j_k + j_{k-1} \cdots j_n$. Similarly, for any set of variables $\mathcal{V}$, we say a string $(\alpha = x_n a^{i_n} x_{n-1} a^{i_{n-1}} \cdots x_1 a^{i_1}) \in (\mathcal{V} \cup a)^*$ is a valuation string if for all $l, k \in [1..n]$, we have $l \neq k \implies x_l \neq x_k$ (i.e. each x_i appears at most once). Firstly, given any valuation string $\alpha = x_n a^{i_n} x_{n-1} a^{i_{n-1}} \cdots x_1 a^{i_1}$ and a set of variable $\mathcal{V}$, we define $\mu_\alpha^\mathcal{V}$ as, for any $j \in [1..n]$, $\mu_\alpha^\mathcal{V}(x_j) = a^{i_j} + a^{i_{j-1}} + \cdots + a^{i_1}$, i.e. it maps the variables x_j, to a value equal to number of a's appearing before it in α. For any $x \in \mathcal{V}$ such that x does not appear in α, we let $\mu_\alpha(x) = 0$.

Given any formula Ψ, we use $Cl(\Psi)$ to indicate the set of all formulas obtained by closing the formula Ψ over subformulas. Note that even if Ψ is a sentence, elements of $Cl(\Psi)$ can have free variables. We now show that satisfiability of first order formula over $(N, <)$ (known to have non-elementary complexity [9]) can be reduced to a parity games over the bounded-phase MPDS.

The informal idea is to construct an MPDS, in which the state space contains the subformulas of the given formula Ψ (i.e. $Cl(\Psi)$), along with some intermediary states. The MPDS starts with empty stack and the formula Ψ. At any point in the game, the *MPDS* maintains the unprocessed part of the formula $\phi \in Cl(\Psi)$ as part of its state space and the linear encoding (linearisation) of the current valuation μ (w.r.t. ϕ) in its stack. There are two parts to the game depending on whether the unprocessed part begins with a quantifier or not. If the unprocessed part of formula begins with a quantifier $\forall$, then player-1 strips off the quantifier and assigns a valuation to the corresponding variable by modifying the stack. If it begins with a $\exists$ quantifier then the valuation is provided by player-0. If the valuation that the player wishes to provide is less than the variables already in the stack, the elements are moved to stack-2 till the appropriate position is found, the variable is placed in this position and the elements from stack-2 are moved back to stack-1. If the valuation that the player wishes to provide is greater than all the variables present in the stack, extra a's are appended and the variable is placed. If the outer most operator is $\wedge$, then the player-1 chooses a subformula and the game proceeds. If the outer most operator is $\vee$, then the player-0 selects a subformula. The game proceeds till the unprocessed part is an atomic formula, in which case it can easily be verified based on the valuations in the stack.

We will formally describe the construction of the *MPDS* $M_\Psi = (2, Q, \Gamma = \{a, \perp\} \cup Var(\Psi), \Delta, q_0)$ in two parts. The first part describes the moves till we reach an atomic formula. It contains the following set of states $Cl(\Psi) \cup Cl(\Psi) \times \{\text{lt}, \text{gt}, m_{1,2}, m_{2,1}\} \cup Cl(\Psi) \times \{m_{1,2}, m_{2,1}\} \times (\{a\} \times Var(\Psi))$. The transition relation Δ is defined as follows. We will used $?x$ to denote either of $\exists x$ or $\forall x$.

1. For all $\psi_1 \wedge \psi_2 \in Cl(\Phi)$, the transitions $(\psi_1 \wedge \psi_2, \mathbf{Int}, \psi_1), (\psi_1 \wedge \psi_2, \mathbf{Int}, \psi_2) \in \Delta$. Similarly for all $\psi_1 \vee \psi_2 \in Cl(\Phi)$, the transitions $(\psi_1 \vee \psi_2, \mathbf{Int}, \psi_1)$ and $(\psi_1 \vee \psi_2, \mathbf{Int}, \psi_2) \in \Delta$.
2. For all $?x.\psi \in Cl(\Phi)$, we add $(?x.\psi, \mathbf{Int}, (?x.\psi, \text{lt}))$ and $(?x.\psi, \mathbf{Int}, (?x. \psi, \text{gt})) \in \Delta$, this transition enables guessing whether the current variable x needs to be inserted in between the existing variable (valuation falls below the current maximum) or needs to be inserted on top (is greater than the current maximum).
3. We also add $((?x.\psi, \text{gt}), \mathbf{Push}_1(a), (?x.\psi, \text{gt})) \in \Delta$ (pushes a into stack-1 to increase possible valuation for x) and $((?x.\psi, \text{gt}), \mathbf{Push}_1(x), \psi) \in \Delta$ (Marks position of x and shift to the sub-formula).
4. We add $((?x.\psi, \text{lt}), \mathbf{Int}, (?x.\psi, m_{1,2})) \in \Delta$ (Begin moving from stack-1 to 2), $((?x.\psi, m_{1,2}), \mathbf{Pop}_1(a), (?x.\psi, m_{1,2}, a)) \in \Delta$ and $((?x.\psi, m_{1,2}, a), \mathbf{Push}_2 (a), (?x.\psi, m_{1,2})) \in \Delta, \forall a \in \Gamma \setminus \{\perp\}$ (moves values from stack-1 to 2).
5. Similarly we add $((?x.\psi, m_{1,2}), \mathbf{Push}_1(x), (?x.\psi, m_{2,1})) \in \Delta$ (Begin moving from stack-2 back to 2), $((?x.\psi, m_{2,1}), \mathbf{Pop}_2(a), (?x.\psi, m_{2,1}, a)) \in \Delta$ and $((?x.\psi, m_{2,1}, a), \mathbf{Push}_1(a), (?x.\psi, m_{2,1})) \in \Delta, \forall a \in \Gamma \setminus \{\perp\}$ (moves values from stack-2 to 1). We also add $((?x.\psi, m_{2,1}), \mathbf{Zero}_2, \psi) \in \Delta$ (Move to the next sub-formula).

In the second part, we describe the state space starting at a state of the form $(x = y)$ or $(x < y)$ that determines winner of the game. It contains the following set of states $\{x = y, x < y, a_y \mid x, y \in V\} \cup \{T, F\}$. The transitions are as below.

1. $(x = y, \mathbf{Pop}_1(z), x = y) \in \Delta$, for all $z \in V \setminus \{x, y\} \cup \{a\}$, pop all elements other than x, y.
2. $(x = y, \mathbf{Pop}_1(z), z') \in \Delta$, for $z \in \{x, y\}, z' \in \{x, y\} \setminus \{z\}$, as soon as one of $\{x, y\}$ is seen (say x) goto a state expecting to see the other variable (y if we saw x previously).
3. For $x \in V$, we add $(x, \mathbf{Pop}_1(a), F) \in \Delta$, if we see an a when we are expecting a variable in $x \in V$, we goto the losing state F.
4. For $x, z \in V$, $z \neq x$ we add $(x, \mathbf{Pop}_1(z), x) \in \Delta$, if we see a variable other than x, we skip.

5. For $x \in V$, we add $(x, \mathbf{Pop}_1(x), T) \in \Delta$, if we see a variable x, we goto winning state.
6. We also add $(T, \mathbf{Int}, T)$ and $(F, \mathbf{Int}, F)$ to Δ.

The set transitions needed for $\neg(x = y), (x < y), \neg(x < y)$ are similar. We will now consider the bounded-phase parity game given by $(|\Psi|, \mathcal{C}(M_\Psi), \tau, \sigma)$ where $\sigma : Q \mapsto \{0, 1\}$ and $\tau : Q \mapsto \{0, 1\}$ are defined as:

- We let $\sigma(T) = 0$ and $\sigma(F) = 1$. We let $\sigma((\exists x.\Psi', gt)) = 1$ and $\sigma((\forall x.\Psi', gt)) = 0$ (this will ensure that either of the player cannot simply win by just pushing elements onto the stack). For all other $q \in Q$, we let $\sigma(q) = 0$.
- For any state s such that its subformula component is of the form, $\forall x.\Psi'$ or $\Psi_1 \wedge \Psi_2$, we let $\tau(s) = 1$ (player-1 position). Otherwise, $\tau(s) = 0$ i.e. we let all other states to be player-0 position.

Notice that along any positions in the game, where the state is only a subformula from $Cl(\Psi)$, the stack content of the first stack α is a valuation string. This is easy to see since by nature of the formula we have assumed that along any path, we can never encounter the same variable twice. Clearly such a $\mu_\alpha^\mathcal{V}$ function is a valuation function. We show in Lemma 8, that along positions in game graph where the state is only a subformula from $Cl(\Psi)$, the valuation function constructed out of the content of stack 1 is actually a model of the subformula iff player-0 has a winning strategy from that position.

Lemma 8. *Give any configuration $c \in \mathcal{C}(M)$ which is of the form $(\Psi, \alpha\bot, \bot)$ where $\alpha = x_n a^{i_n} x_{n-1} a^{i_{n-1}} \cdots x_1 a^{i_1} \in (V\Gamma^*)^*$ is a valuation string containing all the free variables of Ψ, then $\mu_\alpha^\mathcal{V} \models \Psi$ iff player-0 has a bounded-phase winning strategy from c.*

Corollary 1. *For any sentence Ψ, Ψ is satisfiable iff $(\Psi, \bot, \bot)$ is winning for player 0 in the game $(|\Psi|, \mathcal{C}(M_\Psi), \tau, \sigma)$. Thus deciding bounded-phase games has a* NON-ELEMENTARY *lower bound.*

References

1. Cachat, T.: Uniform solution of parity games on prefix-recognizable graphs. Electr. Notes Theor. Comput. Sci. **68**, 1–15 (2002)
2. Emerson, E.A., Jutla, C.S.: Tree automata, mu-calculus and determinacy (extended abstract). In: 32nd Annual Symposium on Foundations of Computer Science, San Juan, Puerto Rico, 1–4 October (1991)
3. Kupferman, O., Piterman, N., Vardi, M.Y.: An automata-theoretic approach to infinite-state systems. In: Manna, Z., Peled, D.A. (eds.) Time for Verification. LNCS, vol. 6200, pp. 202–259. Springer, Heidelberg (2010). doi:10.1007/978-3-642-13754-9_11
4. Martin, D.A.: Borel determinacy. Ann. Math. **102**, 363–371 (1975)
5. Qadeer, S., Rehof, J.: Context-bounded model checking of concurrent software. In: Halbwachs, N., Zuck, L.D. (eds.) TACAS 2005. LNCS, vol. 3440, pp. 93–107. Springer, Heidelberg (2005). doi:10.1007/978-3-540-31980-1_7

6. Saivasan, P.: Analysis of Automata-theoretic models of Concurrent Recursive Programs. Ph.D. thesis, Chennai Mathematical Institute (2016)
7. Serre, O.: Note on winning positions on pushdown games with [omega]-regular conditions. Inf. Process. Lett. **85**, 285–291 (2003)
8. Seth, A.: Games on multi-stack pushdown systems. In: Artemov, S., Nerode, A. (eds.) LFCS 2009. LNCS, vol. 5407, pp. 395–408. Springer, Heidelberg (2008). doi:10.1007/978-3-540-92687-0_27
9. Stockmeyer, L.J.: The Complexity of Decision Problems in Automata Theory and Logic. Ph.D. thesis. MIT, Cambridge (1974)
10. Torre, S.L., Madhusudan, P., Parlato, G.: A robust class of context-sensitive languages. In: LICS. IEEE Computer Society (2007)
11. Torre, S., Madhusudan, P., Parlato, G.: Reducing context-bounded concurrent reachability to sequential reachability. In: Bouajjani, A., Maler, O. (eds.) CAV 2009. LNCS, vol. 5643, pp. 477–492. Springer, Heidelberg (2009). doi:10.1007/978-3-642-02658-4_36
12. Walukiewicz, I.: Pushdown processes: games and model checking. In: Alur, R., Henzinger, T.A. (eds.) CAV 1996. LNCS, vol. 1102, pp. 62–74. Springer, Heidelberg (1996). doi:10.1007/3-540-61474-5_58

Reachability Analysis of Dynamic Pushdown Networks with Priorities

Marcio Diaz[1](✉) and Tayssir Touili[2]

[1] LIPN and University Paris Diderot, Villetaneuse, France
marcio.diaz@gmail.com
[2] LIPN, CNRS and University Paris 13, Villetaneuse, France
tayssir.touili@lipn.univ-paris13.fr

Abstract. In this paper, we consider the reachability problem of multi-threaded programs where threads have priorities and are scheduled by a priority based round-robin scheduler. For that, we introduce a new model, called Dynamic Pushdown Networks with Priorities (P-DPNs) that extends the well known DPN model with priorities. We represent potentially infinite sets of configurations of P-DPNs using finite state automata and show that the backward reachability sets of P-DPNs are regular and can be effectively computed.

1 Introduction

Writing multi-threaded programs is notoriously difficult, as concurrency related bugs are hard to find and reproduce. This difficulty is increased if we consider that several software systems consist of different components that react to the environment and uses resources like CPU or memory according to a real time need. For instance, in systems that control automobiles we can have a component in charge of the music subsystem and another component in charge of the braking subsystem. Obviously, the braking subsystem should have a higher priority access to the resources needed, since a delay in the action of the brakes can cost lives.

The programming model used in the vast majority of these embedded systems, used from automobiles to spacecrafts, defines a set of threads that perform computation monitoring or responding to events. Each thread is typically assigned a priority and are scheduled by a priority round-robin preemptive scheduler: if a thread with a higher static priority becomes ready to run, the currently running thread will be preempted and returned to the wait list for its priority level. The round-robin scheduling policy allows each thread to run only for a fixed amount of time before it must yield its processing slot to another thread of the same priority.

Combining threads with priorities and different synchronization primitives can easily leads to a large number of undesirable behaviors. Consider for example the pseudocode of Fig. 1. It consists on five threads that synchronize their access to shared variables using a spin-lock. The program consists of two global variables x and y, and one spin-lock l (lines 1, 2 and 3). The program starts with thread

© Springer International Publishing AG 2017
A. El Abbadi and B. Garbinato (Eds.): NETYS 2017, LNCS 10299, pp. 288–303, 2017.
DOI: 10.1007/978-3-319-59647-1_22

```
 1  int x = 0;                         22      int tmp = x;
 2  int y = 0;                         23      assert(tmp == x);
 3  spin_lock l;                       24      spinlock_unlock(l);
 4                                     25      thread_create(D, 2);
 5  void main() {                      26  }
 6      // Priority 1.                 27
 7      thread_create(A,1);            28  void C() {
 8      thread_thread(B,1);            29      // Priority 2.
 9  }                                  30      spinlock_lock(l);
10                                     31      y++;
11  void A() {                         32      spinlock_unlock(l);
12      // Priority 1.                 33      thread_create(A, 1);
13      spinlock_lock(l);              34  }
14      x++;                           35
15      spinlock_unlock(l);            36  void D() {
16      thread_create(C, 2);           37      // Priority 2.
17  }                                  38      int tmp = y;
18                                     39      assert(tmp == y);
19  void B() {                         40      thread_create(B, 1);
20      // Priority 1.                 41  }
21      spinlock_lock(l);
```

Fig. 1. Pseudocode of a program with threads, priorities and spin-locks.

main (line 5), of priority one, creating two threads A and B (lines 7 and 8), each of them of priority one too. Thread A increments variable x (line 14), holding the spin-lock, and then it creates thread C (line 16), of higher priority of two. Thread B, holding the spin-lock, reads variable x into variable tmp (line 22) and checks if they are equal (line 23). Note that threads A and B can be executed concurrently, but the assert succeeds, since all accesses to variable x are protected by the spin-lock. Thread C is similar to thread A, but this time incrementing variable y and creating again thread A. This creates a loop that executes thread A and C in an interleaved way. Thread D mimics thread B, reading variable y but this time without protecting it with the spin-lock. Thread D also create thread B, making a loop with it.

Now, we may think that the error in this program is the lack of protection to the global variable y on thread D. But the assertion (line 39) will always succeed, since threads C and D will never be executed concurrently. Indeed, either C or D will be created first and will block the creation of the other thread until it finish. However, the program still has a bug. The problem occurs when thread B owns the spin-lock (lines 22 or 23) and it is interrupted by thread C trying to acquire it (line 30). In this case we have a deadlock, since the only thread that can make progress is thread C, for having higher priority, but it cannot acquire the spin-lock.

Deadlock freedom and absence of conflicts, like data races, are among the most crucial properties that need to be checked for multi-threaded programs. The previous example shows that there is a real need for formal methods to find automatic verification techniques for *multi-threaded programs with priorities.*

Dynamic pushdown networks (DPNs) were introduced in [1] as a suitable formalism to model multi-threaded programs. DPNs generalize pushdown systems by rules that have the additional side effect of creating a new thread that is then executed in parallel. The key concept for analyzing DPNs is computation of predecessor sets. Configurations of a DPN are represented as words over control and stack symbols, and for a regular set of configurations, the set of predecessor configurations is regular as well and can be computed effectively [1]. Predecessor computations can be used for various interesting analyses, like kill/gen analysis on bit-vectors, context-bounded model checking.

However, DPNs cannot model multi-threaded programs with priorities. In a DPN model all the threads have the same priority to make a transition to another configuration independently of other threads. Previous research [2,3] on verification of multi-threaded programs with priorities using pushdown systems has focused on threads scheduled under a FIFO policy, on which each thread can only be interrupted by another thread of highest priority (threads of the same priority cannot interleave).

Here we consider multi-threaded programs with priorities where threads with the same priority can interleave as well. For this, we extend the DPN model allowing the creation of threads with different priorities. In this new model, called P-DPN, only threads in a configuration with highest priority are allowed to make transitions. Threads with the same priority can interleave their executions, imitating the round-robin scheduling.

The paper is organized as follows: first we introduce the definition of P-DPNs and give its semantics (Sect. 2); then we show how to model programs with threads and priorities, in particular we give the P-DPN model for the program of Fig. 1 (Sect. 3). Next, we show a way to see executions of P-DPNs as trees (Sect. 4) and present a finite abstraction over these executions trees (Sect. 5). This abstraction allows to determine whether a DPN execution satisfies the priority semantics or not. Then we show how to represent infinite sets of configurations of a P-DPN, using a finite automaton, and show how to detect data races and deadlocks with them (Sect. 6). Finally, we give the algorithm to compute predecessor sets in P-DPNs (Sect. 7).

2   Model Definition

Definition 1. *A Dynamic Pushdown Network with Priorities (P-DPN) is a tuple $M = (P, \Gamma, \Delta, \eta)$, where P is a finite set of control states, Γ is a finite stack alphabet with $P \cap \Gamma = \emptyset$, $\eta : P \to \mathcal{P}$ is a function from control states to a finite set of natural numbers $\mathcal{P}$ representing priorities, and $\Delta = \Delta_N \cup \Delta_S$ is a finite set of non-spawning rules $p\gamma \hookrightarrow qw \in \Delta_N$ and spawning rules $p\gamma \hookrightarrow q_1 w_1 \rhd q_2 w_2 \in \Delta_S$, where $p, q_1, q_2 \in P, \gamma \in \Gamma$ and $w, w_1, w_2 \in \Gamma^*$.*

A Dynamic Pushdown Network (DPN) can be seen as a P-DPN $(P, \Gamma, \Delta, \eta_0)$ such that $\forall p \in P, \eta_0(p) = 0$. Given a P-DPN $M = (P, \Gamma, \Delta, \eta)$, its DPN M' is defined as $(P, \Gamma, \Delta, \eta_0)$, abbreviated (P, Γ, Δ).

A P-DPN can be seen as a collection of threads running in parallel, each of them being able to perform pushdown operations using non-spawning rules and to create new threads in the system using spawning rules. Using pushdown operations in the stack we can model calls and returns from (possibly recursive) functions.

A *global configuration* of a P-DPN M is a word over the alphabet $P \cup \Gamma$, starting with a symbol in P, representing the state of the P-DPN. A global configuration can be seen as a sequence of words in $P\Gamma^*$ each of them corresponding to the configuration of one of the threads running in parallel on the system, also called *local configuration*. Let $Conf_M$ be the set of all global configurations of a P-DPN M.

The function η assigns a priority to each control state. Intuitively, this means that a thread can be in configurations with different priorities. P-DPNs must execute first the thread in the configuration with highest priority. We overload the function η to configurations as follows: for all $c = p_1 w_1 \ldots p_n w_n \in Conf_M$, $\eta(p_1 w_1 \ldots p_n w_n) := max(\eta(p_1), \ldots, \eta(p_n))$. We say that $\eta(c)$ is *the priority of c.*

Thus, a thread in a local configuration $p\gamma r$ can move to another local configuration qwr if its priority $\eta(p)$ is highest among the others local configurations, as the following definition shows.

Definition 2. *The transition relation* $\longrightarrow_M$ *is defined as the smallest relation in* $Conf_M \times Conf_M$ *such that* $\forall c_1, c_2 \in Conf_M$:

1. $c_1 \, p\gamma r \, c_2 \longrightarrow_M c_1 \, qwr \, c_2$, *if* $\eta(c_1 \, p\gamma r \, c_2) = \eta(p)$ *and* $p\gamma \hookrightarrow qw \in \Delta_N$;
2. $c_1 \, p\gamma r \, c_2 \longrightarrow_M c_1 \, q_2 w_2 \, q_1 w_1 r \, c_2$, *if* $\eta(c_1 \, p\gamma r \, c_2) = \eta(p)$ *and* $p\gamma \hookrightarrow q_1 w_1 \triangleright q_2 w_2 \in \Delta_S$;

where $p, q, q_1, q_2 \in P, \gamma \in \Gamma, w, w_1, w_2, r \in \Gamma^*$. *We denote as* $\longrightarrow_M^*$ *the transitive-reflexive closure of* $\longrightarrow_M$.

The semantics above says that: (1) a thread in a local configuration with control state p and top of stack γ can move to a local configuration with control state q, replacing the top of its stack γ by w, if there is a non-spawning rule $p\gamma \hookrightarrow qw$ and its priority $(\eta(p))$ is equal to the highest priority in the system $(\eta(c_1 \, p\gamma r \, c_2))$; (2) a thread in a local configuration with control state p and top of stack γ can move to a local configuration with control state q_1, replacing the top of its stack γ by w_1 and creating another thread in control state q_2 with stack w_2, if there is a spawning rule $p\gamma \hookrightarrow q_1 w_1 \triangleright q_2 w_2$ and its priority $(\eta(p))$ is equal to the highest priority in the system $(\eta(c_1 \, p\gamma r \, c_2))$. Note that each transition has the power to block and/or unblock others threads according to the priority of the new control states.

Given a configuration c, the set of immediate predecessors of c in M is defined as $pre_M(c) = \{c' \in Conf_M \;:\; c' \longrightarrow_M c\}$. This notation can be generalized straightforwardly to sets of configurations. Let pre_M^* denote the reflexive-transitive closure of pre_M. For the rest of this paper, we assume that we have fixed a P-DPN $M = (P, \Gamma, \Delta, \eta)$. Let $M' = (P, \Gamma, \Delta)$ be its corresponding DPN defined as in Definition 1.

3   Modeling Programs with P-DPNs

It was explained in [1] how to use DPNs to model multi-threaded programs where all threads have the same priority. P-DPN extends the DPN model by

Thread Main:

Thread C:

$p_1 \, m_0 \hookrightarrow p_1 \, m_1 \rhd p_1 \, a_0$

$p_2 \, c_0 \hookrightarrow p_{2,l} \, c_1$

Thread B:

$p_1 \, m_1 \hookrightarrow p_1 \, m_2 \rhd p_1 \, b_0$

$p_{2,l} \, c_1 \hookrightarrow p_{2,l} \, c_2$

$p_1 \, m_2 \hookrightarrow p_0$

$p_{2,l} \, c_2 \hookrightarrow p_2 \, c_3$

$p_1 \, b_0 \hookrightarrow p_{1,l} \, b_1$

$p_2 \, c_3 \hookrightarrow p_2 \, c_4 \rhd p_1 \, a_0$

Thread A:

$p_{1,l} \, b_1 \hookrightarrow p_{1,l} \, b_2$

$p_2 \, c_5 \hookrightarrow p_0$

$p_{1,l} \, b_2 \hookrightarrow p_{1,l} \, b_3$

$p_1 \, a_0 \hookrightarrow p_{1,l} \, a_1$

$p_{1,l} \, b_3 \hookrightarrow p_1 \, b_4$

Thread D:

$p_{1,l} \, a_1 \hookrightarrow p_{1,l} \, a_2$

$p_1 \, b_4 \hookrightarrow p_1 \, b_5 \rhd p_2 \, d_0$

$p_2 \, d_0 \hookrightarrow p_2 \, d_1$

$p_{1,l} \, a_2 \hookrightarrow p_1 \, a_3$

$p_1 \, b_5 \hookrightarrow p_0$

$p_2 \, d_1 \hookrightarrow p_2 \, d_2$

$p_1 \, a_3 \hookrightarrow p_1 \, a_4 \rhd p_2 \, c_0$

$p_2 \, d_2 \hookrightarrow p_2 \, d_3 \rhd p_1 \, b_0$

$p_1 \, a_4 \hookrightarrow p_0$

$p_2 \, d_3 \hookrightarrow p_0$

Fig. 2. Some transition rules corresponding to the P-DPN of the program of Fig. 1.

attaching a priority to each control state and restricting the execution of each thread according to the priority of the control state of his local configuration. Only threads with highest priority can execute, i.e. only threads in a local configuration with the higher priority of the global configuration can make transitions to other local configurations. Then, by giving to all the control states of a thread the same priority, we can model a thread with that priority.

When modeling the termination of a thread, we must make sure that the priority of its final control state does not prevent other threads from making a transition. To ensure this, the control state of the final configuration should have priority zero (the smallest priority).

Thus, the P-DPN of the program of Fig. 1 consists on:

- The set of control states $P = \{p_0, p_{0,l}, p_1, p_{1,l}, p_2, p_{2,l}\}$. The sub-index indicates the priority and the spin-locks of the control state. For instance p_0 is a control state with priority zero and does not hold any spin-lock, while $p_{1,l}$ is a control state with priority one and holds spin-lock l.
- The stack corresponds to program points on each thread:
  $\Gamma = \{m_0, \ldots, m_3, a_0, \ldots, a_4, b_0, \ldots, b_5, c_0, \ldots, c_4, d_0, \ldots, d_3\}$.
- We show some of the transition rules on Fig. 2. For example, there are three rules corresponding to thread Main: the first two representing the creation of threads A and B; and the last one representing the end of its execution (note that it moves to a control state of zero priority). Thread A, for its part, is represented by five transition rules, each one representing (in this order): the acquisition of lock l, the write of variable x, the release of lock l, the creation of thread C, and the end of its execution. The rules for the others threads are created following a similar reasoning. Note that sometimes is not possible to anticipate the locks that each thread holds on each program point. On these cases we should add a rule for each possible subset of locks. We omitted these rules on Fig. 2.

– As said previously, the sub-index of the control states indicates their priority. Thus we have that $\eta(p_0) = 0, \eta(p_1) = \eta(p_{1,l}) = 1, \eta(p_2) = \eta(p_{2,l}) = 2$.

4   Execution Hedges

The executions of P-DPNs can be viewed as trees, in which we specify the order of transitions inside each thread and the father-child relation between threads but we do not specify the order of transitions between different threads running concurrently. Then, a P-DPN execution viewed as a tree can be either:

– only a configuration, representing an execution without transitions;
– a configuration with a child subtree, representing a configuration that makes a non-spawning transition with the subtree representing the remaining part of its execution;
– a configuration with two children subtrees, representing a configuration that makes a spawning transition with the right subtree representing the remaining part of the execution of the father thread and the left subtree representing the execution of the child thread.

Thus, we model an execution of a P-DPN M as a list of trees called *execution hedge*, where each tree represents the execution started from each thread in the beginning of the execution.

Formally, let X be a variable, we define the set $T[X]$ of *terms* over $P \cup \Gamma \cup \{X\}$, inductively, as follows: $X \subseteq T[X]$, $P\Gamma^* \subseteq T[X]$, if $t \in T[X]$, $c \in P\Gamma^*$ then $c(t) \in T[X]$, if $t_1, t_2 \in T[X]$, $c \in P\Gamma^*$ then $c(t_1, t_2) \in T[X]$. Terms in $T[]$ are called *trees*, and will be denoted also by T. A *context* C is a term in which X occurs exactly once. Let t be a tree, then $C[t]$ is the tree obtained by substituting in C the occurrence of the variable X with the tree t. We define a *hedge* as a finite sequence of trees in T, denoted as T^*. Given a hedge $h \in T^*$, we define the *root configuration* of h, $root(h)$, as the configuration formed by concatenating the roots of each tree in h, from left to right. Given a hedge $h \in T^*$, we define the *yield configuration* of h, $yield(h)$, as the configuration formed by concatenating the leaves of h, from left to right. On Fig. 3 we can observe a graphical representation of two of the possible hedges from the P-DPN of Fig. 2. In particular, these hedges are called *execution hedges*, since its edges match transition rules of Δ. Note that the execution hedge of the left is contained in the execution hedge of the right. At the top of the right hedge we can observe the thread *Main* creating thread A. The left subtree corresponds to the execution of thread A, on which it acquire and release the spin-lock l and create thread C. The right subtree corresponds to the remaining execution of thread *Main*, where it creates thread B, and the execution of thread B, on which it acquire and release the spin-lock l and creates thread D.

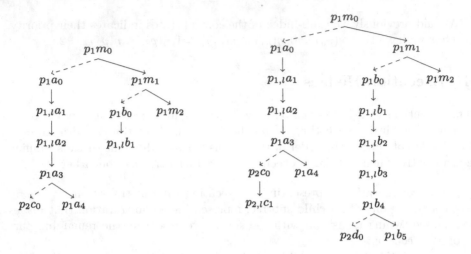

Fig. 3. Two execution hedges corresponding to the P-DPN of Fig. 2.

Note that the configurations p_2c_0 and $p_{1,l}b_1$, can be reached simultaneously from the starting configuration:

$$p_1m_0 \rightarrow p_1a_0\ p_1m_1 \rightarrow p_1a_0\ p_1b_0\ p_1m_2$$
$$\rightarrow p_{1,l}a_1\ p_1b_0\ p_1m_2 \rightarrow p_{1,l}a_2\ p_1b_0\ p_1m_2$$
$$\rightarrow p_1a_3\ p_1b_0\ p_1m_2 \rightarrow p_2c_0\ p_1a_4\ p_1b_0\ p_1m_2$$
$$\rightarrow \underline{p_2c_0}\ p_1a_4\ \underline{p_{1,l}b_1}\ p_1m_2$$

This configuration corresponds to the deadlock mentioned in the introduction: the thread C in configuration p_2c_0 is the only one allowed to execute, but it cannot make progress since it should acquire the spin-lock owned by thread B in configuration $p_{1,l}b_1$. On the otherside, the configurations $p_{2,l}c_1$ and p_2d_0, corresponding to a data race mentioned in the introduction, cannot be reached simultaneously as explained in that section.

We say that a hedge h is *schedulable* if we can interleave the edges of it allowing us to reach the leaves of the hedge $(yield(h))$ from its root $(root(h))$. For instance, on Fig. 3, the left execution hedge is schedulable but the right execution hedge is not.

Definition 3. *Let $\Longrightarrow$ be the smaller transition relation between trees that satisfies:*

$$C[p\gamma r] \Longrightarrow C[p\gamma r(qwr)] \qquad if \quad p\gamma \hookrightarrow qw \in \Delta$$
$$C[p\gamma r] \Longrightarrow C[p\gamma r(q_2w_2,\ q_1w_1r)] \qquad if \quad p\gamma \hookrightarrow q_1w_1 \triangleright q_2w_2 \in \Delta,$$

where C is a context, $p, q, q_1, q_2 \in P, \gamma \in \Gamma, w, w_1, w_2, r \in \Gamma^*$. Its transitive-reflexive closure is denoted by $\Longrightarrow^*$. We extend this definition in the obvious way to hedges.

Then, we can define the execution hedge as the hedge resulting from a sequence of $\Longrightarrow$ transitions starting from a configuration.

Definition 4. *A hedge $h \in T^*$ is an* execution hedge *iff $root(h) \Longrightarrow^* h$.*

The definition of execution hedges guarantees that they represent only valid executions in the DPN M'. The following lemma is straightforward and is intended to state the relation between $\longrightarrow^*$ and $\Longrightarrow^*$.

Lemma 1. *Let $c, c' \in Conf_M$, then $c \longrightarrow^*_{M'} c'$ iff there is an execution hedge $h \in T^*$ such that $c = root(h)$ and $c' = yield(h)$.*

Since we are interested in execution hedges that can be mapped to at least one valid execution path under P-DPN semantics, we define now a *scheduler* relation that schedules the transitions of an execution hedge respecting the priority semantics.

Definition 5. *The scheduler $\rightsquigarrow \subseteq T^* \times (P\Gamma^*) \times T^*$ is the least relation satisfying the following constraints:*

$$h_1\, c(t)\, h_2 \rightsquigarrow h_1\, t\, h_2 \qquad \text{if}\quad \eta(root(h_1\, c(t)\, h_2)) = \eta(c)$$
$$h_1\, c(t_1, t_2)\, h_2 \rightsquigarrow h_1\, t_1 t_2\, h_2 \qquad \text{if}\quad \eta(root(h_1\, c(l_1, t_2)\, h_2)) = \eta(c)$$

where $h_1, h_2 \in T^*, l, t_1, t_2 \in T, c \in P\Gamma^*$. The transitive reflexive closure of $\rightsquigarrow$ is denoted by $\rightsquigarrow^*$.

The transition rules above mean that the scheduler chooses configuration c to execute first since c has the highest priority of the other active threads: the priority of c is $\eta(root(h_1\, c(t)\, h_2))$ for the first rule and $\eta(root(h_1\, c(t_1, t_2)\, h_2))$ for the second rule.

We will say that a hedge h is *schedulable* if the scheduler can schedule all its transitions, i.e. the sequence of $\rightsquigarrow$ transitions end up with the yield configuration of h.

Definition 6. *A hedge h is* schedulable *iff $h \rightsquigarrow^* yield(h)$.*

Then, it is easy to see that a schedulable execution hedge has a valid execution path in M, i.e. under P-DPN semantics. Thus, we can relate $\longrightarrow^*_M$ with $\Longrightarrow^*$ (execution) and $\rightsquigarrow^*$ (schedulable), as follows:

Theorem 1. *Let $c, c' \in Conf_M$, then $c \longrightarrow^*_M c'$ iff there is a schedulable execution hedge $h \in T^*$ with $c = root(h), c' = yield(h)$.*

5   Priority Structures

Given an execution hedge $h \in T^*$, one way to decide whether it is schedulable or not is to try all the possible ways to schedule its transitions until we succeed on executing all of them, i.e. to saturate $\rightsquigarrow^*$ and then to check if $h \rightsquigarrow^* yield(h)$.

We will see now a more efficient and useful way to decide it, by computing a finite abstraction over the execution hedges.

We compute this finite abstraction, called *priority structure*, using a function denoted by Φ. The computation is carried out inductively over the structure of the hedge, from leaves to roots. If the hedge is schedulable its priority structure will be defined as a tuple $[\![x, y]\!]$, where x is the lowest priority of the configurations that make a transition, called *lowest transition priority*; and y is the priority of the yield configuration, called *highest final priority*. Otherwise, if the hedge is not schedulable, its priority structure will be denoted by the symbol $\bot$. The set of all priority structures is defined as $\mathsf{PS} = \{[\![x, y]\!] \mid x \in \mathcal{P} \cup \{\infty\}, y \in \mathcal{P}\} \cup \{\bot\}$, where ∞ is defined as the highest possible priority.

The priority structure of an execution hedge will be computed using two auxiliary functions called *update* and *compose* ($\oplus$). The function *update* updates the priority structure in non-spawning transitions, while the function $\oplus$ compute a new priority structure from the priority structures of a spawning transition.

Definition 7. *Given a hedge $h \in T^*$ we define its priority structure $\Phi(h)$ as:*

$$\Phi(h) := \begin{cases} [\![\infty, \eta(c)]\!] & \text{if } h = c \\ update(\eta(c),\ \Phi(t)) & \text{if } h = c(t) \\ update(\eta(c),\ \Phi(t) \oplus \Phi(t')) & \text{if } h = c(t, t') \\ \Phi(t_1) \oplus \cdots \oplus \Phi(t_n) & \text{if } h = t_1 \ldots t_n \end{cases}$$

$$update(n, s) := \begin{cases} [\![min(n, x), y]\!] & \text{if } s = [\![x, y]\!] \\ \bot & \text{if } s = \bot \end{cases}$$

$$s_1 \oplus s_2 := \begin{cases} [\![min(x_1, x_2), max(y_1, y_2)]\!] & \text{if } s_1 = [\![x_1, y_1]\!] \wedge s_2 = [\![x_2, y_2]\!] \\ & \wedge((y_2 \leq x_1 \wedge x_1 \leq x_2) \\ & \vee(y_1 \leq x_2 \wedge x_2 \leq x_1)) \\ \bot & \text{otherwise} \end{cases}$$

where $c \in P\Gamma^*, t, t', t_1, \ldots, t_n \in T, s, s_1, s_2 \in \mathsf{PS}, x, x_1, y, y_1 \in \mathcal{P}$.

Let us give the intuition behind this definition:

1. If the hedge is a leaf ($h = c$), i.e. a configuration pw without transitions, then it is trivially schedulable. Its priority structure $\Phi(h)$ is the tuple $[\![\infty, \eta(p)]\!]$: its lowest transition priority is set to ∞, since there are no transitions; and the highest final priority, by definition, is the priority of its control state $\eta(p)$.
2. If the hedge is a root configuration with a unique child subtree ($h = c(t)$); then it is schedulable if the subtree t is schedulable, since the first non-spawning transition can obviously be made. This case is handled by the auxiliary function *update* ($update(\eta(c), \Phi(t))$), depending on the schedulability of the subtree t:
   2.1 If the subtree t is not schedulable, then its priority structure is $\bot$. Thus, the hedge is obviously not schedulable and then its priority structure is also $\bot$.

2.2 If the subtree t is schedulable, then its priority structure is $[\![x, y]\!]$ for some priorities x, y. Then, the lowest transition priority will be the minimum between the priority n of the root configuration and x; and the highest final priority will remain equal to y. Thus, the priority structure of h is $[\![min(n, x), y]\!]$.

3. If the hedge is a root configuration with two children subtrees $(c(t, t'))$, then it is schedulable if the subtrees are schedulable, since the first spawning transition can obviously be made. So, we use the function *update* in the same way as the previous item, but over the *composition* of the priority structures of each subtree $(update(\eta(c), \ \Phi(t) \oplus \Phi(t')))$. The composition operator $\oplus$, depending on the schedulability of each subtree, is defined as follows:

3.1 If one of the subtrees is not schedulable ($s_1 = \perp$ or $s_2 = \perp$), then obviously the two subtrees cannot be scheduled together.

3.2 If the subtrees are schedulable, then they have priority structures $[\![x_1, y_1]\!]$ and $[\![x_2, y_2]\!]$ for some priorities x_1, y_1, x_2, y_2. Note that at least one of the subtrees finish its execution first, the one with higher lowest transition priority. Once it finishes its execution, its highest final priority should allow to execute the remaining transitions of the other tree. Thus, in this case, the subtrees are schedulable together if:

3.2.1. The tree with lowest transition priority x_1 finish its execution first, $x_1 > x_2$, and it does it with highest final priority y_1 allowing the execution of the transitions of the other tree, $y_1 \leq x_2$; or,

3.2.2. The tree with lowest transition priority x_2 finish its execution first, $x_2 \geq x_1$, and it does it with highest final priority y_2 allowing the execution of the transitions of the other tree, $y_2 \leq x_1$.

If this happen, then the composition of the priority structures is the priority structure of the hedge tt': the minimum of the lowest transition priorities and the maximum of the highest final priorities, i.e. $[\![min(x_1, x_2), max(y_1, y_2)]\!]$.

4. If the hedge is a sequence of trees $t_1 \ldots t_n$, then it is schedulable if the composition of their priority structures is not $\perp$, i.e. $\Phi(t_1) \oplus \cdots \oplus \Phi(t_n) \neq \perp$. Since the $\oplus$ operator is associative and commutative, the intuition of the previous case, with only two subtrees, can be applied here composing by pairs of priority structures.

The intuition explained in item 3.2 leads to the following lemma:

Lemma 2. *Given two schedulable hedges h_1 and h_2 with priority structures $[\![x_1, y_1]\!]$ and $[\![x_2, y_2]\!]$, respectively, the execution hedge $h_1 h_2$ is schedulable if and only if:*

$$(y_1 \leq x_2 \land x_2 \leq x_1) \lor (y_2 \leq x_1 \land x_1 \leq x_2)$$

Then, we can show the following theorem.

Theorem 2. *An execution hedge h is schedulable if and only if $\Phi(h) \neq \perp$.*

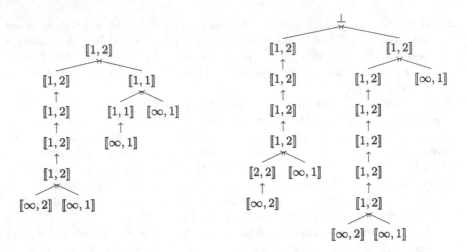

Fig. 4. Computation of priority structures of the hedges of Fig. 3.

On Fig. 4 we show the computation of the priority structures of the execution hedges of Fig. 3, the arrows show the direction of the computation of the priority structures and each node contains the priority structure of the tree rooted by itself. Thus, by the previous theorem, the execution hedge of the left is schedulable since it has a priority structure of $[\![1, 2]\!]$; and the execution hedge of the right is not schedulable since its priority structure is $\perp$.

6 Representing Infinite Sets of Configurations of a P-DPN

Following [1], we use finite automata called M-automata to represent regular (possible infinite) sets of configurations of P-DPNs.

Definition 8. Let $M = (P, \Gamma, \Delta, \eta)$ be a P-DPN, a finite automaton $\mathcal{A} = (S, \Sigma, \delta, s^0, F)$ is an M-automaton if the following conditions hold:

1. $\Sigma = P \cup \Gamma$ is the finite alphabet.
2. The set of states is partitioned into two sets $S = S_c \cup S_s$ s.t. $S_c \cap S_s = \emptyset$.
3. For every $s \in S_c$ and every $p \in P$, there is a (unique and distinguished) state $s_p \in S_s$. Let $S_P = \{s_p : s \in S_c, p \in P\}$.
4. There is a relation $\delta' \subseteq S_s \times \Gamma \times (S_s \setminus S_P) \cup S_s \times \{\epsilon\} \times S_c$. such that $\delta = \delta' \cup \{(s, p, s_p) : s \in S_c, p \in P\}$.
5. The initial state $s^0 \in S_c$.
6. $F \subseteq S$ is the set of final states.

For $\sigma \in \Sigma \cup \{\epsilon\}$ and $s, s' \in S$, we write $s \xrightarrow{\sigma}_\delta s'$ instead of $(s, \sigma, s') \in \delta$. We extend this notation in the obvious manner to sequences of symbols: $\forall s \in S.s \xrightarrow{\epsilon}_\delta s$, and $\forall s, s' \in S. \forall \sigma \in \Sigma \cup \{\epsilon\}. \forall w \in \Sigma^*.s \xrightarrow{\sigma w}_\delta s'$ iff $\exists s'' \in S.s \xrightarrow{\sigma}_\delta s''$ and $s'' \xrightarrow{w}_\delta s'$. Note that requirement (4) encodes a number of conditions on δ:

– Each $s \in S_c$ has s_p as its unique p-successor and no Γ-transitions.
– s is the only predecessor of s_p.
– Only ϵ-moves from states in S_s leads to states $s \in S_c$.
– States $s \in S_s$ don't have p-successors from any $p \in P$.

So, every path in a M-automaton (starting from the initial state) is the concatenation of paths of the form: $s \xrightarrow{p}_\delta s_p \xrightarrow{w}_\delta t \xrightarrow{\epsilon}_\delta s'$, where $s, s' \in S_c, p \in P, w \in \Gamma^*$ and all states in the path $s_p \xrightarrow{w}_\delta t$ are in S_s. Note that for every finite automaton $\mathcal{A}$ over the alphabet $P \cup \Gamma$ such that $L(\mathcal{A}) \subseteq Conf_M$, it is possible to construct an M-automaton recognizing the same language. A set of configurations C is regular if there exists an M-automaton $\mathcal{A}$ such that $L(\mathcal{A}) = C$.

Suppose we want to check that the program of Fig. 1 does not have data races between threads C and D. We can create an M-automaton for each pair of program points that access the same global variable, with at least one write access, compute their predecessors configurations and check if the initial configuration is included. For instance, control points c_1 and d_0 attempt to access variable y, the first one to write it and the second one to read it. So, in order to check if these control points can be reached at the same time, we can create an M-automaton $\mathcal{A}$ that accepts the language $(P\Gamma^*)^* Pc_1(P\Gamma^*)^* Pd_0 (P\Gamma^*)^*$ and $(P\Gamma^*)^* Pd_1(P\Gamma^*)^* Pc_1 (P\Gamma^*)^*$.

In a similar way, we can create another M-automaton $\mathcal{A}$ to check that the program does not have deadlocks as a result of the interaction between the priorities and the spin-locks. This M-automaton will accept the language of global configurations with a local configuration holding a spin-lock, like configuration $p_{1,l}b_1$, and another local configuration, with a higher priority, trying to acquire the same spin-lock, like configuration p_2c_0.

7   Computing pre^* Images of P-DPNs

Given a P-DPN M and a M-automaton $\mathcal{A}$, we will compute $pre^*_M(L(\mathcal{A}))$. The main idea of the algorithm consists on computing the predecessors without taking care of priorities, using the algorithm of [1] over a modified version of M', and then filtering out the unreachable configurations using priority structures. In order to filter or not a configuration $c \in pre^*_{M'}(L(\mathcal{A}))$, we compute the priority structure of the hedge h with root configuration c and yield configuration in $L(\mathcal{A})$. Then, using Theorems 1 and 2, if $\Phi(h) \neq \bot$ we conclude that the configuration c belongs also to $pre^*_M(L(\mathcal{A}))$.

For computing the priority structure of these hedges, we modify M' and $\mathcal{A}$ (steps 1 and 2), embedding the definition of Φ inside the control states of the configurations. We obtain thus a DPN M'' and a M-automaton $\mathcal{A}'$. Then, instead of computing predecessors of $L(\mathcal{A})$ in M', we compute predecessors of $L(\mathcal{A}')$ in M'' (step 3), obtaining configurations of the form $(p_1, s_1)w_1 \dots (p_n, s_n)w_n$. Intuitively, $(p_1, s_1)w_1 \dots (p_n, s_n)w_n \in pre^*_{M''}(\mathcal{A}')$ means that $p_1w_1 \dots p_nw_n \in pre^*_{M'}(L(\mathcal{A}))$ and that $s_1 \oplus \dots \oplus s_n$ is the priority structure of the execution hedge rooted at $p_1w_1 \dots p_nw_n$ and whose yield is in $L(\mathcal{A})$. Finally, we create an automaton $\mathcal{A}_{pre^*_M}$ (step 4) that accepts only the configurations of $pre^*_{M''}(L(\mathcal{A}'))$ with priority structures not equal to $\bot$. Thus, the algorithm consist of four steps that we explain in detail below.

Step 1: Compute $\mathcal{A}'$. First, we create an automaton $\mathcal{A}'$ from $\mathcal{A}$. We want to compute the predecessors of $p_1w_1 \ldots p_nw_n$, for $p_1w_1 \ldots p_nw_n \in L(\mathcal{A})$. Each predecessor should be the root of an execution hedge whose yield is $p_1w_1 \ldots p_nw_n$. To compute the priority structures of such execution hedge, we need, as explained in Sect. 5, to start the computation upward on the hedge, while initializing the leaves $(p_1w_1, \ldots, p_nw_n)$ by their priority structures $(\llbracket\infty, \eta(p_1)\rrbracket, \ldots, \llbracket\infty, \eta(p_n)\rrbracket)$. Thus, we need to transform $\mathcal{A}$ in order to take into account these priority structures. For that, we transform $\mathcal{A}$ into $\mathcal{A}'$, that accepts the language:

$$L(\mathcal{A}') = \{(p_1, \llbracket\infty, \eta(p_1)\rrbracket)w_1 \ldots (p_n, \llbracket\infty, \eta(p_n)\rrbracket)w_n \mid p_1w_1 \ldots p_nw_n \in L(\mathcal{A})\}.$$

It is easy to see that $\mathcal{A}'$ can be computed from $\mathcal{A}$ in a straightforward manner.

Step 2: Compute M''. Now, we continue the computation of priority structures of the hedges with yield configurations in $L(\mathcal{A})$ that we started in the previous step. For that, we create a new DPN M'' from M, attaching priority structures to the control states of P and embedding the definition of Φ (for cases $h = c(t)$ and $h = c(t,t')$) in the transitions rules of Γ. Then, we obtain the control states P' and transitions rules Δ' of M'', as follows:

- For each control state $p \in P$, we add a control state $p_s = (p, s)$ to P', for each priority structure $s \in \mathsf{PS}$. Intuitively, the configuration $(p, s)w \in P'\Gamma^*$ means that s is the priority structure of the execution hedge that starts at configuration $pw \in P\Gamma^*$.
- Given a non-spawning transition $p\gamma \hookrightarrow qw \in \Delta$, we add the transitions $(p, s_p)\gamma \hookrightarrow (q, s_q)w$ to Δ', where $s_p = update(\eta(p), s_q), \forall s_q \in \mathsf{PS}$. This means that if we have the execution hedge $qwr(\ldots)$ with priority structure s_q then we have the execution hedge $p\gamma r(qwr(\ldots))$ with priority structure $update(\eta(p), s_q)$.
- Given a spawning transition $p\gamma \hookrightarrow q_1w_1 \rhd q_2w_2 \in \Delta$ we add the transitions $(p, s_p)\gamma \hookrightarrow (q_1, s_{q_1})w_1 \rhd (q_2, s_{q_2})w_2$ to Δ', where $s_p = update(\eta(p), s_{q_1} \oplus s_{q_2}), \forall s_{q_1}, s_{q_2} \in \mathsf{PS}$. This means that if we have the hedges $q_1w_1r(\ldots)$ and $q_2w_2(\ldots)$ with priority structures s_{q_1} and s_{q_2}, respectively, then we have the execution hedge $p\gamma r(q_1w_1r(\ldots), q_2w_2(\ldots))$ with priority structure $update(\eta(p), s_{q_1} \oplus s_{q_2})$.

Definition 9. *Given the P-DPN $M = (P, \Gamma, \Delta, \eta)$, the DPN $M'' = (P', \Gamma, \Delta')$ is defined as: $P' = \{(p, s) \mid p \in P, s \in \mathsf{PS}\}$ and the transition rules of Δ' are:*

$$(p, s_p)\gamma \hookrightarrow (q, s_q)w \in \Delta' \quad if \quad p\gamma \hookrightarrow qw \in \Delta \wedge s_p = update(\eta(p), s_q)$$
$$(p, s_p)\gamma \hookrightarrow (q_1, s_{q_1})w_1 \rhd (q_2, s_{q_2})w_2 \in \Delta' \quad if \quad p\gamma \hookrightarrow q_1w_1 \rhd q_2w_2 \in \Delta$$
$$\wedge s_p = update(\eta(p), s_{q_1} \oplus s_{q_2})$$

where $p, q, q_1, q_2 \in P, \gamma \in \Gamma, w, w_1, w_2 \in \Gamma^*, s_p, s_q, s_{q_1}, s_{q_2} \in \mathsf{PS}$.

The following lemma is a direct result from Theorems 1 and 2 and the definition of M''. It intuitively says that M'' can compute priority structures.

Lemma 3. $p_1w_1 \ldots p_nw_n \longrightarrow_M^* p_1'w_1' \ldots p_m'w_m'$ *if and only if*
$(p_1, s_1)w_1 \ldots (p_n, s_n)w_n \longrightarrow_{M''}^* (p_1', [\![\infty, \eta(p_1')]\!])w_1' \ldots (p_m', [\![\infty, \eta(p_m')]\!])w_m'$
and $s_1 \oplus \cdots \oplus s_n \neq \bot$.

The next lemma shows that we can use M'', $\mathcal{A}'$ and the algorithm for predecessor sets in DPNs of [1] to compute predecessors sets in P-DPNs by filtering out the configurations with the composition of its priority structures (stored in the control states) equal to $\bot$.

Lemma 4. $p_1w_1 \ldots p_nw_n \in pre_M^*(L(\mathcal{A}))$ *if and only if*
$(p_1, s_1)w_1 \ldots (p_n, s_n)w_n \in pre_{M''}^*(L(\mathcal{A}'))$ *and* $s_1 \oplus \cdots \oplus s_n \neq \bot$.

Step 3: Compute $\mathcal{A}_{pre^*M''}$. Then, we apply the algorithm of [1] to the DPN M'' and the M''-automaton $\mathcal{A}'$. We obtain an automaton $\mathcal{A}_{pre_{M''}^*}$ such that:

$$L(\mathcal{A}_{pre_{M''}^*}) = pre_{M''}^*(L(\mathcal{A}')).$$

Step 4: Compute $\mathcal{A}_{pre_M^*}$. Finally, as we said previously, we need to filter out the configurations accepted by $\mathcal{A}_{pre_{M''}^*}$ with the composition of the priority structures in their control states equal to $\bot$. This corresponds to the case $h = t_1 \ldots t_n$ of the definition of Φ. For doing this, we define a new automaton $\mathcal{A}_{pre_M^*}$ that satisfies:

$$L(\mathcal{A}_{pre_M^*}) = \{p_1w_1 \ldots p_nw_n \mid (p_1, s_1)w_1 \ldots (p_n, s_n)w_n \in L(\mathcal{A}_{pre_{M''}^*})$$
$$\wedge s_1 \oplus \cdots \oplus s_n \neq \bot\}$$

It is easy to see that is straightforward to construct such M-automata.

Finally, we get the main result of the paper that says that backward reachability sets of P-DPNs are regular and can be effectively computed.

Theorem 3. $L(\mathcal{A}_{pre_M^*}) = pre_M^*(L(\mathcal{A}))$.

Note that the time complexity of the proposed algorithm is polynomial on the size of M, $\mathcal{A}$ and the number of priorities.

8 Related Work

Several other models have been proposed for multi-threaded programs with procedure calls and thread creation, like Ground Tree Rewrite Systems [4] and process rewrite systems (PRS) [5]. However, these models cannot deal with priorities. PA-processes, a subclass of PRS and incomparable with DPNs, was extended with priorities in [6]. On the other hand, PA-processes cannot precisely model procedure calls. Other works extend DPNs to model multi-threaded programs [7–12], but none of these extensions handle priorities.

The models of [2,3] do not allow concurrent behavior between threads of the same priority. Kidd et al. introduced in [2] a program transformation that translates a multi-threaded program into a sequential one. The key insight behind their reduction is that because a preempted lower-priority thread is not rescheduled until the higher-priority thread has finished, the two threads can share the same stack. Bouajjani et al. [3] extended multiset pushdown systems with priorities on each task. Multiset pushdown systems is a model where some procedure calls can be stored as tasks to be processed later.

9   Conclusion

We have defined a new formalism called Dynamic Pushdown Networks with Priorities (P-DPN) that extends the well known DPN model by attaching priorities to each control state and restricting the transition relation to threads with highest control state priority.

Then, we show that backward reachability sets of regular (possible infinite) sets of configurations of P-DPNs are regular and effectively computable. Using automata-based techniques, we give a polynomial-time algorithm to compute these sets. Finally, we show how to use our model to rule out false alarms regarding data races and to detect deadlocks.

References

1. Bouajjani, A., Müller-Olm, M., Touili, T.: Regular symbolic analysis of dynamic networks of pushdown systems. In: Abadi, M., Alfaro, L. (eds.) CONCUR 2005. LNCS, vol. 3653, pp. 473–487. Springer, Heidelberg (2005). doi:10.1007/11539452_36
2. Kidd, N., Jagannathan, S., Vitek, J.: One stack to run them all. In: Pol, J., Weber, M. (eds.) SPIN 2010. LNCS, vol. 6349, pp. 245–261. Springer, Heidelberg (2010). doi:10.1007/978-3-642-16164-3_18
3. Atig, M.F., Bouajjani, A., Touili, T.: Analyzing asynchronous programs with preemption. In: FSTTCS, pp. 37–48 (2008)
4. Goller, S., Lin, A.W.: The complexity of verifying ground tree rewrite systems. In: LICS, pp. 279–288 (2011)
5. Mayr, R.: Process rewrite systems. Inf. Comput. 156(1), 264–286 (2000)
6. Cleaveland, R., Hennessy, M.: Priorities in process algebras. Inf. Comput. 87(1–2), 58–77 (1990)
7. Gawlitza, T.M., Lammich, P., Müller-Olm, M., Seidl, H., Wenner, A.: Join-lock-sensitive forward reachability analysis for concurrent programs with dynamic process creation. In: Jhala, R., Schmidt, D. (eds.) VMCAI 2011. LNCS, vol. 6538, pp. 199–213. Springer, Heidelberg (2011). doi:10.1007/978-3-642-18275-4_15
8. Wenner, A.: Weighted dynamic pushdown networks. In: Programming Languages and Systems, pp. 590–609 (2010)
9. Lammich, P., Müller-Olm, M., Wenner, A.: Predecessor sets of dynamic pushdown networks with tree-regular constraints. In: Bouajjani, A., Maler, O. (eds.) CAV 2009. LNCS, vol. 5643, pp. 525–539. Springer, Heidelberg (2009). doi:10.1007/978-3-642-02658-4_39

10. Bouajjani, A., Esparza, J., Schwoon, S., Strejček, J.: Reachability analysis of multithreaded software with asynchronous communication. In: Sarukkai, S., Sen, S. (eds.) FSTTCS 2005. LNCS, vol. 3821, pp. 348–359. Springer, Heidelberg (2005). doi:10.1007/11590156_28

11. Lammich, P., Müller-Olm, M.: Precise fixpoint-based analysis of programs with thread-creation and procedures. In: Caires, L., Vasconcelos, V.T. (eds.) CONCUR 2007. LNCS, vol. 4703, pp. 287–302. Springer, Heidelberg (2007). doi:10.1007/978-3-540-74407-8_20

12. Lugiez, D.: Forward analysis of dynamic network of pushdown systems is easier without order. In: Bournez, O., Potapov, I. (eds.) RP 2009. LNCS, vol. 5797, pp. 127–140. Springer, Heidelberg (2009). doi:10.1007/978-3-642-04420-5_13

Security and Privacy

Monitorability Bounds via Expander, Sparsifier and Random Walks

The Interplay Between On-Demand Monitoring and Anonymity (Extendend Abstract)

Shlomi Dolev[1] and Daniel Khankin[1,2]([✉])

[1] Ben-Gurion University of the Negev, Beer-Sheva, Israel
dolev@cs.bgu.ac.il, danielkh@post.bgu.ac.il
[2] Shamoon College of Engineering (SCE), Beer-Sheva, Israel
daniehe@ac.sce.ac.il

Abstract. *Software-defined networking* (SDN), network functions virtualization (NFV) and network virtualization (NV) build a mini-cosmos inside data centers, cloud providers, and enterprises.

The network virtualization allows new on-demand management capabilities, in this work we demonstrate such a service, namely, on-demand efficient monitoring or anonymity. The proposed service is based on network virtualization of expanders or sparsifiers over the physical network. The defined virtual (or overlay) communication graphs coupled with a multi-hop extension of Valiant randomization based routing lets us monitor the entire traffic in the network, with a very few monitoring nodes.

In particular, we show that using overlay network with expansion properties and Valiant randomized load balancing it is enough to place $O(m)$ monitor nodes when the length of the overlay path (number of intermediate nodes chosen by Valiant's routing procedure) is $O(n/m)$.

We propose two randomized routing methods to implement policies for sending messages, and we show that they facilitate efficient monitoring of the entire traffic, such that the traffic is distributed uniformly in the network, and each monitor has an equiprobable view of the network flow. In terms of complex networks, our result can be interpreted as a way to enforce the same betweenness centrality to all nodes in the network.

Additionally, we show that our results are useful in employing anonymity services. Thus, we propose monitoring or anonymity services, which can be deployed and shut down on-demand. Our work is the first, as far as we know, to bring such on-demand infrastructure structuring using the cloud NV capability to existing monitoring or anonymity networks. We propose methods that theoretically improve services provided by existing anonymity networks, and optimize the degree of anonymity, in addition to providing robustness and reliability to system usage and security.

At last, we believe, that our constructions of overlay expanders and sparsifiers weighted network, that use several random walk trees, are of independent interest.

Keywords: SDN · NFV · NaaS · On-demand · Monitoring · Anonymity · Network · Expander

© Springer International Publishing AG 2017
A. El Abbadi and B. Garbinato (Eds.): NETYS 2017, LNCS 10299, pp. 307–321, 2017.
DOI: 10.1007/978-3-319-59647-1_23

1 Introduction

Software-defined networking (SDN) is a building block and mechanism for realizing network virtualization (NV) and architecture independent network functions virtualization (NFV). Network virtualization allows us to create virtual networks which network's topology is decoupled from the topology of the underlying physical network, and dynamically create policy-based virtual networks [33]. An overlay network is one of many possible forms of network virtualization. Its main idea is to encapsulate a network service decoupled from the underlying infrastructure [33].

Network functions virtualization concerns implementation of network functions in software. Due to increasing demand for dynamic network architectures, network virtualization technology was utilized in Network-as-a-Service (NaaS) models that enabled dynamic deployment of a network service on-demand [7]. Integration of SDN and NFV enables flexible, programmable and dynamic deployment of network services [6], and in [7] one such SDN-based implementation was presented.

Today, companies heavily rely on networking and Internet connection even for simple tasks. As such, traffic monitoring is a common request in private corporate networks. In this work, we describe an on-demand overlay network construction which enforces a defined policy of message sending scheme utilizing Valiant [37] randomization technique. We propose to construct an overlay network over the underlying network in such a way that the overlay network will preserve the expansion properties of the underlying network, moreover, we build the overlay network oriented towards having capacity approximately close to the capacity of the underlying physical network. This requirement makes the overlay network maximally utilize the capacity usage for all sort of network applications.

The monitoring of the network resorts to monitors that are located at the nodes of the constructed overlay network. Monitors are not required to be located at each node of the network but can be placed at selected nodes. This decision depends on selected message sending policy of the network. The combination of the enforced message sending scheme and spectral properties of the overlay network graph provides uniform monitoring abilities such that each monitor supervises uniform fraction of network traffic, and none of the monitors have higher network traffic observation.

Goyal et al. showed in [28] that it is possible to construct an expander graph via random spanning trees. We follow this method of constructing expander graph from random spanning trees. However, we employ this method on weighted graphs in order to build a capacity biased overlay network. Moreover, we show that the constructed graph is a sparsifier of the underlying graph, namely, the constructed graph spectrally approximates the underlying graph. Furthermore, we provide a distributed algorithm for overlay network construction together with an algorithm for verifying the mixing properties of the constructed graph. In contrast to independent sampling methods of sparse graph construction, spanning tree is a connected graph, and as such, using spanning trees results in a connected graph.

By its very nature, the constructed network is robust and is able to recover from congestion and link failures due to expansion properties, and due to path diversity which is achievable by a combination of random spanning trees [28, 31]. Moreover, the overlay network is scalable and may grow linearly in the number of vertices.

We have also identified a possible application of our dynamic network architecture service for anonymity in the network. The proposed network architecture with its spectral properties and enforced messaging policy provides a high degree of anonymity for senders as for receivers. Its on-demand flexibility allows private deployment for an individual or with a trusted party usage.

In the next session, we discuss the related works. Later, we describe the overlay network construction method and distributed expansion verification algorithm used in distributed construction of the overlay network. In Sects. 5 and 6 we describe the use of expander graphs for monitoring, message sending scheme and the probabilities of successful network monitoring. Finally, in Sect. 7 we show a feasible implementation of our on-demand network construction as an on-demand anonymity service, which we believe opens a new scope in the research on communication anonymity. Due to space limitations proofs and some details are omitted. See in [16] for complete proofs and discussions.

2 Related Work

Goyal et al. demonstrated the building process of an expander graph, which expansion depends on the degree of the primal graph, by the union of random spanning trees and showed that the union of the trees approximates each cut of the primal graph within a factor of $O(\log n)$. In our work, we show that the same method can be used to build weighted expanders from a weighted graph, moreover, we show that the union of weighted spanning trees spectrally approximates the primal graph.

Similar result to ours was shown by Fung et al. in [24]. Fung et al. showed that sampling spanning trees while adjusting their link weights, results in a sparsifier. In contrast to their work, we utilize the weights of the given primal graph in order to construct a capacity optimized expander, while including enough edges results in an overlay network which sparsifies the primal graph. Performing random walk on a weighted graph, better preserves the locality[1] of a cut.

In contrast to previously mentioned works, we additionally employ a distributed construction of the expander graph. Our construction method can run in a distributed manner for the concurrent construction of expander graphs. Distributed construction of expander graphs was also shown by Dolev and Tzachar in [18], where the authors introduced the notion of *Spanders*, distributed spanning expanders, and showed a practical way for verifying that the constructed graph is an expander. We use the method of expansion verification presented in [18] in order to optimize the construction of the overlay network and limit the number of constructed spanning trees.

---

[1] We thank Noga Alon for drawing our attention to this observation.

We show that our network architecture is valuable for network monitoring. Altshuler et al. showed an efficient flooding scheme for generating a collaboration between a group of random walking agents which are released from different sources and at different times [3]. This participation of agents results in a collaborative monitoring infrastructure, requiring only a small number of active monitors.

Measures for estimating monitoring capabilities of a vertex (BC, SPBC, LC, FBC) were established in [5,21,22,25]. Routing betweenness centrality (RBC), a network measure for estimating the control probabilities of a vertex or a set of vertices was proposed in [15], generalizes aforementioned network measures. RBC measures the extent to which vertices or group of vertices are exposed to the traffic [15]. As a result, RBC is useful for predicting the effectiveness (and cost) of passive network monitoring. We use the RBC measure to show that each monitor in our constructed network is equivalently effective as a passive monitor.

Chaum introduced the concept of a *mix* [10] and mix-net based protocols, and also a DC-net [9], a broadcast network which provides both sender and receiver anonymity. DC-net scheme suffers from poor scalability and it is unsuitable for large-scale networks [29]. Most notable work based on DC-net is Xor-Trees [17], which was proposed by Dolev and Ostrovsky to provide sender and receiver anonymity, additionally reducing the amount of communication overhead. Additional anonymous communication scheme which provides a high degree of anonymity is Buses [4], which is a network routing based anonymous communication scheme, that can be viewed as a bus system. Buses attempts to hide traffic patterns and to provide an unlinkability for two communicating parties.

Recent work by Hermoni et al. proposed a Peer-to-Peer file sharing system which provides anonymity to all participants, namely, receiver (server) and sender (publisher or reader) anonymity [29]. Hermoni et al. propose the use of anonymity tunnels for each different user. The authors assume a semi-honest adversary in their first provided solution, while the same adversary as the one assumed in Tor for their second solution.

The authors of [12,14] show that restricted topologies provide better anonymity with less cover traffic overhead, additionally they scale better as the number of mix nodes grows. We show that sparse overall network with expansion properties can provide anonymity service with restricted routes and optimal topology.

Our results can be used as the base to provide a flexible and robust network architecture as a service with on-demand deployment. Boubendir describes an implementation of NaaS architecture with SDN-enabled NFV in [6], and shows feasible on-demand dynamic network service based on SDN-enabled NFV [7]. We further exploit the NV, SDN and NFV emerging technologies to enable network architecture as a service for use in private commercial networks, network and service providers, or facilities desiring flexible policy enabled networking to secure their traffic and to monitor network flows for mitigation of misuse or malicious uses.

3   Preliminaries

3.1   Notation

We specify a graph $G = (V, E)$, having a vertex set $V = 1, \ldots, n$ and an edge set $E \subseteq \{(u, v) \mid u, v \in V\}$. If the graph is weighted, it will be specified by $G = (V, E, w)$ where $w_{(u,v)} > 0$ for each $(u, v) \in E$. For each vertex $u \in V$, $w(u) = \sum_z w(u, z)$ is defined as the total weight of edges that are incident to the vertex v. For $S, T \subset V$, we specify the set of edges emerging from S to T by

$$E(S, T) = \{(u, v) \mid u \in S, v \in T, (u, v) \in E\}$$

We denote the *edge boundary* of a set S as ∂S and is defined as $\partial S = E(S, \bar{S})$. The edge boundary is a set of edges emerging from the set S to its complement. We specify the set of neighbors of v for $v \in V$, as $\Gamma(v) = \{u \in V \mid (u, v) \in E\}$. For $A \subseteq V$, $\Gamma(A) = \cup_{v \in A} \Gamma(v)$ and $\Gamma'(A) = \Gamma(A) \setminus A$.

3.2   Graph Expansion

For a good introduction on expander graphs see [26,30]. Here, we describe only the basic definitions of expander graphs. Expansion requires that any set of vertices, of size at most $n/2$, has a relatively large set of neighbors. The edge expansion ratio of G, denoted by $h(G)$, is defined as:

$$h(G) = \min_{\{S \mid |S| \leq \frac{n}{2}\}} \frac{|\partial S|}{|S|}$$

The vertex expansion of graph G is defined as:

$$h(G) = \min_{\{S \mid |S| \leq \frac{n}{2}\}} \frac{|\Gamma'(S)|}{|S|}$$

4   Expander Overlay Network Construction

Assume that the underlying network is represented by a weighted graph $G = (V, E, \omega)$. A random walk begins from a randomly chosen vertex, and moves to one of its neighbors with probability proportional to the weight of the edge, $P[(u, v)] = \frac{\omega(u,v)}{\omega(u)}$. Each time the random walk arrives at a new vertex, a vertex which was not visited before; the edge, through which it arrived, is added to the spanning tree construction. Inspired by the work of Goyal et al. [28], we show that for a weighted bounded degree graph and for the weighted complete graph a small number of spanning trees result in a subgraph with expansion properties comparable to each cut of the original graph. In addition, the generated subgraph utilizes the capacity of the primal network by including edges of greater capacity with a greater probability.

For generating a random spanning tree, we use the algorithm derived by Andrei Broder [8]. However, we modify the algorithm to utilize the probabilities

---

Algorithm 1. Generation of Spanning Tree via Random Walk Simulation

---

input   : $G = (V, E, \omega)$
output : spanning tree T

1 $T = \{\}$
2 Simulate a weighted random walk on graph G starting at an arbitrary vertex s
   until every vertex is visited. $T \leftarrow T \cup e(v, u)$ for each vertex $u \in V \setminus s$ if this is
   the first visit of vertex u.
3 **return** T

Algorithm 2. Expander Overlay Construction

---

input   : $G = (V, E, \omega)$, k
output : union of k random spanning trees U_G^k

1 $U_G^k = \{\}$
2 **repeat**
3 | Generate a random spanning tree T, according to Algorithm 1
4 | $U_G^k \leftarrow U_G^k \cup T$
5 **until** k trees are generated
6 **return** U_G^k

---

of edges (Algorithm 1). Overlay network is created by repeating k times the creation of a random spanning tree (Algorithm 2).

Goyal et al. showed in [28] that for any bounded degree graph, the union of at least two random spanning trees of the graph approximates the expansion of every cut in the graph. Using more trees gives a better approximation. We follow the outline of the proofs in [28] and prove them for weighted graphs. Pemantle proved the following Theorem on the negative correlation property of uniform spanning trees [35]:

Theorem 1. *For any finite connected graph G, let T be a uniform spanning tree. If e and f are distinct edges, then*

$$P[e, f \in T] \leq P[e \in T]P[f \in T]$$

Goyal et al. extended Theorem 1 for any subset of edges in [28]:

Theorem 2 (Negative Correlation of Edges). *For any subset of edges $e_1, \ldots, e_k \in E$ we have*

$$P[(e_1 \in T), \ldots, (e_k \in T)] \leq P[e_1 \in T] \cdots P[e_k \in T] \tag{1}$$

We prove our results using Chernoff bounds, for this, we define the following indicator variables:

$$X_e = \begin{cases} 1 & e \in T \\ 0 & otherwise \end{cases}$$

Now, we can rewrite (1) as

$$E[X_{e_1} \cdots X_{e_k}] \le E[X_{e_1}] \cdots E[X_{e_k}] \tag{2}$$

We can say that $\{X_e\}$ satisfying (2) are negatively correlated for every subset of edges $e_1, \ldots, e_k$. It is possible to apply Chernoff bounds unaltered to negatively correlated variables [19, Proposition 5]. Then, by [2, Theorem A.1.13] it is possible to derive the following version of Chernoff bounds [28]:

Theorem 3. *Let $X_{i_{i=1}}^n$ be a family of $0-1$ negatively correlated random variables such that $1 - X_{i_{i=1}}^n$ are also negatively correlated. Let p_i be the probability that $X_i = 1$. Let $p = \frac{1}{n} \sum_{i \in [n]} p_i$. Then for $\lambda > 0$*

$$P[\sum_{i \in [n]} X_i < pn - \lambda] \le e^{\frac{-\lambda^2}{2pn}}$$

Due to space limitations, the proofs of the next three Theorems are omitted and can be found in [16].

Base graph is a complete graph. We show that the union of two random spanning trees is required to approximate the expansion of a complete weighted graph.

Theorem 4. *The union of two randomly spanning trees of the complete weighted graph on n vertices has constant vertex expansion with probability $1 - o(1)$.*

Base graph is a bounded-degree graph. We consider weighted and irregular graphs with bounded degrees, and we show the probability bounds for the construction process on these graphs. In the following Theorem, p is an average probability for edge e being part of a random spanning tree.

Theorem 5. *For a weighted graph $G = (V, E, \omega)$, let U_G^k be the union of k uniformly random spanning trees. Also, let $\alpha > 0$ be a constant and $\alpha(k-1) > \frac{8}{p}$. Then with probability $1 - o(1)$, for every $A \subset V$ we have*

$$|\partial_{U_G^k} A| \ge \frac{1}{\alpha \ln(n)} |\partial_G A|$$

U_G^k **is a sparsifier.** We show that U_G^k generated by the process defined above is a sparsifier of a weighted graph G, if $|U_G^k|$ is sufficiently large.

Theorem 6. *Let G have Laplacian L and U_G^k have Laplacian L' and $\frac{1}{\sqrt{n}} \le \epsilon \le 1$, $|U_G^k| \in O(n \log n / \epsilon^2)$. With probability at least $\frac{1}{2}$*

$$\forall x \in \mathcal{R}^n \ (1 - \epsilon) x^T L x \le x^T L' x \le (1 + \epsilon) x^T L x$$

4.1 Distributed Construction of Overlay Network

The algorithm for overlay network construction (Algorithm 2) can be modified to a distributed algorithm. This is also beneficial for networks where a centralized entity has several cores that can execute the algorithm in a distributed manner. For example, in software-defined networking, the network control software [23] can execute the iterations of the algorithm concurrently or delegate the execution of some iteration to a different controller. Each controller will execute one or a few iterations of the algorithm until the required approximation of the primal graph is achieved. In such setup, a monitoring algorithm for verification of expander construction is required. The monitoring algorithm can be executed by the main controller in charge of the network (see Algorithm 4).

Algorithm 3. Mixing Rate Based Monitoring

> **input** : U_G^k for some k
> **output** : j: number of counted nodes

1 L: max length of the walk
2 $counter \leftarrow 0$
3 v: arbitrary chosen vertex
4 $length \leftarrow 1$
5 $\Gamma'_{U_G^k} = \{\}$
6 **repeat**
7 | **if** v *was not visited before* **then**
8 | | $counter \leftarrow counter + 1$
9 | | $\Gamma'_{U_G^k} \leftarrow \Gamma'_{U_G^k} \cup \Gamma'(v)$
10 | **end**
11 | $length \leftarrow length + 1$
12 | choose $u \in \Gamma'_{U_G^k}$
13 | $v \leftarrow u$
14 **until** *all vertices are visited or length* $> L$
15 **return** *counter*

We exploit the mixing rate based monitoring algorithm described in [18] which is modified for our construction scheme (Algorithm 3). This monitoring algorithm is used to estimate the expansion of constructed graph, since calculating the expansion is NP hard. The mixing rate based monitoring algorithm employs the rapidly mixing property of expander graphs, $O(\log n)$ mixing rate. It is also known that cover time of expander graphs is $O(n \log n)$ [1,18]. The control software starts a random walk of length $O(n \log n)$ on an arbitrary vertex v, each new visited vertex is marked and counted. The neighbors of the newly visited vertex are added to the set of all neighbors. Afterward, the walk proceeds from one of the randomly chosen neighbors. When the random walk is terminated, the counter is examined by the control software. In case the walk covered less than n nodes, we can conclude with high probability that the graph is not rapidly mixing as was required or there are too many edges in the constructed graph, implying that the construction was not successful [18].

Algorithm 3 can be sped up by performing $O(n)$ random walks of length $O(\log n)$ [1,18]. The controller software, which runs the algorithm, in SDN can perform parallel random walks and possibly delegate to other controller units. Each of the controller units will return the results to the main controller, upon which will be the decision to stop generating random spanning trees (see Algorithm 4).

Algorithm 4 is executed until the expansion of U_G^k, measured by the mixing rate quality, reaches the required value or at most $O(\log n)$ iterations. At each iteration of the algorithm, the number of generated spanning trees is doubled. The algorithm will stop when the required approximation of the expansion is achieved, which results in fewer spanning trees and fewer edges in the expander graph.

Algorithm 4. Distributed Expander Overlay Construction

　　input : $G = (V, E, \omega)$
　　output : union of k random spanning trees U_G^k
1　$U_G^k = \{\}$
2　$k \leftarrow 1$
3　**while** *mixing rate requirement is not satisfied* **do**
4　　　$T \leftarrow$ delegate the generation of k random spanning trees
5　　　**for** T *in* $\mathcal{T}$ **do**
6　　　　$U_G^k \leftarrow U_G^k \cup T$
7　　　**end**
8　　　verify mixing rate requirement using Algorithm 3
9　　　$k \leftarrow 2 \cdot k$
10　**end**
11　**return** U_G^k

5　Sparse Expander Graphs for Monitoring

We propose a message sending scheme similar to the one proposed by Valiant in [37]. Source node s, that sends a message to destination t, performs a random walk of length $l = \log(n)$ to intermediate destination $v \in V$. The set of vertices visited by a length l random walk on an expander graph is a randomly chosen sequence of $v_0, v_1, \ldots, v_l$, where each v_{i+1} is chosen uniformly at random and independently, among the neighbors of v_i, for $i = 0, \ldots, l - 1$ [11]. The sender sends the message along the path from s to v, in such a way that the path is a sequence of vertices chosen by the random walk, and then the random walk is performed again to deliver the message from v to destination t. The message is sent through two paths, each of length $\log(n)$.

In fact, the sender can arbitrary choose the number of several intermediate destinations, such that a message would be sent from source to intermediate destinations $v_1, v_2, \ldots v_r$ for some chosen r. Each path from source to intermediate destination and between the intermediate destinations, including destination t chosen by s, is a random walk of length $\log(n)$. Overall route complexity is $O(\log n)$ overlay edges. If the underlying graph is an expander graph too, then the total route complexity is $O(\log n)$, otherwise it is $O(\log(n) \cdot diam(G))$.

The message sending scheme implements two routing methods; incremental path building (incremental routing) and loose routing. In incremental routing, the sender's application proxy software builds the route hop by hop, corresponding and exchanging keys with each router on behalf of the user. As such, sender's application proxy is aware of each participant in the chosen route. In loose routing [27], a node may decide to extend or change the message's path, this means that the sender may not be aware of all the nodes which constitute the whole path.

On the one hand, it may be preferable for the sender to route a message to a subarea of the network where the local routing policy will decide upon the routing in the subarea towards the receiver. On the other hand, in the former case, the implementation is easier. As well, the sender can negotiate session keys with each router it chooses in the route, as opposed to the latter case where it is left to the router that performs a modification to the route on behalf of the sender.

The full discussion on assessment of different routing strategies is omitted due to space limitations. The reader can find the full discussion and assessment on the success of traffic monitoring in case of both incremental and loose routing in [16], where we use Chernoff bounds to show that there is an exponentially small chance for none of the nodes in a path to be a monitoring node. As a matter of fact, we show that in the expander based overlay network, with very high probability at least one node in the sequence of traveled nodes will be a monitoring node, and we can have a vast majority of non-monitoring nodes whilst with probability no more than $\frac{1}{2}$ the complete path will not be monitored.

These probability calculations show that with high probability in a route of length $O(\log n)$ at least one node is a monitoring node, and consequently, $O(n/\log n)$ monitors are required in order to monitor the traffic in the network with high probability.

6   Measuring Monitoring Success

In this Section, we quantify the monitoring level of the system. Using several approaches, we show that our system is able to uniformly monitor the traffic in the network. Full details of the following discussion can be found in [16].

Traffic analysis. We employ the Bayesian inference method of traffic analysis for extracting the probability distribution over the hidden states of the system [36]. Observation of a system results in obtaining the correspondence between inputs and outputs of each node. This collection of input-output relationships is called the *hidden state* of a system. The hidden state of a system can be described by the path each message has taken [36]. Therefore, the probability of hidden states of a system is proportional to the probability of the paths that were chosen by the user.

A user who is interested in sending a message according to our message-sending scheme is allowed to choose the number of intermediate nodes, which consequently affects the total path length of the message. The number of intermediate nodes is uniformly chosen, and the probability for any sequence of nodes for the chosen length are considered equally likely.

Thus, the probability for every path of a message, and following the probability for each hidden state of the system, would be equally likely too. The obtained samples of the hidden state can be used to compute the probability for monitoring network flows. Since all states are equiprobable, the distribution of the hidden states would be uniform, and as such the distribution of the network flows. Hence, each monitor can uniformly audit the network traffic, and the network traffic is unbiased towards flowing through specific links.

Monitoring avoidance. The maximum degree of monitoring is achieved when the sender sees all monitors as equally likely being the auditors of a message. The entropy of the system, after an observation is performed, is compared against the maximum entropy [13]. This comparison gives a hint of the amount of information that was learned.

The most useful property of expander graphs is that a random walk mixes fast. If a random walk starts at any vertex, after $O(\log n)$ steps the position will be uniformly random. Therefore, without any additional knowledge of the system, and given that the probability for each hidden state of the system is equally likely, each of the, n_{mntr}, monitors is assigned the probability of $p_i = \frac{1}{n_{mntr}}$ being the auditor of the message. Furthermore, without any prior knowledge on the number of monitors, every node in the graph may be a possible monitoring node. Hence, the probability of identifying the monitor node is $\frac{1}{n}$. The entropy of the system is maximized.

Monitors locations. We estimate the monitoring potential of each node in the network, employing routing betweenness-centrality (RBC) measure proposed by Dolev et al. RBC of a vertex represents its potential to monitor and control data flow in the network [15]. The probability for a packet to pass through some vertex, v, on its way from source to destination, can be recursively calculated for the set of immediate predecessors of v. Whilst, the message-sending policy is embedded into the function representing the routing scheme, the probability for a message to be sent from any vertex to its neighbor is equal for every set of vertices and their neighbors. Additionally, all routing decisions in our message sending policy are independent. Thus, we obtain the result that the RBC is equivalent for every node in our constructed network, and there is no preferred location for a monitor, and each node has an equivalent potential for monitoring the network.

7   Anonymity

Anonymity of a subject is defined as being not identifiable within the anonymity set [32]. The anonymity set is the set of all possible subjects who might cause an action. A subject is identifiable if we can get a hold of information that can be linked to the person. In the model proposed by [13], the concept of entropy was proposed to measure the information gained after an attack on a system. Assuming the adversary has no prior knowledge with regard to the anonymity set, in the best case scenario the adversary has no better than $\frac{1}{n}$ chance of identifying a subject within the anonymity set of size n. Therefore, we obtain that all subjects have an equiprobable probability to appear as the source of an action, consequently, obtaining a maximum entropy, and as such, a maximal degree of anonymity.

Anonymity on-demand. Similarly to the case with monitoring nodes (see Sect. 5 and extended discussion in [16]), calculations show that we can have more than half of compromised nodes and yet remain anonymous in the network.

The computation of anonymity is based on computing the entropy of the distribution of all possible sources of action [13,34]. Since all hidden states are equiprobable (see Sect. 6), the distribution of the hidden states would be uniform and the entropy of the system will be maximized.

The on-demand nature of our network architecture can mitigate common attacks on anonymity networks, in particular, onion routing based. Intersection attacks [20] can be mitigated by using cover traffic. Since the constructed overlay network is of a bounded degree, only a linear number of output packets would be sent. Hence, in the worst case, $O(\Delta \cdot n)$ messages are required.

In predecessor timing attack, unknown path length can significantly decrease the success of an attack [38]. As proposed in our message sending scheme, varying number of intermediate nodes and possibly in combination with loose routing can be used for dynamic path length. A number of rounds required to success-fully perform the attack with high probability is $O\left(\left(\frac{n}{c}\right)^2 \ln n\right)$ where c is the number of attackers [38]. The required amount of rounds is greater than the route length, which is of order $O(\log n)$. This means that until the attack is successfully completed, the anonymity network service can be shut down since messages have already arrived at their destinations. Circuit clogging, or conges-tion attack, can be prevented with the policy we proposed for the constructed network. This sort of attack (as also DoS attack) can be inspected as if certain nodes are compromised, as noted above, more than half of nodes in the network can be compromised without significantly affecting the routing of traffic.

8   Discussion

We have presented in this paper methods for constructing a flexible, on-demand network service over SDN-enabled architecture with defined policy of message sending scheme which can be deployed by service providers, commercial com-panies, or private users. We have shown that constructing overlay network with expansion properties in combination with randomized message sending policy, we were able to achieve uniform dispersion of network traffic and consequently with high probability monitoring the whole network requiring relatively small number of monitors, in particular $O(n/\log n)$ monitors are enough to cover the complete overlay network when each path is of length of $O(\log^2 n)$ physical edges. The overlay network can be constructed in distributed manner, converging faster towards the required features. The constructed overlay network graph is a sparse connected graph, approximating the primal weighted graph if $O(n \log n/\epsilon^2)$ edges are included in the construction.

Furthermore, we have shown that our construction method can be applied for providing anonymity network. This work presents first of its kind, as far as the authors know, anonymity on-demand network service. The NaaS architecture of the network can mitigate most of the known attacks on anonymity networks. Notably, attacks that congest the network or result in relay server denial of service can be coped with on-demand nature of the network. If the user, who deployed the anonymity network, suspects that over time the relays were compromised, he/she can periodically shut down the service and re-deploy it with different nodes and even with a different topology. This kind of service can be suitable for private communication use among trusted parties.

Acknowledgment. The research was partially supported by the Rita Altura Trust Chair in Computer Sciences; The Lynne and William Frankel Center for Computer Science; the grant of the Ministry of Science, Technology and Space, Israel, and the National Science Council (NSC) of Taiwan; the Ministry of Foreign Affairs, Italy; the Ministry of Science, Technology and Space, Infrastructure Research in the Field of Advanced Computing and Cyber Security; and the Israel National Cyber Bureau. We thank Noga Alon for the elaborate discussion and valuable comments.

References

1. Alon, N., Avin, C., Koucky, M., Kozma, G., Lotker, Z., Tuttle, M.R.: Many random walks are faster than one. In: Proceedings of the Twentieth Annual Symposium on Parallelism in Algorithms and Architectures, SPAA 2008, NY, USA, pp. 119–128. ACM, New York (2008)
2. Alon, N., Spencer, J.H.: The Probabilistic Method. Wiley, New York (2004)
3. Altshuler, Y., Dolev, S., Elovici, Y.: TTLed random walks for collaborative monitoring in mobile and social networks. In: Thai, M.T., Pardalos, P.M. (eds.) Handbook of Optimization in Complex Networks. Springer Optimization and Its Applications, vol. 57, pp. 507–538. Springer, New York (2012)
4. Beimel, D.: Buses for anonymous message delivery. J. Cryptology **16**(1), 25–39 (2002)
5. Borgatti, S.P.: Centrality and network flow. Soc. Netw. **27**(1), 55–71 (2005)
6. Boubendir, A., Bertin, E., Simoni, N.: NaaS architecture through SDN-enabled NFV: network openness towards web communication service providers. In: NOMS 2016–2016 IEEE/IFIP Network Operations and Management Symposium, pp. 722–726 (2016)

7. Boubendir, A., Bertin, E., Simoni, N.: On-demand dynamic network service deployment over NaaS architecture. In: NOMS 2016–2016 IEEE/IFIP Network Operations and Management Symposium, pp. 1023–1024. IEEE (2016)
8. Broder, A.: Generating random spanning trees. In: 30th Annual Symposium on Foundations of Computer Science 1989, pp. 442–447. IEEE (1989)
9. Chaum, D.: The dining cryptographers problem: unconditional sender and recipient untraceability. J. Cryptology **1**, 65–75 (1988)
10. Chaum, D.L.: Untraceable electronic mail, return addresses, and digital pseudonyms. Commun. ACM **24**(2), 84–90 (1981)
11. Chung, F.: Spectral Graph Theory. Series in Mathematics, vol. 92. American Mathematical Society, Washington, DC (1996)
12. Danezis, G.: Mix-networks with restricted routes. In: Dingledine, R. (ed.) PET 2003. LNCS, vol. 2760, pp. 1–17. Springer, Heidelberg (2003). doi:10.1007/978-3-540-40956-4_1
13. Díaz, C., Seys, S., Claessens, J., Preneel, B.: Towards measuring anonymity. In: Dingledine, R., Syverson, P. (eds.) PET 2002. LNCS, vol. 2482, pp. 54–68. Springer, Heidelberg (2003). doi:10.1007/3-540-36467-6_5
14. Diaz, C., Murdoch, S.J., Troncoso, C.: Impact of network topology on anonymity and overhead in low-latency anonymity networks. In: Atallah, M.J., Hopper, N.J. (eds.) PETS 2010. LNCS, vol. 6205, pp. 184–201. Springer, Heidelberg (2010). doi:10.1007/978-3-642-14527-8_11
15. Dolev, S., Elovici, Y., Puzis, R.: Routing betweenness centrality. J. ACM **57**(4), 25:1–25:27 (2010)
16. Dolev, S., Khankin, D.: Monitorability bounds via expander, sparsifier and random walks. The interplay between on-demand monitoring and anonymity arXiv:1612.02569 [cs] (2016)
17. Dolev, S., Ostrobsky, R.: Xor-trees for efficient anonymous multicast and reception. ACM Trans. Inf. Syst. Secur. **3**(2), 63–84 (2000)
18. Dolev, S., Tzachar, N.: Spanders: distributed spanning expanders. In: Proceedings of the 2010 ACM Symposium on Applied Computing, SAC 2010, NY, USA, pp. 1309–1314. ACM, New York (2010)
19. Dubhashi, D., Ranjan, D.: Balls and bins: a study in negative dependence. Random Struct. Algorithms **13**(2), 99–124 (1998)
20. Erdin, E., Zachor, C., Gunes, M.H.: How to find hidden users: a survey of attacks on anonymity networks. IEEE Commun. Surv. Tutorials **17**(4), 2296–2316 (2015)
21. Freeman, L.C.: A set of measures of centrality based on betweenness. Sociometry **40**(1), 35–41 (1977)
22. Freeman, L.C., Borgatti, S.P., White, D.R.: Centrality in valued graphs: a measure of betweenness based on network flow. Soc. Netw. **13**(2), 141–154 (1991)
23. Fundation, O.N: Software-defined networking: the new norm for networks. ONF White Paper (2012)
24. Fung, W.S., Hariharan, R., Harvey, N.J., Panigrahi, D.: A general framework for graph sparsification. In: Proceedings of the Forty-third Annual ACM Symposium on Theory of Computing, STOC 2011, NY, USA, pp. 71–80. ACM, New York (2011)
25. Goh, K.I., Kahng, B., Kim, D.: Universal behavior of load distribution in scale-free networks. Phys. Rev. Lett. **87**(27 Pt 1), 278701 (2001)
26. Goldreich, O.: Basic facts about expander graphs. In: Goldreich, O. (ed.) Studies in Complexity and Cryptography. Miscellanea on the Interplay between Randomness and Computation. LNCS, vol. 6650, pp. 451–464. Springer, Heidelberg (2011). doi:10.1007/978-3-642-22670-0_30

27. Goldschlag, D.M., Reed, M.G., Syverson, P.F.: Hiding routing information. In: Anderson, R. (ed.) IH 1996. LNCS, vol. 1174, pp. 137–150. Springer, Heidelberg (1996). doi:10.1007/3-540-61996-8_37

28. Goyal, N., Rademacher, L., Vempala, S.: Expanders via random spanning trees. In: Proceedings of the Twentieth Annual ACM-SIAM Symposium on Discrete Algorithms, SODA 2009, pp. 576–585. Society for Industrial and Applied Mathematics, Philadelphia, PA, USA (2009)

29. Hermoni, O., Gilboa, N., Felstaine, E., Dolev, S.: Rendezvous tunnel for anonymous publishing. Peer-to-Peer Networking Appl. 8(3), 352–366 (2014)

30. Hoory, S., Linial, N., Wigderson, A.: Expander graphs and their applications. Bull. Am. Math. Soc. 43(4), 439–561 (2006)

31. Motiwala, M., Elmore, M., Feamster, N., Vempala, S.: Path splicing. In: Proceedings of the ACM SIGCOMM 2008 Conference on Data Communication, SIGCOMM 2008, NY, USA, pp. 27–38. ACM, New York (2008)

32. Pfitzmann, A., Köhntopp, M.: Anonymity, unobservability, and pseudonymity — a proposal for terminology. In: Federrath, H. (ed.) Designing Privacy Enhancing Technologies. LNCS, vol. 2009, pp. 1–9. Springer, Heidelberg (2001). doi:10.1007/3-540-44702-4_1

33. Rao, S.K.: SDN and its use-cases-NV and NFV. Network 2, H6 (2014)

34. Serjantov, A., Danezis, G.: Towards an information theoretic metric for anonymity. In: Dingledine, R., Syverson, P. (eds.) PET 2002. LNCS, vol. 2482, pp. 41–53. Springer, Heidelberg (2003). doi:10.1007/3-540-36467-6_4

35. Snell, J.L.: Topics in Contemporary Probability and Its Applications. CRC Press, Boca Raton (1995)

36. Troncoso, C., Danezis, G.: The bayesian traffic analysis of mix networks. In: Proceedings of the 16th ACM Conference on Computer and Communications Security, CCS 2009, NY, USA, pp. 369–379. ACM, New York (2009)

37. Valiant, L.G.: A scheme for fast parallel communication. SIAM J. Comput. 11(2), 350–361 (1982)

38. Wright, M.K., Adler, M., Levine, B.N., Shields, C.: The predecessor attack: an analysis of a threat to anonymous communications systems. ACM Trans. Inf. Syst. Secur. 7(4), 489–522 (2004)

A Location Privacy Estimator Based on Spatio-Temporal Location Uncertainties

Arielle Moro[✉] and Benoît Garbinato

Université de Lausanne, Lausanne, Switzerland
{arielle.moro,benoit.garbinato}@unil.ch

Abstract. The proliferation of mobile devices and location-based services (LBS) is strongly challenging user privacy. Users disclose a large volume of sensitive information about themselves to LBS. Indeed, such services collect user locations to operate and can thus use them to perform various inference attacks. Several privacy mechanisms and metrics have been proposed in the literature to preserve location privacy and to quantify the level of privacy obtained when these mechanisms are applied on raw locations. Although the use of these metrics is relevant under specific threat models, they cannot anticipate the level of location privacy on the sole basis of the altered location data shared with LBS. Therefore, we propose a location privacy estimator that approximates the level of location privacy based on spatio-temporal uncertainties resulting from location alterations produced when a location privacy preserving mechanism is applied on user raw locations. This estimator also takes into account spatial-temporal user privacy parameters. We also describe the computation of the spatio-temporal uncertainties through the sampling, the Gaussian perturbation as well as the spatial cloaking. Finally, we compare the results of our estimator with those of the success of two localization attacks. The findings show that our estimator provides reasonable or conservative estimates of the location privacy level.

1 Introduction

Over the past few years, we have observed a privacy paradigm shift. Following the constant increase of mobile device users and location-based services (LBS), user sensitive data is not only shared with friends and acquaintances, but also with companies, which provide these services. However, users are not always aware of this privacy issue and they often do not have enough information to properly assess risks and benefits of the use of LBS [12]. We are in a privacy paradox as described in [3]. In this paper, Barnes discusses about privacy issues in a context involving teenagers and social networks. A user can reveal a lot of personal information about herself on a social network. This user obviously thinks that her data is adequately protected according to the privacy settings she chooses. She takes care about her privacy and does not want to disclose her private information to people she does not know on this social network. However, her personal data can be sold to third parties or explored for a variety of goals

© Springer International Publishing AG 2017
A. El Abbadi and B. Garbinato (Eds.): NETYS 2017, LNCS 10299, pp. 322–337, 2017.
DOI: 10.1007/978-3-319-59647-1_24

(e.g., profiling, targeted advertising) by the social network itself meaning that there is probably no privacy any more. Analyzing user information on social network is not the only way to obtain personal data about users. For instance, we can easily extract sensitive user information by exploring the metadata of user's photos shared online and performing attacks on them as demonstrated in [21]. There also exist other subtle ways to infer user's personal information, such as analyzing user's locations collected by a LBS. In the context of location privacy, Krumm [14] describes the main computational threats. According to these threats, various inference attacks can be performed by an adversary to reveal user sensitive information, such as home place, gender, tastes and much more as indicated in [8]. In order to deal with a privacy threat, user locations must be protected by using an adapted location privacy preserving mechanism. These mechanisms belong to different types of location alterations, such as location obfuscation, location perturbation, location confusion and location suppression as described in detail in [6]. A large number of location privacy metrics, presented in the literature, can accurately evaluate the level of protection provided by different location privacy preserving mechanisms by taking into account precise threat models as well as specific inference attacks performed by an adversary. To the best of our knowledge, there is no metric that can estimate the level of location privacy on the sole basis of the altered locations sent to a possible adversary. In addition, existing metrics do not take into account spatial and temporal privacy choice of the user.

To address this issue, we propose a spatio-temporal estimator enabling to approximate the level of location privacy and that only takes as input spatial and temporal uncertainties generated when a location privacy preserving mechanism is applied on the raw data in order to alter and protect them. Moreover, the estimator is user-oriented because it takes into consideration privacy choice of the user as parameters or could automatically define them by exploring the mobility behavior of the user. We consider that extracting spatio-temporal uncertainties from location alterations is crucial to estimate the level of location privacy. In the context of a stream of locations, most of location privacy preserving mechanisms, which modify the space dimension of a location, can also have an impact on the time dimension of the location(s) of this stream. Consequently, it is crucial to take into account these two types of uncertainties in the computation of a location privacy estimate. In order to properly evaluate this estimator, we compare its results and those of the performance of two localization attacks according to specific location privacy preserving mechanisms applied on user raw locations. This comparison enables to highlight if our privacy estimator can reasonably estimate the privacy level by only analyzing uncertainties resulting from the alterations produced after the application of a protection mechanism on raw data. For the experiments, we use a Nokia dataset containing real mobility traces of 185 users as precisely described in [16]. We choose three types of location privacy preserving mechanisms presented in [8,13]: the sampling, the Gaussian perturbation and the spatial cloaking. We also decide to evaluate the success of the two following localization attacks: the discovery of the most frequently visited places of a user (i.e., user's zones of interest) and the discovery of user's home place.

This paper has three main contributions: presenting a new spatio-temporal location privacy estimator, describing the computation of the spatio-temporal uncertainties resulting from location alterations and evaluating our estimator with real user traces.

The paper is structured as follows. We start by describing the definitions and modeling of the main entities of our work in Sect. 2 providing the foundation to introduce the location privacy estimator in Sect. 3. Section 3.1 presents how spatial and temporal uncertainties are computed after applying three types of location privacy preserving mechanism on raw locations. In Sect. 4, we present in detail the evaluation as well as the obtained results in the context of localization attacks. Section 5 provides an overview of the existing location privacy metrics and highlights the links between these metrics and our estimator. Finally, we summarize the most relevant findings and present the future work in Sect. 6.

2   Definitions and Modeling

This section describes the definitions and modeling of the main entities required to introduce the location privacy estimator.

User and Raw Locations. We consider a user who moves in a two dimensional space and owns a mobile device. This device enables to obtain raw locations via an embedded Global Positioning System (GPS) or a WiFi Positioning System (WPS) in order to locate itself. The history of the successive raw locations of the user stored in the device is a sequence $L = \langle loc_1, loc_2, \cdots, loc_n \rangle$, where $loc_i = (\phi, \lambda, t)$ is a 3-item tuple representing a unique location in which $\phi, \lambda \in \mathbb{R}$ are respectively a latitude and a longitude and $t \in \mathbb{N}$ is the time when the location was captured. We use the notation $loc.\phi$, $loc.\lambda$ and $loc.t$ to designate specific parts of loc below. In order to ensure that locations are mostly caught in a regular manner, the duration between two successive locations in L does not exceed a constant Δt_{limit}. Let loc_i and $loc_{i+1} \in L$, $loc_{i+1}.t - loc_i.t \leq \Delta t_{limit}$.

Location Privacy Preserving Mechanism, Altered Locations and Spatio-Temporal Location Uncertainties. A location privacy preserving mechanism is applied on the raw locations of a user in order to protect them and to ensure her location privacy. There exist two main mechanisms to preserve user location privacy: anonymizing the identity of a user and altering the set containing user raw locations before sharing them with third-party entities such as LBS. In this paper, we only focus our attention on the second mechanism. Following this, we introduce a function called $protect(L)$ that modifies the set of user raw locations passed as a parameter by using a specific location privacy preserving mechanism. This function returns an altered set of locations that are sent to a third party entity, which can be seen as an untrusted component. This set is called $L_a = \langle loc_{a_1}, loc_{a_2}, \cdots, loc_{a_m} \rangle$. Applying a location privacy preserving mechanism on the set containing all raw locations L also generates spatial and temporal location uncertainties, which vary depending on the chosen mechanism. We define a zone z that describes a spatial location uncertainty, expressed by a 3-item tuple $z = (\phi, \lambda, \Delta r)$ where $\phi, \lambda \in \mathbb{R}$ represent a latitude and a longitude respectively and $\Delta r \in \mathbb{R}$ represents the radius of the zone. We also introduce $\Delta t \in \mathbb{N}$ that is a duration representing a temporal location uncertainty. Therefore, a spatio-temporal location uncertainty, called u, is a 3-item tuple including z and Δt as well as the number of raw locations of L affected by an alteration, simply called nb, such as $u = (z, \Delta t, nb)$. In the following sections, we sometimes use the notation $u.z$, $u.\Delta t$ and $u.nb$ to designate specific parts of u. Finally, we introduce a function called $uncertainties(L)$ that returns a set containing all the uncertainties computed when the location privacy preserving mechanism was applied on the set L. The output of this function is a set U containing all uncertainties such as $U = \langle u_1, u_2, \cdots, u_m \rangle$. It is important to note that the size of U can differ from the size of L_a and also the size of L. The computation of uncertainties only depends on the location privacy preserving mechanism applied on the set of raw locations and how the mechanism operates. The beginning of the next section will present how spatial and temporal uncertainties are computed in the context of three location privacy preserving mechanisms.

3   Location Privacy Estimator

This section describes both the computation of spatio-temporal uncertainties and the location privacy estimator. The first part is necessary to introduce the estimator, which takes as input the spatio-temporal uncertainties.

3.1   Computation of Spatio-Temporal Uncertainties

There exist various location privacy preserving mechanisms that are described in the following papers [2,7,8]. Amongst them, we only consider the three following mechanisms such as the sampling, which will be performed in two ways, i.e., according to a time window (TW) and a specific number of locations (LN), the Gaussian perturbation as well as the spatial cloaking. All these mechanisms firstly affect the spatial dimension of a location and can also have an impact on the temporal dimension of a location or a subset of locations if we consider the context of a location stream. All new locations mentioned in the explanation below are obviously considered as the altered locations of the location set L_a sent to a LBS.

TW Sampling. The sampling according to a time window is a location privacy preserving mechanism enabling to summarize a subset of successive locations occurring during a specific period of time into a single new location. In a concrete implementation, we divide the entire user raw location set into several location subsets and compute new locations according to them. The latitude of the new location is simply the mean of all latitudes of the original locations of the subset and, in the same manner, the longitude of this new location is the mean of all longitudes of the original locations. Concerning the timestamp of the new location, we consider that it corresponds to the timestamp of the location being in the middle of the subset of locations. Consequently, this location privacy preserving mechanism generates both space and time alterations. We introduce $tw \in \mathbb{N}$ being the duration of the time window. We also consider a subset $L_{sub_i} \in L$ of successive raw locations such as $L_{sub_i} = \langle loc_1, loc_2, \ldots, loc_j \rangle$. This subset is a TW sampling subset iff the two following conditions are met:

- $loc_j.t - loc_1.t <= tw$
- $loc_{j+1}.t - loc_1.t > tw$

Then, the new location loc_{a_i} computed from the subset L_{sub_i} containing j raw locations is a tuple that includes the following elements:

- $loc_{a_i}.\phi = \frac{1}{j} \times \sum_{i=1}^{j} loc_i.\phi$
- $loc_{a_i}.\lambda = \frac{1}{j} \times \sum_{i=1}^{j} loc_i.\lambda$
- $loc_{a_i}.t = loc_{i/2}.t$

Concerning all spatio-temporal uncertainties u_i produced with the TW sampling, we generate an uncertainty for each new location. The centroid of the spatial alteration $u_i.z$ corresponds to the new location and its radius $u_i.z.\Delta r$ is the distance between the new location and the farthest raw location of the subset. The temporal alteration $u_i.\Delta t$ is the duration between the last and the first raw locations of the subset. The number $u_i.nb$ of raw locations affected by the mechanism is equal to the size of the subset L_{sub_i}. Let a function called $distance(loc_i, loc_j)$, which computes and returns the distance between the two locations passed as parameters. In addition, let a function called $farthest(loc_r, \langle loc_1, loc_2, \ldots, loc_n \rangle)$, which finds and returns the farthest location of the set of locations passed as a parameter from a given reference location loc_r. The several items below describe the previous explanations with the subset of raw locations L_{sub_i} introduced before.

- $u_i.z.\phi = loc_{a_i}.\phi$
- $u_i.z.\lambda = loc_{a_i}.\lambda$
- $u_i.z.\Delta r = distance(loc_{a_i}, farthest(loc_{a_i}, L_{sub_i}))$
- $u_i.\Delta t = loc_j.t - loc_1.t$

LN Sampling. The sampling according to a number of successive locations is a location privacy preserving mechanism enabling to summarize a specific number of locations into a single new location. In a concrete implementation, we create several subsets having the same number of successive locations and we summarize each subset into a single one new location. The latitude and the longitude of the new location is computed in the same manner as mentioned above for the TW sampling. The timestamp of this new location also corresponds to the timestamp of the raw location being in the middle of the subset of locations. Consequently, both space and time alterations are also generated when this mechanism is applied.

Gaussian Perturbation. The Gaussian perturbation mechanism modifies each location of the set of the user raw locations by bringing spatial noise to its latitude and longitude. The latitude and the longitude of the raw location are changed according to two parameters: a mean and a standard deviation, which are the latitude or the longitude of the raw location and a value that may be expressed in meters respectively. Consequently, this location privacy preserving mechanism only affects the spatial dimension of the original location because the timestamp of each altered location remains unchanged. We introduce Δd_ϕ and $\Delta d_\lambda \in \mathbb{R}$ corresponding to two distances (i.e., spatial noise) randomly generated and added to the latitude and the longitude respectively in order to spatially blur the original location. Each location loc_i, contained in the set of user raw locations L, generates a new altered location that is sent to the untrusted component and noted loc_{a_i} as follows:

- $loc_{a_i}.\phi = loc_i.\phi + \Delta d_\phi$
- $loc_{a_i}.\lambda = loc_i.\lambda + \Delta d_\lambda$
- $loc_{a_i}.t = loc_i.t$

In this context, the spatial alteration is computed for each new location such as the centroid of the zone $u_i.z$ is loc_{a_i} and its radius is the distance between the loc_{a_i} and the raw location loc_i. The temporal alteration $u_i.\Delta t$ is equal to 0 because the timestamp of the new location remains the same. The number $u_i.nb$ is equal to 1 because the perturbation only affects one raw location. The spatial and temporal alterations generated are summarized below:

- $u_i.z.\phi = loc_{a_i}.\phi$
- $u_i.z.\lambda = loc_{a_i}.\lambda$
- $u_i.z.\Delta r = distance(loc_{a_i}, loc_i)$
- $u_i.\Delta t = loc_{a_i}.t - loc_{a_i}.t = 0$

Spatial Cloaking. As presented in [13], Krumm introduces an implementation of the spatial cloaking algorithm that can be applied on a single user's location dataset. In Krumm's paper, an ambiguity is created around a sensitive location (i.e., user's home place in the paper) by computing a specific cloaked region containing the user's home place and deleting all user raw locations being recorded in this region in order to protect the privacy of the user. A cloaked region is a zone defined by a centroid and a radius. The sensitive location is not the center of the computed cloaked region but it is only contained in this region. Consequently, it is more difficult to find the original sensitive location for an adversary in this case. In our implementation, we do the same around all zones of interest found for a user, which are obviously her sensitive areas. By applying this location privacy preserving mechanism on user raw data, we only delete sensitive locations occurring in a cloaked region without altering the previous or successive raw locations that are not located in cloaked regions. Consequently, all locations being in the set L_a of altered locations and sent to a LBS will be raw, such as $loc_{a_i} = loc_i$.

Spatial and temporal uncertainties are generated for the deletion of the raw locations being in the cloaked regions. Let C the set containing k computed cloaked regions and $C[i]$ a cloaked region in which the raw locations of the subset $L_{sub_i} = \langle loc_1, loc_2, \cdots, loc_j \rangle$ are located. Raw locations are sent to a LBS, consequently, we also compute uncertainties for these raw locations. In the following description, (1) describes the uncertainty of the deletion of raw locations and (2) presents the uncertainty of a raw location. The number $u_i.nb$ of the first uncertainty is equal to the number of raw locations deleted and contained in L_{sub_i} while the number of the second uncertainty corresponds to 1.

- (1) $\langle loc_1, loc_2, \cdots, loc_j \rangle \in C[i]$
  - $u_i.z.\phi = C[i].\phi$
  - $u_i.z.\lambda = C[i].\lambda$
  - $u_i.z.\Delta r = C[i].\Delta r$
  - $u_i.\Delta t = loc_j.t - loc_1.t$
- (2) $loc_i \notin C[i]$
  - $u_i.z.\phi = loc_{a_i}.\phi$
  - $u_i.z.\lambda = loc_{a_i}.\lambda$
  - $u_i.z.\Delta r = distance(loc_{a_i}, loc_{a_i})$
  - $u_i.\Delta t = loc_{a_i}.t - loc_{a_i}.t$

3.2   Estimator

The location privacy estimator takes as input all the uncertainties obtained when a location privacy preserving mechanism is applied on the set of raw locations L and generates the altered set of locations L_a as described in Sects. 2 and 3.1. Since an uncertainty has spatial and temporal dimensions, the estimator includes the privacy evaluations of these two dimensions. A top-down approach is chosen to present the estimator. As detailed in Eq. 1, the final result of this estimator is the sum of each location privacy estimate $Privacy(u_i)$ related to each spatio-temporal uncertainty u_i contained in the set U multiplied by the number of raw locations affected by an alteration. Finally, the sum is divided by the total number of raw locations n of L.

$$Privacy_e = \frac{1}{n} \times \sum_{i=1}^{n} (Privacy(u_i) \times u_i.nb) \tag{1}$$

The computation of the estimate of the location privacy of a single spatio-temporal uncertainty $Privacy(u_i)$ is described in Eq. 2. This second equation is the sum of spatial and temporal location privacy estimates of the uncertainty multiplied by their respective factor (i.e., α for the spatial location uncertainty and β for the temporal location uncertainty) and finally divided by the sum of these two factors in order to normalize the final result. These two factors must be chosen according to the importance of the spatial and the temporal dimensions for the user. If a user considers that her spatial privacy is more important than her temporal privacy, α could have more weight than the temporal factor β, knowing that β must be always equal to $1 - \alpha$.

$$Privacy(u_i) = \frac{(\alpha \times P_{space}(u_i.z)) + (\beta \times P_{time}(u_i.\Delta t))}{\alpha + \beta} \quad (2)$$

The location privacy estimate of the spatial uncertainty $P_{space}(u_i.z)$ is presented in Eq. 3, where the minimum between the area of the zone $u_i.z$ and the area of a zone that we consider as a maximum area called z_{max} is divided by this maximum area z_{max}. It means that, when this area is reached, the user cannot lose more privacy because her privacy is fully ensured when this maximum area is reached.

$$P_{space}(u_i.z) = \frac{min(Area(u_i.z), Area(z_{max}))}{Area(z_{max})}$$
$$= \frac{min(u_i.z.\Delta r^2, z_{max}.\Delta r^2)}{z_{max}.\Delta r^2} \quad (3)$$

The location privacy estimate of the temporal uncertainty $P_{time}(u_i.\Delta t)$ is presented in Eq. 4, where Δt_{max} is a time threshold beyond which the user cannot lose more privacy. The equation is therefore the division of the minimum between $u_i.\Delta t$ and Δt_{max} by Δt_{max}.

$$P_{time}(u_i.\Delta t) = \frac{min(u_i.\Delta t, \Delta t_{max})}{\Delta t_{max}} \quad (4)$$

The two values, z_{max} and Δt_{max}, should also be chosen by the user who is able to know when she considers that the spatial and temporal dimensions of her privacy are considered as entirely ensured. These two values could also be automatically determined by studying the mobility behavior of the user.

4   Experiments and Results

In this section, we present the chosen approach to evaluate the reliability of the location privacy estimator in the context of localization attacks. To reach this goal, we observe the correlation between the evolution of the privacy level predicted with the estimator and the evolution of the success of the chosen localization attacks. In the next sections, we first present the dataset used for the experiments, the localization attacks as well as our findings at the end. It is also important to indicate that we created a dedicated OS X application containing the implementations of all blurring techniques and all localization attacks we chose.

4.1   Dataset

We select a dataset provided by Nokia that contains real mobility data traces collected in Switzerland (Europe) from October 2009 to March 2011. The collecting process of this campaign is explained in detail in [16]. This dataset consists of real data traces of 185 users including GPS location data, GPS WLAN location data, SMS, calls and several other data. Since the duration of the data collection varies from one user to another, i.e., from less than one day to more than 500 days, we decide to only retain 103 users of this dataset who met the following conditions. A user must have a set of raw locations captured during a period of at least 300 days and a Δt_{limit} (defined in Sect. 2) of 600 s on an average meaning that the locations are captured in a frequent manner.

4.2   Localization Attacks

From an adversary viewpoint, an inference attack aims at discovering sensitive information based on user locations. In our context, the adversary is the untrusted component of the mobile device, i.e., a LBS. The data, which is used as input to perform the attack, is the user locations sent to the LBS after applying a location privacy preserving mechanism on raw data. Various threats and inference attacks are presented in [8,13,14,20]. We select two different localization attacks [20] having different goals: discovering zones of interest of a user and discovering user's home place. We describe in detail their goal, the way they operate as well as the quantification of their success in the next sections.

Discovering User's Zones of Interest. This first localization attack is performed by an adversary that wants to highlight all the most frequently visited places, i.e., zones of interest, of a user based on her locations sent from the trusted component, i.e., operating system, to the untrusted component, i.e., LBS. The zone of interest discovery process is entirely based on an algorithm described in this paper [15], with the sole exception that the recent aspect of a zone is not taken into account. In order to calculate the success of this attack, we first compute the reference set of user's zones of interest that is obtained when this attack is performed on user's raw data. Consequently, we decide to quantify the success of this attack as the discovery area percentage of the reference set by comparing it to that obtained with the altered set of locations. Firstly, we consider a set Z_r containing all reference zones of interest of the user obtained with the set L. Secondly, we introduce Z_b that is a set containing all user's zones of interest computed from the set L_a. Finally, we compare Z_r and Z_b to evaluate the success of this inference attack. More specifically, we compute the discovery area mean of all discovery areas linked to the reference zones of interest of the user as described in Eq. 5. In this Equation, we consider that Z_r contains n reference zones of interest such as $Z_r = \{z_i, z_{i+1}, \cdots, z_n\}$ and Z_b has m zones of interest such as $Z_b = \{z_j, z_{j+1}, \cdots, z_m\}$. We simply use z_i and z_j below to refer a zone of Z_r and a zone of Z_b respectively. The result of the success of this attack is a value between 0 (i.e., no zone is discovered) and 1 (i.e., all zones are discovered) included.

$$success_{IA}(Z_r, Z_b) = \frac{1}{n} \times \sum_{i=1}^{n} discoveredAreaSum(z_i, Z_b) \qquad (5)$$

Equation 6 enables to compute the sum of all discovered areas of a specific reference zone of interest z_i by comparing it with all possible zones of interest of Z_b.

$$discoveredAreaSum(z_i, Z_b) = \sum_{j=1}^{m} discoveredArea(z_i, z_j) \qquad (6)$$

Then, we compute the discovered area percentage of a reference zone, also scaled from 0 to 1, in Eq. 7. For this computation, we take into account if there exists a discovered area between a reference zone of interest and a zone of interest of Z_b. Four cases are taken into consideration in order to compute this discovered area percentage. Firstly, if there is no intersection or inclusion between the reference zone and one of the zones of Z_b, the discovered area percentage equals 0. Secondly, in the case where there exists an intersection between the reference zone and one of the zones of Z_b, the discovered area percentage is equal to the area of the intersection divided by the area of the reference zone. Thirdly, in the case where one of the zones of Z_b is fully included in the reference zone, we also compute the discovered area percentage as mentioned previously. And fourthly, if the reference zone is fully included in one of the zones of Z_b, the discovered area percentage corresponds to the area of the intersection divided by the area of the zone of Z_b because the discovery precision is reduced. Since the zone of interest discovery algorithm includes a merging of clusters before the zone of interest discovery, there is no overlap amongst all discovered user's zones of interest. Considering this, we do not need to manage cases where a same specific area of a reference zone is covered by two zones of Z_b. These four cases are summarized in Eq. 7 below.

$$discoveredArea(z_i, z_j) = \begin{cases} 0, & \text{if } z_i \cap z_j = 0 \\ Area(z_i \cap z_j)/Area(z_i), & \text{if } z_i \cap z_j \neq 0 \\ & \text{or if } z_j \subset z_i \\ Area(z_i \cap z_j)/Area(z_j), & \text{if } z_i \subset z_j \end{cases} \qquad (7)$$

Discovering User's Home Place. For this localization attack, an adversary wants to discover the user's home place. Two techniques are used to perform this attack. The first technique is based on the discovery of user's zones of interest with the process explained in the previous section, while the second technique focuses on one heuristic. Regarding the first technique, we use the user's zones of interest because the user's home place is obviously one of them. We start by computing the set containing all user's zones of interest, then we search the home place amongst all of them by highlighting the most likely visited zone of interest of the set during a specific time slice, i.e., from 8:00 PM to 6:00 AM the next day. The second technique is inspired by a heuristic called *last destination*, which is described in [13]. *Last destination* heuristic consists in computing the last destination visited by a user, i.e., at the end of the day. In our implementation, this place is discovered during the time slice starting at 0:00 AM and ending at 4:00 AM. The output of the second technique used is also a zone defined by a centroid and a radius. In order to evaluate these two inference attacks related to the user's home place, we compute a reference user's home place zone z_i with the user raw locations L. Similarly, we also extract z_j, which is the user's home place computed from the altered set of locations L_a. We compute the success of these inference attacks by using Eq. 7 in order to evaluate the discovery percentage between the reference zone z_i and the other computed zone z_j.

4.3   Experimental Settings and Results

In the previous sections, we presented all the key elements used for the experiments. We now describe the experimental settings as well as the main findings.

Experimental Settings. Regarding the location privacy estimator, we first choose equal factors for the computation of the privacy of the spatial and temporal uncertainty meaning that α and β have the same weight for all users, i.e., both are equal to 0.5. Secondly, we consider that the radius of z_{max} equals a value of 1000 m indicating that the user considers that her spatial privacy is fully ensured when this radius is reached or exceeded. This value is determined according to the dataset because users mainly move in cities or areas where a sufficient number of individuals are living. In addition, we select a value of 24 h for Δt_{max}, also meaning that her temporal privacy is entirely ensured if this duration is exceeded. Thirdly, several parameters are selected for each location privacy preserving mechanism. Regarding the TW sampling, we select 68 values for the time window ranging from 5 min to 5 days. About the LN sampling, we choose 24 values ranging from 10 locations to 2500 locations per sample. Concerning the Gaussian alteration, 16 standard deviation values are selected ranging from 0.0001 (i.e., about 12 m) to 0.05 (i.e., 5948 m approximately). And finally, for the spatial cloaking, we take 6 values ranging from 100 m to 10000 m for the radius of the cloaked region. Regarding the localization attacks, we select the following parameters for the user's zone of interest discovery: Δd_{max} equals 60 m and Δt_{min} is 900 s (i.e., 15 min). A value of 6 visits is chosen for the *visitThreshold* in order to highlight the frequent user's zones of interest. We found these values by exploring the Nokia dataset. The time slices used for each inference attacks are described in the previous section. To conclude, the chosen location privacy preserving mechanisms are those described in Sect. 3.1.

Results. For each selected parameter of each location privacy preserving mechanism, we first compute the mean of the success results of all users for each localization attack. Then, we display the evolution of the privacy level according to the evolution of the mean of the success results of all localization attacks in Figs. 1 and 2. In the four graphs, each dot corresponds to a specific parameter that evolves from the lowest value to the highest value of the range of the parameters of each protection mechanism described in the previous section. These graphs allow us to see the evolution trend between the results of our location privacy estimator and the success of the attacks. Regarding the Gaussian perturbation in Fig. 2 on the left, the maximum result given by the location privacy

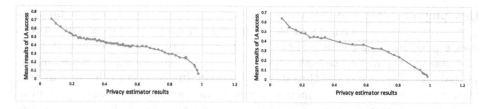

Fig. 1. TW (left) and LR (right) sampling results.

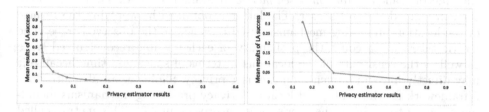

Fig. 2. Gaussian perturbation (left) and spatial cloaking (right) results.

estimator is 0.5 because the temporal uncertainty is equal to 0. The best results are obtained with the TW sampling and the LR sampling because the curves show a negative linear correlation between the success of the attacks and the privacy estimator results. Regarding the Gaussian perturbation and the spatial cloaking, we observe exponential decay curves meaning that our privacy estimator is pessimistic. In the context of Gaussian perturbation, the performance of the localization attacks declines relatively quickly because the added spatial noise has a high impact on the detection of the zone's of interest. In the context of spatial cloaking, the performance of the localization attacks declines sharply because all zone's of interest are considered as cloaked regions. Even if Gaussian perturbation and spatial cloaking results present less accurate estimates than those of TW and LR sampling, the obtained privacy estimates are conservative in that they do not give a false sense of location privacy. This means that there is no outlying curve (i.e., exponential curve) or outlier results such as a high success probability of the localization attacks and a high location privacy estimate at the same time.

5 Related Work

Estimating location privacy is the central aspect of this paper. Therefore, this related work presents a classification of existing privacy metrics found in the literature and the possible links between them and our estimator at the end.

Error-Based Metrics. To begin with the first category, Hoh and Gruteser use two main location privacy metrics to evaluate a path perturbation algorithm they propose in [9]. The first location privacy metric, called *mean location privacy*, computes the accuracy of the estimation of each location contained in a user's path by an adversary (i.e., the expectation of distance error). It takes into account the difference between correct and estimate locations as well as the probability of occurrence of the estimate location. In addition to this first metric, they also consider a second metric, called *mean location error* aiming at evaluating the quality of service provided. Basically, this metric helps to compute the location accuracy difference of each user's paths (i.e., between the original and the observed location). In [19], Shokri et al. introduce a new location privacy metric, called *distortion-based metric*. It evaluates the level of distortion of a reconstructed trace of a user. The latter is obtained by applying the reverse of the location preserving mechanism used to generate the observed trace. The metric takes into account the probability of each possible reconstructed trace as well as the sensitivity of the locations in terms of space and time because it may directly have an influence on the user privacy. Shokri et al. also introduce a framework for the analysis of location privacy preserving mechanisms including a metric to evaluate the user's location privacy in [20]. This metric, called *correctness*, enables to quantify the correctness of the attack by computing the expected estimation error of the distance between the true expected result and all the results contained in the estimate distribution, which is the output of an attack. Moreover, other error-based metrics are presented in [6,17,18].

Uncertainty-Based Metrics. In [4], Beresford and Stajano use a metric computing the level of anonymity ensured by a mix-zone by using the entropy. To summarize, an adversary is confronted with a mapping issue including old and new pseudonyms taken by users in a mix-zone. The entropy enables to compute the level of uncertainty in the mapping set and quantify the number of users that we are not able to distinguish from each other. Hoh et al. also introduce a privacy level measure called *mean time to confusion* in [11]. It highlights the tracking time from which an adversary is no longer able to find the next location sample with a sufficient certainty. In [5], Cheng et al. present a framework enabling to control the location uncertainty aiming at preserving user privacy. They also build a model and queries helping to reach this goal and introduce two means of quantifying privacy. The first is the size of uncertainty region due to the fact that the larger the region size, the higher the privacy. The second is based on the location of the user and its link with sensitive regions such as an hospital or other sensitive places related to the user. More formally, it computes the ratio between the area of sensitive regions discovered (i.e., the intersection between the sensitive regions and the area of the uncertainty of a location) and the area of the uncertainty of a location. The higher the ratio, the lower the privacy. Finally, Ardagna et al. present a metric called *relevance* that represents the relative accuracy loss of the location when a location obfuscation is applied on a raw location in [1,6]. This metric only takes into account the geometric uncertainty generated by a location obfuscation mechanism without defining the adversary's goal and knowledge.

Score-Based Metrics. Hoh et al. evaluate the degree of privacy protection with two metrics in the context of traffic monitoring in [10]. They consider that an adversary could try to infer the user's home and they evaluate the privacy obtained for different sampling frequencies. The first metric focuses on the effectiveness of the detection by computing the home identification rate (i.e., the number of correct estimated homes out of the total number of correct homes) and the second metric computes the false positive (i.e., the number of incorrect estimated homes out of the total number of estimated homes). In [8], Gambs et al. evaluate the impact of different sanitization mechanisms on different means aiming at reaching the same adversary's attack. More specifically, the attack relates on detecting the user's clusters. In order to evaluate this impact, they use well-known metrics called precision and recall. In their analysis, the precision is the number of correct points of interest divided by the total number of points of interest returned by an attack and the recall is the number of area detected divided by the total number of areas.

To finish, there also exist other metrics such as *k-anonymity* and differential privacy-based metrics as discussed in [6]. In this classification, our location privacy estimator could clearly belong to the *uncertainty-based* category. The existing metrics mainly take into account the spatial dimension to compute the privacy while the temporal dimension is equally important and can also be affected by a location privacy preserving mechanism. To the best of our knowledge, there is no user-oriented location privacy metric using spatio-temporal uncertainties resulting from spatial and temporal alterations applied on user raw locations.

6   Conclusion and Future Work

In this paper, we have presented a location privacy estimator taking into account spatial and temporal uncertainties, generated when a location privacy preserving mechanism is applied on user raw data, as well as user privacy preferences. We also introduce how to generate spatial and temporal uncertainties according to three existing privacy mechanisms. We chose to evaluate it by comparing the results of our estimator and those of the success of two localization attacks. This comparison showed that our estimator provides reasonable or conservative estimates of the location privacy level. Future work could focus on implementing other location privacy preserving mechanisms and other localization attacks in order to have a better overview of the behavior of the estimator. Then, we could also try to automatically adapt z_{max} and Δt_{max} to the mobility behavior of each user. Another interesting work could be to add a weight to each uncertainty according to the degree of importance of the raw location(s) affected by an alteration in order to see if it increases the accuracy of the results of the estimator. And finally, a last challenge could be to adapt the computation of the location privacy with our estimator in realtime during the use of a LBS on a mobile device.

Acknowledgment. This research is partially funded by the Swiss National Science Foundation in the context of Project 146714.

References

1. Ardagna, C.A., Cremonini, M., Damiani, E., Capitani di Vimercati, S., Samarati, P.: Location privacy protection through obfuscation-based techniques. In: Barker, S., Ahn, G.-J. (eds.) DBSec 2007. LNCS, vol. 4602, pp. 47–60. Springer, Heidelberg (2007). doi:10.1007/978-3-540-73538-0_4
2. Armstrong, M.P., Rushton, G., Zimmerman, D.L.: Geographically masking health data to preserve confidentiality. Stat. Med. **18**, 497–525 (1999)
3. Barnes, S.B.: A privacy paradox: social networking in the united states. First Monday **11**(9) (2006)
4. Beresford, A.R., Stajano, F.: Mix zones: user privacy in location-aware services. In: Proceedings of the Second IEEE Annual Conference on Pervasive Computing and Communications Workshops, 2004, pp. 127–131, March 2004
5. Cheng, R., Zhang, Y., Bertino, E., Prabhakar, S.: Preserving user location privacy in mobile data management infrastructures. In: Danezis, G., Golle, P. (eds.) PET 2006. LNCS, vol. 4258, pp. 393–412. Springer, Heidelberg (2006). doi:10.1007/11957454_23
6. Damiani, M.L.: Location privacy models in mobile applications: conceptual view and research directions. GeoInformatica **18**(4), 819–842 (2014)
7. Duckham, M., Kulik, L.: Location privacy and location-aware computing. In: Dynamic & Mobile GIS: Investigating Change in Space and Time, pp. 34–51 (2006)
8. Gambs, S., Killijian, M.-O., del Prado, N., Cortez, M.: Show me how you move and i will tell you who you are. Trans. Data Priv. **4**(2), 103–126 (2011)
9. Hoh, B., Gruteser, M.: Protecting location privacy through path confusion. In: SecureComm, pp. 194–205. IEEE (2005)
10. Hoh, B., Gruteser, M., Xiong, H., Alrabady, A.: Enhancing security and privacy in traffic-monitoring systems. IEEE Pervasive Comput. **5**(4), 38–46 (2006)
11. Hoh, B., Gruteser, M., Xiong, H., Alrabady, A.: Preserving privacy in gps traces via uncertainty-aware path cloaking. In: Proceedings of the 14th ACM Conference on Computer and Communications Security, CCS 2007, pp. 161–171. ACM, New York (2007)
12. Kehr, F., Kowatsch, T., Wentzel, D., Fleisch, E.: Thinking styles and privacy decisions: need for cognition, faith into intuition, and the privacy calculus. In: Smart Enterprise Engineering: 12. Internationale Tagung Wirtschaftsinformatik, WI 2015, Osnabrück, Germany, March 4–6, 2015, pp. 1071–1084 (2015)
13. Krumm, J.: Inference attacks on location tracks. In: LaMarca, A., Langheinrich, M., Truong, K.N. (eds.) Pervasive 2007. LNCS, vol. 4480, pp. 127–143. Springer, Heidelberg (2007). doi:10.1007/978-3-540-72037-9_8
14. Krumm, J.: A survey of computational location privacy. Pers. Ubiquit. Comput. **13**(6), 391–399 (2009)
15. Kulkarni, V., Moro, A., Garbinato, B.: A mobility prediction system leveraging realtime location data streams: poster. In: Proceedings of the 22nd Annual International Conference on Mobile Computing and Networking, MobiCom 2016, pp. 430–432. ACM, New York (2016)
16. Laurila, J.K., Gatica-Perez, D., Aad, I., Blom, J., Bornet, O., Do, T.-M.-T., Dousse, O., Eberle, J., Miettinen, M.: The mobile data challenge: big data for mobile computing research. In: Pervasive Computing (2012)
17. Rebollo-Monedero, D., Parra-Arnau, J., Díaz, C., Forné, J.: On the measurement of privacy as an attacker's estimation error. Int. J. Inf. Sec. **12**(2), 129–149 (2013)

18. Shokri, R., Freudiger, J., Hubaux, J.P.: A unified framework for location privacy. In: Proceedings of the 9th International Symposium on Privacy Enhancing Technologies (PETS 2010), pp. 203–214. Citeseer (2010)
19. Shokri, R., Freudiger, J., Jadliwala, M., Hubaux, J.-P.: A distortion-based metric for location privacy. In: Proceedings of the 8th ACM Workshop on Privacy in the Electronic Society, pp. 21–30. ACM (2009)
20. Shokri, R., Theodorakopoulos, G., Le Boudec, J.-Y., Hubaux, J.-P.: Quantifying location privacy. In: Proceedings of the 2011 IEEE Symposium on Security and Privacy, SP 2011, pp. 247–262. IEEE Computer Society, Washington, DC (2011)
21. Xu, H., Wang, H., Stavrou, A.: Privacy risk assessment on online photos. In: Bos, H., Monrose, F., Blanc, G. (eds.) RAID 2015. LNCS, vol. 9404, pp. 427–447. Springer, Cham (2015). doi:10.1007/978-3-319-26362-5_20

AdaGraph: Adaptive Graph-Based Algorithms for Spam Detection in Social Networks

Amira Soliman[✉] and Sarunas Girdzijauskas

School of Information and Communication Technology,
Royal Institute of Technology (KTH), Stockholm, Sweden
{aaeh,sarunasg}@kth.se

Abstract. In the past years, researchers developed approaches to detect spam in Online Social Networks (OSNs) such as URL blacklisting, spam traps and even crowdsourcing for manual classification. Although previous work has shown the effectiveness of using statistical learning to detect spam, existing work employs supervised schemes that require labeled training data. In addition to the heavy training cost, it is difficult to obtain a comprehensive source of ground truth for measurement. In contrast to existing work, in this paper we present AdaGraph that is a novel graph-based approach for spam detection. AdaGraph is unsupervised, hence it diminishes the need of labeled training data and training cost. Particularly, AdaGraph effectively detects spam in large-scale OSNs by analyzing user behaviors using graph clustering technique. Moreover, AdaGraph continuously updates detected communities to comply with users dynamic interactions and activities. Extensive experiments using Twitter datasets show that AdaGraph detects spam with accuracy 92.3%. Furthermore, the false positive rate of AdaGraph is less than 0.3% that is less than half of the rate achieved by the state-of-the-art approaches.

Keywords: Unsupervised spam detection · Social networks · Distributed systems · Evolving graphs algorithms · Community detection

1 Introduction

With the widespread usage of user generated content in Online Social Networks (OSNs), spam has increased and has become an effective vehicle for malware and illegal advertisement distribution. Spam not only pollutes the content contributed by normal users, resulting in bad user experiences, but also misleads and even traps legitimate users. Furthermore, OSNs have also led to new methods of delivering spam, such as spammy apps, social bots, and fake accounts. These methods result in increasing social media spam to 355% in 2013 over 2012[1]. Spotting spammers is very challenging especially with the dynamic nature of social networks where activities and interactions among users evolve rapidly.

---

[1] http://nexgate.com/solutions/nexgate-social-media-security-stat-center/.

© Springer International Publishing AG 2017
A. El Abbadi and B. Garbinato (Eds.): NETYS 2017, LNCS 10299, pp. 338–354, 2017.
DOI: 10.1007/978-3-319-59647-1_25

Additionally, the problem becomes more challenging due to the huge amount of data shared by users. Therefore, researchers have analyzed different spam strategies to design mechanisms to combat the spam activities from different prospectives, including studying the redirection chains of embedded URLs [1–3], analyzing textual content [4–6], as well as analyzing different friendship graph properties of spammers against those of legitimate users [4–6].

The research community has produced a substantial number of mechanisms for automated spam detection based on binary classification mechanisms. The design of such spam detection mechanisms in general is guided by the behavior dissimilarity exhibited by legitimate users than spammers. The central premise as proved in the existing work is that spammer behavior appears anomalous relative to normal user behavior along some features that could be extracted from textual content (i.e., content-based features such as number of URLs, hashtags and mentions used per post) and OSN friendship graph (i.e., graph-based features that are calculated from the friendship graph such as local clustering coefficient and betweenness centrality). However, all of the existing techniques rely on supervised binary classification methods [1,4,6–8].

Although the proposed binary classification methods succeed at detecting spam content, they implicitly require offline training with statistically sufficient and representative labeled training set of different user behaviors in order to achieve good detection coverage. This requirement itself is hard to satisfy, not to mention the difficulty of adapting to different behavior patterns that emerge in the future. Furthermore, the number of features required to discriminate spammers increases due to the diverse users activists in OSNs, the evolving spam patterns, as well as the limited the amount of labeled data. For example, Zhu et al. [8] use 1,680 different user activities in their supervised detection approach. Additionally, binary classification methods result in false positive rate that could range between 5.7% and 0.8% [7,9] resulting in some legitimate users are identified as spammers and get disconnected from the network. Particularly, derived from the remark that spammers hijack trending topics and include many URLs in their posts, content-based classification methods distinguish spammers by the extensive use of URLs, hashtags and mentions. Consequently, legitimate users such as the official news channels that continuously broadcast posts with diverse topics containing URLs and hashtags of the trending topics are going to be classified as spammers.

To address these issues, in this paper we propose AdaGraph[2] that is a novel unsupervised graph-based clustering technique for spam detection. Differently from existing work, AdaGraph constructs a *user similarity graph* that is created by connecting users with edges having weights that quantify their behavioral similarity. The essence of AdaGraph is to construct a user similarity graph that encodes within its topology a holistic view of all behavioral interactions and patterns of OSN users. Afterwards, AdaGraph performs graph clustering by applying community detection on top of the newly created graph.

---

[2] This work is under the umbrella of the iSocial EU Marie Curie ITN project (FP7-PEOPLE-2012-ITN).

In particular, we create a user-based feature vector to summarize both content and graph features associated with every user. Accordingly, the edges are created connecting users having weights equal to the cosine similarity of feature vectors of source and destination nodes[3]. Afterwards, AdaGraph detects communities on top of similarity graph to identify different behavioral patterns existing in the social network, then spots the spam patterns among the detected ones by applying some lexical analysis. Spam detection using graph-based clustering not only diminishes the training cost, but also achieves low false positive rate. Graph-based clustering provides meaningful insights to the existing behavioral patterns, therefore, categorizes the existing patterns into more homogeneous and accurate clusters than binary splitting as illustrated in Fig. 1. Hence, grouping users into multiple communities minimizes the chances of high false positive rates, specially for legitimate users with diverse and highly active behaviors such as news channel accounts. Clustering will group such accounts into a separate cluster with a closer distance to users having legitimate behavior pattern with diverse topics rather than the spam pattern that exhibit high URL and hashtags rate, yet in the same time has high similarity in the content. Hence, graph-based clustering provides more accurate results compared to binary classification without the need of the repetitive cost of maintaining up-to-date labeled training dataset.

However, centralized graph-based clustering techniques are not realistically scalable due to the huge number of users in current OSNs. Therefore, graph-based clustering algorithms must be developed as massively parallel clustering that eliminates the need of single centralized aggregation point. Even better, graph-based clustering can be implemented as fully decentralized solution to be applicable with currently emerging Decentralized Online Social Networks (DOSNs). DOSNs operate as distributed information management platforms on top of networks of trusted servers or P2P infrastructures [10]. Thus, DOSNs provide a privacy preserving alternative to current OSNs, where users have full control of their data. Accordingly, in AdaGraph we allow every node to independently process its data and only communicate with its direct neighbors. Additionally, AdaGraph adaptively updates similarity connections among nodes in the detected communities based on the newly received information integrated with the previously known without the need of recomputing from scratch. Hence, AdaGraph is capable of monitoring the behavioral changes and dynamically adapts to the evolving social activities and interactions among users. We have performed experiments, using Twitter datasets, to show the effectiveness of our proposed approach. The results show that AdaGraph provides more accurate spam detection rate with accuracy up to 92.3% and false positive rate less than 0.3%. Thus, AdaGraph outperforms the state-of-the-art techniques not only in plain performance figures, but also by removing the need of labeled data and offline training effort (since AdaGraph is unsupervised) as well as removing the scalability issues due to the fully decentralized and distributed nature of the algorithm.

---

[3] Users and nodes refer to the same meaning and are used interchangeably.

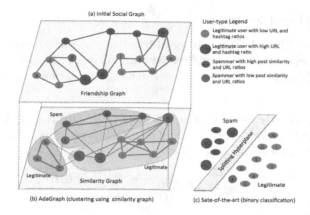

Fig. 1. Similarity-based clustering vs. Binary classification. (a) Initial social graph of OSN users having different behavioral patterns. (b) AdaGraph creates similarity graph and extracts communities that group users with similar behaviors. (c) Binary classification organizes all users in feature space to find the best splitting hyperplane.

Accordingly, our work offers the following contributions to the problem of spam detection:

- We propose unsupervised spam detection approach that requires no a priori labeling while maintaining low false positive rate,
- We propose a novel graph-based spam detection technique that detects spam using graph clustering on top of a constructed user similarity graph which encodes user behavioral patterns within its topology,
- We introduce adaptive algorithms that enable similarity-based community detection to evolve with respect to the behavioral changes of the users,
- Our proposed graph-based spam detection technique out-performs existing centralized binary classification,
- All of the above contributions are performed in purely distributed and decentralized manner.

The remainder of this paper is structured as follows. In Sect. 2 we list the features used for spam detection, whereas, in Sect. 3 we illustrate the core algorithms implemented in AdaGraph. Furthermore, in Section 3 we detail the lexical analysis method adopted to indicate the spammers communities among the detected ones. In Sect. 4 we present evaluation of AdaGraph. Finally, Sect. 5 shows the related work, then Sect. 6 concludes the paper.

2 Spam Detection Features

In this section, we first briefly describe the graph-based and content-based used in AdaGraph to compute user-based feature vectors.

2.1 Graph-Based Features

In this part we utilize the original social friendship graph connecting users. We consider the social network as undirected graph G = (V, E), where V is the set of nodes and E is the set of edges. $e_{ij} \in E$ denotes a relationship between nodes v_i and $v_j \in V$.

Definition 1. *Local Clustering Coefficient (LCC). Given $v_i \in V$, let $DF_i = \{v_j \in V | e_{ij} \in E\}$ be the direct friends of v_i. LCC_i represents the local clustering coefficient of v_i, and equals to:*

$$LCC(v_i) = \frac{|e_{jk} : v_j, v_k \in DF_i, e_{jk} \in E|}{|DF_i|(|DF_i| - 1)} \tag{1}$$

LCC is one of the graph-based features that are hard to fake [6]. LCC of a node is the ratio between the number of existing links among its direct neighbors and the number of links that could possibly exist among them [11]. LCC is used to quantify the extent to which the direct neighbors of a node are connected to each other. Due to decentralized nature of AdaGraph, we assume that every node calculates its LCC locally by keeping track of two-hop neighbors (i.e., neighbors of the neighbors).

Definition 2. *Average Neighbors Clustering Coefficient (ANCC). We define ANCC of node v_i as the average of LCCes computed by DF_i.*

ANCC is used to quantify the connectedness of the neighborhood of a node. Madden et al. [12] show that majority of OSN users are more skeptical regarding the acceptance of new friendship requests from strangers. Therefore, it is hard for spammers to have strongly connected neighborhood surrounding them. Thus, ANCCes of legitimate users are commonly higher than those of spammers.

2.2 Content-Based Features

A recent study [13] shows that spammers generate posts using complex templates such as finite-state machines to evade spam detection methods. Although, finite-state machines increase the number of different spam posts that can be generated, all of the generated posts follow a structured content, for example [mentions of other users + some text + URLs + hashtags of trending topics]. Furthermore, spam posts still have some words in common such as "look at this video" or "gain more", etc. Therefore, AdaGraph adopts the following content-based features.

Definition 3. *Average Posts Similarity (APS). Let P_i be the set of posts shared by v_i, and $pair_{(j,k)}$ be the pair of two posts p_j and p_k in P_i. We define the average posts similarity of v_i as follows:*

$$APS(v_i) = \frac{1}{\binom{|P_i|}{2}} \sum_{pair_{(j,k)} \in P_i} \frac{p_j \cap p_k}{p_j \cup p_k} \tag{2}$$

This feature leverages the similarity among the posts shared by a single user. We define post similarity using jaccard coefficient, such that for every post pair of a user, we divide the intersection (i.e., the number of common words in the post pair) by the total number of words in the post pair. Due to decentralized nature of AdaGraph, we assume that posts are publicly available and can be collected by other nodes.

Definition 4. *Mentions Ratio (MR). Spammers add mentions to random users to increase the visibility of their content. Accordingly, we define MR of a user u_i as the number of mentions which refer to a username not included in DF_i to the total number of posts generated by u_i.*

Definition 5. *URL Ratio (UR). Spammers embed malicious URLs in their posts to direct the users to their websites. Thus, we define UR as the the ratio of the number of posts containing a URL to the total number of posts a user has (i.e., $|URLs|/|P_i|$).*

Definition 6. *Hashtags Ratio (HR). Hijacking trending topics in OSNs has been a widely adopted strategy among spammers to reach wider audience. Therefore, we define HR as the number of trending topics associated with user posts to the total number of posts (i.e., $|Hashtahs|/|P_i|$).*

3   Graph-Based Spam Detection

In this section, we present the core of AdaGraph. First, we illustrate the construction of user similarity graph, followed by the details of the local clustering algorithm. Afterwards, we present the quick community adaptation algorithm used for tracing the evolution of users behaviors represented in detected communities over time. Furthermore, we discuss the computational complexity of AdaGraph and present the adopted lexical analysis approach to spot spammers communities among detected ones.

3.1   Similarity Graph Construction

The first step of AdaGraph is to construct users similarity graph from the social graph. To build a massively parallel approach, we allow every node in the social graph to participate in similarity graph construction. Initially, every node starts by creating similarity edges among itself and its social neighbors. The edges are created by connecting any pair of nodes having cosine similarity of their feature vectors greater than specific threshold. So as, the weight of an edge connecting node i and node j equals to:

$$w(e_{ij}) = \frac{x_i.x_j}{||x_i||.||x_j||} \tag{3}$$

where, x_i is the feature vector of node i and x_j is the feature vector of node j. Particularity, the feature vector of a node has the following values [LCC, ANCC,

APS, MR, UR, HR] as defined in Sect. 2. If the weight $w(e_{ij})$ is greater than the threshold ϵ, then an edge connecting node i and node j is added to the graph with weight equals to $w(e_{ij})$ (see Fig. 1, the thickness of an edge reflects its weight). Afterwards, every node enlarges the similarity graph further by exploring the possibility of creating more similarity edges with the neighbors of its currently direct neighbors.

3.2   Clustering by Community Detection

Our objective is to find the topological communities inside the constructed similarity graph. Let us first define similarity graph as an undirected weighted graph $G = (V, E)$, where V is the set of nodes and E is the set of similarity edges, where $e_{ij} \in E$ denotes cosine similarity between nodes v_i and $v_j \in V$ that is computed as defined in Eq. 3. Commonly, finding communities is well-know as community detection and is defined as:

Definition 7. *Community Detection. A community detection C, also known as graph clustering, is a mapping*

$$C : G \rightarrow G'_1 \times \ldots \times G'_n \tag{4}$$

that partitions G into n non-empty, node-disjoint subgraphs $G'_1 \times \ldots \times G'_n$ representing a set of communities or clusters. A widely used quality measure for community detection is the modularity Q of the clustering $C(G)$ [14], that assigns a quality value q to the clustering $C(G)$ defined by

$$q := \sum_i (w(e_{ii}) - b_i^2) \tag{5}$$

where $b_i = \sum_j w(e_{ij})$, where e_{ij} represents an edge in community i for which the target node of the edge lies in community j. The higher the quality value q is, the better the detected community is. One possible definition for C is to maximize Q over all clustering $C(G)$ [14].

AdaGraph employs recently developed decentralized diffusion-based community detection strategy [15]. In particular, every node in the similarity graph starts by joining the node with the maximum cosine similarity among its direct friends to form a community. Afterwards, in successive iterations every node chooses to quit its current community and join one of its neighbour's if this brings some modularity gain. As described in method *selectCommunity* in Algorithm 1, nodes select the dominant community in their neighborhood to join (i.e., the community with the highest sum of weights). This step is iteratively repeated until no node wants to change its community as it already represents the dominant one of all its neighbors. Thereafter, the topological communities detected in the similarity graph represent the different user behavioral patterns.

Algorithm 1. Community Detection Methods

Result: Community Structure C_{t+1}

Procedure selectCommunity(*node u*)

> **forall the** $C \in NeighborCommunity(u)$ **do**
> > | $q(C) \leftarrow sum(w_{e_{uj}})|C_j = C$
>
> **end**
> $C_u \leftarrow C_j|q(C_j) = max(q(C))$

Procedure changeCommunity(*node u*)

> $C_{u_{new}} \leftarrow$ selectCommunity(u)
> **if** $C_u \neq C_{u_{new}}$ **then**
> > $C_u \leftarrow C_{u_{new}}$
> > **forall the** $x \in Neighbor(u)$ **do**
> > > | changeCommunity(x)
> >
> > **end**
>
> **end**

3.3 Community Structure Adaptation

OSNs are dynamic by nature due to rapidly evolving social activities and inter-actions among users. Therefore, the constructed similarity graph must be contin-uously updated to cope with evolving users' behaviors. Thus, we have integrated adaptive modularity-based methods for identifying and tracing the changes in the communities structure of the constructed similarity graph. The similarity graph is updated by either inserting or removing a node or set of nodes, or by either introducing or deleting an edge or set of edges. We have modeled these graph changes as a collection of simple events namely: *newNode, removeNode, newEdge* and *removeEdge*. AdaGraph starts by extracting initial community structure C_0, by detecting the communities exist in the first snapshot of the net-work. Thereafter, this initial structure is continuously updated for the successive snapshots by applying different adaptation methods as illustrated in Algorithms 2 and 3.

Algorithm 2. Node Simple Events

Result: An updated Community Structure C_{t+1}

Procedure newNode(*node u*)

> | $C_u \leftarrow$ selectCommunity(u)
> | Update $C_{t+1} : C_{t+1} \leftarrow (C_t \setminus C_u) \cup (C_u \cup u)$

Procedure removeNode(*node u*)

> $C_u \leftarrow (C_u \setminus u)$
> **forall the** $v \in Neighbor(u)$ **do**
> > | removeEdge(e_{vu})
>
> **end**

– **newNode(V+u)**: a new node u with its associated edges are introduced, such that u could come with no or more than one new edge(s). When u joins the similarity graph, it assigns itself to the dominant community in its neighborhood as illustrated in method *newNode*.

– **removeNode(V−u)**: node u with its adjacent edges are removed from the graph. As shown in methods *removeNode*, when an existing node u is of a community C is removed, all of its adjacent edges are removed as a result. Consequently, the resulting community structure might change, hence, neighbors of that removed node re-evaluate their community memberships as illustrated in the next method *removeEdge*.

Algorithm 3. Edge Simple Events

Result: An updated Community Structure C_{t+1}

Procedure newEdge(*edge e_{vu}*)

    if *v and u are new nodes* **then**

        | $C_{t+1} \leftarrow C_t \cup \{v, u\}$

    else if $C_v = C_u$ **then**

        | $C_{t+1} \leftarrow C_t$

    else

        | changeCommunity(u)

        | changeCommunity(v)

Procedure removeEdge(*edge e_{vu}*)

    if (v, u) *is a single edge* **then**

        | $C_{t+1} \leftarrow (C_t \setminus \{v, u\}) \cup \{v\} \cup \{u\}$

    else if *either v (or u) is of degree one* **then**

        | $C_{t+1} \leftarrow (C_t \setminus C_v) \cup \{v\} \cup \{C_v \setminus v\}$

    else if $C_v \neq C_u$ **then**

        | $C_{t+1} \leftarrow C_t$

    else

        | changeCommunity(u)

        | changeCommunity(v)

– **newEdge(E+e)**: a new edge e is introduced, we can divide it further into two cases: an intra-community edge (both nodes belong to the same community) or an inter-community edge (connecting two communities). In the first case, no change happens to the community structure (as detailed in method *newEdge*). Yet, the interesting situation happens when e is an inter-community edge, as its presence could possibly make source and destination nodes change their community memberships. Consequently, these nodes notify their neighbors in case of change, so as cascading updates could take place if further changes are required (as detailed in method *changeCommunity*).

– **removeEdge(E−e)**: an existing edge e in the graph is removed. Similarly to edge addition, edge removal can be divided into two case, such that the edge to be removed e is either an inter-community edge or intra-community edge. In the first case, the removal of e will strengthen the current community structure and cause no change to it. However, in the second case, edge removal might cause community split. Therefore, the edge source and destination nodes re-evaluate their community memberships and notify their neighbors in case of change.

3.4   Lexical Analysis of Posts

As aforementioned, the core of AdaGraph is to detect different behavioral patterns in the user similarity graph by performing community detection. However, spotting spam patters among detected ones is not straightforward. So as, further lexical and semantic analysis is required to efficiently spot spammers communities among extracted ones. Specially, spammers can use automated spinning to avoid duplicate detection, such that they can create new versions with vaguely similar meaning but sufficiently different appearance. Therefore, in AdaGraph we apply lexical analysis of the most frequent words to determine if those words or their synonyms are commonly used by spammers. AdaGraph integrates Gavagai lexicon[4] that learns the words synonyms and their related n-grams terms. Accordingly, we identify a set of trusted nodes in the social graph and these nodes are responsible for labeling any of detected communities as spam if the majority of the users belonging to these communities frequently use spam words or their lexical related terms.

3.5   Complexity Analysis

The model cost is expected to be low given that every node performs its local computation independently of the other nodes. We discuss the complexity of AdaGraph in terms of communication traffic among all the nodes in the OSN. By our adopted work for decentralized community detection, the algorithm complexity is $\mathcal{O}(N * D * R)$, where N is the total number of users in the similarity graph, D is the average node degree, and R is the total number of rounds needed for the algorithm to converge[5] [15]. This step requires that all the nodes are online at the time of its execution; however, it is also a process that is performed once and that is incrementally updated only. Moreover, as we demonstrate through experiments on real OSN data, the convergence time of our solution is very realistic and achievable (see Sect. 4.3).

4   Evaluation

AdaGraph applies vertex-centric approach which is proved to be scalable, efficient and fast. Our algorithms are implemented in GraphLab[6], with two different distributed execution modules. In the first module, nodes participate in creating the similarity graph using their feature vectors. Thereafter, the control is moved

---

[4] Available via http://lexicon.gavagai.se/.
[5] R depends on the topological properties of the underlying graph.
[6] https://turi.com/products/create/.

Table 1. Twitter datasets used in our experiments.

Twitter dataset	US_Active	UK_Active	US_Passive
Tweets	453,519	489,484	360,927
Legitimate accounts	17,322	19,312	12,128
Suspended accounts	2,072	1,617	3,109
Social-graph edges	1,357,806	1,187,036	2,349,314
Similarity-graph edges	2,149,414	2,297,150	3,339,617

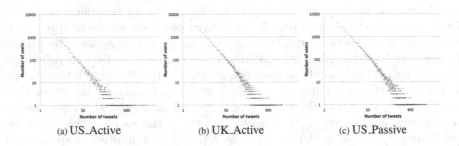

(a) US_Active   (b) UK_Active   (c) US_Passive

Fig. 2. The tweeting distribution in Twitter datasets in log scale.

to the second module that performs the community detection algorithm. In the following subsections, we thoroughly evaluate the performance of AdaGraph in terms of the accuracy of spam detection. We compare AdaGraph with different centralized and supervised binary classification approaches, utilizing the Weka tool[7], namely: K-means (KM) with number of clusters $= 2$, Decision Tree (DT) and Random Forest (RF).

4.1 Datasets

We have collected our dataset from Twitter using Twitter streaming API[8] from May 2015 to July 2016. We have accessed Twitter's API using privileged accounts, collecting users' tweets and the social graph connecting these users. In order to identify the spammers, we have queried the status of all accounts regularly to check if any got suspended for abusive behavior. Upon suspension, we identify suspended accounts as spammers. Table 1 lists the details of the collected datasets. The first two datasets (US_Active and UK_Active) are collected from users with high level of posting tweets located in United States and United Kingdom, respectively. Yet, the third dataset (US_Passive) is collected from users located in United States with low level of posting activity. Accordingly, in Fig. 2 we show the tweeting distribution for the collected datasets in log scale. As shown, tweeting distribution follows power law probability distribution, such that there is uneven distribution of number of tweets being posted

---

[7] http://www.cs.waikato.ac.nz/ml/weka/.
[8] https://dev.twitter.com/rest/public.

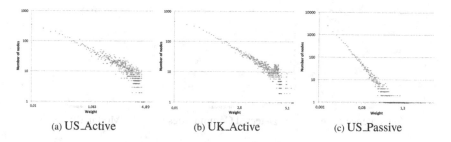

(a) US_Active   (b) UK_Active   (c) US_Passive

Fig. 3. The weight distribution in the generated similarity graphs for Twitter datasets in log scale.

by users. Majority of users post few tweets, whereas there is small number of highly active users who post large number of tweets.

4.2 Generated Similarity Graph

As aforementioned, the user similarity graph is constructed in a fully decentralized manner, such that each node explores its surrounding neighborhood progressively to add further similarity edges. Furthermore, as mentioned in Sect. 3.1, nodes add similarity edges if the similarity weight is greater than the threshold ϵ. We allow nodes to determine freely the value of ϵ, such that each node computes the average weight of its current edges, and sets the average weight as value for ϵ. As shown in Table 1, the average number of added edges in the similarity graph is almost equal to 50% of the existing edges in the social graph. Accordingly, AdaGraph connects only highly similar nodes instead of creating a fully connected graphs.

Figure 3 depicts the similarity weight distribution obtained for each dataset in log scale. As shown, the similarity weight distribution follows power law probability distribution similarly to the tweeting distribution. Furthermore, the similarity weight distribution spans over wider range in US_Active and UK_Active compared to US_Passive. Particularly, in US_Passive 91.5% of the similarity weight is less than 0.25, and this resulted from the low post frequency of users in this dataset. Therefore, we can infer that the more active posting behavior of users, the more strong edges are be added in the similarity graph. Additionally, AdaGraph can successfully adapt to different social activities of the users and accordingly create the user similarity graph to reflect the underlying user behavior.

4.3 Adaptive Community Detection

As aforementioned, every node repeatedly runs the community detection, until communities structure does not change any more (i.e., the convergence is reached). Figure 4(a) depicts the number of rounds required till convergence, and number of extracted communities per round. As shown, in the very beginning

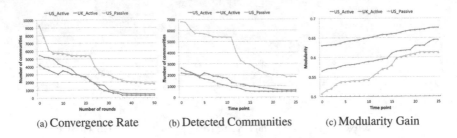

(a) Convergence Rate   (b) Detected Communities   (c) Modularity Gain

Fig. 4. Community detection results of AdaGraph. (a) Number of iterations required for convergence. (b) Number of detected communities per each snapshot. (c) The modularity gain obtained per each snapshot.

the number of communities is very large, every node starts to form a community with one of its direct neighbors. However, over time nodes join the dominant communities in their neighborhood, as a result the communities start to merge and the number of communities continues to decrease. In order to identify the communities that contain spammers, we have construct a list of 500 words that are commonly used by spammers associated with their semantically similar terms and n-grams (see Sect. 3.4). Further, for every node we select the most frequent words used in its tweets. Accordingly, the collected word list per community is checked against a list of common spam words. A community is identified as spam if majority (i.e., more than 50%) of its members use common spam words in their tweets. The results show that the percentage of spam communities is 17.3%, 21.6% and 23.5% in US_Active, UK_Active and US_Passive, respectively.

Additionally, we study the adaptability of AdaGraph with dynamic and evolving graphs. We started by loading 50% to form the basic structure, such that we constructed the similarity graph using only 50% of nodes from the social graph and 50% of their associated tweets. Afterwards, we simulated the network evolution by adding the remaining nodes/tweets via a series of 25 growing snapshots. Figure 4(b) depicts the number of detected communities per snapshot as well as Fig. 4(c) shows the resulted modularity of the detected communities per snapshot. Furthermore, we have noticed that the changes caused by incrementally adding the snapshots are localized, such that on average 15% to 17% of old nodes got affected by the change and re-evaluate their communities membership. Consequently, AdaGraph dynamically adapts to the topological changes of evolving graphs. Moreover, AdaGraph adapts incrementally with no need to start community detection from scratch.

Furthermore, we study the effect of ϵ as a graph sparsification parameter, as well as the ability of AdaGraph to extract communities in denser graphs. Accordingly, we have repeated the community detection experiments with another generated user similarity graphs in which all edges are added even though the weight is less than ϵ. Consequently, the new generated user similarity graphs are denser than those generated having edges with weight greater than ϵ. The obtained results show that AdaGraph maintains the same convergence rate and

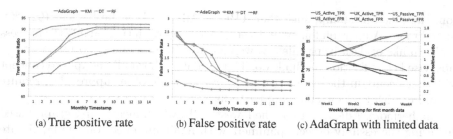

(a) True positive rate   (b) False positive rate   (c) AdaGraph with limited data

Fig. 5. The performance gain achieved by AdaGraph compared with centralized and supervised methods. The reported values are the average of achieved performance across the three datasets. (c) AdaGraph performance using only the first month snapshot of the data.

structure of detected communities with denser graphs, though the execution time is almost double the execution time of ϵ sparsificated graphs. Specifically, with ϵ sparsificated graphs the execution time is 15.4, 17.7, and 13 min for US_Active, UK_Active and US_Passive, respectively. On the other hand, with denser graphs the execution time is 39, 35.9, and 26.9 min for US_Active, UK_Active and US_Passive, respectively. Therefore, by disregarding a large fraction of low-weight edges that are insignificant for the task, running times of community detection algorithms are reduced.

4.4 Performance Comparison

We calculate the accuracy of AdaGraph using True Positive Rate and False Positive Rate, that are defined as the following: (1) True Positive Rate (TPR): we calculate TPR as the fraction of spammers that are successfully detected. (2) False Positive Rate (FPR): we calculate FPR as the fraction of legitimate users that are identified as spammers.

We have updated all of the supervised machine learning algorithms to be performed in online learning fashion. Instead of executing them in batch learning manner that uses the entire training dataset at once, we have used the monthly updates of the data in a sequential order to update the predictors by retraining them with misclassified data points from future data. On the other hand, AdaGraph is already developed to capture the evolving changes in social network. For the comparison, we update the user similarity graph with sequence of monthly data.

Figure 5 depicts the detection performance comparison of AdaGraph with the different centralized and supervised classification methods. As shown, AdaGraph outperforms all binary classification methods especially when limited data is available. Specifically, the gap between AdaGraph and other methods in prediction accuracy for the first month is around 14,1%. Namely, the performance of supervised classification methods gets increased as the available training data increases (i.e., starting from the sixth month). On the other hand, AdaGraph creates an evolving similarity graph and continuously clusters users more accurately from the first timestamp, such that TPR of AdaGraph is the highest (92.3%). Furthermore, AdaGraph follows a decentralized approach that enables to process small chunks of data in parallel, as well as AdaGraph requires no retraining as supervised classification methods do. Thus, AdaGraph rapidly adapts to concept drift that occurs in the system (user behavior), while other approaches require retraining with the new emerging patterns.

Furthermore, AdaGraph has the lowest FPR, which means that graph-based clustering successfully detect spammers with minimum effect on the legitimate users. Specifically, we can see that FPR in AdaGraph can be steadily maintained under 0.3%, as shown in Fig. 5(b), while the rate of RF method (the best binary classification method) starts with 2% and drops to 0.39% with increase of the training data. Consequently, the community detection approach adopted in AdaGraph perfectly categorizes the existing behavioral patterns into more homogeneous and accurate clusters than binary classification.

Additionally, we have further analyzed AdaGraph considering only the data collected in the first snapshot. In this experiment, we want to study the minimum number of posts needed to achieve good TPR meanwhile the FPR is kept low. Figure 5(c) depicts the weekly detection performance of AdaGraph in the first month. As shown, lowest TPR of AdaGraph is more than 75% while the FPR is less than 1.6% during the first week when the average number of available posts is 14 post across the three datasets. Hence, AdaGraph has an acceptable accuracy with very limited data. The first key reason behind AdaGraph good performance is the hybrid features that AdaGraph employs, i.e., the graph-based and content based features. Secondly and most importantly, the community detection algorithm categorizes user into more homogeneous and accurate clusters than binary classification.

5   Related Work

The first family of spam detection mechanisms includes techniques using blacklists to identify URL on OSNs websites directing to spam content [1,2]. However, URL blacklisting has several practical challenges. First, those blacklists are publicly available, hence spammers can evade them by changing their domain names or hiding them behind some redirecting pages. Second, URL blacklisting becomes ineffective with the spread usage of URL shortening services such as bit.ly and t.co. Therefore, different techniques have been proposed to analyze the redirection chains of URLs and their correlations [3]. Yet, those techniques are not designed as online detection tools, since they either have long lag-time or limited efficiency.

Furthermore, a rich corpus of research work lies in adopting supervised machine learning based methods using hybrid features extracted from textual content and OSN friendship graph. For example, Hongyu et al. [4] propose to train a binary classifier with hybrid features including user social degree, yet spammers can increase their social degree by purchasing more followers. Thus, Yang et al. [6] employ graph-based features that are hard to fake such as local clustering coefficient and betweenness centrality. More recently, [16] suggests an unsupervised solution to spam detection based on sybil defense mechanism. The proposed scheme starts by identifying non-spammers (i.e., non-sybils) by applying a clustering algorithm on social graph. The authors focus their analysis on intensive URL sharing, yet instead of using URL blacklisting, they add new user-link edges to the social graph by connecting users sharing the same URL. However, the assumption that sybil nodes form tight-knit communities does not presist as shown in recent studies [17].

6   Conclusion

In this paper, we have introduced AdaGraph that is a novel decentralized and unsupervised spam detection framework in contrast to existing centralized and supervised approaches. AdaGraph resembles graph-based spam detection technique that detects spam using graph clustering on top of a newly constructed user similarity graph which encodes within its topology a holistic view of all behavioral interactions and patterns of OSN users. More importantly, AdaGraph integrates community detection algorithm that categorizes the existing user behavioral patterns into more homogeneous and accurate clusters than binary classification. The proposed approach achieves detection accuracy upto 92.3% and false positive rate less than 0.3%. Additionally, AdaGraph is scalable and massively parallel that suitably fits DOSNs and OSNs environments.

References

1. Thomas, K., Grier, C., Ma, J., Paxson, V., Song, D.: Design and evaluation of a real-time url spam filtering service. In: SP Symposium, pp. 447–462. IEEE (2011)
2. Levchenko, K., Pitsillidis, A., Chachra, N., Enright, B., Félegyházi, M., Grier, C., Halvorson, T., Kanich, C., Kreibich, C., Liu, H., et al.: Click trajectories: end-to-end analysis of the spam value chain. In: SP Symposium, pp. 431–446. IEEE (2011)
3. Lee, S., Kim, J.: Warningbird: detecting suspicious urls in twitter stream. In: NDSS (2012)
4. Gao, H., Chen, Y., Lee, K., Palsetia, D., Choudhary, A.N.: Towards online spam filtering in social networks. In: NDSS (2012)
5. Yang, C., Harkreader, R.C., Gu, G.: Die free or live hard? empirical evaluation and new design for fighting evolving twitter spammers. In: Sommer, R., Balzarotti, D., Maier, G. (eds.) RAID 2011. LNCS, vol. 6961, pp. 318–337. Springer, Heidelberg (2011). doi:10.1007/978-3-642-23644-0_17
6. Yang, C., Harkreader, R., Gu, G.: Empirical evaluation and new design for fighting evolving twitter spammers. Inf. Forensics Secur. 8(8), 1280–1293 (2013)
7. Amleshwaram, A.A., Reddy, N., Yadav, S., Gu, G., Yang, C.: Cats: characterizing automation of twitter spammers. In: COMSNET 2013, pp. 1–10. IEEE (2013)
8. Zhu, Y., Wang, X., Zhong, E., Liu, N.N., Li, H., Yang, Q.: Discovering spammers in social networks. In: AAAI 2012 (2012)
9. Martinez-Romo, J., Araujo, L.: Detecting malicious tweets in trending topics using a statistical analysis of language. Expert Syst. Appl. 40(8), 2992–3000 (2013)

10. Datta, A., Buchegger, S., Vu, L.-H., Strufe, T., Rzadca, K.: Decentralized online social networks. In: Handbook of Social Network Technologies and Applications, pp. 349–378. Springer, New York (2010)
11. Dorogovtsev, S.N., Mendes, J.F.: Evolution of networks. Adv. Phys. **51**(4), 1079–1187 (2002)
12. Madden, M., Lenhart, A., Cortesi, S., Gasser, U., Duggan, M., Smith, A., Beaton, M.: Teens, social media, and privacy, vol. 21. Pew Research Center (2013)
13. Chen, C., Zhang, J., Xiang, Y., Zhou, W., Oliver, J.: Spammers are becoming "smarter" on twitter. IT Prof. **18**(2), 66–70 (2016)
14. Newman, M.E.: Modularity and community structure in networks. Proc. Natl. Acad. Sci. **103**(23), 8577–8582 (2006)
15. Rahimian, F., Girdzijauskas, S., Haridi, S.: Parallel community detection for cross-document coreference. In: WIC, vol. 2, pp. 46–53. IEEE/ACM (2014)
16. Tan, E., Guo, L., Chen, S., Zhang, X., Zhao, Y.: Unik: unsupervised social network spam detection. In: CIKM 2013, pp. 479–488. ACM (2013)
17. Yang, Z., Wilson, C., Wang, X., Gao, T., Zhao, B.Y., Dai, Y.: Uncovering social network sybils in the wild. In: TKDD 2014, vol. 8, no. 1, p. 2 (2014)

Incoercible Fully-Remote Electronic Voting Protocol

Wafa Neji[1]([✉]), Kaouther Blibech[2], and Narjes Ben Rajeb[3]

[1] Laboratory LIP2. The General Directorate of Technological Studies,
ISET Beja, Beja, Tunisia
wafa.neji@gmail.com
[2] Laboratory LIP2, ISTEUB, University of Carthage, Tunis, Tunisia
[3] Laboratory LIP2, INSAT, University of Carthage, Tunis, Tunisia

Abstract. Civitas is the first fully remote e-voting protocol which ensures verifiability and coercion resistance at the same time. In 2011, Shirazi et al. found a security flaw on the credential management process during Civitas' registration phase and proposed solutions to avoid this drawback.

In this paper, we describe some attacks found during the Civitas' registration phase. We show that Shirazi's solutions cannot be used in practical situations and/or doesn't ensure coercion-resistance. Then, we present a fully remote e-voting protocol that addresses these drawbacks.

Our protocol aims to separate voter's registration data from voter's vote into two different bulletin boards. Merging this data will only be done by tallying authorities to identify and tally valid votes. Moreover, our protocol uses a new ballot's encryption function that ensures coercion resistance in a different manner. Compared to Civitas, we use a secure registration phase and we reduce the computational complexity of tallying phase from quadratic to linear time.

Keywords: Electronic voting · Internet voting · Coercion-resistance · Civitas

1 Introduction

Many governments are turning to the use of e-voting systems to ensure the conduct of elections in more efficient, faster, easier, cheaper and attractive way than the traditional voting process.

Fully remote e-voting protocols allow voters to vote anywhere. They must satisfy several security requirements related to voting process. One of the hardest security requirements seems to be the coercion resistance. So, how to ensure that a voter doesn't vote under a threat of a coercer? In 2008, Clarkson et al. [1] define the first fully remote e-voting protocol, called Civitas, which ensures coercion resistance and verifiability at the same time. Civitas protocol is an improvement of the JCJ protocol defined by Juels et al. in 2005 [14].

© Springer International Publishing AG 2017
A. El Abbadi and B. Garbinato (Eds.): NETYS 2017, LNCS 10299, pp. 355–369, 2017.
DOI: 10.1007/978-3-319-59647-1_26

In Civitas, to ensure coercion resistance, each voter owns a credential delivered by trusted registration authorities. This credential is casted by voter within its ballot to validate it. Neither the voter nor the adversary can prove or verify the validity or the invalidity of the credential. Thus, the adversary cannot control voter's choice and is also confused about the validity of the casted ballot. Civitas received much research interest, and several improvements have been proposed in the literature. In [3,10], authors propose solutions to reduce the complexity of Civitas' tallying phase from quadratic to linear. In [11,12], authors propose an implementation of Civitas by the use of smart cards in order to overcome credential management problem. However, they based their solutions on a partially remote registration phase. To register, a voter must at first contact in person a supervised registration authority. Then, he finishes the registration process remotely with other registration authorities. This contradicts the aim to define a fully remote e-voting protocol. In [9], Shirazi et al. found an attack during Civitas' registration phase. This security flaw arises due to the credential management in Civitas. Therefore, Shirazi et al. propose extended versions with intention to overcome this drawback. However, as we will show in this paper, their solutions cannot be used in practical situations and/or violate the coercion resistance in certain cases.

In this paper, we discuss the attacks found in Civitas' registration phase and we propose a fully remote secure registration protocol. We present also a new e-voting protocol based on Civitas. The main idea behind our protocol is to separate voter's registration data from voter's vote. In fact, we use two types of bulletin boards[1]. The first one, called Credential Bulletin Board (CBB) is used for registration and authentication of voters. The second one, called Ballot Bulletin Board (BBB), is used for submitting the votes. Tallying authorities will then merge the data from the boards to identify and tally valid votes.

Our protocol satisfies security requirements of e-voting process, especially verifiability and coercion resistance. It is characterized by the fact that it allows voters to submit valid ballots in the presence of a coercer who forces them to cast a particular vote.

This paper is organized as follows: first, Civitas protocol is introduced. Second, attacks found during Civitas' registration phase are detailed. Then, we present a new e-voting protocol based on a secure registration phase. Finally, we study the security of our e-voting protocol.

2   The Civitas Protocol

In this section, due to the space constraints, we present briefly each phase of Civitas protocol [1]. The participants involved in this protocol are Supervisor Authority SA, Registrar RE, Registration Authorities $RA_1, RA_2, \ldots, RA_l$, Tallying Authorities $TA_1, TA_2, \ldots, TA_n$ and Voters $V_1, V_2, \ldots, V_m$. A Bulletin

---

[1] A bulletin board is a public broadcasted channel in which anyone can read and verify data and no one can erase any information from it.

Board (BB), is used by these participants to publish all the information needed for e-voting process.

Initialization. First, SA starts the election and posts on BB a message (p, q, g) containing the parameters related to cryptosystem ElGamal where p and q are two large prime numbers, such that $q|(p-1)$ and g a generator of the order q subgroup of Z_p^*. Note that Civitas uses ElGamal threshold encryption over a pre-established secret key noted sk shared jointly among tallying authorities. The public key related to this secret key is noted pk. In what follows, the encryption of a message m with ELGamal encryption under the public key pk and a random value r is noted $Enc_G(m, pk, r) = (X_m, Y_m) = (g^r, m.pk^r)$.

Second, the registrar RE publishes on BB the list of legitimate voters with their public keys. Note that each voter owns two keys: a registration key and a designation key. Voter's registration key is used by registration authorities to authenticate voters during the registration phase. Voter's designation key is used by voters to provide fake credentials if they are under a threat of a coercer during the voting phase.

Then, for each voter, registration authorities jointly generate a credential noted C_j used to prove voters' legitimacy. For this, each RA_i chooses randomly a secret credential share $c_{i,j}$ for the voter V_j. The credential C_j related to V_j is computed from the product of $c_{i,j}$. A public credential share $S_{i,j}$ is associated to each private credential share $c_{i,j}$ and published by RA_i on BB using ElGamal encryption, such as $S_{i,j} = (X_{i,j}, Y_{i,j}) = (g^{\varepsilon_{i,j}}, c_{i,j}pk^{\varepsilon_{i,j}})$, where $\varepsilon_{i,j}$ is randomly chosen in Z_q.

After all registration authorities have published $S_{i,j}$, the public credential S_j related to the private credential C_j can be computed as the product of public values $S_{i,j}$, such as: $S_j = \prod_{i=1}^l S_{i,j} = (\prod_{i=1}^l g^{\varepsilon_{i,j}}, \prod_{i=1}^l c_{i,j}pk^{\varepsilon_{i,j}})$.

Registration. During this phase, each voter V_j contacts registration authorities to obtain his credential. Here, it will be assumed that voters and registration authorities are already authenticated[2]. The registration protocol runs as follows:

1. V_j asks each RA_i to send him the share $c_{i,j}$ of his private credential C_j.
2. Each RA_i computes $S'_{i,j} = (g^{\varepsilon'_{i,j}}, c_{i,j}pk^{\varepsilon'_{i,j}})$ where $\varepsilon'_{i,j} \in_R Z_q$.
3. Each RA_i sends secretly to V_j the credential share $c_{i,j}$, the encrypted credential share $S'_{i,j}$, the random value $\varepsilon'_{i,j}$ and a Designated-Verifier Re-encryption Proof ($DVRP$) due to Hirt and Sako [17]. This proof is convincing only V_j that $S'_{i,j}$ is a re-encryption of the public credential share $S_{i,j}$.
4. V_j verifies that $S'_{i,j}$ is computed correctly from the values $c_{i,j}$ and $\varepsilon'_{i,j}$. He also verifies the $DVRP$ proof.
5. After retrieving all credential shares, V_j computes his private credential as $C_j = \prod_{i=1}^l c_{i,j}$.

---

[2] Each registration authority will authenticate voters using their registration keys. Note that we do not detail identification and authentication mechanism used in Civitas protocol.

Vote. To vote, each voter posts on BB an unsigned ballot noted B_{V_j} which contains his encrypted vote v_j and his encrypted credential C_j such that:

$$B_{V_j} = (Enc_G(v_j, pk, r_{v_j}), Enc_G(C_j, pk, r_{C_j}), P_w, P_k)$$

where $r_{C_j}, r_{v_j} \in_R Z_q$, and P_w, P_k are zero-knowledge proofs. P_w shows that $Enc_G(v_j, pk, r_{v_j})$ encrypts a valid vote v_j. It is based on a 1-out-of-L re-encryption proof defined by Hirt and Sako in [17]. P_k shows that V_j knows r_{C_j} and r_{v_j}. It is based on the technique defined by Camenisch and Stadler in [4] and impede an adversary to submit values dependently on previously published B_{V_j}.

If a voter votes under a threat of a coercer, he may submit a fake credential[3] C_j and an invalid encryption $Enc_G(C_j, pk, r_{C_j})$ within his B_{V_j}. The coercer cannot verify the validity of C_j. Then, V_j can submit another B_{V_j} with a valid credential during a secret moment in the absence of the coercer.

Tallying. The Tallying phase involves the following steps:

1. For each casted B_{V_j}, tallying authorities check P_w and P_k. They eliminate ballots with invalid proofs.
2. According to re-voting policy[4], tallying authorities eliminate ballots posted with the same credential C_j by applying the Plaintext Equivalence Test (PET)[5] [5] on each pair $(Enc_G(C_j, pk, r_{C_j}), Enc_G(C_{j'}, pk, r_{C_{j'}}))$ for $j \neq j'$ of encrypted credentials casted on BB.
3. Both the list of submitted ballots B_{V_j} and the list of public credentials S_j are passed as input to a mix-net. For this, each tallying authority apply its own re-encryption and provide a proof of its validity.
4. To eliminate ballots casted with invalid credentials, tallying authorities apply PET on all pairs $(S_j, Enc_G(C_j, pk, r_{C_j}))$. If PET returns true, the ballot will be counted in the tally.
5. Tallying authorities run a distributed decryption on valid ballots and compute the final voting result.

Note that if BB includes N casted ballots, applying PET during step 2 and 4 of tallying process causes worst-case running time. Thus, the tallying process involves quadratic time complexity of $O(N^2)$, which depends on the number of all casted ballots.

3   The Insecurity of Civitas' Registration Phase

In Civitas protocol, during the registration phase, authors do not specify what happens if a voter V_j received an invalid credential share $c_{i,j}$ from a dishonest

---

[3] The voter uses his private designation key to provide, to an adversary, a fake $DVRP$ proof proving the validity of his fake credential.

[4] If voters can re-vote, then only the last ballot with valid credential is counted, the other ones, submitted with duplicate credentials, are eliminated. If voters cannot re-vote, then all ballots casted with the same credential are eliminated.

[5] Given a pair of encrypted credentials $Enc_G(C_1)$ and $Enc_G(C_2)$, PET checks if $C_1 = C_2$ without revealing any information on C_1 or C_2.

registration authority RA_j. If the public credential S_j is computed from public credential shares $S_{i,j}$ published by all registration authorities, a dishonest authority can imped voters from voting simply by sending invalid credential shares. Thus, voters cannot compute their secret credentials and cannot cast valid ballots. This attack has been described by Shirazi et al. in [9]. Two solutions are proposed by the authors in [9] to avoid this attack. In the first solution, the voter must fix a subset of honest registration authorities before requesting his credential shares. This seems to be impracticable in real situations. In the one hand, it is extremely difficult for the voter to decide, from the beginning, on the set of trusted registration authorities. In the other hand, if one of the set of trusted registration authorities is under the influence of an attacker, the described attack will be still possible.

The second solution proposed by Shirazi et al. assumes that each voter must select a random subset of registration authorities and contact them to receive his credential shares. The size of this subset must be greater than one half of the total number of registration authorities. Then, the voter must contact once more each trusted registration authority to reveal the subset of honest authorities whom sent him valid credential shares. This solution don't ensure coercion resistance if the voter is accompanied by a coercer who forces him to select a specific subset of registration authorities. Moreover, an attacker can modify the distribution of the generated credentials if he knows in advance the random subset of registration authorities that the voter will contact. This attack will be described in detail below.

In Civitas' protocol, the authors claim that the protocol used to construct credentials ensures a uniform distribution of the generated credentials. However, in what follows, we show that Civitas' registration protocol allows a dishonest registration authority to influence the distribution of the generated credentials. This attack is similar to the one found by Gennaro on Pedersen's distributed key generation (DKG) protocol [2].

The attack occurs when a dishonest registration authority noted RA_1 wants to modify the last bits of the public credential $S_j = (X_j, Y_j)$ related to V_j. Assume that RA_1 wants to change the value of S_j such that the last bit of X_j and Y_j will be 0. The adversary RA_1 will wait until all registration authorities publish public credential shares $S_{i,j}$. Then he computes $S_j^* = (\prod_{i=1}^{l} X_{i,j}, \prod_{i=1}^{l} Y_{i,j})$. If S_j^* ends with 0, he will submit correct share $S_{1,j}$ to V_j. Otherwise, RA_1 sends either an invalid credential share with an invalid $DVRP$ proof to V_j or simply abstains from sending a credential share. He also can simply copy any share posted by other registration authorities. As described in Civitas, this breaks the execution of the registration process. In all cases, RA_1 will force the interruption of the registration process. All registration authorities will then re-run the registration protocol. In fact, RA_1, or other dishonest registration authorities, can force the re-run of this protocol several times until they get the value S_j^* ending with 0. This breaks the assumption of uniform distribution of the generated credentials.

The attack described above is also applicable in the second solution proposed by Shirazi et al. [9]. Assuming that the voter contacts RA_1 to receive his credential share, and that RA_1 knows in advance the selected arbitrary subset of registration authorities, RA_1 can decide whether he will be or not in the subset of trusted authorities (noted SET) selected by the voter. According to his goal, RA_1 can force S_j to be $S_j^1 = (\prod_{i \in SET} X_{i,j}, \prod_{i \in SET} Y_{i,j})$ or $S_j^2 = (\prod_{i \in \{SET \setminus RA_1\}} X_{i,j}, \prod_{\{SET \setminus RA_1\}} Y_{i,j})$. He can also cooperate with other dishonest registration authorities to force the value of S_j ending with specific bit values.

4 Our Electronic Voting Protocol

In this section, we present the whole process of our e-voting protocol. Our protocol is based on a registration phase which is secure against the attacks described in Sect. 3. In our protocol, we consider the use of a pairwise of credentials for each voter. One credential will be used for authentication, and the other one to hide the vote value during voting phase. We will also consider the use of indexes that are associated to voters in order to reduce the computational complexity during tallying phase. Note that our protocol is based on a new ballot's encryption function which allows voters to submit valid ballots in the presence of a coercer who forces them to cast a particular vote.

In what follows, we describe at first the communication model and the adversary capabilities. Then, we present in detail the process of each phase of our e-voting protocol.

4.1 Communication Model

Our e-voting protocol includes a Supervisor Authority noted SA, a set of l Registration Authorities $RA_1, RA_2, \ldots, RA_l$, a set of n Tallying Authorities $TA_1, TA_2, \ldots, TA_n$ and a set of m Voters $V_1, V_2, \ldots, V_m$. We consider the use of two bulletin boards. The first one is the Credentials Bulletin Board (CBB), the second one is the Ballots Bulletin Board (BBB). During the registration phase, we use an untapabble channel between voters and registration authorities. During the registration and the voting phases, we use anonymous channels for all messages published by voters.

4.2 Adversary Capabilities

We consider that our e-voting protocol is secure against an adversary with the following capabilities:

- The adversary can corrupt up to $t - 1$ of the l registration authorities such that $(t - 1) \leq l/2$. The adversary can also corrupt up to $t - 1$ of the n tallying authorities such that $(t - 1) \leq n/2$. Thus, in both cases, the majority of authorities are honest.

- During the registration phase, an adversary cannot simulate voters. However, voters can be accompanied by a coercer when they submit their public credentials. He can coerce voters by forcing them to abstain or to submit a particular public credentials.
- During the voting phase, voters can be accompanied by a coercer when they cast their ballots. He can coerce voters by forcing them to abstain or to submit a particular vote. He can also force voters to sell or surrender their credentials.
- It will be assumed that an adversary cannot drop or inject messages on CBB and BBB.
- An adversary cannot spy on the network channel between the voter and the registration authorities during the registration phase. During voting and registration phases, we assume the existence of anonymous channels to avoid that an adversary identify the sender of a message casted on CBB and BBB.
- The adversary can perform any polynomial-time computation.

4.3   Notations

Let p and q denote two large prime numbers, such that $q|(p-1)$. Let further G_q denote a subgroup of prime order q in Z_p^*, such that computing discrete logarithms in this group is infeasible. Moreover, g and h denote independently selected generators of G_q. Note that we perform all the computations in Z_q.

In our e-voting protocol, instead of ElGamal encryption, we use a variant of the encryption function defined by Schoenmakers in [6]. In what follows, the encryption of a message m under the public key pk and a random value $r \in_R Z_q$ is noted $Enc(m, pk, r)$ and includes the pair of values A_m and B_m, such as:

$$Enc(m, pk, r) = (A_m, B_m) = (g^r, pk^{m+r})$$

In order to simplify this notation, we omit pk and r when they are clear from context and we simply use $Enc(m)$.

4.4   Our Secure Protocol of the Registration Phase

In this subsection, we define a registration protocol which is secure against attacks described in Sect. 3. During our registration phase, each voter V_j needs to have two credentials. The first one is the authentication credential noted $C1_j$. It's used by the voter to prove its legitimacy. The second one is the ballot credential noted $C2_j$. It's used under the vote encryption to hide the value of vote and to ensure incoercibility.

In what follows, we present at first the modified initialization phase of our protocol. Second, we present the secure protocol of our registration phase. Finally we studied the security of our registration protocol.

Initialization. First, tallying authorities use the DKG protocol defined in [13] to jointly generate a secret and public keys (sk, pk) without resorting to a trusted party. Second, the supervisor SA posts on CBB the list of eligible voters

$V_1, V_2, ..., V_m$ with their public keys. As Civitas, we assume that each voter owns a registration key to authenticate during registration phase, and a designation key used to provide fake credentials. In addition, the supervisor SA publishes on BBB the list of standard encryptions of valid votes. Let L be the total number of candidates. The list $(Enc(v_1), Enc(v_2), ..., Enc(v_L))$ contains encryptions of valid votes $(v_1, v_2, ..., v_L)$.

Therefore, each registration authority chooses randomly secret credential shares $c1_{i,j}$ and $c2_{i,j}$ (related to private credentials $C1_j$ and $C2_j$) for each voter V_j and publishes on CBB the values $S1_{i,j}$ and $S2_{i,j}$ such as:

$$[S1_{i,j} = Enc(c1_{i,j}, pk, \varepsilon1_{i,j}), S2_{i,j} = Enc(c2_{i,j}, pk, \varepsilon2_{i,j})]$$

where $\varepsilon1_{i,j}$ and $\varepsilon2_{i,j}$ are randomly chosen in Z_q.

Our registration protocol. Here, it will be assumed that voters and registration authorities are already authenticated. The registration protocol runs as follows:

1. V_j contacts each RA_i to receive shares $c1_{i,j}$ and $c2_{i,j}$ of his private credentials $C1_j$ and $C2_j$.
2. Each RA_i sends secretly to V_j the shares $c1_{i,j}$ and $c2_{i,j}$, and two proofs $DVRP_1$ and $DVRP_2$ convincing only V_j that $S1_{i,j}$ and $S2_{i,j}$ are valid. $DVRP_1$ shows that $S1_{i,j} = (g^{\varepsilon1_{i,j}}, pk^{c1_{i,j}+\varepsilon1_{i,j}})$ is the re-encryption of $(g^0, pk^{c1_{i,j}})$. Here, it will be assumed that $(g^0, pk^{c1_{i,j}})$ is the initial encrypted credential share and that $(g^{\varepsilon1_{i,j}}, pk^{c1_{i,j}+\varepsilon1_{i,j}})$ is the re-encrypted credential share computed by RA_i[6]. Thus, $DVRP_1$ proves that $(g^{\varepsilon1_{i,j}}/g^0)$ and $(pk^{c1_{i,j}+\varepsilon1_{i,j}}/pk^{c1_{i,j}})$ have the same discrete logarithm for bases g and pk, respectively. In the same manner, $DVRP_2$ convinces only V_j that $S2_{i,j}$ is valid.
3. V_j verifies $DVRP_1$ and $DVRP_2$ proofs. We define the set $QUAL$ of honest registration authorities who sent valid shares and proofs. V_j chooses the set $QUAL$ such that $|QUAL| \geq t$ and computes $Enc(QUAL)$.
4. V_j computes his private credentials $C1_j$ and $C2_j$ from valid received shares $c1_{i,j}$ and $c2_{i,j}$. Note here that $C1_j$ and $C2_j$ are computed as the sum of secret shares $c1_{i,j}$ and $c2_{i,j}$ such that $C1_j = \sum_{i \in QUAL} c1_{i,j}$ and $C2_j = \sum_{i \in QUAL} c2_{i,j}$. Then, V_j computes his public credentials $S1_j = Enc(C1_j)$ and $S2_j = Enc(C2_j)$.
5. V_j computes his encrypted index $Enc(index_j)$. We assume that a specific index noted $index_j$ is assigned for each voter. This index can be considered as the voter's rank in CBB. It will be used by tallying authorities during the tallying phase to find easily on CBB the values $S1_{i,j}$ and $S2_{i,j}$ associated to V_j.
6. V_j provides a zero-knowledge proof noted ZKP_{V_j}, based on the technique of [4], proving knowledge of random values used to compute $S1_j$, $S2_j$, $Enc(QUAL)$, and $Enc(index_j)$. This proof avoid that an adversary publish messages in function of previously submitted values.

---

[6] Compared to Civitas, RA_i doesn't compute an additional encrypted share $S1'_{i,j}$ and V_j doesn't have to verify later the validity of $S1'_{i,j}$.

7. Finally, V_j publishes on CBB, an unsigned message noted D_{V_j} which contains the following elements:

$$D_{V_j} = [S1_j, S2_j, Enc(QUAL), Enc(index_j), ZKP_{V_j}]$$

Note here, that to ensure resistance coercion during the registration phase, we allow voters to submit D_{V_j} more than once. In addition, only a single valid value D_{V_j} can be used by each voter to vote. If a dishonest voter publishes several valid D_{V_j} and used them to cast several ballots, tallying authorities detect this during the tallying phase and eliminate all these ballots.

Security against attacks and coercion resistance. To avoid the attack described by Shirazi et al. (see Sect. 3), we ask each voter to compute his credential from valid credential shares received from a subset $QUAL$[7] of trusted registration authorities. The value of $QUAL$ and the public credentials $S1_j$ and $S2_j$ are computed by the voter and published on CBB in encrypted form under D_{V_j}. In other words, $S1_j$ and $S2_j$ are not computed from all public credential shares $S1_{i,j}$ and $S2_{i,j}$ published by all registration authorities and a dishonest authority cannot imped voters from voting if he send them an invalid credential shares.

To provide a solution for the attack described at the end of the Sect. 3, in our registration protocol, the public credential $S1_j$ and $S2_j$ are not computed from the public values $S1_{i,j}$ and $S2_{i,j}$ published by registration authorities but from a subset of the valid credential shares that voter received such that $S1_j = Enc(\sum_{i \in QUAL} c1_{i,j})$ and $S2_j = Enc(\sum_{i \in QUAL} c2_{i,j})$. Since a dishonest authority cannot re-run the registration process and have no information on the values $c1_{i,j}$ and $c2_{i,j}$, he cannot influence the distribution of the generated credentials beside the values $S1_{i,j}$ and $S2_{i,j}$ that he will publish. Reasoning in the same way, even a set of dishonest registration authorities cannot modify the distribution of the generated credentials.

To ensure coercion resistance during the registration process, we use the same idea proposed by Civitas during the voting process. The idea is based on the fact that voters can reveal fake credentials for their real credentials to a coercer. Note that each voter can re-publish several times D_{V_j}. The coercer may force the voter to register correctly or not in front of him. In both cases, the voter will use fake credentials[8]. The coercer may also wants the voter to abstain from registering. In all cases, the voter behaves however the coercer asks, and submits another valid D_{V_j} when he is alone. It will be assumed that there are secret moments in time wherein a voter is not accompanied by the coercer. Note here that unlike the voting phase, the registration phase can be spread over several weeks or months. Thus, each voter can find a private moment to register.

---

[7] Note that the voter is the only one who can determine the subset $QUAL$. This is due to the $DVRP$ proof which convinces only the voter that the credential share is valid.

[8] In the first case, the coercer knows it and wants to prevent voter from registering, and in the second case, the voter can use fake credentials without being caught by the coercer.

4.5   Voting Phase

To vote, each voter V_j chooses a valid vote v_j and posts on BBB an unsigned message which contains his ballot B_{V_j} such as:

$$B_{V_j} = [Enc(v_j - C2_j), \widetilde{S1}_j, Enc(\widetilde{index}_j), \widetilde{ZKP}_{V_j}]$$

where $\widetilde{S1}_j$ is the encryption of $C1_j$ and $Enc(\widetilde{index}_j)^9$ is the encryption of $index_j$. $\widetilde{ZKP}_{V_j}$ is based on the technique of [4] and proves knowledge of random values used to encrypt $Enc(v_j - C2_j)$, $\widetilde{S1}_j$ and $Enc(\widetilde{index}_j)$.

Resisting Coercion. The coercer may force the voter to submit a valid ballot B_{V_j} or not. If the coercer forces the voter to submit a particular vote, the voter does so with a fake ballot credential and a valid authentication credential[10]. Let coercer vote be v_c. The voter V_j chooses one credential share $c2_{k,j}$ and claims that $c2_{k,j}^{fake} = c2_{k,j} + v_c - v_j$. V_j casts a valid encrypted ballot which contain his real vote v_j in encrypted form such as:

$$Enc(v_j - C2_j, pk, \lambda_j) = (g^{\lambda_j}, pk^{v_c + \lambda_j - c2_{k,j}^{fake} - \Sigma_{i \in \{QUAL \setminus k\}} c2_{i,j}}) = (g^{\lambda_j}, pk^{v_j + \lambda_j - \Sigma_{i \in QUAL} c2_{i,j}})$$

where λ_j is randomly chosen in Z_q. Thus, V_j can submit a valid ballot B_{V_j} despite the presence of the coercer.

Otherwise, if the coercer forces the voter to sell or reveal his credentials, the voter does so with fake credentials. The coercer may also force the voter to abstain from voting. In these cases, the voter behaves however the coercer asks, and votes when he is alone.

4.6   Tallying Phase

This phase is inspired from the modified version of Civitas protocol presented in [3] which reduces the tallying time process from quadratic to linear time. Furthermore, this solution fits perfectly with our protocol and enables us to verify the validity of D_{V_j} and B_{V_j}. Our tallying protocol runs as follows:

A. Regarding BBB
  1. Tallying authorities verify $\widetilde{ZKP}_{V_j}$ in ballots B_{V_j} posted on BBB and eliminate invalid ones.

---

[9] $Enc(\widetilde{index}_j)$ will be used to eliminate invalid ballots with invalid votes or invalid authentication credentials. Note also that the use of this index during the tallying phase reduce the tallying process from quadratic to linear complexity in the number of casted ballots [3].

[10] To prevent a coercer from re-using the authentication credential to submit another vote, it will be assumed that the first valid ballot casted into BBB will be considered. The other ones will be eliminated.

2. Tallying authorities eliminate duplicated ballots B_{V_j} casted with a same authentication credential $\widehat{S1_j}$[11]. For this, we use the linear-time scheme proposed by Smith and Weber [7,8] on values $\widetilde{S1_j}$.

3. Then, tallying authorities add an additional number of fake B_{V_j} for each voter [3]. This prevents discovering who has cast a vote. The resulting list of ballots is passed as input to a first re-encryption mix-net which outputs:

$$(Enc(v_j - C2_j)', \widetilde{S1}'_j, Enc(\widetilde{index_j})')$$

B. Regarding CBB

1. Tallying authorities verify ZKP_{V_j} related to D_{V_j} posted on CBB and eliminate invalid ones.

2. Then, a random number of fake D_{V_j} are added by trusted authorities on CBB to avoid knowing voters who have voted or simply registered when indexes will be decrypted (same as step A.3.). The resulting list is passed as input to a re-encryption mix-net which outputs:

$$(S1'_j, S2'_j, Enc(QUAL)', Enc(index_j)')$$

C. Regarding CBB and BBB

1. Tallying authorities jointly decrypt $Enc(index_j)'$ on CBB and $Enc(index_j)'$ on BBB. Public credentials and ballots with invalid indexes will be removed. They also decrypt $Enc(QUAL)'$ and retrieve for each $index_j$ the values $\widehat{S1_j} = \prod_{i \in QUAL} Enc(c1_{i,j})$ and $\widehat{S2_j} = \prod_{i \in QUAL} Enc(c2_{i,j})$ from BBB. Recall that these values are published by registration authorities during the initialization phase. Thus, tallying authorities create a list of tuples:

$$(Enc(v_j - C2_j)', \widetilde{S1}'_j, S1'_j, S2'_j, \widehat{S1_j}, \widehat{S2_j}, Enc(index_j)')$$

2. These tuples are passed to a re-encryption mix-net which outputs tuples:

$$(Enc(v_j - C2_j)'', \widetilde{S1}''_j, S1''_j, S2''_j, \widehat{S1}'_j, \widehat{S2}'_j, Enc(index_j)'')$$

3. For each tuple, tallying authorities apply PET on $(S1''_j, \widehat{S1}'_j)$, and PET on $(S2''_j, \widehat{S2}'_j)$. This eliminate tuples formed from invalid D_{V_j} submitted by voters during the registration phase, and tuples formed from fakes D_{V_j} added during step B.2.

4. Then, for each tuple, tallying authorities apply PET on $(\widetilde{S1}''_j, S1''_j)$ to remove tuples formed from ballots with invalid authentication credential $C1_j$, and tuples formed from fake ballots generated during step A.3.

---

[11] Note that we keep only the first ballot B_{V_j}, the other duplicated ballots with the same authentication credential are eliminated.

5. Tallying authorities remove all remaining tuples casted with the same index. For this we use the linear-time scheme of Smith and Weber [7,8] on values $Enc(index_j)''$. Note that in this step, if there are tuples with the same index, this implies that a dishonest voter publishes several public valid credentials D_{V_j} and used them to cast several ballots B_{V_j}.

6. Then, for each valid tuple, tallying authorities compute $Enc(v_j) = Enc(v_j - C2_j)'' * S2_j''$ and apply PET on $Enc(v_j)$ and each element in the list of standard encryptions of valid votes. This allows to detect and remove invalid encrypted votes.

7. Finally, tallying authorities jointly decrypt valid ballots and publish the final voting result. Let us take the case of a binary vote in which voters have to answer with 1 (yes) or 0 (no). Suppose that at least M voters cast valid ballots. Tallying authorities collect valid encrypted votes $Enc(v_j) = (A_{v_j}, B_{v_j})$ and use the Lagrange interpolation to compute the value $\prod_{j=1}^{M}[A_{v_j}]^{sk}$. Then, they compute $R = \prod_{j=1}^{M} B_{v_j}/[\prod_{j=1}^{M} A_{v_j}]^{sk} = pk^{\sum_{j=1}^{M} v_j}$. Note that computing the value of $v_1 + v_2 + \dots v_M$ is possible for a reasonable size of M [15]. To prove the validity of the final result, tallying authorities show that R is correct by using proof of the equality of two discrete logarithms [16] proving that $\prod_{j=1}^{M} A_{v_j}$ and $\prod_{j=1}^{M} B_{v_j}/R$ have the same discrete logarithm for bases g and pk, respectively.

Note that if BBB includes N casted ballots, applying PET during steps C.3., C.4., and C.6. does not cause worst-case running time. In fact, if CBB includes K casted D_{V_j} for each ballot B_{V_j} on BBB, then the total number of formed tuples (with merged data from boards CBB and BBB) is $K * N$. Clearly, if K is independent of N for all ballots, then our tallying process runs in $O(N)$ time.

5   Security Analysis

Civitas relies on a set of trust assumptions to ensure the trustworthiness of the whole protocol. We assume that our protocol is based on the same trust assumptions with some modifications. In this section, we first discuss the modified trust assumptions. Second, we present the most important security requirements ensured by our e-voting protocol.

5.1   Trust Assumptions

In Civitas, it was assumed that each voter trusts at least one registration authority. We replace this assumption by a new one, such that:

New Trust Assumption 1. Each voter trusts at least t of the registration authorities and the channel from the voter to the voter's trusted registration authorities is untappable.

It was assumed that the majority of registration authorities are honest, thus at most we have $t - 1$ dishonest registration authorities. In our secure modified registration protocol, the voter must select the set $QUAL$ such that the size of $QUAL$ is greater than t. Otherwise, a dishonest voter may cooperate with a subset of dishonest registration authorities by revealing the values of his private credentials.

In our protocol, instead of ElGamal encryption which is secure under the decisional Diffie-Hellman assumption (DDH), we use the encryption function defined by Schoenmakers [6]. The security of this encryption function is based on the computational Diffie-Hellman (CDH) assumption. Therefore, we add the following assumption:

New Trust Assumption 2. Under the CDH assumption, it is impossible to break the encryption of messages.

The encryption of a message m under the public key pk and a random value r is defined as $Enc(m, pk, r) = (A_m, B_m) = (g^r, pk^{m+r})$. For a dishonest party knowing the public values $pk = g^{sk}$, $A_m = g^r$ and $B_m = pk^{m+r}$, breaking the encryption of m implies computing pk^m (for a reasonable size of m [15]). To be able to do that, the dishonest party have to compute $pk^m = B_m/g^{sk*r}$ from the values B_m, $pk = g^{sk}$ and $A_m = g^r$. This implies computing g^{sk*r} from the values g^{sk} and g^r. Recall that the CDH assumption states that it is infeasible to compute g^{sk*r} given g^{sk} and g^r. Thus, the dishonest party cannot break the encryption of messages.

5.2 Security Requirements

E-voting protocols must satisfy security requirements of voting process. In this paper, we focus our analysis on the following requirements:

- **Privacy.** All casted ballots must be secret and/or no traceability between the voter and his ballot can be established.
  In our protocol, an adversary cannot know values from encrypted elements under B_{V_j} and D_{V_j} published on BBB and CBB (see Sect. 5.1 - New Trust Assumption 2). Moreover, all proofs are zero-knowledge. Thus, any information related to votes cannot be known from these proofs. To ensure anonymity, both the list of D_{V_j} and B_{V_j} are passed to mix-nets during steps A.3., B.2. and C.2. of tallying phase (see Sect. 4.6). In addition, tallying authorities generate fake B_{V_j} and D_{V_j} during steps A.3. and B.2. of tallying phase (see Sect. 4.6) to anonymize ballots and credentials, and to avoid knowing voters who have been registered or voted when decrypting indexes.
- **Coercion-Resistance.** This property defends voters from coercion and prevent selling of votes.
  Our protocol ensures coercion during registration and voting phases. During both phases, if a voter V_j is under the threat of a coercer, he behaves however this coercer asks with fake private credentials. Then, during a private moment, V_j can submit another valid values D_{V_j} and B_{V_j} with his real credentials $C1_j$ and $C2_j$. Only valid values casted with valid credentials will be taken into account by authorities during tallying phase. The coercer cannot detect the real values submitted by the voter because tallying authorities generate additional fake D_{V_j} and B_{V_j} for each voter.

Note that neither the voter nor the coercer can prove or verify the validity or the invalidity of private credentials $C1_j$ and $C2_j$ used under the encryption of D_{V_j} and B_{V_j}. In addition, the encryption of voter's choice $Enc(v_j - C2_j)$ is computed using $C2_j$. Therefore, V_j cannot prove the validity of his choice and cannot sell his vote.

Thus, the coercer cannot control voter's choice and the voter cannot sell his vote. In both cases, the adversary will be confused about the validity of the submitted values.

- **Verifiability.** Verifiability is composed of two sub-properties:
  - **Individual verifiability**: Each voter can check if his ballot has been correctly recorded.

    In our protocol, each voter can verify that submitted values D_{V_j} and B_{V_j} are correctly recorded simply by consulting CBB and BBB.

  - **Universally verifiability**: Any party can check the validity of the tallying process and the validity of the final voting result.

    In our protocol, we assume that tallying authorities use verifiable re-encryption mix-nets based on zero-knowledge proofs. Thus, each tallying authority must provide proofs of his honesty during tallying process. Each voter (or any party) can check the validity of the tallying by verifying the validity proofs of resulted lists obtained from the mix-nets in each step.

6   Conclusion

In this paper, we showed that Civitas' registration phase is insecure and subject to some attacks. For this purpose, we proposed a fully-remote incoercible e-voting protocol based on a new registration protocol which is secure against the described attacks and which ensures a uniform distribution of the generated credentials. In addition, compared to Civitas, we reduce the complexity of tallying phase from quadratic to linear time. Our e-voting protocol becomes then more secure and requires less computational costs than Civitas protocol.

Moreover, the proposed protocol is based on a new ballot's encryption function that prevents voters from proving the validity of their encrypted votes and allows them to vote even if they are under a threat of a coercer.

As future researches, we intend to propose solutions to implement our e-voting protocol from a practical point of view. It is an interesting open issue whether we can contribute to implement a secure fully remote e-voting protocol which can be used within real world elections.

References

1. Clarkson, M., Chong, S., Myers, A.: Civitas: a secure remote voting system. In: Dagstuhl Seminar Proceedings. Schloss Dagstuhl-Leibniz-Zentrum fúr Informatik (2008)
2. Gennaro, R., Jarecki, S., Krawczyk, H., Rabin, T.: Secure distributed key generation for discrete-log based cryptosystems. J. Cryptology **20**(1), 51–83 (2007)

3. Spycher, O., Koenig, R., Haenni, R., Schläpfer, M.: A new approach towards coercion-resistant remote e-voting in linear time. In: Danezis, G. (ed.) FC 2011. LNCS, vol. 7035, pp. 182–189. Springer, Heidelberg (2012). doi:10.1007/978-3-642-27576-0_15

4. Camenisch, J., Stadler, M.: Efficient group signature schemes for large groups. In: Kaliski, B.S. (ed.) CRYPTO 1997. LNCS, vol. 1294, pp. 410–424. Springer, Heidelberg (1997). doi:10.1007/BFb0052252

5. Jakobsson, M., Juels, A.: Mix and match: secure function evaluation via ciphertexts. In: Okamoto, T. (ed.) ASIACRYPT 2000. LNCS, vol. 1976, pp. 162–177. Springer, Heidelberg (2000). doi:10.1007/3-540-44448-3_13

6. Schoenmakers, B.: A simple publicly verifiable secret sharing scheme and its application to electronic voting. In: Wiener, M. (ed.) CRYPTO 1999. LNCS, vol. 1666, pp. 148–164. Springer, Heidelberg (1999). doi:10.1007/3-540-48405-1_10

7. Smith, W.D.: New cryptographic election protocol with best-known theoretical properties. In: Proceedings of Workshop on Frontiers in Electronic Elections, September 2005

8. Weber, S.G., Araujo, R., Buchmann, J.: On coercion-resistant electronic elections with linear work. In: The Second International Conference on Availability, Reliability and Security 2007, ARES 2007, pp. 908–916. IEEE, April 2007

9. Shirazi, F., Neumann, S., Ciolacu, I., Volkamer, M.: Robust electronic voting: Introducing robustness in civitas. In: 2011 International Workshop on Requirements Engineering for Electronic Voting Systems (REVOTE), pp. 47–55. IEEE, August 2011

10. Araújo, R., Foulle, S., Traoré, J.: A practical and secure coercion-resistant scheme for internet voting. In: Chaum, D., Jakobsson, M., Rivest, R.L., Ryan, P.Y.A., Benaloh, J., Kutylowski, M., Adida, B. (eds.) Towards Trustworthy Elections. LNCS, vol. 6000, pp. 330–342. Springer, Heidelberg (2010). doi:10.1007/978-3-642-12980-3_20

11. Neumann, S., Volkamer, M.: Civitas and the real world: problems and solutions from a practical point of view. In: 2012 Seventh International Conference on Availability, Reliability and Security (ARES), pp. 180–185. IEEE, August 2012

12. Neumann, S., Feier, C., Volkamer, M., Koenig, R.E.: Towards a practical JCJ/Civitas implementation. IACR Cryptology ePrint Archive 2013, p. 464 (2013)

13. Neji, W., Blibech, K., Ben Rajeb, N.: Distributed key generation protocol with a new complaint management strategy. Security and Communication Networks (2016)

14. Juels, A., Catalano, D., Jakobsson, M.: Coercion-resistant electronic elections. In: Proceedings of the 2005 ACM Workshop on Privacy in the Electronic Society, pp. 61–70. ACM, November 2005

15. Cramer, R., Gennaro, R., Schoenmakers, B.: A secure and optimally efficient multiauthority election scheme. Eur. Trans. Telecommun. 8(5), 481–490 (1997)

16. Chaum, D., Pedersen, T.P.: Wallet databases with observers. In: Brickell, E.F. (ed.) CRYPTO 1992. LNCS, vol. 740, pp. 89–105. Springer, Heidelberg (1993). doi:10.1007/3-540-48071-4_7

17. Hirt, M., Sako, K.: Efficient receipt-free voting based on homomorphic encryption. In: Preneel, B. (ed.) EUROCRYPT 2000. LNCS, vol. 1807, pp. 539–556. Springer, Heidelberg (2000). doi:10.1007/3-540-45539-6_38

Software Engineering

A Comparative Study of Software Testing Techniques

Meriem Atifi[⊠], Abdelaziz Mamouni[⊠], and Abdelaziz Marzak[⊠]

Faculty of Sciences Ben M'sik,
University Hassan II of Casablanca, Casablanca, Morocco
Meryematif@gmail.com, Mamouni.abdelaziz@gmail.com,
Marzak@hotmail.com

Abstract. Nowadays, software systems have become an essential element in our daily life. To ensure the quality and operation of software, testing activities have become primordial in the software development life cycle (SDLC). Indeed, software bugs can potentially cause dramatic consequences if the product is released to the end user without testing. The software testing role is to verify that the actual result and the expected result are consistent and ensure that the system is delivered without bugs. Many techniques, approaches and tools have been proposed to help check that the system is defect free. In this paper, we highlight two software testing techniques considered among the most used techniques to perform software tests, and then we perform a comparative study of these techniques, the approaches that supports studied techniques, and the tools used for each technique. We have selected the first technique based on the 2014 survey [62] that heighted the motivations for using the Model-based-testing, and by analyzing the survey results we have found that some MBT limits are benefits in Risk based testing, the second technique in our study.

Keywords: Software systems · Software testing · Software testing approaches · Model-based testing · Risk-based testing

1 Introduction

Software system consists of a number of separate programs, configuration files, which are used to set up these programs, system documentation, which describes the structure of the system, and user documentation, which explains how to use the system and web sites for users to download recent product information [59]. Nowadays, software systems have become an essential part of our daily life. We use these software systems daily and have generally tried to keep them updated as much as possible. While in many times these software systems do not work as expected. Therefore, creating high-quality software is an intellectual challenge. Generally this quality is ensured by a test activity. However, this activity is time consuming, and too demanding as far as resources are concerned, and it is essential to ensure a certain percent of software quality. Indeed, a defect in software can have serious consequences for users and companies. These consequences may cause trivial issues viz; loss of money, time, business credibility or even loss of life. This was the case, for example in medicine in 1985, the Therac 25,

A. El Abbadi and B. Garbinato (Eds.): NETYS 2017, LNCS 10299, pp. 373–390, 2017.
DOI: 10.1007/978-3-319-59647-1_27

was a radiation therapy machine for treating cancer. A dysfunction of software has led to an overdose of radiation and was the cause of several deaths. Also the flight 501 failure of Ariane 5 in 1996 caused by a problem in specification, the estimated loss of this failure is 8.5 BILLION dollars. And more recently, on 6 January 2010, the German bank card holders designed by Gemalto had the unpleasant surprise of not being able to use their cards in some terminals. However, even if this bug lasted only one day, Gemalto has estimated the cost associated between 6 and 10 million. These accidents show that regardless of the scope of the software, it is necessary to validate and verify its operation and quality before using it. To ensure the quality and operation of software, testing activities have become primordial in the software development life cycle (SDLC). Indeed, software testing is a process of validating and verifying that a software product works as expected. Recently, the Software testing activity has changed dramatically, the complexity of IT systems has increased, the applications areas have been expanded, and the costs and consequences of bugs became higher, turning testing into an essential activity that should not be overlooked during the software development cycle. Testing is a vital part of software development, and it is important to start it as early as possible, and to make testing a part of the process of deciding requirements [60]. For that, in this present paper, we will present the tools, the processes, and the approaches of existing testing techniques. Also, this paper offers a detailed comparison between these testing techniques, especially, two major techniques viz; the model based testing technique (MBT), which is an application of model-based design to perform software testing or system testing. Models can be used to represent the desired behaviour of a System Under Test (SUT), or to represent testing strategies and a test environment; and the risk based testing technique (RBT), which is a type of software testing that functions as an organizational principle used to prioritize the tests of features and functions in software, based on the risk of failure, the function of their importance and likelihood or impact of failure [61].

The rest of this paper is organized as follows. Section 2 exposes general processes of MBT and RBT techniques, used tools and stockholders of each technique. Section 3 presents a classification of approaches related to each technique. Section 5 present some MBT and RBT Advantages and Limits, Sect. 6 discuss and presents the results of our analysis. Finally, Sect. 7 describes conclusion and future work.

2   MBT and RBT Processes

2.1   Model-Based Testing

The MBT (Model-Based Testing) is a form or a technique that aims to automatically generate test cases from formal specification or models describing the expected behaviour of the system under test. The behaviour model or formal specification are built from requirements and represents the software characteristics. It consists in managing and listing the requirements, creating a behavioural model of the SUT based on this list of requirements in order to generate abstracts tests cases and Requirements Traceability Matrix (RTX) by using the selection criteria that aim the model coverage and detect certain types of fault. The tests cases generated are then concretized, making them executable on the SUT, the actual result and the expected result are then compared in order to get a verdict. Based on MBT application steps, used tools and stockholders, we present the following process.

As shown in Fig. 1 above, the process of Model-based testing can be splitted into five main steps. These steps will be explained further below.

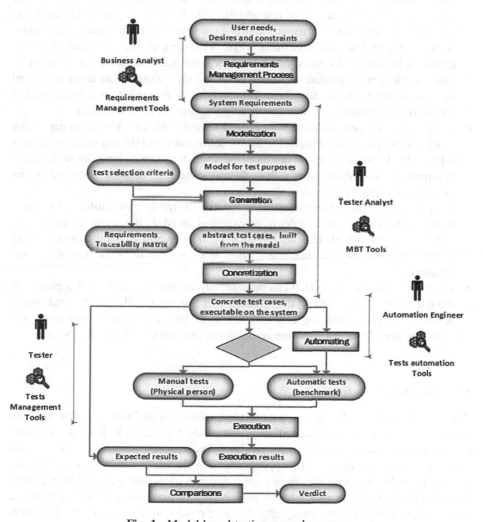

Fig. 1. Model-based testing general process

- Requirements management: The first step of model based testing is to collect customer needs, desires and constraints, manage and classify them as requirements. This first step is potentially the most important step in a process of testing software such as MBT. Requirement management step in MBT involves the collection, analysis, prioritization, validation, definition and control of all customer business requirements, it serves to create a requirement repository that is the basis of communication between analysts and testers and is define in a structured way the expected result for the software, in different terms (functional, technical, security, load and response time…).

- Modelling: The main purpose of the modelling step in MBT is to model the system requirements, it consists in creating a behaviour model that describes the expected behaviour of the system under test and suitable for test purposes, this model is created by a tester analyst using requirements resulting from requirements management step and described in many ways, depending on the discipline. It can be described by use of diagrams, tables, text, or other kinds of notations. It might be expressed in a mathematical formalism or informally, where the meaning is derived by convention kinds of notations. They might be expressed in a mathematical formalism or informally, where the meaning is derived by convention.

- Generation: The generation step is realized on the basis of a test generator which takes as input the model designed in the modelling step and the test selection criteria selected by the test analyst and produces the abstract test cases from the model and a requirements traceability matrix that illustrates the link between tests and model elements covered by the tests.

- Concretization: The concretization step consists to translate the abstracts test cases to executables test cases in order to be executed on SUT. It consists in making the link between the model elements and the system's concrete elements, and involving specific adapters and manual intervention that requires the expertise of the test engineer.

- Execution: The execution step can be manually or automatically. In this phase, all the test cases are executed on the system under test, eventually the obtained results are then compared with the expected results to give a verdict for test cases and consequently give a status on the operation of the product [1, 2, 13, 15–18].

2.2   Risk-Based Testing

When we cannot test exhaustively, we must test selectively and achieve better with less in time and resources and without affecting the product quality. The RBT is a software testing technique or method that uses risk as a basis for test planning, It uses risk to select, prioritize and manage the appropriate tests during test execution and consequently to make sure that the limited time and resources are used to test the most important things [3, 5]. In simple terms, Risk is an undesirable event whose appearance is not certain and having as consequence negative results on the project objectives such as impact on completion date, costs, the quality, the company image, etc. Thus, the risk may be considered as the composition of two factors viz; the probability of occurrence of an undesirable event and the severity of the potential consequences of the undesirable event. Based on RBT application steps, used tools and stockholders [3, 7, 62], we present in Fig. 2 below, the process of risk-based testing that can be divided into five main steps.

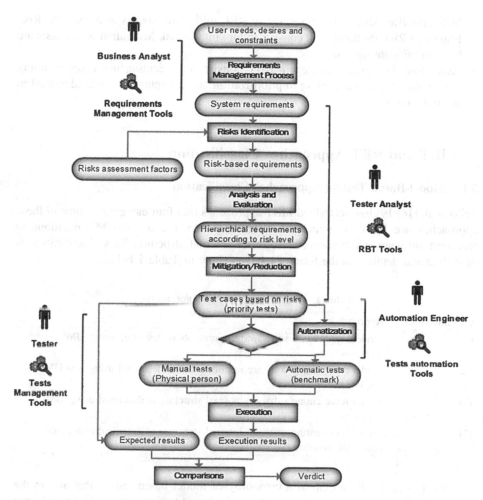

Fig. 2. Risk-based testing general process

- Requirements management: As the MBT process, RBT process start with requirements management step to extract and identify requirements from system specifications.
- Risks identification: Identifying risks is an absolutely essential activity in RBT process, it involves making a list of everything that might potentially come up and disrupt the normal flow of project, and provides the indicators that allows the organization to identify major risks before they impact operations and hence the business. It consists to identify and describe all requirements in terms of risk involved in the project. Thus at the end of this step all risk items are identified.
- Analysis and Evaluation: Risk analysis and evaluation is the second step of risk management in RBT process. It consists in studying the risks identified in risk identification phase, categorizing them, determining the level of risk by specifying likelihood and impact of the risk and then assigning the level of risk to each item.

- Mitigation/Reduction: The objective of Risk mitigation step is to reduce the Risk Impact or Risk Probability. It consists in looking for risk Mitigation where tests are built to mitigate the risk.
- Execution: The execution step in RBT consists in executing test cases resulting from reduction step according to prioritization and acceptance criteria identified in the risks report.

3   MBT and RBT Approaches Classification

3.1   Model-Based Testing Approaches Classification

Arilo et al. [16, 19] have classified MBT approaches into four categories, some of these approaches use UML diagrams, whereas, the others use a non-UML notations to represent software requirements or software internal structure. This classification is described and detailed in the form of table as show in Table 1 below.

Table 1. Classification of MBT approaches

Classifications	Approaches
C1	Model representing software requirements is described using UML diagrams
C2	Model representing software requirements is described using non-UML notation
C3	Model representing software internal structure is described using UML diagrams
C4	Model representing software internal structure is described using any non-UML notation

Utting et al. [2] have defined a taxonomy of model based testing that allows the characterization of different approaches to model-based testing, they have defined three general classes viz; model specification, test generation and test execution. Each of these classes is divided into various categories viz; model specification: It is divided into scope, characteristics and paradigm categories; test generation: It is divided into test selection criteria and technology categories; and test execution: It is divided into online test execution and offline test execution. Based on this taxonomy, Utting et al. have classified a collection of existing approaches in order to show the characteristics of those approaches to target various application domains. They have classified the existing approaches into two main categories: approaches to model-based test case generation and approaches to model-based test input generation. Felderer et al. [6] have defined a novel classification of model-based security testing approaches. They have classified the existing approaches into two dimensions viz; automated test generation and risk. The first dimension describes how much of the system and the security requirements is captured by formal models. The second dimension "risk" can have the values integrated into the model or not integrated into the model. Anand et al. [58] have performed a survey of methodologies for automated software test case generation. They have classified the MBT approaches into three categories viz; axiomatic approaches that use scenario-oriented notations, finite state machine approaches that use state-oriented notations, and labelled transition system approaches that use process-oriented notations.

3.2 Risk-Based Testing Approaches Classification

In other respects, for RBT technique, Erdogan et al. [5] have classified the approaches that use both tests and risks into two global categories, some approaches when risk is used to focus testing, and others when test is used to focus risk. It defines the first category for test-based risk analysis (TR), and the second category for risk-based testing (RT). In Table 2 below we expose the approaches studied by Erdogan et al. [5] and Alam et al. [3] in order of this classification. Otherwise, depending on main focus, Erdogan et al. have classified RBT approaches into eight categories viz;

Table 2. TR & RT approaches classification

TR category	RT category
Wong 2005 [39] Schneidewind2007 [49] Bach Inside-Out1999 [52]	Amland2000 [20], Felderer2012 [21], Felderer2013 [22], Felderer2015, Redmill2004 [23], Redmill2005 [24], Yoon 2011 [25], Gleirscher2011 [26], Gleirscher2013 [27], Ray2013 [28], Kloos2011 [29], Nazier2012 [30], Wendland2012 [31], Xu2012 [32], Zimmermann2009 [33], Chen2003 [34], Chen2002 [35], Entin2012 [36], Stallbaum2008 [37], Hosseingholizadeh2010 [38], Kumar2009 [40], Rosenberg1999 [41], Bai [42, 43], Casado2010 [44], Murthy2009 [46], Zech2011 [47], Zech2012 [48], Souza2010 [50], Bach-Outside-In1999 [51], Paul2002 [52], Stålhane2003 [54] and Palanivel2014 [9]

- Approaches that combine risk analysis and testing at a general level as Amland2000, Felderer2012, Felderer2013 and Redmill2004 and Redmill2005;
- Approaches with main focus on model-based risk estimation as Gleirscher2011, Gleirscher2013 and Ray2013;
- Approaches with main focus on test-case generation as Kloos2011, Nazier2012 and Xu2012;
- Approaches with main focus on test-case analysis as Chen2003, Chen2002 and Entin2012;
- Approaches based on automatic source code analysis as Wong 2005 and Hosseingholizadeh2010;
- Approaches targeting specific programming paradigms as Kumar2009 and Rosenberg1999;
- Approaches targeting specific applications as Bai2009, Bai2012, Casado2010 and Zech2011;
- Approaches' aiming at measurement in the sense that measurement is the main issue as Schneidewind2007 and Souza2009.

4 MBT and RBT Supporting Tools

To benefit fully from any technique or approach as MBT or RBT, the automation supports are required to automate as much as possible and to increase the reliability of the software testing process. In MBT, the challenge is that from a formal, semi-formal or informal models generate complete test cases without human interference. On the other hand, in RBT approach, the challenge is how to manage, select, and evaluate risk in testing process. In this context, when practitioners want to adopt an MBT or RBT approach, they therefore seek associated tools. For MBT, a number of model-based testing tools have been proposed [8, 10–12, 18]. We can classify these tools in different criteria viz; tool category: Commercial (CL), Open Source (OS) or Academic (AC); model type: UML, SysML, FSM, EFSM, Textual Models (TM), and more; and test type: Functional Testing (FT), Non Functional Testing (NFT), Structural Testing (ST). The Table 3 below describes these tools according to these criteria. For RBT, the most used tools are test management systems that support RBT approaches [14]. Table 4 exposes some of the test management tools that support RBT and some tools intended for RBT technique.

Table 3. MBT tools classification

Tool	Category	Model type	Software area	Test type
4Test	CL	TM	All	FT
BPM-Xchange	CL	BPMN	All	FT
Conformiq Creator	CL	Activity Diagrams & DSL	All	FT
Conformiq Designer	CL	UML State Machines and QML	All	FT
DTM	CL	Custom activity model	All	ST
MaTeLo	CL	Markov chains	All	FT
MBTsuite	CL	UML, BPMN	All	FT
RT-Tester	CL	UML, SysML and Matlab	All (embedded real-time systems)	FT
Smartesting CertifyIt	CL	UML, OCL and BPMN	All (Enterprise IT applications)	FT
Microsoft's SpecExplorer	CL	model programs in C#, FSM/ASM	All	FT
TEMPPO Designer (IDATG)	CL	Task flow model	All	FT
TestCast	CL	UML State Machines	All (Embedded Systems)	FT & ST
TestOptimal	CL	FSM & E-FSM	All	FT & NFT
T-VEC	CL	Simulink	All (Embedded Systems)	ST

(*continued*)

Table 3. (*continued*)

Tool	Category	Model type	Software area	Test type
Conformiq's Qtronic	CL	UML, QM & TM	All	FT
Test Designer	CL	UML	All	FT
LTG [2, 57]	CL	UML, OCL and B abstract machines	All	FT
mbt	OS	FSM/EFSM	All	FT
GraphWalker	OS	FSM	All (nondeterministic systems)	FT
JTorX [2, 56]	OS(AC)	LTS	All	FT
Modbat	OS	EFSM	Specialized for API testing of program libraries	FT
ModelJUnit	OS	FSM & EFSM	All	FT
OSMO	OS	Model programming Java	All	FT
PyModel	OS	Python source	All	ST
Tcases	OS	TM	All	FT
JSXM	AC	SXM	All	FT
MISTA	AC	PrT net	All	FT & NFT
MoMuT::UML	AC	UML state machines & OOAS	All	FT
MOTES	AC	EFSM	All (Embedded Systems)	FT
AGEDIS	AC	UML (AML)	All (Component based distributed Systems)	FT
ParTeG	AC	UML & OCL	All	FT

5 MBT and RBT Advantages and Limits

The MBT and RBT solutions are highly effective testing techniques that can be used to perform and manage software testing. Each solution has distinct benefits and limits. In this context, Legeard [4], has classified the major MBT benefits that solved some problems of classical approaches into six areas viz; SUT fault detection, reduced testing cost and time, improved test quality, requirements defect detection, tractability management, and requirements evolution. Also, he discussed some of fundamental limitations that limit the usage areas of MBT approaches. In the other hand, Alam [3] in his paper highlight some benefits and limits of RBT. Table 5 present some major advantages and disadvantages of RBT and MBT Approaches.

Table 4. RBT tools classification

Tool	Category	Model type	Software area	Test type
HP Quality Center	CL	-	All	FT
Kristoffer Tool [14]	AC	-	All	FT & NFT
NORIZZK.COM (SaaS platform)	CL	-	All	FT & NFT
Sonata	OS	-	All	FT & NFT
Casado Framework [45]	AC	Transaction Model	Web services models and standards	NFT
ReQtest(SaaS platform)	CL	-	All	FT & NF
SOASense™ framework [40]	AC	-	Aspect oriented programming	ST
Hosseingholizadeh Tool [38]	AC	-	All	ST
RBTTool [55]	AC-OS	-	All	FT
RiteDAP [37]	AC	Activity diagrams	All	FT

Table 5. MBT and RBT limitations and advantages

Ref.	Remaining problems (Limits)	Solved problems (Advantages)
Hartman et al. [53] Arilo et al. [19] Monalisa et al. [18]	**MBT approach** • Cannot manage outdated requirements when the software evolves • One of practical limitations of model based testing is tester skills; the model designers must be able to design the models, in addition to being experts in the application area • Difficulty to analyze failed tests when any of the generated tests is failed • Difficulty to model some parts of the system under test • Requires a formal specification or model to carry out testing • Test cases are tightly coupled to the model; the change of model gives rise to a generation of altogether different test cases	**MBT approach** • Allows improving the bugs' detection in system under test • Allows reducing testing time and costs • Allows improving testing quality and therefore software quality • The fact that the model is derived from the requirements allows to start very early in system cycle life and so allows to detect defaults in requirements • Allows the traceability management between requirements and the abstract model through the requirements traceability matrix generated in generating step in MBT process

(continued)

Table 5. (continued)

Ref.	Remaining problems (Limits)	Solved problems (Advantages)
	• Writing test cases that cover dynamic aspects of the system dependent on the engineer expertise • Difficulty to detect all the differences between model and implementation	• Allows to easily adapting the model to the new changes contributed to system under test and re-generate test case what makes easy adaptation of requirement's evolution and reduce the maintenance costs • Using MBT approach in testing activity allows to high level of automation and to generate high volumes of non-repetitive useful tests
Mottahir et al. [3] Erdogan et al. [5] Felderer et al. [7]	**RBT approach** • When some risks are not identified or marked as low, may cause problems in future if they become a reality • Managing traceability between requirements and tests is too expensive • Difficulty to associate concretes test cases to risks identified too abstract • Sometimes, some mitigation are very expensive in cost and time • Difficulty to identify and select the right stakeholders for risk assessment	**RBT approach** • Allows optimizing available time and resources without affecting product quality • The RBT activities can be started early in system cycle life and discovered defaults • Test in risk order gives the highest likelihood to discovering defects in severity order and therefore allows risking reducing • When time, money and resources are limited, RBT reduces the number of tests for adapting with available resources without impacting product quality • In RBT the communication is based on risk that is understandable by all stakeholders • Prioritize testing tasks more efficiently • Allows to detect high risk defects in software and therefore to reduce risks

6 Analyse and Discussion

Both studied techniques have their own processes, approaches, tools, merits and demerits. For risk-based testing, all approaches described in this paper use risk to prioritize what to test and focus on activities related to risk identification, analysis and prioritizing. Most RBT approaches are black-box testing that takes as input software requirements. In this category we find some approaches which are intended to functional testing as Amland, Chen, Bach, and others that are proposed for non functional testing as Zech, Xu and Bai. Otherwise, for white-box testing, we find a limited number of RBT approaches which are intended to Structural testing like Wong and

Hosseingholizadeh. For model-based testing, the general idea is that from an explicit behaviour model that represents behaviour of system under test, generate test cases to validate the expected behaviour of the system under test. Based on studied classifications and after analyzing different approaches of model-based testing, we concluded that we can also classify existing MBT approaches according to different criteria viz; testing type, testing level, testing sources, and notation type used to represent testing sources. This classification is very detailed and it facilitates the selection of MBT approaches according to the test context (Table 6).

Table 6. MBT approaches classification

Criteria	Categories
Testing type	• Category approaches which are intended to functional testing • Category approaches which are intended to non functional testing • Category approaches which are intended to Structural testing
Testing level	• Category approaches which are intended to system level testing • Category approaches which are intended to integration level testing • Category approaches which are intended to unit/component level testing • Category approaches which are intended to regression level testing
Testing source	• Category approaches which uses software requirements as testing source • Category approaches which uses software internal structure as testing source
Testing notation type	• They uses Graphical notation to describe and represent testing source • They uses Textual/Scripting notation to describe and represent testing source • They uses Symbolic (completely mathematical) notation to describe and represent testing source

Based on MBT Approaches Characterization proposed by Arilo and Guilherme [19], we expose some approaches in order of proposed classification (Tables 7, 8, 9 and 10).

Table 7. MBT approaches classification in term of testing type

Functional testing	Non-functional testing	Structural testing
Abdurazik2000, Crichto 2001, Chen2002, Cavarra2003, Botaschanjan2004, Andrews2005, Bernard2006, Sokenou2006	Bousquet1999, Garousi2006, Mandrioli1995, Offutt1999b, Parissis1996, Pretschner2001, Richardson1992, Rumpe2003, Felderer2012	• Xu2006 • Kim1999 • Chang1999

Table 8. MBT approaches classification in term of testing level

Unit/Component testing	Integration testing	System testing	Regression testing
• Kim1999 • Dalal999 • Briand2006 • Barbey1996	• Bertolino2003 • Bertolino2005 • Beyer2003 • Chen2005	• Abdurazik2000 • Briand2004 • Crichton2001 • Legeard2004	• Briand2002 • Chen2002 • Den2004 • Tahat2001

Table 9. MBT approaches classification in term of testing source

Software requirements	Software internal structure
Ammann1994, Bernard2006, Belletini2005, Cavarra2003, Friedman2002 and Offut1999	Kim1999, Legard2004, Chang1999, Garousi2006 and Xu2006

Table 10. MBT approaches classification in term of testing notation type

Graphical notation	Textual notation	Symbolic notation
Bertolino2003, Briand2002, Kansomkeat2003, Lund2006, Sokenou2006 and Zhen2004	Bousquet1999, Mandrioli1995, Tahat2001, Hartmann&Nagin2004 and Tan2004	• Legeard2004 • Richardson1996 • Ammann1994

Table 11. RBT approaches classification in term of testing type

Functional testing	Non-functional testing	Structural testing
Amland2000, Bach-Outside-In1999, Bach-Inside-Out1999, Chen2003, Chen2002, Paul2002, Scheafer, Felderer2012, Stallbaum2008, Zimmermann2009, Wendland2012, Stålhane and Souza2010	Bach-Outside-In1999, Palanivel201, Zech2011, Zech2012, Murthy2009, Casado2010, Xu2012, Bai2009	Rosenberg1999, Hosseingholizadeh2010 and Wong 2005

Table 12. RBT approaches classification in term of testing level

Unit/Component testing	Integration testing	System testing	Regression testing
Paul2002, Wong 2005	Paul2002, Wong 2005	Amland2000, Bach-Outside-In1999, Bach-Inside-Out1999, Paul2002, Stallbaum2008, Zimmermann2009 and Wendland2012	Chen2003, Chen2002

For RBT technique, After Analyzing existing approaches, we concluded that we can also classify them according to the following criteria: Testing type, Testing level, Testing sources, and Notation type used to represent testing sources if exist (Tables 11, 12, 13 and 14).

Table 13. RBT approaches classification in term of testing source

Software requirements	Software internal structure
Amland2000, Chen2003, Chen2002, Bach1999, Redmill2004, Redmill2005, Felderer2012, Zech2011, Zech2012, Entin2012, Stallbaum2008, Zimmermann2009, Wendland2012, Stålhane2003, Souza2010 and Bai2009	Rosenberg1999, Hosseingholizadeh2010 and Wong 2005

Table 14. RBT approaches classification in term of testing notation type

UML notation	Non UML notation
Stålhane, Chen2002, Chen2003, Entin2012, Stallbaum2008, Wendland2012, Stallbaum2008 and Wendland2012	Felderer2012, Felderer2013, Zech2012 and Xu2012

7   Conclusion and Perspective

In this paper, we have studied the main two techniques of software testing. The idea of the first technique is to use the abstractions of a system under test and its environment to automatically generate test cases. MBT consists to create an abstract system model that specifies the behaviour of the SUT, and then generate test cases. The key points of MBT are the modelling behaviour of the SUT for test generation, the test generation strategies and techniques, and the concretization of abstract tests into concrete, executable tests. The second is a technique that aims to minimize the software risks and testing problems. RBT consists of a set of activities regarding risk factors identification associated to software requirements. Once identified, the risks are prioritized according to its likelihood and impact and the test cases are projected based on the strategies or approaches for treatment of the identified risk factors. The test efforts are continuously adjusted according to the risk monitoring. Based on our study between MBT and RBT techniques we are identifying the following research tasks in the area of model-based testing and risk based testing viz; Proposition of a meta-model that represent model-based testing technique; Proposition of a meta-model that represent risk-based testing technique; Proposition of a novel testing approach based on model based testing and risk based testing techniques to overcome some testing limitations; and Make some case studies by applying the novel testing approach to obtain empirical results and compare our approach over existing approaches.

References

1. Pretschner, A.: Model-based-testing. In: ICSE, pp. 722–732 (2005)
2. Utting, M., Pretschner, A., Legeard, B.: A Taxonomy of Model-Based Testing, a School of Computing and Mathematical Sciences (2006)
3. Alam, M.M.: Risk-based testing techniques: a perspective study. Int. J. Comput. Appl. **65**, 33–41 (2013). (0975–8887)
4. Utting, M., Legeard, B.: Practical Model-Based Testing: A Tools Approach. ACM, Inc. (2017)
5. Erdogan, G.: Approaches for the combined use of risk analysis and testing: a systematic literature review. Int. J. Softw. Tools Technol. Transfer **16**, 627–642 (2014). Springer-Verlag Berlin Heidelberg
6. Felderer, M.: A classification for model-based security testing. In: The Third International Conference on Advances in System Testing and Validation Lifecycle (2011)
7. Felderer, M.: A taxonomy of risk-based testing. Int. J. Softw. Tools Technol. Transfer **16**, 559–568 (2014)
8. Micskei, Z.: Model-Based Testing (MBT), Online Dictionary. http://mit.bme.hu/~micskeiz/pages/modelbased_testing.html
9. Palanivel, M., Selvadurai, K.: Risk-driven security testing using risk analysis with threat modeling approach, Palanivel and Selvadurai SpringerPlus (2014)
10. Hartman, A.: AGEDIS: Model-Based Test Generation Tools, January 2009. http://www.agedis.de
11. Dranidis, D.: JSXM: a tool for automated test generation. In: Proceeding SEFM 2012 Proceedings of the 10th International Conference on Software Engineering and Formal Methods (2012)
12. Aichernig, B.: MoMuT: UML model-based mutation testing for UML. In: 2015 IEEE 8th International Conference on Software Testing, Verification and Validation (ICST) (2015)
13. Pretschner, A.: One evaluation of model-based testing and its automation. In: ICSE 2005, 15–21 May 2005
14. Kristoffer, L.: A Software Tool for Risk-based Testing. http://www.idi.ntnu.no/grupper/su/fordypningsprosjekt2004/Jorgensen2004.pdf
15. Dalal, S.R., Jain, A., Karunanithi, N.: Model-based testing in practice. In: ICSE 1999, May 1999
16. Dias Neto, A.C., Travassos, G.H.: A survey on model-based testing approaches: a systematic review. In: WEASEL Tech 2007, November 2007
17. Cristi, M.: Using {log} as a Test Case Generator for Z Specifications. GNCS project PICT 2011-1002
18. Sarma, M., Murthy, P.V.R.: Model-based testing in industry – a case study with two MBT tools. ACM, 2–8 May 2010
19. Dias Neto, A.C., Travassos, G.H.: Characterization of model-based software testing approaches, Technical report at PESC/COPPE/UFRJ, Brazil, Published August 2007
20. Amland, S.: Risk-based testing: risk analysis fundamentals and metrics for software testing including a financial application case study. J. Syst. Softw. **53**, 287–295 (2000)
21. Felderer, M., Haisjackl, C., Breu, R., Motz, J.: Integrating manual and automatic risk assessment for risk-based testing. In: Biffl, S., Winkler, D., Bergsmann, J. (eds.) SWQD 2012. LNBIP, vol. 94, pp. 159–180. Springer, Heidelberg (2012). doi:10.1007/978-3-642-27213-4_11

22. Felderer, M., Ramler, R.: Experiences and challenges of introducing risk-based testing in an industrial project. In: Winkler, D., Biffl, S., Bergsmann, J. (eds.) SWQD 2013. LNBIP, vol. 133, pp. 10–29. Springer, Heidelberg (2013). doi:10.1007/978-3-642-35702-2_3

23. Redmill, F.: Exploring risk-based testing and its implications. Softw. Test. Verif. Reliab. **14**, 3–15 (2004)

24. Redmill, F.: Theory and practice of risk-based testing. Softw. Test. Verif. Reliab. **15**, 3–20 (2005)

25. Yoon, H., Choi, B.: A test case prioritization based on degree of risk exposure and its empirical study. Int. J. Softw. Eng. Knowl. Eng. **21**, 191–209 (2011)

26. Gleirscher, M.: Hazard-based selection of test cases. In: Proceeding if the Sixth International Workshop on Automation of Software Test (AST 2011), pp. 64–70. ACM, New York (2011)

27. Gleirscher, M.: Hazard analysis for technical systems. In: Winkler, D., Biffl, S., Bergsmann, J. (eds.) SWQD 2013. LNBIP, vol. 133, pp. 104–124. Springer, Heidelberg (2013). doi:10.1007/978-3-642-35702-2_8

28. Ray, M., Mohapatra, D.P.: Risk analysis: a guiding force in the improvement of testing. IET Softw. **7**, 29–46 (2013)

29. Kloos, J., Hussain, T., Eschbach, R.: Risk-based testing of safetycritical embedded systems driven by fault tree analysis. In: Proceeding of the Fourth International Conference on Software Testing, Verification and Validation Workshops (ICSTW 2011), pp. 26–33. IEEE, New York (2011)

30. Nazier, R., Bauer, T.: Automated risk-based testing by integrating safety analysis information into system behavior models. In: Proceeding of the 23rd International Symposium on Software Reliability Engineering Workshops (ISSREW 2012), pp. 213–218. IEEE, New York (2012)

31. Wendland, M.-F., Kranz, M., Schieferdecker, I.: A systematic approach to risk-based testing using risk-annotated requirements models. In: Proceeding of the Seventh International Conference on Software Engineering Advances (ICSEA 2012), pp. 636–642. IARA (2012)

32. Xu, D., Tu, M., Sandford, M., Thomas, L., Woodraska, D., Xu, W.: Automated security test generation with formal threat models. IEEE Trans. Dependable Secure Comput. **9**, 526–540 (2012)

33. Zimmermann, F., Eschbach, R., Kloos, J., Bauer, T.: Risk-based statistical testing: a refinement-based approach to the reliability analysis of safety-critical systems. In: Proceeding of the 12th European Workshop on Dependable Computing (EWDC 2009), pp. 1–8 (2009)

34. Chen, Y., Probert, R.L.: A risk-based regression test selection strategy. In: Proceeding of the 14th IEEE International Symposium on Software Reliability Engineering (ISSRE 2003), Fast Abstract, pp. 305–306. Chillarege Press (2003)

35. Chen, Y., Probert, R.L., Sims, D.P.: Specification-based regression test selection with risk analysis. In: Proceeding of the 2002 Conference of the Centre for Advanced Studies on Collaborative Research (CASCON 2002), pp. 1–14. IBM Press, New York (2002)

36. Entin, V., Winder, M., Zhang, B., Christmann, S.: Introducing model-based testing in an industrial scrum project. In: Proceeding of the Seventh International Workshop on Automation of Software Test (AST 2012), pp. 43–49. IEEE, New York (2012)

37. Stallbaum, H., Metzger, A., Pohl, K.: An automated technique for risk-based test case generation and prioritization. In: Proceeding of the Third International Workshop on Automation of Software Test (AST 2008), pp. 67–70. ACM, New York (2008)

38. Hosseingholizadeh, A.: A source-based risk analysis approach for software test optimization. In: Proceeding of the Second International Conference on Computer Engineering and Technology (ICCET 2010), vol. 2, pp. 601–604. IEEE, New York (2010)

39. Wong, W.E., Qi, Y., Cooper, K.: Source code-based software risk assessing. In: Proceeding of the 2005 ACM Symposium on Applied Computing (SAC 2005), pp. 1485–1490. ACM, New York (2005)

40. Kumar, N., Sosale, D., Konuganti, S.N., Rathi, A.: Enabling the adoption of aspects-testing aspects: A risk model, fault model and patterns. In: Proceeding of the Eighth ACM International Conference on Aspect-Oriented Software Development (AOSD 2009), pp. 197–206. ACM, New York (2009)

41. Rosenberg, L., Stapko, R., Gallo, A.: Risk-based object oriented testing. In: Proceeding of the 24th Annual Software EngineeringWorkshop, pp. 1–6. NASA, Software Engineering Laboratory (1999)

42. Bai, X., Kenett, R.S.: Risk-based adaptive group testing of semantic web services. In: Proceeding of the 33rd Annual IEEE International Computer Software and Applications Conference (COMPSAC 2009), vol. 2, pp. 485–490. IEEE, New York (2009)

43. Bai, X., Kennett, R.S., Yu, W.: Risk assessment and adaptive group testing of semantic web services. Int. J. Softw. Eng. Knowl. Eng. 22, 595–620 (2012)

44. Casado, R., Tuya, J., Younas, M.: Testing long-lived web services transactions using a risk-based approach. In: Proceeding of the 10th International Conference on Quality Software (QSIC 2010), pp. 337–340. IEEE, New York (2010)

45. Casado, R., Tuya, J., Younas, M.: A framework to test advanced web services transactions. In: Proceeding of the 4th International Conference on Software Testing, Verification and Validation (ICST 2011), pp. 443–446. IEEE, New York (2011)

46. Murthy, K.K., Thakkar, K.R., Laxminarayan, S.: Leveraging risk based testing in enterprise systems security validation. In: Proceeding of the First International Conference on Emerging Network Intelligence (EMERGING 2009), pp. 111–116. IEEE, New York (2009)

47. Zech, P.: Risk-based security testing in cloud computing environments. In: Proceeding of the Fourth International Conference on Software Testing, Verification and Validation (ICST 2011), pp. 411–414. IEEE, New York (2011)

48. Zech, P., Felderer, M., Breu, R.: Towards risk-driven security testing of service centric systems. In: 2012 12th International Conference on Quality Software (QSIC). IEEE (2012)

49. Schneidewind, N.F.: Risk-driven software testing and reliability. Int. J. Reliab. Qual. Saf. Eng. 14, 99–132 (2007)

50. Souza, E., Gusmão, C., Venâncio, J.: Risk-based testing: a case study. In: Proceeding of the Seventh International Conference on Information Technology: New Generations (ITNG 2010), pp. 1032–1037. IEEE, New York (2010)

51. Bach, J.: Heuristic Risk-Based Testing. Software Testing and Quality Engineering Magazine, November 1999

52. Paul, G.: Risk-Based E-Business Testing, pp. 3–29, 51–80 (2002). ISBN: 1580533140

53. Hartman, A.: The AGEDIS tools for model based testing. In: ISSTA 2004 Proceedings of the 2004 ACM SIGSOFT International Symposium on Software Testing and Analysis (2004)

54. Stålhane, T.: Risk Analysis as a Prioritizing Mechanism in EuroSPI (2003)

55. http://promise.cin.ufpe.br/rbttool/

56. Tretmans, J., Brinksma, E.: Côte de Resyste – automated model based testing. In: Progress 2002 – 3rd Workshop on Embedded Systems (2002)

57. Bouquet, F., Legeard, B., Peureux, F., Torreborre, E.: Mastering test generation from smart card software formal models. In: Proceedings of International Workshop on Construction and Analysis of Safe, Secure and Interoperable Smart devices (2004)

58. Anand, S., Burke, E.K., Chen, T.Y., Clark, J., Cohen, M.B., Grieskamp, W., Harman, M., Harrold, M.J., McMinn, P.: An orchestrated survey of methodologies for automated software test case generation. J. Syst. Softw. **86**, 1978–2001 (2013)
59. http://unina.stidue.net/Ingegneria%20del%20Software%202/Materiale/Sommerville%20-%20Software%20Engineering%208e.pdf
60. https://msdn.microsoft.com/en-us/library/jj159342.aspx
61. https://www.dice.com/skills/Risk-based+testing.html
62. Legeard, B., et al.: Model-based-Testing User Survey: Results (2014). http://model-based-testing.info/wordpress/wp-content/uploads/2014_MBT_User_Survey_Results.pdf

Software Project Management in the Era of Digital Transformation

Rachida Hassani$^{(\boxtimes)}$, Younés El Bouzekri El Idrissi,
and Abdellah Abouabdellah

National School of Applied Sciences, Kenitra, Morocco
rachida.hassani22@gmail.com, y.elbouzekri@gmail.com,
a.abouabdellah2013@gmail.com

Abstract. Integrating digital into the DNA of their business model is an essential part of business success for companies across industries today. The digital transformation has become a critical management issue and requires new ways of managerial thinking. In this context, we address the specificity of digital projects compared to IT projects in general, to innovate during the implementation of digital projects following their trends generated by digital transformation, while respecting the triangle "Quality, Price, Duration". To do this, we adopt a methodology based on describing the management tasks and roles of digital project manager to identify obstacles to digital transformation in digital project management, then analyze these obstacles to countermeasure them and propose a new knowledge based system "KBS" based on the feedback of digital experiences.

Keywords: Risk management · Digital project management · Digital transformation · Critical affecting factors · Management innovation

1 Introduction

According to the investigation data announced by the Standish Group International, Inc., in 2003, among the 13,522 investigated projects in terms of the standards Group International, Inc., only 34% of projects were completed successfully, 15% of projects were canceled before completion, and 51% of projects were completed but were doubted, because they were over budget, over schedule and so on [1].

Companies typically ensure that their employees have the technical skills they need to work on whatever tasks they are assigned, but, as Jim Johnson, Chairman of the Standish Group, has said, "When projects fail, it is rarely technical" [2].

Integrating and exploiting new digital technologies are one of the most urgent challenges for companies today. Across industries, they face increasing pressure to make their digital transformation a strategic priority and to embrace the opportunities presented by recent digital technologies.

Digital projects have been hamstrung by numerous issues over recent years: cost, complexity, cavalier management... all have endangered project completion [3]. So what are the barriers to change and what can be done to reduce the risks and improve project management?

© Springer International Publishing AG 2017
A. El Abbadi and B. Garbinato (Eds.): NETYS 2017, LNCS 10299, pp. 391–395, 2017.
DOI: 10.1007/978-3-319-59647-1_28

2 IT Project and IT Project Management

As to IT project, there different definitions. Q. Zhang thinks that in IT project mainly refers to the information management systems of computers. Y. Li mentions three features of IT projects: Urgency, Uniqueness, Uncertainly [1].

Regarding IT project management, there are different definitions as well. According to Z.Y. Li, IT project management based on information technology, a special type of project management, and a new kind of project management that came into being and is being improved continuously with the development of information technology [4].

N. Zhang and P. Wang thinks that IT project management refers to the management practice which ensures the smooth execution of engineering system development methods, based on the theories of management science, and integrating with the development practice of IT products as well as a serie activities. L. Xu puts forward three features of IT project management: abstractness, timeliness of information communication, and uncertainty [5].

3 Project Management in the Era of Digital Transformation

New technologies such as digital projects are becoming commonplace, which is something that has changed consumer's expectations and behaviors for good, services must be fast and easy-to-use, fully transparent, always available and multi-device access.

What does project manager do? Here are some thoughts:

- Optimization of time and modules to be implemented, and which directly impact the planning and the cost of the project;
- Exploring of the potential of feedback to maximize the quality of projects and foster new and innovative ideas;
- Adapting communication approach by providing stakeholders with rapid access to real-time project information.

In this paper, digital project management refers to a series of activities in which cost, personnel, progress, quality, risk file, etc. are analyzed, managed, and controlled so that digital projects can be completed in terms of the budget, scheduled progress and quality [6].

4 Obstacles of Digital Transformation in Digital Project Management

Digital project management is developing rapidly in the era of digital transformation, but it encounters some obstacles. The major ones are as follows:

1. Undefined Goals – When goals are not clearly identified, the whole project and team can suffer. When upper management cannot agree to or support undefined goals, the project in question typically has small chance to succeed [7].
2. Scope Changes – Also known as scope creep, occur when the project management allows the project's scope to extend beyond its original objectives [6].
3. Improper Risk Management – Learning to deal with and plan for risk is another important piece of project management training [8].
4. Ambiguous Contingency Plans – It's important for project managers to know what direction to take in pre-defined "what-if" scenarios [6].
5. Poor Communication – Project managers provide direction at every step of the project, so each team leader knows what's expected [6].
6. Impossible Deadlines – A successful project manager knows that repeatedly asking a team for the impossible can quickly result in declining morale and productivity [6].
7. Resource Deprivation – In order for a project to be run efficiently and effectively, management must provide sufficient and put the right resources in the right way.

5 Analysis of Affecting Factors of Digital Transformation in the Digital Project Management

Fishbone Diagram is a kind of method that is used to analyze factors affecting a certain problem. The factors are found by brainstorming, classified together with the problem to be resolved according to their relevance, and finally form a diagram with key factors marked.

In this paper, Fishbone Diagram is applied to analyze the major factors that affect digital project management. There are two steps: analyzing the problem's structure and drawing the fishbone diagram.

The key factors that affect digital project management in a digital transformation time are shown by the fishbone diagram, i.e. Fig. 1.

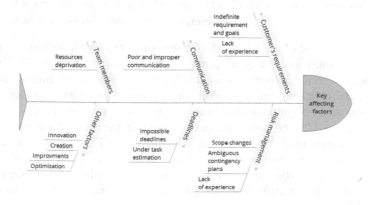

Fig. 1. Fishbone diagram of critical affecting factors of digital project management

6 Countermeasures for the Existing Problems in Digital Project Management

Feedback is a reflection process used to draw positive and negative lessons from ongoing or completed projects. In this process, we look at the approach developed, the methods used, the outputs produced, the role and level of involvement of the actors involved, and the means used.

The main stages of feedback are:

- Choice of project, for which the process will be implemented;
- Definition of the modalities (individual and/or collective information of a grid or a questionnaire);
- Designation and role of the various stakeholders in the process;
- Collection and analysis of information;
- Capitalization of lessons learned;
- Valuing and making available these lessons;
- Possible implementation of an action plan to change practices.

In order to countermeasure the various problems mentioned in the previous paragraphs, and in order to exploit the potential of feedback for the implementation of digital projects. We suggest the establishment of a knowledge base system (KBS) allowing to automatically make available the feedback to all the stakeholders at any stage of the project.

This KBS must have as input an analysis grid, that must be organized by project step, and on each step, it is necessary to specify positive and negative lessons, identify the used technologies, etc. It must be informed by different stakeholders to collect different viewpoints on it. It can also be used as a basis for the construction of analysis or maintenance guides (implemented for strategic projects. Or, in order to draw as many useful lessons as possible from different actors in the project, internal as well as external.). Then, as output, feedback, that can be used to improve and innovate in new digital projects to be implemented, to control project risks, to increase quality and reduce the duration of project implementation, which directly impacts the cost of the project.

In this way, we will overrode the problems already mentioned as follows:

1. Defining goals and objectives: Before communicating with customers, project managers should make a good preparation for requirement work, then ask customers to confirm them. To do this, he must make a preliminary research in the KBS of its entity, to exploit the potential of older experiences that have some same objectives and goals, to reuse and improve them.
2. Project scope: Clients and supervisors may ask for changes on project, and it takes a strong project manager and by using the KBS, he can do a simple research on it to evaluate each request and decide how and if to implement it.
3. Risk management: Risk management is essentially a planning strategy. Then, the KBS help to identify potential problem areas can lead to a smooth and successful project.

4. Communication: In digital project management, project manager's communication includes four aspects, i.e. customers, team members, top management, and other stakeholders involved in the projects. If communication can be conducted as early as possible and as positively as possible, then communication efficiency will be highly improved. So by using the KBS, the manager can reuse some successful communication plans.

5. Deadlines: Digital project consists of a set of modules, some are common, according to the type of projects. The KBS will allow the project manager to identify these modules, consult the time consumed by them to set realistic deadlines or reuse some implemented modules if the feedback is positive to optimize the duration of the implementation.

6. Personnel: The feedback (by using the KBS) can help choose team members carefully according to the cycle length of the projects and assure the continuity of the right people during the process of the projects. So, it will help to place the right people in the right positions.

7. Innovation and creativity: The trick is finding a strategy that allows full sight of the project, but doesn't suffocate creativity and innovation [9]. We highlight three novel ways we can integrate on the digital management project strategy through the KBS: learn from the knowledge base system, consider the company management structure, and automate the project's processes.

7 Conclusion

The major factors that affect digital project management which are illustrated on the Fishbone diagram, must be dealt with by the digital project enterprises through a healthy communication with their project management, and by integrating the Knowledge Based System and constant innovation to explore effectively the potential of feedback and therefore perfect there digital project management.

References

1. Li, Y.: Existing problems and their countermeasures in IT project management. Inf. Res., 115–117 (2007)
2. Gould, M., Freeman, R.: The art of project management: a competency model for project managers. Boston University Corporate Education Center
3. https://www.toplev.com/blog/barriers-to-change-the-obstacles-in-digital-projects/
4. Li, Z.Y.: Solving problems in IT project management by psychology. Sci. Technol. Innov. Herald, 162–163 (2008)
5. Fitzgerald, M., Kruschwitz, N., Bonnet, D., Welch, M.: Embracing Digital Technology. MIT Sloan Manage. Rev. (2013)
6. https://www.projectmanagement.com/blog-post/21925/Project-Management-in-the-Age-of-Digital-Transformation
7. https://www.coursehero.com/tutors-problems/Business/9268757-Hi-would-you-be-able-to-write-this-in-ap-format-please-using-all-ref/
8. http://www.elinkgroup.net/English/englishIndustryInsights/newsDetails.aspx?id=3159
9. http://technologyadvice.com/blog/information-technology/innovative-project-management-strategies/

Using Fuzzy Gray Relational Analysis in the Vertical Handover Process in Wireless Networks

Mouâd Mansouri$^{(\boxtimes)}$ ⓘ and Cherkaoui Leghris

Department of Computer Sciences FST, L@M Lab, RTM Team,
Hassan II University, Casablanca, Morocco
mansouri.mouad@yahoo.com, cleghris@yahoo.fr

Abstract. The use of internet is becoming larger, in more and more diverse situations, going from messaging, e-mailing, video and data transfers, to cloud computing, and internet of things (IoT). Users are willing to connect to any wireless access technology, anywhere and anytime to satisfy the 'ABC' (Always Best Connected). This leads to vertical handovers (VH). VH differs from horizontal handover (i.e., the transfer of connections between two base stations or access points with the same access technology). The transfer must be without session breaks.

In this paper, we propose a new hybrid decision method for VH decision process, named FGRA combining Fuzzy sets and Gray Relational Analysis (GRA) to perform more efficient VH decisions. Moreover, our combination allows the VHs to be seamless, without session ruptures. This new method is compared with the normal MADM methods GRA and TOPSIS, known for their efficiency in this context, in terms of number of handovers, and the QoS offered in every decision point. Our new hybrid method gives better results than the classical ones through the simulation scenarios' results we perform.

Keywords: MADM · Multi-access environment · Mobile networks · Vertical handover · Wireless networks

1 Introduction

Always more users are using internet wirelessly anywhere, to connect to the best access network available anytime, to profit from services like data, voice and video transmission, and IoT. This provokes vertical handovers (VHs), this means changing the network type (e.g., 3G to Wi-Fi). It must be fast and efficient enough, not to cause session breaks, this supposes that the VH must be well managed. This is ensured by Mobile IPv6 (MIPv6), Fast Handover for Mobile IPv6 (FHMIPv6) [4] and "Media Independent Handover" MIH (IEEE 802.21), standardized in 2009. The VH process is divided into three principal steps: VH discovery, VH decision and VH execution. Different techniques were used in this context, like Neural networks, Artificial intelligence, Fuzzy logic and MADM methods. In this work, we combine GRA with fuzzy sets, to deal with imprecisions in the attribute values.

© Springer International Publishing AG 2017
A. El Abbadi and B. Garbinato (Eds.): NETYS 2017, LNCS 10299, pp. 396–401, 2017.
DOI: 10.1007/978-3-319-59647-1_29

The next section is the background of our work, the third section discusses our proposal to optimize the VH decision, using our combination, the fourth section discusses the simulation results, and the conclusion will be the fifth section of this paper.

2 Background

The VH problem was tackled in many works. In [3], the authors present an investigation on network selection criteria's interdependence, and their effects on criteria's importance, and the current research trend in the application of MADM algorithms to network-selection problems in HWNs. [6] introduces a novel utility-based approach supporting multiple client classes, a bandwidth sharing policy and a "controlled unfairness" scheme is achieved by combining distinct priority classes with logarithmic utility functions. Some of the modified MADM algorithms used in the context of VH are cited in [7, 9–11, 13]. In [13], A.T. Gumus et al. propose a fuzzy Analytical Hierarchical Process (Fuzzy-AHP) and Fuzzy-GRA to select the most appropriate Hydrogen Energy Storage (HES) method for Turkey from the alternatives of tank. The steps of GRA are:

1. Decision matrix D_{mn} is filled with the attribute values for every alternative:

$$D_{mn} = \begin{pmatrix} d_{11} & \cdots & d_{1n} \\ \vdots & \ddots & \vdots \\ d_{m1} & \cdots & d_{mn} \end{pmatrix} \tag{1}$$

2. Normalization: We used the sum method, to have the normalized matrix R_{mn} [12]:

$$r_{ij} = \frac{d_{ij}}{\sum_1^m d_{ij}} \tag{2}$$

3. Weighting: The weight of each criterion is determined and multiplied by attributes.

$$V_{ij} = r_{ij} * W_j \tag{3}$$

4. Compute the best and worst ideal alternative:

$$V^+ = \max\{V_{ij}\}; \text{ for benefit criteria, and } \min\{V_{ij}\}; \text{ for cost criteria.} \tag{4}$$

5. Compute the GRA coefficient (GRC) for each alternative:

$$GRC_i = \frac{1}{\sum_1^m |v_{ij} - V_j| + 1} \tag{5}$$

6. Ranking in decreasing order.

3 Our Proposal

We propose a combination of GRA and the fuzzy sets, named FGRA. The decision matrix will be fuzzy, i.e. $d_{ij} = (l_{ij}, m_{ij}, u_{ij})$. The distance between two fuzzy sets $v_{ij}(l_{ij}, m_{ij}, u_{ij})$ and $V_j(L_j, M_j, U_j)$, is Eq. 4. Table 1 shows the linguistic variables.

$$v_{ij} - V_j = (l_{ij} - L_j) + (m_{ij} - M_j) + (u_{ij} - U_j) \tag{6}$$

Table 1. Fuzzy numbers corresponding to linguistic variables used as attribute values

Very poor (VP)	(1, 1, 2)	Fair (F)	(3, 4, 5)
Poor (P)	(1, 2, 3)	Medium good (MG)	(4, 5, 6)
Medium Poor (MP)	(2, 3, 4)	Good (G)	(5, 6, 7)
Very good (VG)	(7, 8, 8)		

Numeric attributes used for TOPSIS and GRA are in the values shown in Table 2, to simulate data gathered during the discovery phase, in a movement scenario designed by IEEE 802.21 tutorial [5]. For FGRA, we used linguistic variables in Table 3.

Table 2. Numeric interval values used to simulate data gathered in the discovery phase

Network	F (Kbps)	Av (%)	S (%)	D (ms)	L ($*10^6$)	EC (1–7)	C (1–7)	J (ms)
GPRS/2.5G	21.4–171.2	50–100	50	50–70	50–80	2	1	3–20
EDGE/2.75G	43.2–345.6	40–100	50	20–60	25–70	2	2	3–20
UMTS	144–2000	40–100	60	20–40	15–65	4	4	3–20
HSDPA/HSUPA	14 Mbps	50–100	60	10–50	10–80	4	5	3–20
LTE	10–300 Mbps	40–100	65	10–30	10–40	7	7	3–20
Wifi a,b,g	8–54 Mbps	40–100	60	130–200	30–70	3	1	3–20
Wifi n	72–450 Mbps	30–100	65	100–140	20–60	3	1	3–20
Wifi ac	433–1300 Mbps	50–100	70	90–110	10–40	5	2	3–20
Wimax	70 Mbps	40–100	60	60–100	10–70	7	5	3–20

Table 3. Linguistic variables used as attribute values in our fuzzy GRA simulation scenario

Network	F	Av	S	D	L	EC	C	J
GPRS/2.5G	VP	P	F	VG	VG	P	P	G
EDGE/2.75G	P	MP	F	G	VG	P	P	MG
UMTS	F	F	G	F	MG	MG	F	F
HSDPA/HSUPA	MG	MG	G	P	F	G	F	MP
LTE	G	G	VG	VP	P	VG	G	P
Wifi a,b,g	F	F	MP	F	F	P	VP	F
Wifi n	G	MG	F	P	MP	MP	P	MP
Wifi ac	VG	G	MG	VP	P	F	MP	P
Wimax	G	G	G	P	P	G	MG	MP

4 Results and Discussion

The Figs. 1 and 2 illustrate respectively the results returned applying TOPSIS and GRA using numeric values as inputs, and FGRA, taking fuzzy sets as inputs.

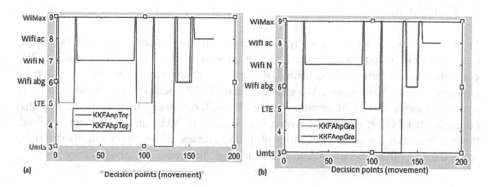

Fig. 1. Results returned by applying TOPSIS (a) method and GRA (b)

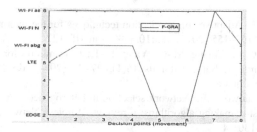

Fig. 2. Results returned by applying the fuzzy GRA method

The results are compared in terms of number of VHs, number of ranking reversals and the QoS offered. FGRA produces less handovers and no ranking abnormality. The number of VHs and the ranking reversals made by each method is shown in Fig. 3.

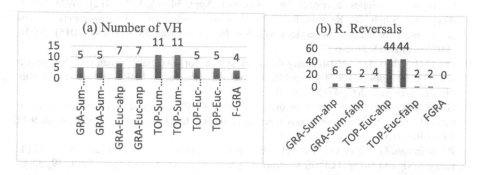

Fig. 3. Number of VHs (a) and rank reversals (b) occurred using different MADM methods

FGRA is the best among the compared methods seeing the QoS, the number of performed VHs (4), and no ranking abnormalities, but this combination is to be verified with real metrics, to see its efficiency in real time conditions.

5 Conclusion

In this work, we propose a new hybrid decision making method named fuzzy GRA, combining GRA and the fuzzy sets, in the context of the VH decision making. We compared this hybrid method with GRA and TOPSIS, which are known for their efficiency in the VH context. We establish that FGRA method isn't sensible to these small variations in weight vectors returned by different weighting methods. We also conclude that FGRA is the best with a low number of VHs, and no ranking reversal, this performance has to be verified for all traffic classes. More combinations still have to be tried to offer a better QoS to users anytime, to access all services they want.

References

1. Du, P., Roussos, G.: Adaptive communication techniques for the internet of things. J. Sens. Actuator Netw. **2**, 122–155 (2013). doi:10.3390/jsan2010122
2. Tsai, C.-W., Lai, C.-F., Chiang, M.-C., Yang, L.-T.: Data mining for internet of things: a survey. IEEE Commun. Surv. Tutorials **16**(1), 77–97 (2014). doi:10.1109/SURV.2013. 103013.00206. First quarter
3. Obayiuwana, E., Falowo, O.E.: Network selection in heterogeneous wireless network using multi-criteria decision-making algorithms: a review. Wireless Netw., 1–33 (2016). doi:10. 1007/s11276-016-1301-4
4. Fernandes, S., Karmouch, A.: Vertical mobility management architectures in wireless networks: a comprehensive survey and future directions. IEEE Commun. Surv. Tutorials **14** (1), 45–63 (2012). doi:10.1109/SURV.2011.082010.00099. First quarter
5. IEEE 802.21 Media Independent Handover, IEEE P802.21 Tutorial, 17 July 2006
6. Tsompanidis, I., Zahran, A.-H., Sreenan, C.-J.: Towards utility-based resource management in heterogeneous wireless networks. In: MobiArch 2012, 22 August 2012
7. Lahby, M., Leghris, C., Adib, A.: New optimized network selection decision in heterogeneous wireless networks. Int. J. Comput. Appl. **54**(16), 1–7 (2012). (0975–8887)
8. Ahuja, K., Singh, B., Khanna, R.: Optimal network selection in heterogeneous wireless environment for multimedia services. Wireless Pers. Commun. **83**, 441–454 (2015). doi:10. 1007/s11277-015-2402-6
9. Do, Q.H., Chen, J.-F.: Establishing the index system for sustainable urban transport project selection: an application of group MCDM based on the fuzzy AHP approach. Int. J. Bus. Manag. Invention **2**(6), 47–57 (2013)
10. Goyal, R.K., Kaushal, S., Vaidyanathan, S.: Fuzzy AHP for control of data transmission by network selection in heterogeneous wireless networks. Int. J. Comput. Technol. Appl. **9**(1), 133–140 (2016)
11. Büyüközkan, G., Çifçi, G.: A novel hybrid MCDM approach based on fuzzy DEMATEL, fuzzy ANP and fuzzy TOPSIS to evaluate green suppliers. Expert Syst. Appl. **39**, 3000–3011 (2012). doi:10.1016/j.eswa.2011.08.162

12. Mansouri, M., Leghris, C.: Towards a better combination of the MADM algorithms for the vertical handover optimization in a mobile network multi-access environment. In: 2015 10th Intelligent Systems: Theories and Applications (SITA) (2015). doi:10.1109/SITA.2015. 7358421

13. Gumus, A.T., Yayla, A.Y., Çelik, E., Yildiz, A.: A combined fuzzy-AHP and fuzzy-GRA Methodology for hydrogen energy storage method selection in Turkey. Energies **6**(6), 3017–3032 (2013). doi:10.3390/en6063017

14. Radhika, K., Venugopal Reddy, A.: Network selection in heterogeneous wireless networks based on fuzzy multiple criteria decision making. Int. J. Comput. Appl. **22**(1), 7–10 (2011). (0975–8887)

15. Charilas, D.E., Markaki, O.I., Psarras, J., Constantinou, P.: Application of fuzzy AHP and ELECTRE to network selection. In: Granelli, F., Skianis, C., Chatzimisios, P., Xiao, Y., Redana, S. (eds.) MOBILIGHT 2009. LNICST, vol. 13, pp. 63–73. Springer, Heidelberg (2009). doi:10.1007/978-3-642-03819-8_7

Concurrency and Specifications

Sequential Proximity
Towards Provably Scalable Concurrent Search Algorithms

Karolos Antoniadis$^{(\boxtimes)}$, Rachid Guerraoui, Julien Stainer,
and Vasileios Trigonakis

École Polytechnique Fédérale de Lausanne, Lausanne, Switzerland
{karolos.antoniadis,rachid.guerraoui,julien.stainer,
vasileios.trigonakis}@epfl.ch

Abstract. Establishing the scalability of a concurrent algorithm a priori, before implementing and evaluating it on a concrete multi-core platform, seems difficult, if not impossible. In the context of search data structures however, according to all practical work of the past decade, algorithms that scale share a common characteristic: They all resemble standard sequential implementations for their respective data structure type and strive to minimize the number of synchronization operations.

In this paper, we present *sequential proximity*, a theoretical framework to determine whether a concurrent search algorithm is close to its sequential counterpart. With sequential proximity we take the first step towards a theory of scalability for concurrent search algorithms.

1 Introduction

Concurrent search data structures (CSDSs), such as linked lists and skip lists, are fundamental building blocks of modern software, ranging from operating systems, such as the Linux kernel [15], to key-value stores, such as RocksDB [6]. A vast amount of work has been dedicated to the development of *correct* and *scalable* CSDS algorithms [3–5, 7–10, 14, 17].

To establish the correctness of such algorithms, several formal tools are available. For instance, *linearizability* [12] helps determine the *safety* of CSDS algorithms. Similarly, in terms of *liveness*, we can prove whether a CSDS algorithm is *lock-free* or *wait-free* [11].

In contrast, no formal tool is available for establishing the scalability of a CSDS algorithm, namely that the algorithm delivers better performance when the number of threads accessing the data structure increases. A non-scalable CSDS that resides in an application's critical path eventually becomes a performance bottleneck that needs to be replaced by an alternative design. Ideally, we would like to be able to prove that an algorithm is scalable without the need to evaluate the algorithm on every single workload and multi-core platform.

Defining a formal theory of scalability is an onerous task, since such a theory would need to take into account a multitude of different architectures, diverse set

This work has been supported in part by the European ERC Grant 339539 - AOC.

A. El Abbadi and B. Garbinato (Eds.): NETYS 2017, LNCS 10299, pp. 405–420, 2017.
DOI: 10.1007/978-3-319-59647-1_30

of workloads, etc. In this work, we follow an indirect approach: Instead of formalizing scalability, we create a formal framework that captures when a CSDS is similar to its respective sequential search data structure. Our work is based on the vast amount of prior practical work that points to a single direction for achieving scalability: Strip down synchronization (i.e., every construct that induces coordination of concurrent threads), which is a major impediment to scalability. To achieve minimal synchronization, all existing patterns for designing concurrent data structures do, directly or indirectly, promote concurrent designs that are close to their sequential counterparts: concrete CSDS algorithms [10,13], RCU [17], RLU [16], OPTIK [8], ASCY [4], etc.

Comparing a CSDS and a sequential search data structure in a formal way is challenging (e.g., how to compare the number of stores or where stores are issued between a CSDS and its respective sequential counterpart, etc.) In this paper, we tackle this challenge by introducing *sequential proximity (SP)*, a theoretical framework composed of ten formal properties that can be used to establish whether a CSDS algorithm is *close* to a reference sequential counterpart. SP can be viewed as a first step towards formalizing the scalability of CSDS algorithms.

Sequential Proximity: Overview. Our ten SP properties (Table 1) are defined with respect to the three basic operations of a CSDS: search, insert, and delete, for retrieving, adding, and removing an element from a set, respectively.

SP_{1-4} concern search operations. In a sequential design, search operations (i) are read-only, (ii) do not block, (iii) do not restart, and (iv) do not allocate any memory. SP_{1-4} enforce the exact same behavior as (i)–(iv) for concurrent search operations. SP_{2-5} concern parsing the set before performing an update (i.e., insert or delete). Essentially, the *parse* phase of an update operation traverses the set to find the node(s) to be modified. In a sequential data structure, parsing is identical to

Table 1. The ten commandments of SP.

	SP#	Name	search	insert	delete
traversal	SP₁	Read-only	✓		
	SP₂	Non-blocking	✓	✓	✓
	SP₃	No back-step	✓	✓	✓
	SP₄	No allocation	✓	✓	✓
	SP₅	Read-clean		✓	✓
modification	SP₆	Read-only unsuccessful		✓	✓
	SP₇	Conflict restart		✓	✓
	SP₈	Number of stores		✓	✓
	SP₉	Region of stores		✓	✓
	SP₁₀	No allocation			✓

searching, hence searching and parsing share SP_{2-4}. SP_5 replaces SP_1 for parsing, to capture the fact that concurrent designs (e.g., [7,9]) might retain some minimal helping strategy in order to "clean-up" the data structure. SP_6 concerns both insertions and deletions. In a sequential design, no writes are issued if the operation is unsuccessful (e.g., a deletion does not find the target element in the set). SP_6 enforces the same behavior for concurrent algorithms: An unsuccessful update cannot perform any stores or atomic operations after parsing. SP_7

restricts the ability of an update operation to restart due to concurrency. SP_7 does not have any correspondence in sequential algorithms, as the latter never restart. Intuitively, an update in a CSDS can only restart when a concurrent update of another thread modifies the same nodes as the current update. SP_8 and SP_9 restrain the amount of synchronization allowed when modifying the structure during insertions and deletions. We define the maximum number of shared memory stores (or atomic operations) and the locations of these stores in a concurrent design with respect to the sequential counterpart per data structure. Finally, SP_{10} captures the fact that deleting an element from a set should not allocate memory.

A CSDS algorithm is said to be *sequentially proximal* if it satisfies SP_{1-4} for search, SP_{2-9} for insert, and SP_{2-10} for delete operations.

Overall, we believe that SP can be used in guiding the design of scalable CSDS algorithms, detecting whether a CSDS algorithm is likely to scale, and optimizing existing CSDS designs by "fixing" one or more SP properties.

Roadmap. The rest of the paper is organized as follows. In Sect. 2, we recall background notions on CSDSs and describe the machinery we use to formulate the SP properties. We describe the SP properties in Sect. 3. We conclude the paper of SP in Sect. 4. Due to space limitations, we defer the reader to the technical report [1] for the precise definitions of some parts of our vocabulary, proofs of relations between SP properties and classic progress conditions, proofs that two known concurrent linked lists are sequentially proximal, related work, as well as concrete examples of the applicability of SP.

2   Preliminaries

In this section, we define sequential and concurrent search data structures and we introduce the formalism used to define our ten SP properties.

2.1   Search Data Structures

A *search data structure* (SDS) corresponds to a set of elements and operations for retrieving, storing, and removing elements. The main operations of a SDS are the search, insert, and delete operations. In this work, we consider linked lists, hash tables, skip lists, and binary search trees, which are all widely-used SDSs. Queues and stacks are not SDSs as they do not provide search operations.

The insert and delete operations are *update operations* used for inserting and removing elements, respectively. An update operation can be divided into two phases: *parse* and *modify*. For instance, an insertion in a sorted linked list first looks for the position where the element has to be inserted. The actual insertion can then happen during a modify phase. The typical flow of an update operation in a SDS is depicted in Fig. 1. The parse phase takes place first and returns a boolean value which indicates whether it can be followed by a modification. If the returned value is true (e.g., deleting an element that exists), the modification can be attempted. Otherwise, if the returned value is false (e.g., deleting an element that does not exist), the parse phase did not find a valid state to apply the subsequent modification. After a successful parse phase, the modify phase takes place (which always returns true in sequential SDSs).

Sequential Specification. The sequential specification of a SDS, denoted $Spec_{SDS}$, can be constructed using the notion of a set. At the beginning of a history of $Spec_{SDS}$ the set is empty, thus every search operation returns false. If an insert operation is called and the element is not in the set, the element is inserted into the set and true is returned. Otherwise, the set remains unchanged and false is returned. If a delete operation is called for an element that belongs to the set, the element is removed from the set and true is returned. Otherwise the set remains unchanged and false is returned.

Concurrent Search Data Structures (CSDSs). In CSDSs, the modify phase of update operations can return two values other than true, namely false and restart. These two additional transitions appear as dashed lines in Fig. 1.

On the one hand, a modification can return false either due to concurrency (e.g., the element was concurrently deleted by another process), or because the algorithm enters the modify phase, although the operation cannot be completed. On the other hand, a modification might return restart due to conflicting concurrency (i.e., another process modifies the same vicinity of the structure).

The sequential and concurrent SDSs that we consider in this work are implementations of $Spec_{SDS}$. We assume they have been proven correct in their respective environments (i.e., when used by one process for sequential and by several for CSDSs). We consider that fulfilling $Spec_{SDS}$ in a concurrent context means ensuring *linearizability* [12].

2.2 Language

To describe CSDS algorithms, we consider a formal language [2] that we extend to capture specific characteristics of CSDSs. We present here a quick overview of its classic features and a more detailed description of the additions we introduce to capture the notions needed to define sequential proximity.

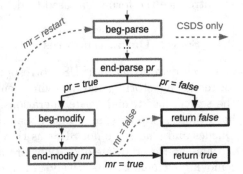

Fig. 1. Flow diagram of an update operation. The transitions in dashed lines are only feasible in concurrent SDSs.

Shared Memory Locations. These are the unit of memory, accessible by every process, on which read and write instructions operate atomically.

Local and Global Instructions. Each process executes a sequential program (of a Turing-complete language) augmented with instructions to interact with the shared memory. The language uses a standard syntax and semantics for boolean and numerical literals, variables, and expressions. It also features pointers, conditionals expressions, and branching (labels and goto instructions).

Each process maintains a *state* (set of local variables and execution context) and executes elementary *local* or *global* instructions. Shared memory allocations, and any instruction that takes as operand a shared memory location, are considered global instructions. There are six types of global instructions: allocate, read, write, compare-and-swap, try-lock, and unlock. A read(l) instruction retrieves the content of the shared memory location l and a write(v, l) writes the value of the local variable v to shared memory location l.

Compare-and-swap. In one atomic step, a compare-and-swap(l, old, new) instruction reads the content v of the shared memory location l, and, if $v = old$, it writes value *new* in l. In any case, compare-and-swap returns v.

Try-lock and Unlock. In one atomic step, the try-lock(l) instruction tests if the value v contained in the shared memory location l is true, and, in this case, it writes false in l. In any case, try-lock returns v. The try-lock instruction can be used to implement a traditional blocking lock operation by repeatedly executing try-lock until it returns true. The unlock(l) instruction writes true in l.

Allocate. allocate takes a list of local variables as argument and fills each variable with the address of a newly allocated shared memory location. Note that the use of allocate is closely related to the notion of *node*, defined below, that plays an important role in the definition of the SP properties.

Operations Delimiters. To capture the implementation of CSDSs, additional dummy statements are introduced to delimit the beginning and the end of search, insert, and delete operations. For update operations (i.e., insert and delete), additional statements are used to localize the beginning and the end of the parse and modify phases: beg-parse, end-parse, beg-modify, and end-modify. The statement end-parse returns a boolean indicating if the update is possible (i.e., the target value is not already present in the set for insert operations, or is present for delete operations). The statement end-modify returns true, false, or restart, indicating respectively that the operation succeeded, failed, or has to be restarted. For $op \in \{$search, insert, delete$\}$ the dummy statement entry op v (resp. exit op b) denotes the beginning (resp. end) of an operation of type op on the data structure (resp. returning a boolean b, indicating success or failure).

States, Transitions, and Executions. A *program state* σ is a tuple ($pc, locals, globals$) where pc associates to each process the current value of its program counter, *locals* associates values to the local variables of each process, and *globals* to shared memory locations. The *transition function* TF associates to a state σ and a process p the program state σ' reached after p executes its next instruction in state σ. A triple (σ, p, σ') s.t. $TF(\sigma, p) = \sigma'$ is called a *transition*.

An *execution* is a sequence of transitions $t_0, t_1, \ldots$ s.t. $\forall i \geq 0, t_i = (\sigma_i, p_{j_i}, \sigma_{i+1})$, where $p_{j_i} \in \{p_0, p_1, \ldots\}$. Furthermore, σ_0 designates the *initial state* in which each process is about to execute its first instruction and all the local variables and shared memory locations are uninitialized.

Histories. A *history* is a sequence of tuples (p, st) where st is an entry or exit statement and p is a process. To any execution π, we associate history $hs(\pi)$ defined as the subsequence of the transitions of π corresponding to entry and exit statements, labelled by the processes taking them.

Given a history H, we denote by $H|_p$ the history formed by the subsequence of the tuples of H taken by p. Statements $s = (p, \text{entry } op \ v)$ and $s' = (p', \text{exit } op' \ b)$ of a history H are said *matching* if $p = p'$, $op = op'$, s precedes s' in H, and if there is no $(p, \text{exit } op \ b')$ statement in H between s and s'. An entry statement of a history H that has no matching exit in H is said *pending*. A history H is said *sequential* if $H = en_0, ex_0, en_1, ex_1, \ldots$ where for all $i \geq 0$, en_i and ex_i are matching entry and exit statements. A sequential history that does not end with a pending entry statement is said to be a *complete sequential history*. A history H is *well-formed* if for each process p, $H|_p$ is sequential.

Consider any execution π s.t. $hs(\pi)$ is a well-formed history, and t_{en} a transition of π corresponding to an entry statement executed by process p. We define $opTrans(t_{en}, \pi)$ as the subsequence of π formed by the transitions of p from t_{en} to the next transition t_{ex} corresponding to an exit statement by p. If the operation entered in t_{en} is pending in $hs(\pi)|_p$, there is no such transition t_{ex} and $opTrans(t_{en}, \pi)$ is defined as the sequence of transition taken by p in π starting from t_{en}.

Parse-modify Patterns. For an execution π s.t. $hs(\pi)$ is well-formed, let us consider a transition t_{en} taken by process p that corresponds to an entry $op \ v$ statement with $op \in \{\text{insert, delete}\}$ and let t_{ex} be the matching exit transition. We defer for the moment the case of t_{en} corresponding to a pending entry statement in $hs(\pi)$. We say that the operation entered in t_{en} *follows a parse-modify pattern* if it follows the flow illustrated by Fig. 1. Formally, if we consider $pm(opTrans(t_{en}, \pi))$ the subsequence of transitions of $opTrans(t_{en}, \pi)$ corresponding to beg-parse, end-parse, beg-modify and end-modify statements, then (a) $pm(opTrans(t_{en}, \pi))$ starts with a beg-parse statement, (b) each beg-parse is immediately followed by an end-parse, (c) an end-parse returning true is immediately followed by a beg-modify statement, (d) if an end-parse or end-modify statement returns false, it is the last transition of $pm(opTrans(t_{en}, \pi))$ and t_{ex} returns false, (e) a beg-modify is immediately followed by an end-modify statement, (f) if an end-modify statement returns true, it is the last transition of $pm(opTrans(t_{en}, \pi))$ and t_{ex} returns true, and (g) an end-modify statement returning restart is immediately followed by a beg-parse statement.

If the transition t_{en} is pending in $hs(\pi)|_p$, we consider that $opTrans(t_{en}, \pi)$ follows a parse-modify pattern if π can be extended to an execution in which t_{en} has a corresponding t_{ex} statement and the (now complete) operation entered in t_{en} follows a parse-modify pattern.

Consider an entry transition t_{en} of an execution π s.t. $opTrans(t_{en}, \pi)$ follows a parse-modify pattern. We define the integer $numberOfParsePhases(t_{en}, \pi)$ (resp. $numberOfModifyPhases(t_{en}, \pi)$) as the number of transitions corresponding to beg-parse (resp. beg-modify) statements in $opTrans(t_{en}, \pi)$. We also define the sequence $parsePhase(t_{en}, \pi, k)$ (resp. $modifyPhase(t_{en}, \pi, k)$), for any k in $1, \ldots, numberOfParsePhases(t_{en}, \pi)$ (resp. $1, \ldots, numberOfModifyPhases(t_{en}, \pi)$), as the subsequence of $opTrans(t_{en}, \pi)$ starting at the k-th beg-parse (resp. beg-modify) statement and ending at the next following end-parse (resp. end-modify) statement (or at the end of $opTrans(t_{en}, \pi)$ if there is no such statement).

Positions of Global Transitions. We say that an execution π s.t. $hs(\pi)$ is well-formed has *no global transition outside operations* if each global transition of π belongs to some $opTrans(t_{en}, \pi)$ with t_{en} an entry transition of π.

Similarly, we state that an execution π has *no global update transition outside parse and modify phases* if, for any entry transition t_{en} of an insert or delete operation, any global transition of $opTrans(t_{en}, \pi)$ belongs to either the set $parsePhase(t_{en}, \pi, k)$ (for some k in $1, \ldots, numberOfParsePhases(t_{en}, \pi)$) or $modifyPhase(t_{en}, \pi, k')$ (for some k' in $1, \ldots, numberOfModifyPhases(t_{en}, \pi)$).

Well-formed Executions. An execution π is *well-formed* if it verifies: (a) $hs(\pi)$ is a well-formed history, (b) transitions never read uninitialized variables, (c) for any transition t_{en} corresponding to an entry *op v* statement with $op \in \{$insert, delete$\}$, the operation entered in t_{en} follows a parse-modify pattern, (d) π has no global transition outside operations, and (e) π has no global update transition outside parse and modify phases.

A program $Prog$ is said *well-formed* if all the executions it allows are well-formed. The set of all the executions allowed by $Prog$ is denoted $[\![Prog]\!]$. The remaining of the paper considers only well-formed programs.

2.3   Nodes and Allocation Sets

Nodes and Shared Memory Management. We assume that a SDS implementation provides the notion of *node* that captures the set of shared memory locations that are allocated and freed/unlinked together. It is assumed that one allocate statement allocates a list of shared memory locations corresponding to exactly one node. For example, in an external tree, a single operation can allocate shared memory locations logically corresponding to an internal node and to a leaf. The SP properties rely on that a separate allocate instruction is used for each of these two nodes.

To capture this relation between nodes and allocate instructions, we define, for any execution π and any transition t_{al} corresponding to an allocate instruction, the set $NodeAlloc(t_{al}, \pi)$ of the memory locations it reserves.

Memory reclamation is orthogonal to designing correct CSDSs and is typically handled by an external garbage collector. For clarity reasons, we do not consider memory reclamation in our model: Once a node is unlinked from the data structure (becomes *unreachable*, see below), the corresponding shared memory area is never reused.

Read and Written Locations. For any execution π and any transition t of π, we denote by $wloc(t)$ (resp. $rloc(t)$) the set that contains the shared memory location written (resp. read) by the instruction corresponding to t. If t corresponds to a local instruction, a global read, or an allocate instruction, then $wloc(t) = \emptyset$. If t corresponds to a write(v, l), try-lock(l), unlock(l), or a compare-and-swap(l, old, new) global instruction, then $wloc(t) = \{l\}$. Similarly, $rloc(t) = \emptyset$ if the instruction executed during t is a local instruction, a global write, or an allocate instruction, while $rloc(t) = \{l\}$ if it is a read(l), try-lock(l), or a compare-and-swap(l, old, new). By an abuse of terminology, we will refer to instructions issued by a transition t s.t. $wloc(t) \neq \emptyset$ as write instructions.

For each transition t_{en} of π that corresponds to a process p executing an entry $op\ v$ statement, we define the set $WrittenLoc(t_{en}, \pi)$ (resp. $ReadLoc(t_{en}, \pi)$) of shared memory locations written (resp. read) during the operation started at t_{en} as follows:

$$WrittenLoc(t_{en}, \pi) = \bigcup_{t \in opTrans(t_{en}, \pi)} wloc(t)$$

$$ReadLoc(t_{en}, \pi) = \bigcup_{t \in opTrans(t_{en}, \pi)} rloc(t).$$

Writing to Nodes Allocated by Others. Consider a well-formed execution π and any entry transition t_{en} corresponding to an entry $op\ v$ statement by a process p. Let S be a subsequence of $opTrans(t_{en}, \pi)$, and let us denote by $w(S)$ the subsequence of transitions of S corresponding to global write instructions. We define $opAlloc(t_{en}, \pi)$ as the set of shared memory locations allocated by p during the operation starting by t_{en}. Formally:

$$opAlloc(t_{en}, \pi) = \bigcup_{t \in al(opTrans(t_{en}, \pi))} NodeAlloc(t, \pi),$$

where $al(opTrans(t_{en}, \pi))$ is the subsequence of $opTrans(t_{en}, \pi)$ transitions that issue allocate instructions.

We now define the set $OtherNodeWrites(S, t_{en}, \pi)$ of the transitions of S writing into shared memory locations that have not been allocated by p during the operation it started at t_{en}. Formally, $OtherNodeWrites(S, t_{en}, \pi)$ is the maximal subset of $w(S)$ such that:

$$opAlloc(t_{en}, \pi) \cap \left(\bigcup_{t \in OtherNodeWrites(S, t_{en}, \pi)} wloc(t) \right) = \emptyset.$$

2.4   Solo Executions, Relative Nodes, and Reachability

Capturing the idea that a CSDS issues stores in a similar region as a respective sequential one is challenging: It is difficult to define what a "similar region" is.

To overcome this challenge, we define the notions of sequential freedom and solo executions and then introduce the concept of relative nodes. We then show how relative nodes can be used to construct sets of read and written nodes. Finally, we define the notion of reachability and the set of nodes that are freed during an operation.

Sequential Freedom. An execution π is in a *steady state*, if there is no entry statement pending in $hs(\pi)$. A program *Prog* is *sequentially free* if, starting from any steady state, an operation taking steps alone terminates.

Solo Execution. A *solo execution* by a program *Prog* of a history $S \in Spec_{SDS}$ corresponds to the execution of each operation of S by *Prog* in a solo (i.e., running the operation alone with no real concurrency) manner. Formally, consider a complete sequential history $S = en_0, ex_0, en_1, ex_1, \ldots, en_n, ex_n$ s.t. $S \in Spec_{SDS}$. Let Σ be the sequence $p_{j_0}, p_{j_1}, ..., p_{j_n}$ of process identifiers that execute operations $en_0, en_1, ..., en_n$, respectively (a process identifier might appear several times). We call *solo execution* of history S by program *Prog*, and denote by $se(S, Prog, \Sigma)$, the execution of *Prog* in which p_{j_0} executes alone the transitions of the operation entered in en_0 and exited in ex_0, then followed by p_{j_1} executing alone the operation entered in en_1, etc.

Relative Nodes. A *relative node* corresponds to a pair $(a, b) \in \mathbb{N} \times \mathbb{N}$ in an execution π, if there is a transition t_{en} in π that corresponds to an entry statement s.t. this entry statement appears in the a-th position in $hs(\pi)$ and the sequence $al(opTrans(t_{en}, \pi_S))$ contains at least b elements. For example, if there exists a relative node $(5, 2)$ in an execution π, then this node has a "one-to-one" correspondence with the second allocate statement that was executed during the fifth operation.

Using relative nodes, we abstract away from memory locations and instead of comparing writes, we can compare the nodes where those writes are issued to. This abstraction allows us to compare writes (by comparing nodes) between a CSDS and a sequential SDS in order to capture property SP$_9$. We use relative nodes only on solo executions. We assume that in any solo execution of a given sequential history S, the operations of the CSDS and those of the respective SDS *allocate the same nodes and in the same order*.

Given an execution π, we define $rel(a, b, \pi)$ for $a, b \in \mathbb{N}$ to be a transition t_{al} of π. If $rel(a, b, \pi) = t_{al}$, this means that there is an entry statement in the a-th position of history $hs(\pi)$ that has a corresponding transition t_{en} in π and there are at least b elements in $al(opTrans(t_{en}, \pi))$ issuing an allocate instruction with t_{al} being the b-th such transition. If there exist no such a and b, then $rel(a, b, \pi) = \bot$.

Read and Written Nodes. For defining the read and written nodes of an operation we first define the set S which contains all the relative nodes of an execution π.

$$S = \{(a, b) \in \mathbb{N} \times \mathbb{N} : rel(a, b, \pi) \neq \bot\}$$

We can now define the sets of read and written nodes that contain relative nodes. $ReadNodes(t_{en}, \pi)$ is the set of pairs $(a, b) \in S$ satisfying:

$$ReadLoc(t_{en}, \pi) \cap NodeAlloc(rel(a, b, \pi), \pi) \neq \emptyset.$$

Similarly, $WrittenNodes(t_{en}, \pi)$ is the set of pairs $(a, b) \in S$ that satisfy:

$$WrittenLoc(t_{en}, \pi) \cap NodeAlloc(rel(a, b, \pi), \pi) \neq \emptyset.$$

These sets are used in defining property SP$_9$ in Sect. 3.

Reachability and the Root Pointer. Consider an execution π and a transition t of π such that, after t, a pointer pt points to a shared memory location l. Since π is well-formed, l was allocated by an allocate statement. Let t_{al} be the corresponding transition in π. l satisfies $l \in NodeAlloc(t_{al}, \pi)$. We define $reachable(pt, 1)_t$ as the set $NodeAlloc(t_{al}, \pi)$. For a set of shared memory locations M, we denote by $pointers(M)$ the locations of M that corresponds to pointers.[1] We define recursively for any $x > 0$:

$$reachable(pt, x + 1)_t = \bigcup_{pt' \in pointers(reachable(pt, x)_t)} reachable(pt', 1)_t.$$

Intuitively, $reachable(pt, x)_t$ captures the set of shared memory locations that are reachable from pt by following a path traversing at most x nodes. Those locations are reachable immediately after transition t has been executed in π but before the transition succeeding t in π has been executed. We additionally define $reachable(pt, \infty)_t = \bigcup_{x>0} reachable(pt, x)_t$ the set of all shared memory locations accessible from pt.

We assume that each data structure provides an init operation that is executed before any other operation. The init operation, as the name implies, is used for initializing the data structure. For example, for a linked list, init could allocate the head and tail of the list to simplify the execution of the upcoming operations. We denote with *root* (and call it *root pointer*) any pointer that points to a memory location that was allocated during the first allocate statement of init. For instance, init for linked list has to first allocate the head node, so the root pointer points to this head node.

Reachable and Freed Nodes. In a sequential setting, freed nodes are the ones removed by a delete operation. In order to define freed nodes, we first have to define the nodes that are reachable from a pointer pt. Using *reachable*, for a transition $t \in \pi$ we define $ReachableNodes(pt, \pi)_t$ as the set of pairs $(a, b) \in S$ satisfying:

$$NodeAlloc(rel(a, b, \pi), \pi) \cap reachable(pt, \infty)_t \neq \emptyset,$$

---

[1] Locations containing pointers could be differentiated from other locations if they contain a pointer type. This could be easily done by for example marking the last bit of the value residing in such a location.

where S is the set of relative nodes defined earlier. *ReachableNodes* includes the nodes that contain at least one location reachable from pt just after transition t.

For a tuple (t_{en}, t_{ex}) in a sequential history $hs(\pi)$, we define $FreedNodes(t_{en}, \pi) = InitialNodes \setminus FinalNodes$, where $InitialNodes = ReachableNodes(root, \pi)_{t_{en}}$ and $FinalNodes = ReachableNodes(root, \pi)_{t_{ex}}$.

The above definition captures the idea that freed nodes are the nodes that were reachable from a root pointer at the beginning of the operation, but are not anymore reachable at the end. Note that the definition of *FreedNodes* makes sense only for solo executions and is helpful when restricting the number (SP$_8$), as well as the region of stores (SP$_9$).

Logical Deletion. Many CSDSs [9,10] perform deletions in two steps: (i) mark the node to be deleted, and (ii) do the actual deletion (i.e., physical removal).

In the technical report [1], we formally define logical deletions. Additionally, we define when a transition is a *cleaning-up* store, meaning a transition that physically removes a marked node from the data structure. Intuitively, a cleaning-up store is defined as a transition that after it is performed in an execution, makes a reachable node of the data structure to be unreachable (based on *reachable*).

3 Sequential Proximity (SP)

In this section, we define the ten SP properties. The first five properties describe characteristics of traversals: search operations and parse phases. The last five describe modifications due to update operations.

3.1 Traversals

Traversals correspond to search operations or parse phases of update operations. More precisely, for an entry transition t_{en} in execution π, we define $traversals(t_{en}, \pi)$. If t_{en} is a search entry transition (i.e., t_{en} executes an entry search v statement), then $traversals(t_{en}, \pi)$ corresponds to $\{opTrans(t_{en}, \pi)\}$. If t_{en} is an update entry transition (i.e., t_{en} executes an entry op v statement where $op \in \{$insert, delete$\}$), then $traversals(t_{en}, \pi)$ corresponds to $\{parsePhase(t_{en}, \pi, k), 1 \leq k \leq n\}$ where $n = numberOfParsePhases(t_{en}, \pi)$.

SP$_1$: Read-only Traversal. No global memory is written during traversals.

Definition 1 (SP$_1$). *A program Prog has op read-only traversals if for each entry op transition t_{en} in $\pi \in [\![Prog]\!]$, there is no transition executing a* write *instruction in any sequence of traversals(t_{en}, π).*

SP$_2$: Non-blocking Traversal. Traversals must not block (e.g., do not wait for a lock to be released). To define this property, we first define the notion of a *non-blocking* process. Intuitively, a process is non-blocking if there is a constant

n such that no global memory location is read more than n times. Also, in every n steps that the process takes, at least one global memory location is read.

In detail, we say that a process p is n *steps non-blocking* in $tr(p) = t_1, t_2, \ldots, t_e$, where $tr(p)$ is a contiguous subsequence of $opTrans(t_{en}, \pi)$ with an entry transition t_{en} taken by process p in execution π, if $\exists n \in \mathbb{N}$ s.t.:

- no more than n transitions from $tr(p)$ execute a global read instruction to the same memory location;
- for all $r \in \{1, 2, \ldots, e\}$, consider $k = \lfloor r/n \rfloor$ s.t. $(k + 1) \cdot n \leq e$, then there is a transition that issues a global read in the sequence of transitions: $t_{k \cdot n + 1}, \ldots, t_{(k+1) \cdot n}$.

Definition 2 (SP$_2$). *A program Prog has op non-blocking traversals if there exists an $n \in \mathbb{N}$ such that: For every entry op transition t_{en} taken by a process p in execution $\pi \in \llbracket Prog \rrbracket$, p is n steps non-blocking in every sequence of traversals(t_{en}, π).*

SP$_3$: No Back-step Traversal. Only forward progress is allowed in traversals: When moving from a node a to a b during traversal, node a is never visited again.

For this property, we first define the notion of no back-steps. More precisely, consider a contiguous subsequence $tr(p)$ of $opTrans(t_{en}, \pi)$ where t_{en} is an entry transition taken by a process p in π. We say that process p has *no back-steps* if, for any pair of transitions $t_r, t_{r'}$ appearing in this order in $tr(p)$ with $rloc(t_r) = rloc(t_{r'}) = \{\ell\}$ and $\ell \in NodeAlloc(t_{al}, \pi)$, every transition t taken between t_r and $t_{r'}$ in $tr(p)$ verifies $rloc(t) \subseteq NodeAlloc(t_{al}, \pi)$.

Definition 3 (SP$_3$). *A program Prog has op no back-step traversals if for every entry op transition t_{en} taken by a process p in $\pi \in \llbracket Prog \rrbracket$, in every sequence trav in traversals(t_{en}, π), process p has no back-steps in trav.*

SP$_4$: No allocation Traversal. Traversals do not allocate any memory.

Definition 4 (SP$_4$). *A program Prog has op no allocation traversals if for every entry op transition t_{en} in $\pi \in \llbracket Prog \rrbracket$, there is no transition executing an allocate instruction in any sequence of traversals(t_{en}, π).*

SP$_5$: Read-clean Traversal. Traversals might issue stores only for cleaning-up purposes.

Definition 5 (SP$_5$). *A program Prog has op read-clean traversals if for every entry op transition t_{en} in $\pi \in \llbracket Prog \rrbracket$, if a transition t_w executes a write instruction in a sequence of traversals(t_{en}, π), t_w is a cleaning-up store.*

3.2 Modifications

For an update entry transition t_{en} in π, we define $modifications(t_{en}, \pi)$ to be the set of sequences $\{modifyPhase(t_{en}, \pi, k), 1 \leq k \leq n\}$ where $n = numberOfModifyPhases(t_{en}, \pi)$.

SP$_6$: Read-only Unsuccessful Modification. An unsuccessful operation (e.g., trying to insert an element that is already present) does not issue any write in a solo execution.

Definition 6 (SP$_6$). *A program Prog has op read-only unsuccessful modifications, if, for any complete sequential history $S \in Specs_{SDS}$ and any sequence of processes P, the solo execution $\pi = se(S, Prog, P)$ verifies that: For every entry op transition t_{en} in π that has a matching* exit op false *statement in $hs(\pi)$, it is the case that $modifications(t_{en}, \pi) = \emptyset$.*

SP$_7$: Conflict Restart Modification. The modify phase of an update operation can restart if there is a conflict with a concurrent operation. This type of conflict corresponds to the modification of similar nodes by concurrent operations. To capture when concurrent operations are allowed to conflict and restart, we check if such a conflict exists in the underlying sequential data structure.

We first introduce some auxiliary definitions. Two entry transitions t_{en_0} and t_{en_1} are said *conflict-free* in a solo execution π, if $(WrittenNodes(t_{en_0}, \pi) \cup FreedNodes(t_{en_0}, \pi)) \cap (WrittenNodes(t_{en_1}, \pi) \cup FreedNodes(t_{en_1}, \pi)) = \emptyset$. An entry transition t_{en} is called *restart-free* in an execution π, if $opTrans(t_{en}, \pi)$ does not contain an end-modify transition with a restart result. Given an execution π and two operations op_1 and op_2, we say that an execution π' is an *extension* of π by op_1 and op_2, if π is a prefix of π' followed by the transitions of the operations op_1 and op_2 executed by two processes (possibly concurrently) until their corresponding exit transitions.

Consider two programs $Prog_S$ and $Prog_C$ and $S' = S, en_0, ex_0, en_1, ex_1$ a complete sequential history, where S is a history and for every $i \in \{0, 1\}$, en_i corresponds to an entry statement and ex_i is its matching exit statement. Let us consider the following notations:

- $\pi_S = se(S', Prog_S, P_S)$ and $\pi_C = se(S, Prog_C, P_C)$, for P_S and P_C any sequences of processes;
- t_{en_0} and t_{en_1} the transitions corresponding to the entry statements en_0 and en_1 in π_S.

The triple $t = (S', Prog_S, Prog_C)$ is said to be a *valid restart triple* if t_{en_0} and t_{en_1} are not conflict-free in π_S or if, for any extension $\pi_{C'}$ of π_C by operations en_0 and en_1, the transitions corresponding to the entry statements en_0 and en_1 in $\pi_{C'}$ are restart-free.

Definition 7 (SP$_7$). *A program $Prog_C$ has valid conflict restart modifications, with respect to a sequential search data structure $Prog_S$, if for all complete sequential histories S with at least four tuples, triple $(S, Prog_S, Prog_C)$ is valid restart triple.*

SP$_8$: Number of Stores per Modification. SP$_8$ defines the number of stores allowed per modification. SP$_8$ depends on a respective sequential SDS and on whether the operations of the concurrent algorithm are blocking or not. The distinction between blocking and non-blocking is made due to the fact that a

Table 2. SP$_9$: Upper bounds on the number of writes (i.e., stores, lock acquisitions, and CAS operations).

insert	$\lvert CASOps(modi)\rvert + \lvert AcquiredLocks(modi)\rvert \leq MaxOtherNodeWrites(\text{insert})$
	$\lvert OtherNodeWrites(modi, \pi)\rvert \leq MaxOtherNodeWrites(\text{insert})$, for lock-based.
	$\lvert OtherNodeWrites(modi, \pi)\rvert = 0$, for non-blocking.
delete	$\lvert CASOps(modi)\rvert + \lvert AcquiredLocks(modi)\rvert$ $\leq MaxOtherNodeWrites(\text{delete}) + MaxFreedNodes(\text{delete})$
	$\lvert OtherNodeWrites(modi, \pi)\rvert$ $\leq MaxOtherNodeWrites(\text{delete}) + MaxFreedNodes(\text{delete})$, for lock-based.
	$\lvert OtherNodeWrites(modi, \pi)\rvert = 0$, for non-blocking.

lock-based algorithm needs to acquire a lock and then issue its modification store. In contrast a non-blocking algorithm applies its modification simultaneously with a compare-and-swap statement.

Definition 8 (SP$_8$). *A program $Prog_C$ has a sequential number of stores per modification, with respect to a sequential search data structure $Prog_S$, if the number of stores per modify phase is bounded by the maximum number of sequential writes and freed nodes, as defined in Table 2. Specifically, the upper bounds of Table 2 hold for all $modi \in modifications(t_{en}, \pi)$ where t_{en} is an update* entry op *transition in $\pi \in [\![Prog]\!]$. $CASOps(S)$ corresponds to the set of transitions that execute a* compare-and-swap *instruction in the sequence of transitions S. $AcquiredLocks(S)$ corresponds to the transitions from S that successfully acquired a lock (i.e., transitions that executed a* try-lock *statement that returned* true*). $MaxFreedNodes(typ)$ is defined as the maximum number of freed nodes during the sequential execution of an operation of type typ. $MaxOtherNodeWrites(typ)$ is defined as the maximum number of writes issued during the sequential execution of an operation op of type typ to nodes that were not allocated by operation op. The number of stores are constrained depending on whether the CSDS operation is blocking or not.*

SP$_9$: Region of Stores per Modification. The following property restricts the nodes that an operation writes during a modification, with respect to a sequential SDS.

We first define the written nodes during all the modify phases of an operation. To do this, we define all the memory locations that were written during all the modify phases:

$$WrittenMLoc(t_{en}\pi) = \bigcup_{t \in modi\,:\,modi \in modifications(t_{en}, \pi)} wloc(t)$$

$WrittenMNodes(t_{en}, \pi)$ is the set of pairs $(a, b) \in \mathbb{N} \times \mathbb{N}$ s.t. $rel(a, b, \pi) \neq \perp$ that satisfies:

$$WrittenMLoc(t_{en}, \pi) \cap NodeAlloc(rel(a, b, \pi), \pi) \neq \emptyset.$$

Definition 9 (SP$_9$). *A program $Prog_C$ has a valid region of stores per modification with respect to a sequential search data structure $Prog_S$ if it writes to similar nodes as $Prog_S$ during modifications. Formally, for every complete sequential history S and any sequence of processes P_C and P_S, consider the solo executions $\pi_C = se(S, Prog_C, P_C)$ and $\pi_S = se(S, Prog_S, P_S)$. Since $hs(\pi_C) = hs(\pi_S)$, for every entry transition t_{en} in π_C, there is a corresponding entry transition $t_{en'}$ in π_S. SP$_9$ is satisfied[2] if the following holds for every update transition t_{en} in π_C:*
If t_{en} executes

- *an insert statement, then $WrittenMNodes(t_{en}, \pi_C) = WrittenNodes(t_{en'}, \pi_S)$;*
- *a delete statement, then $WrittenMNodes(t_{en}, \pi_C) \subseteq WrittenNodes(t_{en'}, \pi_S) \cup FreedNodes(t_{en'}, \pi_S)$.*

SP$_{10}$: No Allocation Modification. No memory is allocated during modifications.

Definition 10 (SP$_{10}$). *A program $Prog$ has op no allocation modifications if for every entry op transition t_{en} in $\pi \in [\![Prog]\!]$ there is no transition executing an allocate instruction for any sequence in $modifications(t_{en}, \pi)$.*

Definition 11: Sequential Proximity

A concurrent search data structure $Prog_C$ is called **sequentially proximal** if it satisfies SP$_{1-4}$ for search, SP$_{2-9}$ for insert, and SP$_{2-10}$ for delete operations.

---

4 Concluding Remarks

In this paper, we defined sequential proximity (SP), a formalization that captures the closeness of concurrent search data structures (CSDSs) and their sequential counterparts. Based on prior work, we argued that sequentially-proximal algorithms, namely algorithms which follow SP, are scalable. As a result, we claim that SP is the first step towards a formal theory for proving that a CSDS algorithm is likely to be scalable. We believe that from a practitioner's point of view, adherence to the SP properties can lead to scalable implementations and help avoid commonly introduced bottlenecks in CSDSs.

---

[2] For randomized data structures, such as skip lists [18], we assume that the underlying random number generator produces the exact same sequences of numbers for both $Prog_S$ and $Prog_C$.

References

1. Antoniadis, K., Guerraoui, R., Stainer, J., Trigonakis, V.: Sequential proximity: towards provably scalable concurrent search algorithms. Technical report, EPFL (2017)
2. Attiya, H., Guerraoui, R., Hendler, D., Kuznetsov, P. Michael, M.M., Vechev, M.T.: Laws of order: expensive synchronization in concurrent algorithms cannot be eliminated. In: POPL (2011)
3. Bronson, N.G., Casper, J., Chafi, H., Olukotun, K.: A Practical Concurrent Binary Search Tree. In: PPopp (2010)
4. David, T., Guerraoui, R., Trigonakis, V., Concurrency, A.: The secret to scaling concurrent search data structures. In: ASPLOS (2015)
5. Ellen, F., Fatourou, P., Ruppert, E., van Breugel, F.: Non-blocking binary search trees. In: PODC (2010)
6. Facebook: RocksDB. http://rocksdb.org
7. Fraser, K.: Practical lock-freedom. Ph.D. thesis, University of Cambridge (2004)
8. Guerraoui, R., Trigonakis, V.: Optimistic concurrency with OPTIK. In: PPopp (2016)
9. Harris, T.L.: A pragmatic implementation of non-blocking linked-lists. In: Welch, J. (ed.) DISC 2001. LNCS, vol. 2180, pp. 300–314. Springer, Heidelberg (2001). doi:10.1007/3-540-45414-4_21
10. Heller, S., Herlihy, M., Luchangco, V., Moir, M., Scherer, W.N., Shavit, N.: A lazy concurrent list-based set algorithm. In: Anderson, J.H., Prencipe, G., Wattenhofer, R. (eds.) OPODIS 2005. LNCS, vol. 3974, pp. 3–16. Springer, Heidelberg (2006). doi:10.1007/11795490_3
11. Herlihy, M.: Wait-free synchronization. In: TOPLAS (1991)
12. Herlihy, M., Wing, J.: Linearizability: a correctness condition for concurrent objects. In: TOPLAS (1990)
13. Herlihy, M., Lev, Y., Luchangco, V., Shavit, N.: A simple optimistic skiplist algorithm. In: Prencipe, G., Zaks, S. (eds.) SIROCCO 2007. LNCS, vol. 4474, pp. 124–138. Springer, Heidelberg (2007). doi:10.1007/978-3-540-72951-8_11
14. Howley, S.V., Jones, J.: A non-blocking internal binary search tree. In: SPAA (2012)
15. Linux Kernel: Linux Kernel. https://www.kernel.org
16. Matveev, A., Shavit, N., Felber, P., Marlier, P.: Read-log-update: a lightweight synchronization mechanism for concurrent programming. In: SOSP (2015)
17. McKenney, P.E., Slingwine, J.D.: Read-copy update: using execution history to solve concurrency problems. In: PDCS (1998)
18. Pugh, W., Lists, S.: A probabilistic alternative to balanced trees. In: CACM (1990)

An Executable Sequential Specification for Spark Aggregation

Yu-Fang Chen[1], Chih-Duo Hong[1], Ondřej Lengál[1,2(✉)], Shin-Cheng Mu[1],
Nishant Sinha[3], and Bow-Yaw Wang[1]

[1] Academia Sinica, Taipei, Taiwan
[2] Brno University of Technology, Brno, Czech Republic
lengal@fit.vutbr.cz
[3] IBM Research, New Delhi, India

Abstract. Spark is a new promising platform for scalable data-parallel computation. It provides several high-level application programming interfaces (APIs) to perform parallel data aggregation. Since execution of parallel aggregation in Spark is inherently non-deterministic, a natural requirement for Spark programs is to give the same result for any execution on the same data set. We present PURESPARK, an executable formal Haskell specification for Spark aggregate combinators. Our specification allows us to deduce the precise condition for deterministic outcomes from Spark aggregation. We report case studies analyzing deterministic outcomes and correctness of Spark programs.

1 Introduction

Spark [1, 29, 30] is a popular platform for scalable distributed data-parallel computation based on a flexible programming environment with concise and high-level APIs. Spark is by many considered as the successor of MapReduce [15, 25]. Despite its fame, the precursory computational model of MapReduce suffers from I/O congestion and limited programming support for distributed problem solving. Notably, Spark has the following advantages over MapReduce. First, it has high performance due to distributed, cached, and in-memory computation. Second, the platform adopts a relaxed fault tolerant model where sub-results are recomputed upon faults rather than aggressively stored. Third, lazy evaluation semantics is used to avoid unnecessary computation. Finally, Spark offers greater programming flexibility through its powerful APIs founded in functional programming. Spark also owes its popularity to a unified framework for efficient graph, streaming, and SQL-based relational database computation, a machine learning library, and the support of multiple distributed data storage formats. Spark is one of the most active open-source projects with over 1000 contributors [1].

In a typical Spark program, a sequence of transformations followed by an action are performed on Resilient Distributed Datasets (RDDs). An RDD is the principal abstraction for data-parallel computation in Spark. It represents a read-only collection of data items partitioned and stored distributively.

© Springer International Publishing AG 2017
A. El Abbadi and B. Garbinato (Eds.): NETYS 2017, LNCS 10299, pp. 421–438, 2017.
DOI: 10.1007/978-3-319-59647-1_31

RDD operations such as map, reduce, and aggregate are called *combinators*. They generate and aggregate data in RDDs to carry out Spark computation. For instance, the aggregate combinator takes user-defined functions *seq* and *comb*: *seq* accumulates a sub-result for each partition while *comb* merges sub-results across different partitions. Spark also provides a family of aggregate combinators for common data structures such as pairs and graphs. In Spark computation, data aggregation is ubiquitous.

Programming in Spark, however, can be tricky. Since sub-results are computed using- multiple applications of *seq* and *comb* across partitions concurrently, the order of their applications varies on different executions. Because of indefinite orders of computation, aggregation in Spark is inherently *non-deterministic*. A Spark program may produce different outcomes for the same input on different runs. This form of non-deterministic computation has other side effects. For instance, the private function AreaUnderCurve.of in the Spark machine learning library computes numerical integration distributively; it exhibits numerical instability due to non-deterministic computation. Consider the integral of x^{73} on the interval $[-2, 2]$. Since x^{73} is an odd function, the integral is 0. In our experiments, AreaUnderCurve.of returns different results ranging from -8192.0 to 12288.0 on the same input because of different orders of floating-point computation. To ensure deterministic outcomes, programmers must carefully develop their programs to adhere to Spark requirements.

Unfortunately, Spark's documentation does not specify the requirements formally. It only describes informal algebraic properties about combinators to ensure correctness. The documentation provides little help to a programmer in understanding the complex, and sometimes unexpected, interaction between *seq* and *comb*, especially when these two are functions over more complex domains, e.g. lists or trees. Inspecting the Spark implementation is a laborious job since public combinators are built by composing a long chain of generic private combinators—determining the execution semantics from the complex implementation is hard. Moreover, Spark is continuously evolving and the implementation semantics may change significantly across releases. We therefore believe that a formal specification of Spark combinators is necessary to help developers understand the program semantics better, clarify hidden assumptions about RDDs, and help to reason about correctness and sources of non-determinism in Spark programs.

Building a formal specification for Spark is far from straightforward. Spark is implemented in Scala and provides high-level APIs also in Python and Java. Because Spark heavily exploits various language features of Scala, it is hard to derive specifications without formalizing the operational semantics of the Scala language, which is not an easy task by itself. Instead of that, we have developed a Haskell library PURESPARK [4], which for each key Spark combinator provides an abstract sequential functional specification in Haskell. We use Haskell as a specification language for two reasons. First, the core of Haskell has strong formal foundations in λ-calculus. Second, program evaluation in Haskell, like in Scala, is lazy, which admits faithful modeling of Spark aggregation. Through the use of Haskell we obtain a concise formal functional model for Spark combinators without formalizing Scala.

An important goal of our specification is to make non-determinism in various combinators explicit. Spark developers can inspect it to identify sources of non-determinism when program executions yield unexpected outputs. Researchers can also use it to understand distributed Spark aggregation and investigate its computational pattern. Our specification is also *executable*. A programmer can use the Haskell APIs to implement data-parallel programs, test them on different input RDDs, and verify correctness of outputs independent of the Spark programming environment. In our case studies, we capture non-deterministic behaviors of real Spark programs by executing the corresponding PURESPARK specifications with crafted input data sets. We also show that the sequential specification is useful in developing distributed Spark programs.

Our main contributions are summarized below:

– We present formal, functional, sequential specifications for key Spark aggregate combinators. The PURESPARK specification consists of executable library APIs. It can assist Spark program development by mimicking data-parallel programming in conventional environments.
– Based on the specification, we investigate and identify necessary and sufficient conditions for Spark aggregate combinators to produce deterministic outcomes for general and pair RDDs.
– Our specification allows to deduce the precise condition for deterministic outcomes from Spark aggregation.
– We perform a series of case studies on practical Spark programs to validate our formalization. With PURESPARK, we find instances of numerical instability in the Spark machine learning library.
– Up to our knowledge, this is the first work to provide a formal, functional specification of key Spark aggregate combinators for data-parallel computation.

2 Preliminaries

Let A be a non-empty set and $\odot : A \times A \to A$ be a function. An element $i \in A$ is the *identity* of $\odot$ if for every $a \in A$, it holds that $a = i \odot a = a \odot i$. The function $\odot$ is *associative* if for every $a, a', a'' \in A$, $a \odot (a' \odot a'') = (a \odot a') \odot a''$; $\odot$ is *commutative* if for every $a, a' \in A$, $a \odot a' = a' \odot a$. The algebraic structure $(A, \odot)$ is a *semigroup* if $\odot$ is associative. A *monoid* is a structure $(A, \odot, \bot)$ such that $(A, \odot)$ is a semigroup and $\bot \in A$ is the identity of $\odot$. The semigroup $(A, \odot)$ and monoid $(A, \odot, \bot)$ are commutative if $\odot$ is commutative.

Haskell is a strongly typed purely functional programming language. Similar to Scala, Haskell programs are lazily evaluated. We use several widely used Haskell functions (Fig. 1). **fst** and **snd** are projections on pairs. **null** tests whether a list is empty. **elem** is the membership function for lists; its infix notation is often used, as in 0 '**elem**' []. (++) concatenates two lists; it is used as an infix operator, as in [**False**] ++ [**True**]. **map** applies a function to elements of a list. **reducel** merges elements of a list by a given binary function from left to right. **foldl** accumulates by applying a function to elements of a list iteratively, also

fst :: $(\alpha, \beta) \rightarrow \alpha$
fst (x, _) = x

snd :: $(\alpha, \beta) \rightarrow \beta$
snd (_, y) = y

null :: $[\alpha] \rightarrow$ **Bool**
null [] = **True**
null (x:xs) = **False**

elem :: $\alpha \rightarrow [\alpha] \rightarrow$ **Bool**
elem x [] = **False**
elem x (y:ys) = x==y || **elem** x ys

(++) :: $[\alpha] \rightarrow [\alpha] \rightarrow [\alpha]$
[] ++ ys = ys
x:xs ++ ys = x:(xs ++ ys)

map :: $(\alpha \rightarrow \beta) \rightarrow [\alpha] \rightarrow [\beta]$
map f [] = []
map f (x:xs) = (f x):(**map** f xs)

reducel :: $(\alpha \rightarrow \alpha \rightarrow \alpha) \rightarrow [\alpha] \rightarrow \alpha$
reducel h (x:xs) = **foldl** h x xs

foldl :: $(\beta \rightarrow \alpha \rightarrow \beta) \rightarrow \beta \rightarrow [\alpha] \rightarrow \beta$
foldl h z [] = z
foldl h z (x:xs) = **foldl** h (h z x) xs

concat :: $[[\alpha]] \rightarrow [\alpha]$
concat [] = []
concat (xs:xss) = xs ++ (**concat** xss)

concatMap :: $(\alpha \rightarrow [\beta]) \rightarrow [\alpha] \rightarrow [\beta]$
concatMap xs = **concat** (**map** f xs)

lookup :: $\alpha \rightarrow [(\alpha, \beta)] \rightarrow$ **Maybe** β
lookup k [] = **Nothing**
lookup k ((x, y):xys) = **if** k == x
    then Just y **else lookup** k xys

filter :: $(\alpha \rightarrow$ **Bool**$) \rightarrow [\alpha] \rightarrow [\alpha]$
filter p [] = []
filter p (x:xs) = **if** p x
    then x:(**filter** p xs) **else filter** p xs

Fig. 1. Basic functions

from left to right. **concat** concatenates elements in a list. **concatMap** applies a function to elements of a list and concatenates the results. **lookup** finds the value of a key in a list of pairs. **filter** selects elements from a list by a predicate.

In order to formalize non-determinism in distributed aggregation, we define the following non-deterministic shuffle function for lists:

shuffle! :: $[\alpha] \rightarrow [\alpha]$
shuffle! xs = ...   *-- shuffle xs randomly*

A random monad can be used to define random shuffling. Instead of explicit monadic notation, we introduce the *chaotic* **shuffle!** function in our presentation for the sake of brevity. Thus, **shuffle!** [0, 1, 2] evaluates to one of the six possible lists [0, 1, 2], [0, 2, 1], [1, 0, 2] [1, 2, 0], [2, 0, 1], or [2, 1, 0] randomly. Using **shuffle!**, more chaotic functions are defined.

map! :: $(\alpha \rightarrow \beta) \rightarrow [\alpha] \rightarrow [\beta]$
map! f xs = **shuffle!** (**map** f xs)

concatMap! :: $(\alpha \rightarrow [\beta]) \rightarrow [\alpha] \rightarrow [\beta]$
concatMap! f xs = **concat** (**map!** f xs)

Chaotic **map!** shuffles the result of **map** randomly, **concatMap!** concatenates the shuffled result of **map**. For instance, **map! even** [0, 1] evaluates to [**False**, **True**] or [**True**, **False**]; **concatMap! fact**[2, 3] evaluates to [1, 2, 1, 3] or [1, 3, 1, 2] where **fact** computes a sorted list of factors (note that the two subsequences [1,2] and [1,3] are kept intact).

repartition! :: $[\alpha] \rightarrow [[\alpha]]$
repartition! xs = **let** ys = **shuffle!** xs ...
                 in yss $--$ ys $==$ concat yss

The function **repartition!** shuffles a given list and partitions the shuffled list into several non-empty lists. For instance, **repartition!** $[0, 1]$ results in $[[0], [1]]$, $[[1], [0]]$, $[[0, 1]]$, or $[[1, 0]]$. The chaotic function can be implemented by a random monad easily; its precise definition is omitted here.

3 Spark Aggregation

Resilient Distributed Datasets (RDDs) are the basic data abstraction in Spark. An RDD is a collection of partitions of immutable data; data in different partitions can be processed concurrently. We formalize partitions by lists, and RDDs by lists of partitions.

type Partition $\alpha = [\alpha]$ **type** RDD $\alpha = [\text{Partition } \alpha]$

The Spark **aggregate** combinator computes *sub-results* of every partitions in an RDD, and returns the aggregated result by combining sub-results.

aggregate :: $\beta \rightarrow (\beta \rightarrow \alpha \rightarrow \beta) \rightarrow (\beta \rightarrow \beta \rightarrow \beta) \rightarrow$ RDD $\alpha \rightarrow \beta$
aggregate z seq comb rdd = **let** presults = **map!** (**foldl** seq z) rdd
                              in foldl comb z presults

More concretely, let z be a default aggregated value. **aggregate** applies **foldl** seq z to every partition of rdd. Hence the sub-result of each partition is accumulated by folding elements in the partition with seq. The combinator then combines sub-results by another folding using comb.

Note that the chaotic **map!** function is used to model non-deterministic interleavings of sub-results. To exploit concurrency, Spark creates a task to compute the sub-result for each partition. These tasks are executed concurrently and hence induce non-deterministic computation. We use the chaotic **map!** function to designate non-determinism explicitly.

A related combinator is **reduce**. Instead of **foldl**, the combinator uses **reducel** to aggregate data in an RDD.

reduce :: $(\alpha \rightarrow \alpha \rightarrow \alpha) \rightarrow$ RDD $\alpha \rightarrow \alpha$
reduce comb rdd = **let** presults = **map!** (**reducel** comb) rdd
                       in reducel comb presults

Similar to the **aggregate** combinator, **reduce** computes sub-results concurrently. The chaotic **map!** function is again used to model non-deterministic computation.

Sub-results of different partitions are computed in parallel, but the **aggregate** combinator still combines sub-results sequentially. This can be further parallelized. Observe that several sub-results may be available simultaneously from distributed computation. The Spark **treeAggregate** combinator applies comb to pairs of sub-results concurrently until the final result is obtained. In addition to concurrent computation of sub-results, **treeAggregate** also combines sub-results from different partitions in parallel.

In our specification, two chaotic functions are used to model non-deterministic computation on two different levels. The **map**! function models non-determinism in computing sub-results of partitions. The **apply**! function (introduced below) models concurrent combination of sub-results from different partitions. It combines two consecutive sub-results picked chaotically, and repeats such chaotic combinations until the final result is obtained. Observe that the computation has a binary-tree structure with comb as internal nodes and sub-results from different partitions as leaves.

apply! :: $(\beta \rightarrow \beta \rightarrow \beta) \rightarrow [\beta] \rightarrow \beta$
apply! comb [r] = r
apply! comb [r, r'] = comb r r'
apply! comb rs = **let** (ls', l', r', rs') = ... $-- \; rs == ls' + [l', r'] + rs'$
  in apply! comb (ls' + [comb l' r'] + rs')

treeAggregate:: $\beta \rightarrow (\beta \rightarrow \alpha \rightarrow \beta) \rightarrow (\beta \rightarrow \beta \rightarrow \beta) \rightarrow$ RDD $\alpha \rightarrow \beta$
treeAggregate z seq comb rdd = **let** presults = **map**! (**foldl** seq z) rdd
  in apply! comb presults

The **treeReduce** combinator optimizes **reduce** by combining sub-results in parallel. Similar to **treeAggregate**, two levels of non-deterministic computation can occur.

treeReduce :: $(\alpha \rightarrow \alpha \rightarrow \alpha) \rightarrow$ RDD $\alpha \rightarrow \alpha$
treeReduce comb rdd = **let** presults = **map**! (**reducel** comb) rdd
              in apply! comb presults

Pair RDDs. Key-value pairs are widely used in data parallel computation. If the data type of an RDD is a pair, we say that the RDD is a *pair* RDD. The first and second elements in a pair are called the *key* and the *value* of the pair respectively.

type PairRDD $\alpha \; \beta$ = RDD (α, β)

In a pair RDD, different pairs can have the same key. Spark provides combinators to aggregate values associated with the same key. The **aggregateByKey** combinator returns an RDD by aggregating values associated with the same key. We use the following functions to formalize **aggregateByKey**:

hasKey :: $\alpha \rightarrow$ Partition $(\alpha, \beta) \rightarrow$ **Bool**   **hasValue** :: $\alpha \rightarrow \beta \rightarrow$ Partition $(\alpha, \beta) \rightarrow \beta$
hasKey k ps = **case** (**lookup** k ps) **of**   **hasValue** k val ps = **case** (**lookup** k ps) **of**
  Just _ → **True**   Just v → v
  Nothing → **False**   Nothing → val

addTo :: $\alpha \rightarrow \beta \rightarrow$ Partition $(\alpha, \beta) \rightarrow$ Partition (α, β)
addTo key val ps = **foldl** (λr (k, v) → **if** key == k **then** r **else** (k, v):r) [(key, val)] ps

The expression **hasKey** k ps checks if key appears in a partition of pairs. **hasValue** k val ps finds a value associated with key in a partition of pairs. It evaluates to the default value val if key does not appear in the partition. The expression **addTo** key val ps adds the pair (key, val) to the partition ps, and removes other pairs with the same key.

The **aggregateByKey** combinator first aggregates all pairs with the value z and the function mergeComb in each partition. If values vs are associated with the same key in a partition, the value **foldl** mergeComb z vs for the key is pre-aggregated. Since a key may appear in several partitions, all pre-aggregated values associated with the key across different partitions are merged using mergeValue.

aggregateByKey :: $\gamma \to (\gamma \to \beta \to \gamma) \to (\gamma \to \gamma \to \gamma) \to$ PairRDD $\alpha\ \beta \to$ PairRDD $\alpha\ \gamma$
aggregateByKey z mergeComb mergeValue pairRdd =
   let mergeBy fun left (k, v) = **addTo** k (fun (hasValue k z left) v) left
      preAgg = **concatMap!** (**foldl** (mergeBy mergeComb) []) pairRdd
   in repartition! (**foldl** (mergeBy mergeValue) [] preAgg)

In the specification, we accumulate values associated with the same key by merge-Comb in each partition, keeping a list of pairs of a key and the partially aggregated value for the key. Since accumulation in different partitions runs in parallel, the chaotic **concatMap!** function is used to model such non-deterministic computation. After all partitions finish their accumulation, mergeValue merges values associated with the same key across different partitions. The final pair RDD can have a default or user-defined partitioning. Since a user-defined partitioning may shuffle a pair RDD arbitrarily, it is in our specification modeled by the chaotic **repartition!** function.

Pair RDDs have a combinator corresponding to **reduce** called **reduceByKey**. **reduceByKey** merges all values associated with a key by mergeValue, following a similar computational pattern as **aggregateByKey**. Note that every key is associated with at most one value in resultant pair RDDs of **aggregateByKey** or **reduceByKey**.

reduceByKey :: $(\beta \to \beta \to \beta) \to$ PairRDD $\alpha\ \beta \to$ PairRDD $\alpha\ \beta$
reduceByKey mergeValue pairRdd =
   let merge left (k, v) = **case lookup** k left **of Just** v' $\to$ **addTo** k (mergeValue v' v) left
                                     Nothing $\to$ **addTo** k v left
      preAgg = **concatMap!** (**foldl** merge []) pairRdd
   in repartition! (**foldl** merge [] preAgg)

Spark also provides a library, called GraphX, for a distributed analysis of graphs. See [12] for a formalization of some of its key functions.

4 Deterministic Aggregation

Having deterministic outcomes is desired from all aggregation functions. If a function may return different values on different executions, the function is often not implemented correctly. A program with explicit assumptions on the input data is also desirable. Otherwise, the program may work correctly on certain data sets but produce unexpected outcomes on others where implicit assumptions do not hold [27]. We now investigate conditions under which Spark aggregation combinators always produce deterministic outcomes. Proofs of the given lemmas can be found in [12]. Proofs of some crucial lemmas have also been formalized using Agda [4].

We first show how to deal with non-deterministic behaviors in the **aggregate** combinator. Consider a variant of the formalization of **aggregate** from Sect. 3:

aggregate' $:: \beta \to (\beta \to \alpha \to \beta) \to (\beta \to \beta \to \beta) \to$ RDD $\alpha \to \beta$
aggregate' z seq comb rdd = **let** presults = perm (**map** (**foldl** seq z) rdd)
  in foldl comb z presults

Observe that we changed the application of the chaotic **map**! function with an application of the permutation perm after the regular **map** function. The function composition perm(**map** ...) is a concrete instantiation of **map**!, that is, a function that permutes its list argument. Notice that perm can be pushed inside **map**:

perm (**map** f xs) == **map** f (perm xs).

Assume that rdd was obtained from a list xs by splitting and permuting, that is, rdd == perm' (split xs) where split $:: [\alpha] \to [[\alpha]]$ satisfies xs == (concat . split) xs. We can therefore rewrite the computation of presults in **aggregate'** to

let pres = perm (**map** (**foldl** seq z) (perm' (split xs))),

After pushing perm inside map, we obtain

let pres = **map** (**foldl** seq z) ((perm . perm') (split xs)).

Since perm . perm' is also a permutation perm", we have

let pres = **map** (**foldl** seq z) rdd'

where rdd' is another RDD obtained from xs by splitting and shuffling. Let us call (deterministic) instances of **repartition**! as *partitionings*. As a consequence, we focus only on proving if calls to **aggregate**^{D} defined below have deterministic outcomes for different partitionings of a list into RDDs:

aggregate$^D :: \beta \to (\beta \to \alpha \to \beta) \to (\beta \to \beta \to \beta) \to$ RDD $\alpha \to \beta$
aggregate^D z seq comb rdd = **let** pres = **map** (**foldl** seq z) rdd
                      in foldl comb z pres

Moreover, we define deterministic versions of **reduce**

reduce$^D :: (\alpha \to \alpha \to \alpha) \to$ RDD $\alpha \to \alpha$
reduce^D comb rdd = **let** presults = perm (**map** (**reducel** comb) rdd)
  in reducel comb presults

and also **treeAggregate**^{D} and **treeReduce**^{D} in a similar way.

In the following, given a function f that takes an RDD as one of its parameters and contains a single occurrence of the chaotic **map**! (respectively **concatMap**!) function, we use f^D to denote the function obtained from f by replacing the chaotic **map**! (respectively **concatMap**!) with a regular **map** (respectively **concatMap**). A similar reasoning can show that it suffices to check whether calls to f^D have deterministic outcomes for different partitionings on a list into RDDs.

For better readability, standard mathematical notation of functions is used in the rest of this section. We represent a Haskell function application f x1 ... xn as $f(x_1, \ldots, x_n)$.

4.1   aggregate

In this section, we give conditions for deterministic outcomes of calls to the aggregate combinator **aggregate**$(z, seq, \oplus, rdd)$ for $z :: \beta$, $seq :: \beta \times \alpha \to \beta$, $\oplus :: \beta \times \beta \to \beta$, and $rdd :: \text{RDD } \alpha$. We first define what it means for calls to the **aggregate** combinator to have deterministic outcomes.

Definition 1. *Calls to* **aggregate**$(z, seq, \oplus, rdd)$ *have* deterministic outcomes *if*

$$\textbf{aggregate}^D(z, seq, \oplus, part(L)) = \textbf{foldl}(seq, z, L) \tag{1}$$

for all lists L and partitionings part.

Conventionally, **aggregate** is regarded as a parallelized counterpart of **foldl**. For example, the sequential **aggregate** function in the standard Scala library ignores the $\oplus$ operator and is implemented by **foldl**. This is why we characterize deterministic **aggregate** as **foldl** in Definition 1. Our characterization, however, does not cover all **aggregate** calls that always give the same outputs. In particular, it does not cover an **aggregate** call where $\oplus$ is a constant function, which is, however, quite suspicious in a distributed data-parallel computation and should be reported.

We give necessary and sufficient conditions for **aggregate** calls to have deterministic outcomes in several lemmas, culminating in Corollary 1. The first lemma allows us to check only conditions on seq and $\oplus$ over all possible pairs of lists instead of enumerating all possible partitionings on lists. For brevity, we use $\langle p_1 \rangle$ for **foldl**(seq, z, p_1), and $img()$**foldl**(seq, z) for the image of **foldl**(seq, z, L) for any list L. That is, $img($**foldl**$(seq, z)) = \{y \mid$ there is a list L such that **foldl**$(seq, z, L) = y\}$.

Lemma 1. *Calls to* **aggregate**$(z, seq, \oplus, rdd)$ *have deterministic outcomes iff:*
1. $(img($**foldl**$(seq, z)), \oplus, z)$ *is a commutative monoid, and*
2. *for all lists $p_1, p_2 :: [\alpha]$, $\langle p_1 +\!\!+ p_2 \rangle = \langle p_1 \rangle \oplus \langle p_2 \rangle$.*

Note that condition 2 in Lemma 1 is equivalent to saying that $\langle \cdot \rangle$ is a list homomorphism to the monoid $(img($**foldl**$(seq, z)), \oplus, z)$ [6].

The lemma below further helps us reduce the need of testing conditions over all possible pairs of lists to conditions over elements of $\alpha \times img($**foldl**$(seq, z))$.

Lemma 2. *Let $\oplus$ be associative on $\gamma = img($**foldl**$(seq, z))$ and z be the identity of $\oplus$ on γ. The following are equivalent:*

1. *for all lists $p_1, p_2 :: [\alpha]$,*

$$\langle p_1 +\!\!+ p_2 \rangle = \langle p_1 \rangle \oplus \langle p_2 \rangle, \tag{2}$$

2. *for all elements $d :: \alpha$ and $e :: \gamma$,*

$$seq(e, d) = e \oplus seq(z, d). \tag{3}$$

Summarizing the lemmas, we get the following corollary:

Corollary 1. *Calls to* **aggregate**$(z, seq, \oplus, rdd)$ *have deterministic outcomes iff*
1. $(img($**foldl**$(seq, z)), \oplus, z)$ *is a commutative monoid and*
2. *for all $d :: \alpha$ and $e :: img($**foldl**$(seq, z))$, it holds that $seq(e, d) = e \oplus seq(z, d)$.*

4.2   reduce

This section explores conditions for deterministic outcomes of calls to **reduce**$(\oplus, rdd)$ for $\oplus :: \alpha \times \alpha \to \alpha$ and $rdd :: \mathsf{RDD}\ \alpha$. We use the function **reduce**^{D} defined in the introduction of Sect. 4. For **reduce**, we assume that for any non-empty list, all partitions of its partitioning are non-empty (otherwise the result of **reduce** is undefined).

We define deterministic outcomes for **reduce** as follows.

Definition 2. *Calls to* **reduce**$(\oplus, rdd)$ *have* deterministic outcomes *if*

$$\mathbf{reduce}^D(\oplus, part(L)) = \mathbf{reducel}(\oplus, L) \tag{4}$$

for all lists L and partitionings part.

We reduce the problem of checking if **reduce** has deterministic outcomes to the problem of checking if **aggregate** has deterministic outcomes by the following lemma.

Lemma 3. *Calls to* **reduce**$(\oplus, rdd)$ *have deterministic outcomes iff calls to* **aggregate**$(\mathsf{Nothing}, seq', \oplus', rdd)$ *have deterministic outcomes, where seq' and $\oplus'$ are as follows:*

seq' x y = **case** x **of** $(\oplus')$ x y = **case** (x, y) **of** (**Nothing**, y') $\to$ y'
  Nothing $\to$ **Just** y   (x', **Nothing**) $\to$ x'
  Just x' $\to$ **Just** (x' $\oplus$ y)   (**Just** x', **Just** y') $\to$ **Just** (x' $\oplus$ y') .

Combining Corollary 1 and Lemma 3, we get the condition for deterministic outcomes of **reduce**$(\oplus, rdd)$ calls.

Corollary 2. *Calls to* **reduce**$(\oplus, rdd)$ *have deterministic outcomes iff $(\alpha, \oplus)$ is a commutative semigroup.*

4.3   treeAggregate and treeReduce

This section gives conditions for deterministic outcomes of calls to the following two aggregate combinators:

1. **treeAggregate**$(z, seq, \oplus, rdd)$ for $z :: \beta$, $seq :: \beta \times \alpha \to \beta$, $\oplus :: \beta \times \beta \to \beta$, and $rdd :: \mathsf{RDD}\ \alpha$; and
2. **treeReduce**$(\oplus, rdd)$ for $\oplus :: \alpha \times \alpha \to \alpha$, $rdd :: \mathsf{RDD}\ \alpha$.

Different from **aggregate** and **reduce**, the tree variants have another level of non-determinism modeled by **apply**!. The chaotic function effectively simulates non-deterministic computation with a binary-tree structure (Sect. 3).

To define calls to **treeAggregate** and **treeReduce** to have deterministic outcomes, we use the functions **treeAggregate**^{T} and **treeReduce**^{T} obtained by adding an explicit deterministic instantiation of **apply**! to **treeAggregate**^{D} and **treeReduce**^{D}.

Definition 3. *Calls to* **treeAggregate**$(z, seq, \oplus, rdd)$ *and* **treeReduce**$(\oplus, rdd)$ *have deterministic outcomes if*

$$\textbf{treeAggregate}^T(apply, z, seq, \oplus, part(L)) = \textbf{foldl}(seq, z, L) \qquad (5)$$

and

$$\textbf{treeReduce}^T(apply, \oplus, part(L)) = \textbf{reducel}(\oplus, L) \qquad (6)$$

respectively for all lists L, partitionings part, and instantiations apply of **apply !**.

The following two propositions state necessary and sufficient conditions for the **treeAggregate** and **treeReduce** combinators to have deterministic outcomes.

Proposition 1. *Calls to* **treeAggregate**$(z, seq, \oplus, rdd)$ *have deterministic outcomes iff calls to* **aggregate**$(z, seq, \oplus, rdd)$ *have deterministic outcomes.*

Proposition 2. *Calls to* **treeReduce**$(\oplus, rdd)$ *have deterministic outcomes iff calls to* **reduce**$(\oplus, rdd)$ *have deterministic outcomes.*

4.4   aggregateByKey and reduceByKey

We proceed by investigating conditions for the following combinators on pair RDDs:

1. **aggregateByKey**$(z, seq, \oplus, prdd)$ for $z :: \gamma$, $seq :: \gamma \times \beta \to \gamma$, $\oplus :: \gamma \times \gamma \to \gamma$, and $prdd :: \textsf{PairRDD } \alpha \ \beta$; and
2. **reduceByKey**$(\oplus, prdd)$ for $\oplus :: \beta \times \beta \to \beta$ and $prdd :: \textsf{PairRDD } \alpha \ \beta$.

We define an auxiliary function **filterkey** that obtains a list of all values associated with the given key from a list of pairs.

filterkey $:: \alpha \to [(\alpha, \beta)] \to [\beta]$
filterkey _ [] = []
filterkey k (k, v):xs = v:(**filterkey** k xs)
filterkey k (_, _):xs = **filterkey** k xs

Deterministic outcomes of calls to **aggregateByKey** are now defined using the function **aggregateByKey**^{D} as follows.

Definition 4. *Calls to* **aggregateByKey**$(z, seq, \oplus, prdd)$ *have* deterministic outcomes *if*

$$\textbf{lookup}(k, \textbf{aggregateByKey}^D(z, seq, \oplus, part(L))) = \textbf{foldl}(z, seq, \textbf{filterkey}(k, L))$$

for all lists L of pairs, partitionings part, and keys k.

Finally, the following proposition states the conditions that need to hold for calls to **aggregateByKey** to have deterministic outcomes.

Proposition 3. *Calls to* **aggregateByKey**$(z, seq, \oplus, prdd)$ *have deterministic outcomes iff calls to* **aggregate**$(z, seq, \oplus, rdd)$ *have deterministic outcomes.*

We define when calls to **reduceByKey** have deterministic outcomes via **reduceByKey**^{D}.

Definition 5. *Calls to* **reduceByKey**$(\oplus, prdd)$ *have* deterministic outcomes *if*

$$\mathbf{lookup}(k, \mathbf{reduceByKey}^D(\oplus, part(L))) = \mathbf{reducel}(\oplus, \mathbf{filterkey}(k, L))$$

for all list L of pairs, partitioning part, and key k.

Proposition 4. *Calls to* **reduceByKey**$(\oplus, prdd)$ *have deterministic outcomes iff calls to* **reduce**$(\oplus, rdd)$ *have deterministic outcomes.*

4.5   Discussion

Our conditions for deterministic outcomes are more general than it appears. In addition to scalar data, such as integers, they are also applicable to RDDs containing non-scalar data, such as lists or sets. In our extended set of case studies, we will prove deterministic outcomes from a distributed Spark program using non-scalar data [12].

Corollary 1 gives necessary and sufficient conditions for calls to **aggregate** to have deterministic outcomes. Instead of checking whether **aggregate** computes the same result on all possible partitionings on any list for given z, seq, and $comb$, the corollary, instead, allows us to investigate properties for all elements of $img(\mathbf{foldl}(seq, z)) \times img(\mathbf{foldl}(seq, z))$ and $\alpha \times img(\mathbf{foldl}(seq, z))$. Our precise conditions reduce the need of checking all partitionings to checking all elements of Cartesian products. It appears that deterministic outcomes from calls to combinators can be verified automatically. The problem, however, remains difficult for the following reasons:

(a) The domain $img(\mathbf{foldl}(seq, z))$ can be infinite and in general not computable.
(b) Even if α and $img(\mathbf{foldl}(seq, z))$ are computable, seq and $\oplus$ may not be computable. Naïvely enumerating elements in α and $img(\mathbf{foldl}(seq, z))$ would not work.
(c) Testing equality between elements of $img(\mathbf{foldl}(seq, z))$ can be undecidable.

Given $seq :: \beta \times \alpha \to \beta$, recall that $img(\mathbf{foldl}(seq, z))$ is a subset of β. A sound but incomplete way to avoid (a) in practice is to test the properties of $\oplus$ on all elements of β instead. If a counterexample is found for some elements of β, the counterexample may not be valid in a real **aggregate** call because it may not belong to $img(\mathbf{foldl}(seq, z))$. In practical cases, the sets α and β are finite (such as machine integers) and equality between their elements is decidable. Even for such cases, checking if outcomes of **aggregate** are deterministic is still difficult since seq and $\oplus$ might not terminate for some input. In many real Spark programs, however, seq and $\oplus$ are very simple and thus computable (for instance, with only bounded loops or recursion). A semi-procedure to test these conditions might work on such practical examples.

5   Case Studies

We evaluated advantages of our PURESPARK specification on several case studies. In this section, we first analyze a Spark implementation of linear classification. Using the **treeAggregate** specification and its criteria for deterministic outcomes, we construct inputs yielding non-deterministic outcomes from the Spark implementation. Second, we analyze an implementation of a standard scaler and find a non-deterministic behavior there, too. Yet more case studies are provided in [12].

5.1   Linear Classification

Linear classification is a well-known machine learning technique to classify data sets. Fix a set of *features*. A *data point* is a vector of numerical feature values. A *labeled* data point is a data point with a discrete label. Given a labeled data set, the *classification problem* is to classify (new) unlabeled data points by the labeled data set. A particularly useful subproblem is the *binary* classification problem. Consider, for instance, a data set of vital signs of some population; each data point is labeled by the diagnosis of a disease (positive or negative). The binary classification problem can be used to predict whether a person has the particular disease. Linear classification solves the binary classification problem by finding an optimal hyperplane to divide the labeled data points. After a hyperplane is obtained, linear classification predicts an unlabeled data point by the half-space containing the point. Logistic regression and linear Support Vector Machines (SVMs) are linear classification algorithms.

Consider a data set $\{(\vec{x}_i, y_i) : 1 \leq i \leq n\}$ of data points $\vec{x}_i \in \mathbb{R}^d$ labeled by $y_i \in \{0, 1\}$. Linear classification can be expressed as a numerical optimization problem:

$$\min_{\vec{w} \in \mathbb{R}^d} f(\vec{w}) \quad \text{with} \quad f(\vec{w}) = \xi R(\vec{w}) + \frac{1}{n} \sum_{i=1}^{n} L(\vec{w}; \vec{x}_i, y_i)$$

where $\xi \geq 0$ is a *regularization parameter*, $R(\vec{w})$ is a *regularizer*, and $L(\vec{w}; \vec{x}_i, y_i)$ is a *loss function*. A vector $\vec{w}$ corresponds to a hyperplane in the data point space. The vector $\vec{w}_{opt}$ attaining the optimum hence classifies unlabeled data points with criteria defined by the objective function $f(\vec{w})$. Logistic regression and linear SVM are but two instances of the optimization problem with objective functions defined by different regularizers and loss functions.

In the Spark machine learning library, the numerical optimization problem is solved by gradient descent. Very roughly, gradient descent finds a local minimum of $f(\vec{w})$ by "walking" in the opposite direction of the gradient of $f(\vec{w})$. The mean of subgradients at data points is needed to compute the gradient of $f(\vec{w})$. The Spark machine learning library invokes **treeAggregate** to compute the mean. Floating-point addition is used as the comb parameter of the aggregate combinator. Since floating-point addition is not associative, we expect to observe non-deterministic outcomes (Proposition 1).

Consider the following three labeled data points: -10^{20} labeled with 1, 600 labeled with 0, and 10^{20} labeled with 1. We create a 20-partition RDD with an equal number of the three labeled data points. The Spark machine learning library function LogisticRegressionWithSGD.train is used to generate a logistic regression model to predict the data points -10^{20}, 600, and 10^{20} in each run. Among 49 runs, 19 of them classify the three data points into two different classes: the two positive data points are always classified in the same class, while the negative data point in the other. The other 30 runs, however, classify all three data points into the same class. We observe similar predictions from SVMWithSGD.train with the same labeled data points. 37 out of 46 runs classify the data points into two different classes; the other 9 runs classify them into one class. Interestingly, the data points are always classified into two different classes by both logistic regression and linear SVM when the input RDD has only three partitions. As we expected from our analysis of the function, non-deterministic outcomes were witnessed in our Spark distributed environment.

5.2   Standard Scaler

Standardization of data sets is a common pre-processing step in machine learning. Many machine learning algorithms tend to perform better when the training set is similar to the standard normal distribution. In the Spark machine learning library, the class StandardScaler is provided to standardize data sets. The function StandardScaler.fit takes an RDD of raw data and returns an instance of StandardScalerModel to transform data points. Two transformations are available in StandardScalerModel. One standardizes a data point by mean, and the other normalizes by variance of raw data. If data points in raw data are transformed by mean, the transformed data points have the mean equal to 0. Similarly, if they are transformed by variance, the transformed data points have the variance 1.

The StandardScaler implementation uses **treeAggregate** to compute statistical information. It uses floating-point addition to combine means of raw data in different partitions. As in the previous use case, since floating-point addition is not associative, StandardScaler does not produce deterministic outcomes (Sect. 4.3). In our experiment, we create a 100-partition RDD with values $-10^{20}, 600, 10^{20}$ of the same number of occurrences. The mean of the data set is $(-10^{20} \times n + 600 \times n + 10^{20} \times n)/(3n) = 200$ where n is the number of occurrences of each value. The data point 200 should therefore be after standardization transformed to 0. In 50 runs on the same data set in our distributed Spark platform, StandardScaler transforms 200 to a range of values from -944 to 1142, validating our prediction of a non-deterministic outcome.

6   Related Work

MapReduce modeling and optimization. In the MapReduce (MR) computation, various cost and performance models have been proposed [16,18,25,31]. These models estimate the execution time and resource requirements of MR jobs. Karloff et al. developed a formal computation model for MR [21] and showed how a variety of algorithms can exploit the combination of sequential and parallel computation in MR. We are not aware of a similar work in the context of Spark. To the best of our knowledge, our work is the first to address the problem of formal, functional specification of Spark aggregation. Verifying the correctness of a MR program involves checking the commutativity and associativity of the reduce function. Xu et al. propose various semantic criteria to model commonly held assumptions on MR programs [28], including determinism, partition isolation, commutativity, and associativity of map/reduce combinators. Their empirical survey shows that these criteria are often overlooked by programmers and violated in practice. A recent survey [27] has found that a large number of industrial MR programs are, in fact, non-commutative. Recent work has proposed techniques for checking commutativity of bounded reducers automatically [13]. Because it is non-trivial to implement high-level algorithms using the MR framework, various approaches to compute optimized MR implementations have been proposed [17,23,24]. Emoto et al. [17] formalize the algebraic conditions using semiring homomorphism, under which an efficient program based on the generate-test-aggregate programming model can be specified in the MR framework. Given a monolithic *reduce* function, the work in [23] tries to decompose *reduce* into partial aggregation functions (similar to *seq* and *comb* in this paper) using program inversion techniques. MOLD [24] translates imperative Java code into MR code by transforming imperative loops into *fold* combinators using semantic-preserving program rewrite rules.

Numerical Stability under MapReduce. Several works try to scale up machine learning algorithms for large datasets using MapReduce [14,25]. To achieve numerically stable results across multiple runs [5,26], for example, preventing overflow, underflow and round-off errors due to finite-precision arithmetic, a variety of techniques are proposed [26]: generalizing sequential numerical stability techniques to distributed settings, shifting data values by constants, divide-and-conquer, etc. We showed that simulating machine learning algorithms using our specification enables early detection of points of numerical instability.

Relational Query Optimization. Relational query optimization is an extensively researched topic [11,20]: the goal is to obtain equivalent but more efficient query expressions by exploiting the algebraic properties of the constituent operators, for instance, join, select, together with statistics on relations and indices. For example, while inner joins commute independent of data, left joins commute only in specific cases. Query optimization for partitioned tables has received less attention [2,19]: because the key relational operators are not partition-aware, most work has focused on necessary but not sufficient conditions for query equivalence. In contrast, we investigate determinism of Spark aggregate expressions, constructed using partition-aware *seq* and *comb* combinators. We describe necessary and sufficient conditions under which these computations yield deterministic results independent of the data partitions.

Deterministic Parallel Programming. In order to enable deterministic-by-default parallel programming [7–10,22], researchers have developed several programming abstractions and logical specification languages to ensure that programs produce the same output for the same input independent of thread scheduling. For example, Deterministic Parallel Java [7,8] ensures exclusive writes to shared memory regions by means of verified, user-provided annotations over memory regions. In contrast, deterministic outcomes from Spark aggregation depend on algebraic properties like commutativity and associativity of *seq* and *comb* functions and their interplay.

7   Conclusion

In this paper, we give a Haskell specification for various Spark aggregate combinators. We focus on aggregation of RDDs representing general sets, sets of pairs, and graphs. Based on our specification, we derive necessary and sufficient conditions that guarantee deterministic outcomes of the considered Spark aggregate combinators. We investigate several case studies and use the conditions to predict non-deterministic outcomes. Our executable specification can be used by developers for more detailed analysis and efficient development of distributed Spark programs. We also believe that our specifications are valuable resources for research communities to understand Spark better.

There are several future directions. The conditions for deterministic outcomes of aggregate combinators could be used for: (i) creating fully mechanized proofs for properties about data-parallel programs; (ii) developing automatic techniques for detecting non-deterministic outcomes of data-parallel programs; and (iii) synthesizing deterministic concurrent programs from sequential specifications. We have formalized the proofs of some crucial lemmas in Agda [4]. Using Scalaz [3], verified Haskell specifications can be translated to Spark programs to ensure determinism by construction.

Acknowledgement. This work was supported by the Czech Science Foundation (project 17-12465S), the BUT FIT project FIT-S-17-4014, the IT4IXS: IT4Innovations Excellence in Science project (LQ1602), and Ministry of Science and Technology, R.O.C. (MOST projects 103-2221-E-001-019-MY3 and 103-2221-E-001-020-MY3).

References

1. Apache Spark. https://github.com/apache/spark
2. IBM DB2 Version 9.7. Partitioned Tables. https://ibm.biz/BdHyYR
3. The Scalaz project. https://github.com/scalaz
4. PureSpark. https://github.com/guluchen/purespark
5. Bennett, J., Grout, R., Pebay, P., Roe, D., Thompson, D.: Numerically stable, single-pass, parallel statistics algorithms. In: CLUSTER, pp. 1–8 (2009)
6. Bird, R.S.: An introduction to the theory of lists. In: Broy, M. (eds) Logic of Programming and Calculi of Discrete Design. NATO ASI Series (Series F: Computer and Systems Sciences), vol. 36, pp. 5–42. Springer, Heidelberg (1987)
7. Bocchino Jr., R.L., Adve, V.S., Dig, D., Adve, S.V., Heumann, S., Komuravelli, R., Overbey, J., Simmons, P., Sung, H., Vakilian, M.: A type and effect system for deterministic parallel Java. In: OOPSLA, pp. 97–116 (2009)

8. Bocchino Jr., R.L., Heumann, S., Honarmand, N., Adve, S.V., Adve, V.S., Welc, A., Shpeisman, T.: Safe nondeterminism in a deterministic-by-default parallel language. SIGPLAN Not. **46**(1), 535–548 (2011)
9. Budimlic, Z., Burke, M.G., Cavé, V., Knobe, K., Lowney, G., Newton, R., Palsberg, J., Peixotto, D.M., Sarkar, V., Schlimbach, F., Tasirlar, S.: Concurrent collections. Sci. Program. **18**(3–4), 203–217 (2010)
10. Burnim, J., Sen, K.: Asserting and checking determinism for multithreaded programs. Commun. ACM **53**(6), 97–105 (2010)
11. Chaudhuri, S.: An overview of query optimization in relational systems. In: PODS 1998 (1998)
12. Chen, Y., Hong, C., Lengál, O., Mu, S., Sinha, N., Wang, B.: An executable sequential specification for Spark aggregation arXiv:1702.02439 [cs.DC] (2017)
13. Chen, Y.-F., Hong, C.-D., Sinha, N., Wang, B.-Y.: Commutativity of reducers. In: Baier, C., Tinelli, C. (eds.) TACAS 2015. LNCS, vol. 9035, pp. 131–146. Springer, Heidelberg (2015). doi:10.1007/978-3-662-46681-0_9
14. Chu, C., Kim, S.K., Lin, Y., Yu, Y., Bradski, G.R., Ng, A.Y., Olukotun, K.: Map-Reduce for machine learning on multicore. In: NIPS, pp. 281–288 (2006)
15. Dean, J., Ghemawat, S.: MapReduce: a flexible data processing tool. Commun. ACM **53**(1), 72–77 (2010)
16. Dörre, J., Apel, S., Lengauer, C.: Modeling and optimizing MapReduce programs. Concurrency Comput. Pract. Experience **27**(7), 1734–1766 (2015)
17. Emoto, K., Fischer, S., Hu, Z.: Generate, test, and aggregate. In: Seidl, H. (ed.) ESOP 2012. LNCS, vol. 7211, pp. 254–273. Springer, Heidelberg (2012). doi:10.1007/978-3-642-28869-2_13
18. Herodotou, H., Babu, S.: Profiling, what-if analysis, and cost-based optimization of MapReduce programs. Proc. VLDB Endowment **4**(11), 1111–1122 (2011)
19. Herodotou, H., Borisov, N., Babu, S.: Query optimization techniques for partitioned tables. In: SIGMOD 2011, pp. 49–60 (2011)
20. Ioannidis, Y.E.: Query optimization. ACM Comput. Surv. **28**(1), 121–123 (1996)
21. Karloff, H., Suri, S., Vassilvitskii, S.: A model of computation for MapReduce. In: SODA, pp. 938–948 (2010)
22. Leijen, D., Fähndrich, M., Burckhardt, S.: Prettier concurrency: Purely functional concurrent revisions. In: Haskell, pp. 83–94 (2011)
23. Liu, C., Zhang, J., Zhou, H., McDirmid, S., Guo, Z., Moscibroda, T.: Automating distributed partial aggregation. In: SoCC, pp. 1:1–1:12 (2014)
24. Radoi, C., Fink, S.J., Rabbah, R.M., Sridharan, M.: Translating imperative code to MapReduce. In: OOPSLA, pp. 909–927 (2014)
25. Sakr, S., Liu, A., Fayoumi, A.G.: The family of MapReduce and large-scale data processing systems. ACM Comput. Surv. **46**(1), 11:1–11:44 (2013)
26. Tian, Y., Tatikonda, S., Reinwald, B.: Scalable and numerically stable descriptive statistics in SystemML. In: ICDE, pp. 1351–1359 (2012)
27. Xiao, T., Zhang, J., Zhou, H., Guo, Z., McDirmid, S., Lin, W., Chen, W., Zhou, L.: Nondeterminism in MapReduce considered harmful? an empirical study on non-commutative aggregators in MapReduce programs. In: Companion Proceedings of ICSE, pp. 44–53 (2014)
28. Xu, Z., Hirzel, M., Rothermel, G.: Semantic characterization of MapReduce workloads. In: IISWC, pp. 87–97 (2013)
29. Zaharia, M., Chowdhury, M., Das, T., Dave, A., Ma, J., McCauly, M., Franklin, M.J., Shenker, S., Stoica, I.: Resilient distributed datasets: a fault-tolerant abstraction for in-memory cluster computing. In: NSDI, pp. 15–28 (2012)

30. Zaharia, M., Xin, R.S., Wendell, P., Das, T., Armbrust, M., Dave, A., Meng, X., Rosen, J., Venkataraman, S., Franklin, M.J., Ghodsi, A., Gonzalez, J., Shenker, S., Stoica, I.: Apache spark: a unified engine for big data processing. Commun. ACM **59**(11), 56–65 (2016)
31. Zhang, Z., Cherkasova, L., Verma, A., Loo, B.T.: Performance modeling and optimization of deadline-driven Pig programs. ACM Trans. Auton. Adapt. Syst. **8**(3), 14:1–14:28 (2013)

Long-Lived Tasks

Armando Castañeda[1]($\boxtimes$), Sergio Rajsbaum[1], and Michel Raynal[2,3]

[1] Instituto de Matemáticas, UNAM, 04510 México D.F, Mexico
armando.castaneda@im.unam.mx
[2] Institut Universitaire de France, Paris, France
[3] IRISA, Université de Rennes, Rennes, France

Abstract. The predominant notion for specifying problems to study distributed computability are *tasks*. Notable examples of tasks are consensus, set agreement, renaming and commit-adopt. The theory of task solvability is well-developed using topology techniques and distributed simulations. However, concurrent computing problems are usually specified by *objects*. Tasks and objects differ in at least two ways. While a task is a one-shot problem, an object, such as a queue or a stack, typically can be invoked multiple times by each process. Also, a task, defined in terms of sets, specifies its responses when invoked by each set of processes concurrently, while an object, defined in terms of sequences, specifies the outputs the object may produce when it is accessed sequentially.

In a previous paper we showed how tasks can be used to specify one-shot objects (where each process can invoke only one operation, only once). In this paper we show how the notion of tasks can be extended to model any object. A potential benefit of this result is the use of topology, and other distributed computability techniques to study long-lived objects.

Keywords: Distributed problems · Formal specifications · Tasks · Sequential specifications · Linearizability · Long-lived objects

1 Introduction

A predominant formalism for specifying one-shot distributed problems, especially in distributed computability, is through the notion of a *task* [12]. Tasks are *one-shot* because each process invokes exactly one operation, and receives exactly one response. We think of the operation invoked by the process as its proposal, or its *input value*, and of the response, as its *output value*. Informally, a task is specified by an input/output relation, defining for each set of processes that may run concurrently, and each assignment of inputs to the processes in the set, the valid outputs of the processes. A central task is *consensus*, where processes agree on one of the proposed input values. In *k-set agreement*, processes agree on at most k different input values. Thus, 1-set agreement is the same as consensus. Tasks have been intensively studied in distributed computability, leading to an understanding of their relative power [8], to the design of simulations between

© Springer International Publishing AG 2017
A. El Abbadi and B. Garbinato (Eds.): NETYS 2017, LNCS 10299, pp. 439–454, 2017.
DOI: 10.1007/978-3-319-59647-1_32

models [2], and to the development of a deep connection between distributed computing and topology [7].

In concurrent computing, problems are typically specified sequentially, instead of as tasks, because it is harder to reason about concurrent specifications. Tasks and objects model in a different way the concurrency that naturally arises in distributed systems: while tasks explicitly state what might happen when a set of processes run concurrently, objects only specify what happens when processes access the object sequentially.

An *object* is specified in terms of a sequential specification, i.e., an automaton describing the outputs the object produces when it is accessed sequentially. There are various ways of defining how the object behaves when it is accessed concurrently by several processes. The *linearizability* [11] consistency condition is a way of producing a sequential execution out of a concurrent execution, which then can be used against the object specification. Linearizability is very popular because it is *local*, namely, one can consider linearizable object implementations in isolation, and their composition is guaranteed to be linearizable. Also, linearizability is a *non-blocking* property, which means that a pending invocation (of a total operation) is never required to wait for another pending invocation to complete.

Contributions. In a previous paper [4] we showed how tasks can be used to specify one-shot objects (where each process can invoke only one operation, only once). In this paper we show how the notion of tasks can be extended to model any object. More precisely, for any object X, we describe how to construct a task T_X, the long-lived task derived from X, with the property that an execution E is linearizable with respect to X if and only if E satisfies T_X. Then we explore the opposite direction, namely, transforming long-lived tasks to sequential objects. As shown in [4,13], there are tasks (in the usual sense) that cannot be expressed as objects. Notable examples are the set agreement and immediate snapshot tasks. Interval-sequential objects, introduced in [4], are a generalization of sequential objects, which can describe any pattern of concurrent invocations. We show that from any long-lived task T can be obtained an interval-sequential object X_T such that an execution E satisfies T if and only if E is interval-linearizable with respect to X_T. Thus, interval-sequential objects and long-lived tasks have the same expressive power.

Related work. Tasks and objects have largely been independently studied. The first to study the relation between tasks and objects was Neiger [13] in a brief announcement in 1994, where he noticed that there are tasks, like *immediate snapshot* [1], with no specification as sequential objects. An object modeling the immediate snapshot task is necessarily stronger than the immediate snapshot task, because such an object implements test-and-set. In contrast there are read/write algorithms solving the immediate snapshot task and it is well-known that there are no read/write linearizable implementations of test-and-set. Therefore, Neiger proposed the notion of a *set-sequential* object, that specifies the values returned when sets of processes access it simultaneously.

Then, one can define an immediate snapshot set-sequential object, and there are *set-linearizable* implementations. Much more recently, it was again observed that for some concurrent objects it is impossible to provide a sequential specification, and *concurrency-aware* linearizability was defined [9], and studied further in [10]. In [4] we initiated an in-depth study of the relation between tasks and objects. We introduced the notion of *interval-sequential* object, and showed that it can model any task. Also, we showed that a natural extension of the notion of a task is expressive enough to specify any one-shot object.

Set linearizability and concurrency-aware linearizability are closely related and both are strictly less powerful than interval-linearizability to model tasks.

Transforming the question of wait-free read/write solvability of a one-shot sequential object, into the question of solvability of a task was suggested in [6]. That transformation takes a sequential object X and produces a task T_X such that X is solvable in the read/write wait-free crash-failure model of computation if and only if T_X is solvable in that model. In T_X, processes produce outputs for X and an additional snapshot. Our construction here and in [4] is reminiscent to the construction in [6].

2   Tasks and Objects

2.1   Tasks

A *simplicial complex*, or complex for short, is a generalization of a graph. A complex is a collection of sets closed under containment. The sets of a complex are called *simplices*. A graph consists of two types of simplices: sets of dimension 1, namely edges (which are sets of vertices), and sets of dimension 0, namely vertices. A 2-dimensional complex consists of simplices of 3 vertices, simplices of 2 vertices, and simplices of 1 vertex. It is always required that if a simplex is in the complex, all its subsets also belong to the complex.

Formally, a *task* is a triple $\langle \mathcal{I}, \mathcal{O}, \Delta \rangle$, where $\mathcal{I}$ and $\mathcal{O}$ are complexes, with $\mathcal{I}$ containing valid input configuration to the processes and $\mathcal{O}$ containing valid output configurations. Each simplex of $\mathcal{I}$ has the form $\{(\mathrm{id}_1, x_1), \ldots, (\mathrm{id}_k, x_k)\}$, where the $id_i's$ are distinct ID's of processes and the $x_i's$ are inputs. The vertices of $\mathcal{I}$ are its singleton sets. The meaning of an input simplex σ is that the processes in σ might start with those inputs in the simplex. The output complex $\mathcal{O}$ is defined similar.

In Fig. 1 part of the input complex $\mathcal{I}$ for 2-set agreement, for 3 processes, is illustrated. It is the part where each process proposes as input its own id. The simplex σ represents the initial configuration where each processes proposes as input its own id. Inside a vertex is the id of the process, and outside is its input value. The edges of σ are input simplexes, where only two processes participate, and the third process never wakes up. The vertices of σ represent initial configurations where only one process participate.

Each simplex of the output complex represents the decisions of the processes in some execution solving the task. Vertices are labeled, on the inside with ids, and on the outside with decision values. For instance, in σ_1 the decisions are p, r

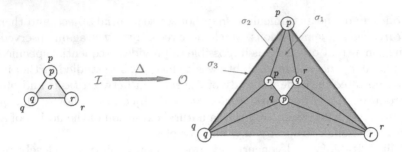

Fig. 1. An input simplex σ and the corresponding output complex $\Delta(\sigma)$, for 2-set agreement task.

and p, respectively for p, q, r. Notice that there is no simplex in the center, there is a hole, because the processes are not allowed to decide 3 different values in 2-set agreement. An example of a 1-dimensional simplex is σ_3, where p decides p and q decides q.

The relation Δ states that if a process sees only itself in an execution, it should decide its own input value. For instance, Δ of input vertex for p contains only the output vertex of p labeled p at the top corner of $\mathcal{O}$. Similarly, if p and q see each other in an execution, where r does not participate, Δ of the input edge for p and q contains only σ_3. Finally, $\Delta(\sigma)$ contains *all* triangles of $\mathcal{O}$, because it specifies output values when all three processes see all input values.

The function Δ is the artefact that relates valid inputs and outputs. Formally, Δ is a function mapping each input simplex $\sigma \in \mathcal{I}$ to a subcomplex $\Delta(\sigma) \subseteq \mathcal{O}$ such that each output simplex $\tau \in \Delta(\sigma)$ has the same cardinality as σ and both simplexes, σ and τ, contain the same ID's of processes. In words, $\Delta(\sigma)$ describes all possible output configurations in executions in which only the processes in σ participate in the computation and all of them run to completion.

Tasks have their own notion of solvability, that is, a mechanism to distinguish between valid from invalid executions, with respect to a given task. Let E be an execution in which every participating process decides an output value (to its unique invocation). Namely, there are no pending invocations in E. Let σ_E be the set with all pairs (id_i, x_i), where x_i is the input of process id_i, and, similarly, let τ_E be the set with all pairs (id_i, y_i), where y_i is the output of process id_i. Then, we say that E *satisfies* a task T if $\tau_E \in \Delta(\sigma_E)$, i.e., the processes decide an output assignment that agrees with the specification of the task.

2.2   Objects

A *long-lived sequential object,* or object for short, allows each process to invoke any number of times any of the operations provided by the object. For example, in a stack, each process can invoke push and pop operation as many times as it wants, in any order. Typically, a long-lived object is formally specified in terms of a sequential specification, i.e., an automaton describing the outputs the object produces when it is accessed sequentially. Thus, an execution with concurrent operations needs to emulate somehow an allowed sequential behavior of the automaton.

There are various ways of defining what it means for an execution to be valid with respecto a sequential specification (or the meaning of emulating a sequential behavior of the automaton). One of the most popular consistency conditions is *linearizability* [11].

Given a sequential specification of an object, an execution is *linearizable* if it can be transformed into a sequential one such that (1) it respects the real-time order of invocation and responses and (2) the sequential execution is recognized by the automaton specifying the object. Thus, an execution is linearizable if, for each operation call, it is possible to find a unique point in the interval of real-time defined by the invocation and response of the operation, and these *linearization points* induce a valid sequential execution.

Linearizability is very popular to design components of large systems because it is *local*, namely, one can consider linearizable object implementations in isolation and *compose* them without sacrificing linearizability of the whole system [5]. Also, linearizability is a *non-blocking* property, which means that a pending invocation (of a total operation, i.e., an operation that always can be invoked regardless of the state of the automaton) is never required to wait for another pending invocation to complete.

2.3 Limitations of the Standard Semantics of Task

It has been observed [4] that tasks are too weak to represent some objects, under the usual semantics of a task described above. We briefly recall the following example from [4].

Consider a restricted queue O for three processes, p, q and r, in which, in every execution, p and q invoke $enq(1)$ and $enq(2)$, respectively, and r invokes $deq()$. If the queue is empty, r's dequeue operation gets $\perp$.

Suppose, for contradiction, that there is a corresponding task $T_O = (\mathcal{I}, \mathcal{O}, \Delta)$, that corresponds to O. The input complex $\mathcal{I}$ consists of one vertex for each possible operation by a process, namely, the set of vertices is $\{(p, enq(1)), (q, enq(2)), (r, deq())\}$, and $\mathcal{I}$ consists of all subsets of this set. Similarly, the output complex $\mathcal{O}$ contains one vertex for every possible response to a process, therefore it consists of the set of vertices $\{(p, ok), (q, ok), (r, 1), (r, 2), (r, \perp)\}$. It should contain a simplex $\sigma_x = \{(p, ok), (q, ok), (r, x)\}$ for each value of $x \in \{1, 2, \perp\}$, because there are executions where p, q, r get such values, respectively. See Fig. 2.

Now, consider the three sequential executions of the figure, α_1, α_2 and $\alpha_\perp$. In α_1 the process execute their operations in the order p, q, r, while in α_2 the order is q, p, r. In α_1 the response to r is 1, and if α_2 it is 2. Given that these executions are linearizable for O, they should be valid for T_O. This means that every prefix of α_1 should be valid:

$$\{(p, ok)\} = \Delta((p, enq(1))$$
$$\{(p, ok), (q, ok)\} \in \Delta(\{(p, enq(1)), (q, enq(2))\})$$
$$\sigma_1 = \{(p, ok), (q, ok), (r, 1)\} \in \Delta(\{(p, enq(1)), (q, enq(2)), (r, deq())\}) = \Delta(\sigma)$$

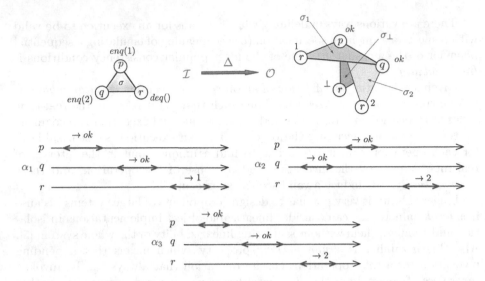

Fig. 2. Counterexample for a simple queue object

Similarly from α_2 we get that

$$\sigma_2 = \{(p, ok), (q, ok), (r, 2)\} \in \Delta(\sigma)$$

But now consider α_3, with the same sequential order p, q, r of operations, but now r gets back value 2. This execution is not linearizable for O, but is accepted by T_O because each of the prefixes of α_3 is valid. More precisely, the set of inputs and the set of outputs of α_2 are identical to the sets of inputs and set of outputs of α_3.

3   Long-Lived Tasks

Tasks provide a compact and static formalism for specifying one-shot distributed problems. Could it be that long-lived objects can be specified as a task? Is it possible to have a static representation of a queue or list? As explained above, tasks are not expressive enough to model even restricted queues or stacks in which each process can execute at most one operation. However, the task formalism can be extended to handle long-lived objects.

In order to model long-lived objects, the task formalism has to be extended to deal with two issues: (1) each process might invoke several operations (in any order) and (2) model valid executions, i.e., executions that are linearizable with respect to the object (which in the end involves modeling the interleaving pattern in a given execution).

A *long-lived* task is a triple $\langle \mathcal{I}, \mathcal{O}, \Delta \rangle$, where $\mathcal{I}$ and $\mathcal{O}$ are input and output complexes and Δ is a function from simplexes of $\mathcal{I}$ to subcomplexes of $\mathcal{O}$. A main difference with regular tasks is the meaning of input and output vertices and the solvability condition, which will be slightly modified. Roughly speaking, for a long-lived task, a vertex of $\mathcal{I}$ represents the invocation of an operation by a particular process. Then, an input simplex $\sigma \in \mathcal{I}$ represents a collection of invocations (maybe all of them by the same process) that are to be performed on the object, and $\Delta(\sigma)$ is the subcomplex containing all allowed responses the invocations in σ might obtain, in all sequential interleavings. We will use Fig. 3 as a running example.

3.1 Modeling Multiple Invocations

Let X be any sequential object. To make things simple, we will treat each invocation as unique by tagging each of them with an invocation ID made of a pair composed of the ID of the invoking process and an additional integer which makes invocations of the same process to the same operation type unique.

Let Inv be the infinite set with all invocations to X. Each element in Inv has the form $Inv(\mathrm{id}_i, op\_type, input_i)$. Then, $\mathcal{I}$ is the complex containing every finite subset of Inv as simplex. Thus, $\mathcal{I}$ is a simplex of infinite dimension whose faces are of finite dimension. Note that simplices in $\mathcal{I}$ might contain invocations by the same process.

The output complex $\mathcal{O}$ has the responses to the invocations in $\mathcal{I}$. Let Res be the infinite set with all response values X might produce to the invocation in Inv.

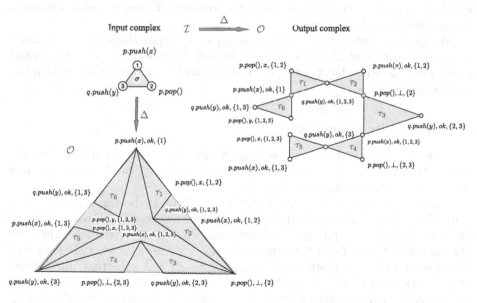

Fig. 3. An input simplex of the long-lived task modeling the stack in which p executes a push and a pop and q a push. Two ways of drawing the output complex are shown. The one on the bottom emphasizes the role of the map Δ: input vertices are sent to corner output vertices, edges are sent to edges on the boundary of $\mathcal{O}$, and σ is sent to all of $\mathcal{O}$.

The output complex $\mathcal{O}$ is the complex containing every finite set in $Inv \times Res \times 2^{Inv}$, where 2^{Inv} is the power set of Inv. Thus, each vertex in $\mathcal{O}$ is a triple with an invocation, a response to the invocation and set of invocations. This set is called *set-view* and is the mechanism to model valid sequential executions, as explained below.

3.2   Modeling Valid Executions

Let E be sequential execution accepted by X in which every invocation has a matching response. We would like to represent that execution and its interleaving pattern as an output simplex in $\mathcal{O}$, that is, we identify that sequential interleaving and the output values as correct and encode it somehow in $\mathcal{O}$. It turns out that this can be easily done by adding to each response in E, the set of invocations preceding the response in E. These are the *set-views* mentioned before. Intuitively, the set-view of a response is the set of all invocation a process sees when computing the output for its invocation. Thus, the set-view of a response is a subset of the set of all invocations in E.

Let σ_E be the set with all invocation in E and τ_E be set of all pairs invocation, response in E, each of them with its corresponding set-view. The importance of the set-views is that they together fully capture the interleaving pattern in E. More precisely, two executions E and E' (not necessarily sequential) induce the same set of set-views (namely, $\tau_E = \tau_{E'}$) if and only if they have the same interleaving pattern, i.e., they are the same execution. Therefore, using set-views, we can model valid executions.

We can now define the mapping Δ: for every input simplex $\sigma \in \mathcal{I}$, $\Delta(\sigma)$ is the subcomplex of $\mathcal{O}$ containing τ_E, as defined above, for every sequential execution E accepted by X with only invocations in σ and every invocation has a matching response.

3.3   Solvability Condition

Se far we have encoded all valid sequential executions with the help of the set-views. Now we need a way to identify any execution as valid, namely, as one which is linearizable with respect to X.

For a given sequential object X, let $T_X = \langle \mathcal{I}, \mathcal{O}, \Delta \rangle$ be the long-lived task constructed from X as described above. Consider any execution E without pending operations let σ_E and τ_E be the simplexes defined above from E. Then, we say that E *satisfies* T_X if there is a simplex $\lambda \in \Delta(\sigma_E)$ such that for every $(inv, resp, view) \in \tau_E$ there is a $(inv', resp', view') \in \lambda$ such that $inv' = inv$, $resp' = resp$ and $view' \subseteq view$. Intuitively, E satisfies the task if its set-views can be sequentially arranged so that the sequence induce an execution in $\Delta(\sigma_E)$, hence, by construction, accepted by X.

Theorem 1. *Let X be any sequential object and let T_X be the long-lived task derived from X. Consider any execution E without pending operations. Then, E is linearizable with respect to X if and only if E satisfies T_X.*

Proof. We first show that if E is linearizable then E satisfies T_X. By linearizability, E can be transformed into a sequential execution S accepted by X such that S respects the real-time order of E. Consider the simplexes $\sigma_E, \sigma_S, \tau_E$ and τ_S obtained from E and S. We have that $\sigma_E = \sigma_S$ because E and S have the same invocations. Also, $\tau_S \in \Delta(\sigma_E)$, by the definition of T_X and because S is accepted by X. Pick any $(inv, resp, view) \in \tau_E$ and let $(inv', resp', view') \in \tau_S$ with $inv' = inv$. Since S is a linearization of E, it must be that $resp' = resp$. Observe that if we prove that $view' \subseteq view$, then it follows that E satisfies T_X. For the sake of contradiction, assume that $view' \supset view$. Then, in the sequential execution S, the invocation inv appears after the response of an invocation inv^* in $view' \setminus view$. However, since $inv^* \notin view$, hence, the response of inv occurs before inv^* in E, from which follows that S does not respect the real-time order in E. A contradiction.

We now show that if E satisfies T_X then E is linearizable. Let σ_E and τ_E be the simplexes induced by E. Since E satisfies T_X, there is a $\lambda \in \Delta(\sigma_E)$ such that for every $(inv, resp, view) \in \tau_E$ there is a $(inv', resp', view') \in \lambda$ such that $inv' = inv$, $resp' = resp$ and $view' \subseteq view$. By definition, λ is induced by a sequential execution S accepted by X. Let σ_S and τ_S be the simplexes induced by S. Note that E and S contain the same invocations and responses. If we prove that S respects the real-time order in E, then S is a linearization of E. By contradiction, suppose the opposite. Then, there are invocations inv and inv' such that the response of inv appears before inv' in E but the response of inv' appears before inv in S. Let $view_E$ and $view_S$ be the set-views of inv in E and S. Thus, $inv' \notin view_E$ and $inv' \in view_S$, and hence $view_S \nsubseteq view_E$. A contradiction. Then, S is a linearization of E.   □

We stress that set-views are not output values produced by processes, they are a mechanism to identify executions as correct. An alternative way to think of set-views is that they model the memory of a long-lived object in a static manner. It is also worth to stress that the set-views of any execution (possibly non sequential) are essentially snapshots: each set-view contains its corresponding invocation and every pair of set-views are comparable under containment.

Remark 1. If a long-lived task is restricted so that each process executes at most one operation and every set-view is the empty set, then we obtain a regular task and the solvability condition is equivalent to the usual solvability condition for tasks.

4   Interval-Sequential Objects

A natural question is if we can do the opposite direction of the construction described in the previous section. Namely, if for every long-lived task there is an object such that any execution satisfies the task if and only if it is linearizable with respect to the object. As shown in [4,13], there are tasks (in the usual sense) that cannot be expressed as objects, e.g., the set agreement and immediate snapshot tasks. Generally speaking, the reason is that tasks (and hence also long-lived tasks) have the ability to describe executions in which there are concurrent invocations, which cannot be naturally described with sequential objects (this can be done at the cost of getting counterintuitive objects, like objects that can predict future invocations).

Interval-sequential objects, introduced in [4], are a generalization of sequential objects. Intuitively, they allow concurrent invocations by more than a single process in some states. As we shall see later, these objects can model long-lived tasks.

4.1   The Notion of an Interval-Sequential Object

To generalize the usual notion of a sequential object e.g. [3,11], instead of considering sequences of invocations and responses, we consider sequences of *sets* of invocations and responses. An *invoking concurrency class* $C \subseteq 2^{Inv}$, is a non-empty subset of the set of invocations Inv such that C contains at most one invocation by the same process. A *responding concurrency class* $C, C \subseteq 2^{Res}$, is defined similarly, where Rev is the set of possible responses.

Interval-sequential execution. An *interval-sequential execution* h is an alternating sequence of invoking and responding concurrency classes, starting in an invoking class, $h = I_0, R_0, I_1, R_1, \ldots, I_m, R_m$, where the following conditions are satisfied.

1. For each $I_i \in h$, any two invocations $in_1, in_2 \in I_i$ are by different processes. Similarly, for $R_i \in h$ if $r_1, r_2 \in R_i$ then both responses are from distinct processes.
2. Let $r \in R_i$ for some $R_i \in h$. Then there is $in \in I_j$ for some $j \leq i$, such that *res* is matching response for in and furthermore, there is no other in' such that in and in' are from the same processes and $in' \in I_{j'}$, $j < j' \leq i$.

In words, an interval-sequential execution h consists of matching invocations and responses, perhaps with some pending invocations with no response.

Interval-sequential object. An *interval-sequential* object X is a (not necessarily finite) Mealy state machine $(Q, 2^{Inv}, 2^{Res}, \delta)$ whose output values R are responding concurrency classes R of X, $R \subseteq 2^{Res}$, are determined both by its current state $s \in Q$ and the current input $I \in 2^{Inv}$, where I is an invoking concurrency class of X. There is a set of *initial states* Q_0 of X, $Q_0 \subseteq Q$. The transition relation $\delta \subseteq Q \times 2^{inv} \times 2^{Res} \times Q$ specifies both, the output of the automaton and its next state. If X is in state q and it receives as input a set of invocations I, then, if $(R, q') \in \delta(q, I)$, the meaning is that X may return the non-empty set of responses R and move to state q'. We stress that always both I and R are non-empty sets.

Interval-sequential execution of an object. Consider an initial state $q_0 \in Q_0$ of X and a sequence of inputs $I_0, I_1, \ldots I_m$. Then a sequence of outputs that X may produce is $R_0, R_1, \ldots R_m$, where $(R_i, q_{i+1}) \in \delta(q_i, I_i)$. Then the *interval-sequential execution of X* starting in q_0 is $q_0, I_0, R_0, q_1, I_1, R_1, \ldots, q_m, I_m, R_m$. However, we require that the object's response at a state uniquely determines the new state, i.e. we assume if $\delta(q, I_i)$ contains (R_i, q_{i+1}) and (R_i, q'_{i+1}) then $q_{i+1} = q'_{i+1}$. Then we may denote the interval-sequential execution of X, starting in q_0 by $h = I_0, R_0, I_1, R_1, \ldots, I_m, R_m$, because the sequence of states $q_0, q_1, \ldots, q_m$ is uniquely determined by q_0, and by the sequences of inputs and responses.

Notice that X may be non-deterministic, in a given state q_i with input I_i it may move to more than one state and return more than one response. Also, sometimes it is convenient to require that the object is *total*, meaning that, for every singleton set $I \in 2^{Inv}$ and every state q in which the invocation *inv* in I is not pending, there is an $(R, q') \in \delta(q, I)$ in which there is a response to *inv* in R. In what follows we consider only objects whose operations are total.

Our definition of interval-sequential execution is motivated by the fact that we are interested in *well-formed* executions $h = I_0, R_0, I_1, R_1, \ldots, I_m, R_m$. Informally, the processes should behave well, in the sense that a process does not invoke a new operation before its last invocation received a response. Also, the object should behave well, in the sense that it should not return a response to an operation that is not pending.

Representation of interval-sequential executions. An interval sequential execution $h = I_0, R_0, I_1, R_1, \ldots, I_m, R_m$ can be represented by a table, with a column for each element in the sequence h, and a row for each process. A member $in \in I_j$ invoked by p_k (resp. a response $r \in R_j$ to p_k) is placed in the kth row, at the $2j$th column (resp. $(2j+1)$th column). Thus, a transition of the automaton will correspond to two consecutive columns, I_j, R_j. See Fig. 4.

Interval-sequential objects include as particular cases sequential objects and the set-sequential objects and its corresponding set linearizability consistency condition suggested in [13].

Remark 2 (Sequential and Set-sequential objects). Let X be an interval-sequential object, $(Q, 2^{Inv}, 2^{Res}, \delta)$. Suppose for all states q and all I, if $\delta(q, I) = (R, q')$, then $|R| = |I|$, and additionally each $r \in R$ is a response to one $in \in I$. Then X is a *set-sequential* object. If in addition, $|I| = |R| = 1$, then X is a sequential object in the usual sense.

4.2 An Example: The Validity Problem

Consider an object X with a single operation validity(x), that can be invoked by each process, with a *proposed* input parameter x, and a very simple specification: an operation returns a value that has been proposed. This problem is easily specified as a task. Indeed, many tasks include this apparently simple property, such as consensus, set-agreement, etc. It turns out that the validity task cannot be expressed as a sequential object. As an interval-sequential object, it is formally specified by an automaton, where each state q is labeled with two values, $q.vals$ is the set of values that have been proposed so far, and $q.pend$ is the set of processes with pending invocations. The initial state q_0 has $q_0.vals = \emptyset$ and $q_0.pend = \emptyset$. If in is an invocation to the object, let $val(in)$ be the proposed value, and if r is a response from the object, let $val(r)$ be the responded value. For a set of invocations I (resp. responses R) $vals(I)$ denotes the proposed values in I (resp. $vals(R)$). The transition relation $\delta(q, I)$ contains all pairs (R, q') such that:

- If $r \in R$ then $id(r) \in q.pend$ or there is an $in \in I$ with $id(in) = id(r)$,
- If $r \in R$ then $val(r) \in q.vals$ or there is an $in \in I$ with $val(in) = val(r)$, and
- $q'.vals = q.val \cup vals(I)$ and $q'.pend = (q.pend \cup ids(I)) \setminus ids(R)$.

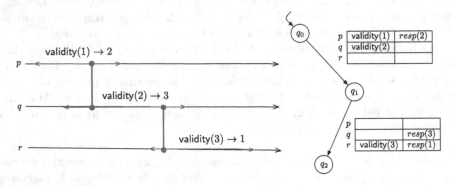

Fig. 4. An execution of a validity object, and the corresponding part of an interval-sequential automata

On the right of Fig. 4 there is part of a validity object automaton. On the left of Fig. 4 is illustrated an interval-sequential execution with the vertical red double-dot lines: I_0, R_0, I_1, R_1, where $I_0 = \{p.\mathsf{validity}(1), q.\mathsf{validity}(2)\}$, $R_0 = \{p.\mathsf{resp}(2)\}$, $I_1 = \{r.\mathsf{validity}(3)\}$, $R_1 = \{q.sfresp(3), r.\mathsf{resp}(1)\}$.

The interval-linearizability consistency notion described in subsection 4.3 will formally define how a general execution (blue double-arrows in the figure) can be represented by an interval-sequential execution (red double-dot lines), and hence tell if it satisfies the validity object specification. The execution in Fig. 4 roughly shows that the validity object has no specification as a natural sequential object: if one tries to transform the execution into a sequential one respecting real-time order, then always an invocation outputs a value that has not been proposed, namely, the invocation "predicts" the future.

4.3   Interval Linearizability

Interval-sequential come with its own consistency condition, called *interval linearizability*, that generalizes the linearizability condition of sequential objects.

Given an interval-sequential specification of an object, an execution is *interval linearizable* if it can be transformed into an interval-sequential execution such that (1) it respects the real-time order of invocation and responses and (2) the interval-sequential execution is recognized by the automaton specifying the object.

In other words, an execution is interval-linearizable if, for each operation call, it is possible to find two points, defining an interval, in the interval of real-time defined by the invocation and response of the operation, and these *linearization intervals* induce a valid interval-sequential execution. Although being more general, and hence expressive, interval linearizability retains the good properties of linearizability of being local and non-blocking.

We can now complete the example of the validity object. In Fig. 5 there is an interval linearization of the execution in Fig. 4.

	init	term	init	term
p	validity(1)	resp(2)		
q	validity(2)			resp(3)
r			validity(3)	resp(1)

Fig. 5. An execution of a validity object

Remark 3 (Linearizability and set-linearizability). When restricted to interval-sequential executions in which for every invocation there is a response to it in the very next concurrency class, then interval-linearizability boils down to set-linearizability. If in addition we demand that every concurrency class contains only one element, then we have linearizability.

5   Interval-Sequential Objects = Long-Lived Tasks

In this section, we finally show that long-lived tasks and interval-sequential objects have the same expressiveness power, i.e., they are able to describe the same set of distributed problems.

5.1   From Interval-Sequential Objects to Long-Lived Tasks

Let X be an interval-sequential object. Using the construction in Sect. 3, one can obtain a long-lived task T_X modeling X. The only difference is that, when defining $\Delta(\sigma)$, we consider all valid executions of X in which only the invocations in σ appear. Some of these executions might be non-sequential, i.e., they might be strictly interval-sequential executions but that is not a problem, the interleaving pattern in those executions can be succinctly modeled by the set-views. The solvability conditions remains the same.

The proof of the following theorem is almost the same as the proof of Theorem 1, we just need to replace the word linearizability by interval linearizability.

Theorem 2. *Let X be any interval sequential object and let T_X be the long-lived task derived from X. Consider any execution E without pending operations. Then, E is interval-linearizable with respect to X if and only if E satisfies T_X.*

5.2   From Long-Lived Tasks to Interval-Sequential Objects

Let $T = \langle \mathcal{I}, \mathcal{O}, \Delta \rangle$ be a long-lived task. We require the task is well-defined in the following sense. We say that T is *well-defined* if its set-views have the *snapshot* property: for every $\sigma \in \mathcal{I}$, for every $\tau \in \Delta(\sigma)$, the set-views in τ satisfy the following: (1) for every $v \in \tau$, its set-view contains the invocation in v and (2) for every $u, v \in \tau$, the set-views of u and v are comparable under containment.

In what follows we consider only well-formed long-lived tasks. It can be checked that the tasks constructed from interval-sequential objects above are well-formed.

We define an interval-sequential object X_T from T as follows. The set of invocations, Inv, is the infinite set with all invocations in $\mathcal{I}$ and the set of responses, rev, is the infinite set with all responses in $\mathcal{O}$. The set of states Q contains every pair (I, R) where I and R are finite sets of Inv and Res, respectively. The interval-sequential object X_T has one initial state: $(\emptyset, \emptyset)$.

The transition function δ is defined as follows. Let E be an execution without pending operations that satisfies T. Let σ_E and τ_E be the simplexes induced by E. Since E satisfy T, there is a simplex $\lambda \in \Delta(\sigma_E)$ such that for every $(inv, resp, view) \in \tau_E$ there is a $(inv', resp', view') \in \lambda$ such that $inv' = inv$, $resp' = resp$ and $view' \subseteq view$. Since T is well-defined, the set-views in λ can be ordered $V_1 \subset V_2 \subset \ldots \subset V_m$ (with $V_m = \sigma_E$). Set $W_0, V_0 = \emptyset$. For $i = 1, \ldots, m$, let $I_i = V_i \setminus V_{i-1}$, $R_i = \{resp : \exists inv \in V_i, (inv, resp, V_i) \in \lambda\}$ and $W_i = \cup_{j=1,\ldots,i} R_i$. One can check that the sequence $S = I_1, R_1, I_2, R_2, \ldots, I_m, R_m$ has the form a interval sequential execution. The reason is that R_i contains every matching response, $resp$, to an invocation, $inv \in V_i$, whose set-view is precisely V_i. Then, inv can be completed with $resp$ right after I_i because, at that point, the set-view of inv is the needed one, i.e., V_i (see Fig. 6). Then, for every $i = 1, \ldots, m$, $\delta((V_{i-1}, W_{i-1}), I_i)$ contains $((V_i, W_i), R_i)$. In other words, X_T accepts the interval-sequential execution S obtained from λ. We repeat the previous construction for every such execution E.

Theorem 3. *Let T be any long-lived task and let X_T be the interval-sequential object derived from T. Consider any execution E without pending operations. Then, E satisfies T if and only if E is interval-linearizable with respect to X_T.*

Proof. We first show that if E satisfies T then E is interval linearizable with respect to X_T. Let σ_E and τ_E be the simplexes induced by E. Since E satisfies T, there is a $\lambda \in \Delta(\sigma_E)$ such that for every $(inv, resp, view) \in \tau_E$ there is a $(inv', resp', view') \in \lambda$ such that $inv' = inv$, $resp' = resp$ and $view' \subseteq view$. By construction, λ induces an interval sequential execution S accepted by X_T. Note that E and S contain the same invocations and responses. If we prove that S respects the real-time order in E, then S is an interval linearization of E. By contradiction, suppose the opposite. Then, there are invocations *inv* and

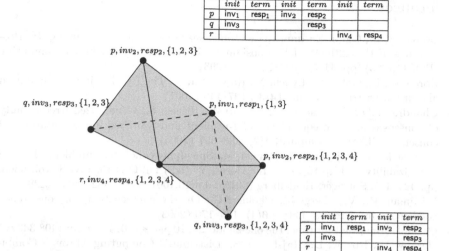

	init	term	init	term	init	term
p	inv₁	resp₁	inv₂	resp₂		
q	inv₃			resp₃		
r					inv₄	resp₄

	init	term	init	term
p	inv₁	resp₁	inv₂	resp₂
q	inv₃			resp₃
r			inv₄	resp₄

Fig. 6. From output simplexes to interval-sequential. The two simplexes have set-views with the snapshot property. Each invocation in a set-view is represented by its subindex. The corresponding interval-sequential executions are shown at the right.

inv' such that the response of inv appears before inv' in E but the response of inv' appears before inv in S. Let $view_E$ and $view_S$ be the set-views of inv in E and S. Thus, $inv' \notin view_E$ and $inv' \in view_S$, and hence $view_S \not\subseteq view_E$. A contradiction. Then, S is an interval linearization of E.

We now show that if E is interval linearizable with respect to O_T then E satisfies T. By interval linearizability, E can be transformed into an interval sequential execution S accepted by X_T such that S respects the real-time order of E. Consider the simplexes σ_E, τ_E obtained from E. We have that E and S have the same invocations. By construction, there is a $\lambda \in \Delta(\sigma_E)$ that induces S in X_T. Since S is an interval linearization of E and the execution S is induced by λ, for any $(inv, resp, view) \in \tau_E$, there is a $(inv', resp', view') \in \lambda$ with $inv' = inv$ and $resp' = resp$. Observe that if we prove that $view' \subseteq view$, then it follows that E satisfies T_O. For the sake of contradiction, assume that $view' \supset view$. Then, in the interval sequential execution S, the invocation inv appears after the response of an invocation $inv^* \in view' \setminus view$. However, since $inv^* \notin view$, the response of inv occurs before inv^* in E, from which follows that S does not respect the real-time order in E. A contradiction. $\qquad\square$

Acknowledgements. Armando Castañeda was supported by UNAM-PAPIIT project IA102417. Sergio Rajsbaum was supported by UNAM-PAPIIT project IN109917. Part of this work was done while Sergio Rajsbaum was at École Polytechnique and Paris 7 University. Michel Raynal was supported the French ANR project DESCARTES (grant 16-CE40-0023-03) devoted to distributed software engineering. This work was also partly supported by the INRIA-UNAM *Équipe Associée* LiDiCo (at the Limits of Distributed Computing).

References

1. Borowsky, E., Gafni, E.: Immediate atomic snapshots and fast renaming. In: Proceedings of the 12th ACM Symposium on Principles of Distributed Computing (PODC 1993), pp. 41–51. ACM Press (1993)
2. Borowsky, E., Gafni, E., Lynch, N., Rajsbaum, S.: The BG distributed simulation algorithm. Distrib. Comput. **14**(3), 127–146 (2001)
3. Chandra, T.D., Hadzilacos, V., Jayanti, P., Toueg, S.: Generalized irreducibility of consensus and the equivalence of t-resilient and wait-free implementations of consensus. SIAM J. Comput. **34**(2), 333–357 (2004)
4. Castañeda, A., Rajsbaum, S., Raynal, M.: Specifying concurrent problems: beyond linearizability and up to tasks. In: Moses, Y. (ed.) DISC 2015. LNCS, vol. 9363, pp. 420–435. Springer, Heidelberg (2015). doi:10.1007/978-3-662-48653-5_28
5. Friedman, R., Vitenberg, R., Chokler, G.: On the composability of consistency conditions. Inf. Process. Lett. **86**(4), 169–176 (2003)
6. Gafni, E.: Snapshot for time: the one-shot case, 10 pages (2014). arXiv:1408.3432v1
7. Herlihy, M., Kozlov, D., Rajsbaum, S.: Distributed Computing Through Combinatorial Topology, 336 pages. Morgan Kaufmann/Elsevier (2014)
8. Herlihy, M., Rajsbaum, S., Raynal, M.: Power and limits of distributed computing shared memory models. Theoret. Comput. Sci. **509**, 3–24 (2013)
9. Hemed, N., Rinetzky, N.: Brief announcement: concurrency-aware linearizability. In: Proceedings of the 33th ACM Symposium on Principles of Distributed Computing (PODC 2014), pp. 209–211. ACM Press (2014)
10. Hemed, N., Rinetzky, N., Vafeiadis, V.: Modular verification of concurrency-aware linearizability. In: Moses, Y. (ed.) DISC 2015. LNCS, vol. 9363, pp. 371–387. Springer, Heidelberg (2015). doi:10.1007/978-3-662-48653-5_25
11. Herlihy, M., Wing, J.: Linearizability: a correctness condition for concurrent objects. ACM Trans. Program. Lang. Syst. **12**(3), 463–492 (1990)
12. Moran, S., Wolfstahl, Y.: Extended impossibility results for asynchronous complete networks. Inf. Process. Lett. **26**(3), 145–151 (1987)
13. Neiger, G.: Set-linearizability. Brief announcement in Proc. 13th ACM Symposium on Principles of Distributed Computing (PODC 1994), p. 396. ACM Press (1994)

Communication

Joint Price and QoS Competition with Bounded Rational Customers

Driss Ait Omar[1]([⊠]), M'hamed Outanoute[2], Mohamed Baslam[1],
Mohamed Fakir[1], and Belaid Bouikhalne[3]

[1] Information Processing and Decision Support Laboratory, Faculty of Sciences
and Technics, Sultan Moulay Slimane University, Beni Mellal, Morocco
aitomard@gmail.com, baslam.med@gmail.com, fakfad@yahoo.fr
[2] Interdisciplinary Laboratory of Research in Sciences and Technologies, Faculty
of Sciences and Technics, Sultan Moulay Slimane University, Beni Mellal, Morocco
mhamed.outanoute@gmail.com
[3] Interdisciplinary Laboratory of Research in Sciences and Technologies,
Polydisciplinary Faculty, Sultan Moulay Slimane University, Beni Mellal, Morocco
bbouikhalene@yahoo.fr

Abstract. Recently, there has been an increased research interest in
telecommunication network pricing, which leads to many proposals for
new pricing schemes motivated by different objectives namely: to maximize service provider's revenue, to guarantee fairness among users and
to satisfy QoS requirements for differentiated network services.

In present paper, we consider a Bertrand model with N rational Service Providers (SPs) that offer homogeneous telecommunication services
to customers. We assume that all SPs offer the same services and seek to
persuade more customers in the same market, we model this conflict as
a non-cooperative game. On the one hand, each SP decide his policies of
price and Quality of Service (QoS) in order to maximize his profit. On
the other hand, we assume that the customers are boundedly rational
and make their subscription decisions probabilistically, according to Luce
choice probabilities. Furthermore, they decide to which SP to subscribe,
each one may migrate to another SP or alternatively switch to "no subscription state" depending on the observed price/QoS. In this work, we
have shown that the SPs have an interest in confusing customers i.e.
more than the customers are irrational, the SPs earn more.

Keywords: Pricing · QoS · Bounded rationality · Nash equilibrium ·
Luce choice probabilities

1 Introduction

Currently the theory of games is widely used to analyze the behavior of customers
and service providers in the telecommunications market. The competition in
terms of prices and QoS among SPs entails the formation of non-cooperative
games.

© Springer International Publishing AG 2017
A. El Abbadi and B. Garbinato (Eds.): NETYS 2017, LNCS 10299, pp. 457–471, 2017.
DOI: 10.1007/978-3-319-59647-1_33

In this paper we consider that the market consists of N SPs and boundedly rational customers. In order to optimize his revenues, each rational SP decide a best responses of his price p_i and his QoS q_i. As SPs share the same market, therefore, behavior of each depends on those of his opponents and those of customers. In this work, we present a model to calculate a single criteria Nash equilibrium (price) for several SPs, taking into account Bertrand's model in game theory, which implies that players (SPs) only choose prices. Our model is mainly inspired from the paper [3], where the authors have considered that the rationality of SPs and have constructed a Markov model that derive the behavior of customers depending on the strategic actions of the SPs, to study a non-cooperative game for pricing problem considering QoS as an extra decision parameter. But in our case, we will write that the demand for a SP is related to the size of the market (number of consumers) and the probability of choosing it; to make the model of the application non-linear, and take into account the degree of irrationality of users (λ).

Rationality implies that each customers has to reason to increase his own payoff. In other words, he possesses all the information on the market that allow him to rationalize his choice, so he is able to maximize his own gain. John V. Neumann and Morgenstern justified the idea of maximizing the excepted payoff in their work [13]. In the real world, the assumption of "full rationality" almost never holds. This real world "Bounded rationality" is one of the major impediments to applying conventional game theory in the real world.

Bounded rationality of consumers means that: rather than choosing the optimal action, customers choose an action that gives them a higher payoff with higher probability. In particular, we adopt the Luce model of probabilistic choice, that determines the probability with which a customer will decide to subscribe with a given SPi. We consider also that the bounded rationality of consumers can be measured by a degree of irrationality that can be expressed by, λ, with $\lambda = 0$ corresponding to the rational behavior and $\lambda \to 1$ corresponding to the totally random choice.

In related works, bounded rationality of the players (SPs) have studied in many researches. The authors of papers [14–17] proposed that partial information can be modeled as marginal profiles. Namely, players decide their strategy according to their respective marginal profit. In the paper [3] the authors have modeled the behavior of customers towards the telecommunications market and the bounded rationality of the services providers, the migration or the dynamic behavior of customers in the field of telecommunications is formalized in the form of a chain of markov; In this dynamic system the authors have shown to demonstrate theoretically and numerically the stability of the equilibrium between the players who are the SPs. But the concept of bounded rationality on customers are little studied especially in telecommunication market. The authors of the article [1] considered a Bertrand oligopoly model by modeling the rationality of consumers who make their purchasing decisions in a probabilistic way, according to the Luce model; This business model is aimed at companies of all kinds; that is more general. In the article [22], the authors proposed a model of sales prices by taking into account the way the company follows to present its prices to consumers and it is this way that confuses them. The authors of the article [2] were able to introduce the concept of confusion of customers in the telecommunications market and proposed a competitive price model between two rational SPs; The model proposed in this work is based on the price parameter without using the other pole of the strategies of SPs which is QoS quality of service. The authors investigated the impact of customer confusion on a market of two SP s. In our work we will extend the study by proposing a new competitive model between N SPs that take their strategies according to price and quality of service QoS. Our model will be based on a new formulation of the demand which is made nonlinear and we will adapt the probabilistic model of Luce used in the article [1] for the case of the telecommunications market.

This rest paper is organized as follows: In Sect. 2, we present the modeling of customer behavior using the Luce probabilistic model. Next, we describe the utility model of SP s and the gain of users in the telecommunications market in the sense of the Bertrand model in Sect. 3. Finally, we give a theoretical and numerical analysis obtained on the models proposed in this study and we conclude this paper with perspectives in Sects. 4, 5 and 6 respectively.

2   Customer Behavior Model

The modeling of customer behavior is a very important task when one is studying economically a market. In the telecommunications market, the authors P. Maille, M. Naldi and B. Tuffin [18] modeled this behavior in the form of a Markov chain. In this study, we use the Luce model to mathematics the discrete choice of clients by exploiting the softmax function or the normalized exponential function [19], as in the article [20].

2.1   The Luce Model

The Luce model is a first probabilistic choice model that incorporates boundedly rational choice of customers [4,5]. By using this model, customers can select the SP that maximize their payoff with higher probabilities, but not necessarily the best response with probability one. More precisely, the choice probabilities for specific strategies are proportional to the expected payoffs associated with such strategies. We augment this framework by including a free parameter λ that determines a degree of customers irrationality.

When customers faced with a choice among different alternatives $i \in \{1..N\}$, the perfectly rational decision maker always chooses the most preferred option(s) $i \in \{arg \max_i(u_i)\}$, where u_i is a profit of users who have chosen SP i. In contrast, to capture bounded rationality, we assume that customers choose alternative $i \in \{1..N\}$ with probability, as in [21], is given by:

$$\rho_i = \frac{\exp(u_i/\lambda)}{\sum_{j=1}^{N} \exp(u_j/\lambda)} \tag{1}$$

where, $\lambda \in [0, 1]$, is a degree of irrationality of customers to the telecommunications market. As λ increases (approximates 1), the customer is less likely to choose the offer (the SP) with the highest expectation and he will not explore other offers from other SPs; So in this case the choice is random and t is said that the customer choice is irrational. But, If λ decreases (approaches 0); the client is likely to make a rational choice.

2.2   Utility and Behaviors Models

We consider that the utility u_i of customers that are subscribed with SP_i is a function that depends on the strategies price p_i and QoS q_i of SP i:

$$u_i(p_i, q_i) = v_i(q_i) - p_i \qquad (2)$$

where $v_i(q_i)$ are a revenues of customers that are subscribed with SP i.

We assume that the customers never decide to subscribe with more than one SP, i.e. each consumer has $(N + 1)$ different choices, so, the probability a customers will decide to subscribe with SP i is:

$$\rho_i(\mathbf{p}, \mathbf{q}) = \frac{\exp\left(\frac{v_i(q_i) - p_i}{\lambda}\right)}{1 + \sum\limits_{j=1}^{N} \exp\left(\frac{v_j(q_j) - p_j}{\lambda}\right)} \qquad (3)$$

3   The Bertrand Model of the Market

In telecommunication market the SPs can compete on several variables, for example, they can compete based on their choices of prices and QoS. The most basic and fundamental competition pertains to pricing choices. The Bertrand Model is examines the interdependence between rivals decisions in terms of pricing decisions. In this section, we present the utility for all the SP s that offer homogeneous services to customers, as well as the gain of customers in the telecommunications market.

3.1   Utility Model

We consider a population of, n, customers, therefore the expected demand of, SP i, is given by, $n\rho_i(\mathbf{p}, \mathbf{q})$. So, the utility function of, SP i, is exactly the difference between his revenues, $n\rho_i(\mathbf{p}, \mathbf{q})p_i$, and the fee paid to buy a given amount of bandwidth μ_i:

$$\Pi_i(\mathbf{p}, \mathbf{q}) = n\rho_i p_i - F_i(\rho_i, q_i)$$
$$= n\rho_i p_i - \vartheta_i \mu_i(n, \rho_i, q_i) \qquad (4)$$

where ϑ_i is the price of unit of bandwidth and $\mu_i(\rho_i, q_i)$ is the amount of bandwidth required by SP i to guarantee the promised QoS q_i, which has the following form:

$$\mu_i(n, \rho_i, q_i) = (n\rho_i)g_i(q_i) + h_i(q_i) \qquad (5)$$

where n is a number of customers in the market and $g_i(q_i)$ and $h_i(q_i)$ are positive increasing functions.

The profile function of SP i becomes:

$$\Pi_i(\mathbf{p}, \mathbf{q}) = \frac{n \quad \exp\left(\frac{v_i(q_i) - p_i}{\lambda}\right)}{1 + \sum\limits_{j=1}^{N} \exp\left(\frac{v_j(q_j) - p_j}{\lambda}\right)}(p_i - \vartheta_i g_i(q_i)) - \vartheta_i h_i(q_i). \tag{6}$$

3.2 The Profit of Users in This Market

The real gain of users in the telecommunication market is normally not depended only at his subscription in SP_i, but it's depended in secondary at the strategies of anothers SP_{-i}. We propose in this part the modelisation of this profit.

The revenue of user u if he chooses the subscription at SP_i is:

$$R_i^u(P^*) = u_i(p_i, q_i) - \sum_{j=1, j \neq i}^{N} \beta_j^u (p_i^* - p_j^*) \tag{7}$$

Where:

- $\beta_j^u \in [0, 1] \ \forall j \in [1, N]$ *and* $j \neq i$ is the sensitivity of the user u at the motivating strategies of adversaries of its SP_i. If $\beta_j^u \to 0$ then the user u is faithful to his SPi, but if $\beta_j^u \to 1$ then the user u is totally attracted by the offer of the operator SPj and in this case we are not talking about the fidelity of u.
- P^* is the vector of Nash Equilibrium Prices.

Then, the profit (welfare) of user u in the telecommunication market is the accumulate of his revenue in the all SPs, its presented in this equation:

$$G_u(P^*) = \sum_{i=1}^{N} R_i^u(P^*) \tag{8}$$

4 Analyse of the Non-cooperative Game

The noncooperative game between rational SPs is formulated as follows: consider a market with, N, SPs, who decide their price and QoS strategies in order to maximize their individual utility/payoff, $\Pi_i(.)$. These SPs are selfish, hence they do not cooperate with each other to manage their policies. We consider that P_i and Q_i are respectively the price and QoS strategy set of SP i.

4.1   Learning Nash Equilibrium Price

Definition of Nash equilibrium of the price game: We consider a game of strategic form of N -players

$$\Gamma = \{\mathcal{N}, P_1, ..., P_N, \Pi_1, ..., \Pi_N\}, \tag{9}$$

where P_i is the set of price strategies of player i and Π_i its utility function.

Definition 1. *Nash equilibrium specifies a strategy $p_i^* \in P_i$ for each player i (with $i = 1, .., N$) in such a way that:*

$$\Pi_i(p^*, q) = \max_{p_i \in P_i} \Pi(p_1^*, ..., p_{i-1}^*, p_i, p_{i+1}^*, ..., p_N^*, q), \tag{10}$$

When the vector of QoS parameters, q, of all providers is fixed to a certain predetermined point.

Below, we analyze the competitive prices for N SPs that maximize their utilities. To do so, we demonstrate the existence and uniqueness of the game equilibrium between N SPs, after we calculate the equilibrium point. To analyze equilibrium of the game, we need to find properties on the utility function.

Algorithm 1. Best Response algorithm

1: Initialization of price vectors;
2: For each SP_i $i \in \mathcal{N}$ at iteration t:

$$- \quad p_i^{t+1} = \operatorname*{argmax}_{p_i \in P_i} \left(\Pi_i(p^t, q) \right)$$

Algorithm 2 describes how to algorithmically and graphically determine Nash equilibria.

Algorithm 2. Graphically finding the Nash equilibria of the game

---
1: Initialization of price vectors p_1 and p_2 ;
2: For all possible values of p_2, find the set $BR_1(p_2)$ of p_1 values maximizing $\Pi_1(p_1, p_2, q)$.
3: For all possible values of p_1, find the set $BR_1(p_1)$ of p_2 values maximizing $\Pi_2(p_2, p_1, q)$.
4: On a same graphic, plot the best response functions $p_1 = BR_1(p_2)$ and $p_2 = BR_2(p_1)$, as illustrated Fig. 1.
5: The set of Nash equilibria is the (possibly empty) set of intersection points of those functions.

4.2   The Price Equilibrium

In this part, we consider that SPs have fixed their QoS, $\mathbf{q}$, at some predetermined point, $\bar{\mathbf{q}}$, and we consider only the price game. The utility function (6) become:

$$\Pi_i(p_i, \mathbf{p}_{-i}) = \frac{n \quad \exp\left(\frac{\bar{v}_i - p_i}{\lambda}\right)}{1 + \sum\limits_{j=1}^{N} \exp\left(\frac{\bar{v}_j - p_j}{\lambda}\right)}(p_i - \vartheta_i \bar{g}_i) - \vartheta_i \bar{h}_i. \tag{11}$$

where $v(\bar{q}_i) = \bar{v}_i$, $\bar{g}_i = g_i(\bar{q}_i)$ and $\bar{h}_i = h_i(\bar{q}_i)$ are positive real constants. An important derivative property of relation (3) is that:

$$\frac{\partial \rho_i}{\partial p_i} = -\frac{\rho_i(1 - \rho_i)}{\lambda},$$

Proof

$$\frac{\partial \rho_i}{\partial p_i} = \frac{\partial\left(\dfrac{\exp\left(\frac{\bar{v}_i - p_i}{\lambda}\right)}{1 + \sum\limits_{j=1}^{N} \exp\left(\frac{\bar{v}_j - p_j}{\lambda}\right)}\right)}{\partial p_i}$$

$$= \frac{\dfrac{\partial \exp\left(\frac{\bar{v}_i - p_i}{\lambda}\right)}{\partial p_i}\left(1 + \sum\limits_{j=1}^{N} \exp\left(\frac{\bar{v}_j - p_j}{\lambda}\right)\right) - \dfrac{\partial\left(1 + \sum\limits_{j=1}^{N} \exp\left(\frac{\bar{v}_j - p_j}{\lambda}\right)\right)}{\partial p_i} \exp\left(\frac{\bar{v}_i - p_i}{\lambda}\right)}{\left(1 + \sum\limits_{j=1}^{N} \exp\left(\frac{\bar{v}_j - p_j}{\lambda}\right)\right)^2}$$

$$= \frac{\dfrac{-\exp\left(\frac{\bar{v}_i - p_i}{\lambda}\right)}{\lambda}\left(1 + \sum\limits_{j=1}^{N} \exp\left(\frac{\bar{v}_j - p_j}{\lambda}\right)\right) + \dfrac{\left(\exp\left(\frac{\bar{v}_i - p_i}{\lambda}\right)\right)^2}{\lambda}}{\left(1 + \sum\limits_{j=1}^{N} \exp\left(\frac{\bar{v}_j - p_j}{\lambda}\right)\right)^2}$$

$$= -\frac{\exp\left(\frac{\bar{v}_i - p_i}{\lambda}\right)}{\lambda\left(1 + \sum\limits_{j=1}^{N} \exp\left(\frac{\bar{v}_j - p_j}{\lambda}\right)\right)} + \frac{\left(\exp\left(\frac{\bar{v}_i - p_i}{\lambda}\right)\right)^2}{\lambda\left(1 + \sum\limits_{j=1}^{N} \exp\left(\frac{\bar{v}_j - p_j}{\lambda}\right)\right)^2}$$

$$= -\frac{\rho_i}{\lambda} + \frac{\rho_i^2}{\lambda} = -\frac{\rho_i(1 - \rho_i)}{\lambda}$$

therefor, the profit derivative for SP i is:

$$\frac{\partial \Pi_i(p_i, \mathbf{p}_{-i})}{\partial p_i} = -n\,(p_i - \vartheta_i \bar{g}_i)\frac{\rho_i(1 - \rho_i)}{\lambda} + n\rho_i, \quad \forall i = 1..N \tag{12}$$

with second derivative

$$\frac{\partial^2 \Pi_i(p_i, \mathbf{p}_{-i})}{\partial p_i^2} = -n\,(p_i - \vartheta_i \bar{g}_i)\frac{\rho_i(1 - \rho_i)(2\rho_i - 1)}{\lambda^2} - 2n\frac{\rho_i(1 - \rho_i)}{\lambda} \tag{13}$$

Lemma 1 (Existence of Equilibrium). *Considering the game of levels of price which arose when the QoS vector is fixed to all SPs, there exists at least a Nash equilibrium price, of SPs game, if the price he satisfied this condition:*
$p_i > \vartheta_i \bar{g}_i - \frac{2\lambda}{2\rho_i - 1}$

Proof. Equation 13 represent the second derivative of the utility function 11 relative to the price. The condition for this function as strictly concave is:

$$\frac{\partial^2 \Pi_i(p_i, \mathbf{P}_{-i})}{\partial p_i^2} < 0,$$

$$then \quad -n(p_i - \vartheta_i \bar{g}_i) \frac{\rho_i(1 - \rho_i)(2\rho_i - 1)}{\lambda^2} - 2n \frac{\rho_i(1 - \rho_i)}{\lambda} < 0,$$

$$Finally \quad p_i > \vartheta_i \bar{g}_i - \frac{2\lambda}{2\rho_i - 1},$$

Lemma 2 (Uniqueness of Equilibrium). *The most common method to show uniqueness is the following condition of Rosen [11]. Moulin [12], (see, for example, [6]):*

$$\frac{\partial^2 \Pi_i}{\partial p_i^2} + \sum_{j \neq i} \left| \frac{\partial^2 \Pi_i}{\partial p_i \partial p_j} \right| < 0. \tag{14}$$

Proof. To prove the uniqueness of equilibrium, we check the correctness of the following inequality:

$$\frac{\partial^2 \Pi_i}{\partial p_i \partial p_j} = \left(\frac{n(p_i - \vartheta_i \bar{g}_i)}{\lambda^2} (2\rho_i^2 - \rho_i) + \frac{n}{\lambda} \rho_i \right) \rho_j,$$

so:

$$\sum_{j \neq i} \left| \frac{\partial^2 \Pi_i}{\partial p_i \partial p_j} \right| = \left| \frac{n(p_i - \vartheta_i \bar{g}_i)}{\lambda^2} (2\rho_i^2 - \rho_i) + \frac{n}{\lambda} \rho_i \right| \sum_{j \neq i} \rho_j$$

$$= \left| \frac{n(p_i - \vartheta_i \bar{g}_i)}{\lambda^2} (2\rho_i - 1) + \frac{n}{\lambda} \right| \rho_i(1 - \rho_i), \tag{15}$$

from (13) and (15) we have:

$$\frac{\partial^2 \Pi_i}{\partial p_i^2} + \sum_{j \neq i} \left| \frac{\partial^2 \Pi_i}{\partial p_i \partial p_j} \right| = \rho_i(1 - \rho_i) \left(-\frac{n(p_i - \vartheta_i \bar{g}_i)(2\rho_i - 1)}{\lambda^2} - \frac{2n}{\lambda} + \left| \frac{n(p_i - \vartheta_i \bar{g}_i)}{\lambda^2} (2\rho_i - 1) + \frac{n}{\lambda} \right| \right),$$

if $\left(\frac{n(p_i - \vartheta_i \bar{g}_i)}{\lambda^2} (2\rho_i - 1) + \frac{n}{\lambda} \geq 0 \right)$, i.e. $p_i \geq \vartheta_i \bar{g}_i - \frac{\lambda}{2\rho_i - 1}$ then

$$\frac{\partial^2 \Pi_i}{\partial p_i^2} + \sum_{j \neq i} \left| \frac{\partial^2 \Pi_i}{\partial p_i \partial p_j} \right| = -\frac{n\rho_i(1 - \rho_i)}{\lambda} < 0,$$

if $\left(\frac{n(p_i - \vartheta_i \bar{g}_i)}{\lambda^2} (2\rho_i - 1) + \frac{n}{\lambda} \leq 0 \right)$, i.e. $p_i \leq \vartheta_i \bar{g}_i - \frac{\lambda}{2\rho_i - 1}$ then

$$\frac{\partial^2 \Pi_i}{\partial p_i^2} + \sum_{j \neq i} \left| \frac{\partial^2 \Pi_i}{\partial p_i \partial p_j} \right| = \frac{-n\rho_i(1 - \rho_i)}{\lambda} \left(\frac{2(p_i - \vartheta_i \bar{g}_i)}{\lambda} (2\rho_i - 1) + 3 \right)$$

when $p_i > \vartheta_i \bar{g}_i - \frac{3\lambda}{2(2\rho_i - 1)}$

4.3   Price of Anarchy

The concept of the social surplus [7] or total cost [8], is defined as the maximum of the sum of utilities of all agents in the systems (i.e. Providers). It is well known in game theory that selfishness of the agent, as in a Nash equilibrium, typically does not lead to a socially effective situation. As a measure of efficiency loss due to divergence of interests of users, we use the price of anarchy (*PoA*) [9], the latter is a measure of the loss of efficiency due to the selfishness of the actors. This loss was defined in [9] as the ratio of the worst comparing the measure of the overall efficiency (to be selected) at the end of non-cooperative game played between the actors, to the optimum value of this measure efficiency. A *PoA* close to 1 indicates that the equilibrium is about socially optimal, and then the consequences of selfish behavior are relatively benign. The term price of anarchy was used by Koutsoupias and Papadimitriou [9]. As in [10], measuring the loss of efficiency due to the selfishness of the actors as the quotient of the social welfare obtained at the Nash equilibrium and the maximum value of social welfare:

$$PoA = \frac{\min_{p,\bar{q}} W_{NE}(p,\bar{q})}{\max_{p,\bar{q}} W(p,\bar{q})} \tag{16}$$

where $W(p,\bar{q}) = \sum_{i=1}^{N} \Pi_i(p,\bar{q})$ is a function of welfare and $W_{NE}(p,\bar{q}) = \sum_{i=1}^{N} \Pi_i(p^*,\bar{q})$ is a sum of utilities of all actors in the Nash equilibrium.

5   Numerical Analysis of the Game

In this section, we turn now to discuss how to take gain from our analytical findings. We propose to numerically study the gaming market taking account of previous expression of utility of the SPs. For illustrative purpose, we consider two homogeneous SPs seeking to maximize their earnings. Until we contraindicate, the parameter values are summarized in Table 1.

Table 1. Parameters setting used for numerical examples

n	N	$\bar{v}_1$	$\bar{v}_2$	λ	$P_1 = P_2$
100	2	25	20	0.7	[1 : 1000]
$\bar{g}_1$	$\bar{g}_2$	$\bar{h}_1$	$\bar{h}_2$	ϑ_1	ϑ_2
5	10	4	6	1.5	1

We used the Algorithm 2 for plotting the best response curves of both providers on the same graph highlights the Nash equilibria of the game. Those curves are shown in Fig. 1. This figure shows that Nash equilibria of the game

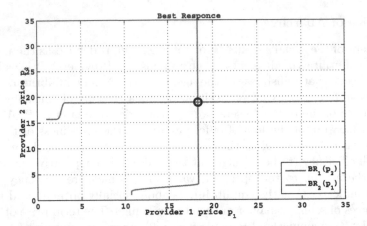

Fig. 1. Graphical determination of nash equilibria. One solution here (circled point).

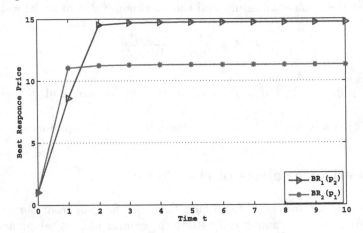

Fig. 2. Convergence to the price nash equilibrium

is unique and this reflects what we found in the theoretical study of the unique-ness of the Nash equilibrium. The equilibrium obtained graphically is exactly the point of intersection between the curve of the vector $BR_1(P_2)$ and that of the $BR_2(P_1)$.

The Fig. 2 represent the convergence curves Nash Equilibrium Prices for both SPs. The best dynamic response algorithm used in this framework converges to a unique Nash equilibrium. We also notice that the algorithm has turned approx-imately 10 iterations, which shows the rapidity of the speed of convergence. Then this simulation of Algorithm 1 is able to converge efficiently to the Nash equilibrium price.

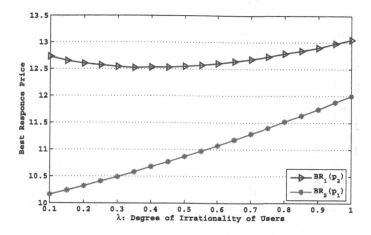

Fig. 3. Equilibrium prices w.r.t degree of irrationality of users

5.1   Impact of Users Degree of Irrationality on the Equilibrium Price

In this simulation, we have undergone a discretization, at regular step, at the interval of λ. Figure 3 shows the influence of the degree of irrationality on price equilibrium. In the interval where the degree of irrationality is low ($\lambda < 0.35$) i.e. the choice the users is often rational; the SP_1, which starts the games with proportionately high prices, has decreased its price to attract more customer and increased his PayOff. While, the SP_2, which starts the games with motivating prices, began to increase its price to ensure its profit. And with high degrees of irrationality, the SPs raise their prices without worrying about the opponent's strategy as clients make irrational decisions.

5.2   Impact of Unit of Bandwidth on the Equilibrium Price

In this simulation, we have undergone a discretization, at regular step, at the interval of ϑ_i $i \in \{1, 2\}$. Figure 4 shows the influence of price of unit of bandwidth on price equilibrium. The figure shows that it is clear that when the unit price of bandwidth increases, all SPs are obliged to increase their price strategy with the goal of keeping at least their current beneficence.

5.3   Impact of Users Degree of Irrationnality on the Their Gain

To validate our model of user gain to the telecommunications market presented in the Eq. 8, we simulate by varying the degree of irrationality of the users and calculating their gain. Figure 5 shows that when users make decisions about the choice of SP in a rational way, their gain in the market increases. While, during a random selection of the SP from users, their gain decreases. In summary, the more customers are confused by their SP s, more their gain decreases in this market.

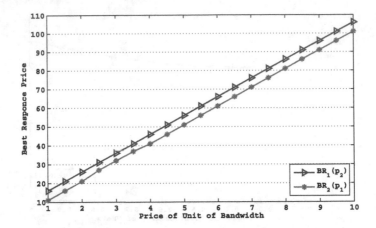

Fig. 4. Equilibrium prices w.r.t degree of unit of requested bandwidth

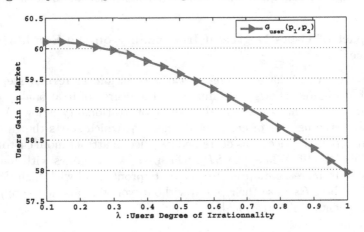

Fig. 5. Users gain w.r.t degree of irrationality

5.4 Impact of Users Sensitivity on the Their Gain

In this section, we consider a user u that subscribes to the services of the SP_1 (i.e. $\beta_1^u = 0$) and we vary the sensitivity β_2^u, To the strategy of SP_2, to see its impact on the user's gain u. We notice from Fig. 6 that when the sensitivity β_2^u of user u increases, the social gain of u decreases in the telecommunications market. And this result is actually seen in this market, So that when a user subscribes to the services of a SP_i and as soon as the SP_j offers services more motivating than the SP_i, The user u feels bad about his choice.

5.5 Equilibrium Efficiency

In this part, we will use the concept of the anarchy price presented in the Sect. 4 to discuss the effectiveness of the Nash equilibrium. The Fig. 7 shows the PoA

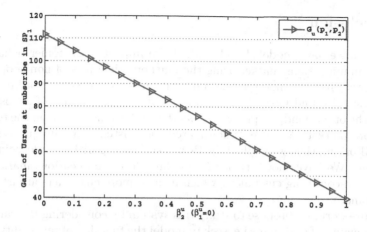

Fig. 6. Users gain w.r.t sensitivity

variation curve as a function the λ which represents the users degree of irrationality.. In that figure, we first notice that the price of anarchy increases when λ increases. When the degree of irrationality is low, i.e. users make their choice decisions rationally, the price of anarchy is low and what shows that the sum of the optimal utilities is greater than the sum of utilities to equilibrium; which shows that the SPs are selfish and each one seeks to maximize its profit. While in the case where the price of anarchy approaches 1, the SPs are not selfish and each one takes consolidation the strategy of his opponent to finally fall into the state of equilibrium.

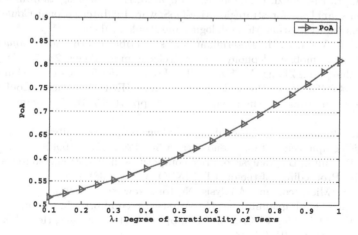

Fig. 7. Price of anarchy w.r.t degree of irrationality

6   Conclusion

In this work we have modeled and studied the impact of customer behavior in the telecommunications market using the mathematical tool of non-cooperative game theory. First, we modeled the competition between SPs according to two parameters: price and QoS taking into account the probability of choosing the SPs. On the other hand, we proposed a model of the gain of users in the telecommunications market. We have demonstrated the existence and uniqueness of the Nash equilibrium, then we applied the Best response Algorithm for learning Nash equilibrium. We have shown that SPs in the telecommunications market have an interest in confusing customers, which means; more customers are irrational, SPs earn more.

In future work, we propose to study this system by considering the variability of the rationality of customers i.e. seek to model the function of rationality. Client rationality is a function to be modeled that depends on a set of parameters such as those related to customer behavior themselves and those related to offers trapped or confused by the SPs in the telecommunications market.

References

1. Basov, S., Danilkina, S.: Bertrand oligopoly with boundedly rational consumers. The BE J. Theor. Econ. **15**(1), 107–123 (2015)
2. Mouhyiddine, T., Sabir, E., Sadik, M.: Telecommunications market share game with ambiguous pricing strategies. In: Fifth International Conference on Next Generation Networks and Services (NGNS 2014), Casablanca, Morocco, 28–30 May 2014. IEEE, Piscataway (2014)
3. Baslam, M., El-Azouzi, R., Sabir, E., Bouyakhf, E.: New insights from a bounded rationality analysis for strategic price-QoS war. In: International Conference on Performance Evaluation Methodologies and Tools (2012)
4. Kim, H.-S., Yoon, C.-H.: Determinants of subscriber churn and customer loyalty in the Korean mobile telephony market. Telecommun. Policy **28**, 751–765 (2004)
5. Qi, J., Zhang, Y., Zhang, Y., Shi, S.: TreeLogit model for customer churn prediction. In: APSCC 2006: Proceedings of the 2006 IEEE AsiaPacific Conference on Services Computing, Washington, DC, USA, pp. 70–75. IEEE Computer Society (2006)
6. Milgrom, P., Roberts, J.: Rationalizability, learning, and equilibrium in games with strategic complementarities. Econometrica **58**, 1255–1277 (1990)
7. Maille, P., Tuffin, B.: Analysis of price competition in a slotted resource allocation game. In: Proceedings of the of IEEE INFOCOM (2008)
8. Varian, H.: Microeconomic Analysis. Norton, New York (1992)
9. Koutsoupias, E., Papadimitriou, C.: Worst-case equilibria. In: Meinel, C., Tison, S. (eds.) STACS 1999. LNCS, vol. 1563, pp. 404–413. Springer, Heidelberg (1999). doi:10.1007/3-540-49116-3_38
10. Guijarro, L., Pla, V., Vidal, J., Martinez-Bauset, J.: Analysis of price competition under peering and transit agreements in internet service provision to peer-to-peer users. In: IEEE Consumer Communications and Networking Conference (CCNC2011), Las Vegas, Nevada USA, pp. 9–12 (2011)

11. Rosen, J.: Existence and uniqueness of equilibrium points for concave N-person games. Econometrica **33**, 520–534 (1965)
12. Gabay, D., Moulin, H.: On the uniqueness and stability of Nash-equilibria in noncooperative games. In: Bensoussan, A., Kleindorfer, P., Tapiero, C.S. (eds.) Applied Stochastic Control in Econometrics and Management Science. North-Holland, Amsterdam (1980)
13. von Neumann, J., Morgenstern, O.: Theory of Games and Economic Behavior. Princeton University Press, Princeton (1944)
14. Ahmed, E., Agiza, H.N., Hassan, S.Z.: On modifications of Puu's dynamical duopoly. Chaos, Solitons Fractals **11**, 1025–1028 (2000)
15. Bischi, G.I., Naimzada, A.: Global analysis a dynamic duopoly game with bounded rationality. In: Advanced in Dynamics Games and Application, Birkhauser, Basel **5**, (1999)
16. Yassen, M.T., Agiza, H.N.: Analysis of duopoloy game with delayed bounded rationality. Appl. Math. Comput. **138**, 378–402 (2003)
17. Elsadany, A.A.: Dynamics of a delayed duopoloy game with bounded rationality. Math. Comput. Model. **52**(9–10), 1479–1489 (2010)
18. Maille, P., Naldi, M., Tuffin, B.: Price war with migrating customers. In: 17th Annual Meeting of the IEEE/ACM International Symposium on Modelling, Analysis and Simulation of Computer and Telecommunication Systems (MASCOTS 2009), IEEE Computer Society, London, UK, September 2009
19. Bishop, C.M.: Pattern Recognition and Machine Learning. Springer, New York (2006)
20. Pleskac, T.J.: Decision and choice: Luce's choice axiom. In: Wright, J.D. (ed.) International Encyclopedia of the Social and Behavioral Sciences, 2nd edn., vol. 5, pp. 895–900. Elsevier, Oxford (2015)
21. Sutton, R.S., Barto, A.G.: Reinforcement Learning: An Introduction, 2nd edn. MIT Press, Cambridge (2012)
22. Chioveanu, I., Zhou, J.: Price Competition and Consumer Confusion, Department of Economics, University College London, 1 September 2009

Profiling and Modelling of HEVC Intra Video Encoder's Energy Consumption for Next Generation WVSNS

Achraf Ait-Beni-Ifit[1](✉) (iD), Othmane Alaoui-Fdili[1], Patrick Corlay[2],
François-Xavier Coudoux[2], and Driss Aboutajdine[1]

[1] LRIT-CNRST URAC29, Faculty of Sciences,
Mohammed V University, Rabat, Morocco
mr.ifit@gmail.com
[2] IEMN UMR 8520, Department OAE, UVHC, Valenciennes, France

Abstract. Energy consumption is of main concern in the field of Wireless Video Sensor Networks (WVSNs) where energy resources are limited, consisting only in the battery of the sensor nodes that determines their lifetime. In this paper, we propose an empirical parametric model to predict the energy consumption of a High Efficiency Video Coding (HEVC) based video encoder in its intra-only mode, used in the context of the next generation WVSNs. Such model is of great interest to adapt the waste of energy of the encoding phase to the remaining energy budget of the node, while meeting the required video quality. The proposed model predicts the energy consumption, considering the adopted Quantization Parameter (QP) and the Frame Rate parameter (FR). A Raspberry Pi 2 card based video sensor node is used for modelling and validation, considering different configurations and spatial resolutions. The obtained results demonstrate that the proposed model describes well the occurred energy dissipation during the video encoding phase, with an average prediction error of 4.5%.

Keywords: Profiling and modelling · Energy consumption · Video compression · H.265/HEVC · Next generation wireless video sensor network · Raspberry Pi 2

1 Introduction

Wireless sensor networks (WSNs) have attracted a wide range of disciplines, where close interactions with the physical world are essential. WSNs are new tools to capture information from the environment at a scale, both in time and space, previously hard to achieve [4]. Each node is battery powered and changing this component is, in general, undesirable and even impossible in some applications. Therefore, many efforts have been made in order to propose energy-efficient communication protocols in order to extend node's lifetime as much as possible [7,10]. The availability of low-cost CMOS image sensors has enabled

© Springer International Publishing AG 2017
A. El Abbadi and B. Garbinato (Eds.): NETYS 2017, LNCS 10299, pp. 472–482, 2017.
DOI: 10.1007/978-3-319-59647-1_34

the emergence of the field of next generation Wireless Video Sensor Networks (WVSNs) [15,17]. Each node in a WVSN captures pictures or video sequences from the environment, processes it, then routes it towards the destination. Such nodes have allowed the development of new applications for the WVSNs, an example is given by Karlsson et al. [8] for Zoo video monitoring system called The Digital Zoo, funded by the EU regional development. The approach uses the WVSNs to collect multimedia information about animals and their surrounding. The WVSN have introduced new research challenges to the field of WSN. In fact, the amount of data generated by an image sensor is much higher than other types of sensors. A QVGA image (320×240) at 12 bits per pixel will generate 115 200 bytes of data as presented by Karlsson et al. [8]. This exceeds by far the available RAM memory on a typical wireless sensor node. Moreover, a video sensor node spends its lifetime encoding and transmitting the video signal. According to Lu et al. [9], the video encoding phase consumes a significant amount of energy. Therefore, in order to extend the video node lifetime, the consumed energy during the video compression should be decreased, while maintaining the desired video quality. Consequently, a mathematical model is needed in order to predict the consumed energy by the video encoder. This model enables the node to adapt its configuration, considering its remaining energy as well as the targeted video quality, in order to extend its lifetime.

In this paper we propose an empirical energy consumption model for a High Efficiency Video Coding (H.265/HEVC) intra-only video encoder considering the QP and the FR parameters. The HEVC video coding standard is the last compression standard finalized in late 2012 and designed to achieve multiple goals, including coding efficiency, ease of transport system integration and data loss resilience, as well as implementability using parallel processing architectures. Furthermore, since the motion compensation and the motion estimation in inter GOP generate a significant energy consumption, we adopt the intra video coding for more energy efficiency. In addition, intra coding is essential for high quality mobile video communication and industrial video applications since it enhances video quality, prevents error propagation, and facilitates random access [18]. One can intuitively say that the energy decreases with the increasing of QP and when lowering FR. However, the main question that we are trying to answer is how does energy decrease when only intra-image coding is used? The answer will help to model the consumed energy by any HEVC intra-only mode based encoder, and will further allow us to optimize the consumed energy in WVSNs.

The rest of this paper is organized as follows: in Sect. 2, a brief overview of the previous works given on the subject is presented. In Sect. 3, the proposed mathematical model for energy consumption prediction during the video compression is derived. In Sect. 3, we validate the proposed model under different configurations. Finally, Sect. 5 concludes the paper.

2   Related Works

Several studies have contributed on energy consumption analysis of video-coding standards.

Vanne et al. [16] analyse the rate-distortion-complexity of HEVC reference video codec (HM) and compare the results with AVC reference codec (JM). Profiling results show that the average software complexity ratios of HM and JM encoders are 3.2x in the All-intra case. This paper also reveals the bottlenecks of HM codec and provides implementation guidelines for future real-time HEVC codecs.

Alaoui et al. [1] propose a model to predict the energy consumption of a H.264/AVC intra-only based encoder designed for the WVSNs, with respect to the considered QP and FR values. In fact, in this paper, the authors compare the energy consumption of the intra-only mode against the inter mode (i.e. GOP IPPPP) and prove the energy efficiency of the first mode. Finally, the proposed model is applied on the encoder under different configurations (i.e. resolution, QP and FR). However, the authors perform the tests as simulations on a computer and not on an actual sensor node.

Bossen et al. [2] present an overview of the complexity in both HEVC encoder and decoder and recommend to use the HM implementation of the HEVC standard. However, the authors do not propose a model for complexity behaviour in the HEVC encoder.

Hergoltz et al. [5] propose a model that describes the energy consumption of the HEVC decoder for intra coded videos with a prediction error of 3.2%. However, we are interested by the encoding phase.

Saab et al. [13] propose the profiling of the HEVC standard using the Valgrind tool [14] to determine the cost of each function and instruction of the encoding phase. The results show that, in an HEVC encoding process, about 48% of the instructions are memory related and about 20% are arithmetic operations. Except that, the author did not propose a model of energy consumption in HEVC standard.

Finally Rodr et al. [12] present an energy model for an intra-only HEVC video encoder. It estimates the energy consumed by the HEVC encoder, in a frame by frame basis, considering two factors: the QP and the spatial information of each frame. Experimental validation reports prediction errors that are, on average, below 10% for full HD videos and 5% for 832×480 videos. However, the proposed analytic expression of the model remains complex.

3   The Proposed Model

The main purpose of this section is to find the analytic expression of $f(.)$, defined as follows:

$$E(QP, FR) = f(QP, FR) \tag{1}$$

In order to find the appropriate analytic expression, we adopt the approach that is based on profiling the HEVC using Perf in a Raspberry Pi 2 (RPI2) Card. Figure 1 shows the RPI2 card we used for testing with the camera module. Perf is a profiling tool dedicated to Linux 2.6+ systems. The Perf tool offers a rich set of commands to collect and analyse performance and trace data, especially "perf stat". An execution example of "perf stat" command is presented in Fig. 2.

Fig. 1. Raspberry Pi 2 Card and the camera module

```
Performance counter stats for './TAppEncoderStatic -c in.cfg -c intra.cfg -q 10':

    4667189,435610      task-clock (msec)          #    1,000 CPUs utilized
             2 565      context-switches           #    0,001 K/sec
                 1      cpu-migrations             #    0,000 K/sec
            22 180      page-faults                #    0,005 K/sec
 3 853 429 415 529      cycles                     #    0,826 GHz
      <not supported>   stalled-cycles-frontend
      <not supported>   stalled-cycles-backend
 2 303 511 972 109      instructions               #    0,60  insns per cycle
   174 163 875 700      branches                   #   37,317 M/sec
    52 220 027 760      branch-misses              #   29,98% of all branches

    4667,404334245 seconds time elapsed
```

Fig. 2. Execution example of "perf stat" on an encoding process

Such an approach will provide us an accurate overview of the number of the consumed clock cycles. Then, according to Dai et al. [3], the energy consumed during the video encoding could be approached by:

$$E(N) = N * C * V_{dd}^2 + V_{dd} * (I_0 e^{\frac{V_{dd}}{nV_T}} (\frac{N}{f}))$$ (2)

where N is the number of clock cycles, C is the average capacitance switched per cycle, V_{dd} is the supply voltage, I_0 is the leakage current, f is the clock speed, V_T is the thermal voltage and n a processor dependent constant.

In order to derive the appropriate model, extensive tests were carried out for energy measurements using several video sequences. The ITU-T [6] recommends for the selection of appropriate video test sequences to consider the spatial and temporal perceptual information of the scenes, noted in the following SI and TI respectively. In fact, these parameters reflect the compression difficulty as well as the level of impairment that is suffered when the scene is transmitted. Furthermore, it is important to choose sequences that span a large portion of the spatial-temporal information domain.

Figure 3 presents several sequences of different resolutions providing TI-SI pairs that cover several regions of the SI-TI domain. In fact, four video sequences were selected: Container and Mother-daughter in QCIF size, Foreman and Mobile in CIF size. As can be seen, the considered set of video sequences covers a large area, showing its TI-SI diversity. In fact, according to the Fig. 4,

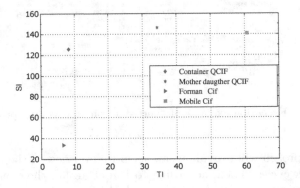

Fig. 3. Illustration of the chosen video sequences of different resolutions and content features

Fig. 4. The TI-SI diagram

this set includes video sequences representing contents with a moderate TI and SI ranging from low to high (i.e. Foreman and Mobile), while others represent contents with a moderate SI and TI ranging from low to high (i.e. Mother-daughter and Container).

3.1 Modelling the Consumed Energy as a Function of QP

To achieve the H.265/HEVC profiling we have carried out several compression operations considering six values of QP ranging from 0 to 51 via the HM-11.0 implementation. Profiling is achieved through the Perf tool under RPI2 Card to estimate the total number of clock cycles. With the use of Perf, we managed to gather the exact number of cycles of each type of operation in all functions of HEVC (i.e. prediction, transformation, quantization and entropy coding). Figure 5 illustrates the behaviour of the normalized consumed cycles during the video compression of the tested video sequences. We can notice that the number of cycles, and hence the consumed energy, decreases when the QP is

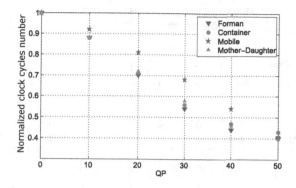

Fig. 5. Normalized number of clock cycles while varying QP

increased. This can be explained by when increasing the QP value, the quantization becomes more severe, generating macroblocks with more null coefficients. Having many null coefficients leads to the reduction of the complexity of the entropy encoding process.

Figure 5 shows the behaviour of a reduction factor dependent on QP, we call it $\alpha(QP)$. This factor decreases the maximal consumed energy E_{max}, which is reached at $QP = 0$. Furthermore, $\alpha(QP)$ reaches its maximum value of 1 at $QP = QP_{min} = 0$ and its minimum value at $QP = QP_{max} = 51$. Based on all the above mentioned arguments, we propose to model $\alpha(.)$ as follows:

$$\alpha(QP) = \exp(-a * QP) \tag{3}$$

where a is a coefficient dependent on the content obtained by minimizing the Root Mean Squared Error (RMSE) between the measured and the predicted data.

The corresponding value of a in Eq. 3 for each sequence, is determinated by curve fitting optimisation [11]. The results of this operation is reported by Fig. 6. Points are the measured coefficients and the curves are the predicted ones by the proposed model of Eq. 3. As can be seen, the proposed model describes well the behaviour of the measured coefficients.

3.2   Modelling the Consumed Energy as a Function of FR

The FR parameter is the second factor that we consider to predict the energy consumption of our video encoder. We can change the FR in the HM implementation by varying the parameter named Frame Skip (FS). The relationship between these two parameters is given as follows:

$$FS = \left\lceil \frac{FR_{max}}{FR} \right\rceil - 1 \tag{4}$$

Figure 7 represents the number of normalized clock cycles while varying the FS. As can be seen, energy decreases with the increasing of the FS, leading to

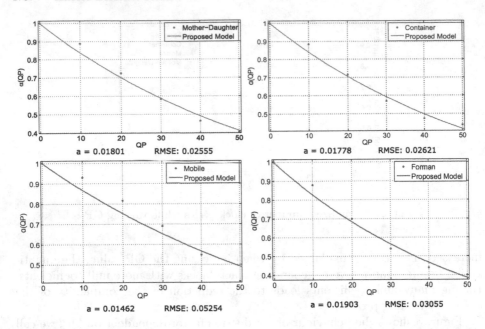

Fig. 6. Measured data and its approximation using the proposed model of Eq. 3

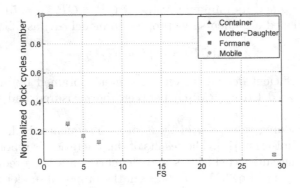

Fig. 7. Normalized number of clock cycles while varying FS

the decreasing of the FR. This can obviously be explained by when reducing the FR, the FS is increased and hence less frames are encoded. Consequently, a considerable reduction of the consumed energy is observed. Note that the FR_{max} of the tested video sequences is 30 fps and using Eq. 4 one can deduce the tested FRs. Also, we notice that the incrementation of the FS by one reduces the energy by about the half and so on, which is an obvious and expected behaviour.

Figure 8 shows the behaviour of a reduction factor that is FS-dependent. We name it $\beta(FS)$. This factor actually reaches its maximum value of 1 at $FS = FS_{min} = 0$ and quickly decreases toward its minimum value at

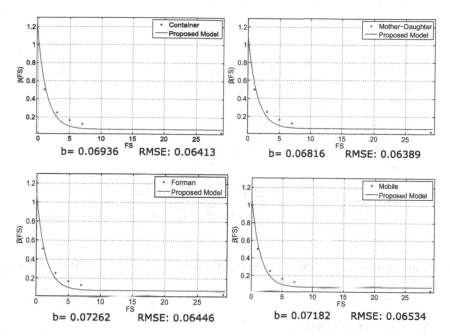

Fig. 8. Measured data and its approximation using the proposed model of Eq. 5

$FS = FS_{max} = 29$. In addition, this factor does not attain the zero value since there is at least one frame to be encoded. Based on the above mentioned arguments we propose to model $\beta(.)$ as follows:

$$\beta(FS) = \frac{1}{2^{FS}} + b \tag{5}$$

where b is a content dependent parameter obtained by minimizing the RMSE between the measured and the predicted data. As shown in Fig. 8, the proposed model in Eq. 5 can model the behaviour of the reduction factor $\beta(FS)$ accurately.

3.3   The Global Model

The energy consumed is reduced by a QP-dependent reduction factor and an FR-dependent reduction factor. Therefore we propose the following formulation of the global model:

$$E(QP, FR) = E_{max} \times \alpha(QP) \times \beta\left(\left\lceil \frac{FR_{max}}{FR} \right\rceil - 1\right) \tag{6}$$

E_{max} is the maximum value of energy, reached for the pair (QP_{min}, FR_{max}). Summarizing, we expose in Fig. 9 the overall behaviour of the normalized video encoding energy consumption while varying QP and FR, using the model of Eq. 6.

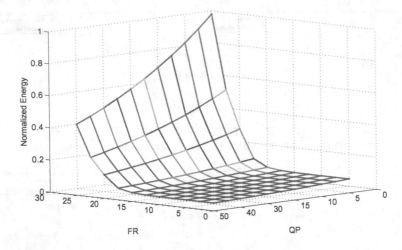

Fig. 9. Illustration of the normalized energy consumption considering QP and FR using the model of Eq. 6

4   Model Application

In this section, we apply the proposed model on seven other sequences using seven different values of QP and FR. The model parameters a and b values of each sequence are set, as a first approach in this paper, to the average values of $a = 0.01736$ and $b = 0.07049$. We report in Table 1 the Measured Value (MV), the Predicted Value (PV) and the Prediction Error (PE) for each sequence and considered configuration. MV is obtained by normalizing the measured number of clock cycles for each configuration in terms of QP and FR. PV is obtained using the proposed model in Eq. 6, for each of the pairs (QP,FR) listed in Table 1. As can be seen, the PE varies from 1.8% for the Basketball-drill sequence to 10% for the Bosphorus sequence, even if the the model parameters values are not the

Table 1. The tests results considering different sequences, of different resolutions under different configurations

Seq	Res	QP	FR	MV	PV	PE
Bus	QCIF	15	1	$0,038$	$0,059$	2%
Hall	QCIF	25	7.5	0.126	0.158	3.2%
Soccer	QCIF	25	3.75	$0,050$	0.101	5%
News	CIF	15	30	$0,368$	0.439	7%
Tennis	CIF	40	6	$0,075$	0.050	2.5%
Basketball	832×480	30	3.75	0.046	0.064	1.8%
Bosphorus	Full HD	15	30	0.711	0.818	10%

optimal ones. As shown in Table 1, the average prediction error of the proposed model in Eq. 6 is about 4.5%.

5   Conclusion

In this paper we have proposed an empirical parametric model to predict the energy consumed by the encoding phase, considering the HEVC intra-only video encoding standard, used in an energy constrained context such as the WVSN. Specifically, we have demonstrated that this energy, given a configuration of (QP, FR), could be approximated by the maximum consumed energy value undergoing QP-dependent then FR-dependent reductions. Finally, the proposed model was validated and applied on different sequences of different resolutions and considering different configurations. This model can be even better by automating the selection of the models parameters a and b; this is actually our ongoing work.

References

1. Alaoui-Fdili, O., Fakhri, Y., Corlay, P., Coudoux, F.X., Aboutajdine, D.: Energy consumption analysis and modelling of a H.264/AVC intra-only based encoder dedicated to WVSNs. In: 2014 IEEE International Conference on Image Processing (ICIP), pp. 1189–1193. IEEE (2014)
2. Bossen, F., Bross, B., Suhring, K., Flynn, D.: Hevc complexity and implementation analysis. IEEE Trans. Circ. Syst. Video Technol. **22**(12), 1685–1696 (2012)
3. Dai, R., Wang, P., Akyildiz, I.F.: Correlation-aware qos routing with differential coding for wireless video sensor networks. IEEE Trans. Multimedia **14**(5), 1469–1479 (2012)
4. Fahmy, H.M.A.: Wireless Sensor Networks: Concepts, Applications, Experimentation and Analysis. Signals and Communication Technology, vol. 1. Springer, Heidelberg (2016)
5. Herglotz, C., Springer, D., Eichenseer, A., Kaup, A.: Modeling the energy consumption of HEVC intra decoding. In: 2013 20th International Conference on Systems, Signals and Image Processing (IWSSIP), pp. 91–94. IEEE (2013)
6. ITU-T RECOMMENDATION, P.: Subjective video quality assessment methods for multimedia applications (1999)
7. Kafi, M.A., Djenouri, D., Ben-Othman, J., Badache, N.: Congestion control protocols in wireless sensor networks: a survey. IEEE Commun. Surv. Tutorials **16**(3), 1369–1390 (2014)
8. Karlsson, J.: Wireless video sensor network and its applications in digital zoo. Ph.D. thesis (2010)
9. Lu, X., Wang, Y., Erkip, E.: Power efficient h. 263 video transmission over wireless channels. In: Proceedings of 2002 International Conference on Image Processing 2002, vol. 1, pp. I-533. IEEE (2002)
10. Pantazis, N.A., Nikolidakis, S.A., Vergados, D.D.: Energy-efficient routing protocols in wireless sensor networks: a survey. IEEE Commun. Surv. Tutorials **15**(2), 551–591 (2013)
11. Pilotte, P.: Curve fitting toolbox, 17 December 2015. http://www.mathworks.com/products/curvefitting/

12. Rodr, R., Alonso, M., Mart, J., Mayo, R., Quintana-Ort, E., et al.: Time and energy modeling of an intra-only hevc encoder. In: 2015 Visual Communications and Image Processing (VCIP), pp. 1–4. IEEE (2015)
13. Saab, F., Elhajj, I., Kayssi, A., Chehab, A.: Profiling of hevc encoder. Electron. Lett. **50**(15), 1061–1063 (2014)
14. Seward, J., Nethercote, N., Weidendorfer, J.: Valgrind 3.3-Advanced Debugging and Profiling for GNU/Linux applications. Network Theory Ltd., Bristol (2008)
15. Soro, S., Heinzelman, W.: A survey of visual sensor networks. Adv. Multimedia (2009)
16. Vanne, J., Viitanen, M., Hamalainen, T.D., Hallapuro, A.: Comparative rate-distortion-complexity analysis of hevc and avc video codecs. IEEE Trans. Circuits Syst. Video Technol. **22**(12), 1885–1898 (2012)
17. Yap, F.G., Yen, H.H.: A survey on sensor coverage and visual data capturing/processing/transmission in wireless visual sensor networks. Sensors **14**(2), 3506–3527 (2014)
18. Zhang, Y., Kwong, S., Zhang, G., Pan, Z., Yuan, H., Jiang, G.: Low complexity hevc intra coding for high-quality mobile video communication. IEEE Trans. Industr. Inf. **11**(6), 1492–1504 (2015)

Author Index

Printed in the United States
By Bookmasters